CRM
in financial
services

a practical guide to making
customer relationship
management work

Bryan Foss & Merlin Stone

IBM®

KOGAN
PAGE

Bryan Foss
To my wife Carol and my children Simon and Helen, for their continued understanding and support.

Merlin Stone
To my wife, Ofra, and especially my daughters Maya and Talya, without whose needs I would never have understood the importance of financial services.

First published in 2002

Kogan Page Limited
120 Pentonville Road
London N1 9JN
UK

Kogan Page US
22 Broad Street
Milford CT 06460
USA

British Library Cataloguing in Publication Data

A CIP record for this book is available from the British Library.

ISBN 0 7494 3696 4

Typeset by Saxon Graphics Ltd, Derby
Printed and bound in Great Britain by Bell & Bain Ltd, Glasgow

Contents

About the authors

BRYAN FOSS

Bryan is CRM Solutions Executive for IBM Global Financial Services. He is currently leading an IBM business providing and integrating application-based CRM solutions for retail banks and other financial services companies worldwide. Typical B2C and B2B projects have included pragmatic customer management consulting, data warehouse and marketing database build, data analysis and data mining, and integrated customer campaign communications, including contact centre, Web and mobile e-business through direct and intermediated channels.

Over many years Bryan has worked primarily with key banking, insurance and other financial services companies globally, including large and innovative companies, composites and new directs. Prior to his global market management and solution development and delivery role, Bryan was responsible for IBM's business relationship with the Prudential Corporation, worldwide, over a 6-year period. Previous experience in financial services also includes a similar period working as IBM's technical management contact with American Express Card and Travel services, supporting all non-US operations.

Prior to joining IBM in 1980, Bryan held responsibility for marketing and financial systems in Nestlé UK, and before that at Gateway Foodmarkets (a major UK retailer).

Bryan's qualifications include an Executive MBA from London City University Business School focused on financial services marketing and CRM, Chartered Marketer and Fellow of the Chartered Institute of Marketing (CFCIM), Postgraduate Diploma in Marketing (DipM), Chartered Engineer (C Eng Information Systems) and Member of the British Computer Society (MBCS) and a Certified Diploma in Accounting and Finance (C Dip AF Certified Accountancy). Bryan has represented IBM on the MBA advisory boards of City and Surrey Universities and is currently a member of the Court of Surrey University.

Bryan is IT editor of the *Journal of Financial Services* and a co-author of the Policy Publications 'Close to the Customer' executive briefing series and the *Financial Times* CRM report. Bryan contributed the 'systems and data' chapter to Merlin Stone's *Up Close and Personal?: CRM @ Work* (Kogan Page, 2000) and launched a new book *Successful Customer Relationship Marketing* (Kogan Page, 2001), co-authored with Merlin Stone. Bryan is a frequent presenter at CRM and Financial Services conferences in the UK and elsewhere.

Bryan can be contacted as follows:

Bryan Foss
IBM United Kingdom Ltd
Knolly's House, 17 Addiscombe Road
Croydon CR9 6HS
UK

Tel: +44 (0) 20 8681 4402 (direct line and voicemail)
Fax: +44 (0) 20 8681 4307
E-mail: bryan_foss@uk.ibm.com (contact preference)

MERLIN STONE

Merlin is the IBM Professor of Relationship Marketing at Bristol Business School, an Executive Consultant with IBM's Business Innovation Services, Financial Services Sector and a Director of QCi Ltd, Swallow Information Systems Ltd and Viewscast Ltd. His consulting experience covers many sectors. He is the author of many articles and author or co-author of 20 books on marketing and customer service. He is a Founder Member of the Institute of Direct Marketing, a Fellow of the Chartered Institute of Marketing and is on the editorial advisory boards of many journals. He has a first-class honours degree and a doctorate in economics.

List of contributors

Philip Aitchison	Student at University College Dublin at time of writing
Ed Aspinall	Royal Mail
Tamsin Brew	IBM
Christopher Cannon	IBM
John Carter	Hoggett Bowers
Paul Clutterbuck	IBM
Dave Cox	Swallow Information Systems
Paul Crick	PricewaterhouseCoopers
Emma Cullen	IBM
Stuart Degg	Royal & Sun Alliance
Colin P Devonport	IBM
Abdelouahed El Marouani	IBM intern at time of writing
Martin Evans	Cardiff Business School
Genevieve Findlay	IBM
Gerard de Graaff	IBM
Paul Greensmith	Royal & Sun Alliance
Rich Harvey	IBM
Martin Hattenbach	IBM
Tim Hughes	Bristol Business School
Barry Jerome	IBM
Chandra Kiran	IBM
Fola Komolafe	IBM
David La Bouchardière	IBM
Kevin La Croix	IBM
Matt Leonard	IBM
Paris de L'Etraz	Mathias CMS

Richard Lowrie	IBM
Vikram Lund	IBM
Liz Machtynger	Mummert + Partner
Maureen Madden	IBM
Vince Mason	Mummert + Partner at time of writing
Peter Mathias	Mathias CMS
Paul McDaid	IBM
Barry McEnroe	IBM
Tess Moffett	IBM
John Mullaly	IBM
Clive Nancarrow	Bristol Business School
Michael Page	Acxiom
Rohitha Perera	IBM
Cathy Pickering	IBM
David Port	Callidus
Ann Rodrigues	Hoggett Bowers
Peter Routledge	Royal & Sun Alliance
Fabian Sander	Student, Regensburg University, Germany
Brian Scheld	IBM
Greg Scorziello	Bi-tech
Clare Seah	IBM
David Selby	IBM
Roy Sheridan	Viewscast
Alison Spottiswoode	IBM
Michael Starkey	De Montfort University
Ted Strader	IBM
John Stubbs	Chartered Institute of Marketing
Alan Tapp	Bristol Business School
David Taylor	IBM
Joy Terentis	IBM at time of writing
Ica Van Eeden	Dimension Data
Berenice Winter	Acxiom at time of writing
Neil Woodcock	QCi
Tony Woods	Insight 4

Foreword from the Industry General Managers of IBM's Financial Services Sector

Customer relationship management, customer loyalty, customer centricity. These are all variations of a great idea – knowing your customers and understanding their needs. It is an idea that IBM has been working on with financial institutions worldwide for many years. During this time we have gained many insights into CRM: what works and what does not, what things need to work together, how long things take and what traps we need to watch out for. One lesson learnt is that there is no simple, universal recipe for managing financial services customers better, to mutual benefit. However, we have begun to assemble 'best practices', drawing on the collective experiences of our global team. This book brings together that knowledge, drawing on the breadth and depth of IBM's own expertise and that of our clients and business partners.

We're pleased at the storehouse of knowledge and practical advice reflected in this book, and we hope it helps you. Treat it like a resource book, not a recipe. Please give us your feedback on ways to make this material even more useful.

Mark N Greene PhD, General Manager, Global Banking Industry
William N Pieroni, General Manager, Global Insurance Industry
Elaine Sullivan, General Manager, Global Financial Markets

Acknowledgements

BRYAN FOSS

It is personally very rewarding to see the contributions of so many experienced colleagues and business associates combined into a tangible form, which can be shared widely as the basis for planning and implementing more successful CRM projects in financial services companies worldwide. Hopefully the resulting projects will in turn provide further learning and accelerated achievements for others. These experiences really are culled from across the financial services globe, with almost no geography, region or country left unrepresented. In my own role I have been fortunate enough to have the enviable opportunity to learn and to share from involvement in leading projects across the world.

My City University MBA and ongoing coaching involvement introduced me to an approach to business thinking with reusable models but 'without walls' – Ronnie Lessem, Robert Lalor and Liz Machtynger (who also worked with me on many projects while at IBM) are worthy of special mention for their help during this time. Further work on the board of the global MBA programme of Surrey European Management School (SEMS) also influenced me, through the wise thinking of Patrick Dowling and Michael Baker and the business enthusiasm of Paul Gamble. The Chartered Institute of Marketing (CIM) has played its role too, with particular thanks to Tess Harris and Alan Pulford.

IBM colleagues are too numerous to mention in full, but must certainly include Tom Romeo, whose original ideas and support have provided a legacy of CRM strength, although he has since moved to another executive role. The interest and support of industry general managers Elaine Sullivan, Bill Pieroni and Mark Greene continue to be important, along with the personal support and contributions of colleagues Richard Lowrie, Brian Scheld, Rich Harvey, Paul Clutterbuck, Mark Chetwood, Bryan Lee, Paul McDaid, John

Bond, Jonathan Miller, David Selby, John Garrett, Kathy Holoman, John Moon (now retired), Adrian Bird and the entire management team of the IBM Dublin Financial Services Centre.

Influence has also come through with close working relationships with alliance partners including Neil Woodcock and the management team of QCi, Lacy Edwards and Paul Buckley of Evoke Software and Kevin Carroll of Carroll Communications.

Finally, special recognition goes to Pauline Goodwin and the team at Kogan Page, who have worked closely with Merlin and myself through an increasing number of successful business publications, and of course to Merlin himself, who has proved to be such a terrific whirlwind of ideas and energy as well as a source of contacts during the eight years or so since we first met and started working together.

MERLIN STONE

This book is the culmination of a lot of hard work, not just by Bryan and myself, but also by the many colleagues at IBM and other companies and organizations who have contributed to the book, so thanks are due to all the contributors, many of whom I had to hound to produce their contributions on time.

However, all the experience that enabled us to produce this book has come from working with our clients all over the world. Naming individual clients would be inappropriate, and in some cases it would breach confidentiality agreements, so I hope those clients who read this book feel properly appreciated by us!

A book like this could never have been produced without the support of Daryn Moody of Henry Stewart Publications, whose journals (particularly the *Journal of Financial Services Marketing*, the *Journal of Database Marketing* and the *Journal of Targeting, Analysis and Measurement for Marketing*) have provided the forum where many of the ideas in this book have been aired, so thanks are due to Daryn for all his support. Similar thanks are due to Gabriel Engelhard of Winthrop Publications in relation to the *International Journal of Customer Relationship Management*. James Lawson of *Database Marketing* has every month given me the licence to express my views in a monthly column, and I have often then taken the resulting material and incorporated in into a chapter.

The university context in which I work is vital, and many thanks are due to Professor Charles Harvey, Dean of Bristol Business School, and my colleagues there – especially Professor Clive Nancarrow and Dr Alan Tapp, who have also contributed to this book. The Chartered Institute of Marketing has always been a strong supporter of my work, and my thanks are due to John Stubbs, its CEO, for sponsoring some of my work at Bristol and allowing us to publish a financial services version of it in this book.

My manager at IBM, Paul Clutterbuck, has given me the time to produce this book, but has unfortunately not benefited from the long periods of e-mail silence from me that he might have expected as a result – the book probably added to the volume of correspondence. My thanks are also due to the rest of our small business research team at IBM – Fola Komolafe, Marina Parshikova and Maureen Madden, who have helped with background research and editing. Strong support for our efforts has also come from IBM senior management, in particular Bob Spooner, David John and Mike Steinharter, and from our marketing team led by Denise Holland. Special thanks are also due to Eddie Keal and Craig Jones, who lead IBM's CRM sales efforts in the region in which I work, and who have been too busy to write anything, but have given me lots of opportunities to discuss the ideas in this book with clients.

The directors of the various companies which I also direct – QCi Ltd, Swallow Information Systems Ltd and Viewscast Ltd – have helped me over the years by giving me access to additional research and consulting material. Special thanks are due to QCi for allowing use – on a strictly confidential basis – of the database arising from the deployment of QCi's Customer Management Assessment Tool (CMAT). Phil Anderson of Citigate has been a great supporter, identifying clients with whom I could cooperate to develop research for mutual benefit. Other companies such as Close Wealth Management, Acxiom and the Royal Mail who sponsored research which led to chapters in this book, also deserve recognition.

Finally, no acknowledgement would be complete with reference to Mike Wallbridge, who brought me into what was called 'database marketing' in the 1980s when we both left Xerox together, and who has remained a staunch supporter – as client and friend – ever since.

Other titles available from Kogan Page:

Successful Customer Relationship Marketing: New Thinking, New Strategies, New Tools for Getting Closer to Your Customers
Merlin Stone and Bryan Foss

'Merlin Stone's new book is the most detailed analysis of CRM I have come across, its in-depth studies are most illuminating. It is sure to become the definitive "must have" guide to CRM. Every practitioner should have one. Merlin stakes his claim as the Kotler of CRM.'
Ray Perry, Director, Brand Marketing, Chartered Institute of Management Accountants

'This book provides a practical guide to gaining return-on-investment from CRM, highlighting the requirements to develop from prescriptive marketing to a real understanding and development of the customer experience.'
Nigel Howlett, Chairman and CEO, OgilvyOne London

Up Close and Personal?: Customer Relationship Marketing @ Work
Paul R Gamble, Merlin Stone and Neil Woodcock

'Merlin Stone brings to this subject a deep intellectual insight backed up by years of real front-line experience working with the senior business officers across many industries, countries and cultures.'
Adrian Bird, IBM EMEA Marketing Manager, CRM & ISV Solutions

'Always invigorating and challenging, Merlin has that rare blend of hard-earned wisdom and clarity of vision that makes his work so significant – and so effective.'
Charles Arthur, Director, Artorius Consulting

Customer Relationship Marketing: Get to Know Your Customers and Win Their Loyalty
Merlin Stone, Neil Woodcock and Liz Machtynger

'… extensively updated due to the impact of technologies and the new models of customer management they make possible, [the book] also remains faithful to the practical and quality-oriented view of the first edition.'
Jerry Cole, General Manager, IBM Global Financial Services Sector

Introduction

Bryan Foss and Merlin Stone

The past few years have seen an outpouring of books and articles on the subject of customer relationship management (CRM). During these years, we have carried out a programme of research, sponsored by IBM and other companies, examining different aspects of CRM – overall and in particular industries, especially financial services. The latter has become a focus for many CRM projects and providers.

In this book, we have brought all our financial services-related material together, as promised in our previous book. The authors of this book and others at IBM have led the extended research team that produced this book. QCi Ltd has also played a very important role in establishing, through the company's Customer Management Assessment Tool, a database of current practice in CRM, strongly biased towards financial services. QCi's directors have also made a substantial contribution to developing knowledge about implementing CRM. We have drawn extensively on this database and these ideas for many chapters in this book.

The theoretical and empirical foundations for this book are contained in three previous books of which Merlin Stone is co-author. These are *Successful Customer Relationship Marketing* by Bryan Foss and Merlin Stone (Kogan Page, 2001), *Customer Relationship Marketing* by Merlin Stone, Neil Woodcock and Liz Machtynger (Kogan Page, 2000) and *Up Close & Personal: CRM @ Work* by Paul Gamble, Merlin Stone and Neil Woodcock (Kogan Page, 1999). The most recent empirical works that our extended research team has produced are *The Customer Management Scorecard* by Michael Starkey, Neil Woodcock and Merlin Stone (Business Intelligence, 2000) and *The State of the Nation II* by Neil Woodcock, Michael Starkey, Merlin Stone, Paul Weston and John Ozimek (Ogilvy, 2001).

To this, we have added material from leading experts on implementing CRM and e-business in financial services, from all over the IBM world and from some of the extended team of colleagues outside IBM with whom we have worked over the past few years.

This book aims to show the value of thinking before, during and after you act – in the world of CRM, this seems to be relatively rare. It gives companies lots of practical ideas about how they can improve their CRM strategy *and* execution, through best practices and case studies. It shows how companies can develop and implement the required competencies. It provides a well-researched and carefully considered view about the role of systems in CRM. It shows how to avoid failure. It has a specific and in-depth focus on the practical deployment of CRM in financial services.

However, the book does not pretend to be a 'cook-book', 'How to get CRM right in financial services'. Getting anything right in management is not easy, and it would be very arrogant of us to claim that we had *the* recipe for getting CRM right in financial services. What we have done is to give readers access to a wide range of interesting and challenging views on CRM in financial services. We have also included some coverage of e-business in financial services, as the topic is so closely related to CRM. Readers should not therefore expect a completely consistent or comprehensive coverage – we preferred to present the best material available to us and not to force it into a completely consistent picture.

This book is divided into 10 parts, as follows:

1. Where are we now in CRM?
2. Where are we now in e-business?
3. Sector situation
4. Understanding customers
5. Systems and data
6. Risk and compliance
7. Channels and value chain issues
8. Implementation
9. Making the most of your (most valuable?) customers
10. Strategic implications

The detailed coverage is listed below, to help you decide which chapters are most relevant to your needs.

PART 1   WHERE ARE WE NOW IN CRM?

Rather than start with definitions and theory, we decided to start the book with the best empirical material available to us on the state of financial services CRM.

Chapter 1 summarizes a qualitative research study by a leading executive recruitment and search firm, Hoggett Bowers. In this study, those responsible for the CRM programmes of many leading financial services companies were interviewed. The chapter demonstrates the gap between theory and reality, but gives strong encouragement to companies that are taking a balanced approach to CRM, with systems, people and processes combined to drive strategy forwards.

Chapter 2 summarizes the results of a qualitative study led by IBM's Business Innovations Services team. This one covers several countries, and covers not just CRM but some aspects of e-business. It confirms the message of Chapter 1, that implementation factors are the key to success, but has a slightly worrying message that it is precisely in this area that some companies see themselves as having significant weaknesses.

Chapter 3 ranges most widely of all, with results from all over the world of research and assessments using QCi's Customer Management Assessment Tool (CMAT). This chapter is written by the QCi team, and provides the strongest possible confirmation that CRM in financial services is at a relatively early stage of evolution, with much scope for improvement. Once again, implementation and programme management issues are singled out as those needing most attention.

PART 2   WHERE ARE WE NOW IN E-BUSINESS?

E-business is always in the background in CRM in financial services. Rather than spread our coverage of e-business throughout the book, we decided to concentrate it into one of the first parts, and to cover both theory and the current situation.

Chapter 4 describes IBM Business Innovations Services' framework for analysing the impact of e-business on the financial services sector.

Chapter 5 summarizes the implications for financial services company of a recent study, carried out by the Chartered Institute of Marketing and Bristol Business School, on the impact of e-business on marketers.

Chapter 6 describes IBM Business Innovations Services' framework for determining overall e-business strategy for financial services companies.

Chapter 7 describes the detailed implications of e-business practice for managing marketing communications in financial services companies. It is based upon research cooperation between IBM and Pricewaterhouse Coopers.

Chapter 8 gives the results of case study work from the Bristol Business School on e-banking.

Chapter 9 is a case study from IBM, demonstrating how a major Dutch bank is planning to implement e-business.

PART 3   SECTOR SITUATION

In this part, we summarize how CRM is evolving in four major sectors of financial services. Many of the themes in these chapters derive directly from issues described in the first two Parts, and are developed in detail in subsequent parts.

In Chapter 10, the IBM team discusses the development of CRM in the life and pensions industry, against a background of rapidly changing customer needs, evolving demography and frequent regulatory intervention.

In Chapter 11, the IBM team discusses trends in general insurance CRM, where the drive towards cost-effectiveness is putting considerable strain on companies' ability to deliver improved customer service.

In Chapter 12, the IBM team discusses trends in banking CRM, where the drive to improve value per customer is often frustrated by customers' desire to spread value between different suppliers.

In Chapter 13, IBM and Mathias experts on the implementation of CRM in investment banking investigate why so many companies in this sector have had serious difficulty in achieving their CRM objectives, and provide a case study of success.

PART 4   UNDERSTANDING CUSTOMERS

Understanding customer needs is a theme that runs throughout this book. For this part, we have avoided basic analysis, and selected three studies that focus on some of the most difficult areas.

Chapter 14 explains some analytical work carried out by IBM and Insight 4 on the difficult issue of cross-selling. It explains why many companies' strategies in this area are poorly thought-through and suggests how they can improve their performance in this area.

Chapter 15 describes some UK empirical research on customer retention carried out by Bristol Business School and the Royal Mail, with some additional work on the implications for financial services companies by the IBM team.

In Chapter 16, the IBM team discusses the application of market segmentation principles to business-to-business financial services.

PART 5   SYSTEMS AND DATA

Chapter 17 is one of a pair with Chapter 1, but in this case the qualitative research by Hoggett Bowers was carried out with senior information systems management. The chapter shows how major companies are changing their IT plans.

Chapter 18 describes the IBM framework for implementing CRM systems and accelerating ROI. It explains the importance of having a clear systems model, and what can be achieved with today's integration products.

In Chapter 19, one of IBM's data management partners, Acxiom, explains some of the issues involved in managing customer data in an e-environment.

PART 6   RISK AND COMPLIANCE

This part covers some of the most challenging issues facing financial services companies globally, in a world where governments want financial services companies to meet customers' needs for privacy while guarding against many customer-based risks.

Chapter 20 provides an overview of risk issues, written by the IBM team together with Bi-Tech, the leading IBM storage solutions partner in Europe.

In Chapter 21, the IBM team combines with Swallow Information Systems, providers of complaints management systems in Europe and the USA, to investigate the extent to which financial services companies are compliant with UK regulatory requirements for complaints management. This chapter is based on empirical research, and includes analysis of relevant CMAT scores.

In Chapter 22, the IBM team describes research sponsored by Acxiom into how far companies comply with data protection law.

Chapter 23 is an IBM analysis of money laundering, which has become a CRM topic because of the need to focus on how customers can systematically break the law by exploiting banks' attempts to facilitate customers' financial lives.

PART 7   CHANNELS AND VALUE CHAIN ISSUES

Channels of distribution and value chain issues are at the heart of many of the e-business issues covered in Part 2 and the sector-specific issues discussed in Part 3. However, we needed more in-depth coverage of this topic, because many of the barriers to obtaining good financial returns from financial services CRM lie in this area.

In Chapter 24, the IBM team describes how bank branches can be managed to improve returns from customers. This chapter establishes clearly that the banking industry has recovered from dot.com insanity and that classic good retailing and database marketing practices are the key to improved performance in this area. This chapter complements Chapter 12.

Chapter 25 describes research into the intermediation situation with life and pensions customers. This piece includes in-depth interviews with leading experts and analysis of how government intervention is affecting distribution in the industry. This chapter complements Chapter 10. The research was originally undertaken as a student dissertation at University College, Dublin.

In Chapter 26, global research carried out by Royal & Sun Alliance and IBM into the deconstruction of the value chain in general insurance is analysed. This chapter complements Chapters 11 and 27.

In Chapter 27, the IBM team discusses the development of the global direct insurance industry. This chapter shows how often inappropriate lessons about disintermediation were drawn from the early successes of companies such as Direct Line. The chapter is completed by a study by Viewscast of how new technology can improve direct feedback from insurance customers.

Chapter 28 builds upon the conclusions of Chapter 27 by showing how insurers working with banking distribution can improve mutual performance. This chapter was based upon case study research done at Mummert + Partner.

Chapter 29 describes research originally funded by the Royal Mail into the use of direct mail in financial services, and shows how a relationship-stage approach can be used to increase CRM effectiveness.

PART 8   IMPLEMENTATION

This part focuses on how to make CRM a management and financial success, starting with business case development and ending with payment systems.

Chapter 30 summarizes IBM's business case methodology and gives an example from the US insurance industry.

Chapter 31 is drawn from the extensive global research and consulting work on CRM implementation done by IBM, QCi and Mummert + Partner. It describes the different factors that need to be brought together, including people, processes, systems and strategies, and how to construct an implementable CRM programme.

Chapter 32, from Callidus, covers a much-neglected area of implementation, payment systems. It shows how changing the way people who manage customers are paid can assist implementation and improve CRM performance.

PART 9   MAKING THE MOST OF YOUR (MOST VALUABLE?) CUSTOMERS

This part focuses on issues related to wealth management, one of the supposedly hot topics of CRM in financial services, but one conspicuous for the number of failures.

Chapter 33 is a challenge from the IBM team to financial services institutions that believe they are involved in managing their customers' wealth. It suggests that most companies would not consider this to be the case.

Chapter 34 is an extensive study by IBM of wealth management practices throughout the world. It suggests that some companies are succeeding, but many have not really understood their customers' needs in this area.

Chapter 35 is a brief study by IBM customers' needs in the private banking area, and how financial services companies can meet them.

Chapter 36 is an extensive study sponsored by Close Wealth Management of how 'mid-worth' customers' needs for managing discretionary assets are met, and includes a case study of Close Wealth Management.

PART 10   STRATEGIC IMPLICATIONS

Strategy is an ever-present theme of this book, but in this final part we have included some IBM views on how companies should approach strategizing in a world of constantly changing customers' needs, economic and social relativities and government intervention.

In Chapters 37 and 38, we present thinking by one of IBM's leading strategic experts on how to gain competitive advantage and close service gaps.

In Chapter 39, we present IBM E-business Innovations Institute's framework for strategic decision making in the area of customer focus.

Finally, in Chapter 40, the IBM team summarizes the issues facing financial services companies and provides some senior management recommendations.

We hope that you find the contents of this book useful, and in particular that they allow you to benefit from the experience of the many companies that, through their involvement with the extended research team, have allowed the development of the knowledge base which this book represents.

Part 1

Where are we now in CRM?

1

The state of CRM in financial services in the UK: promise vs reality

Ann Rodrigues and Merlin Stone

INTRODUCTION

This chapter describes a qualitative survey by the author, a senior member of the global financial services practice of Hoggett Bowers, a leading recruitment consultancy. The second named author helped with the survey and has added some interpretation of the results.

OBJECTIVES

As one of the leading players in financial services recruitment, Hoggett Bowers is continually being confronted by the term CRM. When Hoggett Bowers is briefed by clients to recruit people for senior marketing or operational roles, 'CRM' usually makes an appearance somewhere in the job description. However, when Hoggett Bowers probed the meaning of 'CRM', there seemed to be a staggering variety of interpretations of the term, as there is in the degree of endorsement by the company's senior management and in the extent of uptake, with in many cases only lip-service being paid.

So Hoggett Bowers wanted to find out what is really going on, partly because its clients (rightly) expect it to be at the leading edge of current thinking and knowledge. Secondly, the proliferation of articles, white papers, conferences, seminars and even books (such as this!) on the subject, often sponsored by CRM systems suppliers, has led to some scepticism in many organizations as to the value of CRM to shareholders and management. As an objective third party, Hoggett Bowers is well placed to separate fact from fiction (or aspiration).

THE SURVEY

For the purposes of the survey, we focused on the business to consumer (B2C) sector, and interviewed in depth nearly 30 leading financial services organizations across all sectors – credit and charge cards, insurance, banking, building societies – as well as one or two CRM service providers. In most cases Hoggett Bowers interviewed Marketing, Commercial and Database Marketing Directors. The participants' objective was always to find out 'who is really making it work and how they are doing it'.

Obviously, some of the topics covered were confidential and so cannot be covered. The following organizations participated in this survey, and we would like to thank them for their frank and open participation – and some lively comments!

Abbey National Bank
AIT
Britannia Building Society
CACI
cahoot
Carlson Marketing Group
Churchill
Cigna
Citibank International
Cornhill
Direct Line
Eagle Star
GE Capital – Global Consumer Finance

Halifax Retail
First Direct
HSBC Group
JP Morgan Fleming Asset Management
Lloyds TSB Group
Morgan Stanley Cards
PPP
Royal & Sun Alliance
Royal Bank of Scotland – Retail
Royal London Group
Scottish Widows
Woolwich

Also interviewed were a leading card company and a major insurer, who both wish to remain anonymous.

OVERVIEW OF RESULTS

Participants see CRM (or its other manifestations) as a relevant issue, and one they want to get right. With a small handful of exceptions, few have what can be described as a sophisticated CRM programme, though all are starting to put, or already have, some elements in place. However, on a scale of 0–6 (6 being near-perfect CRM), most participants rated themselves at 2/3. Of the very small number of organizations who would rate the top mark of 4/5, they have some or all of the following in common:

- activities started at least three, usually five, years ago;
- CRM not started by design, but because of acquiring in-depth customer information, which has evolved into CRM;
- driven (not just supported) by the CEO as a corporate strategic objective.

Time-scale is significant. Developing an effective CRM approach will take at least three years of consistent focus and effort. Good quality data and data mining is the vital first step. However, IT is very much an enabler. While infrastructural systems can be built up relatively inexpensively from existing equipment, investment is necessary in front-end systems and software and customer data, to allow the organization to have a 'joined up' view of the customer from every channel/'touch point', and also to give customer-facing staff access to this information at every touch point. This supports the findings throughout this book – CRM is not to be undertaken in a hurry.

Even those organizations at the early stages of developing their CRM approach feel, from hard experience, that the commitment of the CEO is essential both to get the organization as a whole behind it and to ensure CRM is given a high priority in time and financial investment. Not one respondent regarded CRM as an IT initiative. In most cases, there is agreement that it is a cultural/organizational issue, which also relates to business processes. In recognition of this, a few more progressive organizations recognize the importance of people issues and have tightly integrated CRM and human resource policies. In others where the CRM initiative is driven through cross-functional teams, the human resources function participates in these.

Let us now examine the findings in greater detail.

WHAT IS CRM?

In many organizations, CRM is a dirty word ('a way of flogging IT kit'), with Marketing – which is usually responsible for driving the initiative – being sensitive to criticisms that it might be seen as the province of 'marketing luvvies', and therefore not of relevance to the rest of the organization, or merely a passing fad. The term is therefore frequently replaced by other terms, including Customer Management, Customer Experience Management and Customer Solutions. Every one of the nearly 30 participating companies believes that CRM is not an IT initiative, and several that it has been 'hijacked' by IT companies. In the view of a North American banker, familiar with the more sophisticated US model of CRM, 'marketing is sales multiplied', and just as any good salesman in a car dealership would be asking potential customers lots of questions, including lifestyle-based ones, so CRM plays a similar role in B2C marketing. Similarly, there is a perception amongst a few of the organizations that CRM is a way of replicating the bank branch manager of 40 years ago (or the direct salesman) who knew every one of his customers by name and their personal circumstances.

A comprehensive definition comes from one of the leading retail banks: 'The business strategy and mode of operation deployed to maintain and develop relationships with profitable customers, and manage the cost of doing business with less profitable customers.'

Others talk of 'giving power to the customer', 'managing the value and profitability of the customer base, and having a single view of the customer', 'adding value to the company by enhancing the customer's experience of the company's service and product offering, and improving profit', and 'managing relationships across all channels, and getting to the holy grail of one-to-one marketing'. However, one of the leading and generally admired direct banks is certain that CRM is an inappropriate concept because it does not manage customers, but 'customers manage us'. At the same time, one of the UK banks cautioned against being too 'woolly' about customers and not focusing in a hard-headed way on profit. Similarly, another respondent feels that 'CRM is about mutual benefit, not cuddling the customer at any cost'. This point echoes the findings elsewhere in this book, that a hard-headed approach to the identification and management of customer value (see Chapter 14) can destroy many a dangerous illusion.

Those organizations truly committed to making CRM an effective business tool pay as much attention to employees as to customers. A leading direct insurer views CRM as 'the activities required to help frontline staff to deliver a service and to listen', though the same insurer is also known for its proactive selling! For them, CRM is 'more a philosophy and mind-set than a specific programme. There's no CRM solution as such'. And for another, CRM is ' a philosophy of the business – it shows whether the organization truly believes in the customer or not'.

WHY DO CRM?

There seems to be broad agreement that CRM is a mechanism for knowing who your customers are, and using this as a way of acquiring high value (as opposed to high net worth or affluent) customers, increasing cross-selling and reducing lapse. It is also a way of achieving greater operational efficiency in sales and lead generation, and achieving increased customer satisfaction because the processes will be more 'joined up' (retail bank). Significantly, in those few organizations that are investing much management time and financial resource in CRM, this is a direct consequence of the CEO going public on the strategic aim of 'becoming customer-obsessed' (global composite insurer), or of 'doubling profit in three years' (leading UK bank). In another, the CEO visited the USA and found and brought back to his business in the UK a product proposition that could be tailored to individual customers.

To meet the objective of identifying/acquiring valuable customers, data is obviously a key requirement. In two of the most progressive organizations from a CRM perspective (a building society and a top retail bank), CRM developed out of a major strategic business change, in one the need to protect its 'mutual' status and in the other a merger, both of which necessitated building an in-depth customer database. In both cases, development of the database was commenced five years before the study, giving these organizations a head start in what has now evolved into embedded CRM.

PEOPLE AND ORGANIZATION

Perhaps not surprisingly in a service industry, the single most important factors are people/organizational issues. These are the greatest contributors – and in many cases the greatest obstacles – to successful adoption of CRM practices. The drivers to success are:

- a strategic priority, driven by the CEO – in a number of organizations the CRM initiative had stalled or was moving ahead frustratingly slowly because of other business priorities and lack of commitment across the organization;
- an inherent customer service culture in the organization (bank, credit card company, specialist insurer, etc);
- 'internal and external cultures have to match', ie keep staff happy and they will keep customers happy – in one very successful direct banking operation, people issues, 'or rather leadership issues' as they see it, are routinely discussed at board meetings;
- cross-organizational collaboration – it is vital that CRM is owned by all departments, though in most companies it is led by marketing;
- at the most basic level, recognition that 'the call centre agents, or other frontline staff, are king';
- consistency between how frontline staff are rewarded and how their managers are rewarded;
- significant investment in training and development;

- communication – this is very important: 'a constant and iterative process' (retail bank). 'Communication is an investment, sometimes it is difficult to see the short-term benefit' (retail bank).

In two of the most progressive (from a CRM perspective) organizations, the CRM programme is led by Marketing and HR jointly. In another, a global insurer, where the CRM model was developed in conjunction with a specialist consultancy, the organization itself has taken it one step further and developed a comprehensive PRM (People Relationship Management) approach covering all aspects of progressive HR strategies such as reward / recognition, succession planning and career development. It has been warmly received across the organization and will be a significant contributor to the speedy take-up of CRM. One of the acknowledged leaders in CRM deliberately did not put CRM within the Marketing Department because 'it would have been corrupted by Marketing and it is more strategic than that'. The point confirms the need to ensure that CRM is not seen merely as the responsibility or province of Marketing.

Organizational structure is seen as a major issue, particularly if the company is organized by product, as is usually the case, or by channel, rather than being customer-centric. Since to be truly customer-centric would probably mean major organizational change, the solutions adopted include:

- appointing a data-driven CRM team that champions the customer and sets the business and marketing targets, by customer segment, for the Marketing department to achieve (building society leader in CRM);
- appointing a CRM team to work in a matrix with the product teams (several organizations);
- appointing a multi-functional Practice Board for each major customer group, each led by a Board Director (global insurer).

However, it was apparent in discussion with CRM managers, where these existed, that unless they are very senior, they lack real influence, and can feel isolated and frustrated. Appointing a CRM manager and letting him or her get on with it is not the answer. Indeed, in the experience of the second author, such managers do not last long, and become frustrated through their inability to influence the organization. This may lead to adversarial behaviour, which results in the swift departure of the individual concerned.

In summary, making CRM work is effectively a major culture / business process change programme, and treating it as such should ensure that it is given the time, financial investment (in people, and probably to a lesser extent systems) and priority it requires.

DATA

Two of the leading CRM 'stars' share the importance given to data quality, comprehensiveness, analysis and modelling. One of these invests in hiring econometricians and is seen as an employer of choice amongst this community, reaping benefits in propensity modelling and cost reductions, eg in eliminating wastage in direct mail. A North American banker confirmed the value of data collection in the USA, where CRM is more advanced and was led by the automotive industry. A relationship marketing agency took over the retail customer databases of both Bank of America and Chrysler, giving robust data on attitudinal and purchasing behaviour of 48 million households.

IT

It was apparent from practically every discussion that there is a degree of hostility towards the IT industry pushing 'CRM kit'. At the same time, investment in IT is essential: a) to gain robust data on the customer at every touch point; b) to 'join up' this data and give a 'single customer view'; and c) to make this information immediately available to frontline staff during their interaction with the customer, both in order to deliver a better service and to facilitate proactive selling. Only a small handful of companies had already invested in a pure CRM system. The majority were working with what they already had (sometimes a cause of frustration) and one or two were about to install CRM as part of a total overhaul of the IT infrastructure.

OBSTACLES TO SUCCESS

These included:

- 'Approaching CRM piecemeal – but to do it properly is a big investment'.
- Acquisition vs Retention: 'CRM hasn't taken off in the UK because the emphasis has always been on acquisition rather than retention' (new credit card entrant to the UK). There is also the view that acquisition is easier to quantify and attracts investment more easily because it relates to marketing spend. Retention (ie relationship building) is more difficult because it is more intangible, it requires investment in *people* and is more long-term.
- Size – bigger is not better in CRM. In the largest organizations, CRM has not been adopted as rapidly as it might because of the sheer scale and complexity of the project.

The answer seems to be to break down the project into 'bite-sized chunks', or start with a pilot, measure it thoroughly and gradually expand from there (retail bank, credit card company, global insurer).

- 'Changing the mindset of the organization', gaining the buy-in of all the departments concerned, some of whom have conflicting priorities, eg the need to deliver sales versus the need to deliver customer service (eg service-rewarded Operations Manager to sales-focused Marketing: 'that'll cost you 15 FTEs').
- Getting consistent treatment for customer service across all the channels (a systems issue).

TIME-SCALES

It is very clear that in the handful of organizations that are well on the way to establishing a CRM-led approach, the groundwork has been done over several years, and to get to a fully customer-centric organization will take 5–6 years of constant effort and refinement.

WHO DO RESPONDENTS FEEL DOES IT WELL?

The most commonly held statement was 'no one in financial services'. Yet in industry as a whole, the sector is held to be one of the most advanced in CRM, being traditional users of direct mail and other direct marketing channels, and having extensive data on their customers. Most of the comments were a result of personal experience, and a few from feedback from consumer research. The most admired organization is First Direct, 'particularly in its early days', followed by Direct Line, though the latter is felt sometimes to lose the balance between sales and customer service. Britannia Building Society, American Express and some of the newer credit card entrants were also mentioned. Some companies are rated for part of their activities, eg American Express for the best physical delivery, cahoot for its enrolment and fulfilment, whilst Abbey National is seen as particularly innovative in its branch developments. Outside the sector, Tesco is the most frequently mentioned.

FINANCIAL BENEFITS

A number of organizations admit that it is difficult to identify the financial benefits to the organization of a 'proper' CRM approach. Concepts such as Life Time Value are bandied about, but are difficult to measure and not entirely understood by those championing

CRM, ie Marketing. This may explain why only a few of our respondents pointed out the need to submit the business case for CRM – perhaps a surprising omission. However, as Chapter 30 shows, construction of a business case requires many assumptions about how customers will react to CRM initiatives, so it may be better to develop the case through a series of structured tests.

In the majority of cases it is simply too soon to say whether they have realized the benefits, though some can demonstrate quick wins, for example excellent customer service leading to measurable increases in retention and referrals. Two of the direct financial services companies regard their customers as their best salespeople, generating up to one-third of new business in referrals.

CRM and customer segmentation are used by a number of companies, mainly in retail banking, as a way of providing a differentiated service (sometimes covertly) by *channel*, achieving lower costs while maintaining service levels. Thus lower value customers are diverted to the lowest cost channel, the Web, whilst high value customers can have face-to-face service in the branch (the most costly form of service) if they wish. In the case of a global insurer, this approach led to an immediate turnaround in profits in one of its international subsidiaries.

THE FUTURE

In the light of the current downturn, it would be interesting to see whether financial services companies treat CRM as a continuing business imperative, or subject to halted investment. We believe that if undertaken properly, CRM has undoubted benefits for the customer, for the employee and therefore for the service provider. However, our research shows that this is most likely where CRM is undertaken as a part of, and fully integrated with, a wider programme of change over a longer, less hurried period, with a strong focus on the human resources and organizational aspects, from senior management through to the point at which customers are managed.

2

Uncertain directions in Europe and South Africa

Paul Clutterbuck, Rohitha Perera and Merlin Stone

INTRODUCTION

This chapter brings together the opinions of 70 leading executives from 45 different major institutions across the financial services industry – in banking (retail and private) and insurance. The majority of data was collected via face-to-face interviews between IBM Principals and industry executives over the period January–April 2001. In total, the sample comprised 73 senior executives, from some 45 businesses, drawn approximately equally from the retail banking, insurance and private/non-retail banking sectors. Just over a quarter represented non-UK countries, including Eire, Finland, South Africa, Sweden and the Netherlands. It is worth noting that many of the companies that took part have their headquarters elsewhere in Europe (particularly France, Germany, Switzerland and Italy) or in the USA.

Against a background of rapid change, we invited them to discuss a range of key topics. These included disintermediation, the very significant impact of new technology and, perhaps most crucially, the potential of the mass affluent (or mainstream) market and the opportunities it offers for the progressive deployment of wealth management services.

The main focus of this chapter is a complex battleground. Looking on, we find the players of the financial services industry competing fiercely as they seek to acquire new, and retain old, customers. But the 'smoke' conceals some very different policies and outcomes. On the one side, where today the conflict appears toughest, are two much-disputed territories: the 'wealthy' (the top segment) and the 'affluent' (the second layer in the terminology of this chapter). In this struggle, we hear that one current winning strategy aligns the delivery of ever-sharper customer focus with strong reassurance about personal privacy and data protection. Far over on the other side, an eerie silence reigns. Here the players have all but deserted the territory of the 'least affluent' (the last and fourth of the segments). Indeed, they expect the social problem of the 'unbanked' to increase over the next few years. In between, the *mainstream* is at once the largest and most complex of the disputed areas and reveals the widest disparity of approach among the players. Most committed to the territory are the retail banks. Over 80 per cent highlight this ground as 'core/significant' (twice the private bankers' rating) and the majority believes that the potential prize in the mainstream is 'larger/far larger' than in the adjacent wealthy/affluent areas. Insurers largely agree with this assessment of potential, as do nearly 40 per cent of private bankers.

So how will these conflicts resolve themselves? As a useful starting point, the acute observer finds the players by and large curiously (and poorly) motivated. They begin from a core belief that they are 'sustained in business by apathy'. They do believe something can be done and appear to understand what it is. Yet they hesitate. They have little confidence in the power of conventional tools and options: fully half, for example, assert that the practice of many key players of offering an 'ever-widening range of products confuses customers and destroys credibility'. They are also only marginally more comfortable with the next gener-ation: only 45 per cent believe that the much-touted call centres deliver on their CRM-inspired promise to improve customer relations. Meanwhile what are the drivers? Yesterday, they say it was the impact of regulation and legislation. Today, surprisingly, this gives way to the *impact of new technology* (such as the Internet) and a *strong focus on customers*. And tomorrow? Tomorrow (meaning over the next three to four years), the players expect to encounter six major waves of change – each increased in potency over today (although differently weighted in terms of the affluent and mainstream areas). They are:

- sharper customer focus/personalization (strongest in the affluent zone);
- increasing effectiveness of processes (strongest in the mainstream);
- faster new product introduction;
- increasing effectiveness of people;
- product cost reduction;
- levels of merger and acquisition (M&A) activity.

Within these waves, customer focus and the impact of technology remain powerful forces. However, they are joined by four others – each expected to *gain* significantly in strength over the next three to four years:

- a drive to real-time and straight-through processing;
- a progressive disintermediation of the financial value chain;

- anticipated creation of *new wealth management* (or integrated personal financial) services packages; this is seen as a critical departure and, according to most, is quite unlike the old bancassurance concept in a new guise (although many commentators see it that way in practice!);
- increased significance paid to the *power of brand*.

But while technology, customer focus and brand lead the way, the players face many issues – particularly in regard to the last. Fully half express concern that 'many customers have lost their respect for traditional financial sector brands'. They link this with what they see as a 'lack of trust' among younger customers.

So what finally of the outcomes? It is not this chapter's purpose – or place – to try to pick winners and losers; however, two warnings emerge:

1. Any industry whose majority acknowledges that it does not know how to '*grow shareholder value except by acquisition*' is admitting tacitly that, for all its talk of 'customer focus', it is uncertain how best to operate in a 'customer-centric' world. And, as one indicator, its (at best) loose approach to segmentation in this area looks seriously unrefined by the standards of other consumer-facing industries.
2. Among those seeking to exploit the mainstream opportunity, the industry reveals serious uncertainty about the best way forward. Indeed, the players believe they are led by senior managers who 'can barely handle today's pace of change and will be overwhelmed in the near future'.

If, then, there is much to back the pessimists' case, the industry may take greater comfort from the attitudes revealed by our respondents. They have moved well beyond *awareness* to serious *concern*. Looking around and ahead, the executives (whether in private or retail banking or insurance) showed remarkable candour about their situation, accompanied by wholly unexpected congruity in their viewpoints. They clearly understand the road ahead – both its challenges and its opportunities – and in classic behavioural models, such concern is a precursor to effective *action*. It promises to make the next few years in financial services extremely interesting ones.

THE AFFLUENT AND THE MAINSTREAM

Recently, the methodology of customer segmentation has become a major talking point in the FS industry as a whole. For simplicity, in this chapter we use four segments:

- wealthy;

- affluent;
- mainstream;
- least affluent.

This section provides a review of today's major conflicts and tomorrow's key trends, beginning with today's hot-spot – the wealthy and the affluent, followed by the complex and much-disputed mainstream – the larger prize tomorrow on most people's view, and concluding on a cautionary note with a view of the least affluent.

Affluent priorities: management and development

There is widespread agreement about the importance of the affluent segment. Seventy-five per cent of players rate it as 'core/significant' today – a proportion rising to 90 per cent on a three- to four-year view. This prioritization is marginally highest among retail bankers and, geographically, the UK group. As regards business strategy, in perhaps the most significant finding, respondents expect *increasing* levels of change to occur in *all six* key dimensions: product cost reduction, product time to market, customer focus, people effectiveness, process effectiveness and M&A. In this frenetic context, the most significant anticipated shift lies in much greater emphasis on *customer focus*. This aligns closely with a perceived need for strong reassurance about personal privacy and data protection. It is also strongest among those concerned with growing lack of trust among younger customers. *Customer focus* is followed closely by a stress on *process* and, next, not surprisingly in a heavily personalized segment, by the need to make *people* increasingly effective. Least change is expected in (the admittedly already very high) levels of *M&A activity*. Among sub-groups, insurers expect most activity in product cost reduction while the non-UK group place greater emphasis on reducing time to market for new products.

But what do affluent customers want in terms of services? If the industry has done its homework thoroughly, then the future top priority (agreed equally by both private and retail bankers as well as insurers) is *asset management*. Life insurance and pensions, private banking, and share dealing and brokerage follow this with anticipated differences of emphasis: insurers stressing life and pensions most, etc. Finally, planned affluent-segment communications strategy appears wholly conventional at first sight. Overall, 'personal recommendation' leads the way, followed by 'cross-selling of other financial services' and 'home or office visits'. (All three are rated as *critical* by between 35 and 50 per cent of the sample – with the last running second outside the UK.) However, in a key shift of emphasis, both types of bankers place 'personal telephone contact' second to 'personal recommendation'.

On the overall critical/significant indicator, new technology advocates will be delighted by the high rating for the communications power of the Internet/PC but disconcerted, but perhaps not surprised, by the low rating for both 'telephone call centres' and 'automated lobby branches' in this sector. Traditional marketers, meanwhile, will take little comfort from a below 15 per cent 'significant' rating for that old staple 'mailings' (the only tool rated 'critical' by no one!).

Strategies for the mainstream: 'large opportunity, larger prize'

Alongside the affluent segment, the *mainstream* is the largest and most complex of the disputed areas, provokes most debate, and reveals the sharpest contrast in approach among players. Most notably, as a headline finding, whereas players predict *increased importance* for the affluent segment, the *reverse* applies to the mainstream. Today's 'core/significant' rating in the high 70s declines gently to around 70 per cent (via the three- to four-year view and then a five-year projection). This trend is *sharpest* among retail bankers (who start above 80 per cent), shows *little difference* across geographies, and is of least concern to private bankers whose rating *barely shifts* from 40 per cent. Yet despite this gently declining view of long-term importance to their businesses, nearly 60 per cent (of the overall sample) assesses the opportunity in the mainstream market as being '*larger/much larger*' than in the affluent segment. This view is strongest among retail bankers and slightly magnified outside the UK.

So why does the segment's perceived importance decline? *Is it defeatism, uncertainty or practical viewpoint?* The survey evidence supports a mix of all three explanations of this striking contrast between assessed value and prioritization. Practically, timing may be critical. Nearly 60 per cent expect that it will require at least three to four years to 'adapt *current* technology and expertise' (from the affluent segment) in order to develop fully the potential of the mainstream market for wealth management (or integrated personal financial) services. The proportion rises to 80 per cent among private bankers. This may well reflect a highly educated understanding of the difficulties of rolling out solutions designed for a global private banker (with accounts numbered in tens of thousands) to largely domestic retail bankers whose customers are tallied in millions. Equally, no matter the potential 'wealth management' opportunity, respondents (across geographies and with only minor differences among the three industry groups) seem uncertain how to proceed. *In fact, as a whole, they revert to the conventional.*

Where product and service development priorities for the mainstream are concerned, asset management tumbles from its No. 1 priority slot in the development of affluent service strategy to a poor fifth; retail banking, life and pensions, and mortgages vie for the top slot (out of nine), while share dealing and brokerage slips from fourth to seventh.

This shift is mirrored, second, in the anticipated communications mix for the mainstream segment. Compared to the affluent strategy, conventional direct mail, call centres and automated lobby branches rate as more important. The personal touch (physical and electronic

– home visits, personal telephone contact, personalised Web sites) rates less. Notably, those expecting *most* from direct mail are *most* concerned about the potential impact of legislation on data protection. This view is broadly shared across the sample. However, outside the UK, the technology spin is stronger, notably in a higher perceived value for mobile applications. There is considerable divergence among the three industry groups. Private bankers see the need for *greatest* change in the mix. They also elevate technology (including Internet/PC) and reduce the personal element. Insurers, meanwhile, report the *least* differentiation in the mix required by the two segments. Finally, and perhaps conclusively, respondents' business strategy for the mainstream market is much more traditional than for the affluent. Gone is the emphasis on customer focus (it slides away to fourth among the six dimensions proposed). Instead, process rates highest, followed by the need for product cost reduction.

Social issues and the least affluent

Away from the major affluent and mainstream battlegrounds, an eerie silence reigns. Here the players have all but deserted the territory of the '*least affluent*' (the last and fourth of the segments). Indeed, they expect the social problem of the 'unbanked' to increase over the next few years – a process which may have major PR ramifications for the industry.

LOOKING INWARD: FROM MIS-SELLING TO BRAND POWER

In parallel to the major customer-side changes reviewed in the preceding section, this one looks *inward* at the players themselves. It sets out to answer key questions about major trends affecting their organizations, structures and managements recently (over the past three to four years), currently, and in the near future (over the next three to four years).

Past trends: ebb tide for regulation

Respondents estimate that the impact of four out of the top five drivers in the recent past is ebbing rapidly today and will continue to reduce in the near term. First (and perhaps optimistically) they foresee a significant decrease in the rate at which competition arises from *new market entrants*. This force they assessed as *strongest* in the immediately recent past as wholly new players (eg Tesco, Sainsburys) and new intersegment players such as the Internet banks (eg egg) joined the fray. Next, if they are correct, the massive tidal shift of emphasis from the classic branch (or distributed) banking networks to *call centre style* centralization has peaked. They say that (at least relatively) it will be far less important in the future. But, as regards the actual value of call centres, today the 'jury is out'. They may achieve cost-efficiencies in customer administration but do they improve the customer interface? Over one-third agree, or strongly agree, that 'call centres were promoted as a means to improve customer relations: [but] usually achieve the reverse'! Thirdly, the drive to build critical mass (usually via M&A) is perceived as fading. This is less true among insurers and the non-UK group, while perhaps for UK retail bankers there is a shortage of worthwhile opportunities remaining. Finally, and perhaps most intriguingly, senior executives expect that the impact of *regulation and legislation* (felt most strongly among the insurers) will decline in the near future also. We believe that this is wishful thinking!

However, in exploring this area, respondents reported much less concern in the immediate past with, say, new social and employment legislation or European Union harmonization measures than with issues such as security, risk and mis-selling. The disparity of reported attitude is wide in terms of a *significant/critical* rating. Topics such as 'equal opportunities' or the clearing monopoly barely reach 30 per cent. The EU, notwithstanding wide public debate/controversy, hovers between 50–60 per cent; but mis-selling and Internet security issues were rated highest, with almost 40 per cent rating them critical.

Current trends: the customer is king

Today, two factors are reported as much more prominent. First, the *impact of new technology* is perceived as today's strongest change factor in the market. Next comes the customer, most significantly in terms of the need for increasing *customer focus*, backed by the perceived presence of increasingly *demanding customers*. The industry sees today's customer behaviour driven particularly by:

- a shortage of time to understand and navigate the market;
- expectations of reliable professional advice;
- an increasing need to be self-reliant for pensions, etc;
- consequently, a wish for tailored individual products.

From the *customer's* perspective, factors such as brand, risk and even cost-transparency are far less significant – most especially the willingness to embrace new technologies.

Tomorrow's trends/disconnect: customer focus or brand/technology?

There appears to be a major 'disconnect' at work. As shown later in this chapter, this understanding of customer behaviour (and its importance) aligns very closely with the core competencies that respondents select as priorities for their ideal of the future Financial Services Corporation. *They hear – and understand.* However, it diverges sharply from their expectation of tomorrow's most powerful forces, the impact of technology and the significance of brand. But they don't act (or continue to follow conventional thinking). This conflict, or contrast, coupled with the wide (and for this survey unusual) variations in data, highlights both the intensity of debate about the best way forward and underscores the high level of uncertainty. Certainly, respondents expect that the need for customer focus will remain strong tomorrow. It is strongest among private bankers and aligns closely with their expectations that very high levels of change in customer focus will be required in terms of future affluent business strategy. However, major efficiency drivers – the progressive *disintermediation of the financial value chain* and the shift to *real time* and *straight-through processing* – are expected to power the development of new wealth management (integrated personal financial) services (especially among insurers/private bankers) and the increasing focus on the significance of brand. (In fact, insurers and the non-UK group are ahead of the rest of the sample in placing major emphasis on developing wealth management services – and specifically the potential power of brand.)

BUSINESS, BRAND AND PRODUCT STRATEGIES: THE IDEAL AND THE REALITY

At the intersection of the external market situation (described in the section on 'The affluent and the mainstream', p22) and the industry trends and internal changes (set out in the section on 'Looking inward', p25) is a 'crucible'. Here strategy is formed. This section outlines the players' strategies at three levels:

- high-level business strategy;
- brand;
- product/service.

It finds uncertainty about all three. There is also sharp contrast between a perceived *ideal* and a perhaps less than encouraging *reality*.

Business strategy: acquisition or bust?

At the top level, what is the players' high-level business strategy for the financial services market? There is certainly a very clear *ideal*. Asked to assess desirable competencies, they focus on change skills and organic growth factors. As noted earlier, they relegate the execution of M&As to 12th out of 13 options. But the *reality*? There is a frank majority acknowledgement that the industry does not know how to 'grow shareholder value except by acquisition'. This is strongest among insurers and private bankers, and a small majority of retail bankers actually disagree. Overall, though, this suggests that all the talk about 'customer focus' is just that – *talk*. They are uncertain how best to operate in a 'customer-centric' world; and even less how to build and exploit brands.

Brand strategy: power or panacea?

So what of brand? Building a brand is often said to be the fundamental goal of contemporary marketing (in any industry). Its power – positive or negative – may be enormous. Yet, by common consent, the financial services industry has been tardy in this area. So firms' elevation of 'brand significance' as the leading factor over the next three to four years has a clear textbook logic. It is underlined by their assessment of 'brand and reputation' as the key enabler in facilitating change in both affluent and mainstream markets. Yet, if this is the *ideal*, how insubstantial is the *reality* if the goal of customer focus is to build loyalty – which the players say today depends largely on apathy; and if the measure of loyalty is brand, which, they add, is neither respected by the majority nor trusted by the young.

Product and service strategy: short on ammunition

At the product strategy level, or *implementation* level, players have little confidence in the power of conventional 'tactics'. Fully half (with a weighting to the retail bankers), for example, assert that the practice of many key players of offering an 'ever-widening range of products' confuses customers and destroys credibility. They are only marginally more comfortable with the next generation. Only 45 per cent believe that the much-touted call centres deliver on their CRM-inspired promise to improve customer relations. Possibly this level is seen as relatively unimportant? Among proposed financial services' core competencies, 'innovating time to market' ranks only 5th out of 13, while 'product range' obtains only a minor rating as an enabler of change.

MANAGING THE WAVES OF CHANGE

Broadly, the three preceding sections have reviewed the external environment in which players find themselves, the internal impact, and some of their strategies for best approaching the conjunction. This section is concerned with what is likely to happen as the industry seeks to manage the 'waves of change'. It finds that, unreservedly, the industry understands, and acknowledges fully, the importance of change. It questions whether it is ready to take the significant level of action required.

Uncertain beginnings, refreshing candour

The industry starts unpromisingly, but with refreshing candour:

- It has core beliefs that it is 'largely sustained in business by apathy'.
- It is led by senior managers who 'can barely handle today's pace of change and will be overwhelmed in the near future'.
- It is expecting to cede the greater part of the mainstream market over the next 10 years to 'firms whose core business is not financial'.

The waves of change

Accordingly, it meets the six identified waves of change more than a little off balance. Without exception, respondents project massive levels of change in their business, whether facing the mainstream or the affluent segment. Activity is expected to increase in all six nominated business areas over the next three to four years, although with differing emphases (as noted earlier). For the affluent, the emphasis will be on customer focus; for the mainstream, the emphasis will be on process. It's worth noting that M&A appears *least* active. But 85 per cent predict that current frenetic levels of activity will stay the same or actually increase over the period! For those players seeking to straddle both affluent and mainstream segments, this difference of emphasis may present practical issues.

Competencies to manage the waves

Financial services players clearly grasp the need to manage change effectively and by what other factors it should be supported in tomorrow's ideal financial services' institution. Specifically, they rate the 'ability to manage and respond to change' their top core competency for a future successful financial services institution. They also have a clear sense of an ideal direction. Their next-rated competencies define a soft and organically focused view of future development. These include:

- managing the personal relationship with customers;
- knowing each customer and their changing needs;

- being easy to do business with (a special priority for insurers);
- innovating time to market;
- continuously learning and adapting.

In this context, although the differences are mostly fine grain, it's worth noting that three key factors – managing brand strategy, technology excellence and the ability to execute M&As successfully – all *lag*.

Navigating change successfully: inhibitors and enablers

So what will help and hinder as they seek to manage the 'waves'? How does financial services management assess the industry's strengths and weaknesses in terms of either inhibiting or enabling change? Notably, only the impact of regulation and legislation is seen as a potential 'inhibitor'. The jury, meanwhile, is out in regard to 'shareholders and the City' (who are viewed negatively by insurers). Some surprise, however, attends the top three enablers (given the ideal sketched out in the preceding sub-section):

- *brand and reputation* (whose potential is widely lauded but much questioned elsewhere in the survey);
- *vision and purpose*;
- *senior management* (which is expected to be *overwhelmed by change*!).

There is considerable confidence in senior managers' competence to define the strategy/vision but less confidence in their ability to handle the softer culture and communications issues. There is, then, much to back the pessimists' case, but the industry may take greater comfort from the attitudes revealed by our respondents. They have moved well beyond *awareness* to serious *concern*. The executives (whether in private or retail banking or insurance) showed remarkable candour about their situation and wholly unexpected congruity in their viewpoints. They clearly understand the road ahead – both its challenges and its opportunities – and in classic behavioural models such concern is a precursor to effective *action*. It is time, then, for managers to convert concern to clear action. It promises to make the next few years in financial services extremely interesting ones.

3

Assessing the quality of customer management in financial services

Michael Starkey, Neil Woodcock and Merlin Stone

QCi's Customer Management Assessment Tool (CMAT) is becoming one of the simplest ways to measure the quality of customer management. In its approach to assessing customer management, QCi started by developing a simple model for assessing customer relationship management practice. The starting point for this work was QCi's consulting practice, the ideas behind which have been published in several books.[1] These ideas were developed further through university research, which was published in various academic journal articles.[2] Two full reports of findings of assessing customer management all over the world have been published – the Customer Management Scorecard I and II.[3]

THE ASSESSMENT MODEL

The assessment model uses customer management stage analysis described in Table 3.1. The model is summarized in Figure 3.1.

QCi also developed a smart little piece of software for helping companies give a structured response to our 260 questions about how they manage their customers. The scoring for each factor is shown in Table 3.2.

The model encompasses all of the essential elements of practical customer management. It assumes that a company knows which market it is in and where it wants to be – but that

Table 3.1 Customer management stage analysis

Stage	Definition	Typical problems and opportunities
Targeting	When the customer is targeted as being an appropriate customer for the company, and induced to 'join'	• Targeting is not precise enough. So, if the company tries to cross-sell to all its existing customers, irrespective of their suitability, cross-selling can be a loss-making activity. • Very large numbers of customers are targeted, using a variety of approaches – direct mail, off the page, TV. This leads to overlapping coverage and wasted promotional budgets. At worst, if the activities of different product managers are not coordinated, the same person may be targeted for several different products at the same time, with the same names being rented more than once.
Enquiry management	The customer is in the process of joining	• Usually a very short stage, but of critical importance. • In many cases, failure to manage enquiries properly leads to many customers being lost before they join. • Sometimes this process is just too expensive compared with subsequent customer value. • At this stage, customers' expectations are often set for future treatment, yet they are often disappointed.
Welcoming	After the customer has joined, depending on the complexity of the product or service, it is important to ensure that the customer is 'securely on board', eg knows whom to contact if there are problems, knows how to use the product or service	• This is also often a very short stage, yet it is clear from what happens when a customer has problems or makes a claim, that they often do not know who to call or what to do. • For decisions involving significant outlays, customers may need to be reassured that they have made the correct decision, and given the opportunity to say whether they felt they could have been handled better during the buying cycle.
Getting to know	This is a crucial period, when both sides exchange information with each other. Additional customer needs may become apparent, and the customer's profile of use of the product or service becomes known. More is also learnt about the customer's honesty, ability to pay, etc	• Many companies assume that this stage does not exist, and that their customers go straight into a mature state of account management. Yet the early cancellation that applies to many types of insurance policy and loans indicates that this is clearly not so. We cannot expect that no customers will cancel early, but we can expect to be able, through data analysis, to identify customers most likely to, and implement preventative action. Experience in financial services shows that if we try, we will have some success. • Analysis from other industries with long-term relationships with customers indicates that communications behaviour, brand attitudes and satisfaction with the category are good predictors of loyalty, and these can be formed quite early on in the relationship, eg if they respond to your communications, rate your brand highly and are satisfied with how you have arranged their portfolio of products or services, then they will be more likely to stay with you.

Table 3.1 Customer management stage analysis *(continued)*

Stage	Definition	Typical problems and opportunities
Customer development	The relationship is now being managed securely, with additional needs being identified in time and met where feasible	• This is the ideal state, though quite a few customers never reach it, and often dip into the next stage or remain in the previous stage for a long time. This is best detected by short questionnaires – which can be administered by mail, telephone or by sales staff.
Managing problems	The customer has such severe problems that special attention is needed to ensure that the customer returns safely to account management. If this attention is not given, the customer is so dissatisfied that divorce is imminent. If the customer does leave, the customer will usually, after a cooling-off period, be ready for 'win-back'	• This stage is defined in terms of what the supplier should do, but of course the need for it is often missed and the customer goes straight into pre-divorce, eg after a mishandled service event or a change in the customer's need which remains undetected. If a company does not handle the initial problem well, and the customer considers leaving, companies often fail to recognize that this is happening. Surprisingly, many companies give up here, and even pride themselves that they make it easy for customers to cancel. If the reason for cancellation or termination of the relationship was a change in circumstances or a move by the customer out of the category, then brand loyalty may be intact, and in some cases enhanced if the supplier made termination easy.
Win-back	Sometimes, the relationship ended because of high price or the wrong product, so win-back can be initiated when these issues are resolved. Win-back is hardest if the customer left due to poor service, unless the competitors' service is even worse!	• The targeting of win-back campaigns is made difficult because many companies are poor at defining and identifying lost customers and because they have no reliable customer database.

Table 3.2 CMAT scoring process

No real progress: nothing/very little happening, possibly isolated small initiatives	0
Isolated activity: something happening, not systematic, not broadly deployed	15
Some commitment and some progress: concept understood, plan to implement, resource allocated	30
Full commitment and real progress: plans exist, resources allocated, implementation begun	60
Clear evidence and being implemented: doing it, can be seen, no evidence of effect yet	80
Fully implemented and having an effect: company is doing it, it can be seen, proper evidence it is working	100

is all it assumes. Each assignment costs the client around $70–120,000. Those interviewed include people responsible for analysis, for setting policy, for implementing it – right through to customer-facing staff. This enables us to comment on intention and reality. QCi insists upon seeing evidence where appropriate, and evaluates whether a given practice or behaviour is widespread and not isolated.

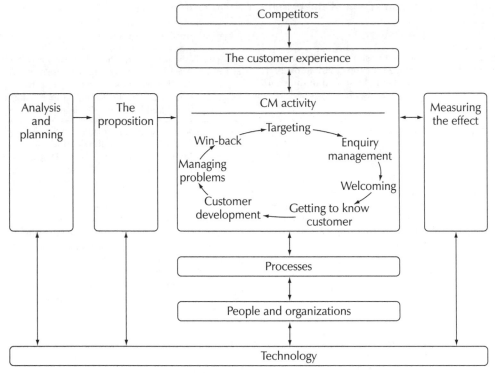

Figure 3.1 The CMAT customer management model

ASSESSMENT RESULTS

The average results of these assessments are shown in Table 3.3. Interestingly, branch banking performs relatively well, although the scores in all areas are quite low, indicating that lots of companies plan to implement CRM, but few succeed. This evidence supports intuition and personal experience that, despite ever-increasing consultancy and research support, companies are not applying the common-sense business practices that will really allow them to manage customers profitably. The lack of applied best practice occurs right through the model of customer management.

Notice that banking scores higher than average, and better than insurance, most of which is intermediated, so insurers focus on getting their products right, while intermediaries manage the customers. Banking, as we would expect in a retail business, scores well in the people area, and also in measurement.

There is a correlation between business performance and CMAT score.[4] We have probed this a bit further, and discovered that the correlation was strongest with these areas:

1. People – a clear winner! Having the right leadership, customer management competencies, people with clear objectives related to customer management and well

Table 3.3 Average assessment scores

	Overall Average	Insurance	Other finance	Retail banking
Overall scores	32	28	30	41
Analysis and planning – knowing which customers you have, which you want, planning to win and keep customers	28	27	19	37
The proposition – why customers should join, stay, and buy more	30	26	24	36
People and organization – structure, motivation, communication, etc	38	31	40	49
Information and technology – systems and data	37	32	38	46
Process management – methodical approaches to all aspects of CRM	29	27	36	35
Customer management activity – the actual process of managing customers, as described in the customer management stages above	31	26	30	37
Measuring the effect – whether what was planned was implemented and the results it achieved	35	29	36	49
Understanding the customer experience – ie knowing what the company and its competitors do to customers, seen from the customers' point of view	28	20	16	42

managed suppliers appears to have the biggest correlation with overall business performance.

2. **Measurement** – regularly measuring actual performance against specific customer behaviours, not just high-level financial targets, *and* having the policy deployment processes in place to action the results from the measurement also correlates well.

3. **CM (customer management) activity** – actually doing something! Implementing some sensible customer management practices such as targeting high lifetime value customers, managing enquiries well and quickly, welcoming new customers and proactively monitoring the initial transactions with your company, handling complaints well and learning from them, etc, has a positive correlation.

The comments below represent the essential components that we look for in each area. A quick scan of these points will show that this is not rocket science – it is just sensible business practice.

Analysis and planning

Customer management starts with understanding the value, behaviour and attitudes of different customers and customer groups. This understanding, derived from internal and external information sources, will drive more questions, which will in turn define the research programme:

- **Value** – on the positive side, margin includes actual value (database), realistic potential value (database or research) and future or strategic value (customer is in a segment which is, for instance, increasing in value). On the negative side, you cannot extract value without investing in your proposition to that customer. We look for some application of 'cost to serve' in determining strategy.
- **Behaviour** analysis will look at retention rates for different value cells, the type of customer you are acquiring and the share of wallet you get from the customer (your penetration).
- **Attitudes** will look at realistic surveys around what the customer looks for in a supplier and how well you match up versus the competition.

Once value, behaviours and attitudes are understood, planning can start for the cost-effective acquisition, retention and penetration of the customer base. We look for sales and marketing plans that reflect specific retention, acquisition, penetration and efficiency objectives at customer or product group levels.

Companies with a low overall score on CMAT tend to have poor scores in the analysis and planning area. Poor customer management almost always begins with unfocused, incomplete analysis. While some customer value analysis is almost always carried out, incomplete data sets and/or a lack of knowledge prevent further analysis taking place. Cost to serve is rarely used in calculations of customer value, and customer management strategies are relatively inefficient in these larger organizations.

Poor customer analysis leads to unclear high-level planning which provides little direction as to how the sales, marketing and service operation should alter behaviours and deploy resource in order to react to retention, acquisition and penetration issues. There is little guidance in the plan as to how the operation can manage the whole customer base efficiently, resulting in customer groups that are either over-managed or under-managed.

The proposition

The enhanced understanding derived from analysis and research will help identify the groups or segments of customers whom we want to manage. Our next step is to define the proposition to each of the segments and plan the appropriate value-based offers. The aim is to identify whether true customer commitment is realistic and, if it is, how we should deliver it. This is done through focused 'needs' research, mapped against the values and behaviour discovered during analysis. The proposition is normally defined in terms of price, service, transactional interactions, relationship, logistics and product, and for each element of the proposition a service standard (performance 'footprint') is defined in terms that can be measured. It must involve all functions within the operation that impact on the proposition and customer experience – it cannot successfully be developed by Marketing and imposed on the organization.

One the proposition is defined, it must be communicated effectively to both customers and the people responsible for delivering it. Many large organizations find it hard to examine their overall proposition to a customer group and to be able to define the full set of needs and experiences that affect customer repeat purchase. If the overall proposition to customers is unclear, undefined in service performance terms, or poorly communicated to others in the organization, more problems become apparent. When this happens, key customer management processes such as enquiry management, welcoming, billing, technical support and managing dissatisfaction – essential moments of customer experience – may be managed separately from other customer management activities and by managers with process, not customer, objectives. Separate management is not necessarily an issue and in some large organizations it is essential, but non-aligned objectives are clearly a problem and can lead to service conflicts and customer dissatisfaction.

Customer management activity

This is the delivery of customer management. Plans and objectives, based on the retention, acquisition, penetration and efficiency findings of the analysis, and the needs of the customer groups, will drive the activity through the whole of the customer life cycle, from prospect, through new customer and on into mature customer. This will involve the day-to-day working practices of the marketing, sales and service support functions in the following key areas:

- targeting of acquisition and retention activity;
- handling of enquiries;
- specific support for new and upgrading customers;
- getting to know customers and how they want to be managed;
- key account management and account management by sales (field, third party, telephone);
- identifying and managing dissatisfaction;
- winning back lost customers.

People and organization

People deliver the activity. We look at the work the organization does, to identify and develop competencies, and at how well the customer management objectives of the company are supported by leadership within an organizational structure that enables good customer management. Suppliers support the organization with the skills not available within the organization, or those that are non-core. What processes are in place to ensure that suppliers are well selected, briefed, managed and evaluated?

Measuring the effect

Measurement of people, processes, profitability, channels and customer activity (eg campaigns) must underpin the vision and objectives as well as enable the assessment of success and failure. Feeding back success and failure enables refinement and redefinition of future plans and activity. Most companies performed poorly in this area.

Customer experience

Customers experience our customer management activity across all of their 'moments of truth'. It is critical to understand from customers questions like 'How well are we doing? What can we improve? What do competitors do better than us?' for each experience they have with us, especially the ones that they rank as most important. We need to look at not just measuring satisfaction but trying to get at what defines true customer commitment to your organization, assuming it is a viable goal in the first place (see The proposition).

Information and technology

Information and technology underpins the whole model. Information needs to be collected, stored and used in a way that supports the way people work and the way customers want to access the organization. Technology needs to be used to enhance the way that customers are managed (from analysis to data at point of contact) and *enable*, rather than disable these core customer management practices.

CONCLUSIONS FROM CMAT ASSIGNMENTS

So a mixed picture. What is perhaps more startling is the gap between the perceptions of senior management and the reality of the way the operations manage customers. It is common to find that basic, common-sense business practices are simply not being applied by companies, but senior managers do not even know it and will, in companies with protective cultures, even go into denial when challenged. It is worth saying here that the boards of the companies we have assessed have always, without exception, accepted our findings. What is implied by our findings is large-scale organizational *ineffectiveness* (lost business) and *inefficiency* (wasted cost) running into millions of pounds for most companies.

Key areas to focus on for most large companies

Our interpretation of these findings is as follows: 1) companies are not particularly smart in the way they manage customers; and 2) there is much to be gained in simplifying what your company does and how it does it and re-focusing on the key principles of customer management described above.

The key principles are:

- Adopt a model of customer management that makes sense to you and your organization.
- Understand customer value and behaviour.
- Be really clear, as a whole organization, about your core (profitable) customers' core needs and how these needs can be delivered efficiently without error, in a way that allows the customers to enjoy the experience. Set and measure service standards around the proposition.
- Double-check that the core processes and policies which affect your customers' experience are robust, customer friendly and measured. This includes you and your suppliers.
- Ensure that your day-to-day activities are driven by the strategy by being clear about targets based on linking retention, penetration, acquisition and efficiency objectives to your overall business goals.
- Check that staff/supplier behaviours that affect achieving the only four things that matter – retention, acquisition, penetration and efficiency – are encouraged and rewarded. This is a leadership issue as well as a remuneration issue.
- Take a fresh look at the key job roles in your or your suppliers' organizations (not necessarily customer facing) that influence the customer experience and ensure that the jobholders are competent to enhance that experience.
- Ensure that processes and technology are not over-engineered but designed within a holistic system vision to support all aspects of the customer management model, focused around delivering the core proposition to customers.

- Ensure that customer experience monitoring takes place and that the results actually influence policy.
- Re-evaluate and simplify where effort is being spent and why (a necessity in most organizations).

Making 'best practice' happen

Whether you are implementing a major new computer system, a key account management process, an analysis discipline or a new planning system, one or more of these points will confront you at some time. Our interpretation of these findings leads us to list the following essential principles of best practice implementation:

- Understand now where you have best practice gaps. Do you really know what the priorities are?
- For the opportunities you uncover, develop a simple business case for the investment you are making. Don't believe advice unless it makes clear practical sense to you.
- Don't worry about what your competitors say they are doing; focus on what makes good sense for you.
- Assign good leadership to the project. The leader must have the authority and budgets to make things happen and alter already existing priorities if necessary.
- Do not over-engineer processes or systems. Use experienced and vocal users to work with you throughout the project as a practical sounding board for ideas.
- Get practical right away. Start small and build on successful beginnings (quick wins).
- If you need external help, work with consultants and agencies who have done it before.
- Target the process change at key influencers within the user community. Involve them in design and let them become the initial users and even trainers.
- Consider changing other processes, policies (eg remuneration, performance contracts, appraisal systems) and people management (eg management styles) to encourage change in behaviour and adoption of best practice.
- Assign sufficient budget to post-implementation coaching and review.

CMAT FINANCIAL SERVICES RESEARCH IN THE USA AND CANADA

Twenty-three leading Canadian and US organizations in the banking (retail), credit card, and e-broking industry sectors were interviewed in July 2001 to measure their competence in managing relationships with their customers. The CMAT research (CMAT R) assessment consisted of a two-hour face-to-face interview with one or more customer management (CM) or marketing executives from each organization. The CMAT R assessment uses an abbreviated subset of the full CMAT assessment (which would normally require 2–4 weeks and interviews with approximately 30 managers from each organization). This consists of 49 *best practice* questions (out of the full 260 questions). While a full CMAT assessment requires *evidence* of each customer management practice, the CMAT R relies on the discussion with the interviewee. Therefore, this research is not 'evidence based' – that is, the researchers did not collect documentary evidence to show that a company actually complied in the way reported. However, the participants in this and all CMAT R surveys were senior management representatives with broad-based knowledge of their organizations' customer management activities. It should be noted that CMAT research scores are generally reduced when a full assessment is carried out. In fact, the difference between intention (what senior managers believe happens) and reality (what actually happens) can be significant. Recent research conducted by QCi revealed that 64 per cent of senior managers were surprised by how low their actual scores were.[5]

While financial services typically outperform the average CMAT database score, results differ between North American and other geographies as well as between regions within North America. Key differences between the top performances in financial services in North America also exist, relative to the CMAT model. Table 3.4 shows the highest scores as compared to the average and median scores.

As suggested by the mean and the median results, the standard deviations are relatively low. However, the highest performance scores are not a single institution, suggesting differing capabilities and focus on customer management. The ranking of the highest scores also suggests the critical priorities in establishing an effective customer management

Table 3.4 North American Financial Services CMAT R scores – highest (and rank), mean, and median

	Highest	Mean	Median
Analysis and planning	73 (=2)	48	50
The proposition	86 (1)	37	40
People and organization	73 (=2)	46	45
Information and technology	72 (3)	43	42
Process management	62 (6)	39	38
Customer management	65 (5)	41	41
Measuring the effect	67 (=4)	50	53
Understanding the customer experience	67 (=4)	36	38
Overall	**60**	**44**	**44**

Table 3.5 Comparative CMAT scores

	Canadian banks	US banks	Other US financial services	Overall section ranking and score
Sample size n =	*6*	*13*	*4*	*23*
Analysis and planning	1 (51%)	3 (47%)	2 (48%)	2 (48%)
The proposition	1 (59%)	3 (31%)	2 (26%)	7 (37%)
People and organization	1 (55%)	2 (44%)	3 (40%)	3 (46%)
Information and technology	1 (55%)	2 (42%)	3 (28%)	4 (43%)
Process management	1 (43%)	2 (38%)	3 (36%)	6 (39%)
Customer management activity	2(41%)	3 (40%)	1 (45%)	5 (41%)
Measuring the effect	1 (55%)	2 (49%)	3 (47%)	1 (50%)
Understanding the customer experience	1 (45%)	3 (31%)	2 (37%)	8 (36%)
Overall sector performance	**1 (50%)**	**2 (42%)**	**3 (41%)**	**44%**

business model, over and above the researched correlation to business performance of people and organizations, customer management activity and measurement of the effect. The sequence suggests that key priorities are the value propositions, built from analysis and planning supported by information. Additionally, people and organization must be addressed, even ahead of the process and customer management activities, as typically people and organizations deliver on the proposition and can compensate for process or other weaknesses. Also critical are the measurements to evaluate the results as well as the ongoing assessment of the customer experience.

In terms of inter-country performance, Table 3.5 illustrates that Canadian banks outperform US banks by 8 per cent and are ranked 1st in all sections of the model except for customer management activities. US banks are in 2nd place for people and organization, information and technology, process management, and measuring the effect and 3rd place for all other elements of the model. Other US financial services (e-brokerage and credit card issuer) are in 1st place for customer management activities, but in 3rd place for people and organization, information and technology, process management and measuring the effect.

Canadian banking performance

Canadian banks report a solid understanding of the value of customers and know the main drivers of loyalty for each of their customer segments. Most carry out research that includes a ranking of their performance against the competition for key elements of the proposition. They also report an understanding of the nature of potential systems/technology necessary to support customer management functions in the medium to long term.

Key areas of strength in Canadian banks surveyed include:

- Analysis and planning:
  - understanding and using retention rates in customer management;
  - identifying which customers should be actively developed;
  - calculating and using customer value;
  - understanding competitor ranking across key dimensions.
- Proposition:
  - understanding loyalty drivers;
  - creating a proposition to match customer needs.
- People and organization:
  - incorporating customer management metrics in formal job descriptions;
  - cascading customer management objectives down the corporate hierarchy;
  - providing leadership from senior management.
- Information and technology:
  - publishing and using data quality standards for imported data;
  - publishing and using a customer information plan;
  - identifying the necessary scope of system support;
  - providing appropriate availability of the customer database.
- Measurement:
  - having and using REAP (retention, efficiency, acquisition and penetration) measures across their business;
  - developing and managing campaign KPIs;
  - holding a formal review of all campaigns.
- Customer experience:
  - using the results of customer satisfaction research to improve the customer proposition.

The priority areas for action (*mean* CMAT question score (50 per cent) in the Canadian Banking sector) are as follows (in priority order, highest priority listed first in each section of the model):

- Analysis and planning:
  - providing more availability of detailed transaction information (for at least three years);
  - developing contact strategies for prospect segments;
  - recognition of acquisition, retention and development goals;
  - aligning the organizational structure with the customer segmentation schema (or at least making them compatible);
  - developing 'game plans' for key customers;

- identifying and utilizing retention rates in business decisions.
- The proposition:
  - articulation of the customer proposition throughout the organization.
- People and organization:
  - providing organizational support for implementing strategies;
  - identifying competency gaps (and developing plans to fill those gaps);
  - understanding and engendering employee loyalty.
- Information and technology:
  - publishing and enforcing data quality standards for imported data;
  - creating and implementing incentives/sanctions around information quality.
- Processes:
  - identifying those processes which most impact the customer experience;
  - developing internal compliance standards;
  - measuring the 'customer acceptability' of all processes.
- Customer management activities:
  - identifying and storing the reason for customer attrition/defection;
  - developing lead distribution agreements;
  - capturing key CM-related information for new customers;
  - fully utilizing existing customer information;
  - establishing and implementing processes for managing 'key accounts';
  - creating service standards for customer enquiries;
  - establishing a 'no blame' culture;
  - being able to identify new customers.
- Measuring the effect:
  - understanding the volume/margin managed by each channel;
  - measuring each of the individual REAP measures (retention, efficiency, acquisition and penetration).
- The customer experience:
  - conducting regular 'mystery shopping' for each customer interface;
  - performing and acting on event-driven customer research;
  - developing and articulating an enterprise-wide definition of and position on customer management.

US retail banks – where performance was good

The US Retail Banking sector did not, as a whole, generally score above 70 per cent in any of the CMAT R questions. However, the top quartile did well in the following areas (highest scoring listed first):

- Analysis and planning:
  - developing game plans for key customers;
  - understanding and using retention rates in customer management;
  - identifying which customers should be actively developed;
  - recognition of acquisition, retention and development measures in marketing plans;
  - using segmentation as a means to align the way business is managed;
  - measurement of customer worth.
- People and organization:
  - organizational support for implementing strategies;
  - cascading customer management objectives down the corporate hierarchy;
  - providing senior management leadership for customer management.
- Information and technology:
  - availability of the customer database;
  - scope of system support for customer management.
- Customer management activities:
  - enquiry handling service standards;
  - identifying a new customer for welcoming activities;
  - applying key account management principles.
- Measuring the effect:
  - measurement of channel cost to serve;
  - clarity of measurement criteria for customer management roles;
  - REAP (retention, efficiency, acquisition and penetration) measures across the business.

US retail banks – where performance needs improving

The priority areas for action (*mean* CMAT question score (50 per cent) in the US Banking sector) are as follows (in priority order, highest priority listed first in each section of the model):

- Analysis and planning:
  - developing contact strategies for prospect segments;
  - providing more availability of detailed transaction information;
  - competitor ranking.
- The proposition:
  - loyalty drivers;
  - clear articulation of the customer proposition throughout the organization;
  - researched customer proposition match to needs.
- People and organization:
  - customer management ownership;

- identifying competencies gap analysis (and developing plans to fill those gaps);
- understanding and engendering employee loyalty;
- documented job descriptions reflecting customer management goals.
- Information and technology:
  - creating and implementing information quality incentives/sanctions;
  - documented customer information plan;
  - data quality standards for imported data.
- Process management:
  - measuring the customer acceptability of processes;
  - identifying those processes which impact the customer experience;
  - continuous improvement in customer management processes.
- Customer management activity:
  - identifying and storing the reason for customer attrition/defection;
  - targeting of high life time value customers;
  - establishing and monitoring time-scales for complaint resolution;
  - establishing a 'no blame' culture;
  - fully using existing customer information;
  - developing and monitoring lead distribution agreements;
  - establishing an information capture structure for new customers.
- Measuring the effect:
  - having and using individual REAP (retention, efficiency, acquisition and penetration) measures in individual mandates and appraisals;
  - developing and managing consistent campaign key performance indicators (KPIs);
  - identifying and managing volume/margin managed by channels.
- The customer experience:
  - assessing and using event-driven customer research;
  - researching and using customer satisfaction levels to develop and improve value propositions;
  - researching and leveraging positioning in customer management;
  - mystery shopping of customer interfaces.

Other US financial services – where performance was good

The top company within sector scored >80 per cent in the following:

- Analysis and planning:
  - recognition of acquisition, retention and development measures in marketing plans;
  - researching and leveraging competitor ranking;
  - segmentation to way of business match.

- People and organization:
  - organizational support for implementing strategies.
- Customer management activities:
  - lead distribution agreements;
  - time-scales for complaint resolution;
  - enquiry handling service standards;
  - identifying new customers.
- Measurement:
  - channel cost to serve.

Other US financial services – where performance needs improving

The priority areas for action (*mean* CMAT question score (50 per cent) in the US other financial services sector (e-brokerage and Credit Card)) are as follows (in priority order, highest priority listed first):

- Analysis and planning:
  - game plans;
  - contact strategies for prospect segments;
  - retention rates;
  - transaction information availability;
  - identifying which customers to actively develop.
- Proposition:
  - loyalty drivers;
  - interpretation of the customer proposition;
  - proposition match to needs.
- People and organization:
  - job descriptions;
  - competencies gap analysis;
  - objectives cascade;
  - customer management ownership.
- Information and technology:
  - customer information plan;
  - information quality incentives/sanctions;
  - availability of the customer database;
  - data quality standards for imported data;
  - scope of system support.
- Processes:
  - continuous improvement in customer management;

- – identifying processes;
- – customer acceptability of processes;
- – internal compliance standards.
- Customer management activities:
  - – key account management principles;
  - – information capture structure for new customers;
  - – targeting of high life time value customers;
  - – use of customer information;
  - – reason for loss storage;
  - – 'no blame' culture.
- Measuring the effect:
  - – campaign KPIs;
  - – formal review phase of campaigns;
  - – individual REAP measures.
- The customer experience:
  - – event-driven customer research;
  - – positioning on customer management;
  - – mystery shopping of customer interfaces.

Areas for North American financial services companies to improve customer management

In this section some of the key strengths and best practices of global financial services relative to the CMAT model (with scores > 70 per cent) are drawn out as North American opportunities:

- The proposition:
  - – Each element of the customer proposition is interpreted in terms of benefits so it can be communicated to each staff person responsible for its delivery and also to customers.
- People and organization:
  - – Customer management being owned as a main job role by senior managers who then give clear, visible leadership in achieving excellence in customer management.
  - – Having an organizational structure design to ease creating new customer strategies through to implementation.
  - – Customer management competencies clearly defined in all job descriptions for customer-facing staff, followed by competencies gap analyses undertaken in order to identify any shortcomings in key skills and competencies.

- Employee satisfaction surveys regularly conducted to measure whether or not employees are happy at work, are highly motivated, and have an overall positive attitude to work and their colleagues.
- Information and technology:
  - Fully consider and document the scope and outline nature of potential system and technology support to customer management functions in the medium to long term.
- Process management:
  - Adopt a continuous improvement process for improving and evolving all customer management activity.
- Customer management activity:
  - Define the customer development activity and clearly understand which customers should be actively developed and which should definitely not be developed.
  - Develop formal contact strategies for each identified prospect segment.
  - Set up clear time-scales for resolving all customer complaints, having a no-blame culture, and developing appropriate targeting and reporting that encourages staff to record all customer complaints as a positive means of improving customer service.
- Measuring the effect:
  - Ensure all marketing campaigns have formal review phase and clearly defined KPIs so that campaign performance can be compared.
  - Have a clear top-level set of measures that define customer management performance in terms of the REAP (retention, efficiency, acquisition, and penetration) measures and cascade these down to customer-facing people, and ensure they understand and accept the performance criteria on which they are measured.
  - Understand the relative cost of serving customers through the various channels, the proportion of their business in terms of volume and margin managed by each channel, and seek and store on the customer database the reason for customer loss.
- The customer experience:
  - Market research to capture in-depth customer satisfaction information for each of the key elements of the product/service proposition and then mystery shop all main customer interface points so that processes are seen and understood from the customers' perspective.
  - Use event-driven research that covers all customer management stages and key moments of truth for both customers and prospects.

HOW NORTH AMERICAN FINANCIAL SERVICES COMPANIES COMPARE WITH THE GLOBAL CMAT R DATABASE

Overall customer management performance

If North American financial institutions do want to differentiate themselves based on developing relationships, the weaknesses and opportunities identified in the survey may suggest that they are still early in their evolution compared to European financial institutions. The US banking industry, though undergoing extensive consolidation, is still highly fragmented, and many banks that are leading players in one region are non-existent in the next. This has driven many US banks (even the 'super-regionals') to manage their franchises and their customers regionally, rather than consistently throughout the enterprise. Also, the consolidation that has occurred in recent years has forced many banks to focus on near-term financial goals – either to ward off potential suitors or to inflate the value of their stock – which is, after all, the real currency used to acquire other institutions. In either case, the investment of money, human resources and executive focus needed to achieve a truly customer-centric business model have often precluded US banks from taking the steps necessary to keep up with their European counterparts.

As the economics of mergers and acquisitions have changed over the past few years, more and more focus is given to 'organic growth' – that is, boosting revenues and profits by increasing the wallet share of existing customers rather than 'buying' a customer portfolio via a merger or acquisition. We suspect that this new emphasis on organic growth will lead US banks to close the customer management gap on their European counterparts. In contrast, according to a recent Forrester research study,[6] Canada's consumer banking industry had supported a history of contrived competition until the mid-1990s. However, the past five years have been characterized by waning customer loyalty, largely in light of online developments, failed mergers (based on the federal government's denial of two proposed bank mergers in early 1998), new competitors (particularly those offering online full service banking as well as specialized services), and recent legislation – making it easier for foreign entrants and increasing direct access to the Canadian payment system. As a result, banks have taken or are projected to use different strategies for sales and customer service than for internal processing and technology.

Therefore, Canada's national banking environment, without consolidation opportunities, is viewed as having acted more proactively in customer management. This is reflected in scores higher than in the USA. Canadian banks lead the North American results with an overall score of 50 per cent (average CMAT R Score) with US Banks (42 per cent) and other US financial (credit card and e-broking) organizations (41 per cent) trailing (see Table 3.6). However, the Canadian score of 50 per cent is still under the European average of

Table 3.6 CMAT scores of Canadian and US retail banks

	Canadian banks %	Rank	US retail banks %	Rank
Analysis and planning	51	5	47	2
The proposition	59	1	31	=7
People and organization	55	=2	44	3
Information and technology	55	=2	42	4
Process management	43	7	38	6
Customer management activity	41	8	40	5
Measuring the effect	55	=2	49	1
The customer experience	45	6	31	=7
Overall sector position	**50**		**42**	

57 per cent, indicating that most Canadian and US banks can leverage developments from their mainland European counterparts.

While analysis of the results shows that customer management scores are actually consistent (low standard deviation of overall scores), the top decile of companies researched in North America did perform well, although again several points below the top decile of companies in Europe (see later inter-regional comparisons).

The profile of scores (which shows the relative competency of companies in different areas of the CMAT model) in North America were, interestingly, very different from Europe and not well aligned with the profile for best business performance (Table 3.7). Actual results differ between sectors, but overall in North America, the critical people and

Table 3.7 CMAT retail banking scores North America and Europe

	Canada	US	Switzerland	Germany	Austria	All
n =	*6*	*13*	*12*	*13*	*12*	*56*
Analysis and planning	4 (51%)	5 (47%)	=2 (63%)	1 (68%)	=2 (63%)	**=2 (59%)**
The proposition	4 (59%)	5 (31%)	1 (76%)	2 (69%)	3 (64%)	**=2 (59%)**
People and organization	4 (55%)	5 (44%)	1 (79%)	3 (72%)	2 (75%)	**1 (66%)**
Information and technology	4 (55%)	5 (42%)	2 (64%)	3 (56%)	1 (66%)	**5 (57%)**
Process management	4 (43%)	5 (38%)	=2 (59%)	1 (62%)	=2 (59%)	**7 (53%)**
Customer management activity	4 (41%)	5 (40%)	1 (65%)	3 (57%)	2 (60%)	**6 (54%)**
Measuring the effect	4 (55%)	5 (49%)	1 (72%)	3 (57%)	2 (63%)	**= 2 (59%)**
The customer experience	=3 (45%)	5 (31%)	2 (51%)	=3 (45%)	1 (62%)	**8 (47%)**
Overall	**4 (50%)**	**5 (42%)**	**1 (66%)**	**3 (63%)**	**2 (64%)**	**57%**

organizational area was only ranked third in overall performance (although second in Canada). In most of Europe, this is the number one area. Measurement was the primary focus of most North American financial services companies assessed in this research. Measurement is critical to support business performance, and shows a commitment to performance reporting and accountability. The second most important area of focus in North America was analysis and planning, a fundamental starting point for customer management. Actually carrying out customer management activities ranked fifth in priority. Interestingly, North American financial services companies did not consistently capture and feed back their customer experience in order to improve the way customers are managed (position eighth, and last). European companies were also inconsistent in this area. The significance of this profile is that North American financial services companies appear to spend a lot of time concerned with numbers and, to some extent, customer research, but less on developing the organization and actually implementing customer management activities.

North America

The overall score for North American financial institutions is 44 per cent, which is 13 per cent below the European average. Canadian banks lead the North American results with 50 per cent, with US banks (41 per cent) and other US financial (credit card and e-broking) organizations (42 per cent) behind.

How do North American financial services companies perform in the top three areas associated with business performance? The best North American score is in measurement, but this is 9 per cent below the European average and 17 per cent below the best performing country in Europe.

North America is weak in people and organization (46 per cent, 21 per cent below the European average, and 28 per cent below the best performing country in Europe) and customer management activity (41 per cent, 14 per cent below European average, and 24 per cent below the best the best performing country in Europe).

Analysis and planning is the area in which North America's performance is most similar to Europe's. Analysis and planning means determining customer worth, behaviour, attitudes and segmentation. We believe this similarity indicates a standard global approach to this area, typical of a 'first pass' approach. In other words, a company may appear to carry out a first-level analysis of analysis, sometimes with customer analytic suppliers, which begins to offer insight into customer behaviour, but due to lack of investment in data and analytics, this analysis stops short of providing real strategic input to the company. Typically, this first-pass analysis uses a partial customer data set available within the company. This would normally include basic customer geo-demographics, product sales volume, and revenue. Sometimes gross profit is included, but it is often incomplete and error ridden. It also involves some data tidy and enhancement work (*note*: 'tidy and enhancement work' is not a phrase common in the USA), although the client rarely pays for enough of this, and includes a first set of customer behaviour analysis, which may range from simple counts and rankings to the use of regression models, CHAID and clustering techniques. This analysis will provide some interesting observations around customer value groups and basic retention/acquisition issues. It may begin to offer insight into what *'best customers'* look like.

The client normally carries out a first pass at this but does not delve further into the data. It is rarely combined with attitudinal (eg satisfaction/commitment), activity (eg marketing, service, complaint, credit) or potential (eg future worth of customer) analysis, to develop real insights. The first-pass analysis often focuses discussion around definitions (eg how do you define a lost customer? what is margin? what is a customer?) and data integration (why haven't we got this data? why can't we pull customer data together more easily?) and may lead to the definition of data enhancement projects. More often than not, however, the data enhancement projects are not progressed, and the first-pass analysis is carried out again next year, with the same incomplete observations.

Companies that progress beyond this first pass obtain a more realistic view of the customer profitability of different segments. These companies are able to:

- understand the impact of cost to serve on customer profitability;
- gain additional insight into the role of different channels;
- identify potential high value segments in their base (amongst lower deciles of 'current profitability');
- look at the retention of different types of customers (different need groups), predictors of defection, subtler acquisition and targeting issues;
- quantify the impact of switching behaviour, the switching 'norms' to be expected and predictors of switching;
- develop programmes around the customer behavioural progression (development) over time;
- investigate the relationship between behaviour and attitude and the impact of process issues (eg impact of sub-standard delivery of 'moment of truth' areas) on acquisition, retention and penetration.

A small number of financial institutions have shown that these activities provide an excellent return on investment.

The proposition score for North American Financial Services overall is low (although this is misleading because for Canadian companies it is much higher). This indicates that propositions (a set of brand values cascading into how the organization must behave to deliver the experience) are undefined and no doubt similar, with mainstream organizations offering much the same undifferentiated product and service. Customers typically demonstrate little loyalty to this approach, with any apparent loyalty due to apathy or inertia.

The score for information and technology is also low, but this is acceptable considering that the other scores indicate a relatively undefined CRM business model and poorly defined processes. A key learning outcome with CRM systems is that they will not add value unless the business model and processes they need to support are well defined.

Although the picture of customer management in North American financial services may be disappointing, our research work offers direction for those enterprises that are prepared to invest in *practical* customer management. Substantial change and investment are required to improve the scores to European levels, but the rewards will be great in terms of increased business performance. Looking at the consistency of scores throughout the US companies researched, for those companies who begin now to develop the competence in customer management, the opportunity for competitive advantage, growth and profit success is enormous.

Therefore, the core recommendation is to develop competence across the CMAT model, improving the relatively good performance in analysis and planning and measurement, and investing heavily in people and organizational development and implementation of customer management activities supported using appropriate information and technology enablers.

Comparisons between US and Canadian retail banks

A somewhat different picture emerges for Canadian companies (see Table 3.8) although the sample size is small ($n = 6$), so we should treat these results with care.

The ranking analysis shows that Canadian companies have genuinely worked to differentiate themselves through propositions. They have invested more in the people and organizational side of CRM and placed more emphasis on information and technology. Perhaps in common with their European counterparts who have done so, they are challenged to achieve acceptable returns from the IT investment. This is because the day-to-day customer management activities (how can IT support the organization in enabling excellence in customer management?) and processes are not as well defined (low scores).

In fact, the day-to-day implementation of customer management is a key area for improvement in most Canadian companies. They appear to have developed the ideas (relatively good scores for analysis and planning and proposition) but are struggling to put them into operation. They appear to have looked for IT help, but have perhaps underestimated their need to develop more detailed clarity about the role of IT in their organizations.

HOW NORTH AMERICAN AND EUROPEAN RETAIL BANKS COMPARE IN CUSTOMER MANAGEMENT

Table 3.7 on page 51 shows the CMAT retail banking scores in North America and Europe. A first glance at the data suggests almost that the mean scores are bi-modal, with European

Table 3.8 Customer management activities CMAT scores North America and Europe

	Canada	US	Switzerland	Germany	Austria	All
n =	*6*	*13*	*12*	*13*	*12*	*56*
Targeting	3 (57%)	5 (35%)	2 (62%)	4 (54%)	1 (64%)	**4 (54%)**
Enquiry management	5 (45%)	4 (48%)	1 (64%)	=2 (60%)	=2 (60%)	**=2 (56%)**
Welcoming	4 (42%)	3 (53%)	5 (40%)	1 (59%)	2 (54%)	**6 (51%)**
Getting to know / Healthcheck	5 (27%)	4 (44%)	1 (83%)	3 (53%)	2 (59%)	**=2 (56%)**
Ongoing management	5 (47%)	4 (48%)	3 (51%)	2 (55%)	1 (62%)	**5 (53%)**
Managing dissatisfaction	4 (42%)	5 (37%)	1 (86%)	3 (65%)	2 (67%)	**1 (61%)**
Win-back	4 (15%)	5 (11%)	1 (65%)	2 (49%)	3 (46%)	**7 (39%)**
TOTAL	**4 (41%)**	**5 (40%)**	**1 (65%)**	**3 (57%)**	**2 (60%)**	**54%**

scores averaging in the sixties and North American scores averaging in the forties. Swiss banks are the clear leaders, with 66 per cent, followed by Austria with 64 per cent, Germany 63 per cent, Canada 50 per cent, and USA 42 per cent. Switzerland comes first in the proposition, people and organization, customer management activity, and measuring the effect. Switzerland is second in analysis and planning, process management and the customer experience. Austria comes first in information and technology and the customer experience and is placed second for people and organization, process management, customer management activity and measuring the effect. It drops to third place for the proposition. Germany comes first in analysis and planning and process management, and second in the proposition and customer management activity. Canada and the USA are respectively fourth and fifth for all elements of the model, except where Canada equals Germany for the customer experience ranking.

Table 3.8 shows the Customer Management Activity scores for North America and Europe. Switzerland leads in enquiry management and getting to know / healthcheck, managing dissatisfaction and win-back. Surprisingly, Switzerland trails in last place for welcoming. Austria leads in targeting and ongoing management, is in second place for welcoming, getting to know / healthcheck, and is in third place for managing dissatisfaction and win-back. Germany leads in welcoming and is second in ongoing management, enquiry management and win-back. The USA is third for welcoming and in fourth or fifth place for all other customer management activities. Canada is in fourth or fifth place for all customer management activities, except for targeting for which it ranks third.

CONCLUSIONS

Obviously, the market situation varies from country to country, and this causes differences in the requirements for success. However, these studies show that the standards of customer management do vary very widely between countries. This can either be construed as a threat (eg hard to change cultures) or an opportunity (learning across frontiers). The latter interpretation is the one we favour. In the UK, for example, the fact that two out of the five major banks' retail operations are managed by Canadians augurs well for improvements in customer management.

Notes

1 Gamble, P, Stone, M and Woodcock, N (1999) *Up Close & Personal: CRM @ Work*, Kogan Page; Stone, M, Machtynger, L and Woodcock, N (2000) *Customer Relationship Marketing*, Kogan Page; and Stone, M and Foss, B (2001) *Successful Customer Relationship Marketing*, Kogan Page

2 Here are just a few of the articles: Stone, M and Foss, B (1996) Information systems and data mining in personal financial services, *Journal of Financial Services Marketing*, **1** (1), pp 84–104; Stone, M and Lowrie, R (1996) Relationship marketing in consumer banking Part 1, *Journal of Financial Services Marketing*, **1** (2), pp 187–199; Stone, M and Lowrie, R (1997) Relationship marketing in consumer banking Part 2, *Journal of Financial Services Marketing*, **1** (3), pp 277–292; Stone, M, Foss, B and Machtynger, L (1997) The UK consumer direct insurance industry: a role model for relationship marketing?, *Long Range Planning*, **30** (3), pp 353–363; Stone, M, Woodcock, N, Foss, B and Machtynger, L (1998) Segment or succeed – the new 'top vanilla' culture in financial services marketing, *Journal of Financial Services Marketing*, **2** (2), pp 107–121; Stone, M, Woodcock, N, Foss, B and Machtynger, L (1998) Implementing relationship marketing in financial services, *Journal of Financial Services Marketing*, **2** (4) pp 334–350; Stone, M and Gamble, P (1998) Using the mail in customer management in financial services, Part 1, *Journal of Financial Services Marketing*, **3** (1), pp 21–42; Stone, M and Gamble, P (1998) Using the mail in customer management in financial services, Part 2, *Journal of Financial Services Marketing*, **3** (2), pp 117–136; Stone, M and Mason, V (2000) CRM in intermediated financial services markets, *Journal of Financial Services Marketing*, **5** (1), pp 61–72; Stone, M and Woods, A (2000) Making sense of cross-purchasing: a note, *Journal of Financial Services Marketing*, **5** (2), pp 129–134; Stone, M and Foss, B (2001) Business to business: lessons on segmentation and other issues from financial services markets, *Journal of Financial Services Marketing*, **5** (4), pp 308–313; and Stone, M (2001) Managing wealth: a new approach, *Journal of Financial Services Marketing*, **6** (1), pp 84–97

3 Stone, M, Starkey, M and Woodcock, N (2000) The Customer Management Scorecard: State of the nation, *Business Intelligence*; and Woodcock, N, Starkey, M, Stone, M, Weston, P and Ozimek, J (2001) The State of the Nation II – 2002: How companies are creating and destroying economic value through customer management, QCi

4 Stone, M, Starkey, M and Woodcock, N (2000) The Customer Management Scorecard: State of the nation, *Business Intelligence*

5 Unpublished QCi research in Europe and AP, 2000

6 Forrester Research, Inc (2001) *Canada's Big Banks Unravel*, May

Part 2

Where are we now in e-business?

4

E-business impact on customer management in financial services: an overview

Alison Spottiswoode and Abdelouahed El Marouani

WHAT IS E-BUSINESS?

There are many definitions of e-business. In this chapter, we use the definition of Lou Gerstner, former CEO of IBM: 'e-business is a fundamental in the way that business will be done – aided, abetted, supported, and enabled by technology'. E-business is *not* just the World Wide Web. E-business is exploiting e-business technologies (eg intranets, portals, content management, middleware, mobile) to enhance shareholder return by:

- transforming key processes to compete in new, faster, better ways, including via multi-channels;
- breaking traditional business model paradigms;
- creating and leveraging brand experiences;
- optimizing interactions with all stakeholders ;
- leveraging knowledge to establish sustainable competitive advantage.

Whilst many financial services organizations have kicked off scores of e-business initiatives, many are still only scratching the surface in realizing the full value of e-business. Figure 4.1 gives the results of a recent IBM survey.

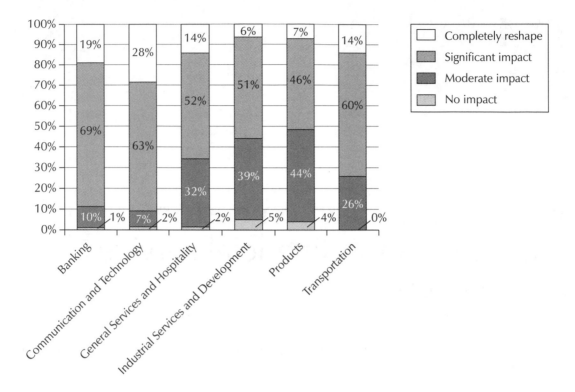

Figure 4.1 Impact of e-business on different industries

E-BUSINESS CUSTOMER IMPACT

Chief executive officers around the world, in all industries, believe that electronic business will significantly affect the way in which business is conducted in the future. Eighty-eight per cent of senior managers in banking believe that e-business will significantly impact or completely reshape their respective industries. Judicious use of e-business impacts an institution's interaction with its customer interactions in a wide variety of areas:

- **New distribution channels** – new distribution channels are created through the use of pervasive technologies – technologies that allow customers to be reached anywhere, from anywhere. E-business also facilitates disintermediation, bypassing existing agency and intermediary networks, and has the power to disrupt existing value chains.
- **New markets** – once a brand has established a significant online following, new markets can be reached, and others can be created. Financial services sites enjoy the luxury of captive repeat business: if companies use a little imagination, it is not too difficult to divert their regular visitors to non-financial marketplaces. Egg, for example, has stretched its brand, and the Prudential's business, from credit cards and bank

accounts into not only a fund supermarket, but also a virtual department store. Egg also has partnerships with Boots and with Microsoft, the latter enabling Egg to market financial products though Microsoft's financial portal. Meanwhile, Microsoft is intent on translating its near-monopoly in PC operating system software into virtual monopoly on the Web, by linking Internet Explorer directly to its Web site. The consequently vast user base of msn.com (41.5 million users in Europe alone) gives the company enormous power to influence which of the billions of Web sites the user visits (such as Egg), influence which is quickly translated to revenue for Microsoft.

- **New business models** – e-business enables direct and simultaneous interaction between all parties in the value chain – buyers, sellers, information providers, regulators, etc. This has the potential to create disruptive business models such as e-marketplace. In financial services we see the most radical impact in the capital markets business, where the economic downturn has only served to accelerate the march of e-business. Much of capital markets' trading is by nature virtual, and, for example, we see expensive brokers rapidly being disintermediated by real-time e-matching of bids and quotes followed by automated trading. Over the past few years we have witnessed the stock trading value chain collapse, accompanied by a loss of millions in revenue from the brokers and market-makers who used to hold sway. Another example of new business models is in insurance, where e-business enables the 'pay-as-you go' business model, where customers pay insurance based on car usage in terms not just of mileage but also location and speed.

- **Transparent marketplace** – in its ultimate incarnation, the World Wide Web offers unlimited information about an unlimited number of products and services to the entire population of the world. Where this is applied to virtual products, such as bank accounts or stock trades, in principle the entire value chain becomes transparent. Buyers can have access to real-time information on current prices, interest rates, commission charges and can at any time select the most advantageous deal. In a transparent market, only the fittest will survive: only those suppliers with the most responsive products and service coupled with the lowest cost bases will be able to compete. One current example is Screentrade, Britain's largest insurance site, which compares prices from multiple insurers providers instantly.

- **E-CRM** – electronic interactions with customers are by nature 100 per cent computer-recorded. Every customer action can be tracked, yielding far more information about customers than available in the past. Coupled with the 'deep computing' capabilities of modern technology, individuals can be analysed and targeted on a one-to-one basis in a way never possible hitherto. Given that the 'transparent marketplace' is some way off, in the meantime e-CRM offers a powerful means of attracting and retaining customers.

- **Reduced costs and improved service** – last but by no means least, e-business facilitates lower prices by reducing operational costs, whilst enabling better customer service and product flexibility through business optimization. E-business has a major impact not just at the point of customer sales and service, as commonly understood. Virtually every process undertaken by a financial institution can be made radically more effective and efficient through rapid, tactical e-automation, knowledge management and self-service. This is probably the most powerful and simultaneously least understood, most under-exploited area of e-business in the financial services arena.

CRITICAL SUCCESS FACTORS

The critical success factors in exploiting e-business to enhance customer management include:

- **Value proposition** – the products and services offered must add up to a truly compelling value proposition for the target audience.
- **Trusted brand** – probably the most undervalued asset in the dot.com boom. Interacting with a computer is of itself highly impersonal – users of financial services on the Internet need far more than the contents of a Web page in which to place their trust.
- **Seamless multi-channel customer management** – Web customers of financial services were until very recently customers of the branch and call centre. Now they also wish to communicate through the Web, e-mail and mobile. To succeed, financial institutions must not only offer sales and services over all channels, both physical and virtual, but also offer seamless service over them all.
- **Web-site quality** – there are many aspects of quality in Web sites, for example usability, 'stickiness', resilience, security, continuity of service. All must be of a high standard if the e-business value proposition is to be well received in practice.
- **Culture/Language/Geography** – despite the global nature of the World Wide Web, the reality is that geography and ethnicity create huge differences in culture and of course language. Successful e-businesses such as AOL and Amazon recognize that different Web sites are required for different audiences, and have both a US and UK version of their sites, recognizing the marked differences between language and culture between these two English-speaking countries.

E-BUSINESS STATES AND TRANSFORMATIONS

Typically, existing businesses progress pragmatically through a number of states in their exploitation of the Internet. These are characterized below as six 'Internet states'. Businesses move from state to state according to their organization's needs or goals. In larger institutions it is quite normal to find different business units in wildly different

Internet states. It is not uncommon to find institutions with an advanced, successful Internet financial services arm, where the vast majority of its employees do not even have access to an intranet.

Internet states

Briefly, the six states may be summarized as follows. Each state assumes the existence of all of the previous ones:

0   Access – some people or everyone has access to the Internet, usually just for e-mail. A very simple Web site may be maintained

I   Publish – a 'static' multi-page Web site for information purposes only.

II   Transact – Web site supports one- or two-way transactions with the end user, but does not imply seamless processing of transactions. For example, for many years Dell Computers retyped Web orders onto their internal systems for processing.

III   Integrate internally – use of e-business to transform internal organization and processes, radically reducing costs and optimizing the business. Very few companies in any industry have made significant progress in this, with the notable exception of IBM, with financial institutions being especially slow to adapt in this area.

IV   Integrate externally – use of e-business to create a seamless, transparent process across the entire value chain, from customer through intermediary through all supplier tiers. This is possibly even more rare, with the shining example of Cisco Systems where 70 per cent of orders are not 'touched' by the organization. Cisco has achieved revenue per employee of nearly twice its nearest rival.

V   Adapt dynamically – use of Internet technologies as the foundation for operating in a digital, virtual community. For example, a fully e- integrated institution can seamlessly in-source or outsource processing functions as demanded by market conditions and changing company structures.

Drivers between states

Primary drivers for continued investment and movement between states are usually organizational capabilities, rather than technical capabilities. The extent to which different factors drive institutions to move between states is illustrated in Table 4.1.

Table 4.1 Factors that drive institutions to move between states of exploitation of Internet

Driver	Issue	0 to I	I to II	II to III	III to IV	IV to V
Market development	Broaden reach of business to new markets, geographies, respond to competitive pressures, etc	◐	●	◐	●	●
Customer support	Improved customer services and with use of self-service application	◐	●	●	●	
Image	Improved customer perception	◐	●	●	●	
Product development	Deliver great product differentiation and new value	◐	●	●	●	
Cost reduction	Reduce costs of sales and marketing, increase bargaining power for purchasing costs, by turning fixed costs into variable costs (out-sourcing)	○	◐	●	●	
Productivity	Improve employee and business productivity by out-sourcing non-core skills and functions	○	◐	●	●	
Competitive positioning	To get there first and to raise barriers to others entering market	○	◐	◐	●	
Financial	Improve revenue and profitability, then create new alliances to manage margins	○	◐	◐	●	
Management focus	Improve management focus by reducing effort on non-core skills	○	◐	◐	●	
Business diversification	Participate new business ventures that exploit core skills – rebirth of re-intermediation and new horizontal integration	○	○	◐	●	
Virtual corporation	Reduce activities of the company to core competencies only	○	○	○	◐	

Barriers between states

There are many reasons why organizations find difficulty in moving between states: the impact of the different barriers is shown in Table 4.2.

THE STATE OF E-BUSINESS IN FINANCIAL SERVICES

E-business in financial services has had a mixed first few years. Generally most financial institutions have progressed to Internet state II, transacting online with their customers, but have had enormous difficulty moving successfully to state III, integrating internally. Succinctly put by the chief operating officer of a large financial institution, 'the essence is properly e-enabling all of our business areas, including HR, finance and everything else. Without this we won't be able to go through to the new world. It's as simple as that.' We believe that success or failure in exploiting e-business technologies will be a major differentiator in financial services shareholder value over the next five years.

Table 4.2 Barriers to moving between states

Barrier	Issue	0 to I	I to II	II to III	III to IV	IV to V
Offerings	Half of all small firms believe they do not have products and/or services that are readily sold via the Web	○	●			
Security	Level of data security currently available on the Internet for busines transactions may limit the scope of those transactions	○	●	◐	●	●
Privacy	The complexity, cost and legal issues involved in managing and delivering privacy to customers	○	●	○	●	●
ROI	Perception that the cost is greater than the benefit	○	●	●	●	●
Skills/ Complexity	Organizations have to have the skills to imagine, understand, build, implement, run and interpret the technology and its benefits	○	◐	●	●	●
Budget cycle	The way the company budgets can be seen to discourage new and reactive projects	○	◐	●	●	●
Technology	Lack of appropriate technology, including common standards and lack of infrastructure needed to facilitate e-business, as well as poor experience of someone else running it for you		◐	●	●	●
Business culture	There is a need to be able, and willing, to focus on and explore new e-business opportunities	○	○	◐	●	●
External relationships	There may be existing relationships, contracts or business deals that inhibit e-business action now. Some key partners may not even be ready	○	○	○	●	●
Competitive pressures	Fear of the commoditization of the products and services, where only price differentiates them or where their business becomes transparent	○	◐	○	●	●
Poor experience	First, second or even third-hand experience of the 'business value' of the Internet	○	◐	○	●	●
Lock-in	Fear of 'lock-in' to a partner or e-market through integration of business-critical processes/applications	○	○	○	●	●
e-market liquidity	Insufficient liquidity (participation) in relevant e-markets to justify the costs of entry	○	○	○	●	●
Legal or governmental	Some legal, governmental or even tax issues can be seen to inhibit e-business opportunity	○	○	○	◐	●

BANKING

Most banks have embraced the concept of transacting online with customers, lured by the obvious advantages of customer self-service. All the major banks have established online banking presence, and provide basic online services to consumers, and many have a strategy to add additional offerings. Some have developed new brands (eg cahoot from Abbey National in the UK) while others have strengthened their brand with online successes (eg HSBC, Lloyds TSB, CIBC in Canada). Many retail banks also offer some online services to corporate customers and are slowly migrating those services to the Web (eg cash management and foreign currency exchange). However, existing banks must wrestle with the dilemma that, whilst online customers transact at low cost, the cost of creating and managing online channels is often merely additive to that of sustaining existing ones. New Internet banks base their value propositions on better rates to consumers, and can happily operate without branches, or perhaps collaborate with existing retail outlet chains, giving them an inherent cost advantage.

Leading banks are now using e-business to integrate internally, transforming their processes to be an e-business. In addition to e-commerce, UK banks are reporting the first impacts of online procurement, Web service delivery, and even more complex processes like trade finance. Whilst many banks have succeeded in the first step of implementing e-systems, very few have made the process and organizational changes required to realize the benefits of internal integration. A few banks recognize the next wave of opportunity in e-markets both as participant in financial e-markets and as supplier of financial services to e-markets such as payments and authentication. IBM believes the trust and confidence typically placed in banks can be leveraged in e-commerce and e-markets in areas such as payments, fraud and privacy, risk assessment, and protection of digital assets. Wise financial institutions will also extend their trusted brand into new markets opened up by the Internet, through judicious partnerships.

Online corporate banks

Corporate banks have used proprietary electronic systems since the early 1980s to exchange data with their clients, mainly for cash management and payment services and custody services. As a result, corporate banks were late in starting to use the Internet and e-business technologies. Online business banking platforms remain poorly developed. However, corporate banking is catching up rapidly with retail banking which had the first-mover advantage.

Online brokerage: the leading edge of innovation

The astonishing growth of online trading in the USA demonstrates how rapidly an online transacting value proposition can move markets and redefine competition. Over the past five years, online trading has grown to encompass one-third of all stock trades by individuals in North America, and it is expected to account for fully half of such trades by 2002.

The leaders in providing brokerage services continually invest in developing their execution and advice capabilities. Charles Schwab is one of the leaders in this practice. In Europe, unlike in the United States, there has been a bypass of the 'full service' brokerages directly to Internet brokerages. Full service brokerage firms are now beginning to compete on the Web, and the innovators are moving to wireless access.

In the USA, the growth of online trading has driven rapid evolution of the market. Price competition has quickly commoditized basic trading executions, driving firms to expand into new services and sectors – including banking, consumer lending, financial planning and insurance – to gather new assets and generate new revenue streams. One of the most important points of competition has turned out to be multi-channel distribution, which has favoured a few incumbent firms that have executed successful hybrid strategies.

At the end of 1999, 40 per cent of all online accounts and 70 per cent of online assets in the USA were controlled by two incumbent firms, discount broker Charles Schwab and mutual fund giant Fidelity Investments.

Online insurance

Leading insurance retailers significantly trail behind their banking and non-financial services retailers in their movement to the Web. Web start-ups such as INSWEB, Screentrade and Charcol On-line have pioneered online insurance sales; however, consumer acceptance has been sluggish in comparison to online banking and insurance telephone sales. In both Europe and the USA, online sales have trailed behind other sectors. At present, a small percentage (approximately 1 per cent in Europe) of insurance sales are made online, although very often the Web is used as source of information and deals are closed off-line (approximately 6 per cent in Europe). In the USA, direct online sales of auto, home and term insurance were only $400 million compared to Internet-*influenced* sales of $1.8 billion in 2000. These figures are projected to reach $4 billion and $7 billion respectively in 2003. However, online delivery has grown rapidly for commodity products like automobile insurance and term life insurance, particularly in countries with well-established direct insurance markets. Sweden and the UK have achieved high penetration rates of 22 per cent and 19 per cent, respectively, for automobile insurance. For life insurance and pension products, which are more complex and consultative, online sales rates have been much lower, with Sweden and the UK leading Europe at 3 per cent. As with mortgage lending, e-business will put increased pressure on insurance prices, as it cuts distribution costs for providers and creates price transparency.

Traditional insurance companies show a marked inability to progress to Internet state III: internal integration. Despite feeling intense competitive and regulatory cost pressures, they find enormous difficulty in taking the cross-organizational actions required to realize the considerable cost and business benefits of becoming an e-enterprise. Culturally, insurance companies find it almost impossible to implement the kind of radical change facilitated by e-business.

We are already seeing aggressive on-line insurance plays by:

- direct brokers, such as Direct Line, who provide most of the sales and servicing capability online;
- traditional banks (such as Lloyds TSB who recently bought the Screentrade brand);
- stand-alone Internet banks such as Egg;
- non-financial players such as Tesco.

Unless traditional insurance product providers commit to being best-of-breed, which means exploiting e-technologies throughout their business, they risk being left high and dry as slowly the off-line tide goes out.

Home lending

New secured lending players are moving into the online marketplace and many existing providers plan to accept online applications by the end of 2000. Leaders in online home lending, such as e-loan, are moving to provide the full breadth of services, surrounding the home buying life event with well-designed user interfaces. Online mortgage is moving toward near real-time approvals, vastly reduced cycle times, performance guarantees, and integration into the overall home buying process. However, there are significant barriers to market growth in this area:

- Low online closing rates: most people still want to close the deal personally with a broker.
- As prices decrease across the board and automation commoditizes mortgages, low prices will no longer guarantee a large market share of new business.
- Lenders are often careful with their own direct selling via the Internet for fear of alienating their brokers, who facilitate most of their business.

Wealth management: a growing online opportunity

An estimated 7 million High Net Wealth Individuals (HNWI) in the world hold more than $1 million in financial assets wealth, totalling approximately $25.5 trillion. This is growing at a great pace. Wealth management is a fast-growing line of business, with many new players challenging traditional service providers in order to capitalize on this highly lucrative market. In Chapters 33–36 we assess this market in depth.

New Web-based financial institutions

Whilst traditional financial institutions are lagging in e-business implementation, a few more dynamic organizations have embraced the technology. They build innovative e-business models, using e-technologies to offer new value propositions, streamline operations, and amputate the traditional way of doing business. They combine this with the best aspects of the traditional infrastructures, thereby achieving cost savings and positioning themselves to compete aggressively and usually with success. One such example is Intelligent Finance, which combines the financial muscle and trusted brand of Halifax with a Web-based proposition, complete with competitive interest rates and low commissions.

E-FINANCIAL SERVICES LANDSCAPE IN THE EARLY 21ST CENTURY

The next few years will witness a fundamental shift in the financial services landscape, away from product-centric, vertically integrated financial services companies towards customer-centric aggregators of diverse products, with many financial services institutions firmly cast in the role of manufacturer. Catalysed by the World Wide Web, we see vertical integration, grounded in selling and servicing a set of products, gradually giving way to companies breaking up to strive for excellence in one or more of three specialist roles:

1. Customer or distribution centric, dedicated to serving customers and agnostic with regard to products, seeking only the best for its customers. This business model will require:

- in-depth knowledge of customers (suppliers and users of funds);
- ability to tailor to customer situations and market appetite;
- premier levels of customer service;
- significant alternative delivery technologies;
- virtual agency capabilities acting on behalf of the customer in accordance with pre-agreed rule sets.

Often financial institutions believe that the customer-centric role is simply the ability to have a 'single view of the customer' and cross-sell their products effectively. This is not what is meant here. Customer centricity involves driving the entire company to serve the customer, deriving profits from relationships with suppliers. Customer-centric e-companies offer the best products for that customer available in the marketplace, irrespective of where they originate.

2. Product/service manufacturer, creating flexible, tailored products at exceptionally good value. This business model requires:

- increasingly dynamic platform;

- instantaneous customized 'shelf' registrations;
- 'best practice' risk management and risk engineering.

3. Information/transaction/infrastructure specialist, processing or managing information faster and more cost-effectively than the competition. This business model requires excellence in:

- information management;
- customer charging mechanisms;
- transaction processing;
- custody and cash management.

The emergence of powerful, customer-centric specialists on the Web, such as AOL and Microsoft, poses a significant threat for financial services companies in the longer term. These sites can take several roles, all of which place traditional financial institutions at risk:

- aggregators, demanding low-cost products and first-class service;
- portals, determining which financial services sites will receive their customers' custom, and which will not;
- virtual agents, demanding high commission rates, leaving little for the product manufacturer (the online equivalent of today's supermarket chains).

Whichever specialist role financial institutions choose to play, they must commit to being the best in that arena, or in the long term they will not be able to compete on the Web.

EMERGING TECHNOLOGIES

Internet technologies have created a seismic shift in 'the art of the possible' in terms of business reach and process efficiency. Emerging technologies – or 'next generation e-business technologies' – have the potential, if wisely applied, to catalyse a transformation in 'the art of the possible' in customer relationship management. In future, customers will grow to expect their online financial services provider to be fast, always on, everywhere, natural, intelligent, easy and trusted. Five emerging technologies will represent an increasingly compelling force for change in financial services customer interactions:

- **Deep computing creating intelligence** – 'deep' computing will provide business decision makers with the ability to analyse customer behaviours in depth and develop new approaches to the marketplace based on solutions to very complex problems.

- **Pervasive computing creating intelligence everywhere** – pervasive computing will enable 'anytime, anywhere' access to information via a panoply of non-PC devices and Europe will lead the way:
  - 'smart devices' and 'smart appliances' are emerging to simplify the delivery of information;
  - computing power will pervade our cars, homes, and coat pockets;
  - mobile access to Internet enabled by WAP, GPRS and UMTS technology.
- **Volume/velocity generating bandwidth** – the development of increasing bandwidth for accessing the network will enable new applications and drive Internet penetration.
- **Universal access via 24/7/365 connection** – continuous, 'always on', access to information.
- **Sensing** – technologies such as the Global Positioning System (GPS) are the first step of the emerging sensing technologies. Using sensing devices will allow automatic interaction between buyers and sellers. For example, embedded sensing technologies in cars provide insurance tools to offer car security, enabling the insurer to offer immediate and accurate information and take appropriate actions in case of emergency.

Existing institutions may feel hampered by large, expensive legacy systems, finding it hard to adapt their business model to the changing requirements for greater efficiency, speed and quality of service. Indeed, financial institutions have often created stand-alone subsidiaries so that they can work with new, independent systems to reduce reliance on legacy systems. However, this need not be the case, since the latest technology architecture allows new and old systems to work effectively together.

The reality is that companies' ability to exploit emerging technologies will be limited only by their imagination. Institutions will be able to create significant competitive advantage through judicious use of emerging technologies, and this should drive business strategy, not simply enable it.

CHALLENGES FACED BY ORGANIZATIONS IN THE FINANCIAL SERVICES SECTOR

Exploitation of e-business in financial services over the past few years somewhat resembles a curate's egg: good in parts. Whilst there have been brave and successful forays into the world of online financial sales and service, and the establishment of efficient new trading marketplaces, institutions by and large have not been able to embrace fully the power of e-business to transform both the external business landscape and the internal organization. Most worryingly perhaps, financial institutions typically have no clear enterprise-wide strategy to position themselves as a major player in the future e-economy and as a result, risk full disintermediation. Traditional financial institutions are lagging in e-business exploitation, and huge threats are looming on the horizon. Typically, financial firms are using e-business technologies only as a new channel of distribution of traditional business. Current slow progress is attributable to a combination of several factors:

- An understandable, but ultimately unsustainable, unwillingness to cannibalize existing business through online competition. The reality is that it is only a question of time before online competition will eat into existing off-line business – the only ponderable is for how long will the existing business stay viable?
- Due to the 'vertically integrated' product-centric business structure adopted by many financial institutions, companies have great difficulty reorienting themselves to the demands of customer centricity inherent in successful, sustainable Web businesses.
- Financial services companies often underestimate the potential contribution to shareholder value of exploitation of e-technologies to transform themselves into an e-business, thereby both cutting costs and optimizing business flexibility.
- The Board has not set the agenda for e-based deployment within the organization and consequently e-initiatives are done in a piecemeal fashion. Often this can lead to multifarious 'e- business' initiatives in different business units, many with overlapping scope and target customers as well as incompatible underlying technologies.
- Where e-initiatives have been implemented, they have often been technology rather than business led, and consequently business transformation aspects of process, culture and organizational change have not been addressed, leading to lower than anticipated benefits.

WHAT SHOULD FINANCIAL SERVICE COMPANIES FOCUS ON FOR A SUSTAINABLE FUTURE E-ENABLED GAIN?

To be a long-term player in this business environment, financial institutions must decide in which business models they see their future, then formulate and execute a clear strategy for excellence in their chosen arena(s). If necessary, new businesses must be created to supplant, over time, existing operations that do not fit with the chosen strategy. Those that do not plan now for their metamorphosis are likely to end up as the hapless 'boiled frog': sitting still whilst the water heats, slowly but surely boiling the blood until it stops flowing. In the short to medium term, there are some golden rules to which financial institutions should adhere to achieve sustainable e-business value:

- Take a coordinated, cross-enterprise approach to e-business initiatives, recognizing similarities in business function and customers exist across different business silos.

- Adopt a common e-infrastructure, which is open and compatible both with legacy systems and emerging technologies.
- Exploit Internet technologies to optimize the business and drive out cost – as Lou Gerstner, CEO of IBM, says: 'It's not about one dot.com, it's about joining up all the dots across the enterprise.'
- Execution is everything – insist that delivery is professionally managed across every aspect of the 'golden triangle' of organization, process and technology.
- Be ruthlessly business-driven in e-business initiatives, and closely measure business benefits arising from them.

CONCLUSION

The impact of the Internet on the financial services industry has already been rapid and profound. The pace of change may not have lived up to the heady predictions of 1999, however, we believe the nature of the change in the financial services marketplace over the next 10 years will be every bit as radical as first predicted.

Financial institutions wishing to survive and thrive into the second decade of the 21st century must recognize that e-business and emerging technologies are not just 'technology enablers': they drive business strategy and 'the art of the possible'. To be successful in gaining e-business value, increasingly synonymous with the value of the business itself, companies must lay a place at the 'top table' of business strategy for e-business and emerging technologies. They must also commit to embedding e-technologies into the very essence of their business to ensure they are positioned as both low-cost operators and, simultaneously, highly responsive to changing customer needs and marketplace conditions.

5

The impact of e-business on financial services marketing and marketers

Alan Tapp, Clive Nancarrow, Merlin Stone, John Stubbs and Bryan Foss

INTRODUCTION AND SUMMARY

In this chapter, we summarize the implications for financial services marketing and marketers of a very recent study carried out for the UK's Chartered Institute of Marketing by Bristol Business School.[1] The research involved analysis of the literature and qualitative research. For the qualitative research participants were drawn from senior marketing management in client companies, systems suppliers, management consultancies and marketing service agencies. The main insights are described below.

New technology is changing both the internal and external landscape of business. Specifically, there are two mechanisms taking place that are acutely important for the marketing role. First, within companies, there is an evolution in the way the value chain is constructed. Electronic technology is acting as a lubricant, helping previously discrete functional areas to work in concert. Internally, 'e' is acting by 'oiling the wheels' and this, along with the accompanying senior management spotlight, will encourage functions to act in concert. Secondly, the Internet has lowered the costs and increased the ease of information gathering by customers, thus shifting market power slowly but inexorably their way.

These forces of change facilitated by new technology mean that the strategic emphasis of marketing must adapt. Whether this necessitates a radical *new* model of marketing is open to debate. We certainly found a body of opinion that two things need to happen. First, as power shifts to customers, the ability to sense what they want and to gain insights into how the firm solves their problems will be vital. Marketers have appropriated the language, but not always the substance, of understanding customer needs. In a world with low levels of churn and high inertia, they may have got away with this, but the balance of power has shifted. Secondly, the philosophy of marketing as a strategic way of doing business – putting customer value at the heart of internal debate – needs to be operationalized. Internally, enabled by new technology, functional areas are breaking down barriers between themselves. This is leading to important debates and decisions about the key processes that deliver customer value – operations, innovation, service delivery. At the moment these debates are largely taking place in a 'marketing vacuum'. It is vital that marketing is at least part of, if not leading, that debate.

Given these imperatives for change, how are those responsible for marketing responding? Some of our research respondents highlighted major concerns about the willingness and ability of marketers to seize the leadership role that many companies are crying out for. Marketers seem to have distanced themselves from the internal changes, and the danger is they will get left behind as the firm moves forward. Respondents told us that the marketing 'mid-life crisis' is far from over. While marketers have taken on board the importance of new media in marketing communications, their role in driving forward the company–customer interface strategy is far from secure. A recent survey found marketers' influence over company Web sites to be declining. Meanwhile, strategically, marketers just do not seem willing to act as facilitators in encouraging a company-wide market orientation. This is a pity, because new technology is providing an impetus and an opportunity for different functional areas to work as teams to a greater extent than was hitherto possible.

Many respondents saw e-business as an opportunity for marketers to 'get back in the game' (improve their place in the political pecking order) but stressed that first marketers must re-invest in their skills in a number of areas. Naturally, the ability to think strategically came high up the list (marketers were collectively advised to 'do an MBA'), but right at the top of the list were *decision-making* skills. In the context of a working environment enabled nowadays by knowledge management systems, research and hi-tech measurement, marketers often exhibit shortcomings in their decision-making processes. They were regarded as having a tendency to 'wing it', perhaps by reacting instinctively or through habit in making decisions. The culture was not to worry about the systematic gathering of information and the tapping of available knowledge and insight. Linked to this was an attitude that measurement and learning from the experiences came a poor second to running another campaign. All very well with the next quarter's targets coming up, but respondents emphasized that senior managers now increasingly expect resource allocation decisions to be made on the basis of sound measurement and intelligent analysis. Directors are increasingly asking themselves: with all this technology, are you telling me you still can't justify your spend?

Together with the shift in power to customers, the pressures on measurement imply that the future requires a different type of person to take up the reins of marketing. The new marketer will need stronger:

- analytical skills to make the most of the increased volume and nature of available data;
- quantitative skills – an ability to test, learn and re-test;
- qualitative skills – to define problems, understand concepts and results.

It is hoped the new 'customer insight' departments springing up will reflect a genuine change rather than a cosmetic change for traditional market research and that eclecticism (the ability to examine phenomena from different perspectives), 'prosearch' (the mindset that considers future scenarios rather than simply researches the past) and bricolage (genuine expertise in a wide range of both traditional and innovative research techniques) will be planned for in HR terms. We must not lose sight of the customers' needs and their likely response to new types of contact via new media and attempts to manage them via CRM. We should also not lose sight of problems in fulfilment and of customers' concerns about privacy. Finally, the shift of power to customers has created the need to seriously consider the concept of 'permission marketing' and in newly created 'customer insight' functions the concept of 'permission customer researching'.

Some respondents felt that knowledge management (KM) was a very important emerging culture. To begin with, the new marketer will need to be proficient at using KM tools and techniques, and be comfortable with KM as a culture of working. More profoundly, however, marketers can use this as a springboard to take a leading role in the supply of customer insights to the firm using company-wide KM systems. It could be that internal KM systems, probably based on the intranet, will be a political battleground in the near future. IBM employees already regard their intranet as their second most important source of information behind the 'grapevine'. The struggle to manage their own tacit knowledge – their own core competences – will be a key growth area over the next decade or two.

The changes outlined so far put into perspective the much-heralded 'paradigm shifts' and 'new models' that accompanied the launch of a thousand dot.coms. Eighteen months later the business world is a sadder and wiser place. In this research project we interviewed leading practitioners who confirmed to us that theories of business change espoused in recent editions of *Harvard Business Review* and elsewhere were, by and large, well ahead of practice. The simple Web-site model has at best a mixed track record, while the much hyped 'infomediary' concept, though still theoretically appealing, has yet to get off the ground. Equally appealing on paper is the notion that new technology will enable the formation of complex networks and alliances between enterprises, redefining value chains at bewildering speed. This was met with raised eyebrows and a weary smile in some quarters. Quite simply, large organizations rarely have the fluidity to move that quickly. One is reminded of the many claims (on a smaller scale) that accompanied the introduction of database and direct marketing into mainstream sectors in the late 1980s and early 1990s. We were told then that all marketing would be data driven within a decade. As we know, that has not happened. It is silly to predict that paradigm shifts driven by new technology will never happen, but it's perhaps sensible to assume that large-scale change will take time to show through.

Tactically too, things have changed for marketing. New media – Web sites, e-mail, mobile media – are already quite well developed, and starting to be used regularly by customers. As channels, these media are providing added customer 'touch points' and added internal complexity for firms to manage. Executives are rightly excited by the continuing opportunities for new ways of doing business that new technology will bring, particularly in the mobile Internet area.

Because it has enabled both external and internal change, new technology has presented companies with a situation of perhaps unprecedented complexity. At the time of writing, many firms are in the position of attempting to make sense of all these changes. Marketers need to be engaging with these debates, but they can only do so if they are listened to. This will only happen if they are prepared to re-invest in traditional skills and subsequently invest in new skills. In the face of change from e-business, marketers do not necessarily need to adopt a major new model of working, instead what many need to do is adapt and implement the existing model more effectively.

THE ROLE OF MARKETING

Our starting premise is that the marketing function is not operating at a high or strategic level in most companies. There is plenty of evidence in support of this assertion; suffice it here to remind ourselves that only 13 out of 100 CEOs of the FTSE top 100 firms have any marketing background, and only about 20 of these firms have a marketing director on the main board. This may be due to the dominance of one type of marketer, focusing heavily on the marketing communications sphere, and 'marketing' to them largely means 'marketing communications'. Arguably most marketing departments are in reality leaning towards this pole. E-business will mean 'e' as a medium or maybe as a channel, but not as a business-wide enabler. It is a rare breed of marketer that has a company-wide perspective. They understand corporate strategy; they see where marketing fits into the wider corporate picture; they see a key marketing role as infusing part-time marketers with an understanding and appreciation of customers' needs and so on.

Of course, these scenarios were true before e-business came along. But e-business has accelerated the need for marketers to do something about them. The impression gained from both very recent literature and our respondents is that the impact of new technology internally within a firm is much greater than its impact on the company–customer interface. E-related technology has and will continue to act as an enabler to faster organizational and strategic change. However, when we asked about the impact of e-business on marketing as a function, the replies fell into two camps. Some felt that all functions were struggling equally in the face of all this change. But those who tended to see marketing from a company-wide perspective felt that while marketing was arguably more important than ever, their concern was that this role was not being carried out by marketers. They felt that it was therefore vital for marketers to engage with the internal debate. Some respondents thought that e-business was acting to break down silos, but marketers are continuing to divorce themselves from business processes.

The respondents argued that new technology is increasing the urgency of solving these problems. They argued that the next few years will be a time of great change in firms, with increased horizontal working, rapidly evolving and dissolving strategies, and technology-led paradigm shifts. They felt that marketers were not engaging as they should be with these *internal* debates. Rather, many marketers were doing what they have always done: fiddling about with customer Web sites and other new media, but *not* tackling the bigger questions: delivering value to the customer, customer service, competitive strategy, positioning. Rather alarmingly, some respondents felt that these deficiencies would become much more apparent in the near future as firms started using new technology to act in a more customer-focused, strategic manner. The danger was that they saw marketing being bypassed.

Discussions revealed that one possible strategy is to concentrate on and look for a leadership role in *internal communications* (for example, the apparent revolution within IBM has been crucially enabled by the intranet). It was felt that if marketers can own this, they can start to lead internally – lead with a compelling story about customers and what they want from the firm, how it can solve their problems for them, and telling and retelling this story to everyone – IT, finance, service, operations, sales, and so on. But first they need to address the credibility question 'Why should anyone listen to marketers'?

Other people implied that the traditional skills of marketing – segmentation, targeting and positioning, and branding – will become even more important. This isn't to imply that all the problems in life lie at marketing's door. Some respondents in financial services sectors took a different perspective:

> I would say it slightly differently. I would say that there aren't enough people with those [e] skills about generally, not just within marketing.

And this led to:

> You are seeing more turnover of staff and more recruitment… recruitment itself is becoming more of a key skill in financial services.
>
> IT consultant, financial sector

Interestingly, the researchers sometimes got the definite impression that increasingly the marketing function is breaking down into other functions – when attempts were made to isolate marketing in the discussion respondents sometimes resisted this and rewrote the question in their minds.

THE SHIFT OF POWER TO CUSTOMERS – IMPLICATIONS FOR MARKETERS

Our start point here is that the Internet has triggered a number of mechanisms that will, over time, shift power from enterprises to customers:

- 'transparency', that is, the ease with which comparisons can be made between competitive offerings;
- the ease with which customers can search for information that will enable them to make these comparisons; and
- the formation of powerful customer communities that are independent of companies.

There is already evidence that these mechanisms are starting to have an effect – evidence of shopping around, better-informed customers, and so on. This power shift is well documented in the marketing literature but it must be said that the issue was not clear-cut with our respondents. While some agreed that power would shift to customers in the future, others felt that consumers in particular would be less inclined to organize themselves effectively. However, respondents exhibited quite a degree of uncertainty in forecasting this future scenario.

THE DIRECT MARKETING ANALOGY

Throughout this research there have been a number of parallels between what forecasters are saying now about e-commerce, and what forecasters and gurus said throughout the 1990s about direct marketing. Amongst other things, these writers predicted that:

- within a few years practically all contact with customers would be data driven;
- 1–1 relationships will be key;
- marketers will be able to measure what they do and relate those measures to customers – new and existing. They will be able to establish the impact on profitability of individual customers. Resource allocation decisions will then be much better informed.

As the last decade drew to a close, these confident predictions began to dry up. As many respondents with experience of CRM were keen to tell us, these revolutionary practices haven't come to fruition because the forecasters and gurus hugely underestimated the practical difficulties of implementing advanced database marketing in the context of large multi-product, multi-channel organizations. In short, the changes didn't happen.

In reading much of the recent literature, it is striking how many similarities there are between what was said 10 years ago about direct marketing and what has been said recently about e-driven marketing (see, for example, reports by consultancies such as Gartner and Forrester). When this context was presented to respondents, overwhelmingly they agreed that there was a large reality gap between, on the one hand, the conference circuit, e-business consultants' report hype and, on the other, the position of most organizations to actually implement these strategies. In summary, and without appearing unduly sceptical, the message seems to be to treat such predictions with some caution.

NEW BUSINESS MODELS FOR OLD?

A plethora of models have been evolved to describe future e-business. They include:

- The basic Web-site model – using the Web to attract custom and sometimes to deliver the customer proposition.
- The rise of customer communities online and the need for real-time/contextual marketing. The picture here is of marketers using wireless Internet technology to send messages to customers that are timed to be appropriate to what the customer is doing at that moment. The C2C model is emerging in which consumers interact with each other, whether or not the community is company hosted. Powerful (and often negative) 'word of mouse' needs to be at least monitored by marketers to track perceptions of their brands.
- Infomediaries who act on behalf of consumers and allow customers, not suppliers, to control the process of going to market.
- Auctions/exchanges – particularly important in a B2B context, and, unlike many e-related models, already widely prevalent.
- The establishment of virtual companies/networks/alliances. Here the Internet facilitates multiple links between sellers, often quite simply by having click-through facilities from one Web site to another. The literature concentrates on a very few case studies such as CD Now and Amazon.com, and extrapolates these models to e-businesses across sectors.
- Slicker supply chain management models. Like auctions and exchanges, the use of e-technology to enable more efficient supply chain management processes appears to be relatively well established.

- 'Non-transaction revenue generation'. These models describe how dot.com firms attempt to make money not through the transaction that attracted the customer in the first place, but through another mechanism based on the customer's presence at the site. This mechanism could be relatively simple like advertising revenue, or a more complex version, for example using customer information as an asset.

In general, respondents were cautious, non-committal, often vague and sometimes indifferent to these supposed paradigm shifts. The authors believe that to some extent this is a symptom of two factors. Firstly, the dot.com crash of 2000 and continuing difficulties of the sector may have generated a more sceptical response to the idea that the Net will change everything. If we had undertaken this research 18 months ago we would have probably got very different responses, but things have changed. Here, we can return to the direct marketing analogy described above: large established firms have been too busy fighting their internal silo-related politics even to contemplate 'paradigm shifts'. For those who can execute these business models, the rewards can be great.

The original report contains much more on these different models. Some important points for financial services are these:

- Intermediation is made easier, because companies' systems can now talk to each other much more simply. Browser interfaces not only make human use easier, but have provided standards for interfacing between systems. So systems will be much less of a barrier to cooperation between companies. Also, the Web makes it easier for customers to browse through to higher-level suppliers, just by a single click.
- Marketers should no longer consider that they can do it all themselves, and consider a variety of alliances, often conflicting, and also realize that they'll often be allying with companies that compete for share of value add. The traditional idea of client–agency and supplier–distributor may start to look a bit ragged. They will stay at the core, but there will be a lot of interesting variations around the edge. This will be particularly true in markets where new media are being used, eg IDTV, mobile, where alliance and experiments are ways of reducing risk.
- In practice, networks/partnerships were very hard to make work at anything other than a transaction level.

Financial services has benefited from exploiting a variety of new models, because so often existing channels have made it hard to improve customer service. New ranges of services, eg wealth management, family management, will be much easier to provide, as the customer will be able to self-manage. This does not necessarily mean that incumbents will suffer, as they are getting quite smart at setting up Web-based operations.

THE IT/MARKETING INTERFACE

One of the key issues that has affected rapid implementation of IT-driven marketing has been the interface between the two silos of marketing and IT itself. Respondents certainly didn't need prompting to raise this important implementation issue. Respondents felt that the need for marketers to know at least something about the IT issues grows more acute. They felt that unless marketers can 'talk turkey' with IT people they have little chance of influencing the IT debate within companies. More fundamentally, marketers cannot control edifices like Web sites unless they know what the problems are.

A CIM survey (see www.cim.co.uk) of UK marketing professionals revealed that from a position of marketers controlling 70 per cent of sites 24 months ago, marketers were responsible for less than half (47 per cent) of company Web sites. While IT departments have made a small gain, customer service departments have more than doubled the number of sites that they are accountable for. The other side of the coin is that IT/e-development people often over-claim about their understanding of business issues and are reluctant to admit they do not know something in front of a big meeting. Is this a case of ignorance on both sides? Perhaps so, but it is interesting to note that IT people are increasingly educating themselves about marketing. A number of respondents, unprompted, pointed out a 'new breed' doing mixed IT/marketing Master's courses.

The sheer pace of technological change has outstripped firms' ability to keep up. Many new software packages have been launched, designed to integrate e-commerce with existing database and call-centre systems, but few companies can change their processes and the way they manage their people to keep pace.

THE WIRELESS INTERNET – REAL-TIME MARKETING?

When reading about the wireless Internet, it is easy to get very excited about the endless possibilities for marketing that this technology brings. There is little doubt that in future, if wireless networks spread to mass markets, they have the potential to change society. At the extreme end of this technology, the social and commercial implications of the so-called 'always on' wearable chip are huge. In brief, the picture being painted is that in the future:

- individuals will carry or wear many devices that have some form of computing capability and some other (multiple) function, for example mobile phones, combined cameras, music players or digital libraries;
- computing/networking will be embedded in a wide range of consumer products other than overt electronics, including clothes, food, toys and cars;

- wireless capability will vary between local personal networking within the home, etc, to worldwide via mobile networks;
- device prices will fall to a matter of a few dollars per item, making them affordable in mass markets;
- display technology will become a lot cheaper and more flexible – for example, retinal projection could allow in-built display in sunglasses;
- built-in global positioning system (GPS) technology will allow positioning to approximately 10 metres.

All this technology may undoubtedly provide exciting playthings for those who are so inclined. However, the notion of us all being receptive to an endless stream of messages – even if they are personalized – needs urgent research and testing before proceeding further. There was agreement that in business planning terms the wireless future is a high-risk one because of the uncertainty regarding the exact form of devices and applications and the uncertainty inherent in predicting consumer behaviour. That said, we were reminded by some respondents that most, if not all, of the above technologies have already been demonstrated in a laboratory. However, the hypothesis we propose is that it will be very difficult to foresee when most companies would be able to use personal data with sufficient precision to avoid mass marketing. Therefore the scenario of 'we know X about you and we see you just passed Y store' is a long way off for most firms (although there are some examples of advanced practice – one drinks company respondent described texting a promotion at certain bars to 'targeted consumers' from databases with mobile numbers). Respondents agreed that a more likely outcome is 'we see you have just passed Y store, here's a message. By the way, sorry if it's not relevant.'

Third-generation mobile technology promises an 'always on' service plus more than 160 characters of text plus video ads. Some debate was held with respondents about the extent to which consumers would actually want such approaches. Once again, the debate seems to centre on proactive marketing (managing customers) versus reactive marketing (let them manage you). The argument may be that with the 'always on' capability, we can plug into the messages as and when we want to. Respondents who travelled internationally had already experienced some 'real-time marketing' from their mobile phone company. 'Welcome to Australia, here's a list of good hotels near you now' is the sort of thing that is fast becoming standard.

However, respondents did not agree with the argument that we will actually want to be 'always on', with 'real time' messages beamed to us about a store while we travel past one. This caution seems justified: surfers are already showing that they do not wish to click on banner adverts while they surf – clickstream data is on a downward path.

MEASUREMENT AND CONTROL

The idea that new technology enables a revolution in the measurement of marketing activity certainly stimulated a lot of debate with respondents. There has been much hype in this area and the IT sector has, true to form, invented a new word for measurement – metrics – implying that a revolution is taking place, that online marketing is now 'scientific': ie there is a closed loop between action and response, due to the precision with which marketing spend can be related, at individual customer level, over time, to gross margin received. Key *strategic* measures are then identified as the cost of acquisition per customer, gross margin per customer over time (lifetime value), percentage of customers repeat-buying over time, and ultimately return on investment. This precision and control then allows tests of different resource allocation decisions.

Some respondents saw it mainly as a hype issue. Chapter 15 describes a study of customer retention in which it was demonstrated that marketers often did not think through the conceptual definitions of loyalty and retention and (so) measures used were of questionable validity. Other respondents argued that behind the hype is an issue of real substance. In short, they agreed that a direct marketing-style culture of measurement – test, think, adapt, test again – will be more widespread as a result of the Net. Many respondents think that we are moving to an age where testing/learning/change is more the norm, and that this cycle is faster than learning cycles used to be. Some also felt that electronics will increase the *visibility* of initiatives to senior managers, and that this will force marketers to become more professional about measurement and about what to measure. However, time after time respondents returned to the key problem – turning theory into practice. Most respondents agreed that measurement was vital in changing the culture of marketing. They linked the visibility of strategic measures (customer satisfaction, repeat purchasing, ROI) as key to changing marketers' focus from tactics to strategy. Views differed as to whether changes will actually happen. Once again there was a divide between the cynics who felt nothing would change, and the optimists whose feeling was that new technology will force more of a spotlight on marketers (it will be easier to see marketers' role in the process and easier to measure) and as a result professionalism will improve.

There is also evidence that in some companies, the 'right' marketers cannot be found, especially in those companies concerned with the technology involved with CRM and database management. There is some criticism that marketers are just not sufficiently numerate or quantitative. Some companies are recruiting geographers on the basis that they are sometimes seen to be able to think strategically but also to be more aware (perhaps through their heavy exposure to Geographical Information Systems (GIS) and related issues) of technical and statistical issues. Marketers might not need to 'do' the number crunching but it appears to be important for them to at least understand the principles in order to interact effectively with those who will – otherwise there is further concern that marketers will be bypassed. The pressure to be more accountable and measurable is perhaps leading to an over-emphasis on short-term returns for shareholders. If this is subordinating the central tenet of the CIM definition of the marketing concept, then it is not surprising that consumers themselves are increasingly cynical about marketing. Marketers are clearly becoming more cynical themselves about it.

So, we are moving towards a '(quantitative) data plentiful but not data rich' culture. The issues won't go away, however, and data skills will become more and more important. Worryingly, marketers remain remarkably poor at the key quantitative skills, data interpretation skills, and lack acumen about what to do with the data. If marketers are not equipped to engage with the new metrics of marketing measurement then others surely will. We do, however, believe that there is a danger of the balance shifting too far in the 'response rate' type of measurement. Indeed the argument proposed by the authors is that moving to a stronger culture of measurement should not blind us to the increased need to improve our culture of understanding. In short, the danger is 'measure everything, understand nothing'.

CUSTOMER INSIGHT

It was felt by many that while marketers do employ customer/market-understanding techniques to gain insights and inform decisions, they don't do as much as they probably should. Marketers' self-image as a profession is that we are the guardians of understanding customer needs and anticipating them: but some respondents felt that this was as much 'spin' as reality. As they put it: what percentage of the average marketer's job is spent gaining insight into customers? Marketing research should be a rich source of *customer insight* that aids decision making and stimulates new ideas; however, the industry may not be delivering as well as it should. The industry is undergoing an intensive period of soul-searching as competitive sources of marketing information bid for the attention and budgets of marketers. These competitors include suppliers of database information, marketing consultancies, independent planners, semiotics analysts and experts, and commentators on human behaviour (popular culture analysts, social psychologists and everyday psychologists).

CASE STUDY – A BANK

The case study below, based on an interview with a respondent, illustrates many of the findings presented in the report so far.

(SOURCE: INTERVIEW WITH RESPONDENT)

How do you/your clients use the Internet and related technology at the moment? Give some examples of the biggest successes and biggest problems/failures.

'Retail banking – biggest use is Online Banking. Going very well. Large number of customers, but not enough using it regularly. Lot have signed up and never used it. The intranet – several of them. Those that do, use it well. E-savings worked phenomenally well. Retention better than usual – easy to transfer it in. Ups activation rate.'

Has it changed the way you or your clients manage your/their marketing and customer service significantly (speed, scope and quality of processes, programmes, management of suppliers, measurement of results, etc)? If so, how? Please give examples.

'Increase in number of channels, split budget. Coherence hasn't deteriorated. Still thought of as an afterthought, but being considered, like call centres used to be. People are pushing boundaries about what they can do online. E-enable whole banking process. Branches aren't Internet-enabled. They don't have access to what customers can see, haven't even got an intranet. E-stuff is all head office. Fear from branches – taking away their jobs. See it as a direct threat, though it's a retention device for the branch.

Biggest grief – slowness in development time – no real acceleration of process. Not aware of how long it takes to set up good infrastructure for e-business and campaigns. Processes are weak, more departments involved than used to be, legal, compliance, IT, security as well as users. Security people are stuffed with work until the end of the year. Won't outsource because of paranoia. History has proved them right, eg savings. E is a small part of a total activity, but our branding seen as progressive. Constant focus on developing new services and features.

No measurement of results – needs a lot of improvement. Lamentable. Vignette (software which links access to Web content to subsequent sales performance) project will help solve this. Still very small proportion of total bank business.

Supplier management processes have been cloned out of marketing communications supplier management. My department now does it. As of January had a briefing process for agencies. Have different online agencies that do banners, some do infrastructure and usability, another one does product pages. What doesn't work well is e-strategy rather e-tactics – tend to be called in too late.'

Do you think it's fairly clear where it's all going, or is there a lot of uncertainty within your company/clients? What do you think will be the most significant developments for marketers?

'Huge amount of uncertainty – makes it a more difficult work environment – a project might never come to fruition, aggregation, e-mail marketing, etc. Creates uncertainty. Also, constant threat of restructure like in xxxxxx!'

How are marketing people coping? Are they adapting their functional activities (product/brand management, pricing, distribution, marketing communication) easily, or struggling? Please give examples.

'They are aware they should be doing something but they don't know what. Some people think they know what they want to do, others very ill-informed (do something on the Web), individual not departmental differences. People who understand it least are traditional advertising people, and their agencies. Direct marketing people want to control it but don't understand it. Feel it should be data driven, but in old ways. Viral marketing not understood, though it's 'member get member' really. Saw an agency today that has very good grip – direct marketing people working with e-people. Not all e is Web, there is also e-mail and mobiles, but onus is on us to demonstrate what you can do.'

Do you think that the characteristics of successful marketers will change? If so, how? Please give examples.

'Yes, very much so. Far more cross-discipline required. Less possible to sit in little silo – I understand direct marketing or advertising, but need people who understand whole communications spectrum. Much more below the line, and more varied below the line. Need to prove cost-effectiveness in different ways. Before we got sign-off for a small campaign, had to feed back weekly results, even for a £50k test. Big area of confusion – what is role of e in branding? Hope that brand values come through in the end.

We become part of operations, so can't separate product from communication – need to have something on the Web that allows people to do "what if's".'

KNOWLEDGE MANAGEMENT

Triggered by the widespread adoption of business process re-engineering with its emphasis on continuous processes and IT-led change, interest in knowledge management (KM) has exploded since the mid-1990s. Unlike organizational learning, KM has been widely adopted by practitioners who have led academics in developing the area. A lot of the interest in KM has been generated by the large management consultancies, who have used KM extensively in their own internal organizations.

One of the problems that has built up in KM has been the over-emphasis on IT-led 'solutions'. They point out that 'the codification of tacit knowledge into formal systems generates its own psychopathy' – that is, the fluid organic informal and intuitive practices (including chance meetings) that are essential in allowing the firm to cope with uncertainty will become rigid. One view is that knowledge travels via language; the more it is pinned down the more it slips away; it does not respond to rules and systems, and the more loosely it is managed the better. Understanding the subtleties of how knowledge transfers and grows will help us avoid the mistake of believing in simple solutions.

One respondent made the point that the intranet/KM system is increasingly important as an influencer of decisions. But he felt marketers weren't engaging with the debate, let alone leading it. Another respondent pointed out the simple but important fact that managers will only use these systems if they have been trained to do so, and it has been made clear how such systems help in decision making. Other respondents implied that the culture of amateurism – 'winging it' – that prevails in marketing prevents us from making proper use of such systems. Our feeling is that KM systems are already important in many companies, and will increase in importance, enabled by cleverer technology. Respondents felt that marketers need to engage with these systems to a greater degree than at present, bringing to them marketers' key asset – customer knowledge. Respondents also felt that politically, KM systems will be vital centres of power in firms in the future.

The following suggestions were seen as the priorities for encouraging (marketers') usage of KM systems:

- thorough training on the systems when you first join the company;
- a culture of working that allows time and space to use KM systems as an everyday way of doing our jobs;
- a reward and motivation structure that encourages usage and penalizes non-usage;
- finally, an as yet undeveloped intelligent filter technology that acts as an electronic aide to reduce the overwhelming volumes of knowledge and directs the user.

A company that takes KM seriously would need to manage the following:

- technology – for example Lotus Notes, chat lines, cams;
- employees – for example a register of employees' skills, areas of knowledge and expertise;
- knowledge – a 'filterer/summarizer/linker' may be needed.

THE EFFECT OF E-MEDIA ON MARKETING COMMUNICATIONS

The dot.com crash may be still ringing in our ears, but it is reassuring for those advocates of new technology that for the time being there is every sign that new media will continue to increase in importance. For traditional companies as well as dot.coms, the Internet and Web-based e-marketing activities provide highly cost-effective means for marketers to communicate with prospective and existing customers. There has also been a great deal of justifiable excitement about the opportunities offered by mobile media linked to the Web. Add to this interactive TV on the cusp of breaking through, and the integration of telephony and Web technology via the evolution of customer contact centres from call centres.

Of course, the level of interest varies widely. One communications agency respondent said that e-media may take up from 5 to 80 per cent of the overall debate with her clients, depending on the sector. A trawl of Web sites indicates that the financial services community is very advanced (especially banking and general insurance), as are many business-to-business users – for both, the Internet is seen to be key to strategy. How has the communications job changed?

Summarizing other observations from our interviews leads us to the following list:

- firstly, the ability to define an internet strategy that de-emphasizes the site itself and emphasizes the contexts in which the customer operates;
- database marketing skills came to the fore – attention to detail, ability to handle data, project management of multiple suppliers, and measurement disciplines;
- new technology skills – eg to create software to change messages according to customer situations.

Of course, the biggest priority of all is to understand the relative strengths and weaknesses of these new media. Agency people were somewhat critical of clients. The complaint was that the key skill lacking was the 'old fashioned' one of understanding the customer/consumer view. In this regard, personal privacy and security are widely regarded as a very important consideration – and more than just lip-service is needed by marketers to address this. E-privacy appears to be much more sensitive than, for example, direct-mail-related privacy. However, the early indications are that some companies are not themselves sensitive to these issues, although efforts have been made to avoid 'spamming'.

Interviews with agency people elucidated a number of insights into the challenges and problems faced by new media agencies. These challenges are acute because new media firms have changed and grown at such a rapid pace. The pace of growth has led to gaps — training is described as poor (there's 'never enough time'), and in general staff are technically oriented rather than customer-oriented. However, this is an industry that is building strong company cultures, for example through knowledge-sharing evenings. Clients may expect Web sites to be turned around very quickly, but a good, fully functioning and appropriate Web site is as hard and complex to design as a direct marketing campaign. Putting too much pressure on the media company can lead to things falling apart. Reward structures have been difficult to put in place. The pressure of time and growth has meant that they sometimes forget to reward their staff for their achievements because they are busy trying to meet deadlines or drumming up new business. An additional problem is a severe shortage of people who are capable of managing in the new marketing media. There appear to be severe recruitment problems in the new media agencies, and reputedly the quality of management is poor. The same may be true in the user-side departments set up to manage this part of the operations.

Thus the issues faced by new media agencies are:

- lots of inexpert clients who keep changing their minds (hardly surprising – everyone is still learning);
- lots of new staff who are trying to work out what they should be doing, and feel a bit insecure;
- both sides (clients and media companies) without much experience of managing people;
- a lack of benchmarks and boundaries, which means that clients' expectations are often unrealistic;
- the fact that it is a new area means that there is a lack of solid processes and procedures that companies should be using to structure how they work – this sort of thing has led to deadlines slipping and so on.

WEB SITES

After the initial hype of a few years ago, it would be fair to say the excitement surrounding the commercial opportunities of Web sites has cooled considerably. High development costs for a good Web site mean that the business plan for Web sites is based on retained customers. This model is fine for financial services companies that will gather lots of information as a natural part of doing business and can use it to provide more value and hence keep customers. But consumer goods sectors can't do this so easily. Respondents seemed to agree that good Web sites need quick download, easy navigation, financial security and convenience. It seems to be conventional wisdom that complicated Web sites that are difficult to navigate are a common mistake and a big turn-off for consumers.

E-MAIL

In contrast to Web sites, respondents were rather more upbeat about e-mail. E-mail marketing is an increasingly popular way of building one-to-one relationships with customers and prospects. To start with, it can be created, executed and measured in-house at much lower cost than traditional direct mail. E-mail newsletters deliver targeted messages that in theory can be tailored to an individual reader at marginal cost. In some companies permission-based e-mail marketing is showing very high returns when well managed. (This is creating stresses in terms of the very cumbersome mechanisms most companies have for marketing communications planning.) One experienced direct marketing-based respondent said that e-mail was a good relationship-building medium because it was so much easier and quicker for customers to respond and for companies to reply to these responses. E-mail can be used to respond quickly to clients' or customers' queries/service requirements. Both client and agency respondents felt these trends will grow and continue. On the other hand, they did not feel e-mail was as good as direct mail at brand image building, lacking as it does the tangibility, colour and visual appeal of direct mail.

Best practice has yet to emerge, but here is a quick 'state of the art' list for e-mail marketing:

- Use permission-based lists only.
- Avoid using e-mail for acquisition.
- E-mail is very powerful and very quickly annoys consumers if used for irrelevant messages. Marketers only have one shot at keeping people's trust.
- Test/develop carefully to get logistics right to avoid spam.
- The temptation is to say let's do HTML e-mail that's 'all whizzy graphics', but many customers' PCs or servers can't handle it, so a lot of money on wonderful creativity can be wasted.
- Bounce-back tactics will work.
- A client who needs time, space, tactility and brand-build capability should use direct mail.

INTERACTIVE TV

At the time of writing, interactive TV (iTV) seems poised on the edge of making a significant impact. Interactive TV looks set to be very important in some sectors, particularly for packaged goods and for less upmarket audiences. However, respondents criticized the iTV industry for over-zealous secrecy that has prevented shared learning of best practice. This is urgently needed: the impression gained was that there is widespread ignorance about the strengths and weaknesses of iTV.

THE IMPACT OF NEW TECHNOLOGY ON CRM

The relatively recent surge of interest in CRM has meant that senior managers are increasingly aware that they need to be able to offer multiple channels to customers. Often the same customer will use different channels; this has given firms the difficult internal job of responding quickly and in an integrated manner. Phone, face-to-face and Internet systems all need to talk to each other in real time so that operatives know the latest customer position. A common customer database needs to sit behind all these systems, enabling the appearance of integrated channels. In many ways, the last thing CRM managers wanted to see coming over the horizon was a flotilla of new media, channels, and ways for a customer to contact the company. But that is the reality, and they are having to deal with it. The term e-CRM has been invented, although this has been criticized.

It is, of course, something of an over-simplification to assume that any implementation of strategic CRM will be achieved by merely buying the latest software. Yet many companies are doing just this. Again there is a real need for marketers to be more informed about IT and database/CRM analysis.

APPENDIX: CASE STUDIES

A pan-European insurance group

This case is a good example to highlight the realities of how a new e-channel fits into a business.

How do you/your clients use the Internet and related technology at the moment? Give some examples of the biggest successes and biggest problems/failures.

We use the Internet for lead creation, direct selling of general insurance, administration of group pensions, property advertising, building communities of interest and corporate advertising. Clients can e-mail us by accessing us through our Internet sites. Success and failure is emotive language – it is hard to generate revenue for financial services through the Internet; we find it hard to manage leads generated off the Net. We are succeeding in building interest on the Net through property advertising and community sites. It pressures us to move more of our communication to an electronic form which is good for the business. Some clients generate their own Internet sites to complain about us.

Has it changed the way you or your clients manage your/their marketing and customer service significantly (speed, scope and quality of processes, programmes, management of suppliers, measurement of results, etc)? If so, how? Please give examples.

No significant changes for the business I am in at present.

Do you think it's fairly clear where it's all going, or is there a lot of uncertainty within your company/clients? What do you think will be the most significant developments for marketers?

I think the whole thing is dogged by uncertainty. We believe that for complex purchases person-to-person advice will be required for some time yet. Changes in regulation affecting margins are more significant and will drive us towards low-cost distribution methods maybe faster than customers would prefer.

How are marketing people coping? Are they adapting their functional activities (product/brand management, pricing, distribution, marketing communication) easily, or struggling? Please give examples.

Marketing people are struggling because their focus remains on products rather than communication. Easy to sell products are being marketed using the Net – eg ISA – but more complex products will not shift this way. E-enablement inside the company is faster and is itself facilitated by cost reduction programmes and the fact that everyone is connected to a network.

Do you think that the characteristics of successful marketers will change? If so, how? Please give examples.

New things to learn – but that is not new. The rate of change is faster – but that is not new either. What you can find out about your clients is now better quality – and that is a change. Client loyalty is more difficult to achieve in a transparent world. Loyalty is becoming a commodity – to be bought and sold.

Case study: alliances

The Internet and Internet/intranet technology or software such as Lotus Notes or e-mail is enabling much closer linkages to be made between partner organizations. One of the best recent examples is that of Delta Lloyd in the Netherlands, part of the NU insurance company. It uses an extranet to provide support to its agents. The Delta Lloyd Digital Domain has four components, as follows:

- the store, where information on its products is found;
- the counter, where users' questions are answered;
- the kiosk, where the latest information is made available;
- the office, for backup information such as telemarketing scripts and advertisements.

This has resulted in a big reduction in Delta Lloyd's agent support costs, as well as an improvement in quality. The use of the Internet to support agents is now becoming so common as to be unworthy of note! Of course, many agents have their own Web sites too, while new intermediaries are springing up offering their services only through the Web.

Notes

[1] Cookham (2001) *The impact of e-business on marketing and marketers*, Chartered Institute of Marketing. The full report can be bought – either through the Institute's Web site (http://www.connectedinmarketing.co.uk) or through CIM Direct on +44 (0) 1628 427427.

6

'E-business strategy' or just 'business strategy'

Barry Jerome

INTRODUCTION

One of the main challenges all companies face when constructing a strategy is how to ensure it is implemented and achieves the results required. Many good strategies become worthless after they are agreed because there is no easily identifiable path to implement them. This is a particular problem for e-business strategies as the rapid pace of change in the financial services industry can mean that a strategy loses its competitive advantage if implementation is delayed.

Another problem is the distinction between e-business strategy and business strategy. An isolated e-business strategy can compete with other parts of a company's strategy, causing conflict and delay. However, for financial services in the foreseeable future, there is no real difference between business strategy and e-business strategy. Financial services are so dependent on electronic means for interfacing to customers, partners and suppliers and for exchanging information that there is really no distinction.

This statement is reinforced by recent events in a number of industries where companies are consolidating or closing Internet-only parts of their business and incorporating them into the mainstream business. For example, AIB decided not to continue with its Internet-only bank, another bank closed its Internet-only subsidiary as it had failed to reach a fraction of its envisaged customer base, and in the motor industry GM is rolling back its e-GM business into the main business.

This chapter describes one approach to creating and documenting an e-business strategy that has a clear path through to implementation. It will identify the focus areas in financial services and highlight where the focus is perhaps different to a traditional business strategy. This approach will include discussion of the components of an e-business strategy and how these components allow a business to move from business vision to implementation of the strategy without ending up as 'shelf-ware'.

KEY ISSUES

An important way of ensuring that a strategy does not end up as 'shelf-ware' is to have a systematic approach. This approach moves logically from the business vision through the value proposition to the capabilities required and then to the implementation plan to make it happen. A component of the strategy is created at each step and forms the base for the next step. In this way the implementation can be clearly shown to be supporting the business imperative and should not then be held up by purely accounting-based return on investment (ROI) arguments on individual projects.

An often-posed statement is that 'everything happens in e-time (or Internet time)' which, because it is much shorter, means that there is no time to spend on developing a strategy as it will have changed by the time it is implemented. This is a fallacy as the lack of a strategy commits a business to reacting to its competition rather than making trade-offs and formulating a strategy that creates sustainable competitive advantage and hence profitability.

Developing an effective strategy for a business that is heavily dependent on e-business activities often requires a change of mindset by the key decision makers. Often the e-business activities have not been a coordinated part of the mainstream strategy. This has resulted in a multitude of unrelated projects. Demonstrating the wasted resources and potential damage to the brand from the disjointed approach can change this mindset. An approach based on developing components of a strategy that build into a comprehensive strategy, allowing the business to make trade-offs and create a practical implementation plan, can then be used to create a coordinated e-business strategy. In particular, this structured approach allows the enablers and capabilities required to implement the strategy to be tied very clearly to the business need.

APPROACH

The components of an e-business strategy that will be discussed in this approach are:

- vision and direction;

- positioning;
- value proposition;
- capabilities required;
- implementation plan.

Each section will discuss the analysis required and construction of that component of the strategy. In particular, it will describe how the thought leadership material, trends, solutions options and value proposition discussed in much of the rest of this book can be exploited.

VISION AND DIRECTION

This component of the strategy is all about understanding what the business wants to do, understanding what competitors and potential competitors are doing, understanding what is possible and also what might soon be possible. This establishes the basis for positioning the business. Understanding potential competitors and what might soon be possible are both critical areas of an e-business strategy.

Technology is a great enabler for a business that wants to extend itself up or down the value system so that it can capture more value. Future competitors should be viewed as any business that is operating in a low-margin commodity area of the value system. The easiest way for that company to capture more value, and hence profitability, is to migrate to adjacent areas.

An example of this can be seen in the automobile industry. Some manufacturers have extended their presence in the value system into financial services. To supply parts, the company has a comprehensive customer database, it has information on credit history and it will already have a relationship, especially with commercial customers. From this, it is fairly easy to extend the value proposition to offer financial services in the form of car loans, financing, insurance, leasing, etc, to the same customer set. Suddenly the financial services industry has a competitor from manufacturing industry.

Throughout this book, we analyse in detail the current situation and likely future trends in the financial services industry, future trends in technology and new business models. The first step when using this information is to construct the 'business landscape'. This analysis sets the scene in which the bank or insurance company is operating. It will enable reasoned thought to take place before setting vision, mission and goal statements, by describing what is happening in the industry and what is possible. This will include analysis to understand which 'wave' the e-business is in, where competitors are, and what options are possible.

Just consider the situation where some banks have created Internet-only banks, some start-ups have set up e-banks, some insurance companies have extended their value system to include banking and some banks have adopted a combined channel strategy to incorporate e-banking. Analysis of these approaches, identifying which are proving successful, will point the way to the 'base zero' position. This is the base that can be considered as the minimum to compete effectively today. It is the base on which to define the value proposition and unique combination of capabilities to compete effectively in the future. Once the 'business landscape' is established, a more detailed analysis of competitors and the way they go to market will be required. Intelligence on competitors is available from a number of sources, but can be time-consuming to assemble. A better option is often to use a company that regularly collects and analyses information from annual reports, analyst and shareholder statements, advertising, press comments, etc. This can provide information quickly on the potential threats in e-space. This type of information is 'secondary' information as it has already been collected and analysed. This is good for establishing what the general competitive environment is like. For more specific information on products and services and segmentation used by competitors it may be necessary to run focus groups or surveys and ask the participants very specific questions about their experience of competitive offerings. Another approach is to analyse specific areas such as competitive Web sites (see Figure 6.1).

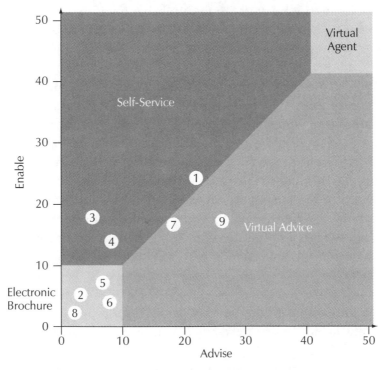

Figure 6.1 Example of an analysis of competitive offerings carried out using a tool that compares different company's Web sites (numbers indicate different company offerings)

For financial services a critical requirement is to understand what type of segmentation is working well, what segmentation strategies are being adopted by current and potential competitors, or what strategies they have said they will be adopting. For example, picking up the banking landscape referred to earlier, where different approaches are being used by incumbent and new entry banks, it is important to understand which customer segments are being addressed in each of the propositions. An understanding of successful current strategies for segmentation can be derived from both the secondary and primary research. 'Base zero' has been established and an understanding has been built of what works today. What will work in the future though? As the small print in financial products states, 'past performance is not necessarily an indicator of future performance; investments can go down as well as up'.

Leading e-business companies invest in research to understand what is happening today, what is influencing the future, what may be possible in the future and hence make projections on what the future will look like. For e-business strategy in financial services there are two key areas of understanding required – the trends in the financial services industry and trends in technology, discussed throughout much of this book. This understanding is very valuable when combined with understanding of the business landscape and of market segmentation as it facilitates creation of a practical strategic vision. This can then be translated into mission and goals, providing the basis for the next component of the strategy – to create a positioning for the company that has a unique competitive advantage that is sustainable over time.

POSITIONING

This relates to selecting the positioning which addresses the business vision and which will give unique competitive advantage, sustainable over time. The positioning provides a framework for defining the value proposition and capabilities needed. In the rapidly moving world of financial services e-business, the only hope of achieving this is by using a systematic approach that considers the combination of all products and services, segments and channels and then makes trade-offs to be able to sustain profitability and advantage. Selecting the main difference in deciding which customer segments to address for e-business strategy is the combination of segment, products and services and channels. Many financial services companies merely extend their channels and offer all products and services to all customer segments through the extended channels. This is not a strategy, as no trade-offs have been made to gain advantage.

Two key considerations in an e-business strategy are: 1) profitability by combinations of segment, product and channel; 2) how focusing segments, products and channels enhances the customer's experience with the company.

A good starting point for addressing these areas is the positioning cube (see Figure 6.2). This cube can be created using the analysis from the vision component of the strategy to highlight the company's position in relation to its competitors and to identify where opportunities exist that can be exploited in the value proposition.

This cube needs to be considered as a set of slices that can be analysed by channel. For each channel consider the current position and what trade-offs should be made for the future to capture more value when delivering products and services to each customer segment. Many companies have put artificial barriers between these slices. For example, start-up banks or insurance companies selling over the Internet are unlikely to have any physical branches; they may have a telephone channel to support the Internet channel. Traditional banks have often launched stand-alone Internet-only spin-offs that have no capability to use their existing infrastructure. This artificial separation of the channels may

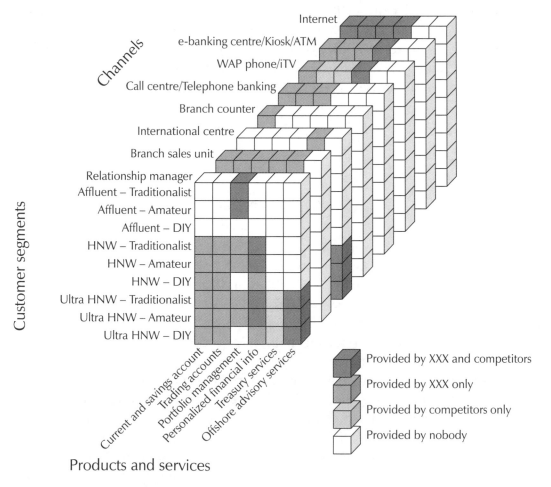

Figure 6.2 Positioning cube

be successful in gaining customers, but it is likely to result in commodity-based competition. The room to manoeuvre and offer a sustainable value proposition has been severely restricted by the imposed barriers. Customers can move easily between different banks, or can keep open accounts with multiple banks. Transfer of savings to the highest interest rate provider, or obtaining loans from those offering the lowest interest rates is simple, and does not result in the loyalty and cross-selling that would be possible through a richer channel proposition.

This cube can also be used to evaluate options for the interaction between the channels. For example, if each slice of the cube is made up of 'cubicles', then analysis shows which cubicles are provided by the company, by its competitors as well, only by its competitors or not by anyone. This can highlight areas to exploit, areas where a presence may be required for a comprehensive service and areas to exit. In Figure 6.3 a wealth management proposition is analysed to indicate which products and services might be offered in the future to which customer segments. This table can then be reconstructed into slices in the cube by deciding which channels to offer the combination of product and segment to maximize profit and positive customer experience.

The decisions on the combinations of channel, segment and products must be based on a customer wants and needs analysis. The customer experience could be completely unsatisfactory without this fundamental research combined with profitability considerations. A combined channel strategy offers the ability to optimize costs to the company and benefits to the customer across channels and hence provide a value-added service with greater opportunity for profitability. Charles Schwab is one of the best-known examples of a successful multi-channel strategy where electronic trading has been combined with a

Example Products and services	Affluent – Traditionalist	Affluent – Amateur	Affluent – DIY	HNW – Traditionalist	HNW – Amateur	HNW – DIY	Ultra HNW – Traditionalist	Ultra HNW – Amateur	Ultra HNW – DIY
Current accounts	✓	✓	✓	✓	✓	✓	✓	✓	✓
Savings accounts	✓	✓	✓	✓	✓	✓	✓	✓	✓
Trading accounts	✓	✓	✓	✓	✓	✓	✓	✓	✓
Portfolio management	✓	✓		✓	✓	✓	✓	✓	✓
Personalized financial info.			✓			✓	✓	✓	✓
Treasury services				✓	✓	✓	✓	✓	✓
Offshore advisory offers							✓	✓	✓

Figure 6.3 Example mapping of products and services to customer segments for a wealth management proposition

branch infrastructure to create a very strong business model which has been difficult to compete with.

A major issue that arises within an e-business strategy that is less likely to occur in a traditional strategy is 'channel conflict'. Take, for example, an insurance company that has dealt exclusively through agents and brokers. A start-up competitor begins to take market share by offering direct insurance at low prices to the most profitable customer segment. How does the incumbent respond without upsetting its agents and brokers? One approach is to re-evaluate which channels to sell and distribute products and services through. Categorizing products into 'simple' and 'complex' is a starting point. Simple products are likely to be commodity items whereas complex products will be value added. The commodity products should then be sold exclusively through the low-cost channels, normally the Internet and call centres, or even supermarkets. The complex products require expertise and should be sold exclusively through agents and brokers. Each channel is then providing the best value to the customer and the most economical way of administering them for the business.

Simple products could still be sold through agents or brokers, but the customer informed that there is a mark-up for the agent's commission. They could alternatively be sold as a value-added tailored product if the individual simple products were sufficiently modular. Several simple products could be grouped together into a portfolio that was configured to the customer's requirement. This would be a value-added product as it requires the agent's or broker's expertise to create the best value product for the customer's needs. As a result of this approach, if the simple products sold through the direct channels are priced competitively then the multi-channel capability should provide a stronger business model to compete effectively against the new entrants.

One way to test positioning conclusions is through the creation of future business scenarios. This is essential preparation for creating a value proposition for the e-business strategy. The business scenarios should consider how the customer would learn about and acquire the products and services, and how the products and services would be administered, eg for an insurance product, how the claims process would fit. It should also consider how the customer would interact with each of the multiple channels, the possible effects of pricing changes and what the competitors' responses might be to the introduction of products and services through the selected channels. If time permits and there are many unknowns, scenario planning can also be used to identify possible futures and potential courses of action for each.

Another critical area to consider in an e-business strategy is corporate governance. This addresses how the products and services will be administered and controlled through the multiple channels, and the interactions ('touch-points') with the selected customer segments. This has been one of the biggest failure areas for Internet companies. These companies often have an excellent sales proposition, but are unable to deliver products effectively or handle complaints. In the financial services industry, this is often shown through a lack of knowledge of the customer or status of customer activities when passing between channels, as well as problems when addressing complaints. Few banks or insurance companies today can claim to have a fully coordinated multi-channel strategy across traditional and electronic channels. The governance model needs to address this. It also needs to address the upstream and downstream interfaces in the value system.

VALUE PROPOSITION

This component of the strategy is about creating a value proposition that is sustainable over time. To be sustainable it needs to be difficult to copy and flexible enough to pre-empt or respond to competitive moves. Chapter 37 discusses sustainability in more detail. The value proposition starts from the company vision, but uses the analysis from the positioning component and the corporate governance considerations to create a proposition that is sustainable over time. Take, for example, a vision that 'the company will double current market share and increase profitability by 50 per cent within five years by transforming to a 'virtual risk manager' model of providing insurance'. This does not sound like a vision for an e-business strategy; however, to be able to realize the vision in the financial services marketplace it requires an e-business strategy. This value proposition is an e-business proposition (see Chapters 4 and 39) for a customer-centric organization. Requirements for the strategy include the need to exploit electronic channels alongside traditional channels, to design straight-through processes (STPs) which run through the organization and which require electronic facilities to control workflow, to provide good quality CRM in all interactions with the customer, to be able to exploit technology to create and sustain the choice of segmentation, to be able to measure profitability at a granular level, to be able to generate flexible products and features using technology to reduce the time to market, and to have electronic links to customers, suppliers of products and the re-insurance market.

The value proposition can be represented using a 'strategic capabilities network' which identifies the statements of value to the customer and to the business, and which then begins to identify which capabilities will help the company to achieve those value statements. Figure 6.4 is not intended to be the answer to the vision statement above, but to illustrate how the vision statement might be developed into a value proposition taking into account the business landscape and competitive analysis from the vision component and using the positioning cube and corporate governance considerations in the positioning component.

The positioning cube will identify the customer segments that will be targeted for the virtual risk manager concept, the channels that will be used to deliver the concept and the services that will be offered. Note that this model is much more of a services-based concept

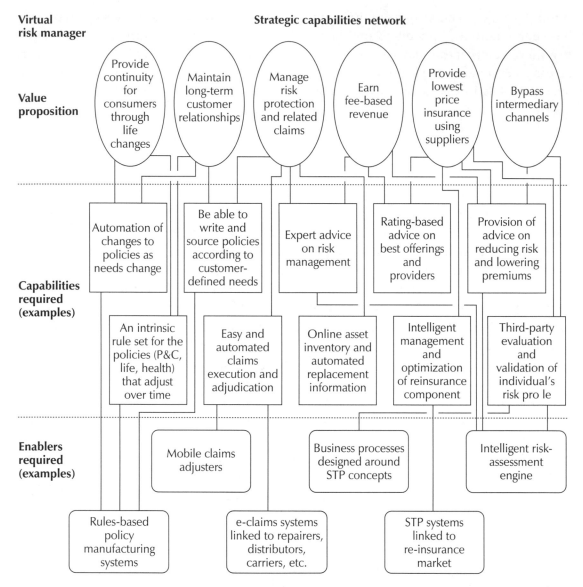

Figure 6.4 Development of a strategic capabilities network to describe a value proposition for a 'virtual risk manager'

than the traditional product-based approach of marketing individual insurance products. A well-coordinated corporate governance model will be required to deliver the service as it needs to be completely seamless from customers through to suppliers and re-insurers. This includes not just electronic links to policy providers, but also to repairers, distributors, carriers, hospitals, etc, in the event of claims.

The value proposition needs to be expanded by developing the detailed products and services strategy that details the types of service and associated products to be offered to the selected customer segments and how they will be offered through the various channels. The services and products offered will be driven by the customer wants and needs analysis for the 'virtual risk manager' concept.

Pricing strategy is the next important consideration. The rationale behind the virtual risk manager concept is that it provides more value to the customer and that it will be fee based. This allows value pricing rather than commodity pricing. Value pricing allows for the value provided to the customer, whereas commodity pricing always has low and diminishing margins. An important consideration in the pricing is the balance between the various channels to be able to achieve the optimum cost structure while still providing excellent customer interaction. Creation of the pricing part of the strategy allows a pricing model to be developed which can be used to test different pricing options. The price points generated need to be verified against the customer wants and needs and competitive analyses.

Another deliverable within the value proposition component of the strategy is the 'channel experience blueprint'. This tells in a story the type of experience that a customer will have in using the various channels when purchasing services (see Chapter 35 for a detailed example of this). Different stories will be required for each segment type and each service and it will need to show the interactions across each of the possible channels. This is another vital piece of an e-business strategy as it describes how the value proposition will be provided across the channels and is one of the best methods of avoiding the problems referred to earlier of uncoordinated channels in a multi-channel proposition.

Brand is also a critical part of an e-business strategy, especially so in financial services. The key question is 'Do I use my current brand or create a new brand?' Each option probably has as many disadvantages as advantages. Providers in the UK have used both approaches to branding. This can be seen in, for example, Egg banking set up by Prudential and cahoot set up by Abbey National. In the former, Egg is a completely different business venture, banking, for an insurance company whereas cahoot is a separate business, but one that overlaps with the existing Abbey National business which is expanding into the same electronic channels. In fact the Abbey National e-saver account is a direct competitor to the cahoot current account. Other financial services providers have adopted the same brand. For example, HSBC has adopted a multi-channel strategy within its existing brand, though they also have the 'First Direct' brand which started as a telephone-banking proposition and expanded into electronic channels. The overlap here is in the Internet channel, where the telephone channels offer different propositions; First Direct provides 24/7 banking over the phone whereas HSBC provides extended banking hours.

It is probably too early for evidence to show definitively which approach is best, although the danger is that restricting the channels will lead to commodity-based competition. It is a balance between offering a service that is different from current services and is re-branded to avoid damaging the original brand, and leveraging an existing brand to promote the new value proposition in electronic channels. These are all questions that need to be addressed in this component of the e-business strategy.

The last key part of this component of the e-business strategy is promotion strategy – how should the value proposition be promoted to the potential customer segments? For the start-up and new brand options this is one of the most expensive parts of the implementation and ongoing costs. Many of the dot.com crashes resulted from haemorrhaging cash through advertising. Establishing a new brand is costly. Creating a promotions strategy is much the same for an e-business as for a traditional business strategy except that it will need to place more emphasis on the electronic channel for promotions. An important action is to include the cost of promoting a new brand into the arguments to decide on branding approach.

CAPABILITIES REQUIRED

This component of the strategy involves taking the capabilities that support the value proposition and identifying the enablers required to implement them. The enablers (see Figure 6.5) are broken down into process, organization, technology and knowledge, and prioritized as the first step in identification of strategic initiatives. The strategic capabilities network (SCN) described in the previous section identified the capabilities required to support the value proposition. Trends in the financial services industry, trends in technology and trends in business models all help to identify the capabilities that will be required. Chapters 39 and 40 also discuss how to make the right choices. Enablers will be required for implementing the capabilities. These enablers may be business process, technology, organization or knowledge and can be a combination of all four.

These capabilities and their associated enablers then become the key design points (KDPs) that will be used for specifying the design of the business processes, organization and change management, IT functionality, IT infrastructure and knowledge management. Once all of the KDPs have been identified, they need to be prioritized according to how important a contribution each KDP makes to the e-business value proposition. KDPs with a similar priority are grouped together as the first step in breaking down the implementation into phases. This phasing is continued in the 'implementation plan' component of the strategy where further considerations from the parts of the strategy developed earlier are overlaid on this. For example, the channel strategy may have identified a preferred sequence for implementing each channel; the product and service strategy may have identified a preferred customer segment to target first. Technology enablers are critical to the success of e-business strategies. A particular focus area is e-business solutions, which can help to 'jump start' the implementation of the strategy. Chapter 18 discusses e-business solutions for financial services in more detail.

Further detail is required for each enabler to be able to gain a perspective of the difficulty and cost to implement. This is essential for creating the implementation plan and constructing the business case.

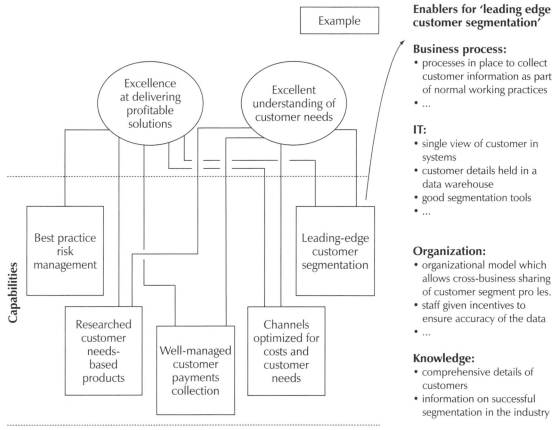

Figure 6.5 Example enablers for a business capability

The business, organization, technology and knowledge enablers need to be prioritized next, based on cost and complexity to implement. This is also where trade-offs can be made between the different enablers. For example, if some IT functionality is particularly difficult or costly to implement, it may be possible to use a process work-around instead; if some business skills are in short supply, it may be necessary to use a modified organizational design to optimize access to available skills. The deliverable from this capabilities component of the strategy is now a comprehensive KDP document that describes the priorities and enablers required to implement the e-business value proposition. It is also the base that will ensure that each initiative, whether following a process, organization, IT or knowledge work stream, will be consistent with each other work stream.

IMPLEMENTATION PLAN

This component of the strategy is about creating a comprehensive plan that remains consistent across work streams during implementation. It includes the initiatives for each work stream in the form of a strategic roadmap, the technology plans to implement the solutions, the marketing plans to reach the selected segments and the regulation and compliance plans. These regulation and compliance plans have become a critical component for e-business strategies as the mechanisms to achieve compliance or gain regulatory approval can be long, whereas e-business implementations are normally short.

The business case is also put together in this component of the strategy. If the value proposition has been well designed, making trade-offs to achieve a sustainable strategy, then the business case should be straightforward as all of the benefits will be traceable back to the original vision. Further trade-offs on costs may be required if some of the enablers are unacceptably expensive to develop or operate. This is achieved by further actions on the KDPs, ensuring that any change to the enablers is assessed for impact on the other work streams. Chapter 30 discusses in detail the management of value for e-business.

The implementation plan component also includes the governance model for the strategic programme, identifying roles and responsibilities for implementing the e-business strategy. This would also include communications plans and the change management approach. The mechanism for creating the implementation plans is not a great deal different for an e-business strategy from creating implementation plans for a traditional strategy. The difference is in the information used. Each of the previous components of the strategy has contributed to building a comprehensive knowledge of what is required to implement the vision and value proposition. Implementing an e-business strategy requires much more coordination between all of the work streams and the plans need to reflect this. An e-business strategy will fail if the business process, technology, organization and knowledge work streams are not all kept aligned throughout the implementation.

CONCLUSIONS

This chapter started with the statement that one of the main challenges when constructing a strategy for financial services is how to ensure it is implemented and achieves its objectives. This is particularly important for an e-business strategy as time-scales are thought of in 'e-' or 'Internet' time. Although the tendency may be to forget strategy and jump straight into implementation to deal with the time-scales, this will lead to failure as there is much greater need in an e-business for everything to run in concert. There are many examples of organizations running an e-business model where there is a breakdown between processes, technologies, organization and knowledge. This is often shown up by inconsistent customer interaction through different channels.

This chapter has attempted to demonstrate that a systematic approach to developing an e-business strategy ensures that the strategy is feasible, has a clear implementation path and clearly supports the business vision when implemented. The description may give the impression that the steps involved are too long for 'e-time', but all of the steps can be achieved quickly if those involved are experienced in developing practical e-business strategies. A factor that may get in the way of developing and implementing the strategy quickly is the potential conflict between e-business and traditional business strategies. In the past, e-business strategies have only addressed part of the business strategy and have often resulted in multiple unrelated initiatives. As the rest of this book shows, to be successful in the future will require a difference approach to business. Organizations will need to become customer, market, fulfilment and/or product centric. Business strategies to address this will be e-business strategies, so that for financial services companies in the future there is really no distinction between the two. This approach will enable a company to develop its business strategy in an e-business world.

7

Managing marketing in the e-world

Tess Moffett, Paul Crick, Merlin Stone and Barry Jerome

INTRODUCTION – CHANGING TIMES, CHANGING TECHNOLOGIES

Financial services companies have started using new customer-facing technologies to complement their classic marketing communications techniques (eg TV, radio, press advertising, sponsorship) and their direct marketing techniques (database marketing, direct mail and questionnaire techniques (such as those used by independent financial advisers (IFAs))). This e-business technology is enabling financial services institutions to share their knowledge and initiatives with agents, brokers and IFAs, as well as making this knowledge available internally. The result is that it is achieving the same status within the company as classic marketing management information. Moreover, the Web, together with pervasive (ie access anywhere) technology (such as the mobile telephone), provides new ways for direct marketing to reach and interact with potential customers.

Marketing managers are using the Web for product marketing. At first, they used branded Web sites and search engines, and now they are beginning to use the Web along with other channels for integrated marketing campaigns. The Internet is relevant for the financial services market because potential customers actively use the Internet to gather information about products and services. This has led to the rise of a new breed of financial services intermediary that specializes in providing online comparisons of products and services, and then provides intermediary services to the end customer.

Potential customers' desire for information also allows financial services marketers to integrate iTV (interactive television) with online selling. The use of iTV will allow marketers to arrange for detailed product information and electronic application forms to be broadcast to set-top boxes prior to an advertisement appearing on the television. When the consumer's interest has been aroused by the advertisement he or she will be able to interrogate the set-top box to find out more information and also be able to complete an application for the product or service. This application can then be sent electronically to the financial services institution, thus capturing new business while interest is still high.

ISSUES – CHANGING EMPHASIS

Owing to the interactive nature of the Internet, the flow of data from individuals has exploded in volume. New types of advanced analytical techniques have been developed so that marketers can now maximize the use of this data. Click-through analysis, for example, enables marketers to evaluate how many potential customers have actively responded to an online ad. Sophisticated business intelligence techniques such as IBM's 'Enterprise Customer Analytics', now enable online campaign design and real-time attuning of responses, plus collaborative filtering. However, these types of analysis will take a long time to be integrated alongside other more traditional marketing techniques and processes. For example, advertising processes are under pressure to change to take advantage of the availability of new ways to analyse customer responses. Hoffman and Novak report that there is significant pressure for large consumer portals to adopt results-oriented pricing models, rather than continuing to use the 'cost per million' exposure-based metrics that have traditionally been used for TV and other mass-market advertising.[1]

Advanced analytics are resulting in financial services companies rethinking how they segment their markets. Traditionally, financial services companies have defined their target market in very broad terms, eg by income and social standing for financial products or by geography, age and claims history for risk-based products. Customer segmentation is now moving beyond demographic variables and is starting to include response and behavioural data. A study by Booz Allen & Hamilton and NetRatings Inc.[2] identified seven online consumer segments based on 'occasionalization', ie how individuals use the Internet on different occasions. They considered that this was the most effective method of segmenting the online market. However, when segmenting their customer bases, marketers should bear in mind the distinction between tactical and response-based segmentation and strategic segmentation. For example, it is becoming easier for the marketer to interact with customers who express an interest in their products, as online data gathering and inter-preting is more straightforward than traditional paper or telephone-based research. However, marketers must be careful how they use the wealth of available consumer online data, and be mindful of data protection requirements.

Our research into the impact of e-business on marketers (see Chapter 5) has shown that many companies are uncertain as to how they should change their processes. The Internet enables financial services marketers to create a dialogue with potential customers and to form a greater bond with them. Financial services companies ignoring the Internet as a way to create and sustain loyalty run the risk of falling behind, as this interactivity can create a greater 'hold' on the consumer. What may seem like small erosions in market share may translate into significant gains in the longer term, as potential customers will be less likely to switch loyalty. One customer segment that is being targeted very strongly for loyalty is the fairly recently defined 'young affluent' segment. This segment has money to spend on many products and services, for example equity trading, travel insurance, personal and secured loans, property insurance, health insurance. They also expect to be able to use technology to spend it, whether by Internet, iTV, WAP phone or other emerging technology. A financial services company that does not have an integrated multi-channel proposition is not going to keep the loyalty of this segment; similarly, they will lose out on the opportunity to market to them through these channels. They will have considerable difficulty in exploiting the 'whole life' experience to gain loyalty by predicting needs based on life events.

New technologies are making new kinds of cooperation possible, resulting in new models for competition in the marketplace – 'co-opetition' is now a reality for financial services! The main achievements have been the developments of classic extranets and portals which give customers access to a variety of sellers of consumer products and services which can be complemented by financial services products, for example credit card purchase, loans and insurance. Barclays Indigo-Square was an early example of this. Results have often been disappointing, however, when consumers have not flocked to the sites in the numbers initially predicted.

To obtain full benefit from these new technologies, financial services marketers should examine how other industries, eg utilities, telecommunications, travel and retail, have created and implemented new processes as they have transformed into e-businesses. Other markets that have embraced new technologies can help companies learn how e-business has changed their market environment and how it might be applied to financial services.

New technologies have:

- reduced costs;
- increased responsiveness – speed and appropriateness;
- enhanced focus on customers;
- enhanced delivery of service;
- allowed competitors to gain entry;
- improved knowledge of customers.

However, a major problem for financial services companies is that most have not updated their approach to knowledge management to take into account learning from new channels of communication. This is key to understanding the behaviour of potential customers and how to respond to them effectively through these new channels.

THE BROADENING ARMOURY

E-business and consumer databases are significantly broadening the options available for marketing managers within the marketing mix. Traditionally, when a marketing manager launched a new product, the options available were limited, as shown in Table 7.1.

In addition to these traditional media, marketing managers can now use interactive options, and also leverage their own and third-party databases for more personalized approaches, as shown in Table 7.2.

These additional options mean that marketers can select from a classic mass-marketing campaign down to an almost individually targeted approach – the funnel of messages to

Table 7.1 New launch support

New launch support: product driven	New launch support: in partnership with third parties (agents, brokers, IFAs)
<ul><li>TV</li><li>Radio</li><li>Press</li><li>Sampling</li><li>Sponsorship</li><li>Vouchers</li><li>Direct mail using own bought lists/own databases</li><li>PR</li></ul>	<ul><li>Point of sale</li><li>Leaflets</li><li>Early sign-up discounts</li><li>Third-party-specific discounts</li><li>Third-party direct mailing</li></ul>

Table 7.2 Interactive marketing options

Additional marketing options: product driven	Additional marketing options with third parties
<ul><li>Promotional Web sites</li><li>E-mail marketing</li><li>E-sampling</li><li>E-discounts</li><li>Online competitions</li><li>Banner ads</li><li>Buttons/interstitials</li><li>Interactive TV</li><li>SMS Messaging/Mobile</li></ul>	<ul><li>Sponsored content/banners on agent and broker sites</li><li>E-promotions on broker and agent sites</li><li>E-mail marketing via broker and agent databases (within the constraints of the Data Protection Act)</li><li>Targeted one-off direct mail via broker and agent databases – could include video, CD ROM</li><li>Discounts only available via third-party Web sites and e-mails</li><li>Targeted advertorials in segment-specific consumer loyalty clubs, eg frequent flier, wine club, etc</li></ul>

the consumer is getting increasingly narrow, and 'direct' marketing now really means direct.

To exploit the marketing opportunities brought by new technology, financial services companies will need to change how they think about marketing today, unfreezing the traditional marketing paradigm, and translating it into a new paradigm. They must allow for the continuing evolution of technology, which will bring with it major changes in level of detail, speed, the degree of customer control, and end-to-end process management. They will also need to distinguish between three discrete levels of marketing process:

- micro-processes (eg managing individual customers);
- macro-processes (eg strategic segment management; financial services partner management);
- highest level of processes – brand, overall customer management, channel management.

THE MARKETER'S DILEMMA

Marketing managers are overwhelmed with choice now that the marketing mix contains so many additional interactive options. Many marketing managers are trained in traditional mass-marketing methods, and are struggling with how to integrate new e-business and database-enabled marketing options into their day-to-day marketing management practices. Even in 1996, Deighton remarked that 'a profession is shaped by its tools and that marketing's toolkit is experiencing unsettling amounts of innovation',[3] However, marketers cannot afford to ignore the Internet in their marketing activity. Uncles considers that 'the Web has become an inescapable part of every marketer's life'.[4] A survey of 40 UK marketers across nine industry sectors in 2000 found that 82.5 per cent of respondents employ the Internet in their marketing activities and that this was the second most frequently employed tool.[5]

Creativity is no longer the main skill requirement for a successful marketing manager. Stroud comments that whilst marketers have always needed to understand how IT supports their activities (customer databases, direct mailing systems, etc), they are concerned that they now need to broaden and deepen their technical knowledge in order to conduct interactive marketing using the Internet. Stroud describes how marketers' lack of knowledge in this area, compounded by the jargon surrounding the Internet, makes it difficult for them to establish common knowledge and understanding both internally with their IT department, and externally, with interactive agencies.[6]

There is no established 'best practice' for using e-marketing and database techniques within marketing management. There is instead considerable experimentation, some of which is not very well justified. Typical reasons for using interactive techniques include:

I need to be seen doing this because it's the hot thing to be in at the moment and I'd like it on my CV.

All my competitors seem to be doing this type of activity, so there must be something in it.

I can try it out to see what benefit it brings!

The agencies are very keen on proposing interactive options in campaigns, so I should be doing this as they know more than I do about this area.

Interactive agencies and marketing managers are learning together as they start to integrate e-marketing techniques into campaigns. As long as agencies can stay ahead of marketing managers in terms of knowledge of this area, they will be perceived as the experts. Understanding how to partner effectively with agencies and other third parties will be increasingly important for marketers. Stroud defines partnering skills as key for the interactive marketer. Understanding, developing and managing alliances are critical for success in e-business, and Stroud considers that partnership skills are the least developed category of the marketer's new skill set.[7]

OUTBOUND VS INBOUND MARKETING

Many marketers still market based on outbound 'news' and messaging to potential customers, but e-business and database techniques may help change this. There are several reasons why this outbound messaging is so prevalent amongst financial services companies. Mitchell suggests that marketing focuses on the seller's rather than the buyer's needs: 'The entire edifice and paraphernalia of marketing as we know it – brands, advertising, direct marketing, market research, public relations, and so on, are affiliated to the seller's interests – they are there to help sellers sell. This is why when companies talk about marketing effectiveness, the sole criteria for measuring it is the degree to which the company's – not the consumer's – objectives are achieved cost effectively.'[8] Relationship Marketing Resource proposes that 'big-budget mass marketers are shooting blanks on the Internet… (because they) are advertisers not marketers'.[9]

Financial services product marketers often communicate to potential customers by product 'trigger points' versus consumer-needs triggers, as shown in Table 7.3.

As databases have become more complex, it is becoming easier to provide the right information that potential customers are looking for at the point in their lives when they need this information, and when they are more likely to try out something new/switch products as a result.

Table 7.4 gives an example of the contrast.

Table 7.3 Product and consumer-driven communication

Product-driven communication	Consumer-needs-based communication (the 'whole life' experience)
• New product launch • New variant launch • Product innovation/facility improvement • Product name change • Product with early sign-up discount • Fixed cut-off date for sign-up to product	• Pregnant • Birth of baby • House move • Becoming a student • Leaving home • Going on holiday • Starting school • Birthday/Christmas/Valentine's Day • Marriage • Seasonal changes – winter/summer • Receiving a bonus or windfall • Retirement

Table 7.4 Example of the contrast between product and consumer needs-driven communication

Product driven	'We have launched this great new mortgage product which allows you to offset your credit balance against your loan.' Communication via press ad.
Consumer-needs driven	'I am three months' pregnant, we live in a one-bedroom flat and do not know how we can afford to move to somewhere larger.' Details of innovative mortgage product together with a voucher to pay valuation fees placed in the *Baby Club* magazine received by mothers in their 3rd–6th month of pregnancy.

Caccavale suggests that many companies use a 'one-shot' marketing model, based on a marketing calendar, with 'events' driven by the organization, not the consumer.[10] He argues that companies should incorporate both customer- and company-driven events into their marketing, and recognize the different mindsets and the technology required to deliver the desired results. He uses the example of a mail-order company that offers good customer-centric service at Christmas, by providing a list of all the recipients of gifts from the customer in the previous year, together with details of the previous gift and five suggestions for this year's gift. A similar approach used by financial services companies would drive the 'whole life' experience, with only a few dates required to be able to predict school starting, travel financing and insurance, health insurance, pension investments, etc.

GLOBAL EXPECTATIONS LOCALLY MET

Customer expectations may be global, but financial services companies should think in terms of meeting needs at a local level. With the growth in global financial services brands, marketers need to consider the global implications of interactive marketing using the Web. Global financial services companies quoting their customer service telephone lines on the Web should not purely use US call centres with US hours of availability, or US address formats on their site. Of course marketers need also to consider using multiple languages on their site, and not just English, if they wish to appeal to a global audience. A further complication for financial services sites is that regulatory and compliance issues can arise if individuals in certain countries are allowed to purchase financial products from a global Web site hosted in a specific country. Disclaimers on the Home page are unlikely to be sufficient. This is another headache for marketing managers – they now need to manage customers to whom they cannot legally market.

LOSS OF CONTROL

The Internet means that marketing managers have less control over the company's image. Traditionally, marketing managers acted as custodians of a company's image in the marketplace, and as such, could largely control all communication about the company in the public domain. With the growth of consumer-to-consumer Web sites, users can voice their own opinions about a company on the Web, without involving the financial services company at all, and these opinions may contradict the company's own messages to the public. De Chernatony highlights how the Internet has enabled potential customers to share information with each other, without involving the company.[11] He cites a retail example – the www.mcspotlight.org site, where potential customers who are against McDonald's share their views. Their home page states 'McDonald's spends over $2 billion a year broadcasting their glossy image to the world. This is a small space for alternatives to be heard.'

PERFORMANCE MEASURES POSE A PROBLEM

Traditional performance measures for marketing managers do not normally encourage consumer-needs-driven (customer want and needs) marketing. Many marketing managers in financial services companies have yet to see the value of needs-driven marketing. Marketing managers are focused on their individual product sales alone rather than on whether the needs of particular types of customers are met. A shift in traditional behaviour and attitudes of marketing managers requires new business performance measures, eg a balanced scorecard. This framework specifically seeks to incorporate measures that assess the progress made in developing the value of a portfolio of potential customers over time (eg relative economic value of individuals over time) together with traditional product-level measures. If marketing managers worked more closely with third parties, this would facilitate them contacting potential customers as their needs are changing and being proactive with promotional materials and information.

KNOWLEDGE MANAGEMENT

Lack of knowledge management processes is slowing the progress in adopting 'best practice' e-marketing management techniques. Without an effective intranet, the opportunity to share the results of experimentation in e-marketing techniques is limited. There is an ongoing risk that marketing budget will be wasted on 'reinventing the wheel'. For example, answering consumer queries can be facilitated by sharing outbound campaign information across the marketing and customer relations teams through a central repository for campaign information. However, Wiedemann points out that marketers now need to understand how to receive responses to campaigns into their organization for maximum benefit, and not just to manage the outbound campaigns.[12]

It is highly likely that many of these companies 'do not know what they know' about their potential customers either explicitly or implicitly. By building knowledge-sharing capabilities, financial services companies can increase their agility to respond to market opportunities in real time rather than the more traditional timings for new product developments or targeted campaigns. In his book *Information Masters*,[13] McKean draws several curves showing how the timing of innovation curves significantly lags behind opportunity – a situation common in many financial services companies today.

However, good KM processes can equally be applied to other parts of the marketing management process. It is too easy to use a third party as a knowledge base! Marketing managers can become reliant on a small, selected group of agencies for news of other areas inside the industry. There is no mechanism for capturing this knowledge inside the organization. Whilst technology addresses the issue of data being located in a central repository, it is the human interaction with the data that generates the understanding needed to keep abreast of developments in the potential customer base. Without close care and attention by the financial services organization, the value of the data can be lost as it becomes corrupt over time through neglect.

Often it is the third party that gains from this, albeit not intentionally. The staff employed to prepare, execute and report on a variety of analyses learn a significant amount through the process of doing the work itself. Passive involvement from the financial services marketing organization, due to shorter-term financial constraints and/or a lack of skills to undertake the work itself, often results in a more superficial understanding of the financial impact of changes in consumer behaviour. This results in a lesser understanding of the opportunities and threats that this presents to a financial services organization at any particular point in time. Once the third party obtains knowledge about a company's potential customers and the initiatives the company is undertaking to meet the needs of those potential customers, the opportunity and competitive advantage are diluted as the information leaks into the market and competitors react to counter any potentially damaging initiatives.

MANAGEMENT PROCESSES

Various marketing processes involve many approvals, both internally and with third parties. Effective use of intranets and extranets to make processes become transparent would reduce 'bottlenecks' in the process and save time and resource. Effective use of intranets/extranets could also simplify complex marketing processes by facilitating heightened levels of collaboration (within the financial services company and with agents and brokers) through improved communication and sharing of information. Intranets and extranets would also enhance competitive advantage. The financial services company that can provide an accurate and timely understanding of potential customer demand in a way that drives purchase behaviour for its products is the one that will secure the competitive high ground. Understanding purchase behaviour through 'whole life' monitoring is one approach to this, although the constraints of the Data Protection Act need to be taken account of when sharing information.

Typical marketing management processes that could be improved through the use of intranets or extranets include:

- Artwork development for new/amended product portfolios. This involves developing and checking copy (involvement of marketing managers), legal approvals, concept generation and artwork development with design houses, final printing approvals with reprographics houses and printing. There is the potential for bottlenecks at every stage in this process, as there are usually several phases of iterations and amendments and the traditional method of avoiding bottlenecks is via persistent chasing through phone/fax/e-mail. With an intranet and extranet to design agencies/repro houses, all parties could see exactly what stage of development the artwork had reached, where the bottlenecks were and suggest contingencies/alternative options.
- Annual promotions budgeting and planning, both internally and with third parties. Using intranets and sharing information across products could facilitate cross-product promotions budgeting and planning. Once promotions plans are agreed, these could be shared with agents, retailers and IFAs through extranets, so third parties could see their specific promotions packages and be kept updated on changes rather than waiting for meetings with the dedicated account managers.

- Promotions implementation with third parties. Vouchers, leaflets, point of sale and advertorials could be developed and approved using intermediaries' or financial services companies' extranets, so that information could be updated more quickly and everyone involved in the process could see changes – saving time, resource and money.
- Media planning. Using an intranet to collaborate across products and categories when planning media spending (annually or by campaign) would facilitate measurement of overall spend and opportunities to make the most effective use of spend (ie purchase of group advertising spots, etc).
- Consumer queries. Queries from potential customers, complaints or suggestions could be logged onto an intermediary extranet, enabling financial services companies to access and act on these (integrate suggestions or complaints into the product improvement processes). Likewise, queries, comments, suggestions and complaints from the financial services company's own contact centres could also be logged on intranets so that product teams can be kept up to date with consumer feedback and also feed these comments into internal processes.
- Product guidelines. Placing product guidelines and policies on financial services companies' intranets/extranets would reduce errors made by teams operating in silos if changes take place to any of the specifications (eg using old logos in leaflets by accident). By incorporating different levels of access in extranets, appropriate information could be streamed to third parties (eg reprographics houses, designers) dependent on the level of detail required.
- Sharing and collaboration. Using intranets and extranets as a way of sharing knowledge about potential customers would help financial services companies streamline the amount of information washing around the organization through a reduction in the number or duplicate market research reports.

THE ROLE OF ACCOUNT MANAGERS IN MARKETING TO INTERMEDIARIES

If marketing to intermediaries is facilitated by e-enabled processes between financial services companies and third parties, this could change the way account managers work. The main role of those who manage big brokerage accounts for financial services companies is to build relationships, facilitate collaboration, share information and enhance buyers' mind-share of their particular products. If brokers can use financial services companies' extranets to access and share information on new product launches, plan promotions and gain approvals on below-the-line activity, how will this impact the role of the account manager? Will this role exist in the future in its current form? In order to maximize opportunities to collaborate with third parties through intranets/extranets, financial services companies may have to change their approach to working with third parties, which may require a change of mindset (and potentially company culture).

Financial services companies often have an uneasy relationship with intermediaries, as they play several roles in the value chain. They fulfil the role of supplier, relying on the broker or independent financial advisor (IFA) to promote and sell their products, whilst knowing that the broker or IFA also stocks their competitors' (ie other financial services companies') products. However, they also compete directly with third parties who produce own-label products.

The third party wants to maximize sales of the financial services company's products, but acknowledges that if another financial services company provides better margins, promotions, and special deals they will focus on the other company. The third party also knows that the financial services company will be trying to build relationships with many third parties, therefore will not build the relationship with them to the detriment of other third parties. This results in a co-dependent but uneasy relationship between financial services company and intermediary, requiring significant collaboration, whilst recognizing that they may be in direct competition with each other.

To maximize efficiencies in marketing processes, financial services companies would need to make greater use of extranets, collaborating with third parties (and other third parties such as design agencies) through sharing large amounts of information. This may require a significant change of mindset in some financial services companies, if their relationship with third parties is currently more adversarial, based on controlling or drip-feeding of information, rather than one of partnership and open data sharing.

CONCLUSION

There are a number of e-business areas that senior marketing management in financial services institutions and third parties should focus on if they are to enhance their competitiveness and the efficiency of their joint efforts. However, it is also clear that progress depends not on technology alone, but also on changes to the way people work and to the processes by which they work.

Notes

1. Hoffman, D L and Novak, T P (2000) When exposure-based Web advertising stops making sense (and what CDNOW did about it), eLab, Owen Graduate School of Management, Vanderbilt University; http://elab.vanderbilt.edu/research/papers/html/manuscripts/cdnow.jan2001.htm
2. Rozanski, H D, Bollmann, G and Lipman, M (2001) Seize the occasion: the seven segment system of online marketing, *Strategy in Business*, Issue 24, Booz Allen & Hamilton
3. Deighton, J (1996) The future of interactive marketing, *Harvard Business Review*, November–December, pp 151–66, quoted in Crick, P (2001) An Exploratory Investigation of Consumer Perceptions towards the Internet as an Enabler of Marketing Relationships, Master's Dissertation, Henley Management College

4   Uncles, M (2001) Interactive electronic marketing and brand management, *Journal of Brand Management*, **8** (4–5), May (Editorial), pp 245–54

5   Abbot, J (2000) The exploding volume and scope of customer information, theory and practice: a relationship marketing viewpoint, pp 22–55. Taken from Crick, P (2001) An Exploratory Investigation of Consumer Perceptions towards the Internet as an Enabler of Marketing Relationships, Master's Dissertation, Henley Management College

6   Stroud, R (2001) Interactive marketing needs interactive marketers, *Interactive Marketing*, **2** (3), January–March, pp 230–39

7   Stroud, R (2001) Interactive marketing needs interactive marketers, *Interactive Marketing*, **2** (3), January–March, pp 230–39

8   Mitchell, A (2000) In one-to-one marketing, which 'one' comes first? *Interactive Marketing*, **1** (4), April–June, pp 354–67

9   Relationship marketing resource: the role of interactive marketing online. Available (online): http://www.relationshipmktg.com/Freepercent20Articles/ArticleIndex.htm, quoted from Crick, P (2001) An Exploratory Investigation of Consumer Perceptions towards the Internet as an Enabler of Marketing Relationships, Master's Dissertation, Henley Management College

10 Caccavale, M (2000) Exploiting interactive marketing, *Interactive Marketing*, **1** (3), January–March, pp 277–83

11 De Chernatony, L (2001) Succeeding with brands on the Internet, *Brand Management*, **8** (35), February, pp 186–90

12 Wiedemann, G (2001) Optimized marketing in the Internet age, *Interactive Marketing*, **3** (1), July–September, pp 7–10

13 McKean, J S (1999) *The Information Masters*, Wiley

8

The implications of e-commerce for strategy: UK case studies

Tim Hughes

INTRODUCTION

A review of press coverage on financial services and e-commerce reveals that there is plenty of activity going on in both the banking and insurance sectors.[1] Companies with existing sites have been extending the services offered (for example, Abbey National Mortgage Management Service, Lloyds TSB Wealth Management site and HSBC Business Banking). They are also looking to extend the service from PC into interactive TV and mobile telephony (for example, Barclays, Nationwide Building Society and Abbey National have all launched services on mobile phones, while Lloyds TSB and Abbey National have been testing interactive banking on television). In addition, major companies previously with a limited Web presence have recently launched new initiatives, notably Norwich Union and Royal & Sun Alliance with its More Th>n brand. Customer numbers through the Internet have been growing: Barclays claims 1.7 million, Lloyds TSB 1.2 million, and Egg 1.72 million. However the start-up investment can also be considerable; Norwich Union quotes a cost of £250 million for building and marketing its site.

How far will e-commerce alter the nature of these businesses as it evolves and develops? The Internet has been predicted to change business quite fundamentally.[2] The continued growth and globalization of electronic marketing has been described as the single biggest opportunity and threat facing almost every industry, laying the foundation for a new industrial order because it will change the relationship between producers and consumers.

In the new Internet age, it is argued, companies can no longer rely on the traditional bricks and mortar model, and managers need to rethink and reshape their business strategies. These changes apply particularly to service industries, though reducing the cost of interacting with the customer.

The impact that new technology may have on traditional financial services companies is multifaceted. It changes the basic cost dimensions of business. For example, it has been estimated that the cost-income ratio for banks using the Internet as the dominant delivery method is 15 per cent, compared with 55–60 per cent for branch and 35–40 per cent for telephone delivery.[3] It may also change the distribution structure. The need to own a branch network or have a sales force is no longer a barrier to entry. This will present financial services companies with new challenges that go far beyond the technical ones of adopting new technologies. Organizationally, companies may have to restructure to manage efficiently a number of different routes to market. Culturally they may have to change ways of thinking within their businesses to cope with competitors with different brand values. Previous research of banks[4] found that 57 per cent of respondents believed that cultural or resource limitations were restricting the development of e-commerce.

THE CASE DEVELOPMENT APPROACH

This chapter takes a case study approach, involving interviews across a range of different functions, in order to obtain a broad-based managerial view of the way in which these financial services organizations have been developing strategies to respond to these changes. Four case studies were developed from a series of in-depth interviews. The cases were chosen to represent the two major categories of the financial services industry: banking and insurance. The UK retail financial services market covers a wide range of institutions, including banks, building societies, insurance companies, credit card issuers, investment trusts, stock exchanges, leasing companies, national savings, unit trusts and others. Because of this diversity it is difficult to conduct research that covers every sector comprehensively. However, the main distinction is between the two main market sectors of banking (including building societies) and insurance. Traditionally insurance companies sold insurance and pension products and banks and building societies dealt with banking products, but this distinction has become meaningless in recent years, as companies in both sectors have increasingly started to sell both product ranges. In the light of this situation, three criteria were used to guide the selection of organizations for the case studies:

1. The primary business should be in the banking and/or the insurance sector of financial services.
2. They should have an existing involvement in e-commerce.

3. There should be a willing sponsor and access to managers within the business.

The main focus of the research has been on how far marketing principles and practice have been applied in developing e-commerce strategies. How far can the ways that the companies developed strategies for e-commerce be described as market oriented? It has been suggested that as market orientation involves doing something new or different in response to market conditions, it may be viewed as a form of innovative behaviour.[5] While market orientation has been extensively researched in quantitative studies across many countries and industry sectors,[6] there has been little recent, in-depth, empirical research into the operation of the marketing concept in either the banking industry or other financial services sectors, and the fact that the whole industry is changing so rapidly suggests that this is overdue.

THE SIGNIFICANCE OF E-COMMERCE IN FINANCIAL SERVICES

There was an almost universal feeling among respondents that e-commerce would have an immense impact on financial services. However, two important qualifications emerge. With regard to the pace of the change, some media claims concerning the immediate impact of e-commerce must be seen in the context of the hype that generally surrounded e-commerce at the end of the 20th century. The respondents suggest that in consumer markets the pace of change will be dictated by the willingness of customers to utilize the new technology and also the adoption of easier to use technology in the form of digital TV and mobile telephony. Therefore the adoption will probably take the form more of evolution rather than revolution. The second emerging point is that e-commerce is seen to be of fundamental importance right across the spectrum of financial services. While much emphasis has been put on applicability to banking,[7] there is also clearly much potential in the insurance sector to transform the market. Interestingly, it is business-to-business e-commerce transactions that are predicted to be transforming many sectors in other markets at the fastest speed.[8] Much of insurance-based financial services business is already business-to-business, involving independent financial advisers (IFAs), who are rapidly adopting the Internet as a business tool with the encouragement and support of product suppliers.

Probing on the nature of the impact of e-commerce obtained answers that fell into three main categories.

Information

The Internet is seen as a powerful research tool that will allow potential customers to compare product details more easily than in the past. In particular, this is because the

Internet is so capable of aggregating information and giving people the information that they want, as they want it and when they want it.

The provision of information should evolve, in time, from providing standard brochure-type information to something that can be individually configured and tailored to the needs of the individual. Personalized information can be made available faster and more economically. This includes electronic provision of valuations on policies, answers to questions and queries, access to policy details and statements and customer feedback. An important feature of the Internet is seen to be that information can be made available faster and more economically than by traditional means. Customers can perform searches more easily with little cost. This has been predicted to be an important mechanism in shifting power away from suppliers to customers.[9]

From the product suppliers' point of view there are opportunities to share information electronically and information on clients can be accessed far more efficiently, so shortening the supply chain. One respondent gives an example of pension schemes where an insurance company requires payroll information: 'Traditionally this would mean that the employer would collate this information on paper, pass it to the IFA who would then pass it to insurance company. With the technology we've got now, we can take that information directly from the employer's payroll computer and just feed it directly into the insurance company's computer.' The potential of the Internet to transform supply chain management has been described as a Darwinian evolution.[10] While supply chain management is not new, the argument goes that the Internet is transforming the supply chain because it greatly reduces the cost of gaining access to information, it increases the richness of the data that can be exchanged and it greatly increases the size of the audience that can be reached electronically.

Transactions and servicing

This idea of a shortening supply chain also applies in the area of transactions and servicing. The option is opened up for more self-servicing directly by the customer on his or her account and also by IFAs in using electronic forms. In theory it should be possible to provide a seamless system for all aspects of a transaction and for ongoing servicing. It is in self-service manipulation of existing accounts and policies that there is seen to be the most benefit. As one respondent puts it, e-commerce: ' gives customers the power to do many things that used to either take days or weeks, or that quite often customers didn't do because it was too much trouble and [took] too much time'. Self-service is seen as a preferable alternative to customers giving instructions to staff who then execute the transaction, and is quite a fundamental change in the nature of the relationship. The idea of using e-commerce to enable customers to conduct their own transactions does not necessarily mean the end of the bank branch. In the retail banking operation studied there does not seem to be a widespread expectation that e-commerce will lead to many branch closures, rather that the role of the branches and branch staff will change. It is hoped that staff will be able to spend time more productively in developing customer relationships and focusing on more complex products. As one manager puts it, the challenge is to 'find the proper place for e in the world of the branch and the proper place for the branch in the world of e'.

Costs and productivity

The significance of cost reduction as a driver to the adoption of e-commerce in financial services has been stressed by a number of authors.[11] New electronic channels are recognized as more cost-effective than telephone and branch-based networks and this is forecast to change the distribution structure dramatically. The potential for cost savings is demonstrated in its purest form in the case of one of the case-study organizations that had developed a stand-alone Internet bank. There are savings on branch networks and sales forces, and also benefits from the automation of internal processes: 'The straight-through processes, the internal knowledge management, the intranet and extranet capabilities that are quite fundamental when it comes to e-commerce. It's those internal efficiencies, those old processes that banks run, bring those online, making them more efficient, designing them around the channel not around the process means that eventually you will be able to pass some of those benefits on.' Keeping overheads low is partly about enabling customers to do it themselves without having to employ large numbers of staff, but making these cost savings depends on the willingness of customers to operate their account in the way that the bank would like them to do. One of the Internet bank interviewees points out that many customers prefer using the telephone, but it is expensive compared to the Internet. This is mainly because of the logistics of manning customer service units. The Internet bank Customer Services Manager explains: 'It's a lot easier if you are responding to an e-mail within the hour, it's a lot easier to respond to that than responding to a call within 30 seconds. There are real economies of scale.'

There is also much potential for cost savings in the insurance sector. At the time of the research the advent of the stakeholder pension was providing a focus for cost reduction. According to an insurance company sales manager, one of the benefits of e-commerce is that: 'It enables the company, at a high level, to look back at the organization and say – here is a system that will enable us to mechanize a large number of processes which are currently carried out by people.' Clearly this will have implications for the organization and the roles within it. Potentially this means lower costs and a shift in some administration to wherever appropriate labour can be found. One organization had already announced that some jobs previously done in the UK would now be done in India and it is felt that e-commerce will extend this.

However, the cost savings appear to be more theoretical than in practice at the moment. In all case studies it was clear that a lot of work is still required in order to fully automate the back office. The benefits of better supply chain management, through e-commerce, do not seem to be coming through yet. In addition, for banking products, the cost of acquiring customers by paying high interest to entice customers into Internet accounts means that they are not profitable. A banking finance manager points out that on the basis of rates paid at the moment on Internet savings accounts and mortgages the books don't balance and at some stage this will have to change: 'You've got to build up the critical mass of accounts that you've got running on those systems before they can start making money to pay for the system investment we have had. If those accounts that you are running are all loss-making accounts in themselves, again the maths just don't work.' Press reports[12] tend to confirm the lack of profitability in the early years. For instance, Egg ran for a number of years without making a profit.

HOW DIFFERENT COMPANIES ARE APPROACHING E-BUSINESS

Clearly, as outlined above, the perception of the interviewees, across the case studies, was that e-commerce does represent a major change that will have significant implications for their organizations. In the light of this, how was each organization responding? This section provides a short description of this, based on the feedback provided to each organization.

The reluctant approach of a life insurance company

While recognizing the potential significance of e-commerce, this company had not really taken steps to seriously address the issue of how e-commerce could integrate with the rest of the operation. At the time it was felt that many of the senior managers had little hands-on experience of using the Internet and had not really caught up with how this development could be used most effectively for their business. There was no clear strategic direction for the company in this area. Ownership of e-commerce within the organization had proved to be a contentious issue over the previous two years. Initially the marketing function had been responsible for driving strategy and implementation. However, this had been moved away from the marketing function which purely retained responsibility for the Web-site design. Each individual division was given responsibility for driving e-commerce within its area on the basis that this would widen responsibility for taking e-commerce forward across the organization. The result had been a complete lack of strategic or coordinated management of e-commerce and after a short period formal strategic responsibility for e-commerce had been centralized again to a corporate development function. At the time of the interviews for the case study, this organization had not advanced beyond the provision of a basic Web site and was in the process of trying to decide the best way forward in electronic servicing of its primary market – the IFA sector.

The integrated approach of a national retail banking operation

This organization has had a presence on the Internet for several years, but it was only at the end of 1999 that it had really taken the decision to follow an e-commerce strategy in a big way. The chief executive had taken the lead in this and seems to have forced through a rapid e-commerce programme, bypassing many of the normal committees and procedures involved in implementing change. In essence this was achieved through working closely with just two other senior managers, the IT Director and the newly appointed Director of Retail Services, to plan and drive through the change. The strategy for e-commerce seemed to be clear and widely understood. Internet terminals had been provided in many branches and the Internet accounts were designed to promote self-service by customers and in turn to reduce the number of over-the-counter transactions. This integrated approach contrasts sharply with those organizations that have put the majority of their development resources into setting up stand-alone Internet banking operations. The focus on mobilizing resources quickly had been successful in getting this integrated e-commerce operation up and running and this organization is now a major player in Internet banking. Significant efforts had been made in internal communications to manage the message so that branch staff did not feel threatened by this development. However, there was a feeling that there was still a long way to go if the organization is to evolve sufficiently to gain the benefits of shifting the burden of administration work to the customer and reorienting staff to other more profitable customer-oriented activities. In particular, it was recognized that to maintain the momentum, ownership and involvement needed to be deepened across the organization. Reaping the full benefits of a business transformation would only be achieved through a sustained effort over a long time.

The focus for change in an international insurance company

This international company had been through many changes in recent years as a result of a number of acquisitions by the parent company, resulting in the need to merge with other operations. The businesses have been run along distribution channel lines, with each distribution channel claiming 'ownership' of its customers. E-commerce was described as an agent of change within this organization and it was recognized that low-cost distribution would be increasingly important in the future. However, there was little consensus about the strategy for e-commerce and there were a lot of different initiatives happening, often competing for scarce development resources. In addition, there was also a major new e-commerce project under way that had been initiated from the head office. While this organization recognized the need for some fundamental change, there seemed to be some enormous cultural and practical barriers to overcome in effective implementation. Not surprisingly, in this situation, activity seems to have been very internally focused in trying to overcome these barriers, with mixed results in terms of the development of successful e-commerce initiatives to date.

The stand-alone Internet bank

In this case the parent bank had set up a separate Internet operation with a distinct brand. The decision to take this route had been taken following a strategic review on the appointment of a new chief executive. The separate Internet bank provided the opportunity to target a younger group of customers on a national basis. At the same time the links with the parent organization meant that it could call upon the parent company's skills and resources without necessarily being constrained to operate within the same systems or culture. Quite deliberately the Internet bank had been set up with its own distinct culture and ways of operating. The management structure was very flat and all individuals were encouraged to take on extra responsibilities and to run with projects, often extending their range of competencies. The Internet bank was situated in one office and a lot of emphasis had been put on staff working together to improve customer service. All customer feedback came back into this one operational unit and processes existed to collect this feedback and then ensure that changes were made to the way of operating so that service improvement could be effectively implemented. This is a contrast with the parent bank's operation, where communication lines were long, management hierarchies predominated and service improvements could be very difficult to implement. There are undoubtedly some major challenges ahead for the Internet bank. In particular, managing growth would seem to be an issue for the future. The current compact structure encourages a high degree of involvement and loyalty amongst employees. Will it be possible to maintain and foster this culture and manage growth without creating new management hierarchies?

KEY FACTORS IN DEVELOPING EFFECTIVE STRATEGIES

The role of senior management

One theme that is apparent in these case studies is the role of senior management leadership in setting a strategy and securing the focus and resources to implement it successfully within the organization. In the retail banking organization and the Internet bank the chief executives acted decisively to define the companies' approaches to e-commerce and have clearly prioritized this development above other activities. For example, in the retail banking organization a middle manager responsible for aspects of the branch operation described how the chief executive called him in just before Christmas and said: 'I want you to get ready for e-commerce launch and it's going to be big. It's going to be bigger than you can imagine now. It's going to be the biggest thing potentially that we do this year. Just clear the way.' Others describe this chief executive as the main driving force, with a personal involvement and a keen interest in the technology. In the Internet bank the operations manager describes the critical role of the chief executive (of the parent bank) as follows: 'This is his baby, he has driven it, he gives it his full 100 per cent support and it's very comforting running the business, as we're spending money very quickly, to know that we've got his support and that he understands the strategic importance to it.'

The limitations of market intelligence from customers at a time of technological change

The marketing literature stresses that a market-oriented organization is focused on the needs of its customers through the collection and dissemination of market intelligence,[13] but how far can information from an existing market be utilized in setting strategy at a time of technological innovation? The relationship between market orientation and innovation is not clear. It has even been argued[14] that a customer focus could be detrimental to innovation based on the idea that this seduces the business to being narrowly interested in short-term customer needs. The evidence from the case studies appears to be that although an enormous amount of research and intelligence was gathered and used within the companies (particularly in the cases of the life company, the retail banking organization and the Internet bank), it was of only limited applicability in developing strategy. This is because of uncertainty about the future and the difficulty in researching theoretical propositions with customers. Certainly the evidence from the case studies brings into question the degree of influence that intelligence generation and dissemination have on strategic decision making in these circumstances. At the level of strategy development, during a time of technological change, the market-oriented organization requires long-term thinking and the capability to anticipate customers' future needs[15]; however, the mechanics of market sensing in this way still seems to be very vague and it is not clear how it fits into existing models.

Capabilities required in a changing environment

The nature of the decisions on e-commerce strategy being made in the case studies depended on the view taken by management on how the organizations could benefit from the use of e-commerce. In this there was a degree of anticipation of what the future market would be like and a consideration of the resource capabilities and options open to the organizations. The aspect of strategy relating to the way that corporate resources are used and allocated brings up the issue of what has become known as the resource-based view (RBV). This perspective[16] takes the position that successful strategy is mainly about the effective development and utilization of corporate resources. Interestingly, in this view the greater the rate of change in the environment, the more the organization must rely on internal resources and capabilities in taking strategic decisions. An RBV perspective on e-commerce would stress the importance of its potential to change the nature of one of the core assets of the financial services organizations involved; that is, the distribution system. As outlined earlier, there is a belief within the financial services organizations studied that e-commerce enables product information to be far more accessible and many transactions to be carried out remotely through self-service. Potentially this changes the value and the role of existing distribution routes such as branch networks for banks and intermediaries and sales forces for insurance companies. The nature of an important element of the marketing mix is changing and the ability of financial services organizations to compete will depend, in part, on the capability of the firm to build a strong competitive position in this new situation. Achieving success in this would seem to require an ability to anticipate or even encourage the development of new customer behaviour together with the capabilities of the company to deliver to the customer's new agenda.

Choosing a strategy as a creative act

It has been suggested that 'There may be times when choosing a strategy consistent with the resources a firm controls is a creative and even entrepreneurial act'.[17] As such, existing theoretical models have limitations as explanations of the phenomenon. While, as discussed earlier, the mechanics of market sensing are not really explained in market orientation models, RBV theory, as currently conceptualized, can also be criticized for taking an oversimplified view of how resources are connected to the strategies pursued. In reality there may be many routes to achieving competitive advantage and it is wrong to assume that during a time of technological change the actions a firm needs to take to exploit its resources will be self-evident. In this situation it is perhaps understandable that in the two banking case study organizations the chief executives were closely involved in deciding the route to take and in giving the priority and impetus for the developments to happen quickly. Who else in the organizations concerned would be in a sufficiently strong position to take accountability for the level of risk involved in setting out a strategic direction (involving major resource implications) while consumer take-up and success in this area were still uncertain? In the event the paths taken by these two organizations can be seen to be very different.

AN INTEGRATED OR STAND-ALONE APPROACH?

The contrasting strategies being pursued by the two banking organizations involved in the research illustrate an important issue of whether the Internet should be used to set up a separate business with a different brand and management or whether it should be integrated into the existing operation. There is a strong argument[18] that the benefits of integration are almost always too great to be abandoned entirely and that the question that companies should be asking is about degree of integration rather than seeing it as a black or white, all or nothing choice. The choice is primarily about trust (the strength of the existing brand) and flexibility (the opportunity to focus exclusively on a new business model) and this can be seen to be very relevant to the Internet bank. Because the decision had been made to target a new customer segment, it made sense for the Internet bank organization to develop a new brand and a new and separate operation with its own distinct style. However, the separation from the parent bank has not been total and the Internet operation has both capital backing and access to many shared resources (such as IT, Marketing and Human Resources). In addition, the route chosen has allowed the bank to keep its strategic options open for the future. The strategy pursued by the Internet bank has a degree of flexibility that is undoubtedly important in reacting to a rapidly changing situation. In the new digital economy it has been argued that strategy needs to be revisited and revised far more regularly than previously.[19] The potential for regularly changing direction as a result of this would seem to favour the smaller separate operation.

Against this is the argument that it is only by pursuing an integrated strategy that the biggest benefits may be achieved.[20] By viewing Internet operations in isolation, managers are failing to integrate the Internet into their proven strategies and are not harnessing their most important elements of competitive advantage. Integration requires a long-term and highly coordinated implementation of strategy. For example, the retail banking organization will only gain the benefits of its integrated approach by fully automating its back-office processes and by taking advantage of customers' use of self-service to free up staff to take on new roles that add value in different ways; for instance, if branch staff spend more time in offering face-to-face advice, resulting in better customer service or higher sales of other financial services products.

CONCLUSIONS

There appears to have been a remarkable consensus from the case studies that e-commerce will have great implications for the way that many different types of financial products and services will be sold, transacted and serviced. It is generally anticipated that it will fundamentally change the economics of distribution for financial services. There was less agreement, though, on the pace of the change and the degree of uptake amongst different segments. In addition, during a period of rapid change, making strategic decisions can be very challenging. At the early stages of adoption of a new technology there are distinct limitations in how far market information is useful and reliable and there may be a considerable 'leap of faith' in assessing how resources and capabilities can best be deployed to develop a competitive advantage.

There is no one path to follow and the strategy needs to be adaptable to changing circumstances. While it would seem to be important to have a strong impetus from the top in getting the initial momentum for the e-commerce initiative, clearly it is the operational end of the organization that must develop it over time and adapt it to changing circumstances and customer needs. It is too early to say whether this can be more effectively done in the 'hot-house' environment of the Internet-only subsidiary or by integrating Internet distribution with the rest of the operation. While the Internet-only route provides a more focused environment, the integrated approach provides the potential to offer customers more choice to deal with their financial services provider in the way that most suits them at any particular time.

Despite the uncertainties, the danger of not having a strategy for e-commerce may be greater than starting with a strategy that may have to change and develop over time. Internet technology is here to stay and will need to be used by financial services companies if they want to remain competitive. In the life company and the international insurance company case studies there was recognition that they needed a strategic approach, but at the time of the research this was not fully developed in the life company and not communicated or integrated in the international insurance company. In view of the potential of the Internet to change the nature of distribution channels, it would seem to be imperative for all financial services companies to develop a strategic approach, albeit one that will change and adapt over time as the application of the technology develops.

Notes

[1] Review of coverage during 2001 in *Revolution* (www.uk.revolutionmagazine.com)

[2] The expected changes are described in the following papers: Achrol, R and Kotler, P (1999) Marketing in the Network Economy, *Journal of Marketing*, **63** (Special issue), pp 146–63; Hamel, G and Sampler, J (1998) The e-corporation (online e-commerce building a new industrial order), *Fortune*, 7 December, p 80; Lord, C (2000) The practicalities of developing a successful e-business strategy, *Journal of Business Strategy*, 21 March, Vol 21 No 2, p 40; Cross, G J (2000) How e-business is transforming supply chain management, *Journal of Business Strategy*, 21 March, Vol 21 No 2, p 36; Wymbs, C (2000) How e-commerce is transforming and internationalizing service industries, *Journal of Services Marketing*, **14** (6), pp 463–77

[3] Durkin, M and Bennett, H (1999) Employee commitment in retail banking: identifying and exploring hidden dangers, *The International Journal of Bank Marketing*, **17** (3), pp 124–37

[4] Daniel, E (1999) Provision of electronic banking in the UK and the Republic of Ireland, *The International Journal of Bank Marketing*, **17** (2), pp 72–83

5   Jaworski, B J and Kohli, A K (1993) Market orientation: antecedents and consequences, *Journal of Marketing*, **57** (3), pp 53–70. In addition, Hurley, R F, Hult, G and Tomas, M (1998) Innovation, market orientation, and organizational learning: an integration and empirical examination, *Journal of Marketing*, **62** (3), pp 42–54

6   Lafferty, B A and Hult, G T M (2001) A synthesis of contemporary market orientation perspectives, *European Journal of Marketing*, **35**, 1–2

7   Birch, D and Young, M A (1997) Financial services and the Internet – what does cyberspace mean for the financial services industry? *Internet Research: Electronic Networking Applications and Policy*, **7** (2), pp 120–28; Boothroyd, D (1998) A pocketful of change (banking technology), *Computing*, **12** (Nov), pp 46–48; Barnatt, C (1998) Virtual communities and financial services on line business potentials and strategic choice, *International Journal of Bank Marketing*, **16** (4), pp 161–69; Dannenberg, M and Kellner, D (1998) The bank of tomorrow with today's technology, *International Journal of Bank Marketing*, **16** (2), pp 90–97

8   See note 2, Cross (2000)

9   Mitchell, A (2000) 'In one-to-one marketing, which 'one' comes first?', *Interactive Marketing*, **1**(4), April–June, pp 354–68; Tapp, A (2000) *Principles of Direct and Database Marketing*, 2nd Edition, Pearson Education

10 See note 2, Cross (2000)

11 Katz, J and Aspden, P (1997) Motivations for and barriers to Internet useage: results of a national public opinion survey, *Internet Research: Electronic Networking Applications and Policy*, **7** (3), pp 170–188; Stone, M (2000) Editorial, *Journal of Financial Services Marketing*, 4 (2), pp 102–04; Tilden, M (1996) Channel vision, *Retail Banker International*, **28**, pp 12–15

12 *Revolution* (www.uk.revolutionmagazine.com)

13 Kohli, A K and Jaworski, B J (1990) Market orientation: the construct, research propositions, and managerial implications, *Journal of Marketing*, **54** (2), pp 1–18; Kohli, A K, Jaworski, B J and Kumar, A (1993) MARKOR: a measure of market orientation, *Journal of Marketing Research*, **30** (4), p 467; Narver, J C and Slater, S F (1990) The effect of a market orientation on business profitability, *Journal of Marketing*, **54** (4), pp 20–35

14 Hayes, R H and Abernathy, W J (1980) Managing our way to economic decline, *Harvard Business Review*, **58**, July–August, pp 67–77

15 Slater, S F and Narver, J C (1998) Customer led and market oriented: let's not confuse the two, *Strategic Management Journal*, **19** (10), pp 1001–06

16 Grant, R M (1995) *Contemporary Strategy Analysis*, 2nd Edition, Basil Blackwell, Cambridge, MA; Wernerfelt, B (1995) The resource based view of the firm: ten years after, *Strategic Management Journal*, **16**, pp 171–180; Mahoney, J T (1995) The management of resources and the resource of management, *Journal of Business Research*, **33** (2), pp 91–101

17 Barney, J B (2001) Is the resource based 'view' a useful perspective for strategic management research? Yes, *Academy of Management Review*, **26** (1), pp 41–56, quote p 53

18 Gulati, R and Garino, J (2000) Get the right mix of bricks & clicks, *Harvard Business Review*, May–June, pp 107–14

19 Pitt, L (2001) Total e-clipse: five new forces for strategy in the digital age, *Journal of General Management*, **26** (4), pp 1–15

20 Porter, M E (2001) Strategy and the Internet, *Harvard Business Review*, March, pp 63–78

9

Branch and virtual CRM – a Dutch case study: Rabobank

Gerard de Graaff

INTRODUCTION

In this chapter we focus on the 'virtual Rabobank' initiative, which is part of the Rabobank Dutch retail operation. This case study (especially the launch of the new 'virtual Rabobank') in the relatively saturated Dutch market is a good example of the issues and options facing banks in similar markets.

Rabobank Netherlands is the largest retail bank in the Netherlands, with about 7 million customers and 450 local banks all operating under the brand name Rabobank. The Rabobank is a cooperative banking organization with no shareholders and the only 'AAA' bank in the world. The bank can be seen as an 'all-finance' institution, as it includes Rabobank International (corporate and investment banking) and its specialized subsidiary Rabo Securities (Dutch equity), Interpolis (insurance and pensions), De Lage Landen (leasing and trade finance), Robeco Group (asset management and investment funds), Nedship Bank (ship financing), Schretlen & Co (private banking) and Gilde Investment Management (venture capital).

The Dutch banking community is developing many e-commerce activities. Traditional Dutch competitors like ABN/AMRO, ING/Postbank and Fortis have defined and are implementing e-commerce strategies to meet the rapid changing customer demand (anytime, anyplace banking). New foreign banks like the Bank of Scotland are entering the

Dutch market via the Internet. Non-traditional competitors like supermarkets offer financial services while others position themselves between client and bank. These threads as well as the low profit growth of the Dutch retail operation in 1999 (+1 per cent versus +18 per cent at ABN/AMRO) led to the virtual Rabobank initiative.

The virtual Rabobank is defined as the capability of clients to access Rabobank's portfolio of financial services via direct channels (Internet, telephone, mail, ATMs and various new media, including mobiles). The aim is that the virtual Rabobank will be implemented in 2002 and that Rabobank will add value to its customers by being a personalized advice bank. The virtual and real Rabobanks will cooperate to create one combined experience for the customer.

OVERVIEW OF RETAIL BANKING IN THE NETHERLANDS

Four big banking consortia, ABN/AMRO, Rabobank, ING/Postbank and Fortis, dominate the Dutch banking retail market.

ABN/AMRO is the largest bank in the Netherlands, providing all financial services and aiming to use its strong home base to become a truly global player. The bank is expanding internationally – particularly in the USA – and now earns half of its revenue outside the Netherlands. While ABN/AMRO has insurance subsidiaries, it – alone amongst the larger banks in the Netherlands – initially sought to develop its insurance activities itself rather than merging with an existing comparably sized insurance company.

ING/Postbank is the second largest bank in the Netherlands and operates with two distinct identities in the market. ING bank has its own network of branches, own products and market formulas while Postbank operates as a direct writer through local post offices. The ING/Postbank is part of the Nationale-Nederlanden group through merger with one of Europe's largest insurers, Nationale Nederlanden.

The Fortis group is a combination of mainly Dutch and Belgian banking and insurance companies like MeesPierson, AMEV, Belgian AG and ASLK. Within the group a range of specialist companies serve particular product markets and distribution channels. The Fortis group's strategy is 'growth via acquisition'.

Next to these large players, a number of medium and small banks and insurers are present in the Netherlands, such as van Lanschot, Aegon, Ohra bank, etc. Each bank/insurer has an 'All-finance' portfolio of products.

The banking sector in the Netherlands is undergoing rapid change, including increasing competition from insurers in the retail market, very different and changing customer behaviours and needs, new information technologies and strong inroads by niche players. All these result in discontinuous change rather than gradual change, particularly as several challenges require simultaneous attention. Examples include increasing customer focus, innovative services, reduction of costs and the mobilization of employees. The banks are reorienting themselves and transforming to more externally focused and business-directed ways of working. Fundamental reorientation is evident from the perceived necessity to adapt business processes from a customer standpoint, whereby artificial definitions, functional stovepipes and hierarchical layers are broken down. External direction is evident from a greater focus on market objectives and, in particular, relationship management. Business-directed working results in, for example, the strengthening of performance management to get a better grip on the business activities. More and more emphasis is placed on the profitability of product and client segments as well as on the distribution channels.

Under the influence of IT and communication technology the role of the retail office is changing more to a 'personal advice' function for complex financial services, while basic financial services are managed through direct channels. Front-office staffing will stay more or less constant but quality is changing drastically and has a key marketing role. Here the main themes are increasing volumes through cross-selling, competition for deposits and more fee-based, personalized, value-added propositions. The number of retail offices will be cut through concentration. Unmanned automated offices are being set up to save labour costs. Operations are being centralized and, together with extensive automation, will result in strongly reduced back-office staffing. It is, however, evident that cutting costs alone does not provide a long-term foundation for operation. For permanent and significant competitive advantage, selective development of new activities is essential.

In the Netherlands strong competition exists between banks and insurers. To have or attain a strong position in the Dutch retail market a financial institution must have a good geographical spread and a good technical infrastructure with various distribution channels. Foreign financial institutions are not yet considered to be competition, probably because they do not have good distribution channels and the necessary technical payments infrastructure, though the first entrants have arrived, including the Bank of Scotland offering mortgage services over the Web.

Bank clients are maturing fast and increasingly want to make their own product choices, want to negotiate the various costs and shop around. Consequently customer loyalty is at stake. Owing to the technology developments – Internet, GSM, cable/telephone, TV shopping – the Dutch financial institutions will be faced with a huge impact on the bank's processes.

Consumers' behaviour is changing and consumers use various channels to operate with their banks. They do more and more banking by themselves, checking their account status online, using online payment systems, buying and selling shares using online brokerage, etc. They travel around the globe, through many time zones, and they want 24-hour, 365-day service availability. They compare the different available offerings just with a mouse click. They buy products and services from more than one bank and don't hesitate to switch to another bank for more attractive products/services or conditions. Customers nowadays are less loyal to their bank and use financial services from different banks. Consumers are much more knowledgeable about finance and manage their finances more actively, ready to tolerate increased risk for higher returns. They also require new products that match their new lifestyle (earlier retirement, living longer, more interest in products that will build wealth and retirement income).

Financial services are sold through multiple channels. Moreover, the number of new channels is expanding very quickly. While young people have no barrier to using the most sophisticated technology channels (PC banking, Internet, GSM), older people often refrain from contact with their bank other than their local branch. In many cases, consumers use multiple channels to operate with their banks (telephone, credit card, ATM, PC, Internet, branch office, mail, etc), so a consolidated client view across all channels is needed.

The value chain

Production and management of products and services is the most expensive part of a retail bank value chain (see Figure 9.1). Here, financial institutions need to achieve economies of scale. However, the larger the bank, usually the larger the number of customers and the more complex the relationships. This puts the focus on the effectiveness with which customers are managed.

The area of marketing and development offers banks an opportunity to differentiate. Time to market for new products is a key factor. Another important factor is what we call a 'value net', which is an extension of traditional business networks beyond procurement and manufacturing to add new kinds of products and services by building virtual enterprises that include suppliers and partners.

IT/technology is a key element through the entire value chain. Technology is present everywhere, and using technology appropriately adds value to each segment of the chain. Applying technology to help businesses to compete more successfully is a key strategic consideration for today and the future.

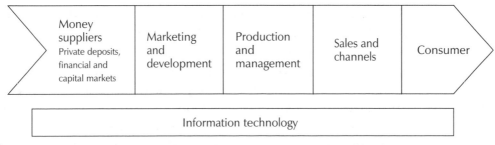

Figure 9.1 Value chain of a Dutch retail bank

PORTER 'FIVE-FORCES' ANALYSIS[1]

Internal rivalry in this industry

The industry restructuring process still continues. Deregulation, globalization and critical mass are factors that encourage concentration. Year after year, more banks disappear than appear, even taking into account new entrants. There is no real product differentiation in universal banking. All universal banks offer more or less similar products at little price difference. Frequent price comparisons by newspapers and consumer organizations tend to increase price competition and have caused banks to reduce profit margins.

Various new competitors are entering this market, including:

- insurance companies targeting niche markets like mortgage or retirement savings (eg Aegon, Ohra);
- e-banks with no other customer infrastructure than the Internet (eg Bank of Scotland);
- venture capitalists financing the creation of new companies (eg financial dot.coms).

In the over-banked Dutch market it is hard to expand market share. Next to innovation, differentiation and internationalization, personal customer relations is *the* way to pursue growth.

Barriers to entry

New entrants to banking include Dutch insurance companies taking over small banks and offering financial services via their own distribution channels. Only a few foreign banks entered the market due to lack of technical infrastructure, adherence to the Dutch payment system and language problems. However, a Turkish savings bank entered the market and focused on a target group of Turkish inhabitants in the Netherlands.

A new entrant needs a well-known brand that is established and trusted, because banking is about money, security and confidentiality. Another reason is the need to create various distribution channels, including the most expensive channel, the branch office channel. A new entrant in this business with local representation would probably prefer to use existing distribution channels through acquisition or merger rather than to build from scratch. The experience and the knowledge that well-established banks have about their customers and their markets are also an inhibitor for new entrants. Incumbents with their knowledge should be able to anticipate their customers' behaviour changes and to respond and adapt very efficiently. So the barriers to enter this business in a traditional manner are high.

This is why new entrants need to come up with a different approach to overcome these barriers. Newcomers have a greater familiarity with the online world and appropriate technologies, whereas banks have the strength of incumbents – capital, established business and extensive relationships. Newcomers leverage state of the art technology and new business models while incumbents are burdened by expensive legacy systems and struggle to migrate to new / redefined business models. New entrants are better positioned to benefit from technology than incumbent banks are, and are not necessarily committed to owning the entire value chain. Some newcomers, like the Bank of Scotland, enter with very focused products (mortgages in this case) and with services accessible only via the Internet and the telephone. Of course, such entrants build specific offerings / products tailored to the Internet.

The Internet opens the door to many new entrants. It permits an entirely new business model and addresses a very large audience from the beginning. It allows any kind of company, brand new firms or bricks and mortar companies (including non-financial companies), to enter the market quickly with one or more financial products aimed at many people around the globe without having to use other distribution channels. Having an established brand or sub-brand still confers significant advantage. Because this industry is still growing and because e-business is expanding at a phenomenal speed, we will no doubt see further new e-entrants, posing a real threat to the incumbent's profits.

Buyer power

The individual buyer has very low power to negotiate with sellers, but despite this markets are still price-competitive. This is true in the retail banking market which offers commoditized, undifferentiated products. The typical consumer (whether retail or small business) of the universal bank does not represent a sufficient fraction of the bank's business to be able to negotiate to any extent. However, because switching costs are low, the buyer has flexibility and no barrier to switch to competition. With e-business, things change. The Internet allows consumers to combine into communities of interest that have access to information that was previously only available to producers. The consumer can now easily compare available offerings, selecting the most attractive proposal. This transparency gives real power to the consumer. Here, power has moved further from the services provider to the consumer and we see a continuing radical shift in boundaries between buyers and sellers.

Supplier power

Supplier power has not changed much over time. The financial / capital market is composed of many firms. All have the same objective – to get the best possible interest rate for the duration of their investment. They supply large amounts of money to other financial institutions. There is room for bargaining in each transaction between buyer and supplier, but since there are so many alternative sources of money around the globe, we cannot say that suppliers have power. When the money supplier is the consumer (savings), they have low power because their investment is so small. The only power the consumer has is to compare with other savings institutes and to select the most attractive offering. This is due more to market rivalry than to supplier power. The suppliers in this case have low power.

Substitutes and complements

Venture capitalists offer a substitute to banks for financing the creation of new companies, especially start-ups. Insurers offer a substitute to banks in the mortgage market. They offer a life insurance complement that may contain different options, including premium waivers in case of invalidity, automatic amortization, revenue tax deduction and so on. The variety of complementary offering is growing. Substitutes and complements represent medium to high factors that influence the demand while affecting the internal rivalry.

   Table 9.1 summarizes the five force analysis.

Conclusion

Because this industry is still growing, it will continue to attract new entrants, especially e-entrants, mainly external to the financial industry. These newcomers, combined with deregulation, globalization, mergers and acquisition, convergence, e-business and the growth of substitutes and complements, will dramatically extend the competition and threat to profits. On the other hand, the new economy and the e-market offer new opportunities to expand market share, even outside national borders, indeed globally. New e-entrants in this industry, as well as incumbents, do not face problems with suppliers, who have weak power. However, buyers now have e-power and they will use it increasingly.

Table 9.1 Five-forces analysis of the Dutch banking industry – summary[1]

Force	Threat to profits
Internal rivalry	Very high
Entry	High (e-competition)
Supplier power	Low
Buyer power	Medium
Substitutes and complements	Medium

THE IDEA BEHIND THE RABOBANK

In the late 19th century Europe was in turmoil. Socially conscious pioneers encouraged people to stand up for their rights by organizing themselves into political parties, unions and cooperatives. It is here that the Rabobank story begins, inspired by Friedrich Wilhelm Raiffeisen. Raiffeisen, mayor of a small German town named Heddesdorf around 1850, was deeply concerned with the lot of its citizens. Farmers in particular had a hard time, for after a poor harvest there was little left to enable them to survive, much less buy new seed. For many, borrowing money was the only solution and they were left to the mercies of lenders who would only extend life-saving credit at exorbitant interest rates. Consequently most rural areas were poverty stricken. Raiffeisen came up with a solution that was both effective and simple: self-sufficiency through self-organization and self-management. He called on the farmers to unite and set up their own bank, an agricultural bank.

A bank of and for the people

Towards the end of the 19th century a string of small banks run by the people for the people sprang up in various towns and small cities – cooperatives that lent money at reasonable rates of interest and whose members clubbed together jointly to bear the credit risk. People would use the bank to borrow money for their business and to save whatever they might have left. By working together and helping one another to secure funds at crucial moments they were able to develop their businesses, to escape the poverty trap and improve their standards of living. The Netherlands spawned hundreds of such tiny credit cooperatives, which acted as forerunners of the local Rabobanks of today. Through the power of working together these small credit cooperatives, which later became known as Raiffeisen, and agricultural banks grew into one of the strongest banks in the world: the Rabobank.

A cooperative bank

The Rabobank works only in the interests of its members. It has no shareholders demanding a share of its profits. Instead, it has members: clients who want to actively participate in shaping the policy of the bank in their area and who have an interest in how it functions. The Rabobank Group is democratically structured, with local banks having a say in its domestic and international policy. Rabobanks were created and grew through local Cupertino. They are banks that were built by their customers for their customers.

Rabobanks are vital links in the local economy. The savings entrusted to them locally are largely extended as credit at a local level – for corporate investments, as housing loans and for initiatives that benefit the local community. In this way each Rabobank contributes to the economic activity and well-being of its own area of operations. Rabobanks are strongly rooted in the local community, familiar with regional circumstances and intimately involved in local and personal concerns. All these independent Rabobanks share a daughter company: Rabobank Nederland. Rabobank Nederland gives them all the facilities required in a modern banking organization. It monitors the liquidity and solvency of the local banks and forms the centre of all their international activities. At the same time it manages the joint interests of the Rabobanks in a string of subsidiaries – companies such as Interpolis (insurance), de Lage Landen (leasing and factoring), Schretlen (private banking) and the Robeco Group (investment funds).

An 'AAA' bank

The Rabobank pursues a sound policy. Reliability and continuity are strongly anchored in the organization through meticulous procedures, the direct influence of management and supervisory board members and a strict regime of internal controls. Rabobank Nederland supervises all its member banks on behalf of the sector regulator, the Dutch Central Bank, De Nederlandsche Bank. The individual member banks, in turn, maintain high standards in order to safeguard their creditworthiness. At Rabobank, the interests of members and customers enjoy maximum protection. Extended credits are backed by substantial reserves, and because Rabobank has no external shareholders, all profit is added to reserves. As a result, equity built up over the years far exceeds that stipulated by De Nederlandsche Bank, making Rabobank one of the world's most creditworthy banking institutions. Rabobank is the only commercial bank in the world to enjoy the highest credit rating from all the major ratings institutes, the so-called triple A-status.

Profile of the Rabobank Group

The Rabobank Group comprises about 425 autonomous local Rabobanks with about 1,800 branches, their umbrella cooperative Rabobank Nederland and a number of specialized subsidiaries. Rabobank is an all-round provider of financial services on a cooperative basis. In addition to the local Rabobanks, the Group's other business units include:

- Rabobank International (corporate and investment banking) and its specialized subsidiary Rabo Securities (Dutch equity);
- Interpolis (insurance and pensions);
- de Lage Landen (leasing and trade finance);
- Robeco Group (asset management and investment funds);
- Nedship Bank (ship financing);

- Schretlen & Co (private banking);
- Gilde Investment Management (venture capital).

These specialized service providers within the Rabobank Group provide financial services and products to local Rabobanks on the one hand and direct to their own clients on the other.

THE VIRTUAL RABOBANK INITIATIVES

Rabobank and e-commerce

The Rabobank has focused on the e-commerce developments from the angle of 'the customer and market' as well as 'the competition'. Customers are becoming more demanding. At one time they may look for convenience and lowest price of banking services while at another time they may want in-depth personal financial advice (for instance for initiating a pension scheme). The number of 'I want it all and I want it now' customers is growing rapidly. They want to determine for themselves how and when they want to make use of financial services. The behaviour of these customers is supported by developments in IT and communication technology. The customer can determine how and when he or she communicates with the financial institution (via PC, GSM, Internet). Some customers want an institution that delivers a day-to-day personalized financial service. This financial guidance function will be of more significance in the near future as the number of financial products and institutions grows.

Traditional competitors in the Dutch marketplace like ABN/AMRO, ING/Postbank and Fortis all have e-commerce strategies in place and are in various implementation phases addressing the customer's changing needs. Their strategies do not differ much from Rabobank's but each has a different market formula, focus areas and priorities. Foreign (niche) players are entering the market after establishing a suitable technical payments infrastructure and an appealing commercial formula. Non-traditional competitors are positioning themselves between customer and banks. Internet search services like Yahoo! can help customers find the right financial service.

Rabobank action programme

The 'Virtual Rabobank' is defined as the way customers access the Rabobank financial services via direct channels (including telephone, Internet, mail, GSM and other new media). It is Rabobank's ambition to be recognized as a personal advice bank rather than as a discounter, direct writer or independent agent (see Figure 9.2).

The Rabobank wants to add value to its customers by supplying the broadest range of financial services (all-finance product range) and offering tailor-made financial solutions for complex personal situations (*advice*), an extensive branch network for servicing the mass market (*service*) and easy and quick direct access to their financial services (*self-service*) (see Figure 9.3).

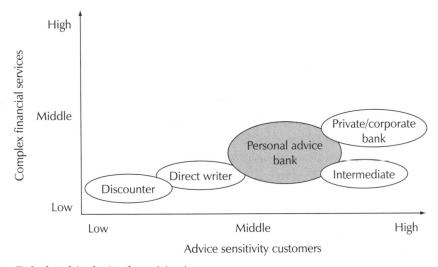

Figure 9.2 Rabobank's desired positioning

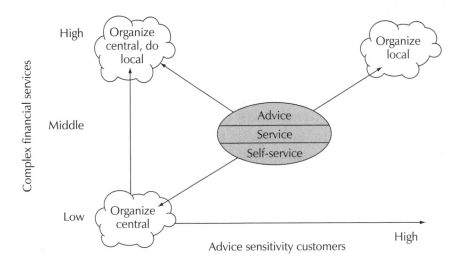

Figure 9.3 Components of Rabobank's positioning: advice–service–self-service

The business objectives for the virtual Rabobank are:

- Maintain market share of private customers, small and medium companies and lower the cost of their financial services by 20 per cent.
- For corporates, keep the cost of the financial services at the same level and grow market share by 1 percentage point per annum by attracting new customers.
- Grow the number of active customers for the virtual Rabobank to 2.5 million by end 2002.

The Virtual Rabobank should add f 190 million to the profitability of the Rabobank. To meet its objectives a number of initiatives were taken:

1. Develop and implement a distinguishing market proposition – a particular product–market–channel combination. It is a relationship arrangement, which will meet customers' needs and lifestyles, providing Allfinanz service and rewarding customer loyalty.
2. Renew sale and transaction processes – customers must experience the physical and virtual Rabobank as one bank. To design the required processes, the bank must decide which products to offer via which channels.
3. Establish the desired channel mix (see Figure 9.4). This entails:
   - developing profitable channel combinations which are logical and attractive to customers;
   - ensuring that the channel mix agreed with the customer is implemented;
   - ensuring that direct communication channels function properly;
   - developing channels taking into account customer requirements and technical possibilities.
4. Enhance the supporting processes and IT systems – for efficiency reasons, and to consolidate customer information across all channels and establish contact management and fulfilment, it is planned to implement the physical and virtual Rabobank on one technical platform.
5. Organize a virtual branch policy – the physical Rabobank has an extensive branch network. The virtual Rabobank must have the same prominent presence on the Web and create meeting places/portals for general and specific events tailored to customer needs.
6. Organize selective new intermediaries – the new intermediates/portals will be based on the competencies the Rabobank already has, like getting customers together around events (like travel or holidays) or needs (eg students). The Rabobank Group already has its own portal named 'Trefpunt' (meeting point). Trefpunt will be enhanced to meet the requirements of the virtual Rabobank and partnerships for content and financials will be engaged.

7. Provide access to Rabobank's financial services – Rabobank provides access with existing devices like the telephone, PC and the Internet. New access devices will be offered if they add value, including getting information about customers, popularizing the virtual Rabobank or encouraging the use of certain channels.

8. Supplement the portfolio of the Rabobank financial services – the Rabobank should constantly check its customers' needs for new financial products. A business case will determine whether these products are profitable and fit in Rabobank's product portfolio. Product/market units can determine through which channel they will be offered.

9. Organize a client policy for the Rabobank product/market units – the development of portals offers product/market units the chance to deliver their products to other non-Rabobank portals. These products will not have the brand name Rabobank. It is expected that this will increase the transaction volume of the product/market unit and lower the transaction costs.

10. Organize the competencies of self-service and manage them from one control point.

The Rabobank has launched five action programmes in order to meet the defined business objectives:

1. 'Formula' – the programme defines how the contact between a customer and the virtual Rabobank will take place and will develop and implement the 'user-interfaces'.

2. 'Assortment' – all products, services and facilities of the physical Rabobank have to be offered via the virtual Rabobank.

3. 'Market development and communication' – to meet the objective of 2.5 million customers for the virtual Rabobank, an extensive market development and communication programme must be carried out.

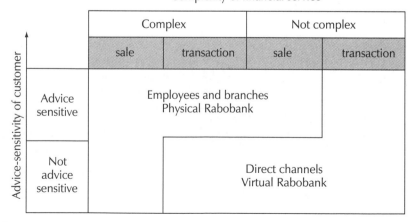

Figure 9.4 Channel mix for different types of product

4. 'Intermediate' – Rabobank wants to be as prominent and present in the virtual world as in the physical world. This programme will carry out a Web advertising programme, the set-up of a extensive virtual branch network, and organize portals in conjunction with partners.
5. 'Prerequisites' – The action programmes can only be implemented if three prerequisites are met, namely processes and systems, security and organization.

THE NETWORK FINANCIAL INSTITUTION

IBM has developed the Network Financial Institution (NFI) model to help its clients address market issues such as Rabobank's. The NFI model is used to understand the core business processes in financial institutions. IBM uses this model (see Figure 9.5) to design integrated e-business solutions for the financial services industry. The following points are worth noting:

1. Senior managers are focusing strongly on access points – the ways a customer can interact and transact business with the financial institution, whether that be bank-operated or customer-operated.
2. Networking and processor technologies have enabled a more complex and multi-faceted access point strategy, which allows customers, business partners, and service providers to exchange information with the financial institution.
3. Operational systems are experiencing increasing demand from front-end access systems. Thus, the trend towards real-time settlement in financial markets requires very efficient securities transaction processing systems that do not exist today. Many of these systems were developed 10 to 15 years ago and, over time, many other components have been added. If these systems break they can be very difficult to repair. These application systems have always lagged hardware in terms of reliability and performance, so business applications have not been able to take full advantage of the advances in processor, storage, and networking technology for reliability, availability and scalability benefits.
4. Knowledge management includes business intelligence systems which financial institutions can use to understand and manage their risk position, understand customers' buying patterns, and manage profitability.

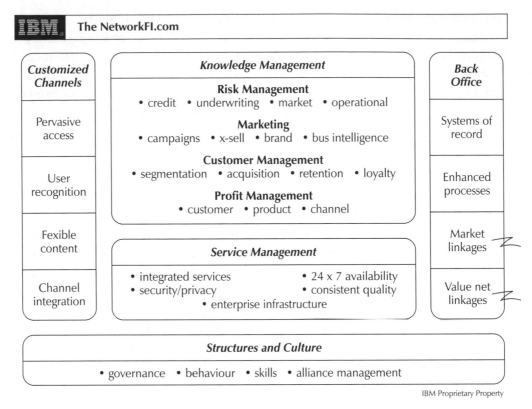

Figure 9.5 The network financial institution model

COMPARISON BETWEEN RABOBANK AND NFI MODEL

The following are the main areas of focus in the model (see Figure 9.6):

1. Develop and implement a distinguishing market proposition – the Rabobank proposition will be a product–market–channel combination. It's a relationship arrangement that will meet customers' needs and suit their lifestyles, covering all-finance service and rewarding customer loyalty.
2. Renew the sale and transaction processes – customers must experience the physical and virtual Rabobank as one bank, which has to be implemented. In order to design the new processes, it has to be decided which product will be offered via which channel.
3. Establish the desired channel mix – channel management has to be implemented, as follows:
   - It develops channel combinations which are logical and attractive to customers and profitable for the bank.
   - It ensures that the agreed channel mix with the customer is implemented.

Rabo-NFI model

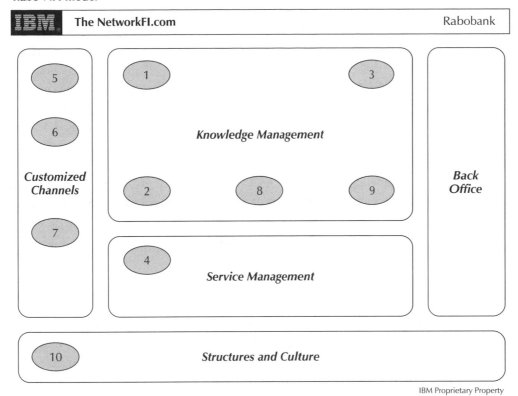

IBM Proprietary Property

Figure 9.6 Main focus areas

- It ensures that the right direct channels are available.
- It develops individual channels on the basis of customer requirements and technical possibilities.

4. Enhance the supporting processes and IT systems – for efficiency, customer information must be consolidated across all channels to establish good contact management and fulfilment. This means implementing the physical and virtual Rabobank on one technical platform.

5. Organize a virtual branch policy – Rabobank has an extensive branch network. The virtual Rabobank should have the same prominent presence on the Web and create meeting places/portals for general and specific events tailored to customer needs.

6. Organize selective new intermediates – the new intermediates/portals will be based on the competencies the Rabobank already has in managing customer groups around events and needs.

7. Provide access to Rabobank's financial services – the Rabobank provides access using existing and accepted devices like the telephone, PC and the Internet. New access devices will be offered as long as they add value to the Rabobank.

8. Supplement the portfolio of the Rabobank financial services – the Rabobank should constantly check customers' needs for new financial products. A business case should determine if these products are profitable and logical in the Rabobank product portfolio. The product/market units can determine through which channel the services will be offered.

9. Organize a client policy for the Rabobank product/market units – the development of portals offers product/market units the chance to deliver their products to other non-Rabobank portals. These products will not have the brand name Rabobank. It is expected that this will increase the transaction volume of the product/market unit and lower the transaction costs.

10. Organize the competencies of self-service and manage them from one control point – in the underlying model the initiatives of Rabobank are set into the NFI model to put them in perspective.

RABOBANK AND CRM

One of the main objectives of the virtual Rabobank is to attract 2.5 million new customers in 2001–03. These objectives are highly challenging for the Rabobank group due to the cooperative culture of the Rabobank group. All Rabobank group subsidiaries have and own their client base. Although arrangements exist to share customer information between the different parts of the Rabobank group, there is no corporate client view in place. For instance, a Rabobank client could have an insurance policy via an Interpolis direct writer while the local Rabobank is not aware of the transaction. There are about 7 million Rabo retail bank clients. The customer data (ie name, address, financial products) is spread across the Rabobank subsidiaries and can be redundant and not synchronized across the different IT systems. Emotional and behavioural customer data is based on the contacts that exist between the customer and the Rabobank employees at the local Rabobank. On a corporate level it is very difficult to explore customer profiling and to determine profitable customer groups.

The bank will be faced with three types of virtual bank customers:

1. New customers, who do not have a Rabobank account yet. The challenge here is to deepen the relationship with the customer and offer the appropriate service and financial product set.

2. Transferred customers, who have changed from physical to virtual Rabobank. The 'transferred' customer will demand the same financial care as in the old days so the challenge here is how to organize the appropriate service and financial product set for this 'new service' customer.

3. Duplicate customers, who will use the physical as well as the virtual Rabobank. The challenge here is how to make the duplicate customer experience the virtual and physical Rabobank as one banking organization.

A key strength of the physical Rabobank is its strong local presence, the face-to-face relationship with the customer and having customer emotional and behavioural data. The virtual Rabobank has no human contact so the challenge is how to contact virtual customers, obtain emotional and behavioural data from them and use it to make and manage a financial services offer via the Web, telephone or email.

The virtual Rabobank initiative is not only put into place for attracting new customers but also retaining existing customers of the Rabobank. The challenge here is how to keep the virtual customer loyal to the virtual Rabobank. When the virtual Rabobank initiative is launched, there will be requirements for measuring the success of the initiative – financial performance, market share and customer satisfaction.

REQUIREMENTS FOR SUCCESS

General

Rabobank has set very challenging business objectives for the 'virtual Rabobank'. As it aims to find 'knowledge' partners in the marketplace, these 'knowledge' partners should carry shared responsibility in meeting the Rabobank's business objectives. The Rabobank is known as a bottom-up organization and has a widely spread consensus culture. Since the market and customer environment is rapidly changing, customer and competitive needs may run ahead of the capabilities of Rabobank. So Rabobank plans to have cross-functional project teams (business and IT) reporting to senior management so as to speed up the decision-making process. Successful implementation of the 'virtual Rabobank' relies heavily on the internal Rabobank organization. Employees must be pointed in the same direction, so it is planned to enhance the Rabobank intranet with in-house e-business applications and a critical mass of content in order to create involvement of the employees as well as establishing communication between the various Rabobank departments. The 'virtual Rabobank' initiatives will result in many more business and IT interrelated, even interdependent, projects. Coordination and priorities are key to meeting objectives. So Rabobank plans to develop a detailed business and IT planning programme that will act as a guideline for all activities and is supported by senior management. During and after the implementation process, senior management expects to receive management information on which it can make decisions to keep the 'virtual Rabobank' on track. So Rabobank plans to put measurement systems in place early to supply up-to-date management information during deployment.

CRM recommendations

The 'virtual Rabobank' is aimed at its customers. Crucial to the success of the initiative will be lifting customer ownership from a subsidiary to a corporate level. Besides this fundamental change for a cooperative financial institution, it is planned to align all customer information systems and set up a central customer information base on which the virtual Rabobank can operate. Building on the corporate customer information, Rabobank plans to put customer profiling and profitability measurement in place in order to offer the optimal product/channel mix to its virtual customers. It plans to offer new customers a basic product/channel set in order to establish a customer profile and profitability, while campaign management can be used to broaden the uptake of additional services. Transferred customers expect that they will be offered the same (financial) products and services offered by the physical bank. It is planned that the Rabobank group communicates to transferred customers which financial products and services will be going 'virtual' and which will not. It is expected that mass financial products and services will go 'virtual' and sophisticated financial products and services will stay 'physical' because of the need for face-to-face contact. Duplicate customers will have to experience the virtual bank in the same way as the physical bank (clicks = bricks). Rabobank plans to focus on uniform customer treatment in both environments.

The strong local Rabobank presence and customer relationship must be extended to the virtual Rabobank. It is planned to set up virtual personalized banking on which one-to-one marketing can be enabled and where the customer feels virtually and financially at home. The success of the virtual Rabobank depends on the loyalty of its customers. Rabobank plans to develop a customer loyalty programme offering benefits for customers who use the optimal product and channel mix and/or stay tuned to the Rabobank offerings.

The virtual Rabobank initiative is a huge investment in money and people. Rabobank plans to put measurement systems in place to track through predefined performance indicators its performance, market share and customer satisfaction.

Notes

[1] This analysis is based on that in Porter, M E (1985) *Competitive Advantage: Creating and sustaining superior performance*, Free Press, New York

Part 3

Sector situation

10

The life and pensions industry: the UK situation compared with other countries

David Taylor, Clare Seah and Christopher Cannon

INTRODUCTION

The UK life and pensions industry has grown strongly in recent decades, supported by booming equity returns in the 1990s and a relative immunity to competitive pressures. In recent years this has been offset with increasing demands from successive governments to regulate the industry and, in the eyes of the consumer, offer protection from miss-selling, maladministration and poor investment strategies. Also, the euphoria of high returns in the early 1990s, with huge terminal bonuses for endowments, has been more than reversed, with life offices potentially unable to meet the returns required to cover endowment-based mortgages.

The life and pensions industry is at a crossroads. On the one hand, several providers are recording record new business figures and strong profits, with record growth in the numbers of IFAs and new products being sold. On the other hand, we have seen the advent of 1 per cent charge caps, possible depolarization, the problems of Equitable Life, falling equity returns, interest rates at their lowest for over a generation, an increasingly enthusiastic Financial Services Authority focusing on the sector, and now stakeholder pensions failing to achieve government goals.

It has been argued by Anthony Hilton, City Editor of London's *Evening Standard* newspaper, that 'just as equity markets are heading for a probably lengthy period of stagnation, the industry faces a consumerist government which is convinced that its basic products – with-profits life assurance and pension plans – perpetrate a fraud on the customer and which has imposed de facto price control by introducing stakeholder pensions backed by all the marketing muscle of government and with a ceiling of 1 per cent on charges.'[1] All this was before the significant market adjustment after the tragic events of 11 September.

The retirement market is forecast to change dramatically over the next 30 years, as shown in Table 10.1. This chapter will explore the broader impacts of these challenges on the life and pensions marketplace.

Table 10.1 Forecast growth in retired population

Age group	2001	2031
Working (16–64)	36.4m	34.6m
Retired (65+)	10.8m	16.1m
Retired as % of working	29.7%	46.5%

Source: Office of Population Census and Surveys population projections

TRENDS

Figures 10.1 and 10.2 illustrate the current and expected future focus of providers. Larger providers have been focusing on market share and revenue. This is due to a number of factors:

- dominant market share is needed for survival;
- 'easy' pickings from Equitable Life;
- operational cost levels are a real challenge for most large providers, particularly because of M&A legacies.

With the next focus for larger providers being the 1 per cent cost challenge, and with major providers seeking to meet this partly through economies of scale, medium-sized providers are unlikely to survive, while smaller providers have focused on operational effectiveness to survive as niche operations.

THE 1 PER CENT WORLD

Over the years, the life industry has grown 'fat' in the eyes of the government and the consumer lobby. It has been running at a cost level of around 2.6–3.0 per cent of assets in

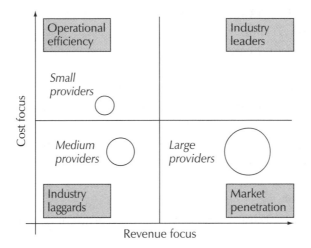

IBM Strategic Alignment Model
UK Life Offices: current effective focus

Figure 10.1 The current focus of life and pension providers

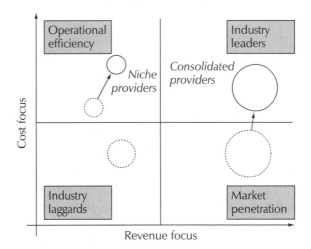

IBM Strategic Alignment Model
UK Life Offices: future focus

Figure 10.2 Expected future focus of providers

recent years. To counter this, and to encourage the democratization of pension savings, the government has introduced product charge caps of 1 per cent for stakeholder pensions and CAT-marked products. The stakeholder model has been seen in other markets with similar products, the most often quoted being the United States with the 401k product which has been around for a number of years, and more recently the launch of the compulsory Superannuation Choice in Australia. In the UK compulsion has yet to raise its head, with the government possibly waiting for a third term before pushing what is likely to be an unpopular move on the consumer.

There are some instructive lessons on compulsion from the Australian experience:

- Regulation – pensions uptake was marginal until compulsion was introduced.
- Products – defined benefit schemes have declined significantly in favour of defined contribution. Retail sales declined in favour of group schemes.
- Competition – large multi-employer schemes driven by industry and trades unions came into being, posing a significant threat to incumbent insurers.
- The difficulties in running multi-employer schemes were underestimated (eg chasing contributions from reluctant employers).
- Unbundling of administration – two large administrators dominate the industry fund market.
- Account numbers proliferated, as every spell of work, no matter how short, resulted in a new account being set up. This increased the cost base.

With, or without, compulsion the introduction of a stakeholder pension scheme in the UK has far-reaching consequences for the industry as a whole. Many providers believe, probably rightly in the longer term, that a 1 per cent charge cap will set the benchmark for other products. A number of the key providers have already committed to limit charges on personal pensions to the 1 per cent seen on stakeholder pensions.

Recent research (October 2001) carried out by the Finance Technology Research Centre and MORI has shown that consumers are less aware of these changes than the providers and the regulators. Consumers who were looking to buy a pension or ISA were asked how aware they were of the charges applicable to stakeholder pensions. Figure 10.3 gives the results. When probed further, nearly half the same consumers indicated a propensity to consider paying high fees for better returns (Figure 10.4), and a significant number indicated a propensity to pay more if quality advice were part of the overall proposition (see Figure 10.5). Additional research, also carried out by FTRC and MORI in the summer of 2001, indicated that less well-off consumers would seek higher returns from an investment product, whereas better-off consumers were more interested in appropriateness (see Figure 10.6).

This research suggests that providers will need to vary offers by segment. The real challenge is that for consumers targeted for stakeholder pensions, the expectation is that quality means higher returns, which consumers think they can obtain by paying for it! As Chapter 36 shows, this is unrealistic.

The real impact of the 1 per cent world on the provider will be the big reduction in costs required to make products such as stakeholder pensions successful. Some life offices expect to need to reduce costs by up to 70 per cent to meet the basic cost targets. One cost on which the spotlight has fallen is commission paid to the intermediary, sales force or channel

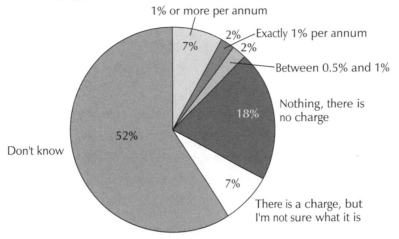

Q *How much, if any, does your pension provider charge you for managing your money?*

Figure 10.3 Awareness of charges

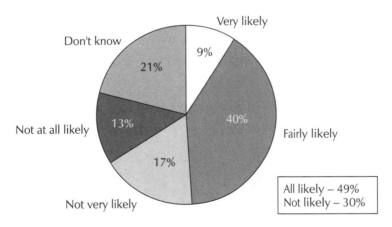

Q *If charges were set at 1%, would you pay a higher charge if there was a higher rate of return?*

All likely – 49%
Not likely – 30%

Figure 10.4 Willingness to pay charges

partner. In the years 2000–01, many life offices did their sums in this area and the result was that most rejected the direct sales force. This led to a further quandary for a number of the life offices as distribution is now at a premium, and the IFA channel currently has the lion's share.

Government strategy has left consumers in the lurch, as those targeted with these low-cost products are the very consumers who need quality advice to manage apparently unrealistic expectations, and to educate them in the need for long-term savings. The advent of the 1 per cent charge cap will not allow for the providers, or the distribution channels, to

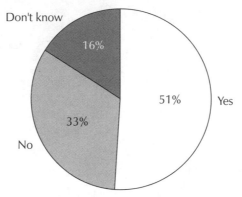

Q *Would you be prepared to pay additional charges of up to 0.5%*
   p.a. to cover the cost of you receiving professional advice on
   finding the right product and managing it in the future?

Figure 10.5 Willingness to pay additional charges for advice

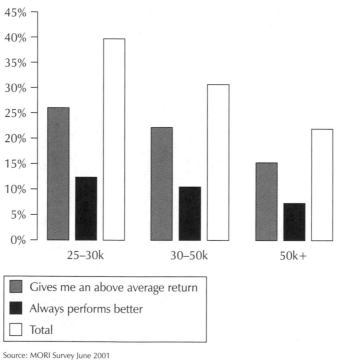

Lower incomes are more concerned with 'above average' products

Source: MORI Survey June 2001

Figure 10.6 Variations in responses by income

provide the luxury of advice funded through commissions, so fees are the only realistic way forward, except that they need to be levied on consumers who can least afford to pay.

The conundrum faced here is very real. Recent analysis of the FSA comparative tables indicates that even for those in the target marketplace, a stakeholder pension may not be the best option for the consumer. Without appropriate advice, a consumer could well end up being worse off. Alison Steed of the *Daily Telegraph* (24 November 2001) observed, 'For example, a 25-year-old saving £100 a month and hoping to retire at 65 would find that Standard Life – Europe's biggest mutual insurer – provided the cheapest pension with its Personal Pension One plan. This plan, if you invested in the with-profits fund, would cost you £28,920 in management charges during the 40-year life of the contract. Another surprise is that Standard Life's cheapest pension costs almost half as much as its stakeholder plan. So, even after the introduction of 'cheap and cheerful' stakeholders, choosing a pension remains a complex task to be approached with care. You even need to consider how you buy the product to make sure that you are not paying unnecessary fees.'[2]

At least two life offices have set out a strategy to dominate the provision of stakeholder pensions to create a critical mass so as to achieve economies of scale. Other markets teach us that commoditization of products will lead to a much smaller number of 'manufacturers' even if there are multiple branded products in the market. Detergents are a prime example of this. In this market in the USA the 401k provision has led to one fund manager taking the majority of funds, and another provider taking the majority of the product servicing. Both of these organizations do not see 401k as a source of profit. However, the relationship with the consumer that the product enables leads to other more profitable products being cross-sold.

In the UK the distribution of regulated products remains highly fragmented (see Figure 10.7), with much expense in the value chain. Again in the USA, increased consumer awareness and a more mature marketplace have seen a shift in provider marketplace, with disintermediation occurring at all levels. This can be evidenced in the rise of direct investment in mutual funds and in the higher level of personal share ownership. The consumer in the UK still has some way to go to reach this level of financial awareness.

To succeed in the 1 per cent world a life office needs to make a number of choices. If it is to remain a 1 per cent product manufacturer then:

- back-office costs need to be radically reduced;
- straight-through processing needs to be enabled through investment in technology;
- distribution friction needs to be removed from the value chain;
- critical mass needs to be achieved;
- cross-selling of products must be enabled either directly, or by working with chosen channel partners.

In terms of the back office a number of expense areas must be restructured (see Figure 10.8).

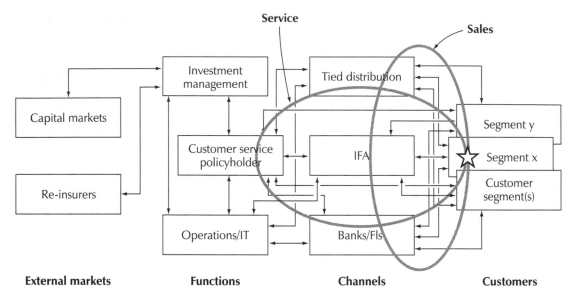

Figure 10.7 Distribution of regulated products in the UK

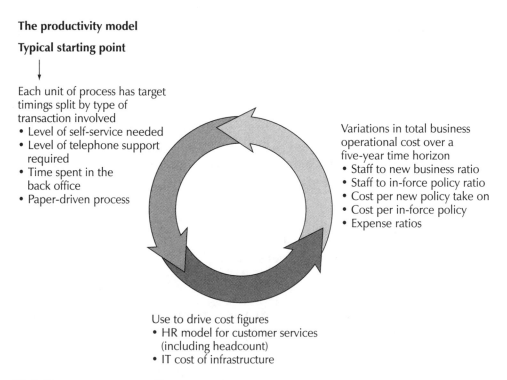

Figure 10.8 Expense areas needing restructure

Providers that cannot achieve low cost goals will need to exit from manufacturing. This pressure, combined with the pressure on access to distribution that depolarization may bring, will lead to a rapid consolidation of the life industry into a significantly smaller number of players than today. For the consumer, 1 per cent may lead to a reduction in the provision of quality financial support. The products may not be the best and consumers may be prevented from obtaining the advice that they need.

ALLIANCE MANAGEMENT

Research IBM has done into alliance management by insurance providers has some interesting and relevant headlines for the UK:

1. A provider's use of alliances is positively correlated to value creation.
2. Providers are entering into alliances for three primary reasons:
   - revenue growth;
   - expense optimization and reduction;
   - strategic positioning.
3. Alliance formation is growing at an increasing rate, both globally and in the UK.
4. The value from alliances in the insurance industry is expected to grow significantly.

DEPOLARIZATION

The first stage of depolarization – in which intermediaries formerly obliged to recommend the best product from all suppliers or to align themselves 100 per cent with one supplier can select a limited number of manufacturers with whom to deal – has already occurred with the advent of stakeholder pensions. Life offices can resell stakeholder products of other organizations. The next stage of depolarization may have a much greater impact on the market. Full depolarization may enable distributors to have multiple ties with life offices. In some cases this just recognizes current practice – the panel approach taken by many IFAs. However, it will enable banks to have multiple ties with life offices and to offer a choice of brand-leading life products.

The summer 2001 research by FTRC and MORI tells us that consumers will be more open to this approach. It seems that this propensity to use banks offering a choice of products may be at the expense of IFAs. Figure 10.9 shows the propensity to buy from:

- IFA offering independent advice on a range of products in the market;
- banks offering products it has selected as best;

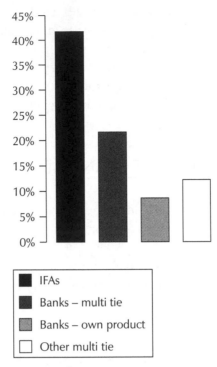

Figure 10.9 Propensity to use different channels

- banks offering their own products;
- other channels.

IFAs are biding their time, waiting to see what the model of depolarization will be. The challenge that IFAs face in their battle with the banks will be relative lack of capital to develop propositions and brand in the marketplace. Pauline Stoffberg wrote in *Money Marketing*[3] (22 November 2001) with some advice for IFAs considering their future:

> Are the majority of your clients high-net-worth or mass-affluent? Are they largely corporate? Do you rely heavily on professional introducers? Do you or your clients value your independence beyond anything else? Can your business survive without external support? Do your life and pension sales follow on the back of your mortgage or general insurance work? If your answer to any of the first four questions is yes, then far from considering multi-ties, your energies would best be deployed joining an organization lobbying regulators, the Treasury and providers… But if you answer no to the first four and yes to five and six, multi-ties may afford you improved support.

Some life offices have recognized this and are considering a strategy of taking minority stakes in IFAs, first of all to enable the IFA to invest and develop its business, but more importantly to protect a key channel of distribution. For the smaller life offices this will create a tremendous challenge. IFA panel sizes have already shrunk significantly, with quality providers being more likely to survive. This will be mirrored if the model of depolarization introduced leads to 'bancassurance' growth. The net result of these changes will be that the top four or five life offices will develop a tighter grip on both product provision and access to distribution.

For the consumer, depolarization may well be a step forward. Despite protestations from the Association of Independent Financial Advisers that the consumer is very aware of the advantages of polarization, our research indicates that most consumers (other than the most important customers of IFAs) are not aware. The majority of consumers, those the government is trying to target with products such as ISAs and stakeholder pensions, are not clear about the role of the IFA, or the cost that they pay an IFA for advice. The potential advantage to the consumer in a depolarized world is that tied salesmen have typically met government targets for charge-capped products in the past. Although many of these sales forces are now gone, access to a choice of quality products through multi-tied intermediaries, such as a bank, may well be a step in the right direction.

RATIONALIZATION

The combined effect of the low-cost operating environment and depolarization squeezing out competition for distribution may be acceleration of rationalization in the life industry. This has already been an area of great activity in the UK, but there is still some way to go. There is simply not a good enough return on equity to support the 40 or so stakeholder manufacturers. Those not absorbed may move to a different business model of reseller of others' products. The remainder are likely to move into niche plays, if they survive at all.

One concern is that those seeking a good return on capital will not find the UK life industry an attractive place to invest. This will also be a challenge for UK-based offices that want to expand abroad, especially into Europe. The reduction in returns and the restructuring for the leaner market in the medium term in the UK market will be a drain on capital that will slow down expansion abroad. Also the failure of government and the FSA to prevent the problems seen at Independent Insurance and Equitable Life will lead to a question mark in overseas markets over the capability of British insurers to operate successfully. It is therefore possible that government will intervene yet again, with cost pressures and technology forcing more consolidation, this time pan-European or even global. It is unlikely that British firms will benefit.

EFFECTIVE IFA DISTRIBUTION

For several years life offices have recognized the benefits of creating a more effective, automated link between themselves and the multitude of IFAs in the market. The IFAs come in many forms and so the creation of some form of common trading platform is of increasing interest. In recent years two strategies have emerged. The Exchange, which provides a basic common trading platform, is the most widely used to obtain quotes. However, the service is basic and once a quote is obtained the IFA then has to resort to contacting the life office directly to transact new business. This is not in line with cost reduction through straight-through processing.

The second strategy of life offices is to launch extranets offering increasingly sophisticated servicing and work-tracking services. The majority of the larger IFA firms now regularly use these extranets. However, the IFAs were generally frustrated with the services offered. This is because each extranet is proprietary, so an IFA or IFA administrator working with several providers must log in separately to each extranet, and learn how to navigate on each site. IFAs are frustrated by this, particularly those who themselves have invested in e-commerce and cannot easily integrate their own systems with those of the providers. IFAs report that they find providers frustrating to deal with as they generally do not show much interest in working with IFAs to learn how to better work together. Providers typically develop extranets to meet their own needs, rather than those of the marketplace or specific IFAs. A small number of providers have carried out 'clinics' with small numbers of IFAs, to work together on joint propositions. However, this is not the norm. The development of e-commerce solutions will continue to be thwarted unless this barrier is resolved.

On a more positive note, several providers are developing more sophisticated Web services that enhance an IFA's offering. Skandia's MyMultiManager is a service that can be embedded in the IFA's own Web site, offering a full-service fund supermarket. The offering creates a servicing capability for the IFA to assist with portfolio management, which in their own words provides:

- sophisticated portfolio tools to build and manage model portfolios and rebalance those portfolios;
- total view of clients, enabling valuing and bulk switching of all Skandia investments as one;
- data download service to help in servicing your clients;
- online applications for many investment and pension contracts, through different tax wrappers;
- unparalleled range of multi-manager funds across the Skandia platform.

Similar offerings are being brought to the market, for example Selestia from Old Mutual, offering IFAs a portfolio management service. Another provider has created a policy-servicing capability that can be embedded to enable consumers to service their policy through their IFA's Web site. There is a big opportunity to use this approach to get the industry to move to the 1 per cent world and effective, efficient distribution. However, fragmentation of the market – both IFAs and providers – creates a big barrier to progress. The creation of offerings such as MyMultiManager is a big step forward for the IFAs. However, it may accelerate what we have seen in other markets, eg the switch to direct investment in mutual funds, away from long-term savings products.

DIRECT

The direct telephone-based approach has been successful for some products, typically high margin, or simple, execution-only commodities, for example guaranteed term plans or ISAs and bonds. Providers that have tried to sell complex products such as pensions have struggled to make such offers compelling. The focused fact-find approach has made the task a little easier, but consumers are unwilling to spend a long time on the telephone, and in many cases do not have the information to hand needed to complete the transaction. Some larger IFAs have been successful in running off-the-page direct marketing activities, with direct fulfilment via call centres. These operations run with a very low ratio of registered individuals to cover key client questions or more complex transactions. For the moment, an approach via direct channels such as the telephone in support of direct marketing activity will remain profitable in only a few product areas.

ALTERNATIVE MARKET ACCESS – WORKSITE MARKETING; CHANNEL OF OPPORTUNITY?

The selling of financial products through the workplace is not new. Many companies offer pension, health and other products and services through workplace schemes. However, the landscape is changing as the boundaries between work, play and home begin to blur, driven by changing consumer demand and new technological capability. Employers are looking for more innovative, flexible and affordable benefits provision whilst employees want choice and convenience. Today, what they both often get is disjointed, inflexible, labour-intensive benefits provision. Many industry players provide some of the answers but it appears that none can do it all. What organizations need is a 'solution integrator', a provider that can consolidate various products and services into a single proposition, through a single interface, which attracts and keeps its most valued employees working for it.

Worksite marketing is receiving increasing attention from providers seeking to exploit low-cost alternative distribution options in the battle to grow and keep market share. Providers with existing worksite operations are considering how technology can differentiate them and drive higher penetration rates. Rapid advances in network and mobile technologies continue to give consumers more choice on how and where they buy financial services products, at home or at work, extending the reach of the traditional worksite market.

The US worksite market has matured and the growth in worksite sales of financial products has beaten growth in traditional sales by a factor of four during the 1990s. There are similarities in worksite dynamics between the US and UK markets, most notably in the areas of pension reforms and the increasing consumer adoption of e-commerce. This suggests that rapid growth in the worksite distribution channel is set to occur in the UK. The introduction of stakeholder pensions has encouraged increased worksite activity, if not full-blown worksite marketing. Several providers have worksite offers, and employers have retained IFAs for fee-based advice, with fees paid by the employer on behalf of employees. This approach may accelerate the acceptance of a more integrated worksite offering.

Although technology can be a key enabler of worksite marketing with products and advice being offered through intranets, a barrier to this is the expense of creating integrated payroll and human resource systems. This is vital in creating straight-through processing, which significantly reduces the cost of scheme and product administration, as the employer carries out much of the employee administration. A leading provider of 401k in the USA has invested heavily in establishing this integration. This has enabled it to 'break even' for core product provision. The provider now has the advantage of a direct link to its customer base and is now increasing its revenues and profits through low-cost cross-selling.

From an employer's perspective, a key proposition that will help embed the worksite offer will be the introduction of 'cafeteria benefits', where employees take responsibility for selecting their own balance of benefits, perhaps trading holiday or car allowances for better life cover or pension provision. This highlights one of the key elements of ensuring that the worksite offering is successful. As with the market at large, any large employer will have employees with widely differing needs, from executives to blue collar workers. Segmentation of treatment, proposition, advice and products is an important dimension for any worksite scheme.

INTEGRATED MULTI-CHANNEL DISTRIBUTION

Historically the life offices have typically been dependent on a single main channel to market, Allied Dunbar with its sales force and Standard Life and its dominance of the IFA channel being two examples. The number of channels has been condensed even more recently. Many offices that had a secondary or even primary channel based on the sales force have seen the economics of this channel look weak and the majority of sales forces have been dropped. However, some providers have achieved greater productivity through integrating several channels into a single combined proposition. An approach such as this will use Web services to provide product information and advice on financial management, call centres to coordinate customer activities, and sales to execute transactions. Organizations taking this approach have successfully driven greater sales productivity.

A similar model may well emerge for intermediaries. Some life offices already provide additional marketing and database analysis services to IFAs for renewals and life stage events. In the future, a multi-tied intermediary will allow (assuming no infringement of benefit-in-kind regulations) a more significant 'tripartite' relationship to be formed – with the intermediary and the provider working in collaboration to derive value from the customer base. This will improve yield management of the customer base, something that the life industry has not done well in the past.

REGULATION

It would be impossible to write about the life and pensions marketplace without a word on regulation. Regulation has placed a huge burden on the industry in terms both of actual cost and of opportunity. Regulation that has focused on the point of sale has, not surprisingly, increased the cost of sale. The cost of implementing regulation is great – scarcely a year has gone by without some mandatory change to the sales process, reducing the ability of life offices to invest in infrastructure and propositions for tomorrow. Regulation has usually been applied mainly to fix problems retrospectively, eg mis-sold pensions. The regulator has fared less well in creating positive solutions to help companies and consumers manage risk. A more forward-looking approach might have identified the problems at Equitable Life or Independent Insurance.

There has been a shift over the past two or three years from point of sale regulation to product regulation, with the introduction of CAT-marked products.

The future of regulation for the industry still remains bleak as the FSA now has new-found teeth and is looking closely at the industry again, to ensure that it is not caught out as it has been over the past couple of years. There will be a significant increase in personal accountability for life office executives, although it is not certain where this will lead. However, it is clear that regulation of the financial services industry as a whole will increase. An example of potential worry for the life industry is CP98, which explores making mortgage providers responsible for all sales compliance, irrespective of the channel. If this principle were applied in life, it would significantly change the landscape of the life sector, which is currently increasingly dependent on IFAs who carry the burden of compliance today.

The FSA may be pressured to control rather than empower the industry. It is also evident that there are key stakeholders beyond the FSA, such as the Treasury, which has different interests. To deal with this potentially disruptive situation, we believe the life offices should join forces to lobby government and its agencies effectively.

KNOW WHERE YOU ARE

As a life office this is a time for strategic choices. Many offices have already begun to make choices, with Standard Life focusing on being a mutual product manufacturer, Norwich Union focusing on market dominance, especially for stakeholder pensions, Legal and General developing a multi-channel approach including IFA, Bancassurance and Direct.

The first step in making these key strategic choices lies with an exploration of the core competencies of the organization, as discussed in Chapters 6 and 39:

- Customer centric – Organizations that have a strong relationship with customers should focus on enhancing their relationships to get further value from these relationships and increase the share of wallet. Few life and pensions companies are truly customer centric.
- Production centric – Many large life and pensions organizations believe that their real strengths lie in production, with the large-scale operation of product factories. This is because of the intermediated nature of the life and pensions marketplace. The exemplar of a production-centric business in the Insurance sector is Direct Line who have demonstrated that effective and efficient operation of scale can result in an operating ratio of nearly half the sector average. What remains to be seen in the Life sector is whether large players can emulate this production focus and reduce cost ratios by the required 50–70 per cent.
- Fulfilment centric – Several life providers are not manufacturers and are focusing on creating leading-edge fulfilment models, specifically in the IFA arena, eg Skandia's mymultimanager.com that enables an IFA to provide a fund supermarket service to its customers, as well as providing portfolio management services for the IFAs themselves. Selestia.com optimizes the delivery of services and products to the client from a range of providers. The focus is on optimizing the fulfilment and service to the end consumer, in addition to providing the IFA with a strengthened service proposition.
- Marketplace centric – There are several marketplace-centric offerings in the life and pensions sector. However, these are not core businesses, but typically small-scale service providers. A key problem with this model is the ability to charge for the services offered. A number of reinsurers have marketplace-centric offerings running alongside a production centric model.

STRATEGIC EVALUATION

Life offices must now reassess their position in the marketplace, specifically their role in the value chain (see Figure 10.10), investing and developing the core competencies outlined above. The key areas are production, distribution and retail. In our view, few players have the brand and infrastructure to be truly retail oriented. This may pave the way for more significant partnerships emerging, with logic, if not history, seeing banks at the top of the list. The remaining options are distribution to channel partners (the Skandia approach) or low-cost manufacture (eg Fidelity).

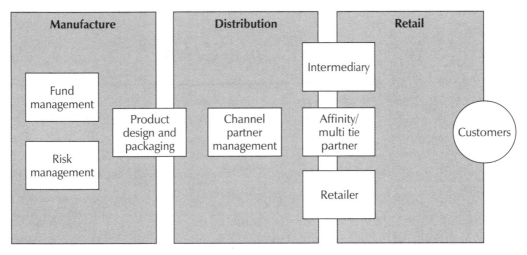

Figure 10.10 Roles in insurance value chain

Notes

1 Anthony Hilton (2001) *Evening Standard*, London, 2 August
2 *Daily Telegraph*, 24 November 2001: 'Cheap and cheerful' might not be such a bargain after all: new league table has some surprises on the relative costs of stakeholders. Alison Steed reports
3 Pauline Stoffberg (2001) *Money Marketing*, 22 November

11

Trends in insurance CRM

Bryan Foss, Merlin Stone and Fola Komolafe

All around the world, one of the major issues exercising senior managers of insurance companies and banks is the convergence of banking, insurance and other financial services. The convergence and blending of the different elements of the retail financial services industry is enabled by many recent technological developments, not the least of which is the Internet. We discuss the impact of the Internet in one of our later briefings. All leading financial services companies are keen to explore what online provision can do for them, and are frightened to be the last to work it out. Most have Web pages, and many now have application forms on them, but few allow customers to manage their entire relationship with the supplier over the Internet.

Countries with a very high usage of the Internet may be becoming models of the electronic commerce world of the future. But the Internet is only one manifestation of a possible entirely screen-based marketplace, in which virtual and real agents also compete for the customer's attention. Most companies are looking forward to having the ability to transact on the Internet or other network in the next few years – whether in the customer's home or workplace or via a kiosk, and other companies are looking at how to help consumers organize their search for better value. All this must affect the way business is done in insurance and banking. However, we must also remember that most financial services companies are still not too good at using the telephone and the mail!

We also need to bear in mind that the future always holds surprises. Today we only discuss all-risk insurance for the consumer, while the world's suppliers continue to see the consumer as the recipient of a number of different products, occasionally combined either as add-ons to each other or, very rarely, as true combination products. In some cases, this concept can be extended to total asset provision (as it already has been with cars and other items of equipment, such that the insurance cost is only part of the total payment to the asset supplier). Some insurance companies and data providers are beginning to explore the idea of all-risk guarantees for named customers – effectively a form of insurance for the supplier, which involves outsourcing the identification and management of an individual's risk pattern across a variety of situations. Putting it simply, the idea is to move away from outsourcing data to outsourcing risk, not in the traditional reinsurance way, but rather by very advanced analysis of comprehensive, possibly cross-product, data sets relating to individual consumers over their life cycle to develop a picture of total lifetime risk and value. This is based on the fundamental idea that the leopard does not change its spots, and that there are correlations of risk or value across product areas. A concept today, it may be a reality tomorrow.

Today, we observe with interest the early experiments of insurance companies in creating or participating in loyalty schemes. However, we are aware that the future might be one in which lack of customer benefit in return for loyalty effectively rules a product or supplier out of consideration – a world where in effect loyalty management paradoxically is no longer a loyalty factor but just a hygiene factor, as it has become with airlines.

Today, we observe government's tentative first steps to shift the burden of longer-term risk onto the customer, favoured by (and perhaps partly causing) a generally rising savings ratio in the Western world. But tomorrow, under scenarios that IBM has actively researched using experts from all over the world,[1] the burden of longer-term individual risk may be carried in many community ways as well as by the state and the individual.

Our research shows that in every sector, although customers do want to be managed better, many customers' nirvana of a relationship with a supplier is for the supplier to provide the customer with ways to manage them. In other words, instead of thinking about distribution channels, companies should think about access channels – and the Internet obviously has a strong role to play here. Research shows very clearly the desire of consumers to use electronic access channels.[2] In our research on complaints and compliments, we introduced the idea of 'customer controlled contact' to express this need. However, today's world is still composed largely of customers hoping (sometimes against hope) to be managed better, with the occasional opportunity to manage their supplier! This hope extends to how suppliers use the most basic communications media – the telephone and the mail – to communicate with them. So the prime focus of this briefing is on helping insurance companies cope with today's markets and customers and tomorrow's, but not quite the day after tomorrow's.

CUSTOMER VALUE MANAGEMENT ANALYSIS

Customer value management (CVM), a methodology created and used by the IBM Consulting Group, can be used as a comprehensive approach to re-engineering a business as well as a tool to identify specific ways to improve customer management. Starting from their previous position as deposit takers, lenders and retail and computer-based transaction-enablers, banks have found it hard to move into an era where understanding customers' needs for value is an essential prerequisite for doing business. The main difference between the banking and insurance sector is the sheer frequency of transactions. Opportunities to add (or lose) value are so much more frequent in banking. However, in many ways, successful customer value management in banking will derive from making a very large number of interactions that little bit friendlier and easier.

In general insurance, however, with an average of around two or three interactions a year on average, customer value management leads companies in the direction of major process re-engineering to radically simplify these transactions so that they take seconds instead of hours. In banking, most of the transactions already take seconds at most (unless you are the unfortunate customer in the queue). Here, the need is twofold, and may also involve a degree of re-engineering. For simple transactions the challenge is to encourage customers to use the most cost-effective methods for simple transactions while not losing touch, by emulating the values delivered by state-of-the-art retailing and electronic commerce. For more complex transactions, such as loan set-up, the needs are very similar to insurance, involving improved (and perhaps automated) diagnosis of customer needs, flexibility of solution, and keeping in touch as the customer's need changes.

CVM in insurance would involve:

1. Identifying the key moments of truth at every stage of the relationship between the supplier and the customer. For example, when the customer looks in the telephone directory to find a supplier, when the customer contacts a call centre to enquire about a product, when the customer signs a contract, when the customer claims. This can be done by interviews, research of customers (particularly focus groups and in-depth interviews), brainstorming (ideally in groups of staff representing every aspect of customer contact). Each area identified, eg taking out a new policy, complaints, claims handling, should itself be subject to intensive examination, as it is likely to reveal many (often connected) moments of truth within it. For each moment of truth, the following areas should be examined:
    - relative importance of this moment of truth in determining whether customer will buy/stay;
    - current practice – not just policy, but actual practice, in its full range (ie not just the average);

- customers' perceptions, expectations and ideal value (by type of customer, in particular taking into account different psychological types, eg does the customer want to retain or give control; by current and past relationship);
- competitive performance, which can be identified by market research or mystery shopping;
- parallel industry performance, ie of companies that set the expectations of the company's target customers, irrespective of the field they operate in;
- the company's aim, ie how far to go towards ideal value – this depends partly on competitive performance and partly on resources. The target may be to achieve the delivery of customer ideal value eventually, but there may be steps along the way, dictated by resource constraints and other feasibility issues. In particular, some moments of truth may be more important than others. This might be broken down into immediate target and subsequent targets.

2. Identifying the ideal value target customers would like during and as a result of this contact. This of course may differ by type of customer. For example, if the customer begins the relationship by looking in the phone book, the value required might be that of finding information about a strongly branded company (branding reduces the uncertainty associated with buying), including an accessible telephone number, ie one that is available when the customer looks in the directory. The kinds of contact that might be included are: first media contact, eg TV advertisement, telephone directory, press advertising; first direct contact, eg telephone call (inbound or outbound), mail, branch; follow-up contact, eg completion of fulfilment form, second telephone call (where fulfilment packs are used, not that a key moment of truth is in fact longer – while the customer is waiting to receive the pack); diagnostic work (fact-find, discussion of options, revisiting fact-find etc); receipt of contract; signature of contract; completion of direct debit; receipt of first bank statement containing direct debit; renewal; receipt of annual benefits statement; claims – notification, authorization, execution and payment; cross-sell letter received; enquiry made to same company through different route. The kinds of ideal value that market research by insurance companies has revealed include:

- clear route of access;
- quick responses to any contact;
- prior given data available at any point of contact, where this can speed/improve quality of transaction (includes avoidance of 'double-give' of data);
- clear documentation/explanation – in particular making clear customer commitment and benefits;
- timely approach (attempt to sell only when customer has relevant need);
- clear diagnosis of requirement for all the family;
- inclusion of family in benefits at reasonable costs (ie recognition of additional business generated through one contact);

- recognition of loyalty when additional products/services bought;
- acknowledgement of all contacts;
- feeling of trust;
- competitiveness of offer.

3. Identifying the gap between what the company currently offers and what the customer values most.

4. Specifying the capabilities (and their underlying enablers) required to close the gap. In our simple directory example it might be the ability to buy media appropriately and to design advertisements well. Here are some other examples of the kinds of capabilities required to deliver these ideal values, including the ability to:
   - identify, hold, access and use data on relevant events in the customer's life and relationship with the insurance provider;
   - propose relevant offers to customers at all stages of their relationship with the company and life-stages;
   - respond quickly and relevantly to all contacts, whether or not solicited;
   - measure the effectiveness of all actions, in customer terms (for value) as well as company terms (for cost-effectiveness);
   - customize any offering to meet customer needs.

5. Identifying the enablers required to deliver the capabilities. In our example, both might be enabled through outsourcing, eg to a media buyer and an advertising agency. Here are some examples of the kinds of enablers required to support these capabilities:
   - data warehouse;
   - data sources;
   - data communications to supply customer data to all points of contact;
   - modularized products, with criteria to match module mix to customer needs;
   - full customer management facility in call centre (to collect and update data as well as to sell/handle queries);
   - model of customer management, to provide clear management processes for customers;
   - media buying and analysis;
   - staff competencies and behaviour (gained by appropriate hiring criteria and employee retention practices);
   - staff trained to manage customers as required by their particular contact role;
   - scripts and processes for attuning the company offer to customer needs;
   - mail sorting and handling capability.

6. Evaluating the costs of providing the capabilities and enablers against the additional value that would be created for customers, and then the value (revenue, profit) that could be obtained from customers for providing that value.

WHAT INSURANCE CUSTOMERS WANT

In the research undertaken for this chapter and in many insurance consulting and CRM deployment engagements, we have reviewed the main conclusions reached by insurance companies from their market research into their customers' needs – for value and for relationships. Here are our conclusions.

Life and pensions

Customers' buying attitude is often passive

Customers still display a high degree of inertia in almost every category of decision. Most customers show a low level of involvement – the risk against which they are insuring and the savings they are building up are simply seen as so far away that it is hard to get excited about them. The products themselves are seen as intangible and often very complex. This leads to the situation where even as some products get an awful press – as endowment mortgages did in the UK in recent years – they continue to sell well.

Customers place a high value on company reputation

In the end, most customers select a life insurance company in terms of trustworthiness, financial security and customer service but a minority believes that there is a substantial difference between companies concerning the above attributes. The differentiation is therefore weak. The reputation of the company has therefore become a key differentiator, with corresponding implications for branding. Credibility is a more important barrier to entry than price.

Most customers fail to see the value of a 'fee for service' financial adviser

Most customers are not keen to pay a fee for financial advice as they simply are not certain about the benefits. The more that direct techniques are used, the more customers will feel that they could have done just as well by replying to a direct response advertisement. Despite this, the complexity and the number of policies available on the market mean that consumers *are* willing to take independent financial advice. However, most consumers still expect it to be paid for out of commission, as is all the other advice that they receive as consumers. Nonetheless, they are often surprised if/when they see the levels of commission paid, ie the monies not invested in their policy fund in initial years.

In some cases, consumers are not even sure when they are getting truly independent advice or when they are buying from a tied agent. This applies especially to banks. In the rare cases that a customer insists on independent advice, the bank then introduces the consumer to the specialist division of the bank that provides the untied service. Usually only more mature investors are aware that such services exist.

The value and benefits of advice by itself are not obvious to consumers and therefore not distinct from the act of purchase. However, a few customers are aware of the benefits, and do respond to tangible demonstrations of these benefits. Compare, for example, the continued success of travel agents in providing information and advice when direct booking has become much easier, but note that for many consumers, the annual holiday is much more important than pensions, insurance or long-term savings. In some situations, customers effectively end up paying for advice because they feel they need to reward the salesperson or agent for the time they have spent investigating their needs.

Customers favour medium-term tax-advantaged products over longer-term commitments

These schemes have proved very popular, although most of the funds invested here have arguably been diverted from other forms of saving, and may be diverted to other uses within the medium term (for example, early mortgage repayment). The very long-term benefits of pension investments seem too remote for many customers, despite their immediate tax advantages. As the first consumers begin to benefit from these long-term pension decisions, they also start to recognize and share their new knowledge of limitations, including current regulatory restrictions on annuity transfer decisions and options for fund inheritance.

One of the most severe attitude problems of customers, from the viewpoint of insurance companies, is that many customers consistently base their decisions on a time horizon that is significantly shorter than most insurance companies would consider optimal. The best example of this today is that most customers only consider long-term care insurance at or near retirement, when it is very expensive. Of course, for prudent customers, this is optimal, as they will have invested enough money in tax-advantaged pension products, the value of which will have grown with tax advantages. This will usually (depending on the country) yield a lump sum that is available for reducing financial commitments (eg mortgage, if it is not already paid off) and investing in a single-premium long-term care policy. However, these are the very people whose prudence will usually have yielded pension revenue which can cope with the demands of long-term care. It is precisely those who have not invested in other long-term assets that need to invest in long-term care insurance.

There is no substitute for a solid long-term brand

Customers will respond to attempts to differentiate by product or service (ie non-price), but the branding that needs to go with this (to establish the differentiation in the customer's mind) can take a long time to establish unless based on a pre-existing brand (eg retail).

Customers are willing to consider as suppliers of financial services trusted companies from different product areas

Given the weak differentiation between suppliers, customers are now considering companies outside the traditional market such as Marks & Spencer and Virgin as well as others from sectors like retail, car manufacture, telecommunications and utilities. Customers welcome these entrants into the insurance and financial services industries. They trust these strong, customer-oriented brands at least as much as the traditional life insurance companies, and often much more.

Buying from these non-traditional companies will increase, particularly if supported by special offers, discounts or improved access and services. These new entrants will continue to threaten established companies, particularly if they have a strong brand image associated with trustworthiness and high quality customer service, and pursue a low-cost strategy supported by product and service simplification and use of direct media, processes and systems. These entry strategies have not only lowered the barrier to entry, but have also found a quick way to the customer's heart and mind. Often the product providers, even through non-traditional channels, are the traditional companies.

Market segments are becoming less well defined in the customer's mind, eg credit may come from a motor company (GM), life insurance from a retailer. However, this threat can also be an opportunity, as by forming strategic alliances with non-traditional outlets, sales opportunities can be created. Here, the strong performance of the 'affinity banks' (eg MBNA) is a clear indicator of the way forward.

Younger customers are more receptive to the idea of buying from these types of companies, but there is relatively little variation of attitude across socio-economic groups.

Customers are concerned about trust and government policy changes

In the UK, there have been strong debates on pension fund accountability, on over-selling of endowment-linked mortgages and on transfers from occupational pension schemes. There have also been many government pronouncements about the needs for individuals to fund more of their own retirement, the imminence of new government pension schemes and reductions in the tax benefits accruing to pension funds. These have combined to stimulate consumer fears about their long-term financial future – even as far as doubts about the government's ability to meet its obligations. Similar waves of uncertainty have broken over consumers in other countries. These pressures should perhaps combine to drive customers towards advisers (either financial services or lawyers and accountants), but because of uncertainty about the value added by the latter, the net result may be to drive customers towards very simple 'low commission' pension offerings such as those of the direct providers.

Customers want improved customer service, but generally don't expect it

Companies have tried to solve problems of customer management by simply introducing more and more new products or by changing their existing products. The focus on customer service has been weak, and customers have noticed this. So most customers have a low level of respect for both company representatives and independent advisers. In fact, many customers do not know which they are dealing with, just as in direct motor insurance they are unaware whether the company is a direct writer or simply using direct marketing techniques.

Customers are becoming increasingly price sensitive

This applies even in areas such as retail banking. As customers cannot really differentiate companies on the basis of reputation or service, differentiation tends to be based on price. Faster, more accurate access to competitive pricing (eg over the Internet) will reduce price disparities and increase competitiveness amongst surviving companies. The simpler the product, eg term life, the stronger this tendency will be. However, this is less true for complex investment products such as pensions, where price usually features as an entry fee plus annual commission rate on the value of the fund and is therefore evaluated against the expected gain in value of the fund.

Customers prefer 'direct' – especially the telephone – and want quick mail fulfilment

Customers are increasingly willing to deal with companies over the telephone and the Web, even for more complex transactions. This is putting pressure on traditional distribution channels.

This tendency is particularly strong in, but not exclusive to, younger consumers, and is mainly because this form of distribution is convenient and quick and can therefore meet the needs of full-time employees, for instance. There is a strong psychological influence – a strong relationship between customers' self-confidence and their comfort in using the phone and then receiving by mail completed fulfilment documentation which they just need to sign. However, simplifying what is being delivered can increase this comfort. This creates a particular opportunity for execution-only services (ie no advice). As regulatory issues require a longer telephone call for more than execution only, the latter is likely to grow and be well accepted by customers. Also, the telephone gives the caller the opportunity to control the relationship, for example avoiding the intrusion of physical presence, ability to start and terminate the call at the customer's convenience, and more easily 'shop around' for alternatives.

The reduction in contact with the supplier created by the telephone allows the customer to contact more suppliers to investigate options, and also makes the contact harder to differentiate from other contacts. This can make the customer more focused on price. To overcome this lack of differentiation, companies may only be able to increase customer retention and loyalty by creating other forms of contact, eg better use of direct mail, telephone updates. A particular opportunity is derived from the fact that most customers' confidence in dealing with long-term insurance matters is relatively low. Only the more confident ones use the telephone – hence the success of the retail proposition. There is still a need to make the buying process much simpler and more accessible from the customer's point of view. Provision of clear information in moderate volumes is one key to this.

Non-life, property and casualty or general insurance

Most of the research results here are virtually the same as with life and pensions. Below, we highlight the main points of emphasis.

Branding and customer service

Branding and customer service are, if anything, more important to customers, and becoming more so because suppliers are working harder to achieve this limited differentiation. The chances of making a claim are much higher than with life (eg perhaps once every 4–5 years in motor – more often if it is a company car, perhaps once every 10 years with household). Actual claims experience is likely to be more recent, so customers actually have an experience other than the one-way flow of money. The renewal experience is of course annual. However, despite this, research on motoring clients suggests that most are concerned mainly with obtaining the policy at the lowest price to satisfy the law. This strong focus on price has made it hard for insurance companies to communicate real product benefits – most benefits are perceived as being of little value as when customers take out the policy, they do not intend to make a claim. Perhaps if insurers paid no-claims bonuses by explicit rebate certificates or even tokens the perceived benefit might be stronger and the tie-in would be created.

Brand is important because most customers make their decisions with limited or imperfect information. If your brand is strong you have more chance that they will include you on their list of three or four price enquiries. Customers cannot possibly trawl the whole market so tend to restrict their search or rely on an intermediary's search capabilities.

Impact of compulsory nature of some general insurance

For those categories of consumer insurance that are compulsory (legally or under loan or mortgage terms), price sensitivity will always be higher because most customers see their buying task as cost or risk minimization under duress. Most categories of commercial insurance are not compulsory, so there is more opportunity for companies to add value here.

Customers usually do not know who is the ultimate supplier of their insurance

Direct methods appeal very strongly to all ages and social classes, because the frequency of interaction makes the simple approach of direct more attractive. However, most buyers are unaware of whether the supplier is a direct writer or just a direct marketer, or indeed what difference this might make to them. Sometimes the brand of product provider is evident, other times minimally or not at all.

Customers don't understand the idea of renewal pricing and customer acquisition pricing

Most customers cannot understand why they can get a better deal from another company than from their existing company – who should know them better and be encouraged to retain them as customers. They are becoming used to the idea of loyalty bonuses, and wonder why financial services companies cannot follow this practice in a manner that directly affects the comparative net premium. Insurance companies have taken part in loyalty consortia. The main focus of a consortium is on gaining more behavioural data and seeking other opportunities to sell, but only time will tell whether being part of a generalized loyalty scheme actually helps retention.

Customers increasingly use competitive quotes to benchmark their existing supplier

The number of companies customers seek quotes from usually rises and falls with the insurance cycle. The new entrants who enter when premia are high spend on advertising to encourage customers to ask for a quote from them. However, as companies begin to offer loyalty bonuses, these requests for quotes will increasingly be undertaken for benchmarking purposes, with the customer being keener to stay with their current supplier because of the bonus.

Customer prefer simpler claims processes

Customers respond very well to attempts to make the claims process easier. Traditionally, they have found the complex administrative work around the claim to be time consuming and stressful. However, the need to control fraud will impose limits to easing the difficulties associated with the claims process.

The key for suppliers is therefore to:

- implement a well-managed claims process, with minimal administration and good feedback to customers on claims' progress;
- manage more of the claims process, leaving less to the client/others;
- ensure that the customer believes he or she has been treated fairly.

Until recently, none of these was a focus for many insurers.

Good customers (higher value or lower risk – often difficult to target because risk tends to rise with value) will be retainable by adjusting the claims process to allow for (probably) lower levels of fraud from this kind of customer. In other words, good customers expect to be trusted a little more.

Most customers respond well to the idea that the claims process can be taken off their hands – those likely to object are those most likely to commit fraud, and therefore will not be customers the company wants to retain.

In markets where most policies are sold through agents, one traditional agent role was to 'see the customer right' at the time of claim, possibly even bending the rules against the insurer. Most insurers are centralizing the claims process, not only to reduce fraud (by customers, agents or repairers) but also to cut costs. This means that a prime source of agent value to the customer has been removed.

CURRENT MARKETING STRATEGIES

Customer strategy

Despite customers' desire for improved service, better prices and some recognition of loyalty, many insurance companies generally focus much more on prospecting for and recruiting new customers than on retaining and developing them. For most insurance companies, the idea of 'customer group' is translated into 'customers for a particular product', or basic geographical, age or risk groupings. Marketing strategy is normally determined by product, and then by risk group within product. Geographical targeting is quite common – typically for test marketing – partly because of the geographical structure of most insurance companies, and partly because risk and value factors are closely corre-lated with local geography. Primary marketing focus is on lead generation and acquisition. The potential longer-term value of the customer is rarely assessed.

Most systems and accountabilities are focused on products rather than customer groups. This tendency seems even greater in companies that are the product of recent mergers, which perhaps could be better described as creating a larger assembly of products. This creates inertia both in systems and marketing. Some companies are trying to make the leap towards customer marketing, partly because of the margin pressure they are experiencing (the idea being to make more margin per customer – by improved retention and cross-selling). However, with the market opportunities being taken by new entrants, by building customer-based multi-product databases and using innovative direct channel approaches, there is a risk that older companies will be relegated to underwriting and claims, unless they develop a process for managing customers which includes their agents. The same tendency is noticeable in credit card markets, where affinity-based marketing is threatening the classic single-product credit card company.

There are, however, a few exceptions:

- A Swiss insurance company focuses on small businesses and higher risk consumers. A complete small business package was developed, including property, vehicles, product liability and so on.
- Some insurance companies have begun to realize that their most valuable personal customers are also smaller business owners or managers, and good prospects for business schemes. This represents a significant departure from classic product targeting.
- A major insurance company in Sweden segments its portfolio by profitability and risk to see whether it is charging the right rate for the right customer segment, by identi-fying attributes which suggest higher claims or lower profit or more propensity for fraud.
- The UK subsidiary of a French insurance company has developed an underwriting system that uses value as well as risk factors.
- A company that deals exclusively through agents is focusing on a total household package for higher net worth customers, making it worthwhile for the agent to visit the house and assess all its risks.

Despite the fact that few such approaches have emerged onto the market, many insurance companies have begun to consider a different approach to strategy. This focuses less on product and more on total customer share – the aim being to meet a wider range of the customer's total insurance and investment needs, in order to improve retention and maximize long-term customer value. As we have seen in our analysis of market research, a prerequisite of this is a strong brand, but the heritage of strong product selling makes it hard for insurance companies to develop their brand – a key asset required for relationship marketing. In fact, strong product selling on price, as in the motor insurance industry, has been very destructive of brand strength, for those companies who initially led by their brand. The only exceptions to this are companies who made low price part of their brand (eg Geico in the USA). Of course, where the price is opaque, as in life and pensions, much purchasing is done on trust – whether of the company or the adviser. This makes a relationship easier to develop, though in practice it has been only the best advisers and companies that have achieved this.

A key aspect of this relationship is the demonstrated professionalism of the supplier in gathering and using customer information at the point of contact with the customer. This has been shown to be feasible (but often not achieved) for simpler insurance items, but in life and pensions, the infrequency of buying decisions combined with the complexity of decisions has made performance generally weak. The attempts being made by non-traditional suppliers to simplify the purchasing process – using execution only and inbound telemarketing – should result in improvements here, not least because in these circumstances customers will have lower expectations about the quantity of information required and its use during the buying process.

Segmenting by channel propensity

Today, one segmentation approach that interests insurance companies is segmentation according to the customer's propensity to buy through different channels. While with simpler products such as motor insurance the propensity to use diverse channels is fairly widespread – across all age groups and social classes – this is less so with the more complex life, pension and long-term savings products, where many consumers still prefer the face-to-face contact with the agent or branch. Some companies are discovering that they generate a much higher telephone response from more aware investors, typically from the higher social classes than from others, who tend to depend upon branches. In Australia, a new direct life insurance company found (some months after launch) that average premium per policy was many times the industry average. They believe this was because their 'execution only' service attracted mature investors who knew their needs.

The customer relationship

The relationship between company and customer is normally quite weak – and is considered so by both parties, though it may experience peaks when a new policy is written, or during a claim. The major exceptions to this are relationships based upon affinity groups, such as trade unions, older people's associations, charities, interest clubs and the like. The workplace basis is still strong, particularly for pension-based relationships involving the deduction of additional contributions (an opt-in relationship), although this is not normally as strong as an affinity-based relationship.

From the supplier's point of view, one of the key benefits of affinity-based relationships is the very high retention rate, often over 90 per cent even for annual contract business such as motor and home contents insurance. This leads to very low marketing costs and higher profit, some of which is of course shared with the affinity group in the form of discounts to individual members and rebates to the scheme sponsor. This retention rate contrasts with about 85 per cent for the very best motor insurance companies. The high retention rate of affinity groups is a lesson for those building societies that were mutual in status but behaved as limited companies in every other sense, losing the feeling of mutuality and its associated benefits for both parties.

If we examine different country markets, it is clear that the strength of the relationship varies according to contractual terms and the type of policy. In the UK, motor insurance experiences high levels of attrition because most contracts are annual and can be cancelled at any time. In contrast, in Germany, many policies last five years and can only be cancelled if the car is sold or if the price is increased above a specified rate. So, in the UK, the only sign of any deepening of a relationship is the customer's increasing hope of a discount for renewal or no claim – not a very solid foundation for relationship marketing.

However, successful financial advisers have developed strong relationships with their clients. Interestingly, these are often based upon the adviser's shrewd appreciation of the customer's likely value – either lifetime or during specific periods. It is this appreciation of relationship value that large companies are trying to emulate through the use of databases and data analysis. However, only the very best financial advisers (and companies) have the endurance to manage the relationship well over generations. This is most common with financial advisers in settled communities, eg rural areas.

What the new direct insurance has done to old relationships

The emergence of direct providers with lower operating costs has put the agent relationship at risk through the pricing transparency that has been created. This applies particularly in certain personal lines such as automotive. Price is much more salient than it was, and the subject of discussion between consumers. If a consumer discovers that the price at which his or her household insurance has been obtained is much higher than that obtained by a neighbour from a direct supplier, the entire relationship may be at risk. However, for certain risk categories, such as motor, a consumer may accept that this higher premium might be due to companies' differing perceptions of risks. However, that consumer might still feel that the high price was a signal that the company did not really want the business, in which case, what hope for the relationship? Suppose the response of the incumbent company is to drop the price when told of the lower quote. The consumer may feel annoyed that he or she has paid a very high price for years, and his much-loved insurer only chose to drop the price when informed of a lower quote. In this case trust lost is unlikely to be easily regained.

Most insurance companies have now identified that good service and consistency of handling is the foundation of good reputation. One direct company has identified that it gets nearly half of its new business from recommendation. The claims process is therefore being managed much more smartly, particularly in motor insurance, where the chances of an individual customer experiencing a claim in any one year can be as high as 40 per cent.

Customer retention in insurance

One of the main reasons for customers seeking alternative quotes and then switching is still price, followed by change of car. Customer service and incorrect cover are less important. This shows that direct insurers have succeeded in attracting price-buyers. The vast majority of customers are satisfied (or at least not dissatisfied!) with their existing insurer, and are just seeking a lower price. This demonstrates the old marketing truth – that it is very easy for major suppliers to destroy branding by price, but very hard to build it up. In many countries consumers have been exposed to a media barrage persuading them to buy on price. It is not, therefore, surprising that they are responding as they have been encouraged to do. Hence the strong emphasis placed by direct insurers in the USA, the UK and in continental Europe, most of whom claim high retention rates on price grounds, on customer service, including: 1) added-value services, service contracts with refunds if target times for processing are not met; 2) rapid (even one-step) approval of claims by phone.

This is likely to start paying off once most of the market has experienced this new claims behaviour. In fact, it needs to pay, given the generally high costs of acquiring customers that are at least as profitable as existing customers and the relatively low costs of retaining them. Note, however, that the furious competition in general insurance has increased the costs of both.

Meanwhile, direct insurers have realized that their hold on the market depends upon developing deeper and deeper knowledge of their customer base and ever more precise targeting, allowing them to: 1) tailor products and services to customer risk and value; 2) retain customers on price as well as on service.

In this respect, the insurance industry cannot be criticized for its marketing practice, because the dream of precisely targeted products priced to individual customers is one that many other industries would like to achieve but are decades away from doing.

Another ploy used principally by the direct insurers is expanding the risk tiers that they serve, giving customers who might otherwise have been priced off the option of staying with the company. Thus, in the USA, Geico historically focused on the preferred market but added a standard and non-standard company. This has allowed them to improve customer retention.

In life and pensions, the complexity of the product and service and problems with the sales process have together caused severe problems in terms of cancellation. One Canadian company therefore decided to offer a six-month product guarantee, allowing any customer to cancel within six months without penalty. The value of this approach is not the guarantee itself, but the change in marketing and sales behaviour. This kind of guarantee has two effects: 1) the company is much more careful to ensure that the product and the financial commitment are right for the customer; 2) the company focuses more strongly on the six months immediately after the sale, ensuring that any queries are handled excellently, and problems solved quickly, and so on. This is the 'welcoming' and 'getting to know' period, which has proved such a graveyard for so many financial services companies.

This type of guarantee is in line with the guarantees that consumers are being offered more and more in their normal retail purchasing. It has great benefits for the brand – provided it is adhered to without question. The key difference, however, between the retail product situation and financial services is that the consumer gains by returning money, but a consumer who cancels must normally go through a buying process again, unless the reason for taking out the policy in the first place has disappeared.

Cross-selling

As part of their retention strategy, companies are aiming to cross-sell products, in the belief that this will help build the 'total relationship', and therefore aid retention. However, this approach is not always as easy as it sounds (see Chapter 14 for more on this).

Improved agent management

The much closer targeting for customer acquisition and the strong focus on retention by all financial services institutions is changing the relationship between product providers and their agents. For years, all users of agents have been aware of the very long tail of what are considered to be poorly performing agents, attracting high administration costs but yielding little in profit. Slowly, insurance companies in particular are beginning to realize that precisely the same methodologies that are being used for customer management can be used for agent management. Low volume agents do not need to be deleted, but they certainly need to be managed differently – usually through a lower cost strategy. The first step in this process is therefore to classify agents by their current performance and by their potential, and develop a complete relationship management proposition for each group – typically:

- high performers – where the need is to sustain performance and increase loyalty;

- middle performers with potential to become high performers, where the need is to develop potential but sustain loyalty;
- middle performers with no prospects for growth – where the need is to sustain loyalty while reducing costs;
- new, recently recruited but currently low performing agents who could perform much better with help, where the need is to invest to obtain greater rewards;
- low performing agents who are going nowhere or about to leave, where the need is to absolutely minimize management costs, or even terminate their employment.

Customer management policies, contact strategies and targets can be set up for each group in order to grow the business from the highest potential agents while minimizing the costs of dealing with low performing agents. Agent retention is a major issue with many insurers. This has led to a focus on automation (to provide better service to agents and to capture customer data as a corporate asset), training and an improved customer prioritization and account management approach, aiming at creating a true long-term business development partnership rather than a short-term and arm's length relationship.

Information and the relationship

Because of the strong product orientation in the insurance business, and the common failure to create cross-product databases and supporting systems, most companies are only now beginning to be able to recognize a customer who comes across from another product or through a different channel. Even those insurance companies that have built their databases are not yet sure how they will use them, whether strategically or at the point of sale (particularly in the call centre). If the database cannot in some way be integrated with the existing point of sale systems, it is unlikely to achieve its supposed benefits. The costs of achieving this integration can be up to $15 million and three years of hard work, as well as the absorption of much management time. The benefits of such an investment need to be examined carefully. Many insurance companies do not even have the capability to make such a decision because they have not worked out the categories of benefit and how to deliver them.

In many markets, customers have developed a degree of suspicion about insurance companies' requests for information. They have relatively clear views about which information they consider is relevant to each buying decision, and are unwilling to give information outside these limits. The limits tend to be quite narrow for motor insurance, but for health products they are wider, because customers believe that they need to give more to enable the underwriting to take place. In many cases, buying information may be a better option as the customer may be less distressed and the data sources can sometimes be more accurate.

In many cases, customers' suspicion that the insurance company knows little about them as individuals is entirely correct, because although the company may have gathered information about them, it has little understanding of their behaviour as customers. Much of the market research that we have seen is product-oriented, or focusing on the most basic customer characteristics. However, in a few companies, the quality of market research is very high, but the market research managers in these companies often find it difficult to get their marketing colleagues to respond to their findings. This is particularly the case if they relate to such uninteresting (for most financial service marketers) topics such as customer service and customer retention. In a few really tragic cases, the insurance company has a strong view – a mental image – about who its customers are which is totally unsupported by any evidence – whether from the database or market research. This image is often based on the volume of responses that they obtain from different media, but there is usually little analysis of which readers or viewers actually responded or whether they will be convertible, profitable or retainable. It is on such shaky foundations that massive cross-selling and other marketing programmes are often based.

It is worth noting that insurance marketing is still dominated by *a priori* segments and clusters rather than the attributes of a particular customer. The idea of focusing, for example, on customers who have experienced good service (or perceive that they have done so) is still rare. Improvements to customer service are still largely based on general ideas of fulfilling service standards rather than on the idea that improved service can lead to improved conversion and retention rates for particular customers.

However, in a few advanced companies, much better use is made of information. Data from one or more customer databases is heavily analysed, perhaps using data mining techniques for propensity modelling and segmentation, and merged with market research findings, to derive conclusions for areas such as:

- targeting for propensity to respond and then buy;
- channel propensities – increasingly important as most companies are now using multiple channels to access and manage their customers;
- fraud detection or prioritization of fast tracking, second-level investigation, etc;
- loss control;
- new product development.

Managing stages of the relationship

Most insurance companies focus almost exclusively on the initial stages of the relationship – targeting and welcoming (see Chapter 3), although welcoming is usually poorly managed. Rapid fulfilment is the key objective today, with the focus on speed after the initial enquiry. This is sensible, as without this the prospect will not become a customer.

However, afterwards, in most cases, the customer is left to his or her own devices. Focus on better welcoming would increase profitability, as a typical direct writer loses 10 per cent of new business between 'conversion' and first payment.

There are some exceptions to this. These include the various insurers that have issued customer magazines. However, some companies do it on a trial basis, not realizing that a successful customer magazine is the outcome of many attempts to get the editorial and advertising right, and to establish its place in the customer's mind as a reliable source of information. So the returns to investment in it usually increase over time. In this respect, a customer magazine is like any other magazine – lending credibility to advertisements in it. The fact that it is free is irrelevant.

At the other end of the relationship, some companies have established telephone hot-lines and help desks, focused on retaining business. However, this depends upon the customer understanding that it is worth calling before cancelling. In most cases, the first the company hears of the customer's intention to end the relationship is non-renewal or notice to cancel. Only a few advanced companies are considering how past response and purchasing patterns may enable prediction of cancellation or non-renewal. Some companies now have outbound calling programmes to aid retention, but these need to be deployed carefully, as incorrectly targeted or poorly scripted calling can stimulate an inert customer to cancel.

However, one of the problems in this area is the cost pressure to keep the number of calls and their length down, despite the fact that well-managed calls usually lead to improvements in the relationship and subsequent retention and cross-selling. If customers were discouraged from leaving by the thought of a bonus on renewal, then perhaps this problem might be easier to solve.

In many countries, the very high commission paid to life and pension agents and sales forces, combined with high staff turnover rate, reinforces the poor attention given to existing customers. This creates a very short-term approach. However, this makes it all the more urgent for companies to use the customer database as a 'backup' to remedy poor field customer management. One possibility insurance companies could consider is to transfer the customer to a customer service unit, targeted on retention and development. In the UK and in other countries the government is watching closely how much business is retained and how much is cancelled. If too much is cancelled, the regulator will assume that it was wrongly sold in the first place, and will threaten withdrawal of the company's licence.

What companies are doing – conclusions

Insurance companies include some of the most advanced practitioners of relationship marketing, and the most retrograde. The gradual switch from customer acquisition to customer retention is very noticeable in some companies, but others still have not learnt to combine these disciplines in one organization. The situation of a direct subsidiary largely responsible for acquisition and the main company battling manfully to retain customers is not unusual. We believe that most insurance companies will need to change their strategies, systems, organizations and marketing and service policies so as to combine the two in one company, to contain costs and reduce customer confusion.

THE WAY FORWARD – SOME STRATEGIES FOR SUCCESS

Our research indicates that successful companies tend to use a few simple concepts to analyse how they manage their customers, and to define better ways of doing so. In the rest of this briefing, we summarize some of these concepts. They are:

1. relationship stages;
2. customer value management;
3. loyalty / value matrix;
4. life-stage analysis.

Stages of customer management

In marketing, as opposed to marriage, binary relationships (in which a customer is 100 per cent loyal to one company or to another) are rare. Most relationships develop in stages (see Chapter 3), with customers sampling different products and often remaining 'switchers' or 'multi-sourcers'. The model of relationship development described in Chapter 3 can be used by companies to understand their customers better and to develop policies for improving the relationship. The relationship is described as a series of stages. In Chapter 3, we explain these stages, their definitions and the problems some companies have in managing them. The key here is to recognize that:

1. Customers don't simply move from being 'prospects', to '100% loyal' and then to 'lost'.
2. Stages of the relationship can be identified and managed; and data can be used to manage this activity.
3. Some of the worst failures occur at the earliest stages of the relationship, when the company thinks that the customer is safely on board – but the customer doesn't! Failures later on in the relationship are often due to poor quality in the first stages, eg failure to welcome or get to know means that information for handling the customer later on is low quality.
4. Success can be achieved by defining the stages that contribute most to success – or

failure, and focusing management attention on improving customer management at these stages.

Loyalty–value matrix

The answer to the above question is to be found partly in loyalty–value analysis. This is based on the simple idea that insurance companies usually want more good customers, and fewer bad customers. The loyalty–value matrix is in fact a simplified version of a more complex analysis, usually carried out by profiling and scoring. In this analysis, customers are better or worse according to their value, loyalty, morality, responsiveness to communications, and propensity to cross-buy. Table 11.1 provides a simplified matrix suggesting how to manage customers in each cell.

Table 11.1 The loyalty–value matrix

Customer value	CUSTOMER TYPE			
	Loyal	Switchers/ multi-sourcers	Competitive loyals	All
High	Work hard to maintain Monitor quality of service Identify new needs Communicate & manage cost-effectively	Identify reasons for switching or multi-sourcing Improve service Work hard to substitute your products & services	Ensure you are visible, accessible & strongly branded for them Ensure excellent welcoming if they contact you	Monitor value and ensure costs of management are in relation to expected lifetime value
Medium	Work hard to maintain Monitor service quality Identify new needs Communicate & manage cost-effectively	Identify reasons for switching or multi-sourcing Improve service Work hard to substitute the company's products and services	As above	As above, but watch for signs of growth or decline
Low	As above, but at low cost and as automated as possible	As above, but at low cost and as automated as possible	As above, but at very low cost	As above, plus watch for signs of growth or decline
Negative	Seek to increase charges or let down slowly	Deter by higher pricing	Guard against entry	Define meaning of 'bad' customer Ensure data is to hand to identify bad customers

Figure 11.1 The developing customer life-cycle and relationship and how to manage it

WHAT CUSTOMERS ALWAYS WANT	Strong branch/direct relationship	Good service during sale	Error-free, quick and friendly service	Reliability and security Convenience and simplicity	Supplier help with problems	Keep informed
WHAT CUSTOMERS WANT AS RELATIONSHIP DEVELOPS	Good targeting	Attractive offer (added value) Product range Competitive initial price	Loyalty incentive	Good needs identification Tailored relationship No pressure selling	Accessibility Flexibility Two-way trust Respect	After-service call or questionnaire – how was it for you Acceptance of occasional mistakes by customers Loss-preventing call
RELATIONSHIP STAGES	Targeting	Enquiry management/recruitment	Welcoming	Getting to know	Customer development – retention, up-sell and cross-sell	Managing problems – intensive care, pre-divorce, divorce win-back
VALUE	ENTHUSIASM FOR BRAND →	→	INVOLVEMENT →	→	LOYALTY →	→
ATTUNEMENT TO PERSONAL LIFE CYCLE	Son/daughter Student	Young worker Single or married No kids	Young married, with kids	Married, older kids, school, then at college	Empty nest, then retired, healthy	Retired sick Death and inheritance
ATTUNEMENT TO BUSINESS LIFE CYCLE	Feasibility study, then formation	Solid foundation	Growth, reorganization	Expansion of scope Internationalization	Taking over or takeover Transfer to next generation	Decline Cessation Sale Bankruptcy
WHAT CUSTOMERS NEVER WANT	Increasing charges Poor perceived value	Poor, repetitive, untargeted, communication	Supplier only communicates when needs to Over-contacting	Poor service Poor staff attitude and skills	Inaccessibility	Deceitful Untrustworthy

Life-stage analysis

Of course, the key to managing customer value – in insurance as in any other industry – is to identify their future value, not their past value. Future value is closely connected with life stage, so it makes sense to use research to define typical customer life cycles and then to see how value changes during these cycles. This is a topic of great complexity, but if the right data is collected at the welcoming stage and then refreshed regularly, managing customers' value over their life cycle becomes possible. Figure 11.1 suggests how needs may vary with the life cycle.

USING THESE CONCEPTS TO DEVELOP A SUCCESSFUL INSURANCE MARKETING STRATEGY

In the insurance industry, relationship marketing and managing customer value are becoming more important for business success. Despite the success of the direct insurers, most insurance customers are still managed through a more complex value chain, with responsibility for quality and customer retention shared by two or more participants. Paradoxically, even some direct players have found the need to work closely with other companies in order to develop a successful customer management proposition, whether 'upstream', eg in marketing or product development, or 'downstream', eg in claims management.

So, for all companies, we recommend the process outlined below. This process has been applied in many companies with success:

1. Identify the different types of customers who need to be managed, their different relationship and value requirements, how these are delivered through interactions with the customer ('moments of truth') and the capabilities and enablers (including data and systems) required by the different participants in the value chain to meet these requirements.
2. Identify business partners at different levels of the value chain who are likely to be most sympathetic to a joint approach, and to have the best skills and capabilities.
3. Identify the technical, managerial, competitive and political barriers to sharing accountabilities and possibly data amongst value chain participants, how these barriers can be overcome, and how risks can be controlled. Where data sharing down the value chain may raise problems, identify possible third parties who may facilitate cooperation, where there might otherwise be problems concerning hosting data.
4. For 'shared value chain' companies, identify the risks of entry by the 'integrated proposition' and any possible weaknesses in the approach.

5. Develop a vision of the customer management proposition across the value chain, and share it with selected partners.
6. Develop a process for managing the vision.
7. If appropriate, pilot the vision to iron out problems.
8. Implement fully.

Notes

[1] IBM (1995) Landscaping the future: insurance scenarios
[2] Bound, Bill and Rhys-Evans, Sophie (1997) Back to the future for screen-based distribution, *Insurance Digest*, Coopers & Lybrand, Spring, pp 8–12

12

The evolution of CRM in banking

Merlin Stone, Richard Lowrie, Bryan Foss and Fola Komolafe

Most sectors of the financial services industry are trying to use CRM techniques to achieve a variety of outcomes.

In the area of strategy, they are trying to:

- create consumer-centric culture and organization;
- secure customer relationships;
- maximize customer profitability;
- align effort and resource behind most valuable customer groups.

When it comes to implementing their strategies, they are trying to:

- integrate communications and supplier – customer interactions across channels;
- identify sales prospects and opportunities;
- support cross- and up-selling initiatives;
- manage customer value by developing propositions aimed at different customer segments;
- support channel management, pricing and migration.

In their efforts, it is possible to identify four stages, as follows:

1. building the infrastructure and systems to deliver customer knowledge and understand customer profitability;

2. aligning corporate resource behind customer value – developing segment management strategies to maximize customer profitability and satisfaction;
3. incorporating a market perspective into understanding of customer value, so that any possibly adverse affects from the market or from economic and social developments are managed, and so that customer relationships are maintained;
4. integrating strategic planning and customer value management.

These stages are usually sequential, but not always so. In many banks there have been a series of different moves, with a start being made on stage 1, then a movement to stage 2, at which point the bank realizes that its systems cannot support stage 2 fully, so there is a pause while there is more development of stage 1. However, in many Western banks the situation now is that stage 1 is more or less complete. But there are still real problems in translating this progress into implementation.

Often, first-stage insights were focused on customer profitability, once banks learnt how to use the new tools and technology they had just acquired, not just the marketing database, but also data warehousing and mining. This led to the classic discovery that value was concentrated in a comparatively small proportion of the customer base, and also – in the case of long-term investments and pensions – this value was in general committed to other suppliers. From this followed the understanding that the distribution of service effort and cost was not well aligned with customer value, with wiser banks realizing that aligning with current value might be fruitless, as alignment with near-term future available value might be much more productive. This is particularly true in the wealth management segments.

Now that many banks understand where customer value is to be had – often not in the most obvious places, they are looking for marketing and systems tools that facilitate implementation rather than insight. Leading practitioners of bancassurance have segmented their customer base by potential and have tried to design customer management strategies and service propositions either around maximization of sales opportunities or control of costs to match current and likely future value. They often succeed more with the latter than the former. Pricing for channel costs and customer value is one element of this, with active channel migration increasingly a feature (eg encouraging the customer to deal with the bank via call centre or Web).

There is also very poor use of fact-finds, which are carried out within a legitimate 'needs analysis' process. A large proportion of the facts collected (key dates, competitor products, attitude to risk, etc) are never held as reusable data. As a result it becomes impractical to target wealth management and other customer development techniques effectively. Targeting projects often resort to the use of external data (which can never be as personal or effective) as data already known by the company is not available for use. The use of sales laptops is slowly improving the situation, although the integration of this key data is often not in place. This problem may be due to the short-term view often taken – with the bank focusing on the immediate sale. Bancassurers are typically more focused on acquisition than development. Minimum data is collected in order to maximize and complete the current sale, not to support the later development of the customer relationship. Key future dates are often ignored and little attempt is made to maintain the currency of key data.

One of the interesting features of stage 2 is the new requirement for external data to supplement insights gained from internal transactional data. As banks realize how little of the available profit per customer they make, they increasingly adopt share of customer wallet as a target. However, this shows them that their existing data sources do not tell the whole customer story, particularly as many customers switch away from branch-based organizations (insurance or banking) to remote or intermediated channels, with their focus on transaction efficiency rather than personal relationship or, at the other extreme, in-depth advice. As customers broaden their portfolio of financial products, the data relating to customer dealings with a single organization (typically for only one or two products) provides less of an insight into the wider behaviour and value of customers. For banks, it becomes clear that transactional and behavioural data are only indirect indicators of customers' attitudes and needs. So many banks become very big users of all available external profiling data sets, including public access lifestyle databases and a new generation of individual-level value and customer-type indicators introduced to replace the post-code based geo-demographics. In the UK at least, this has produced a number of competing individual-level indicators informed by market research with a large sample of financial consumers and modelled out to the wider UK population. Customer databases are then tagged with new individual-level codes. Of course, external data is no substitute for data collected directly from customers and managed properly, but few banks do this well. Still, attitudinal data will never be more than indirect indicators of propensity to buy a particular product from a particular supplier. There is also never any way to *know* the attitudes of more than a small minority of customers.

A highly analytical approach with its strong focus on customer profitability sounds optimal from a marketing point of view. Unfortunately, in today's aggressive competitive scenario it has not always produced the results banks expected. This is because new players, particularly the global insurers and the US new-breed banks, are prepared to buy market share and customer base with loss-leading products or to exploit the propensity of customers (particularly higher value ones) to use new low-cost channels. This leads to a 'value drain' from traditional players to new entrants selling keenly priced products through new channels. Of course, it is the most valuable customers who are the best equipped to process and access information and to take advantage of these 'best in market' offers. This trend is most advanced in comparatively simple products, where pricing is relatively transparent, but the approach is spreading rapidly across sectors into wealth management. Many banks have discovered to their cost that they have not fully understood, let alone managed, the implications of a new channel that adds cost and channel conflict.

The financial services industry has undergone a fundamental redefinition of its products, markets and distribution infrastructures. The traditional sector differences in skills and culture have been largely eliminated. Most financial institutions today do business within interwoven business clusters; in very few businesses is any perceptual, regulatory or banking licence-based structural advantage retained. As a result of competitive pressure, many of the financial industry's leading players adopted a vertically integrated product business cluster structure to emphasize operating efficiency and product business profitability.

CHANGING INDUSTRY STRUCTURE

The industry's primary businesses hold a set of predominantly mature, commoditized products; net revenue growth is coming from fee-based services, industry consolidation and opportunities in emerging e-business offerings. Over the next 5–7 years, 75 per cent of the lines of businesses within the finance sector are subject to explosive market-based reinvention. Without new value capture, we expect a decline in overall revenues for the industry.

E-business and related technologies have unleashed powerful forces redefining the financial services industry, producing a business reinvention pattern that can enable the needed new value to capture opportunity. These forces are changing the dynamics of industry maturation, enabling explosive reinventions of businesses that produce a redistribution of industry enterprises. For example, the traditional brokerage industry in the 1980s was a mature business; the subsequent explosive growth of the discount brokerage business model split the industry. Online brokerage had a similar impact, splitting the industry again and rapidly aging the discount business model. In the networked economy, anticipating this phenomenon becomes a primary management responsibility.

The future will witness the emergence of a global marketplace and the continuing contraction of portfolio-based intermediaries, displaced by market makers and technologically enabled direct intermediaries. In response, viable business models that create acceptable levels of return on investment and demonstrate the capacity for such over time are being created and new relationship models are emerging. IBM sees B2C and B2B e-business as a series of transformation waves moving through global commerce (see Chapters 4, 6 and 39 for more detail on this). The second and third 'wave' opportunities will involve a more significant part of total revenues and value capture:

- Wave 1 companies use the Internet to improve performance of existing business processes and models, seeing it primarily as a new electronic channel to create efficiencies in supply chains and distribution systems.

- Wave 2 companies build innovative e-business models on the Web, using network technology to offer new value propositions, streamline operations, and/or disintermediate traditional market structures.
- Wave 1/2 hybrid enterprises are now being created, blending the innovation of Wave 2 business models with the best aspects of the more traditional Wave 1 infrastructures.
- Wave 3 will produce a realignment and redefinition of entire industries as network-based access to any/all information and proliferation of 'virtual agency' offerings shifts power from producers to consumers.

The role of the executive team will be to ask the right questions and participate in developing the right answers, and to ensure that the right choices are made in selecting the key models for success.

Based on IBM's experience, one of the key points arising from the ongoing research is that the creation of viable business models is dependent on marketing strategies founded upon customer data. Many banks have started with the assumption that data from their existing customers is the foundation for success.

CUSTOMER VALUE MANAGEMENT

We introduced this technique in Chapter 11. The use of Customer Value Management (CVM) is very similar for both banking and insurance; however, slight differences in the approach are highlighted in the following example. CVM in banking would involve:

1. Identifying the key moments of truth at every stage of the relationship between the supplier and the customer; for example, when the customer looks in the telephone directory to find a supplier, when the customer contacts a call centre to enquire about a product, when the customer calls in at the branch to open an account or complete a transaction. This can be done by interviews, research of customers (particularly focus groups and in-depth interviews), brainstorming (ideally in groups of staff representing every aspect of customer contact). Each area identified (eg for banking: opening an account, depositing and withdrawing money, buying an additional savings or investment product, complaining) should itself be subject to intensive examination, as it is likely to reveal many moments of truth within it. For each moment of truth, the following areas should be examined:
   - relative importance of this moment of truth in determining whether customer will buy/stay;
   - current practice – not just policy, but actual practice, in its full range (ie not just the average);

- customers' perceptions, expectations and ideal value (by type of customer, in particular taking into account different psychological types, eg does the customer want to retain or give control; by current and past relationship);
- competitive performance, which can be identified by market research or mystery shopping;
- parallel industry performance, ie of companies which set the expectations of the company's target customers, irrespective of the field they operate in, eg supermarkets;
- the company's aim, ie how far to go towards ideal value – this depends partly on competitive performance and partly on resources. The target may be to achieve the delivery of customer ideal value eventually, but there may be steps along the way, dictated by resource constraints and other feasibility issues. In particular, some moments of truth may be more important than others. This might be broken down into immediate target and subsequent targets.

2. Identifying the ideal value target customers would like during and as a result of this contact. This of course may differ by type of customer. For example, if the customer begins the relationship by calling in at the branch, the value required might be that of quickly providing correct and clear information about the available options, saving the customer time and removing doubt and uncertainty. The kinds of contact that might be included are: first media contact (eg TV advertisement, telephone directory, press advertising); first direct contact (eg telephone call (inbound or outbound), mail, branch); follow-up contact (eg completion of fulfilment form, second telephone call); diagnostic work (fact-find, discussion of options, revisiting fact-find etc); completion of account-opening form; first and subsequent counter transactions; receipt of first and subsequent statements; making a complaint; using the ATM; asking for balance information; cross-sell letter received.

3. Identifying the gap between what the company currently offers and what the customer values most.

4. Specifying the capabilities required to close the gap. In our branch example it might be the ability to deliver the right information in a customizable form.

5. Identifying the enablers required to deliver the capabilities. In our example, it might be enabled through a kiosk

6. Evaluating the costs of providing the capabilities and enablers against the additional value that would be created for customers, and then the value (revenue, profit) that could be obtained from customers for providing that value.

Customer value management can therefore be used to home in on the critical moments during a relationship where your company can add value. The conclusions from this analysis can then be used to define a competitive set of policies for acquiring more customers and retaining them. But which customers?

THE VIEW FROM CUSTOMERS

Today, new sources of data are therefore exciting a lot of interest among banks, eg privatization and demutualization shareholders. Retailers' loyalty cards are providing useful insights into the patterns of purchasing of very large numbers of customers – hence the interest shown by many banks in developing partnerships with these retailers. This same motivation underpins the desire of credit and charge card companies to become involved with airline frequent flyer schemes.

Most bankers aim to improve how they manage their customer relationships. However, today most European banks do not have coherent long-term strategies for recruiting and retaining consumer customers. One reason for this lack of a strong approach to managing customers is that even today banks still only accept 50–60 per cent of applicants for accounts. This is a criticism of the products they market or of their poor targeting, as implicitly the product/targeting combination is only right 50 per cent of the time. It also has the effect of building up resistance to the brand and to banks in general – a scorned customer is a dangerous one. Pre-screening of offers and more detailed prospect definition, so that appropriate offers are made, would help. The rest of the applications fail on risk or other grounds.

Once accepted by banks, customers are remarkably unwilling to change, although attrition rates are still too high for many banks. Typically, at any one time, between 5 and 15 per cent of their customers would like to change banks, but in practice a much lower proportion changes, and this is often related to life-cycle events. However, as the consumer culture that demands a high level of service continues to develop, willingness to change is rising. An increasing proportion of customers buy transaction services and loans from other sources and channels – eg point of sale loans, store charge cards, credit cards from non-traditional banks. The result is higher attrition of bank customers, and lower wallet share for the banks.

One difficulty most banks have is managing their marketing department as an integral part of the sales and customer process. In many banks, marketing departments are quite remote from customers, rarely receiving feedback from them, except as distilled through market research. Many marketing staff are product managers, who live on a diet of highly distilled customer feedback. The failure of bank marketing staff to interact with customers often leads to customers being confronted with unintelligible product information in the bank branch itself. Without these feedback channels, banks will continue to develop products and services which look very attractive from the marketers' point of view, and use the latest information and transaction systems, but which are unintelligible to customers.

Part of the problem is that the people serving the customers themselves often do not understand the product. If they do not understand the product, they do not sell it actively, unless they are measured on it. They are under pressure because of the cost cutting. Some banks view their marketing departments as having performed so poorly that they have produced no value, and have closed them or reduced them considerably in size. However, this has led many of them to struggle with the idea of customer management, which is based on marketing ideas, although *not* product marketing. Banks that have succeeded in this area have redefined the role of marketing. Behind all this confusion lies uncertainty about the role of branches. Branches are very expensive to maintain, and either more business must be obtained from them, or they must be closed. However, some banks have now realized that branches must be treated as a total multi-channel proposition on retail principles, if they are to survive – using the best self-service techniques and not just ATMs.

Banks consider that it is their business to have relationships with customers; however, the main component of the banking relationship is still transactional. With most telephone banks, 80–90 per cent of each call is taken up with the transaction, eg giving a balance, moving funds. The main problem for banks today is managing immediate customer requirements cost-effectively. Moving to the next level, the value-added level or the 'show me what I can/should do' level, the profitable element for banks, is more difficult, particularly via ATMs and telephone banking. Banks find it hard to manage resources to do this while remaining cost-effective. Worse, the information they need to move to the higher level may have been given to the bank in earlier transactions but is either not available at the point of transaction or was not captured at all.

One of the central problems of banks is that customers do not see the relationship as mutual. Banks have not been very good at the lifetime value estimation to handle the risks associated with managing lifetime relationships. Once again, they often have not asked for the information they need to assess lifetime value, of if they have, they do not know how to use it. As for actually anticipating customer needs rather than waiting for them to be expressed, this is an art that is confined to rural banks. The general experience of the financial services is that customers have fairly straightforward requirements as they pass through their life cycle and through their relationship cycle with banks. But because banks have tried to manage customers through these cycles by a series of pre-packaged products, their success in managing their customers, in particular in retaining them, has been much less than they would want.

At the other extreme, companies that at one time or other allowed product marketing to dominate the relationship with customers experience product failures and higher attrition rates. For example, bank advertising is still very oriented to products and recruitment of new customers via products. It is almost as if banks were frightened of developing a relationship with customers, and they would rather concentrate on starting a new relationship, because this is easier. It is easier to let customers close an account because they are not very happy and simply recruit another one to keep the total the same. The numbers can be enormous, for example closing and opening 750,000 accounts each year

The antithesis of good relationship marketing is forcing the customer through a series of transitions just at the time when the customer is vulnerable, ie in the first few years of leaving education, when financial needs evolve rapidly and risk profile is high. This policy is often adopted by banks for two related reasons:

1. Their information systems and culture do not allow them to manage customer groups, but do allow them to manage products. So they are only able to approximate meeting of customer needs by forcing them to adopt different products.
2. They want to reclassify their customers to allow reimposition of risk control, as the customer passes through life stages. Here, because the classification criteria banks use are fairly restricted – usually limited to simple traditional risk assessment variables – they are unable to 'give credit to' customers who might look poor risks in the near future but have high expected lifetime values.

The resulting product management culture in marketing departments combined with a risk-control culture at branch level leaves many customers 'out in the cold', or putting together their own portfolio of services from a variety of suppliers. Meanwhile, product managers are left 'fiddling while Rome burns', trying to find the ideal feature set for their product – a series of bells and whistles which cannot compensate for the general failure of banks to meet customers' lifetime relationship needs.

Further, consumers are gradually becoming used to a culture in which they are given reasons for staying (as opposed to the reasons for leaving proffered by competitive companies and most evident in the UK mortgage and motor insurance markets until recently). These incentives may cost next to nothing and in some cases are self-funding (eg if they reveal patterns of expenditure that can be used for direct marketing targeting, or if the take-up of the incentive actually yields revenue, eg free travel insurance if card used for booking a holiday).

Loyalty can be earned by a brand and lost by inappropriate offers to existing customers or no offer to them whilst new customers are offered better terms. Incentives to stay become a substitute for reasons to stay loyal, eg lack of services, short opening hours, long queues, not listening, poor, slow or wrong responses. All these can lead customers to feel that the bank is just taking them for granted. Even a surprise offer or gift on reaching five years with a bank can delight a customer at a cost which is a fraction of the benefit of retention.

Increasing numbers of banks realize that life cycle management holds the key to managing customers in practice. For example, unless a customer is classified as a 'new customer who needs special care' (which most new customers do), there is no way of ensuring that the organization and systems treat the customer appropriately. A key area for banks is spotting when the relationship is in the 'pre-divorce stage'. Remedying service problems is usually the best way to ensure customer retention. If a customer has ceased transacting through a bank, but still holds the account, there may be an issue that is festering. Customers consider themselves in pre-divorce while the bank thinks they have already divorced. In such circumstances, making contact with the customer, eg by telephone, and identifying and resolving the problem can reactivate the relationship.

Banks are improving their system-supported identification of customers at the point of contact. Curiously, this means that centralized transactions, via computer or telephone, have a higher level of customer recognition than many branch transactions – where there is no recognition until a transaction actually takes place. With system-supported transactions, the recognition takes place as soon as the customer 'enters' the system. However, the branch is alive and well, though its future may be uncertain (see Chapter 24 for more on this).

More and more customers want to be identified and managed as individuals, because they are learning that companies that do this well give customers more benefits and often reduce customers' transaction and relationship costs (eg by speeding up transactions, not asking for the same data twice). Regular customers in up-market hotels expect just to have to sign the bill – and possibly not even that. First Direct achieves this for mortgage processing. The interview is given over the telephone and all the customer has to do is to sign the form when it arrives in the post.

An important part of being recognized is giving enough information to be recognized. Most banks' research tells them that customers are happy to do this, provided that the information capture is efficient (ideally by the customer giving it over the phone and not having to write it) and they are sure that the information is relevant, of the right quantity and will be used well. The telephone seems to be the best tool, and the culture and training of inbound telemarketers supports this. But many banks have not thought clearly about how they will ensure that the customer benefits from giving information. This contrasts with retailers, who have had to motivate customers to join and stay active in loyalty schemes.

Most banks try to categorize customers into groups in some way. Often it is a broad segmentation, based on salary level or a similarly straightforward variable, and very commonly delivered to the customer by the product, eg account type, preferential interest rate, colour of credit card, rather than any other aspect of the relationship. For customers that are completely unresponsive to attempts to develop the relationship beyond transaction management, banks are deliberately creating a plastic-product-based, automated relationship, using ATMs, voice response, and any other technology that eases and minimizes the cost of transactions.

The number of different customer groups banks define is usually below 10, and around 5 on average for retail bankers. Of course, this does not mean that they have not defined many more segments, but this is the number they are trying to manage differently.

Typical segmentation is:

- transaction-only (managed via the plastic automated product);
- lower private banking segment (eg the Barclays Premier customers);
- true private banking;

- small and medium enterprises;
- very large and often multinational businesses and their staff (for example, Citibank has created a worldwide product set for a segment they identified from external data, demographic data, salary data, etc, who travel a lot and want to bank all over the world, 24 hours a day).

The limit here is not analytical, but the capability of the organization and its staff and systems to manage each segment. Branch structure imposes limits. For example, most branches are too small to be able to manage every segment their bank targets, so they focus on the mass transaction customer and perhaps the small business. As banks become more sophisticated in telephone and Web management of customers, they will be able to deliver a more varied segment management to the market, starting with the issuing of different numbers to different customer groups and delivery of different point-of-contact service. A simple example might be a longer waiting time for mass-market customers who call very rarely. Treating each customer fully as an individual is a remote objective. But most customers would like at least to be recognized and spoken to in a diagnostic fashion as if whom they are talking to actually did know them well enough to have a sensible conversation.

13

CRM in investment banking and financial markets

Genevieve Findlay, Peter Mathias, Paris de L'Etraz and Merlin Stone

INTRODUCTION

In this chapter, we discuss just a few of the considerations involved in implementing CRM in investment banking or financial markets. Although nearly all of the rest of this book focuses on retail financial services, we thought it appropriate to cover briefly some aspects of a research programme focusing on investment banking and financial markets CRM that was being undertaken at IBM at the time of writing this book.

In the past few years, insurers and retail banks have made most of the running in CRM. Increased competition and shrinking margins have forced them to deploy CRM strategies and technologies in order to respond to the needs of shareholders and clients. More recently, investment banks have begun to realize the intrinsic value of CRM. The principles of CRM hold true for this sector. Just because investment banking is a business-to-business application does not take away the fact that recognition of the client is still key for CRM success. However, most of CRM in investment banking is still work in progress. It is a missed opportunity since it offers banks a chance to rethink their fundamental approach to client management, to redesign their coverage strategies and to use technology to bring this about.

Better client management is no longer optional. In nearly all business-to-business markets in which clients are as large as, or as in this case, often much larger than their suppliers, the latter must respond quickly to pressures from their clients to improve client management processes and systems. Banks can no longer rely on an information advantage over clients. Clients are better informed than ever and are hence more discriminating. Awareness of the full spectrum of what can be offered (and at what price) leads to increased needs and more stringent demands but lower brand loyalty. To keep their clients, banks need to manage relationships with them better, for mutual advantage. Even if banks themselves are not working hard to manage clients better, through analysis, segmentation, design and delivery of the proposition, and tracking performance, clients themselves are often focusing on how to manage their suppliers to their own advantage. In particular, leading-edge clients are concentrating their business with fewer stronger suppliers that seem likely to provide them with a cost, capital and competitive advantage for their own marketplace.

THE CRM CHALLENGE

Corporate investment banks differ from retail banks in that a few large clients have a big impact on the bank's business performance. This means that CRM techniques will only help investment banks if they improve the bank's ability to:

1. select and then manage the right client set (coverage);
2. determine which products and services should be sold to which client, profitably, and then help the bank implement this sales plan (profit planning and implementation);
3. reduce the cost of coverage, in particular by improving the productivity of sales professionals covering those with small wallets, while maintaining quality of coverage (one day the wallets may be big!);
4. coordinate the multi-product, multi-country relationship in real time.

Coverage is an area of great weakness for many investment banks. They rely on the instinct and energy of their sales and research people to determine which clients to focus upon and then to win business from them. This approach – which has worked for many years – is now unsustainable. The marketplace is changing. Margins are constantly being squeezed. Consolidation of the sector and better information have increased transparency of internal operations. Clients' expectations about levels of service and cost-effectiveness are rising all the time.

Investment banking is characterized by two very different types of relationships with clients, as follows:

- *Share of mind relationships* focus the bank on doing a few large high-impact transactions for the client. While these deals are often opportunistic, they require intense investment of time by key people in the bank so as to build strong and differentiated relationships with key decision makers. The aim is to build access and influence with the right clients within the client organization before the deal.
- *Share of wallet relationships* involve very large-scale coordination of many people, each of whom is operating separately from the others. As banks have merged and clients have become larger (also because of mergers on their side of the market) the scope and complexity of these relationships have increased. The challenge for banks is to transform individual relationships into a broader institutional relationship.

There are many variations on these two types of relationship, and each of the businesses – debt, equity, asset management and banking – have a different view of this.

A central need for client management is to align objectives across products and functions. This is hard to do. Most firms find it hard to agree a process to make trade-offs between differing product, functional and geographic objectives.

Of course, CRM is not the only requirement. Two of the main determinants of business success in investment banking are client satisfaction and product quality. We believe that these two variables account for well over 90 per cent of the differences in financial results over time. CRM plays a key role – but by itself only makes a marginal difference. When used to increase client satisfaction its effect is much greater. When used to make sure clients have access to the right products at the right time, its effect is greater still. However, the quality of people and the discipline with which they are managed and measured, the quality of products, the infrastructure of the bank – all these have much larger impact on financial performance.

WHAT CLIENTS WANT FROM THEIR BANKS

For CRM to work, banks must have a very clear view of what their clients want from them. Four of the most important needs of clients are:

1. cost reductions and efficiencies in services delivered;
2. better control and transparency resulting in accountability for delivering results;
3. greater convenience in having to deal with fewer banks;
4. banks knowing the needs of clients intimately, so that the latter are offered the right products, at the right time and the right price, with appropriate associated service.

CORE PROVIDERS

As clients have merged and consolidated, they have come under increasing pressure from their shareholders to deliver higher returns. As a result, clients seek greater efficiencies from banks they regard as their 'core providers' of services. Clients want fewer banks that will help them achieve these new levels of performance while reducing their costs and risks. By concentrating their business with fewer banks, clients hope to achieve higher degrees of control over their banks, greater accountability for results and improved transparency in financial terms. They want to see new levels of bank commitment associated with this privileged core relationship position.

Clients require a tight linkage between all the following variables:

- long-term commitment and leading market position;
- geographic and product spread;
- ability to provide global coverage and delivery.

Most clients classify banks on the basis of ability to deliver on certain criteria, in particular: 1) long-term ability to deliver results; 2) impact on the client's performance.

Clients are concerned that many banks may not survive today's mergers and consolidations. Developing and sustaining solid working relationships requires an investment on the part of the client. Increasingly, clients are looking to make a strategic choice of core providers, rather than just making opportunistic and tactical decisions. They want to be supplied by banks for whom they are core clients and for whom their business is a core business. They expect a consistent, long-term commitment to market leadership. For example, clients involved in mergers or acquisitions need to extract value from these mergers or acquisitions by breaking down product and geographic boundaries, and this requires coordinated coverage from their core service providers. Global clients require consistent product delivery across geographies. The ability of the bank to execute a meaningful role in terms of geographic presence and product footprint is critical to being a core provider. Finally, in order for this to be effective the bank must provide the level of coverage and delivery infrastructure so as to make the whole process efficient, accountable and transparent to the client.

More demanding expectations of core providers are forcing clients to take coverage issues more seriously. They are beginning to evaluate banks more critically, on the basis of their ability to provide them with this necessary increased level of commitment and coverage. Just as banks cover many of their strategic clients using client service teams as part of key account management programmes, many clients are creating team coverage models for relating to their banks more efficiently. Large clients are increasingly reorganizing themselves so as to achieve performance enhancements and lower costs. There is a direct correlation between their ability to achieve these performance benefits and their success in managing and integrating with their banks more efficiently.

At many clients today, all team members within the buying organization, regardless of location, require and expect the same high standard of service from internal resources as well as from their external providers. The new internal structures of many global clients involve matrix organizations with a number of people having more than one reporting line and a number of functions having global and local activities. If the 10 people at the bank covering a particular client are not organized and aligned so that they work jointly on the coverage of that client, then it will be apparent to the client. Clients want to know:

- how client coverage officers are assigned to them;
- how many clients they cover;
- how often they are reassigned;
- who will assure them of consistency of service.

Client coverage discipline at banks has moved from being an internal efficiency consideration to being driven by their top-tier clients. As a result, many banks are entering a phase of change, in which their understanding, shared knowledge and focused communication will be significant factors in the share of wallet they win. Banks that can deliver these efficiencies will command relationship premiums that will differentiate them from their peers in terms of status as well as profitability. The relationship premium is based on the bank's ability to provide connectivity, communication and client focus.

A core provider's primary objective is to help its client achieve its strategic goals. Once a bank becomes a core provider, it must define a strategy for maintaining its position as well as for gradually increasing its share of the strategic client's wallet over time. As a core provider, a bank is 'permissioned' by the client to present its case for adding value across a range of products, geographies and needs. Clients are optimizers and they know what a bank is good at. Banks must build a 'role' for themselves that maximizes exploitation of their capabilities. The bank's objective is to increase the level of 'permissioning' to the point where it has influence over the buying behaviour. As a core provider the client feels that the bank is adding value. It has been 'permissioned' to provide a service or product of which it is perceived to be an excellent provider. So, it is the bank's challenge to position itself strategically in the mind of the client and maximize its share of the client's wallet. As it increases its level of permissioning its relationship becomes more important to the client and its edge against its competitors grows.

To maximize this benefit a bank must:

- align product and coverage functions;
- define overall objectives for the client;
- measure performance against objectives;
- continuously validate strategy with the client.

Clients want core providers that will help them achieve their strategic goals. They need to be convinced of that. The client's perception of the deliverables and their benefits / value must be very clear. They want to be involved in shaping the deliverables. They want the provider to have formalized and definable objectives that will translate into mutually agreed deliverables. Below is an example request for information (RFI) from a global client. The information is intended to help the communication between the two parties to be more efficient as well as to convince the client of the bank's degree of commitment. It would typically be sent with an organization chart describing client roles and responsibilities by product and location so that the bank knows the key decision makers as well as those that may require their services or products.

Sample checklist of an RFI from a global client to a bank

Overview

- Do you categorize your clients into tiers? Explain.
- Is there a process by which you assign the importance of a client's relationship?
- Do you have any proprietary information that you can share with us periodically that could benefit our relationship?
- How do you rate yourself versus your competitors? Strengths? Weaknesses?

Coverage

- Who is the main contact person on the relationship? List each member of the client service team by role and responsibility.
- What access will we have to senior management?
- What do you expect to achieve from a core relationship with our firm?
- What business do you do with us by product, location (aggregates)?
- Are you prepared to work with us on a research project on a success basis?
- What is your rationale for assigning each member of the coverage team?
- How often are members reassigned?
- How do you compensate them?

Commitment

- What are your product or service areas of greatest commitment? List the individuals and relevant expertise.
- Do you know our strategic goals? How can you demonstrate your commitment to our strategic goals?

Objectives

- What are your critical account objectives for this year with us?
- What is your estimated present share of wallet with us by product or service?
- What would you like it to be by product or service?

NON-CORE PROVIDERS

Being a core provider is increasingly imposing levels of client commitment that may make the economic feasibility of the relationship less attractive. Increasingly, clients will be willing to remove providers from their top-tier lists if they are unable to meet these challenges with more than the traditional lip-service. For those left out, this will mean that their relationships and role will increasingly come under pressure from top-tier providers who can provide a similar product or service.

Clients expect from their non-core providers: 1) focus and excellence in a narrow product set; 2) superior execution, pricing and value. In order to remain competitive, non-core providers need to achieve the following:

- lower cost of coverage than their competition;
- very competitive pricing;
- high share of wallet in a narrow product set;
- opportunistic cross-selling from areas of product strength.

THE TECHNOLOGY TRAP

To support core-provider status, IT systems must support a client-centric approach to information. They need to allow the bank to create virtual client service teams providing their members with access to all relevant client information across products and geographies. To do this, they need to:

- connect existing CRM systems and legacy systems efficiently so that all information around the client can be shared securely between client service team members;
- allow client service team members to engage in CRM without leaving their e-mail systems;
- be very cost-effective; achieving relationship premiums in current market conditions must be done without spending millions on CRM.

Many investment banks have already attempted to implement CRM. This usually involves either the IT division anticipating a requirement for a system and supplying what it thinks will be the answer, or the request to implement 'CRM' being made by the business with a broad idea as to what should be delivered but with little idea as to how to make it work once implemented.

We regard both of these approaches as poor practice and likely to lead to failure – as has indeed been the case with most CRM initiatives in financial services markets of any kind. Putting the technology at the heart of CRM strategy is problematic for a number of reasons, listed below.

Trying to solve CRM issues with technology

CRM technology is complex to build. It requires different systems to work in harmony to deliver the right information at the right time to the right people. In addition to this, it needs to be user-friendly to people in a range of different roles with different levels of technical literacy. In the highly complex world of investment banking this requires a major change to IT architecture, which would take many person-years to complete. As a consequence, most organizations have chosen to buy an off-the-shelf CRM package and build the interfaces into it. There are a number of problems with this approach:

- The package is not bespoke. The depth and breadth of the technology dazzles, but users' real needs are often forgotten, because of obsession with the capabilities of the whole system. Users are expected to work with the technology provided rather than specify what they really need. The package is not seen as an enabler but as a basis for reorganizing the business.
- There has been a tension in the implementation of CRM systems between helping individual bankers/sales people versus helping the bank become productive in cross-selling. In one case, the system was designed to 'make sales people more productive' with little focus on the coverage team. It is quite unlikely that sales people would enter data on their own accounts – they already know them well. This kind of data might only be of value to others on the coverage team. This trade-off between individual and institution goes all the way through the design process.
- Many packaged systems have no direct link to driving client satisfaction, share of mind or any other strategic sales variable. In addition to this, there are a number of other operational problems for individual sales people, eg failure of the system to integrate with their e-mail and diary/scheduling package (eg Lotus Notes or Microsoft Outlook), lack of protection of confidentiality (simplistic approaches are common, in which fields can be viewed either just by the owner or by all), although these deficiencies are now being remedied.

- As Chapter 31 shows, CRM system implementation is most likely to be successful when the organizational capacity for change is taken into account. 'Too much too soon' causes confusion and distrust of the system, leading to problems with uptake. Many CRM solutions require a complete implementation for the system to be effective. This is generally too much for the organization to take and the expensive package ends up being a glorified contact management system, with few of the management information, client planning or client intelligence benefits.

The politics of CRM

There are several organizational issues associated with putting technology at the heart of a CRM solution. These issues arise partly from the unique nature of the sales environment of an investment bank, where primarily individuals rather than the company are responsible for delivery:

- There is internal resistance to the solution because sales are bonus-driven and individuals believe they own the relationship, so are reluctant to put (as they see it) their bonuses (which they see as derived from ownership of the relationship) at risk. The CRM system is perceived to threaten this relationship ownership.
- Client-facing users suspect that the value of the system is mainly its ability to create management information rather than to increase efficiency and profitability.
- CRM installations have not been selective enough in dissemination of information. So much data is pushed towards users that much valuable time is spent sifting through it in order to be able to use it.

So, the ultimate challenge is to deliver a CRM solution that supports sales and account management, for example by providing the right information at the right time, so that it is seen as an essential business tool both for the client-facing staff and their management. The technology should be seen as an enabler, not the starting point for an organizational redesign.

SEEING REAL RETURN ON CRM INVESTMENT

Technology is clearly not the whole answer. There are several other requirements for success in managing clients, and these must be present before the CRM system is implemented (and ideally before it is specified). These include:

- developing a global account management strategy;

- streamlining the bank to meet the needs of the client;
- aligning a set of measures and related incentives to respond to client needs;
- institutionalizing the breadth of client knowledge;
- closing the loop: incorporating client feedback.

Developing a global account management strategy

The main activities of investment banks include arranging major loans for corporate clients, organizing rights issues, performing financial engineering, advising on or carrying out mergers and acquisitions and setting up initial public offerings. The rewards and prestige to the banks of executing such assignments are very great, as are the costs and salaries of the individuals doing such business. Knowing one's clients and the markets that they operate in is absolutely essential. Revenue growth can be achieved if relationships with core clients are strengthened through innovative service models that deliver the optimal mix of products to each segment. This involves assessing the overall profitability of each client to determine the appropriate service and delivery model. This requires a bank-wide understanding of each client's situation, to anticipate future trading and banking needs (with an understanding of inherent profitability and future value). A needs-based analysis must be pursued, to understand the optimal product mix for each client segment, and the outcome of the analysis should be used to create tailored offerings for specific segments.

Getting the right coverage model with the right client set is fundamental to the future profitability of the business. Questions the global account teams must ask themselves during planning include:

- Is this a strategic relationship?
- Has this client historically made us money, or is it a 'prestige' client that we want to see on our books?
- Will this client make the bank money?
- What is the *potential* worth of this client?
- How can cross-subsidization work?

The ability to anticipate demand from specific clients increases loyalty, facilitates successful cross-selling and reduces the length and cost of the sales cycle. However, to reap such benefits, the bank must ensure that its client management objectives are understood and observed right through the bank, in terms of the structure through which it manages its clients and in the setting of objectives, incentives and measurements.

Streamlining the bank to meet the needs of the client

The bank's structure must respond to the needs set by account management strategy, taking into account both geographic and business needs. This is both cost-effective and logical, as this allows the bank to jettison or restructure unprofitable and non-strategic client relationships, whilst focusing on those that are most important strategically. Once the bank is organized around what clients need and want, it becomes clearer which units of the bank are adding substantially to the value proposition and to the bank's profitability, and lines of business can be rationalized accordingly. However, it is important to determine where key cross-business interdependencies exist before finalizing decisions to remove or absorb particular parts of the bank.

Providing sophisticated added value – such as risk analysis and mitigation advice/products – to the same client is not only a way of generating loyalty and retaining the client but also allows for transparency of cross-subsidization across the bank. The ultimate aim is that the bank acts as a homogenized whole – across product lines and between geographies. The current and future value of the account must be recognized so that business opportunity is maximized. For example, a bank may offer a corporate client a large loan at favourable rates in anticipation of helping it with future bond issues or foreign exchange transactions.

Most investment banks are (and may always be) organized mainly by product rather than by market. Delivering specialized information and product advice or creating new and more sophisticated financial instruments requires product focus from dedicated specialists. However, this requirement must be balanced by the need to serve the client as an institution. CRM technology alone is not enough to ensure sharing of information, account planning and account servicing.

Historically, relationship managers have acted as the coordinators between the different parts of the bank and the client. Owing to the organizational structure and measurement systems, this has tended to be a reactive role – an attempt to reduce sub-optimization and wasted opportunity, rather than a high profile business management position. However, best practice suggests that the benefits of client management can only be maximized if this role becomes critical to the business. One of the leading investment banks has been developing and implementing its global relationship bank operation over many years. Its strategy is detailed in the case study at the end of this chapter. Its experience shows how important it is to get organizational design right. Client-focus is maintained through a global account team that leverages the different sources of client value available across the global network to meet client needs.

Aligning a set of measures and related incentives to respond to client needs

Measurement of people, processes, profitability, channels and clients' attitudes must underpin vision and objectives as well as enable assessment of success and failure. Feeding back success and failure enables refinement and redefinition of future plans and activity. A balanced business scorecard biased towards client-based measures of relationship strength, momentum and innovation is the ideal tool to ensure that CRM is being effectively monitored. It should focus on relationship returns over time, not just on revenue. It also needs to measure and manage 'return on effort'.

Carefully weighted incentives need to be developed to ensure that the business responds properly to client-management initiatives. These incentives need to be cascaded down through the bank, covering not only the global account team, but product specialist areas too. This is fundamentally important if a bank is to see continued superb execution in each of the product areas. Moreover, there needs to be alignment of action and objectives across products and a process to coordinate and allocate resources to the clients.

Institutionalizing the breadth of client knowledge

Client knowledge must include quantitative as well as qualitative information that must be shared across the organization. Although different parts of the business are likely to rely on different CRM legacy systems, there must exist a connectivity layer above these initiatives that provides all relevant parts of the organization with a common client identifier and knowledge taxonomy so as to provide everyone with a common language for developing institutional client knowledge.

Any knowledge-gathering exercise must include seamless e-mail integration. The capture of knowledge about clients must be an extremely simple exercise and preferably a natural by-product of the daily workflow. Existing CRM investments must be protected in individual units. Client-management processes vary across different business units and hence may require different CRM solutions.

Closing the loop: incorporating client feedback

For CRM initiatives to succeed, efforts must be rewarded (see Chapters 31 and 32 for more on this). Clearly, balance sheets and broker lists will show at one level whether relationships are growing in the right direction, but these are rather blunt and indirect instruments. A bank seeking to understand whether it is achieving client management objectives must work proactively with the client to gain feedback. Best practice shows that regular relationship reviews with clients allows the bank to:

- understand first hand client attitude and satisfaction (and the relationship between satisfaction, loyalty and profitability);
- understand client commitment;
- experience what clients experience;
- develop benchmarks and understand the competitive environment better.

CASE STUDY: IMPLEMENTING AND MAINTAINING A GLOBAL CRM STRATEGY

Several years ago, an investment bank realized the value of CRM and undertook a radical reorganization that would allow it to serve global clients at a worldwide level, whilst still developing and strengthening local relationships. This initiative marked a new twist to the focus on relationship management. The client was made 'the organizing principle'. Table 13.1 describes the change.

Organizational design

Recognizing the dangers of the diseconomies of complexity, the bank adopted a matrix structure for serving its global clients, as follows.

Table 13.1 Moving to a global focus

Prior to initiative	As a consequence of initiative
The bank was organized outside-in: first by geography, then by product and finally by client.	The bank reorganized on an inside-out basis: around client first, then by product and finally by geography.
There was a myopic focus on revenue – measured from product silos in individual geographies – little emphasis on cross-subsidization across products and intra-country. Revenue was the key business driver.	Focus became broader – the bank aimed for higher growth and higher return. It looked to maximize cross-border opportunities via global clients. A balanced business scorecard was deployed to measure performance.
Businesses was defined by broad geographical areas (little integration).	Business became truly global: • New organizational hierarchy was adopted throughout the bank. • Processes were standardized and well communicated. • Re-education programme was undertaken as part of change management. • Products were rationalized on the basis of what was important to global clients.

Key account managers

Highly experienced relationship managers were appointed to the role of key account manager. These individuals now act as the focal point of the account, being the chief link to the client's head office with a focus on the Chief Financial Officer (CFO)/treasury buying centre. Unlike the original role of relationship manager, a key element of the job is to be proactive – to create and identify opportunities, rather than to react to suggestions from the client. In addition to this, they must watch out for and manage alliance referral opportunities. The key account manager has prime responsibility for the coverage model for that client.

The virtual account teams

The key account manager is responsible for orchestrating virtual global account teams who serve the global client locally. Skills within the teams include industry analysis, risk management, market management, product and service delivery teams. The teams are responsible for delivering to subsidiaries of the client. Their intimate knowledge of the local client requirements, specific market conditions, laws and regulations allows them to deliver to the individual client needs. These teams are flexible enough to reform in order to be able to create bespoke solutions quickly.

Account planning

The bank has recognized the need for a disciplined approach to relationship development. It has developed an understanding of the relationship between level of effort/time expended and the share of wallet achieved. Their clients are plotted on a relationship development curve and segmented accordingly, and potential revenue can be assessed (eg they may rate as a high priority prospect or a strategic partner delivering over $1m with much more to come). This model provides the basis for further analysis, industry planning, relationship planning, activity and scarce resource tracking, and finally for deal tracking and a single integrated pipeline.

Support processes – measures, feedback and technology

The bank follows many of the best practices suggested in this chapter. It runs a balanced business scorecard that is directly linked to incentives and regularly reviewed. Clients are frequently approached for a relationship review and the output of this is fed back directly and efficiently into the client management processes. A single CRM system was developed to support the entire CRM process globally.

Lessons learnt

The bank learnt some simple yet powerful lessons:

1. Have a knowledge of the client at the micro-level. Understand not only the company and the industry that it is a player within (macro level), but endeavour to understand the individuals within the company, the competitive pressures they are under, their strategies and direction, their strengths and weaknesses (micro level). The bank aims to have a better conscious awareness of this than the client does.
2. Anticipate requirement at the micro-level. Through an understanding of the client, issues can be addressed before they become needs. The bank always attempts to allocate employees' time according to these anticipated requirements.
3. Consistently deliver as promised. Aim to deliver to need and ensure delivery of what the client values, eg intellectual property, speed of response, value for money, etc.
4. Aim to be a top-three provider. The bank believes that points 1–3 above give them competitive advantage. It aims to ensure that it is deemed to be one of the top three providers, since this is where clients spend most of their money.

Part 4

Understanding customers

14

Making the most of your customer base

Merlin Stone and Tony Woods

THE PROBLEM

In most of the world, banks sell a variety of non-banking financial services products – investments, property, casualty, health and life assurance, endowments, unit trusts, investment bonds, pensions and so on. The fact that they can do it is not in doubt. What is in doubt is:

- Whether they can do it profitably.
- Whether enough customers want to buy other products from banks to make the effort profitable.
- Whether there are other objectives that should be taken into account (eg if a customer who buys insurance from a bank is more likely to stay as a bank customer, or whether selling insurance to the customer works as a defensive strategy).
- Whether being a bank gives an advantage. This may be a classic marketing advantage such as having a relevant financial services brand image, or a relationship marketing advantage, such as having a database of known customers with known needs, or a combination of the two (eg customers on the database may pay more attention to messages from the bank because of the brand).
- Notwithstanding any advantage banks may have through branding, whether tough competition from existing insurers or new entrants will win customers away from banks. These new entrants may include insurers who set up banks.

- Whether the commissions banks have to charge to make bancassurance profitable will lead to customers getting such poor value that in the end customers will resist banks' attempts to sell non-banking products to them.
- Whether because of competitive factors and past problems (perhaps poorly targeted or executed, or even mis-selling), customers will want to buy insurance from banks.

Insurance companies are heavily involved too, not just as providers to the banks, but because they have been merging with each other on an unprecedented scale. One of their objectives (and indeed justifications for their mergers) is to improve their penetration of their customer base. When they create their first data warehouse, they normally see the good news and the bad news. The bad news is that they have barely penetrated their own customer base – their share of wallet is very low. The good news is that this means – they think – a big opportunity.

Today, cross-selling for banks is focused at least as much on securities (trading) as on insurance. The estimates for growth show that the UK (and other countries in Europe shortly behind) will boom as they have in the USA. Most banks see this as a key aspect of wealth management services. This is shown by the acquisitions and joint ventures that are taking place all over the world. Many banks and other financial institutions are setting up Web portals that combine banking with products for 'wealth management'.

This chapter examines the idea of making the most of your customer base from a relationship marketing perspective.

THE GENERAL SITUATION OF CRM IN FINANCIAL SERVICES

Financial services may exist as an industry category for the companies that are in it, but for consumers, this is doubtful. The reason for this is that the strong product focus of the industry – still evident today – led to companies pushing their products 'at' customers, with a very strong focus on the particular characteristics of each product. There is nothing wrong with this – indeed the most successful and enduring consumer marketing models have tended to do this. The best examples are the packaged consumer goods marketed by companies such as Unilever, Procter & Gamble, Mars, Coca-Cola and the like. Up until the 1980s, it seemed that the cosy world of giant, product-pushing specialists would last for ever.

The first signs of breakdown in this came from companies such as Direct Line in the UK, which combined a very customer-oriented (though still single-product) approach. This involved the use of direct marketing and true disintermediation (direct writing meant bypassing insurance brokers) and its associated information technology to break into the motor insurance market. Interestingly, a bank (Royal Bank of Scotland) owned Direct Line, but nobody called this 'bancassurance', because the relationship was just a funding one. Throughout the world, this approach has been repeated, not necessarily disintermediating as Direct Line did. Indeed, Direct Line (in the form of its Privilege subsidiary) is the writer behinds Barclays Bank's motor insurance, and Direct Line also sells though building societies (Bradford and Bingley Building Society) and retailers (such as Tesco).

This approach has been rapidly extended to all financial services products, with predatory global companies such as AIG, ING, Zurich and AXA seeking to undermine the classic financial services business model of cross-subsidization (often based on hidden or shared marketing costs). They do this by cherry-picking vulnerable customers with a 'top vanilla' proposition.[1] One of the favourite targets of insurance companies is large traditional banks, particularly by offering high interest accounts (Standard Life, Prudential, and ING amongst many), often in league with smaller, more predatory banks (to avoid the need for a banking licence). Banks, subject to this sustained attack, wonder whether they can repay the compliment by attacking large, traditional insurance companies (often in partnership with smaller insurance players or large foreign players wanting to gain a foothold in the market). They are particularly interested in the higher value part of the market (pensions, life assurance and long-term savings), where margins are higher and customer attrition lower. However, they have also targeted property and contents, motor and travel insurance (although almost always as a sales channel rather than as risk-carrier). In response insurers are targeting 'low interest' credit cards, savings and other banking services.

Both parties view the distribution networks of the other as unwieldy and expensive (insurance agents or bank branches). Both also consider that Web distribution offers unparalleled opportunities in terms of ease of addressing their target market – and also unparalleled threats to their many channels. Meanwhile, the process of product commoditization and consequent falling margins continues, in most cases aided by the regulatory authorities' insistence on clarity of reporting of benefits, terms, commissions etc.

Social differences come very strongly into play in market developments. For example, in Sweden, where customers are used to adopting new technologies, direct services were also quickly adopted, with customers moving business between suppliers for better rates. In Germany and Switzerland the change was much slower. Not only were they much more conservative in adopting new technologies, but they were also less willing to accept any change in supplier or product structure – despite price benefits.

One of the most dangerous beliefs of global banks is that their experience in markets where they have achieved higher cross-selling is transferable to markets where cross-selling is lower. This would only be so if the competitive and regulatory situation were the same in each market. In fact, lower cross-selling ratios tend to be associated with having had more years of less-regulated competition. Having a high cross-selling ratio is therefore more likely to be a consequence of recency of competitiveness and the associated customer inertia. There is evidence that global companies are, in general, poor at transferring international knowledge, and this would be a prime example. Transferring knowledge includes determining whether practices can be relevantly transferred.

The advent of deregulation, and the resulting spree of acquisitions and mergers, has led to a situation where although there are fewer players, customers have more choice because virtually all the players now supply a full product range. In particular, the mass-market customer, who traditionally was of little value to most financial services providers, is now seen as having reasonable potential because if (the dream goes) 'we could only improve our cross-selling ratio to these customers, and hold onto them longer, they would become more profitable'.

In Australia and New Zealand, there are no outstanding examples of bancassurance, although many aspire to it or have committed and commenced efforts to achieve it. There are also a few trumpeting their offerings but these are principally pre-emptive strikes to establish a presence and capture customer intent. There are examples going in both directions, ie banks expanding into the insurance arena and insurance companies into banking. The latter are more enthusiastic because they have more to gain. Examples of insurance to banking are NRMA, Mercantile Mutual, National Mutual. 'Banking' here is used in the wide sense of 'financial services', with the traditional banking service provided as a vehicle, and to complete the capture of the customer. Most stay away from health insurance in Australia because it is a minefield. There are many health insurers in Australia, but only a few dominant ones, and they all will soon converge to less than 20. AXA is driving bancassurance and aggregation forcefully, initially through National Mutual and its brand, but now 'National Mutual' has been replaced by 'AXA'. Similarly, ING is doing this through Mercantile Mutual, albeit more slowly. A key facilitator for this and other developments has been the deregulation of banking and financial services that took place in the late 1980s in the UK.

In the UK, banking, insurance, building societies and other financial services have been brought under the same regulatory umbrella. Most of the smaller banks have been taken over by the bigger four. In Australia, as elsewhere, banking, insurance, health insurance, mortgages, and other financial services are still perceived as separate entities. This stems from history, from mistrust, and from a 'don't put all your eggs in one basket' value. It has also been reinforced in the past five years or so by the appearance of independent and attractive mortgage providers emphasizing the gap and the appeal of separate services.

CROSS-SELLING

The cross-selling aspiration, which is the basis of most thinking about the benefits of bancassurance, has for some companies turned out to be a nightmare, for a variety of reasons. These include the following.

Supplier–customer relationships

For many customers, these relationships have been much shallower than banks believed – even non-existent. The customer has had a single transactional product from the bank, perhaps two (if a credit card has been included). The relationship will have been coloured by all the problems of a transactional product – incorrectly registered transactions, un-authorized overdrafts, lost cheque books and debit cards with slow replacement, queues at peak hours, difficulties in getting through by telephone. None of this is unusual, and although many banks have developed very strong customer service propositions, the foundation required for selling insurance products is often weak. In some cases, customers deliberately choose suppliers that are different from the bank – they take the view that they do not want to be too dependent on one supplier, unless there is significant financial or service benefit to them. The service benefit tends to be strongest in areas such as private banking and financial advice – here customers are happy to take several products from a supplier, though usually only when the supplier is an intermediary.

Intermediation

Many insurance markets are strongly intermediated, in the sense that the intermediaries perform a function that is perceived to be valuable by the customer as well as the supplier. This may be under threat from new forms of intermediation. This is the case with the long-term advisory function through Web-based approaches or through new approaches to wealth management (see Chapter 36). However, it is not clear that banks always have the correct branding and knowledge of customers to rival these old or new intermediaries. In some countries, the branding is very strong. Still, banks should be careful not to rest on their laurels, as many banks that have strong general financial services brands have them as a result of lack of past competition. If consumers have had nothing better on offer, then they will tend to rate a bank that has had a reasonable shot at bancassurance quite well. Branding is relative. When new competition arrives, the brand can all too quickly dissolve, and with it the customer base.

In fact there can be several other effects: 1) Many of the most profitable customers may leave, while other customers remain as they are not 'cherry picked' and are better off staying. 2) Inertia. For example, many customers retain their property insurance with their mortgage company despite better offers being available elsewhere. This inertia effect is also evident in the deregulated utilities market.

Customer value – uncertainty and variations

Much of the discussion on the possibilities of cross-selling in bancassurance assumes that a customer base consists of a number of customers, each of known value, propensity to purchase, media preferences, etc. In fact, as many banks have discovered when trying to analyse their database to discover its potential for conventional banking products, this ideal world just does not exist. It is only in the past few years that most banks have organized their databases such that the data in them is high quality and subject to a reasonable updating process. Once this takes place, potential gross customer value in relation to property and casualty insurance is relatively easy to determine in most countries. This is because it is usually possible to establish, either from data collected as part of the normal account management process, from inferences from payments made on the account, or from purchased data used to enhance the database, what assets (property) or individuals (casualty) are available to be insured. It can also be inferred that these customers are in the market quite frequently, eg once every 2–3 years for motor insurance.

However, when it comes to longer-term savings and insurance, this is less easy. Here, whether a customer is a good value prospect depends on various factors. These include:

- the availability of funds;
- the customer's priorities and perceptions concerning provision for the future;
- whether the client has already made relevant commitments;
- whether the customer would consider an approach from any bank – as the customer may have particular views about which suppliers or channels are appropriate;
- whether the customer would consider an approach from that bank in particular (when branding considerations come into play);
- whether the value looks good but is in fact risky, eg does the customer have a propensity to cancel commitments?

In some countries, because following deregulation the development of database marketing in insurance rapidly outpaced that of banks, banks are clearly at a disadvantage in terms of customer knowledge, and are trying to catch up. However, it seems that in some countries the strong ties that mutual banks or mortgage providers have with their customers have allowed them to develop much stronger customer databases (whether through mail questionnaires, branch interviews or similar). In its most mature state, this led to tough competition for the 'free' cash flow of higher value individuals. This means that by the time banks wake up to the possibilities of bancassurance, most of the potential clients of the current generation have been well served by the insurers, so the banks then have to focus on the needs of the next generation. Where this is so, banks will have to be more patient about the time it will take for these customers to be valuable, meanwhile managing them as cost-effectively as possible.

Also, customer value is not evenly distributed, particularly in wealth markets, also when the longer-term view is taken, and for liquid assets. The Pareto rule applies very strongly to financial services. However, within-product Pareto analysis may differ strongly from cross-product analysis. In other words, a customer who is high value for one product is not necessarily high value for another. One simple reason for this is that financial services products are a mixture of transaction products, short-term and long-term asset/credit and liability/debt products. Finally, *net* value (ie net of costs of management, claims, credit default) can differ yet again. A high gross value customer who defaults on a large debt is at one extreme on negative value. This means that simplistic targeting for one product based upon gross value for another is likely to be weak and at worst risky, until proper analysis has been done of the correlation of net value across products.

However, in the area of credit products and property and casualty insurance, there is evidence of correlation of value between different products, simply because a customer who is low risk in insurance seems to have a higher probability of being prudent financially. This of course may just be a reflection of the customer having a lower propensity to commit fraud on creditors or insurers!

Apart from product cost, the cost of managing a customer, for instance, will vary depending on:

- the type and quantity of financial transactions;
- which channel the customer uses for regular contact (eg retail, Internet, telephone);
- how often the customer contacts the bank with complaints or queries (statement queries, timings, re-prints, overdraft limits, interest rates);
- how often the customer requires non-typical service (special permission to do things out of normal policy arrangements, ceased trading, wind-up orders, bankruptcy, extensions to limits).

Although the transaction numbers are smaller, the cost of dealing with lower value customers is often proportionally higher because:

- they prefer to use higher cost channels;
- they are less used to dealing with the bank – so bank and customers' procedures are poorly aligned, causing service hassles;
- there are more non-typical service issues, involving high levels of reasonably senior people's time;
- there is a higher default and bankruptcy rate.

This implies that net margin is likely to be skewed, with a large proportion of lower gross value customers into loss. Of course, the Internet can be used to reduce cost to serve. For this reason, many banks are trying to migrate customers to the Internet, and this may have interesting implications for their ability to cross-sell insurance products.

One of the main issues facing banks and other financial services companies is the fact that customers only become profitable either when they use a product extensively (eg a large mortgage kept for many years, a bank current account with a substantial positive balance), and when they behave 'well', eg they do not give payment problems or transact intensively. Because so few customers are profitable on this basis, banks have sought to improve their profitability by cross-selling. Of course, it could be said that customers who behave 'badly' and are charged 'penal' rates but require little additional monitoring are more 'profitable' *and* less likely to be promiscuous – provided of course that they do not default.

THE PROBLEM WITH GENERALIZED CROSS-SELLING

Generalized cross-selling can reduce profits. Let us define product X as the product already held – usually the 'acquisition' product (eg current account) – as the exporting product, and product Y is the product being sold, the importing product – often a car loan, a mortgage or perhaps an investment product). Mass targeting for product Y of product X's holders is likely to be loss-making. Here are just some of the reasons why:

1. Some product X holders have bought on price, not on brand or service. They may have a low propensity to respond to a contact from the same company – at all or for product Y – and may even be anti one-stop shopping, and have a lower than average propensity to respond than non-product holders of the company. This tendency might increase the *larger* the number of products held from the original company.
2. The profile of product X holders may not match the positive profile for product Y (eg according to need value, life-stage, geo-socio-demographics, etc). For example:
   - Some product X holders may be about to lapse, or have already lapsed.
   - Some product X holders may be in the middle of resolving a service issue.
   - Some product X holders may be low value for Y while being high value for X.
   - Some product X holders may be regarded as bad customers – in general or for product Y, because of risk/payment factors. Examples of this include people who have a poor payment record.
3. Additional normal timing factors (ie not just life stage) indicate that most product X holders will not be in the market for product Y. This depends on issues such as expiry date of product Y (if appropriate, eg a fixed term loan)
4. The relationship stage of product X holders needs to be taken into account. Holders at

the early stage of the relationship may be better prospects than holders at later stages of the relationship. The same applies to holders of competitive product Ys.

For these reasons, we suggest that planning for cross-selling must have more precision in targeting. It must also allow for likely lapse in product X during each business year.

Systems to deploy the customer data

Having good quality customer data, which indicates where the opportunity lies, is one thing. Having the business systems and processes to deploy the data so that action can be taken at the right time, in the right place, is another matter. Many banks have been a little confused by this, assuming that because their main contact with the customer was in the branch or through a bank statement, the systems required would all be either supporting customer contact staff in the branch or supporting direct mail. As it turns out, for insurance marketing, although direct mail is absolutely critical, the communication channels that work best to sell longer-term insurance and savings include seminars, the telephone, and of course the Web. Realizing this, banks in many countries have rushed into buying integrated customer contact systems that can serve any communications channel. This decision is probably the correct one technically – but only correct commercially if customers buy – and only time will tell whether this happens! However, although banks have moved into almost every communication channel, they seem to follow fashion, often having poor channel integration and increasing issues of channel conflict and additional operational costs.

The general situation – conclusion

Banks and insurers are very aware of most of the above issues, and have been in the forefront of CRM developments. They are the leading buyers of CRM systems and consultancy, and usually amongst the earliest adopters of new technology. They have certainly devoted enormous amounts of money and management time to CRM issues. The issue for the banks is whether or not all their investments will help them to sell more products, to reduce the costs of handling customers, and provide a capability that allows them to absorb further acquisitions or partnerships. Whether they are likely to achieve their bancassurance objectives seems to depend upon: 1) whether their customers' current propensity to buy additional products and services from them will stay constant or decline (there seems little prospect of an increase given the enormous competitive pressures being exerted by global insurers); 2) where they and their competitors are in terms of the quality of their CRM approach.

THE MIRAGE OF CROSS-SELLING

Many financial services companies have customer bases in which many, usually the majority of, customers hold only a single product. On the other hand, customers who buy more than one product can be very profitable. Such customers may stay longer, although only a properly constructed time-series analysis can show whether this is true, or whether customers who are loyal tend to buy second products. The supposed correlation between holding more than one product and customer profitability has led many companies to justify investment in customer databases primarily on cross-selling potential. The justification is in terms of:

- A lower cost source of leads than other means of identifying and reaching prospects, eg external list rental, media advertising.
- Possibly higher response rates, if customers are assumed to be more receptive to offers from a company whose product they already hold. Note that this cannot be assumed – much depends upon branding. However, it should be noted that most major insurers have invested large sums in establishing a wider financial services branding in order to encourage customers to generalize a supposed positive image from their experience of dealing with their company from whom they only hold one product.
- Reduction in duplicated mailings, ie not trying to sell products to customers who already hold them – this is particularly important if a company has been formed from a series of mergers, or if new products have been added over many years, each product having its own customer database.

There seems to be some anecdotal evidence that disguising cross-selling as up-selling or product improvement may get higher success rates (and may attract higher value customers). On the other hand, there is also some evidence that just focusing on increasing product holdings per customer can also attract larger numbers of unprofitable customers. For example, cross-selling household insurance to motor insurance customers irrespective of their propensity to claim can lead to a higher claims ratio than if prospects were selected primarily on the grounds of low propensity to claim. Although most companies now realize that generalized cross-selling is not advisable, we still find in our consulting work that discussions of cross-selling targets in financial services are devoid of understanding of the simple statistics of cross-selling.

There are two issues here: 1) Does the company have the information needed to pre-select or even pre-underwrite and price? Often not. If pre-selection is not carried out, many respondents to promotions will be turned down by the filtering process. 2) If the volume of customers targeted is too low, then cross-selling may be unprofitable simply because it does not achieve enough volume to offset set-up costs. However, in general insurance, if pricing is customer sensitive, then unselective targeting followed by careful risk pricing can work well.

There is a tendency for financial services marketing managers to have unrealistically high expectations or aspirations about the productivity of cross-selling. This chapter suggests a methodology which involves calculation of a baseline based on what would occur if customers holding more than one product did so not because of specifically targeted cross-selling activity but rather because of their exposure to the marketing activities for each product. Cross-purchasing rates substantially higher than those suggested by the methodology would suggest that either the brand (assuming it to be extended across more than one product) or some cross-selling activities were having an effect.

In many countries, there is no simple way to assess the performance of a company relative to its competitors in this area. Cross-purchase rates are not published, which prevents that comparison. In the UK, the Financial Research Survey gives an indication of holdings of different products from different companies from a large market research panel (this indicator is showing a decline, due to the ferocity of competition as new entrants appear and as companies cross between categories).

However, it should be possible at least to address the question of whether the company is achieving cross-purchase rates better than those that would occur if customers were spreading their purchases randomly. To do this, we need probability models that let us predict what the cross-purchasing patterns would look like if they were random. The appendix to this chapter considers a series of models of increasing complexity and realism and indicates what is the minimum information required to make the model predictions meaningful.

CONCLUSION

Realistically, any sensible model for cross-purchase rates must include elements of both examples C and D (see appendix below), where we acknowledge that not all consumers buy all products and that the markets for different products will be of differing size. Unfortunately, as soon as we allow different sizes of market, the simple binomial model will not suffice. It is trivial but tedious to write out the theoretical result, though the calculations need to be done carefully, particularly when persistence (length of time that the product is held) is added. That is the good news. The bad news is the need to know something about the total size of the market for each product or product area as well as the company's own market share for each product, or type of product.

The time dimension makes the whole issue much more complex to grasp. Retention is normally stated simply (eg 80 per cent). However, it is usually valuable to see which customers are leaving – new customers, those of two years, three years, four years, etc. If this is drawn as a graph, the level of complexity is very much higher and the charts difficult to interpret or draw conclusions from. The charts might show which of each cohort of customers is leaving now, in comparison to last year's position. The current retention figures may even be shown by month, which might show variations in patterns overlaid on each other. The multiple products held by each customer may be lapsing at different times, and so on.

This is not an easy issue to address, but it is one where multidimensional data mining tools can help to extract some key learning points for attention. Combining propensity modelling (propensity to lapse now or later) and segmentation (finding the key attributes that distinguish groups of lapsers for attention) can determine whether these time and product factors are important indicators. Also, in theory, the best approach is to build scoring models which focus directly on the measure of interest, eg to go directly for profitability rather than scoring separately for propensity to purchase and propensity to claim.

The methodology in this chapter will help financial services marketing managers address the question 'Are we doing as well as, better than or worse than average in getting our customers to create combined holdings with us?' The random cross-purchase models allow a company to calculate what its cross-holding rates should be if it were doing as well as the average for the industry. The company could achieve that average in other ways, not necessarily at random, but the model will give a suggestion as to what the rate would be. Without this, or some similar methodology, there is a tendency for companies to have unrealistic goals. Targets that are well above the industry average may be proposed, and even used as part of a business benefits case for investment in the required marketing systems and process capability. Such an approach is likely to lead to disappointment.

APPENDIX: THE ALGEBRA OF CROSS-SELLING

Example A

This very simplistic model is intended to set the scene. Suppose the whole market consists of just 100,000 consumers who all buy the same two products, X and Y. They continue to hold them indefinitely. Suppose a company has 10 per cent of each product market. Then the company has 10,000 customers who hold product X and 10,000 who hold product Y. Suppose further that cross-purchases with the company are random.

Now start with customers who hold product X. The randomness assumption implies that 10 per cent of these will also hold Y. In that case, the cross-purchase rate across the company's whole customer base will be 1/19, just over 5 per cent. There will be 1,000 customers who hold both products (who make up the 10 per cent of Ys who buy X as well as the 10 per cent of Xs who buy Y), 9,000 who have X only and 9,000 who have Y only; in other words there are only 19,000 *different* customers so the cross-purchase rate is 1,000/19,000 = 1/19 or about 5.3 per cent.

To tackle more complex cases we need to calculate using conditional probabilities. We write Prob(A given B) as P(A/B).

All of our customers hold at least one product with us; we are interested in

Prob(hold 2 or more products given they hold at least 1) or P(>1/>0)

The calculus of probabilities tells us that, in general:

$$P(A/B) = P(A \ \& \ B) \div P(B)$$

where the probabilities on the right-hand side are absolute, unconditional, probabilities.

In the current example, this translates to:

$$P(>1/>0) = P(>1) \div P(>0)$$

The assumption that cross-purchasing is random is equivalent to saying that all purchasing is random, given the market share. If all customers own all products then an appropriate probability model for the number of products held by a customer with a given company which has the same share of every product market is the binomial $B(k,n,p)$, where k is the number of products held by the customer, n is the total number of products in the marketplace and p is the market share. More realistic assumptions will be considered later.

For the binomial distribution $B(k,n,p)$, the probability P_k of holding k different products with the same company, out of a possible n products (assuming random purchasing) is given by:

$$P_k = \frac{n!}{k!(n-k)!} \, p^k \, (1-p)^{(n-k)}$$

For the simple example with two products:

$$P(>0) = P(1 \text{ or } 2) = 2 \times 0.9 \times 0.1 + 0.1 \times 0.1 \text{ and } P(>1) = P(2) = 0.1 \times 0.1$$

Hence:

$$P(>1/>0) = (0.1 \times 0.1) \div (\, 2 \times 0.9 \times 0.1 + 0.1 \times 0.1) = 1/19$$

This is the same answer arrived at by the simpler argument, above.

Example B

Now introduce a more realistic number of products. Suppose there are 10 products and that the company has a 10 per cent of each market. Suppose further, for the moment, that every customer holds all of these products, purchased from any supplier.

In this case, the probability that a consumer holds at least one product with the company is:

$$P(>0) = 1 - P(no\ products) = 1 - 0.9^{10} = 0.651$$

and the probability that a customer holds more than one product is:

$$P(>1) = 1 - 0.9^{10} - 10 \times 0.1 \times 0.9^9 = 0.264$$

Hence the cross-purchase rate is $0.264/0.651 = 45\%$. This means that the model predicts that 45 per cent of customers will hold more than one product. Moreover, the same model predicts that the mean number of products per customer would be:

$$Mean\ number\ of\ products = \frac{np}{Prob\ (al\ least\ one)} = 1/0.651 = 1.54$$

$$(n{=}10,\ the\ number\ of\ products,\ and\ p = 0.1)$$

These values are clearly too optimistic so the model assumptions need relaxing.

Example C

In this example, product markets are the same size but consumers do not buy all products. We start with the situation of example A except that the *total* market for each product is only half of the overall population (randomly chosen). Since we have 10 per cent of both markets, we have 5,000 customers with either product. This time, however, *only half of the X holders own Y anywhere*, ie 2,500 own both products. Of this 2,500, 250 own both with us. Therefore, we have a total of 9,750 *different* customers of whom 250 hold both products with us; a cross-purchase rate of $1/39$, just less than half its previous value of $1/19$.

Using the binomial model, we note that any individual from the population has a probability of only 0.05 of holding any product with us (one half of 10 per cent) and, for two products:

$$P(>0) = P(1\ or\ 2) = (0.05 \times 0.05 + 2 \times 0.05 \times 0.95)\ and$$

$$P(>1) = P(2) = 0.05 \times 0.05$$

so that:

$$P(>1/>0) = (0.5 \times 0.05) \div (0.05 \div 0.05 + 0.1 \times 0.95\ ) = 1/39$$

Extend this to the 10-product case by assuming that any product is purchased somewhere by only half of the total consumer population. The probability that a randomly chosen consumer buys a given product from us is now 0.05, although we still have a 10 per cent share of each market:

$$P(>0) = 1 - 0.95^{10} = 0.401 \text{ and } P(>1) = 1 - 0.95^{10} - (10 \times 0.05 \times 0.95^9) = 0.086$$

As can be seen from the above, the multiple holdings rate is $0.086 \div 0.401 = 21\%$ and the mean number of products per customer is $(10 \times 0.50) \div 0.401 = 1.25$. Hence the more realistic assumption that the market for any one product is less than the total market over all products will produce more acceptable values.

Example D

So far, we have assumed that the markets for the different products are all the same size – we need to relax that. Let us return to Example A, but assume that the *total* market for Product Y is only 50,000. This means that the whole population of 100,000 consumers buys X from any supplier but only half of them buy Y from any supplier. Then our 10 per cent share for the latter product will give us only 5,000 people.

Now consider our X buyers. Half of them do not own Y from any supplier; of the other half we can expect 10 per cent. Thus the overlap will be 500 customers only. The same result comes from starting with the Y buyers. All Y buyers (whether or not we own them) also own X; there is a 10 per cent chance that they bought it from us. Of our 5,000 Y buyers, therefore, 500 will also buy X from us.

This means that we have a total of 14,500 *different* customers of whom 500 own both products and the multiple holding rate will be $500 / 14,500 = 1/29$.

In this case, the probability that a random consumer holds X with us is still 0.1 (10 per cent) but for Y it is only 0.05 (5 per cent) because the total market is smaller.

The realistic model

If there are several products with different sizes of market then the simple binomial model will not work whether or not we have the same share of each market. This is because the probability that a given customer holds a product with a given company will vary with the product. Suppose there are M consumers in the market place, of whom M_i hold the Product$_i$ from a given company. Suppose that the company's share of the market for that product is S_i. Then, if purchasing behaviour is random, the probability, P_i, that any consumer holds Product$_i$ with the given company is:

$$P_i = \frac{M_i}{M} \times S_i$$

(Note: S_i is a proportion, not a percentage, in this expression.)

Suppose there are N different products. Then, for a randomly selected consumer and assuming random purchasing behaviour, the probability that they are a customer of ours is:

$$P(>0) = 1 - Prob(no\ products) = 1 - P_1 P_2 \ldots P_N$$

The probability that they hold more than one product is:

$$P(>1) = P(>0) - Prob(exactly\ one\ product)$$

ie:

$$P(>1) = P(>0) - \sum_i \frac{P_i}{Q_i} Q_1 Q_2 \ldots Q_N$$

where $Q_i = (1 - P_i)$

Under these assumptions, the proportion of customers with multiple holdings will be equal to $(P>0)/P(>1)$.

The proportion holding exactly two products will be:

$$P(=2) = Q_1 Q_2 \ldots QN \sum_{ij} \frac{P_i P_j}{Q_i Q_j}$$

with a similar expression for any other size of product holding.

Detailed example

Suppose there are five products for which the values of the following parameters appear in Table 14.1:

- share (market share held by our company);
- penetration (the proportion of the total consumer base that owns the product, wherever it is purchased);
- P_i is the probability that a consumer purchases the product from us;
- Q_i is the probability that he or she does not – they perhaps do not buy it anywhere.

Table 14.1 Product parameters

Product	A	B	C	D	E
Share	10%	6%	12%	8%	4%
Penetration	0.5	0.8	0.6	0.4	0.7
P_i	0.05	0.048	0.072	0.032	0.028
Q_i	0.95	0.952	0.928	0.968	0.972
Just one	4.2%	4.0%	6.1%	2.6%	2.3%

Then, the probability that a randomly chosen consumer is a customer of ours for one or more products is:

$$P(>0) = 1{-}0.95 \times 0.952 \times 0.928 \times 0.968 \times 0.972 = 0.210$$

The probability that the customer holds just one of the products and nothing else is given for each product in the last row of the table, and adding these together gives:

$$P(exactly\ one\ product) = 0.192$$

$$P(>1) = P(>0) -P(exactly\ 1) = 0.018$$

Therefore the rate of multiple holdings is $0.018 \div 0.192 = 0.94$, or 9.4%.

The mean number of products per customer will be 1.093.

Since less than one per thousand customers will hold more than two products, most of the rest of the picture is provided by considering the rates of occurrence for each pair of products among customers who hold exactly two products (see Table 14.2).

Table 14.2 Rate of occurrence of holding two products

Product	B	C	D	E
A	0.21%	0.32%	0.14%	0.12%
B		0.31%	0.13%	0.11%
C			0.20%	0.18%
D				0.08%

Notes

[1] Stone, M, Foss, B and Machtynger, L (1997) The UK consumer direct insurance industry: a role model for relationship marketing?, *Long Range Planning*, **30** (3), pp 353–63 and Stone, M, Woodcock, N, Foss, B and Machtynger L (1998) Segment or succeed – the new 'top vanilla' culture in financial services marketing, *Journal of Financial Services Marketing*, **2** (2), pp 107–21

15

The meaning and measurement of customer retention

Edward Aspinall, Clive Nancarrow, Merlin Stone and Bryan Foss

THE IMPORTANCE OF CUSTOMER RETENTION

Retaining good customers (or those that may become good) is one of the most important topics in customer relationship marketing (CRM).[1] Its importance is not confined to CRM – customer retention has a pedigree that goes way back to the era of classic direct marketing and branding. But how professionally do companies approach this topic?

In financial services this question is particularly appropriate as:

- The acquisition cost (including marketing, sales and administration) of new customers are very high.
- The majority of financial services budgets and management focus have traditionally been directed to acquisition rather than retention.
- Retention rates in financial services vary dramatically by product and channel. In general insurance, with annual contracts, the rates range from 30 to 90 per cent or even more. In investment products with fixed terms, the rate can be well under 10 per cent. Where retention rates are very low, acquisition rates need to be very high for the customer base even to stand still.
- A pervasive brand can support high lead generation and acquisition rates, but the same brand is undermined by poor retention, breaking the 'virtuous business circle'.

● Not all customers have the same value. A small percentage of customers can generate all the profit of a bank or insurer. Retention and development of profitable and marginal customers become a critical success factor in financial services.

THE MEANING OF CUSTOMER RETENTION IN A DATABASE ENVIRONMENT

Success in business is dependent on clear thinking on the fundamental conceptual issues. If customer retention is a major focus, then a key question is what exactly is an organization trying to retain? The list of possibilities is long (see Table 15.1).

Behavioural definitions (such as those listed below) may seem more relevant in some respects but in other respects may blind marketers to underlying weaknesses in the customer franchise or disposition.

Apathy may lead some customers to demonstrate apparent 'loyalty' or 'commitment' based on behavioural measures. Other customers may resent buying from an organization but be locked into the supplier over a long term for various reasons. For example, it has traditionally been difficult to move financial services products such as endowment policies, pensions, mortgages, personal accounts, etc. In such cases, the reason for staying 'loyal' or 'committed' is that the emotional and financial cost of changing supplier at that point in

Table 15.1 The multifaceted nature of retention: some examples

Behaviour	Hearts and minds (attitudinal variables)
Number of customers (including dormant)	Salience of brand proposition and its components
Number of active customers	
Frequency of buying decisions	Brand preference
Recency of buying decisions	Psychological commitment/loyalty (eg NFO/BJM[14] and Millward
Size of expenditure	Brown models[15])
Share of expenditure (wallet share)	
Possibly even extent of cross-sales	Trust
Contract	Empathy
Adjust buying/usage procedures to fit supplier	Propensity to consider buying/use again/contribute resources
Routinized reordering	
Join club or loyalty scheme	Propensity to pay more/a premium (eg RI's Equity Engine model)
Proven advocacy	
Enquiries	Customer satisfaction/delight
Provide information when requested re needs and/or characteristics	Likelihood to recommend/advocate Possibly even top-of -the-mind awareness
Notify of complaints and successes	
Give you more time than competitors/before	
Pay attention to organization's announcements	

time is too great to countenance. However, if one or more competitors identify this weakness and make it not just easy but rewarding for a customer to switch then apparently loyal customers may do so in droves.

Traditional (eg recency, frequency) behavioural definitions of retention have proven to be important in the definition of retention programmes in financial services, for example: 1) The most recent decision made in an insurer's favour by a particular customer may have been 10–20 years ago in the case of a long-term life policy. How should a retention programme address this behaviour of customer relationship? 2) Products previously purchased may now be reduced to a non-prime or dormant status by the customer, for example a personal banking account that is no longer used for regular salary payments or a credit card with no current transaction flow.

There are also customers who do *not* buy but feel some 'loyalty'. Barriers (price, access etc) may prevent a purchase. However, once the barriers are removed, the loyal customer can demonstrate loyalty or commitment in behavioural terms.

Changes in attitudes are more often than not antecedents of changes in behaviour in all but very low involvement product categories. So while behaviour in various forms of purchasing activity understandably attracts the attention of many hard-nosed marketers seeking hard evidence of retention, the value of the attitudinal variables (soft evidence) should not be underestimated.

Behaviour is a reflection of the current or more likely historical situation, whilst attitudes provide clues to *future behaviour*. In a perfect world, one would examine both behavioural and attitudinal variables and at the same time examine the relationships to determine what drives behavioural disposition. A number of marketing research models attempt to do this, for example RI's Equity Engine and the NFO/BJM Brand Equity Model[2, 3]; both link brand attribute ratings to behavioural disposition rather than behaviour itself. It should also be noted that the link between the psychological and behavioural is sometimes far from perfect, as has been noted in terms of customer satisfaction and behavioural measures of retention or loyalty.[4] In an ideal world, management would develop a customer behaviour model that incorporates all the relevant key variables and describes the relationship between them. The model may be a simple qualitative description of how the variables influence each other. In some organizations it might be possible to develop sophisticated statistical algorithms that permit 'what if' analyses.

As financial services companies have embarked on the development and deployment of management models for retention, they have also gained skills in the use of data mining and 'data discovery' techniques. Using this approach it has been possible to predict (typically with a propensity of 60–80 per cent) the likelihood of retention by customer segment within key time periods – for example predicting the likely lapses of long-term life insurance products, within the first 6, 24 or 60 months, or predicting the retention rate of mortgages on completion of an introductory offer period.

This exercise (when supported by current knowledge and segment-focused market research) highlights the key predictive indicators and specific data items that can assist in the development of a common definition of customer or product retention within the enterprise.

From a conceptual and operational viewpoint, it seems that no single variable should be regarded as representing 'retention'. Any one variable is likely to have shortcomings as an operational measure of commitment or brand strength. A fact-based definition of retention can now be developed using current business and data analysis techniques, providing the basis for common operational activities and measurements across the enterprise.

THE CONCEPT OF LOYALTY

Before moving on to the measurement of retention, we need to address very briefly the concept of loyalty. References to brand 'loyalty' can be found in the early years of marketing.[5] The concept of loyalty (allegiance to monarchy, causes and people) fits in with the military terms found in marketing (strategy, targeting, etc). Interestingly, loyalty is subordinate within the concept of a relationship, yet brand loyalty was a term commonly used in marketing before the wide adoption of the principle of relationship marketing.

Brand loyalty often emerges in financial services as a customer device to limit the time and effort involved in comparative searches at key buying times. There are now so many providers of every type of financial services offering that it becomes impractical for the customer to investigate and compare them all. Consumers who are ready to carry out comparisons themselves, rather than rely on an adviser or choose the most recent offer, will typically only review offerings from a shortlist of 3 to 10 'brands' that they already relate to the type of product offering they need at that time.

Both the concept and practicality of brand loyalty would suggest that in early marketing circles, at least, the term may not have had the full metaphorical significance of loyalty as in an interpersonal relationship. It may instead have been interpreted as a positive disposition to a brand that transcends transactions and makes repurchase likely in the face of adversity (competitor brand entreaties). On occasions, the power of such entreaties from competitors may prove too much and disloyal behaviour may be exhibited. In some parts of the financial services marketplace, such as motor insurance, switching benefits vary from year to year and the barriers to switching are low. When competitive mortgage rates are attractive, switching also becomes more frequent, although barriers to switching (mostly effort required by the consumer) are higher here than in motor or household insurance.

However, it is possible that no unpleasant feelings of disloyalty are experienced as might be the case of an interpersonal relationship. Of course, in some intense service categories such feelings may be manifest (local shops, post offices and service providers, hairdressers, restaurants, football clubs, a friendly financial services adviser, etc). Purchasing of foreign goods may also evoke feelings of disloyalty and guilt. In most aspects of financial services the relationship is relatively impersonal and guilt is unlikely to be felt, except where there is a personal financial adviser (tied or independent) involved.

Assuming therefore that we are looking for some form of behavioural or attitudinal mark of allegiance but perhaps without the finer points of loyalty exhibited in its classical settings, then many of the variables we have listed as relevant to customer retention would also be potential manifestations of loyalty. It is quite likely that adopting one criterion for (or measure of) loyalty (or retention) may not be perfectly valid. Many organizations should certainly try to narrow down to a small set of criteria that seem to account for all or most aspects of the phenomenon but look at these in the round. Dependence on one criterion may be misleading in some instances. This may explain why the same customer was defined as 'loyal' in one study and 'not loyal' in another.[6] Therefore, composite measures of retention may be a more sensible approach to determining retention definition and appropriate operational actions. For instance, Stratigos recommends three indices:[7]

- likelihood to use and renew;
- likelihood to contribute;
- likelihood to recommend.

It has been argued that real purchase behaviour and advocacy are appropriate in some categories.[8] A number of authors clearly define loyalty as a two-dimensional construct – behavioural and attitudinal – and on this basis Liddy developed a potentially useful two-by-two matrix for loyalty classification, as shown in Table 15.2.[9]

Classifying and counting the number of customers in each quadrant might be very illuminating in terms of opportunities and vulnerabilities. However, the matrix below may suggest that loyalty is binary when in reality there may be several different categories of loyalty (exclusively buy from one supplier; preferred brand amongst several; one of many regularly buy but not preferred, etc).

In practice financial services companies have also recognized an addition to this matrix, which would represent the negative aspects of customer loyalty – or relationship terrorism

Table 15.2 Framework for loyalty classification

| | | Behavioural loyalty | |
		Low	High
Attitudinal loyalty	**High**	Latent	High
	Low	Low	Spurious

rather than advocacy. An international insurer made efforts to identify the negative influence of a customer that turned relationship terrorist. While a highly satisfied customer may advocate the supplier to a few others (encouraged by member-get-member schemes), a terrorist will typically influence many more against such a relationship.

It is self-evident that retention criteria and their measures will differ in relevance and importance from product category to category, especially as there is so much variation in the relationship length and relative effect of switching barriers between different financial services products. Finding the best definition and measures is clearly vital to how well an organization can evaluate its performance and link this performance to actions in the market.

While much has been written about customer retention definition and measurement, there has not been an extensive survey of UK organizations to establish the extent to which various definitions and measures are in use. In addition, if customer retention is measured it is not clear how retention levels are evaluated (benchmarks used) nor the extent of research related to understanding what drives customer retention. A recent study by KPMG suggested that such research is not always shared within an organization.[10] It would be useful to know the extent to which senior management, in particular, monitor customer retention as a key performance indicator. The Customer Management Scorecard report[11] indicates that many organizations do not fully implement a customer retention strategy, by virtue of weaknesses in preventing attrition by not using customer information, for instance, to alert customer-facing staff of potential problems. It would be interesting to determine the extent to which customer information relevant to retention is collected and, more importantly, used. Finally, it has been argued that cross-selling can build loyalty and retain customers (see Chapter 14). However, the extent of this belief amongst practitioners is not clear, nor whether there is hard evidence to support the proposition.

THE RESEARCH PROGRAMME

The aim and research objectives

The primary aim of the research for this chapter, which was commissioned by the Royal Mail, was to identify where weaknesses in customer information, in particular definitions and measures of retention and the use of the information, are most likely to undermine customer retention strategies.

The main objectives of the research exercise were as follows:

1. To assess the relative emphasis on customer acquisition and customer retention across business sectors and so focus on organizations that are retention oriented.
2. To determine the extent to which organizations have agreed clear definitions of what constitutes customer retention.

3. To determine how customer retention is measured.
4. To determine benchmarks used to help interpret customer retention measures.
5. To determine how well organizations use customer retention information.
6. To determine what other customer information is used.
7. To determine the extent of the belief that cross-selling builds loyalty/helps retain customers and the evidence for this.

Method

Using a centralized telephone interviewing facility, 314 telephone interviews were conducted with employees at managerial/director level who were responsible for the marketing from a customer database(s) within their organization. The fieldwork was conducted by BJM Research & Consultancy, part of the NFO Worldwide group of companies.

The business sectors that were included were selected on the basis that they were more likely to be involved in customer management of some description and that they were likely to have databases of at least 400 customers. In addition, quotas were imposed on larger companies to ensure that a sufficient number of those with 250 or more employees were interviewed. We also included 24 mail order and 24 dot.com companies for analysis. The reader should bear in mind the low sample sizes for these companies when examining the findings. Interviews were conducted with managers and directors who may have a relatively 'rosy' picture as to how well customer retention is implemented within their own organization. When asking about the customer management process, interviewers were allowed to accept practices even if they only applied to certain (key) customers. Therefore the survey will probably show an optimum state of the art. This should be borne in mind when looking at the overall results achieved. By comparison, the individual and more thorough customer management assessment process described in Chapter 3 carefully identifies the differences between intention, reality and effect across many different interview points within each enterprise.

At the analysis stage the retention research data was weighted in order to bring the sample into line with the business universe in terms of number of employees and service versus other sectors. The number of interviews achieved and the weighting used is as follows.

RESEARCH FINDINGS

Importance of retention

To establish which organizations were retention focused we asked respondents to allocate 10 points between customer acquisition and retention, reflecting the weight they put on each. Over half of the sample (54 per cent) considered customer retention to be more important than acquiring new customers. Only 12 per cent rated customer acquisition above retention. Retention was particularly important to larger companies, those involved in mail order and those marketing to business customers rather than consumers.

Interestingly, a similarly high proportion of dot.coms also focused on retention (the median business life of our sample of dot.coms was one year). Perhaps it is not surprising that retention focuses strongly in the minds of dot.coms, given the example set by Amazon and others. It has been observed that 'the success of online marketer Amazon.com can be traced to its emphasis on three all-important business elements'.[12] These are:

- loyalty (the customer side of retention);
- quality;
- dependability.

Most financial services dot.coms have been focused on acquisition rather than retention, in part because these were often new and relatively independent channels within a larger enterprise, or sometimes a completely stand-alone business. However, some financial services companies have focused their use of e-business to provide personal and small business services that reduce transaction and servicing costs while improving the speed and consistency of service. This is achieved through the development of the e-business channel in an integrated and complementary role focused on the retention and value development of the existing customer base.

Definition of customer retention

We asked respondents if their organization or sphere of operation had an agreed definition of what constitutes customer retention, and if so, what this definition is. Interviewers were instructed to encourage the respondents to state the definition 'as fully as possible'. Only a quarter of the sample claimed that the company has a definition as to what constitutes customer retention. Those more likely to have said this were larger organizations (39 per cent), those with larger databases (39 per cent), mail order companies (38 per cent) and dot.coms (40 per cent). At the same time, 20 per cent of those with a claimed definition stated that they did not know what it was. Amongst those who knew, the majority gave behavioural definitions. The results are summarized in Table 15.3.

In a UK financial services retention project, the initial definition of retention was stated very simply in a single sentence. Within weeks of project initiation, and through the experience of analysing data and engaging with operational retention issues, the definition expanded to a full sheet of paper. This definition included indicators and examples (for example, an insurance policy made paid-up due to late or lapsed payments) that were not initially understood and documented as retention issues.

Table 15.3 Definitions of customer retention

Behavioural	%
Keeping customers	23
Repeat/renew	11
Response to activity	6
Attitudinal	
Satisfaction	17

Base: All respondents

Measurement of customer retention

Although relatively few respondents claimed to have an agreed definition of customer retention, 58 per cent stated that their organization measured customer retention. The larger the organization and the bigger the database, the more likely they were to measure retention. Just over three-quarters of mail order companies (76 per cent) claimed to measure retention. Dot.coms were the least likely to measure retention.

Interviewers then probed the nature of measures used and were instructed to seek precise definitions. Examples were given at the briefing as well as for the analysts coding the answers. Once again, behavioural rather than attitudinal measures were more frequently used. Many of the measures were basic rather than sophisticated (if we refer back to the possibilities we listed earlier) and were suspect where retention definitions were immature. The results are summarized in Table 15.4.

Where retention projects are initiated it is important to measure the improvements achieved against a known starting point. Retention business cases in financial services often only require an improvement in retention of 1 per cent or more to provide adequate payback. In a UK direct insurer a small improvement was achieved on top of an already

Table 15.4 Methods of measuring customer retention

	%
Behaviour	**(80)**
Trends in sales etc	34
Sales (unspecified)	6
Sales at individual level	12
% of customers buying	15
Bought in last period (recency)	5
Frequency	3
Attitude	**(12)**
Measure of declared loyalty/commitment	2
Customer attitude	8
Product preference	1

Base: All measuring customer retention = 180

high retention rate, yielding around £1 million bottom-line benefit for each 1 per cent increment.

Benchmarking customer retention levels

Amongst those measuring retention, 38 per cent either did not have a benchmark against which to measure customer retention or did not know what benchmark (if any) was used. The main criterion against which retention was measured was a comparison with past performance (*an introverted perspective*). Only a few compared performance with competitors (*external perspective*). Other external benchmarks used appeared to be more challenging, such as *'comparison with the best'* or *'against national quality standards'*. Benchmark comparisons in financial services are made more difficult by the large variations in retention by product, within and across companies. The results of this research are summarized in Table 15.5.

How well organizations use customer retention information

Amongst those claiming to measure customer retention, almost 3 in 5 (58 per cent) stated that their senior management regularly monitored retention levels (see Figure 15.1) and a further 23 per cent stated that management monitored them occasionally. Fourteen per cent claimed senior management did *not* monitor customer retention levels. Those most likely to monitor retention levels tended to be in larger organizations, in those organizations with a definition of customer retention and, in particular, in companies with a strong campaign

Table 15.5 Benchmarks used to evaluate customer retention

Base: All measuring customer retention = 180

Benchmark	%
Comparison with past performance	27
Arbitrary target set by ourselves	14
Level of sales	14
Comparison with key competitors	7
Comparison with best available	4
Against national quality standards	5
Other	14
None	15
Don't know	23

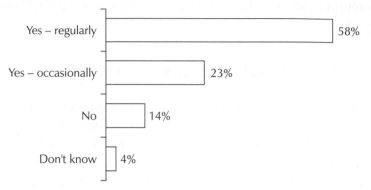

Base: All measuring customer retention = 180

Figure 15.1 Monitoring of customer retention levels by senior management

and mailing culture. Sixty-one per cent of those who measure customer retention claimed that their organization had a process whereby it ensured that retention measures actually have an impact on their business. These tend to be the same company types as those who monitor customer retention levels.

Other customer information from database

The survey was also designed to establish the types of information made available on a regular basis from customer databases to help put the internal distribution of retention measures into context. Trend data that was made regularly available from the customer database covered a variety of customer related issues but mainly concerned:

- frequency of customer purchase (61% mentioning);
- number of customers (58%);
- customer complaints (52%).

Customer defection levels (both actual and predicted) were the least likely trends to be drawn from the database. In financial services, due to long-standing 'silo' organization structures, individual product defections are more often measured than customer defections, and these measurements are based on data from existing administration systems. The results of this research are summarized in Table 15.6.

Interestingly, between 10 and 15 per cent of those focused on retention thought the individual measures above were 'not relevant' or of 'no value'. One wonders about the logic of this. Perhaps, in a few cases, it simply reflects scepticism about the quality of data collection and research in general.

Table 15.6 Trends regularly available from database

Total sample	Sub-groups above the norm
Frequency of customer purchase (61%)	Larger companies (68%), mail order (68%)
Number of customers (58%)	Larger companies (63%), mail order (68%), those with 10,000+ on database (66%)
Customer complaints (52%)	Manufacturers (64%)
Customer retention (47%)	Mail order (70%), charities (60%)
Length of time have retained customers (47%)	Mail order (51%), charities (66%)
Customer satisfaction levels (42%)	Dot.coms (53%)
Customer loyalty levels (39%)	Mail order (65%), charities (49%)
Customer defection levels (30%)	Mail order (49%)
Predicted customer defection levels (15%)	Mail order (30%)

In an attempt to determine how sophisticated the analyses of database data on customers might be, we presented respondents with a prompt list of analyses. The results indicated considerable scope for more sophisticated and potentially useful analyses.

Overall, in the organizations interviewed, the customer database was broken down principally by the status of customers (71 per cent mentioning whether customer was new, current or lost) and type of product bought (63 per cent). In detail, the findings here were as follows:

- The most likely company types to organize databases by customer status were mail order companies (89%), dot.coms (77%), those marketing to individuals (79%), and those with 10,000+ on their database.
- Larger organizations and service-orientated companies were most likely to organize by product/service bought.
- Almost three-quarters (73%) of those with a 10,000+ customer base organized by product/service bought.
- Customer spend (mentioned by 57% in total) was most likely to be used by mail order companies (81%), and those with a 10,000+ database (69%).
- Customer profitability, current and forecast, was mentioned by 39% and 32% respectively.
- Current profitability was most likely to be mentioned by large companies (45%), mail order and dot.coms (54% and 60% respectively).
- Breakdown of customer database by forecast customer profitability was most likely to be mentioned by mail order and dot.coms (38% and 44% respectively).

Of course, some organizations may market to customers who all spend a similar amount *and* are equally demanding in terms of cost-to-serve. However, this seems likely to be a minority of organizations. In financial services the 80/20 rule often applies, where a small proportion of customers generate most or even all of the profit due to the wide variation in spend and servicing costs. The implication is that in the absence of good retention and value, resources are unlikely to be distributed efficiently in many organizations.

Respondents were read out a list of information about named customers that might be collected by an organization. They were asked which, if any, were made available to staff who communicate with customers either on an individual basis (sales rep or service personnel, for instance) or en masse (for direct marketing segmentation strategies, eg customer life-cycle stages). Nearly three-quarters (74 per cent) claimed to pass on the identity of customers who have complained – this was higher amongst small and medium-size companies (91 per cent) and dot.coms (88 per cent).

In financial services companies data has traditionally been shared more frequently when risk avoidance is the objective (ie negative data); however, the more recent focus on CRM has pushed companies to develop the sharing of any data that shows changes in needs, behaviours or customer value and potential value.

The results of this research are summarized in Table 15.7. Note that the figures in Table 15.7 are higher than in Table 15.6. This is because the question in Table 15.4 referred to trend data being made available regularly, while in Table 15.7 we know from respondent feedback that the practice of making information available to staff in contact with customers includes respondents who may do it less than regularly.

Table 15.7 Information made available to staff in contact with customers

Base: All respondents

Identity of customers	%
who have complained	74
who are not satisfied	67
who are likely to be lost (based on past experience)	46
who are not spending as much as expected	45
whose purchase pattern has changed	45
Important dates for customers	60
Competitor activity	60
None of these	7

The special case of cross-selling

One obvious way of using customer information is to look for cross-selling opportunities. Loyal customers, it is argued, buy a larger cross-section of products or services from an organization.[13] This has double significance as it not only provides additional income but can be one way of retaining customers (by increasing dependency between products and on the knowledge and services of a supplier). We examined the latter argument in an attempt to gauge how credible this retention strategy was and whether it was ever tested in practice.

There was overwhelming agreement with the statement *'encouraging customers to buy other products helps your business retain customers'* – 67 per cent agreed strongly, with a further 17 per cent agreeing slightly (Figure 15.2). The level of agreement was highest amongst service organizations and those who market to *both* business and private individuals.

The reason behind the strength of agreement tended to be based on judgement (52 per cent) rather than hard evidence (47 per cent). The most frequent company types to claim to have hard evidence to back up their reaction to cross-selling were mail order and dot.coms, again demonstrating that the marketing culture related to mail and mail-related offerings made the adoption of these processes more likely.

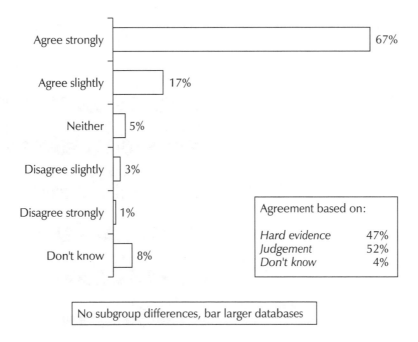

'Encouraging customers to buy other products helps your business retain customers'
Base: All respondents

Figure 15.2 Strength of agreement

Research carried out relevant to customer loyalty

These findings suggest that a substantial amount of research was carried out that is relevant to customer loyalty; however, this research by financial services and other companies is focused much more strongly on customer satisfaction (81 per cent) and follow-up after significant contact than on the relationship between customer satisfaction and retention (64 per cent) or on the impact of retention on profits (55 per cent) (Figure 15.3). Reasons for customer loss are researched in up to 60 per cent of situations.

These findings are consistent with those of Chapter 3, in that many more companies measure customer satisfaction than understand its linkage to customer loyalty, business objectives, or profit. As expected, the percentage of companies measuring each of these factors appears optimistic in this retention research in comparison to the validated research analysed in Chapter 3.

Media

Very strong consistency was observed in the current and planned future use of channels and media to separately retain, develop, update and win back customer relationships. Mail, personal contact and telephone were by far the biggest contributors to each of these objectives, and were anticipated to remain so. The use of e-mail and the Web are growing rapidly,

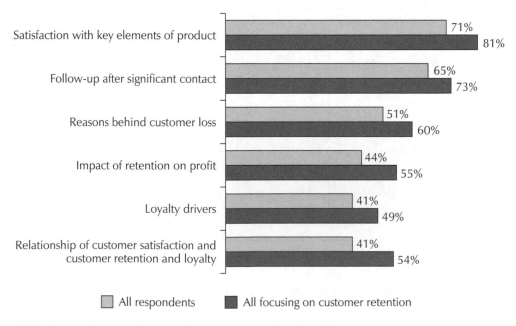

Figure 15.3 Research carried out relevant to retention/loyalty

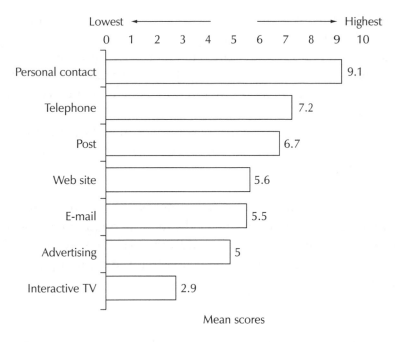

Base: All respondents

Figure 15.4 Rating of medium for building customer relationships

but not expected to topple these primary contact methods. Advertising, fax and digital TV are perceived to be low contributors to retention practices. Figure 15.4 shows a media summary that is consistent with all levels of detailed analysis.

CONCLUSIONS

This chapter shows that despite the enormous attention that has been paid to customer retention in the academic and management press and elsewhere, much is lacking in practice. In particular, many companies that claim to consider customer retention as an important business objective do not define it well or measure it. On this basis, companies' claims to focus on customer retention need to be treated with a pinch of salt. Companies that are serious about needing to improve customer retention should first define it clearly (and most companies may need several definitions of the term), and put in place operational measures that tell them clearly whether they are achieving improvements in it.

The majority now say they focus more on retention than acquisition, yet only around 25 per cent of companies have a clear definition of retention. This may explain why only half of those rating retention as more important than acquisition go on to measure it, and also why retention measures are often basic, behavioural and short-term focused. Database analyses are limited, with profitability and lifetime value rarely calculated, nor are behavioural warnings and signs of disaffection.

When evaluating retention levels, benchmarks are often arbitrary or non-existent or historical. Less than one in six used external benchmarks including best practices, competitors etc. Less than half had activities to understand what drives loyalty or loss, or examined the impact of retention on profit.

Although the optimism of the participants was undermined by the survey findings to a great extent, there seems to be good business potential for many financial services and other organizations if they:

- define customer retention fully and in a relevant way for their business and customer base; good thinking at this point should be the foundation for good practice;
- operationalize the measures, consider also attitudinal and behavioural measures;
- monitor these measures with management attention and meaningful benchmarks;
- act on the above.

Notes

[1] Stone, M (1999) Managing good and bad customers, Part 1, *Journal of Database Marketing*, **6** (3), pp 222–32 and Part 2, *Journal of Database Marketing*, **6** (4), pp 299–314

[2] Morgan, R P (2000) A consumer-orientated framework of brand equity and loyalty, *International Journal of Market Research*, **42** (1), pp 65–78

[3] Wright, L T and Nancarrow, C (1999) Researching international brand equity: a case study, *International Marketing Review*, **16** (4/5), pp 417–31

[4] Kangis, P and Zhang, Yangwei (2000) Service quality and customer retention in financial services, *Journal of Financial Services Marketing*, **4** (4), pp 306–18

[5] Styan, G P H and Smith, H (1964) Markov chains applied to marketing, *Journal of Marketing Research*, February, pp 50–54

[6] Backman, S (1988) *The Utility of Selected Personal and Marketing Characteristics in Explaining Consumer Loyalty to Selected Recreation Services*, Texas A & M, USA

[7] Stratigos, A (1999) Measuring end-user loyalty matters, *onlinemag*, Nov–Dec, p 74

[8] Kangis, P and Zhang, Yangwei (2000) Service quality and customer retention in financial services, *Journal of Financial Services Marketing*, **4** (4), pp 306–18

[9] Liddy, A (2000) Relationship marketing, loyalty programs and the measurement of loyalty, *Journal of Targeting, Measurement & Analysis*, **8** (4), pp 351–62

[10] KPMG (1998) on KMPG Web site (www.kpmg.co.uk)

[11] Starkey, M, Stone, M and Woodcock, N (2000) *The Customer Management Scorecard*, Business Intelligence

[12] Margolis, B (1999) An Amazon.com story: lessons learned?, *Direct Marketing*, **62** (3), p 57

[13] Griffin, J (1996) The Internet's expanding role in building customer loyalty', *Direct Marketing*, **59** (7), p 50

16

Business-to-business segmentation in financial services

Bryan Foss and Merlin Stone

INTRODUCTION

Although much of the work in financial services marketing has focused on the final consumer, most of the value in retail financial services is intermediated. This means that companies that develop a better approach to understanding and managing their intermediaries are likely to make more profit from their marketing. However, most such companies' understanding of segmentation is based on consumer segmentation. This is partly because so many professional direct marketers now work in the marketing departments of these companies. The term 'partner relationship marketing' (PRM) aims to describe CRM efforts focused in this area, although they cannot be detached from other CRM efforts within the enterprise, of course.

The objective of this chapter is to provide business-to-consumer (B2C) financial services companies with an insight into the relevance of business-to-business (B2B) segmentation for their companies. However, the whole area of understanding customers is being turned upside-down by rapidly developing new patterns of intermediation, so almost paradoxically there is a much stronger focus today on 'doing what works' and 'doing what is profitable', rather than trying to optimize. Customers – whether final or intermediary – are simply changing too rapidly to permit the old stable analyses and management of relationships we used to enjoy.

WHY ARE SEGMENTATION AND TARGETING IMPORTANT IN BOTH B2C AND B2B?

The answer to this question is fairly straightforward. Customer value varies – between customers and for individual customers over time. Because marketing budgets are limited, marketing managers are normally under pressure to concentrate their resources where returns are greatest. This does not necessarily mean focusing only on higher value customers, as good money can be made by managing lower value customers cost-effectively and in large volumes. Despite the move towards so-called 'one-to-one marketing', much financial services marketing involves addressing large numbers of customers with common approaches (standard product, high volume channels, etc). So understanding what characteristics are associated with different customer values and behaviour is important. Behaviour is particularly important because willingness to use certain channels has a critical influence on cost to serve.

These challenges exist in virtually all sectors. However, in financial services it is commonly the case that only a small percentage of customer relationships produce all the profit and cover the losses of the others. Put simply, the majority of relationships usually bring no profit and some bring negative profits. In some cases, of course, this apparently poor performance looks better over time, because some of the unprofitable customers become profitable. But in many cases this is not true. There are great rewards to companies that can find ways of attracting and keeping only those customers who are likely to become valuable and/or who are manageable at very low cost. However, as in all sectors, there are *never* sufficient resources, so although in theory it would be nice to invest in understanding all customers, this is not possible either. In financial services we need to focus on those issues or opportunity areas where our customers will reward us with value. This implies segmentation of customers, resulting in stronger focus, improved understanding of needs, improved offers, higher response and conversion rates, and better customer retention.

WHICH COMPANIES SHOULD BE INTERESTED IN B2B SEGMENTATION?

Of course, much business-to-business activity in financial services is directly between 'manufacturers' of financial services and business customers. Even here, though, intermediation is common. In this chapter, we focus particularly on lessons from intermediated markets. These lessons will be relevant to your company if your company manages customers through a combination of channels that may be your own (direct) or owned by partners. This integrated marketing and sales approach is common in financial services and often referred to as 'hybrid marketing' or PRM. As an example, a UK high street mortgage lender known for direct marketing success recently disclosed that 50 per cent of new business comes via mortgage brokers and other introducers.

In insurance, outsourcing is common, including risk assessment and claims management services. This enables companies to make a full service offer with relatively little investment. It may be that your company buys-in part of the offer you make to your customers (products and/or services). For example, manufacturing companies may provide insurance, risk advice, claims management or repair replacement services for their products. In this case, your company will have B2B relationships with both marketing partners (seller side) and suppliers (buyer side), such that your company works simultaneously at different places within the total value (or supply) chain. This kind of complexity is becoming increasingly common because B2B relationships are easier to conduct using e-commerce techniques.

REQUIREMENTS FOR SUCCESS

To manage these complex relationships well, we need to understand customer preferences, needs and behaviours – by market, customer segment or position in the value chain. As we aim to provide a more complete and valued service to our customers, with them returning more frequently, we will need to combine the products and services of others into the 'mix'. Here too, e-commerce has an effect by allowing rapid start-ups, rapid experiences and rapid failures (everything happens at Web speed!). Below, we examine some of the key requirements for success.

Marketing your products to and through other companies – seller side

The classic steps here are as follows.

Defining and analysing your target market

This includes strategic segmentation, definition of key markets, identification of areas where growth can be achieved, where retention is important, where cost reduction is vital, etc. Theoretical segment definitions are helpful, but we have found that undertaking too much analysis before action can be very wasteful. It is worth basing segmentation on success, ie developing from experiences where your company has been able to select, acquire, retain and manage customers through profitable relationships in the past. It is also very helpful to use 'discovery'-based segmentation methods (such as data mining) to identify core segments and their needs, aligning market research efforts to key segments discovered, to understand needs, behaviours and value, etc.

Operational segmentation – targeting resources and efforts into offers

Propensity modelling can identify combinations of right offer, right place, right time, right channel. This combination of factors is sometimes referred to as a treatment. As companies gain experience of identifying and applying segment-based marketing events and key indicators of life cycle or relationship stage, their understanding of these areas will improve. Acting appropriately at relevant times provides improved return on investment (ROI) and shows an increased level of marketing maturity. Customized or even dynamically personalized offers are now possible using this approach. The most advanced practice is to integrate knowledge of customers with operational action. This involves learning how to act in different relationship stages, how to personalize and how to develop value from relationships – sometimes with the application of real-time data-driven personalization. This operational approach is accompanied by setting appropriate business targets, and developing practical and appropriate offers by segment. It also involves setting up measurement systems to track the delivery of that value, so that the company can decide whether to repeat the process, to improve it or invest elsewhere.

Key account management

This involves agreeing the relationship contract with partners/intermediaries and managing the relationship across multiple contact points, to develop value for the customer and the company. New 'account' sales (business to business) are often based on relationships. This implies knowledge of client needs and projection of future value. Cost of sale may be very high in these situations, as major proposal teams might need to be harnessed, using key skills that could otherwise be deployed elsewhere. In such major account relationships value must be delivered as promised, not just once but continually. Such relationships are multi-stage. Traditional game theory tells us that this is the best environment for a continued win–win as compared to one-time purchases, where the balancing influence of a repeat game is not apparent. B2B relationships may be contracted through one responsible account manager but they are delivered through frequent contacts between staff and systems at all levels and over an extended period of time. The relationship needs managing across many points of interaction to ensure value propositions are delivered as expected.

E-business examples – seller side

Current thinking here is much influenced by the introduction of portals. Enterprise portals manage total services to your customer. The aim is to increase 'share of spend', so that the supplier gets increased value from the relationship. To achieve this, portals are designed for stickiness and repeat visits. Intermediaries provide portals – the large ones their own, the smaller ones often with the help of suppliers or in groups. In some cases, competitive comparisons can be provided to discourage customers visiting other portals.

Partner portals provide access to wider markets with selected partners; for example, financial (eg product associated loans or insurance) or delivery and other value-add services (eg package or goods delivery, risk management or maintenance services) can accompany product sales. This approach allows a company's offer to complement (add value to) its partner's primary offer, helping them to provide a more successful market proposition.

Market portals are typically formed by intermediaries (often a financial or infrastructure provider) or jointly with competitors, and may require different offers and prices from the offers made on your enterprise or partner portals.

It is important for companies to focus effort and expense on activities, offers and services that will be valued by customers. An understanding of customers' needs should determine how the offer will be delivered – including what parts are provided by suppliers or partners. It is important at this stage to keep an open mind about combinations that will deliver and derive value, through thinking 'out of the box'.

E-business examples – buyer side

Today complete virtual companies exist – there are many examples of insurance and investment companies that operate in this manner. They often partner in very different ways from their 'bricks' colleagues. They need to be able to make and break alliance relationships as appropriate, focusing as strongly as possible on value because of the highly price-competitive nature of most of their activities. This means that they need to drive changes in the way they operate via continuous measurement against achievement of segmented target market objectives. However, many companies have had poor experiences with managing multiple alliances that may prove to be either short or long term, successful or unsuccessful, so companies have become increasingly careful about this.

It is worth considering what part a company plays, or will play, in the current and future value chain. Companies need to consider the balance of risk and reward and the appropriate role for their particular entity. Perhaps there are arbitrage opportunities to be exploited. Alliances need to be formed and trialled, then developed or deleted. Such flexibility of B2B relationships needs a new culture of risk and reward, new ways of working that appreciate valuable learning from success or failure. This means that these companies need to:

- separately drive change and the operational business against agreed priorities based on strategic segmentation;
- measure and implement corrective actions against these objectives;
- create a closed 'learning loop' through the integration of planning, deployment, results and improvement.

There are some important rules to follow here. It is helpful to develop a customer value index to segment markets and customers. The largest customers may bring revenue but little profit due to their negotiating power. Mid-size customers may be more attractive. So it is important to find the indicators of current and potential profitability and act on them during targeting, acquisition, retention and development. Account should be taken not just of the known skew of customer profitability to just a few customers. Account must also be taken of the fact that the customer base is likely to be changing, with typically 50 per cent or more of customers (final or intermediary) on the way in or on the way out. This requires a focus on future customer profitability and on key decision times, looking for appropriate indicators of decisions and profitability and then responding to them.

Simple segmentation models can be developed and deployed as follows:

- by relationship stage (target, acquire, welcome, get to know, account manage, intensive care, pre-divorce, divorce, win back, as shown in Chapter 3);
- by loyalty / value matrix (negative, low, medium, high value), share of wallet axis;
- traditional life cycle.

SOME WAYS IN WHICH E-COMMERCE CHANGES THE FINANCIAL SERVICES VALUE-CHAIN RULES

A major strategic decision in financial services is the choice between a NetGen approach (stand-alone Web operations) versus multi-channel integration with existing businesses (sometimes called NextGen). 'Greenfield' channels seem attractive and simplified, but new starts of this type are generally proving to be difficult to maintain profitably. In many cases they involve additional costs and channel conflict with traditional operations. However, exploiting a strong brand and traditional marketing channels usually leads to greater success, for stand-alone or integrated operations. New brands are expensive to build and require consistency of investment and attention to continue development.

Gaining a complete view of customers, partners and business dynamics requires new analysis capabilities that combine Web-based data mining with traditional data sources and mining. Active 'agents' can be used for analysis and data-based personalization of response. Practical techniques need to be used to track against top-down customer and intermediary management objectives and scorecards, rather than performing only 'free format' analysis against clickstreams and available data.

E-commerce is changing the rules. Green-field start-ups usually avoid problems with a company's cultural legacy and any negatives associated with the brand. However, they often fail to capitalize on brand strengths and hybrid channels (eg corporate marketing capabilities, value and presence of branch structures, etc). When a new e-commerce channel is designed as an 'integrated' channel, it can more easily avoid additional structural and operational costs. Channel conflict can also be avoided through combining the planning of partnership and direct operations. Customer segmentation and insight need to take into account the evolution between the current and planned hybrid channel environment.

THE DEVELOPING ROLE OF E-MARKETS IN B2B

New e-markets are being developed jointly by suppliers and / or buyers, or even intermediaries (including financial, IT and other partnerships). These e-markets break with the traditional view of marketing and sales management. They reject the idea of 'owning the channel and customer', and tend to adopt the approach of being a place 'where customers will visit'. The company may or may not need to differentiate structure and pricing between direct and indirect or market offers to customers. This implies new board discussions and decisions, such as:

- Should we be there (on a partner or market portal, as well as direct)?
- How should we act (consistently or differently / differentiated in each environment)?
- How does this fit with our other operations (where do we make money now, where will we make money in future)?
- How will our customers and prospects respond (will the same or different customers approach through these additional channels)?

Markets are forming where people believe there is demand. Some markets are formed by the suppliers themselves, some are formed by customers, some by intermediaries of market makers, some by IT or financial clearing companies. Many companies are uncomfortable with trading in markets in which intermediaries participate, preferring 'direct' sales channels. But if a company knows that customers are there, perhaps the new market should be part of future strategy. Initially companies tried to play all market options until the winning strategies became more certain, but this appears too expensive an approach to maintain, and recent withdrawals are obvious. Pricing and / or product structure may need to be different from those available through existing channels, so as to be more comparable with visible offers from others in the same market. Pricing may need to be higher (or lower) to reflect the cost structure of the intermediary channel, or to differentiate from direct operations. Many of these issues require board level discussion and decisions.

TURNING B2B SEGMENTATION AND TARGETING INTO BUSINESS CASES AND PROFIT

There are various techniques for developing B2B business cases, but this is not a 'mature' area. Many B2B e-business investments are not fully justified, rather they are an 'act of faith'. However, some successes include:

- the segmentation and support of intermediaries through 'clubs', grouped and rewarded by value of business, or share of theirs;
- seamless provision of insurance claims handling, even though they are outsourced;
- e-business-based workgroup marketing;
- e-business-based financial services for small businesses.

Many business cases are based on the anticipated financial benefits of change, often extrapolating from existing segment measures. It is usually more difficult to develop business cases for situations in which step changes to marketing strategies are envisaged. The basis for a business case is not always available and act of faith investments may be required, with rapid learning anticipated from pilots and prototypes. This is particularly the case where a company fears that competitors will take the lead.

CHECKLIST FOR ACTION

1. You need to consider the impact of B2B on your B2C business, both buyer and/or seller sides. B2B is probably still for you.
2. E-business is changing the 'rules', but no one is quite sure how (yet).
3. Not all relationships are equal, and you need to find out which ones are best for your company:
   - Prioritize efforts through segmentation, as there will never be enough resources to do everything. But don't expect too much from fine-tuning; focus on how customers move between segments as they increase their take-up of e-business techniques and show willingness to work with new suppliers or partners.
   - New business models are required to understand, select and build the relationships you will need for business success.
4. Become comfortable with uncertainty and change. Be ready to learn and change, as the market, competitive, intermediary and customer rules change.

Part 5

Systems and data

Strategic IT issues in financial services

John Carter and Bryan Foss

INTRODUCTION

This chapter describes a qualitative survey by the author, a senior member of the global financial services practice of Hoggett Bowers, a leading recruitment consultancy. It is commented on by the second author. As one of the leading players in financial services recruitment, Hoggett Bowers has many assignments relating to information technology management. It therefore undertakes research to ensure that it fulfils its clients' expectations of its being at the leading edge of current thinking and knowledge and completely up to date with the current situation.

This chapter describes Hoggett Bowers' research into strategic IT issues in financial services. It is based on interviews with:

- 16 chief information officers (CIOs) or IT directors from across the Financial Services sector, ie retail banking, life and pensions, asset management, investment banking, credit card providers and online banking operations;
- five partners or principals from major consulting firms;
- six practice heads from the financial services consultancy practice of the leading global services provider;
- two heads of capital markets consultancies;

- The marketing director of a leading CRM software provider;
- two resourcing directors from major consultancy firms.

Each was asked to:

- comment on their experience of 2001;
- summarize key challenges, initiatives or, where appropriate, areas of assignment activity;
- offer some thoughts on how the challenges of 1999 and 2000 had been met;
- look ahead and speculate on the major concerns facing financial services IT in 2002 and beyond.

The research updated a study carried out a year previously. The results of this are summarized and updated, and the latest research then covered.

BEYOND 2000

In 1999 the CIOs and IT directors of financial services and financial markets organizations were under pressure. The business mood was one of anticipation and trepidation, the implications of Y2K not yet fully understood. Market volatility had seen the collapse of the Asian markets the previous year. In all sectors of the marketplace margins were under threat. The introduction of stakeholder pensions would see a move in retail financial services from a 4 per cent to a 1 per cent world. Pure-play Internet operations were posing a threat to a whole raft of intermediary activities in the financial markets and threatening to commoditize service offerings in life and general insurance. An established presence and track record were now viewed as a costly legacy environment that acted as a ball and chain to future development.

Yet whilst the need for cost reduction was clear, the cost of IT was spiralling. Businesses were having to swallow the enormous costs of euro conversion and the millennium bug fix. Legacy systems were becoming increasingly expensive to maintain and the business perception of IT service provision was generally poor.

CIOs and IT directors were under pressure to automate processes and reduce costs and to unlock the assets buried in their systems and create information-rich, knowledge-based environments.

Internet companies were demonstrating that it was possible to build lean and mean operations based purely on information and CIOs were tasked with transforming their organizations so that they could respond to this threat. Citibank's strategy at the time, as expressed by one of its IT directors, is representative of thinking in 1999:

- rationalize and streamline processes, ie lose weight;

- offer multiple services to clients;
- enter collaborative joint ventures with niche players;
- get rid of pride of ownership;
- provide segregated Internet provision via the telephone companies.

Whilst 'lose weight' was one response to the challenges of the marketplace, 'acquire scale' was another. Many organizations considered that real economies in claims processing and settlements could only be achieved in organizations of sufficient scale, and 1999 saw acquisitions across all sectors. Cost-cutting targets were in place and, post millennium, these would have to be delivered. High profile mergers and acquisitions on a national level often formed part of more ambitious plans to build 24/7 global operations.

In response to these pressures CIOs and IT directors were developing strategies to address the need for:

- IT architectures that could automate processes, reduce cost and effectively integrate systems and that could provide a basis for further integration;
- service provision models, be they total outsourcing or smart-sourcing, that could address the issues of rising cost and poor service;
- the delivery of information contained in the organization's systems to the business in the form of knowledge management and customer relationship management systems;
- the development of new, IT-based, added-value products, services and channels to market.

These strategies found expression in projects to:

- implement thin-client architectures;
- access legacy data via middleware;
- implement straight-through processing environments;
- establish service delivery functions and strategically outsource;
- implement CRM and knowledge management solutions;
- develop and integrate a full range of delivery channels, with a particular focus on the Internet;
- develop customer segmentation and enable the delivery of more sophisticated, IT-enabled, bundled products to appropriate individuals;
- build portals that would give customers access to a full range – a supermarket – of products as opposed to purely proprietary offerings.

Whilst the Beyond 2000 discussions were full of informed speculation on the future of the financial services sector and the role IT would play in that, few, if any, of the participants could have anticipated the roller-coaster ride that they were about to undertake. The apprehension of the pre-Y2K period gave way to a dot.com-fuelled post-Y2K euphoria, when IT directors were encouraged to pursue value-added initiatives and increase their Internet spend for the favourable effect this would have on the share price. When the Internet bubble burst and the technology stocks slumped, the great bull market came to an end. By mid-2001 the impact this was to have on the sector was apparent to all and the slowdown began, as belts were tightened everywhere.

Given this volatile backdrop and the current uncertainty about the future, it was interesting to revisit the challenges and aspirations of 1999 to see which had been met, which had bloomed like hothouse flowers and failed to thrive, and which had been discarded along the way. Participants in the discussions of 2001 summarized their achievements post-Y2K, underlined current priorities and again speculated on future challenges for their function. From the discussions of both IT directors and external consultants it is possible to assess the progress IT has made in meeting the challenges outlined in 1999 and the status and perception of IT that flows from that progress.

BEYOND 2001

As financial services organizations across the sector struggle to square last year's ambitious revenue forecasts with this year's more sober reality, cost and cost reduction are again immediate and paramount considerations. A partner at one of the leading strategic consultancies summed up the shift in priorities from the heady days of 2000 when he said 'this time last year we were an e-commerce incubator, all our engagements now are focused on cost reduction'. The downturn has forced many organizations into round after round of tactical cost cutting. For IT, this means headcount reduction, the removal of contract staff and the cancellation of projects. At the same time, some organizations are implementing long-term strategic cost reduction exercises in which IT is an enabler, working in partnership with the business. As leading players in the retail financial services sector declare their intention to remove huge costs from their operations to dramatically improve their cost income ratios, one can expect this to have a domino effect. One retail financial services consultant certainly expects this year's emphasis on tactical cost reduction to be replaced by a more considered and strategic approach to the issue, across the sector, next year.

Immediate priorities for IT directors and CIOs therefore are:

- improving and, wherever possible, automating business processes;
- continuing to develop more coherent IT architectures and standard operating environments that avoid costly support and integration issues;
- smart-sourcing specific functional areas, with a view to creating transparent cost models;

- refocusing from the development of external e-channels to the creation of an e-enabled organizational environment that can provide a platform for process improvement.

However, whilst automation and cost reduction are at the top of the agenda, the requirement to leverage information held within business systems is sufficient to demand equal attention. Organizations that are committed to reducing costs by seven-figure sums are, at the same time, prepared to set aside considerable budgets to implement CRM projects. Described by one consultant as 'the only game in town', CRM is now a board-level issue for all financial services organizations, as they struggle to survive in an increasingly competitive world.

Financial services organizations are now aware that they consist of products, channels and customers, and increasingly view CRM as the means to create the best possible relationship between the three. Early software-based, piecemeal approaches to CRM, which had little impact on business processes, are now being jettisoned, as CRM is reassessed as a platform for both business and technical architectures and the interface between back-office processes and product factories and the channels of distribution to customers.

This reappraisal of CRM is having profound consequences for the IT functions in financial services organizations across the sector. For whilst an IT-only solution to CRM implementation has been rejected, CRM remains an IT-enabled strategy. Its ability to deliver the information stored in back-office legacy systems to front-office sales and marketing functions is rewriting the organizational map in financial organizations and repositioning IT as a provider of real bottom-line benefit. Evidence of CRM intentions and activity exist everywhere but few players have fully realized their CRM ambitions. Taking the proposition that financial services organizations consist of products, customers and channels, it is apparent that the majority of initiatives in the last two years have been in the development of distribution channels. Organizations in retail financial services have put a lot of effort into the delivery of a seamless service irrespective of the point of contact. Meanwhile financial markets organizations have acknowledged their intermediary function and support the access to markets they provide to their clients, with CRM-based value-added services.

The imaginative bundling of products to meet customer needs and develop a one-stop-shop approach to the purchasing of financial products has taken place on the fringes. Whilst Egg, Virgin One and the Woolwich have been able to develop innovative offerings, the sheer size of larger retail financial organizations has prevented them from delivering any meaningful offerings in the short term. Large financial organizations are still grappling with the basic issues of integration of customer data and subsequent customer segmentation. Before developing sophisticated product offerings they need to be able to interrogate their data so that they can gain an understanding of the profitability and viability of the relationships they have with their customers. As a result, 'work in progress' is the status of the majority of CRM projects.

What this means in terms of the immediate priorities of CIOs and IT directors in financial services organizations is that they are under pressure to deliver informed customer profiles, competitive product sets and integrated distribution channels. These are no longer the means to massive customer acquisition. The first-mover advantage enjoyed by Egg is over and question marks remain about the acquisition of low- or no-margin customers. The issue now is customer retention through increased customer service. In an increasingly competitive marketplace none can afford to be left behind.

This explains the launch of wealth management initiatives geared to the 'mass affluent', offering access to equity-based products, when market conditions clearly favour none of these initiatives. Organizations have already committed budgets to these projects and don't want to be left behind. 'Me too' remains a business imperative.

THE STATUS OF IT IN FINANCIAL SERVICES

What clearly emerges from the discussions summarized above is that, despite the distractions of short-term imperatives, the IT directors of financial services and markets organizations have made considerable progress in the last two years in meeting the challenges they faced in 1999. They were:

- the delivery of efficient IT architectures to automate processes, reduce cost and provide a platform for successful integration;
- the development of effective service delivery models;
- the leveraging of information assets and their delivery to the business;
- the development of new, IT-based, added-value products, services and channels to market.

In striving to meet these challenges, the perception and status of IT have changed dramatically and it is instructive to assess the transformation that has taken place over the last two years. In 1999 there appeared to be a huge gulf between the IT function and the business across the sector. IT was not appreciated as a strategic contributor to the business and outsourcing and smart-sourcing initiatives were often driven by a desire to downgrade IT to a purely service delivery, operational function. Issues of cost, poor delivery and inflexibility reinforced this negative view. However, it is apparent from current discussions that IT directors and CIOs now enjoy effective working relationships with their boards. This is helped in part by the elevation to board level of a new generation of IT-literate directors. Organizations now appear to have harmonious business and technical architectures and are reluctant to champion business initiatives that fail to conform to these architectures.

A number of factors have conspired to bring about this improvement in the relationship between IT and the business in the financial services sector. However, the bottom line is that IT is now beginning to deliver and is demonstrating that it can meet and overcome the challenges it has faced in the last few years. The need to reduce operational cost and provide effective platforms for enterprise-wide initiatives such as CRM, KM or large-scale systems integration programmes have put infrastructure issues on the business agenda and provided IT directors with the necessary backing and funding to rationalize their systems maps and unravel the spaghetti. Given a more rational architecture and platform, IT has been able to reduce the costs that were so outraging users in 1999 and ensure quicker and more effective delivery.

In addition to providing more cost-effective architectures, IT directors and CIOs have spent the last two years working on the production of more transparent cost models and initiating programmes to reduce those costs. The establishment of service delivery functions is a trend from the United States, enthusiastically taken up by financial services organizations. Not only do these allow IT directors to capture and reduce costs more accurately but they also provide financial services organizations with the flexibility to grow, acquire or change shape with little or no disruption to core services.

The key growth area for IT services organizations this year has been outsourcing and smart-sourcing. Selective outsourcing and the establishment of joint ventures with service providers have again enabled IT directors to capture and therefore reduce costs. The CIO of global settlements within the derivatives area of one of the leading investment banks found that outsourcing the function had introduced a transparency of costs and a financial discipline that transformed the relationship between the front and back office. Front-office personnel, who had previously been accustomed to having their own way, whatever the cost, became aware of the implications of their demands and started to enjoy the prospect of IT costs reducing rather than rising year on year.

Whilst addressing long-term concerns about the cost, quality and delivery of service, CIOs and IT directors have, at the same time, been able to raise the profile of IT within their businesses by delivering information that the businesses really value. The IT director of the leading general insurance provider feels that the data mining/CRM initiatives that allow the firm to calibrate risk at a much greater level of detail have certainly increased the status of his department within the organization. As the value of CRM initiatives begins to impact on many of the organizations currently in the process of implementing CRM architectures and systems, this experience will be duplicated across the sector.

In addition to unlocking information assets and delivering them to the business, the IT functions in the financial services and markets sector have also collaborated at strategic levels with the product development, customer service and sales and marketing functions within their organizations. Bundled product offerings, the multi-channel customer service experience and multi-channel distribution strategies are all products of these close working relationships.

In the year of the dot.com collapse, when former advocates of the 'new economy' are gloating over its demise, financial services organizations seem to have learned a series of lessons from the Internet companies, whose low-cost competitive threat they feared in 1999, and have emerged stronger. Once it was recognized that 'clicks and mortar' rather than 'pure play' propositions were the most attractive, financial services organizations set about transforming themselves into multi-channel, customer-centric, e-enabled businesses and, as a result, elevated IT to the status of strategic enabler.

PRIORITIES FOR FINANCIAL SERVICES IT

It has been taken as given in this chapter that delivery of longer-term strategic goals in financial services IT is often constrained by the need to address more pressing short-term considerations, often the result of market conditions. As organizations consider their strategies for the future, a paramount consideration will be 'getting some visibility on the downturn'. IT directors and CIOs already appear to be, at one and the same time, preparing for a recession and hedging their bets. The financial markets in particular are learning the lessons of 1998, when they were panicked by the collapse of the Asian markets. Major bulge-bracket organizations lost significant momentum as a result of making mass redundancies and canning strategic projects, only to return to the market six months later to hire similar talent. This explains the more cautious approach being adopted at present. In an effort not to lose critical momentum, IT directors are running certain projects with skeleton staff, rather than cancelling then completely. In this environment it is the recruitment agencies, head-hunters and body-shoppers who are suffering.

Whilst the lack of visibility is engendering a 'wait and see' approach, participants are agreed on those initiatives that will flourish:

- Removing cost from the business will clearly remain a priority. However, as has been noted before, this is likely to be driven from a more strategic perspective with the aim of permanently improving processes and reducing costs. Consultancies certainly expect to be working on cost reduction, process improvement and e-enablement engagements across the sector next year, attempting to deliver, and in many cases be remunerated against, some very ambitious cost-reduction targets.
- CRM remains an unrealized ambition in most organizations and will continue to be 'the only game in town'. The number of major 'wealth management' initiatives that will be launched will depend on an upturn in the market. However, as the marketing director of a leading CRM software vendor remarked, 'in the current climate clients can't afford to ignore their customers'.

- Channel development initiatives will continue as clients develop portals that enable them to provide customers with access to competitors' products in an attempt to provide a more complete service.
- In a tighter, more competitive marketplace, customer service will become increasingly important and clients who are seduced by short-term cosmetic goals, driven by analysts concerned only with shareholder value, will continue to suffer.
- The effects of 11 September 2001, combined with the Basel Agreement (new risk, solvency and associated regulation), will see an increased emphasis on operational risk and security. Multi-channel operations are exposed as never before and a new and more strategic approach is required to manage all aspects of risk. Organizations are now appointing chief information risk officers, as well as directors of operational risk, and much thought is being given to where these individuals should sit in the structure. Risk is clearly no longer considered to be only a policing function.

Key areas of demand at an executive level in financial services organizations will continue to be driven by the business transformation initiatives being undertaken, be these process improvement, cost reduction, channel development or CRM based. The majority of IT directors and CIOs who participated in the discussions spoke of the need for programme managers who can:

- proactively identify need and develop appropriate strategies;
- build effective relationships with stakeholders across the business and gain their buy-in;
- manage enterprise-wide programmes with a high element of risk;
- maintain a high-level intuitive feel for the status of a programme and not get too sucked into detail;
- be credible to both business and technical stakeholders.

This requirement echoes the need expressed in our earlier research and in Chapter 2 for:

- people who can manage change as change becomes more complicated and rapid;
- good project managers and programme managers;
- people who sit between the business and IT, or can be both;
- technical people with people skills and strategic overview, and other hybrid skills;
- people with the ability to match business to technology, ie super business analysts.

Beyond 2001, as financial services and financial markets organizations complete their transformation into multi-channel, customer-centric, e-enabled businesses, the requirement for the real hybrid, with one foot in the business and the other in IT, is greater than ever.

18

Achieving ROI from e-business systems in financial services

Bryan Foss, Colin P Devonport and Paul McDaid

THE NETWORKED FINANCIAL INSTITUTION BUSINESS SOLUTION COMPONENTS

The Networked Financial Institution (NFI) is a thorough investigation and representation of the current and future integrated financial services business. The NFI representation identifies the integrated business capabilities required to be successful in the e-business world of financial services. Figure 18.1 represents the major business capabilities required by a leading financial institution. The capabilities apply to banks, insurers and financial markets companies whether in business to consumer (B2C) or business to business (B2B) operations or both. Key alliance partner (value chain) and employee management (B2E) processes are also included to complete the integrated view. NetworkFI.com is also a registered IBM Web-site name, used to represent a fictitious company. Numerous thought leadership materials, including research papers and example futuristic customer experiences, exist under this common branding.

Figure 18.1 is a *representation* of the Networked Financial Institution. It is not a business or systems architecture, but it does provide a checklist of key capabilities and highlights their dependencies visually. Many IBM clients have used this diagram in executive-level

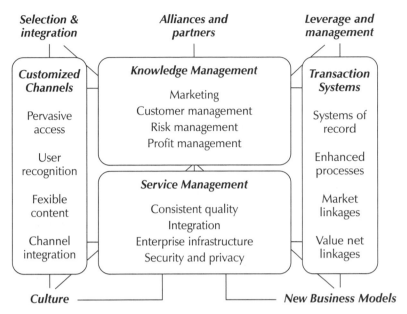

Figure 18.1 The Networked Financial Institution – NetworkFI.com

strategy and planning exercises. This chapter will comment on the NetworkFI structure as a backdrop for implementing e-business and CRM systems projects in Financial Services.

Traditionally, financial services companies have focused on the provision of transaction systems and more recently on an increased selection of customized channels; these are shown in the boxes to the right and left (respectively) of Figure 18.1. Rapid development and deployment of new products and services often force increases in the number of transaction systems, as traditional in-house transaction systems may be relatively inflexible or cumbersome in the development and launch of new products. However, to simplify process operations and to reduce costs, companies usually try to merge and reduce the number of transaction systems. This is especially true where more systems exist than are required, or duplicate systems exist due to previous M&As that have taken place.

Some very substantial projects have been funded to create totally flexible transaction systems that can represent any combination of financial services product or service. However, almost without exception these projects have failed to achieve their design targets and most have been abandoned. A few have achieved production but have failed to absorb more than a limited range of products, leaving the corporation with a continuing mix of transaction systems and very many places (typically 50 to 150) where customer, relationship and event data is held. Some of this data is held by alliance partner systems in the extended 'value net'.

Customized channels have developed from the traditional branch and sales force structures to include mail, call centre, e-business, e-mail, WAP, PDA and digital TV services. In this environment corporations need an integrated view of the customer to enable them to make appropriate offers and service the customer effectively, at the right cost. New channel pilots may need to be implemented through addition to this integrated channel infrastructure. If successful, they can be rapidly scaled up. If not, they can be retained or removed.

To satisfy customer needs, integrated contributions from partners and alliances are increasingly needed. These could be 'sold through' branded goods and services, or 'white label' products with the retailer's own branding. Wealth management operations are an example of such an approach, where aggregation and advice are required to complete the client portfolio. Many financial institutions are just now becoming comfortable with the new business models and culture changes required to integrate such alliances into their operations. Others, such as Legal and General Insurance in the UK, appear to be deploying a 'first mover' alliance strategy.

Customer needs and expectations are met through exceptional service management processes. In addition to current expectations of consistent quality and integrated operations, corporations will be expected to meet exceptional security and privacy requirements in future. As each aims to accelerate its implementation and results from competitive achievements, learning from best practices internally and externally is seen as a speedy and lower risk route to success. Assessing and understanding current capabilities and gaps can be the basis for an enterprise-wide knowledge management programme that launches the company to new and pervasive levels of competitiveness (both broad and deep). The successful networked financial institution will use knowledge management for improved customer management, operational risk management and profit achievement.

GAINING A GOOD RETURN ON INVESTMENT FROM E-BUSINESS PROJECT ACTIONS

There is already substantial research to suggest that the majority of e-business and CRM projects fail (see Chapter 31). Failure can be defined in different ways, depending on the business and situation. Clearly failure to achieve any result at all from an e-business project is one possible outcome. However, more frequently some positive results are achieved but these projects are still not considered to be successful. Failure to achieve anticipated return on investment (ROI) is perhaps the most frequent outcome and biggest potential risk for any e-business project or CRM programme, where a programme is a series of interdependent CRM projects.

As business becomes more competitive, executive management become more focused. Although many priorities are juggled simultaneously, there is evidence that financial services companies are now focused on gaining short- and medium-term ROI through two core objectives: 1) becoming customer centric; 2) becoming more efficient.

A recent AM Best article[1] highlighted the current pressure for North American and European insurers to invest in e-business projects only where internal ROI cases have been proven and accepted. This implies that many previous insurance industry (and no doubt other financial services) investments were made without such ROI cases. Best suggested that the main components of ROI were simply an understanding of costs, benefits and time-scales, which are of course some of the major headings.

The development of the business case is outlined in Chapter 30. But if the ROI approach to e-business programmes is relatively simple to implement, why do so many projects fail to deliver? Our extensive research and global project experience suggests that this is primarily because the broad assessment and management of costs, benefits, time-scales and project risks (marketplace, business and technical) proves much harder than anticipated.

Many more financial services companies are now setting 'hurdle rates' for ROI cases. As shareholder funds are being invested (not investor or policyholder funds), corporate finance departments set ROI objectives which are linked to target rates of return on capital employed (ROCE), market expectations and other commitments. Typical ROI objective rates can be 15, 25 or even 40 per cent using this approach. Of course the process for financial modelling of these internal business cases is usually well known within the executive management team, and cases are often proposed in a manner that demonstrates achievement of ROI targets without sufficient assessment of eventual costs, benefits, time-scales and risks. This effect is lessened if the proposers are rewarded for the ownership and successful achievement of their cases over time. However, even this motivational approach is tough to implement as other factors can and do affect achievement, including management and organizational changes, also dependencies and executive decisions outside of the project team's control.

Our research and experience highlights stages 2 through 5 of the critical path for a business case (described in Chapter 30) as the most common areas for business case failure, including:

- rigorous identification of relevant costs and benefits;
- prior assessment of customer experience and likely responses;
- selection of appropriate IT architecture;
- all aspects of readiness, programme and change management;
- all aspects of risk assessment and mitigation;
- identification of appropriate dependencies and related efforts.

Project costs can be seriously underestimated as it is very common that the full extent of the issues to be tackled is not well known so early in the project. One of the most common current reasons for project failure is the difficulties caused by poor quality and dispersed customer data. Using traditional project approaches, the extent of these problems is normally encountered during the mid or late project stages, rather than in the estimation process. Automated techniques are now available to assess the structure and quality of data sources. These sources are primarily 'legacy' systems (where a legacy system is defined as one that has achieved production status) but can also include database deliverables from previous project stages, for example a marketing database or operational customer database.

There are many other areas where project costs are underestimated. It is critically important that a realistic assessment of costs is made an early stage to avoid projects exceeding time and other resource limitations later on. It is not unknown for project teams to return many times to request the allocation of additional resources to address 'problems not anticipated', until eventually the ROI case is completely undermined, and little or no confidence remains that the project can ever provide any useful deliverable at a reasonable cost. At this point the project and prior investment may be written off. In some cases this is done multiple times before a new approach is taken.

Financial benefits are hard to estimate. The easiest to estimate are probably those that are extrapolations of currently successful activities; for example, where a limited pilot project has demonstrated successful retention or cross-selling and can now be implemented in a more scalable or broad manner. However, many e-business projects are steps into uncharted territory for this or any company. In this case extrapolation of business benefit is not an option. When mobile WAP financial services were first considered, it proved very difficult to gain sufficient confidence of consumer reactions, likely behaviours and business value using market research techniques. For new business areas pilot or 'learning' projects may need to be funded and implemented to increase business understanding and financial confidence. Not all such projects will prove successful, so these pilot projects need to be implemented at low cost (but not necessarily reduced function) to limit financial write-off if they prove unsuccessful. In the event of enormous success the pilot needs to be ready to expand very rapidly to gain extrapolation of benefits.

Where a strong e-business infrastructure is already in place, additional pilots can more easily be put in place, at relatively known costs and risks. Immediate integration will tend to reinforce the achievement of business benefits (for example, by better directing, supporting and measuring the new channel or product) and enable lowest cost entry with rapid exploitation through scalability-on-demand.

The achievement of anticipated benefits usually depends on many factors beyond the immediate control of the project team. This is why it is so important to anticipate risks and dependencies, building a plan to address them where possible or appropriate, or to mitigate and/or keep watch on other risks that are identified. As any project or programme has boundaries, some executive and business management areas may be outside the scope of the project, yet a dependency exists which could limit or nullify the achievement of expected benefits. Despite strong work to anticipate customer response, we cannot prescribe or fully predict the results of our e-business actions on the market. Many benefit-related items remain outside the project team's control, but these can often be anticipated and considered to help assure the achievement of ROI.

E-BUSINESS INTEGRATION DRIVES ROI

In Chapter 3 we discussed the relationship between customer management capabilities and business results. Joined-up capabilities imply a reasonable level of achievement across all the eight customer management capabilities defined in the QCi model, which in turn implies coordination and integration between them as there are mutual dependencies built into a successful business implementation of the model. Of course business systems and processes can hardly be successfully joined up if the underlying systems are not. Breakages in the integration of data (which ensure that the appropriate data is in the right place and of sufficient quality to be used) will undoubtedly cause breakages in business processes.

E-business implementations are very dependent upon integration to achieve ROI. One example is the required integration of customer offers with prior analysis of data to determine the most appropriate and successful promotions to be made. Another example is the integrated service requirements of the customer, supporting the e-business channels with help desks, telephone services, mailings, fulfilment and complaints management. Various assessments of potential ROI and the business and IT actions required to achieve it exist. They are listed below. Each combines a method and tool to help assess current status and potential ROI from improvement and specifically identifies where benefits are derived from integration efforts:

- IBM Becoming Customer Centric – a workshop-based self-assessment of the status of customer centric change and achievement in a financial services organization. This is an excellent place to start when educating the executive management team and involving them in an active discussion about customer centricity efforts and results in their organization.
- QCi Customer Management Assessment as described in Chapter 3 – an interview-based assessment across eight key areas of customer management capability, looking at intention, reality and effect. Both general and e-business versions are available. As evidence is checked and the results are carefully calibrated, benchmark comparisons to a database containing the results of many other leading companies are a practical and useful basis for decision making. This is a very full assessment that makes an excellent starting point (or regular review point) for any major customer management programme.
- IBM Customer Value Management, as described in Chapters 11 and 12. An assessment of the needs of the customers of a given financial services company, the value these customers would attribute to capability and offer improvements and an understanding of the actions required to put these in place. This assessment is often deployed if the Customer Management Assessment identifies lack of understanding of customer needs and the development of appropriate proposition and customer management activities.

- IBM Customer Value Index, which segments and targets the market based on both the current and future value of a customer or segment. This targets customers for cost- or price-appropriate personalized treatment, as well as channel optimization.
- IBM/Siebel Value Maximizer – this assessment looks very specifically at the achievement of enhanced ROI during or following a Siebel e-business, call centre, sales force automation or multi-channel implementation. In practice the same method and tool could be deployed with many other e-business channel solutions, not only Siebel.
- Xchange Customer Value Management ('real-time' rules engine deployment) looks specifically at the ROI case for deployment of a real-time rules engine that provides data-based personalization of e-business channel offers, which may also be made to customers in a consistent manner across complementary channels (eg call centre, branch, etc).
- IBM's Enterprise Customer Analytics services method combines all of the above (as required in any custom situation) from strategy through to execution.

Of course, there are many less tangible or intangible benefits that can eventually form the most significant part of the final business case. These are much more likely to be included, acted upon and achieved if the business case is owned and implemented by a profit centre business unit (eg customer, channel or alliance management) rather than an internal or cost centre such as IT.

ACCELERATING ROI ACHIEVEMENT IN E-BUSINESS PROJECTS

There are tried and tested techniques for accelerating the achievement of ROI from e-business projects or staged e-business programmes. This section focuses on some of the e-business infrastructure fast-start capabilities that can assist.

Rapid assessment of source data

Research and experience suggests that almost all existing source data (for example, in legacy and existing e-business systems) is inadequate for CRM purposes and for additional e-business applications. In a US-based project a three-year-old system was shown to have poorly structured and documented data.[2] Existing processes had allowed data of insufficient quality and accuracy to be captured and stored. In a European project with literally hundreds of existing sources of customer data, the company decided that the only reliable data source was a recent e-business application that encouraged self-maintenance of the data by the customer.

Assessing the quality of these data sources is traditionally a laborious and expensive task taking many months. Rather than delay project start through assessing the situation as input to the sizing and prioritization of project actions, companies normally allowed inherent data issues to be encountered during the project, causing time and cost overrun, rework and eventually many abandoned projects or ROI cases.

Automated tools are now available to achieve the prior assessment of data structure and quality, even recreating missing metadata documentation if required. IBM's internal CRM2000 project deployed Evoke Software to rapidly assess and combine hundreds of sources of customer data to develop a single customer view database (named CII), providing the system of record for probably the largest global deployment of Siebel call centre and sales force systems. Through this approach, accelerated implementation and integration of any new data-based systems component is achieved. With accurate and appropriate data available in the right place at the right time the business process is more effectively supported, accelerating and confirming ROI achievement. Over time a sequence of projects can use the same tools and techniques to add more integrated components into a consistent enterprise integration approach, without being overwhelmed by ever-increasing complexity.

Pre-existing financial services data models

Further project acceleration and ROI can be achieved using proven industry data models. While many CRM and e-business applications (and utilities) are cross-industry, the business problems they need to address are industry specific. Consider for a minute a situation where we make financial services offers to customers based entirely on their likelihood to respond and buy, rather than also considering their value potential or risk to the profitability of our business. Credit or claims risk can easily outweigh other benefits or losses if not considered in the acquisition, retention and development of selected customers. This additional knowledge tends to be based on industry-specific data fields such as fraud or risk indicators, combined with knowledge of the activity-based costs associated with estimating customer value. Over time these data fields have been defined and built into readily available industry models, usually in the operational and analytical common data stores. Most cross-industry applications can be made to allow ready access to these more effective data sources with only limited integration effort.

Pre-designed data models are available to validate existing data models. In staged projects where ROI is expected within months, there is no time to redevelop existing models – without even considering the additional costs and risks involved in this redevelopment. An example of such a pre-designed model is IBM's Insurance Application Architecture (IAA), which is a combination of data and process models for insurers. IAA development was based on the shared models and efforts of 40 insurers, and is now deployed by over 100 insurers worldwide. A similar approach is available for banks and financial markets players from IBM's Information Framework (IFW).

Originally industry data models were deployed to redevelop core systems, although this approach has generally been overtaken by a move to packaged application purchases as rapid deployment of multiple new product systems has been seen as the way to launch new products and new lines of business rapidly. More recently, industry data models are being deployed to accelerate e-business and CRM application component deployment, for example where a campaign management tool requires a data mart to be developed as its data source, or where real-time customer management applications require the existence of a single operational view of the customer (operational data store, or ODS) to integrate the management of multiple customer channels.

Perhaps the most recent and most forward-thinking deployments of industry data models are to support the integration of many existing core systems and new CRM systems to provide a consistent enterprise-wide approach as the basis of a customer-centric business – as outlined earlier in NetworkFI.com. The three major industry data-model-based components of such an approach are:

- operational single view of the customer (ODS), enabling consistent and integrated management of the customer relationship across multiple touch points (eg IBM's Customer Information Integration Solution, CIIS);
- analytical single view of the customer (enterprise data warehouse or EDW), enabling consolidated planning of customer development activities (eg IBM's Banking or Insurance Data Warehouse offerings);
- standards for message or data interchange formats, enabling the linkage of any or all past, present and future systems as required (eg IBM or Acord industry XML standards).

As integration proceeds, companies start to realize the business value of systems integration at higher functional levels. Integration of disparate data is only the start. Soon it becomes apparent that the business processes that span systems provide an end-to-end workflow approach that supports the operational business model more directly. The reusable process steps (or functions) are already defined in these same industry models and are being consolidated with various integration tools (batch, real-time and asynchronous) to support the achievement of maturity in systems integration in the time-scales required.

As companies merge or acquire others, they often look for the ability to link the increased number of current systems and share the combined set of customer data for analysis and operational use as required. This is exactly the stage where they realize the need for the approaches and assets listed above; however, it is almost inevitable that they also consider: 1) the global applicability of locally developed versions of these models; 2) the relative cost and value of developing them in-house.

Most locally developed models tend to be applicable primarily to the country business in which they were developed, often with very limited ability to be expanded or applied elsewhere (eg to other countries, to manage multi-currencies, multi-languages, etc). As a result, an externally purchased data model usually provides a more mature, future-proof and commonly acceptable base for all countries or businesses to migrate to.

Development costs for operational data store, for data warehousing and for integration of existing and new systems are almost always underestimated. In practice not only are these estimates usually unrealistic, but many such projects (as they are very large developments) fail to deliver the expected solution or ROI. As data models become more widely used and prevalent in the marketplace, they are tending to fall in price and be made more widely available to both users and suppliers as a potential development or integration standard. These models can contribute to the control of development costs and acceleration of project implementation.

So, substantial project and ROI acceleration can be gained from the use of industry data models, both at the component implementation stage but also as disparate systems are integrated to leverage much higher ROI from an enterprise approach.

Pre-assembly can accelerate custom CRM projects – data models

Enough projects have been run in financial services to demonstrate that the NetworkFI.com model and underlying technical architecture can be used as a common basis for most, if not all, financial services companies. The challenge is to accelerate the development of CRM capabilities through acceleration of each project stage. However, there are many potential starting points and prioritized routes depending on the company and customer set involved. Using a custom mix of existing, current and future systems has been proven to be practical. However, this is best achieved around common industry data stores (operational and analytical) and a through deployment of reusable approaches to integration (combining batch, asynchronous and real-time connectivity). Re-use of proven methods can help with any combination of CRM systems projects in any sequence. However, where combinations of assets can be predicted as likely, pre-integration by suppliers is practical. This pre-integration can reduce time, cost and risk even further. It is important for most financial services companies that they achieve this without becoming committed to proprietary asset combinations, which reduce future options.

IBM has pre-integrated some of these most likely asset combinations already. For example, as Siebel Systems is so prevalent as a call centre and SFA systems choice, this application has been pre-integrated with IBM's Banking Data Warehouse for complementary customer analytics and the delivery of a closed-loop marketing process. While this type of pre-integration can provide a fast start to any project, it does not restrict further customization or extension, as the data mapping and pre-integration are carried out using methods and tools that the financial services company can extend itself to other CRM project deployments.

Source data analysis is carried out using Evoke Software applications, which can be deployed by financial services companies to rapidly assess existing legacy data and other data sources. Target data models such as Siebel, SAP, IBM's CIIS, Banking Data Warehouse and Insurance Information Warehouse have been pre-loaded into the Evoke Software metadata repository. These data models can still be customized (in fact they are expected to be) by the financial services company, but without undermining any benefits of pre-integration from previous efforts. Using this approach it is much faster and lower risk to integrate the common CRM data stores (operational and analytical) with existing and future systems of all types. As the value of this approach is recognized by more financial services companies and additional software vendors, more pre-integration work is being carried out using this model.

Pre-assembly can accelerate custom CRM projects – integration

In most CRM programmes, very different methods, tools and techniques are used to integrate disparate CRM and legacy systems, so as to link the channels, administration and analytics required to complete closed-loop business processing. As a result, the full benefits of integration remain out of reach for many companies. Of course integration is not achieved overnight, but if a company does not work to a consistent view of how it will be achieved over time, using common approaches at each programme stage, it will fail.

To get the 'right data to the right place at the right time' to support the defined CRM activities, data needs to be moved and restructured in one of three ways:

1. Batch. This is used where the data can be moved overnight, usually in large quantities, and still be sufficiently timely for the business activity. Processes that use this approach may be weekly or monthly, for example revenue results, or overnight updates. Batch implementation is usually achieved using various ETL (extract, transform, load) tools. The choice of batch movement of data is usually for one of these reasons:
    - The data is not required by the business user/process to be updated in a more immediate manner (for example, quarterly or annual regulatory reporting).
    - The data sources are not updated more frequently than this (for example, data updates are only received from some intermediaries on a daily, weekly or monthly basis).
    - The costs of complexity of other types of data movement outweigh (so far) the value of more timely data provision.
2. Asynchronous. This is used where the data needs to be moved in a timely manner, usually in small quantities, the timeliness may be sub-second, or some longer time.

Implementation is normally achieved using a message switching technology such as IBM's MQ Series integrator and/or Crossworlds. Examples of when to use this approach include:

- when (like real-time) a process waits on a rapid response, for example when a customer service representative is entering an address change;
- when a change is propagated to multiple systems, for example the customer's address change causes multiple systems to be updated; this can be achieved *after* the customer is informed that his or her request has been captured and acknowledged;
- when a process requires multiple transactions to be completed, as a workflow process, over a short or extended time (for example, a complete customer application for an additional product).

3. Real-time. This is used where the data needs to be moved immediately, and the process must wait on confirmation that the data is successfully moved (for example, a real-time ordering or other transaction process, with immediate confirmation). E-business implementation would normally be achieved using a Java tool such as IBM's Websphere. Examples of use include 'straight-through processing', or STP, of trading transactions requiring confirmation of settlement price and authority, and teller transactions with immediate effect on working account balances.

These integration options could take place within a company's own systems, or to provide connections to the systems of external companies (eg in business-to-business applications, for wider access to customers through intermediaries, or for a wider product and services portfolio through additional supplier relationships). In practice all three types of integration need to be combined in planning and implementation, whereas they have normally been considered and implemented very separately in different CRM-related projects. For example, a Siebel Systems, PeopleSoft or SAP implementation could require the batch build of a core database, with later update through a combination of batch, asynchronous and real-time updates for different data types with different requirements for timeliness of update. The same is true for new analytical or administrative systems components within the CRM programme.

As a result, a common approach to planning integration needs to be taken, so that:

- different build and update techniques can be deployed against the same systems and databases;
- a variety of update techniques can be implemented cooperatively against the same systems and databases;
- update frequency and methods can be more easily changed at a later date when business requirements change or cost/benefit equations change (for example, due to the reducing costs of technology over time);
- over time all the disparate systems (legacy, CRM, analytical, external, etc) can be integrated without being thwarted by horrendous complexity.

To enable a common integration approach to be taken IBM has combined the asynchronous and real-time integration capabilities of MQ Series and Websphere into a single offering. This can more easily take advantage of common industry data and process models to support the rapid and thorough implementation of the transaction examples mentioned above. In fact, further developments with financial services companies are sure to produce ever-improving levels of pre-packaging that take advantage of recognized data and process models for project acceleration and cost/risk reduction.

A common approach to industry data mapping and metadata management has been developed (using Evoke Software) to be deployed across all of batch, asynchronous and real-time integration, supporting the required mix and match and migration between these techniques. While batch integration requires direct mapping from source to target data models, asynchronous and/or real-time connectivity require mapping from source to target via an interim message format (eg XML or EJB standard); each of these can be achieved using common industry models and rapid 'drag and drop' data mapping techniques.

In summary, pre-integration of best practice and customizable components is practical when a common method and architecture are employed. The next part of this chapter outlines the proven e-business infrastructure that provides a checklist for any financial services CRM integration programme.

PULLING IT ALL TOGETHER ON THE SCREEN – THE INTEGRATED PORTAL

The portal provides integration 'on the screen' to users. Although 'portal' is a term most commonly associated with customer access to multiple services, the same portal technologies are now exploited for any e-business user, including:

- employees providing supported service to customers, for example call centre sales and service agents, advisers, key account managers and others;
- employees with non-customer-facing roles, including supply chain managers (aggregated product and service suppliers in financial services), administrative support staff, help desks, etc;
- customers accessing direct self-service systems, offering a combined and full support service;
- business partners and intermediaries, offering services to their customers that include your services;
- business partners and intermediaries using the company's sales and support systems.

A typical portal application that demonstrates an 'on the screen' integration example could be that of a financial adviser to high net worth individuals. The adviser needs to view the customer's aggregated investment position; carry out a needs analysis and risk assessment; and search for, price, propose and contract appropriate financial offers with automated fee or commission management. To achieve this in real time during a customer conversation, it is important to link seamlessly between these steps, often requiring data and function (process) integration. It is also important for the adviser (and perhaps the customer) to be able to view a number of these different work items, or 'portlets', simultaneously and to move data between them to avoid making notes and re-keying data.

Within the user screen or portal, each task has its own part of the screen and is a separate portlet; each portlet is supported by a separate application. As these applications are disparate (it is likely that a number of them are applications accessed in external company systems), they may have limited data or function integration. A utility capability, such as IBM's Websphere portal server, can assist in the accelerated deployment of a portal that combines these many disparate application sources.

Eventually integration is required at multiple levels:

- data level, where consistency of interchange data is required;
- function level, where reusable functions build towards unbroken processes;
- portal or on-the-screen integration, where a single and appropriate user view is provided.

EBI – E-BUSINESS INFRASTRUCTURE

In *Up Close and Personal?*, the systems chapter[3] reflects proposed terminology of a few years ago. At that time most commentators and analysts considered the scope of CRM systems to address customer contact channels only (whether assisted, self-service or, exceptionally, B2B). In our writings we were already proposing that the closed loop needed to include analytics and administration systems too, to act as the 'brain' to the CRM systems 'hands'. Over time, research and experience have shown that closed-loop integration of complete business processes (eg retention) is key to achieving return on investment. Commentators have updated their boundaries and terminology to reflect this. We now use the terminology that has become most accepted and explanatory, although it has not changed our view and experience of the boundaries of CRM integration. Figure 18.2 introduces an updated and more detailed representation of this architecture.

Analysis (to the right of Figure 18.2), sometimes called analytics or business intelligence (BI), is probably the place where the process should start. For example, in a retention exercise we would need to aggregate holdings to determine which customers were most

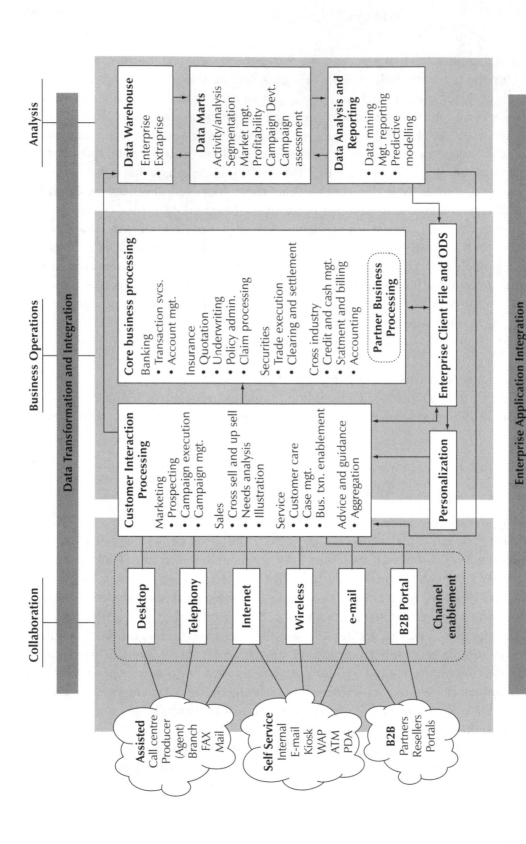

Figure 18.2 E-business infrastructure

Author Paul McDaid, IBM

valuable, which were most likely to leave, how best to recognize these customers and predict lapsing, how best to address their needs to retain them while remaining profitable. This knowledge (the brain) could then be deployed for benefit through the most appropriate customer touch points (the hands). The analysis area typically contains a common data warehouse (preferably with an industry data model), data extracts and/or views (data marts) and applications (data mining, OLAP, etc) to analyse and present or prepare data (reports, interchange tables, etc) for subsequent stages of the closed loop. IBM's Banking and Insurance data warehouses are implemented here, accompanied by analysis and data mining tools (eg IBM's Intelligent Miner, Searchspace or SAS Enterprise Miner) and OLAP tools (including Business Objects, MicroStrategy, Cognos, Brio and many others). Enterprise marketing campaign management tools include Xchange Dialog, Unica, Siebel Marketing, SAS Intrinsic, Chordiant Vantage, e-piphany and others.

Collaborative channels (to the left of Figure 18.2) suggest more than a multi-channel operation. Collaboration implies integrated channels working cooperatively to acquire, retain and develop customer relationships in the most productive and cost-effective manner. Collaborative channels may be self-service, assisted or B2B, although these channels often share the same technologies beneath (eg e-business, telephone, wireless, etc). Examples of application and/or technology e-business components in this area include IBM Websphere (including Web, voice, wireless, etc), Siebel Systems, PeopleSoft, SAP, Cisco, Genesys, Chordiant, S1 banking, Relavis, Amacis, Kana, DWL, Swallow complaints systems and many others. Branch systems renewal is a major focus of banks and insurers, as basic transactions are moved to call centre and Web, allowing the new branch to focus skilled resources on productive advice for consumers (see Chapter 24 for more on branch banking).

Business operations imply the core systems which will account for financial services transactional business, including product structures, pricing tables, transaction logs, etc. These systems are the core of business operations, from wherever accessed. They are often referred to as 'legacy systems' as if these are the systems that we are stuck with. There is an increasing recognition that the opposite is true, that these systems are valuable assets, often providing the rugged, reliable and scalable characteristics of the business. In fact a recently offered definition of a legacy system was 'any system that had achieved production', highlighting the fact that many new or replacement systems still do not make the grade. A core banking systems example is owned by Alltel, previously developed and deployed by IBM; others are provided by Sanchez, Temenos and Fiserv. An increasing priority in this area is new compensation systems to refocus employee effort – examples here include Callidus and SAP, each of which requires close integration with product systems and channel applications.

To develop a true collaborative channel approach, which supports consistent customer knowledge and personalization across all touch points (or varies it deliberately rather than by omission – for example to value price differently when assisted or self-service), certain components need to be common across all touch points. These components are the *enterprise client file* (or ODS), any real-time *personalization* or *rules* engine (such as Xchange realtime), and the common control of *customer interaction processing* that assures consistent customer management as an enterprise. Unfortunately, most channel-related applications are developed with one or more of these capabilities within the channel, where it is impractical in a large and complex financial services organization to expect that one application or channel technology will meet all current and future needs. Sharing these capabilities across channels, and deploying the common integration methods already outlined in this chapter, provides an enterprise-wide solution that can be justified and developed in stages, but also allows achievement of the collaborative goal.

Behind and below Figure 18.3 lies the consistent batch, asynchronous and real-time integration required to gradually complete each example of closed-loop processing, to develop aggregated views of customer relationships, and to be able to deploy this knowledge most effectively across integrated channels and transact using high performance and reliable and secure systems.

Figure 18.3 introduces a real closed-loop implementation example, using many of the full-scale applications provided as examples above. This example has been implemented as the basis for demonstrations and financial services proof-of-concept projects in IBM Dallas and IBM La Gaude (European centre, Southern France).

While these diagrams can look too idealized, or seem unrealistic or unachievable for your organization, they can provide:

- a checklist to assess what components are already in place in your business;
- a checklist for projects under way, including integration dependencies;
- an opportunity to highlight where effort would be better rewarded if focused on integration of existing components rather than the addition of more components;
- a map for the long term, which can include past, current and future systems;
- a common language for a cross-enterprise CRM programme;
- a checklist and map for further mergers and acquisitions;
- a checklist for supplier decisions, and/or standard components to be shared across an enterprise;
- a mature and proven approach to delivering ROI from an otherwise disparate application set.

CRITICAL SUCCESS FACTORS AND CONCLUSIONS

Research and experience suggest that return on investment is difficult, limited, and even impractical for most stand-alone CRM projects. Integrated and closed-loop business processes, including the 'brain and hands', are required to obtain and leverage ROI.

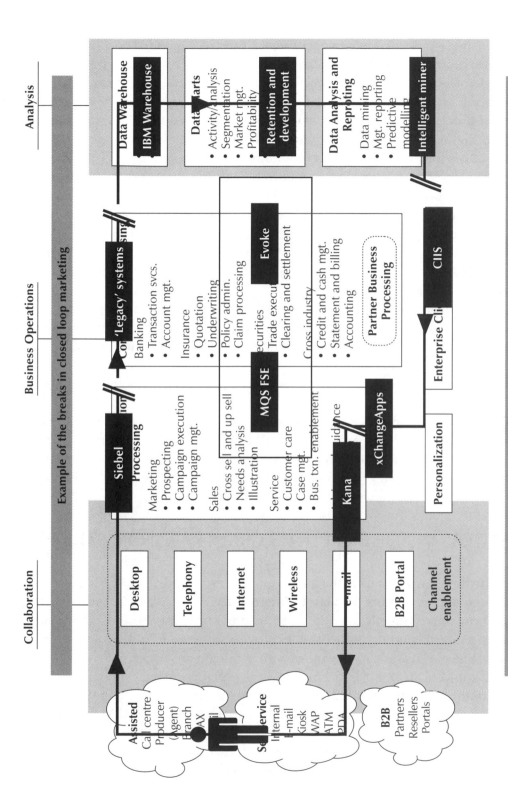

Figure 18.3 Example implementation (based on Figure 18.2 – see page 294)

Author Paul McDaid, IBM

Integrated business processes in complex financial services organizations require integrated systems to deliver the most appropriate and supporting data at the 'right place, right time'. If the systems linkages are broken, then the business processes will be broken too.

As the financial services customer is encouraged to use more self-service systems, the inadequacies of processes, systems and data will become more apparent to the customer and limiting to the organization's development. Poor productivity and high costs result from the same issues in a customer-assisted environment. B2B relationships and value will suffer when the same issues become apparent to alliance partners who act as channels, intermediaries or suppliers to your business.

Many, if not most, CRM projects fail to deliver anticipated ROI. A practical and experienced focus needs to be applied to business cases, projects and programmes.

Industry data models are required for best practice CRM, for the development of common data stores (operational and analytical) and for the definition of data interchange formats between disparate systems and businesses (eg via XML).

Combining and customizing best-of-breed applications with existing systems, while keeping options open for future systems selection, does not mean a company cannot take advantage of pre-integration and reuse benefits. Methods, tools, skills and reusable application combinations are available to help. Sufficient research, experience and supplier developments are available to avoid most issues faced previously, although experienced skills are in short supply.

Finally, IT is critically important for large financial services companies, but at the same time is only an enabler. Many other management, cultural, people, learning and sharing of knowledge, programme management and other aspects of CRM programmes must also be addressed to achieve success. Make some good mutual support contacts, you will need them.

CASE STUDY: INSIDE BIG BLUE'S CRM TRANSFORMATION[4]

IBM is currently implementing one of the most comprehensive, integrated CRM systems in the world. Expected to serve more than 80,000 internal IBM users, 30,000 business partners and millions of customers directly over the Web, the project represents one of the broadest deployments of sales, marketing and customer service software in history and the most extensive use of Siebel eBusiness Applications within a single organization to date.

Gary Burnette, IBM's Director of CRM Architecture, explains the company's vision: 'IBM is totally integrating the company around its customers so they can see, and IBM can see, everything the company does in an integrated fashion. At the same time, IBM is integrating the company within itself, so that it won't matter who within IBM has to respond to a particular customer need; everyone who interacts with customers can use the same system and the same processes to respond as quickly as possible.'

As of November 2001, the company had made significant progress toward its CRM goals, having deployed Siebel eBusiness Applications and critical legacy interfaces to 6,800 employees in 30 countries worldwide. To guide the rollout, IBM has formed a clear set of principles that form a best-in-class approach to implementing an integrated enterprise-wide CRM solution.

Principle number 1: centralize management of the project

To manage its Siebel eBusiness deployment, IBM is using a three-tiered governance structure – the same structure the company uses to manage all of its business transformation efforts. The governance structure consists of:

- An executive investment review board. The board defines strategic direction and manages portfolio spending. 'This model establishes personal accountability with senior management for implementation success,' says Burnette.
- A management team of business leaders, IT leaders and CRM alliance partner leaders. This team ensures that the project stays focused on meeting each functional group's specific needs.
- The CRM project team. This team is accountable for the day-to-day execution of the project plan, including mapping business processes, planning organizational change activities, defining system requirements, and allocating resources. Also within this layer is a centralized architecture team that is responsible for data modelling and building interfaces with legacy systems.

Because there are so many sub-teams involved in the various aspects of IBM's Siebel eBusiness implementation, IBM has developed a comprehensive methodology that defines how these teams operate together. The methodology enables the teams to act in parallel, with minimal supervision. As a result, the company is able to implement the Siebel eBusiness Applications in an integrated fashion and at an accelerated pace.

Principle number 2: execute the implementation in phases

IBM is executing its Siebel eBusiness project as a series of releases, in which additional Siebel eBusiness functions are rolled out to the existing end-user community approximately twice a year. With each release, a new user community is also brought on board. To supplement the major releases, IBM rolls out smaller 'dot' releases as needed to enhance the system's functions.

To accelerate the deployment cycle, IBM avoids developing prototypes before each release. Instead, the company follows a rigorous methodology that enables it to configure a release without prototyping and then deploy the new functions to end users immediately. 'At the end of every major point in the implementation,' says Burnette, 'there is a review of this methodology to submit the lessons learned and refine the methodology for the next phase of the project. This enables the project team to continue moving forward rapidly, taking advantage of knowledge gained along the way.'

Principle number 3: prioritize breadth over depth

With each release, IBM deploys base functions to the largest set of users possible, rather than providing deep functionality to any one particular user audience. This approach allows IBM to reap the benefits of Siebel eBusiness Applications as quickly as possible. In addition, deploying Siebel eBusiness Applications incrementally to a broad user base helps the company gain deeper insight into the ways in which the systems can be used. Burnette explains:

> The natural human instinct is to configure the system so that it supports what users do today. Yet a major goal of this project is to migrate users into a new world. Thus, if you try to define all functional modifications prior to deploying the system, the likelihood of doing that correctly is low. The notion is to deliver enough out-of-the-box function in the first pass to introduce the new world. Once people experience the new world, the requirements a design team can generate from users will be very different than those from users with no understanding at all of the new world. Of course, even the first release must deliver value to the business and to end users.

Principle number 4: minimize application customizations

Keeping customizations to a minimum both accelerates the phased rollout and mitigates future upgrade complexity. Cher de Rossiter, Project Executive CRM2000, explains:

> IBM has a lot of software implementation experience, and one of the things we know is that it takes longer to create custom-developed, stand-alone applications than it does to implement a package out of the box. More important, with custom-developed applications, it's very difficult to manage the proccss of defining requirements, and they're a lot more expensive to maintain. Upgrading and adding functions to custom-developed applications becomes very difficult over time.

The Fit/Gap process, part of IBM's formal implementation methodology, has played an instrumental role in helping the company minimize applications customization. As Burnette explains:

Fit/Gap is a methodology in which we bring end users into a room with a set of business scenarios. We run those business scenarios and we document where the software supports the scenarios and where there are gaps. Then we make a concerted decision about what we're going to do about those gaps. We may choose to wait to resolve the gaps until a later release of the software, or we may decide we have to do some customization. The overall goal is to keep the customization to an absolute minimum so we can deploy more quickly and migrate easily to the next release when it becomes available.

Principle number 5: manage change

IBM takes organizational change management seriously. To gain end-user support for Siebel eBusiness Applications, IBM involves end users in all phases of the implementation, from requirements documentation, through feature design, to application testing and validation. 'Adoption relates to whether individual users personally derive value from the system', explains Burnette. 'By involving users in all phases of the project, we're able to implement a system that serves their specific needs. When you provide people with a tool that helps them succeed, they will use it.'

As IBM continues to roll out Siebel eBusiness Applications to an increasingly diverse user population, these implementation principles will continue to play a key role in ensuring the success of the project. 'One of the most important things IBM has learned,' says Burnette, 'is that transforming the way we do business isn't a destination, it's a journey. It's about centring the entire organization around the customer – and that's a process that never ends.'

Notes

[1] Gorski, Lorraine [online] Insurers want to see payoff from technology investments, *Best's Review*, gorskil@ambest.com, www.ambest.com/bestline order#301825

[2] IBM 'GreatRisk Insurance White Paper', available directly from Bryan Foss (bryan_foss@uk.ibm.com). Note that the actual company in this case study is anonymous: GreatRisk is a fictitious name

[3] Gamble, P, Stone, M and Woodcock, N (1999) *Up Close and Personal*, Chapter 10, Kogan Page, London

[4] Extracted with permission from *The Siebel Journal*, reference http://www.siebel.com/journal/1201/implement_ibm.shtm

19

Data management – moving from CRM to e-business customer management

Berenice Winter and Michael Page

INTRODUCTION

Managing data in a financial services company using e-business techniques for customer management has many of the problems associated with existing data management systems in a more 'traditional' environment, as well as a few new ones. Data management involves ensuring that the organization:

- has control of data flows into and out of the business;
- knows what data it is collecting and why; where it is held;
- knows how the data is used in the organization, and by whom;
- knows what value the data brings to its business processes.

Recently, many financial services companies have made significant investments in e-business initiatives. The first step was to ensure that in their new e-guise their operational systems met functional requirements and performed to acceptable standards. Many companies had to re-engineer their first launches to improve security, allow increased scale and accelerate systems as they were accessed by ever-larger and more unpredictable flows of customers. With these objectives achieved by most companies, many companies are now focusing on using their systems to manage customers for increased profitability.

BUILDING BETTER RELATIONSHIPS

There are three ways to increase the profitability and value of these customer relationships:

1. acquire new relationships;
2. enhance existing relationships;
3. extend the relationship duration.

To be able to derive increased value from the relationship, companies need to ensure that there is:

- minimal wasted effort in acquiring or maintaining customers;
- an understanding of data available to determine which customers to nurture and keep, and those to let go;
- use of technology to store and manipulate data.

Out of this, a number of issues arise in the area of data management:

- **Data capture** – understanding what data needs to be captured and at what stage in the relationship, in what way and how frequently.
- **Data systems** – reviewing the needs for changes to data systems to manage e-business.
- **Data quality and maintenance** – understanding the way the data is held, knowing what you have and how good it is.
- **Data analysis** – appreciating the data that exists and how to make the most out of it, the ways in which the data can be manipulated using statistical and analytical techniques. In an e-business environment, the extent of the data that can be analysed includes not only the standard details about customers, but also the ways in which those customers use the e-business channels.
- **Data security** – including data privacy and fraud.

DATA CAPTURE

Financial services companies made many attempts at data warehousing during the 1990s, but there are still many companies that are 'data rich, information poor'. One of the main reasons for this is lack of attention to data capture. The principles of data capture are similar for all businesses. Businesses have to collect certain data, such as customer name and address, in order to manage the account. However, there is much other data that can and should be captured, relating not just to who customers are, but also to their lifestyle, habits, personal preferences, behaviour in relationship with the company, etc. This information can come from a number of different sources, such as:

- customers/prospects themselves;
- how they interact with different channels;
- analysing their usage behaviour (transaction, claims etc);
- external data – eg lifestyle, geo-demographics, market research.

Failures in data capture may come from:

- Failing to help the customer to provide all of the information that is needed. For example, call centre systems usually allow the customer to supply house number/name and postcode, with the rest supplied by the system. Few e-business systems use this facility on their on-screen application forms.
- Inadequate systems or processes.
- Inadequate storage capabilities.
- Inefficient processing, leaving much data unavailable for analysis.
- Inappropriate or inadequate people skills, preventing release of the full value of the data.

The types of data that should be collected vary by business and by product. However, there are some basic data items that all financial services businesses are likely to want to capture. These are detailed below.

Customer data

Much data can be obtained directly from customers, just by asking them. Customers and prospects are usually willing to supply data provided they feel that they are relevant and pertinent to the business process.

Internal data

Data held internally about customers might include:

- name and address, e-mail, telephone;

- accounts held;
- account balances;
- transaction data;
- promotion history;
- customer service;
- profitability/lifetime value.

External data

There is a vast array of external data that is now available to the marketer. This includes:

- demographics;
- socioeconomic data;
- purchase behaviour;
- lifestyles/psychographics;
- geography.

This external data has two main uses: 1) it can be matched to the customer record to enrich the data directly, and; 2) it can also be used to build models to be used for a wide range of marketing activities.

More specifically, the benefits of using a combination of internal and external data include:

- maximizing customer value;
- improving targeting of messages, through better understanding of which customers have which needs;
- using communication channels more productively by understanding which customers respond to different types of communication through different channels;
- improving customer satisfaction and loyalty;
- increasing cross-sell/up-sell;
- product and service development through deeper customer understanding.

For some businesses, there are problems of using e-business techniques to collect data across borders that have not been an issue when traditional data collection techniques are used. In Europe, these include:

- Different name and address formats. Whilst in some countries such as the UK one can identify if an address exists and offer alternatives if it does not look correct, this is not universal. Thus, in Germany and the Netherlands, the house number is placed after the street name. In Russia, the name of the town comes at the beginning of the address. Postcodes are not universally available across the EU.

- Currency variation, which affects analysis of customer value across borders (the Euro reduces this problem a bit).
- Differences in data protection laws, affecting how data can be collected and processed.

Examples

An insurance company identified a number of differences between running a traditional business and an e-business. Qualities particular to e-business include:

- Data management is seen as fundamental to e-business.
- Faster responses and more frequent refreshes are required by customers.
- Tracking of call centre activity becomes much more important.
- Volumes of information are much greater.
- Costs rise, due to the greater amount of information that needs to be handled and stored.

One financial services company found that people react differently online and functions that are the most popular via the call centre are not necessarily the most popular online. For example, the most popular reason for calling the call centre was to change name and address details. However, the most popular function online was to pay the account by direct debit. This shows how a new channel can change people's behaviour.

Other e-data

Behavioural data can come in many forms. It will include how customers use their account, how frequently, etc. However, in addition to this there is a range of new e-data. These include:

- cookies;
- Web passwords;
- Web user login;
- e-mail – outbound promotions;
- e-mail – outbound promotion – response;
- e-mail – inbound;
- Web-site visit: pages viewed (Web log file data);
- ads/promotions served;

- ads / promotion – response;
- Web user input – orders;
- Web user input – information requests;
- Web user input – questionnaire data;
- Web user input – call back request;
- Web user input – text chat question;
- referring or source site.

The main problem with clickstream and e-data generally is the sheer volume. Many sites might be generating several gigabytes, even terabytes of data a day. Yet the resources to analyse this data are usually one or two analysts at most. Clickstream data types and uses are described in Table 19.1.

Table 19.1 Clickstream data types and uses

Data type	Usefulness
How people get to a site	Helps understand quality of marketing campaigns and links from search engines
The most popular pages	Allows marketers to modify pages to meet customer likes and dislikes
Where they leave a site	Shows which pages are seen as closing pages, and whether they are the expected ones
How they navigate through the site	Shows whether people are taking the expected route and if not, why not
The percentage of visits that lead to an enquiry or sign up to an account	Shows the success of the offering and its presentation
How much time visitors spend on a site	Shows whether spending more time on the site generates value
Which country visitors are visiting from	Shows appeal across borders
Which browser they are using	Shows whether use of different browsers (which see screens in different ways) is affecting customers' reaction to screens
How successful are banner and advertising campaigns	Shows whether cutomers are clicking through company's banner ads on other sites and whether they are leaving company's site via other banner ads.

DATA SYSTEMS

The Internet has created an information overload that many companies find it hard to come to terms with. Customer information is streaming into businesses via e-channels at rates hitherto considered impossible. In the past, most of this Internet data could not be attributed to individuals. Now (with cookies/Web redirection/CGI script parameter flexibility/Web registrations/customer URNs) almost all Internet marketing data can be attributed to individual customers. Marketers also now realize that one does not need to know a person's name and address in order to engage in targeted electronic communications. Many companies have sprung up offering targeting without name and address.

Most financial services companies have marketing databases for use in off-line marketing. These were built mainly to aid segmentation and targeting for direct marketing campaigns. These systems represent a significant investment – in both technology and processes. Their challenges are now to:

1. Use the off-line database's data for online marketing. One approach is to make data from this database available during the first occasion a customer visits a Web site. After all, the organization has often spent $40–80 to generate the enquiry in the first place from a mixture of off-line and online media. Every effort must be made to maximize the response and conversion rates. By pre-populating an online database with customer data from the marketing data warehouse a company can modify the Web communication to maximize response. If fewer key-strokes are needed then customers are more likely to complete registration or application and less likely to abandon their actions before the end.

2. Transfer online customer data to the off-line marketing database. Online data marts collect valuable data for customer modelling, segmentation, site navigation and product development. Most companies need to make design changes to their marketing databases to accept new data types. For example:
   - data without name address – just e-mail address;
   - data without name, address or e-mail address – just cookie and clickstream or Web log data;
   - e-mail opt-in and e-mail preferences;
   - multiple e-mail addresses per customer with links to varying level of opt-ins each related to opt-in topics;
   - e-mail click through activity;
   - deliverability of each e-mail address;
   - e-mail media type.

3. Synchronize both databases with changes as they occur from separate channels. This is specifically important for: 1) opt-outs to ensure privacy compliance, and; 2) customer service data to ensure appropriate customer messaging.

Companies are currently at one of five stages:

1. no data transfers;
2. data from on to off only;
3. data two-way – weekly;
4. data two-way – daily;
5. real-time access.

Real-time access

Many financial services companies are trying to move to daily database updates. However, this is difficult and costly. Typically companies need to push the new records from the online file and the whole of the off-line customer database through a de-duplication or fuzzy matching process to consolidate customer data. For example, a company with 5 million existing customers and 300,000 new customers coming in from its e-business will need to process just under 60 million records a year. Data bureau rates for the matching range from $3–23 per thousand. Even when this is achieved the data is still 24 hours out of date. This will be visible to customers as they can view their profile online. Customers are also more aware of what the company knows about them, in different channels. This may lead to poor service, and also can lead to fraud exposure.

For example, a leading insurance company has set up a separate dot.com business. This part of the business collects data separately into its own database that is then matched back to the main company customer database once a week. The aim is to update on a daily basis and eventually move to real-time using Acxiom's Abilitec. A credit card company has set up a Web presence that reflects its high street presence. The Web site allows existing customers to register to manage their account online as well as apply to become a card-holder. The data is managed by a separate data warehouse which is updated daily. Online applications are sent a physical application form that is already filled in but requires a signature under the UK Consumer Credit Act. These forms are then re-keyed into the main data capture system. This is possible at present due to low volumes, but will need to be reviewed in future.

Recently, new customer recognition and matching technology has been launched by technology companies Acxiom and Experian that enables real-time customer recognition and access. The technology involves databases applying a link identifier to customer records from a common external reference base (see Figure 19.1). These common keys allow customer data to be retrieved in real time from different systems. By using common links the need for high frequency database integration can be avoided. This technology is invaluable for financial services e-businesses, because different products usually have different operational systems and consequently isolated islands of customer information.

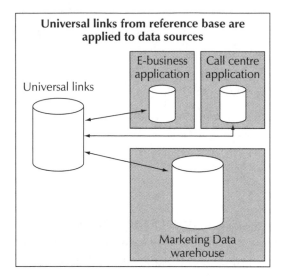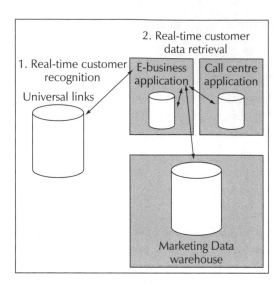

Figure 19.1 Updating data in real time

Systems performance

For new e-business companies, particularly those that are subsidiaries of existing companies, establishing a suitable database to hold all of this new information has been a major challenge. Approaches have varied, but a common approach has been to create a separate data warehouse to hold all the 'new' customer data related to the e-business channel. This data is then matched back to a central data warehouse to ensure that the customer data is kept in line across the business. The different business models adopted will affect the type and quantity and difficulty of managing these data flows. Companies that are purely e-business driven, or with separate product lines from their parent company, do not have the same needs for matching customer data and behaviour across the business as those that operate e-business channels as just another channel within their overall business structure.

Legacy systems developed to hold information about individual products or groups of products still exist. Most of the data warehouses of the past decade were not designed to hold the vast volumes of data now available. CRM systems must now hold not only name, address and product data, but also segmentation, value, geo-demographic, lifestyle, and the vast amounts of behavioural data that can now be collected. Indeed many systems will also try to hold data over a number of years for historical analysis.

Keeping financial services e-business operational sites responsive is a major challenge. The Web sites of today are complex applications and much more processor intensive than the early Web sites serving up static pages. The potential audience is growing rapidly, generating heavier and unpredictable server loads. Promotions can create dramatic spikes of demand on servers. This has caused a number of servers to fail. We believe it will soon be accepted that operational e-commerce systems should not be slowed down by building in marketing functions and processes such as ad-serving, personalization, e-mail campaign management, and Web mining and analysis. It is necessary to create separate databases (digital marketing databases) and systems so that the operational e-commerce infrastructure remains free to support operational functions.

In many cases a company's main off-line marketing databases were designed with a direct mail and analytics focus. These databases are often not designed to manage the real-time interactive demands of e-business. For example, a major insurance company's existing marketing database couldn't be used because the database logged off users at 8.00 pm each night in order to run batch routines. Its database model and indexing meant that record retrieval query times were unacceptable for the response times needed for the Internet application.

The role of the digital marketing/e-CRM database

The digital marketing database provides the data repository to drive a number of online marketing applications. For example:

- implementation of personalization systems will serve specific content (eg special offers) to particular customers, improving customer satisfaction and response rates;
- personalization systems and online databases which identify when to serve incentives and streamline user experience – to avoid shopping cart abandonment and therefore increase sales;
- increasing relevance of the site to the consumer based on the consumer profile, to induce longer site visits and improve levels of enquiry;
- customizing and targeting e-mail communication to increase sales, minimize e-mail channel opt-out and foster customer loyalty;
- sending e-mail newsletters with personalized topics to increase total volume of promotion impressions and raise sales;
- a viral e-mail function to increase the prospect pool through referral.

Data trapped in databases because there is too much of it to handle, or insufficient skill within the organization to release it, means lost competitive advantage. One approach to the problem of data overload is to ensure that the company only uses data that is either needed to manage the account or is going to tell the company something. In other words, it needs to be significant in business models, or actionable in an event-driven marketing strategy. For event-driven marketing, data ideally needs to be in real time. Real-time reporting speeds up the decision-making process, but is hungry for processing capability. Real time is best used in customer service activities, where customers usually expect the customer service representative, virtual or real, to have a complete and up-to-date understanding of their account. However, for activities that do not need these immediate approaches, batch processing may be more appropriate.

DATA QUALITY AND MAINTENANCE

It is no good collecting data about customers unless you have some way of verifying that the quality of that data is good enough for your purposes. If a dot.com financial services business is using customer data from another part of the business, or simply collecting data via the company's main site, there are some distinct advantages to considering the use of CDI software. These include the following.

Prospecting

CDI enables multiple prospect lists to be more effectively de-duplicated and thereby reduces the volume and costs of holding excess data. Also, more effective identification and suppression of existing customers from prospect lists ensures that prospect marketing messages are not sent in error to current customers.

Risk assessment of new customers

For companies needing new customers to be screened for risk management purposes, the ability to use consumer and address links enables a higher percentage of details for previously known bad or fraudulent customers to be identified. This information can be used to screen new applicants and can be used to reject the application or to price the products and services accordingly.

Administrative customer communications

CDI enables more effective de-duplication of existing customers. This helps reduce duplicate communications, saving in administrative contact costs. This is important when setting up a new channel.

Customer marketing communication

By using CDI to provide more effective de-duplication, the cost of outbound marketing communications using mail or telephony will be significantly reduced. Savings can also be made in the reduction in wasted data capture costs for gone-aways through more accurate suppression matching by using customer data integration (CDI) processing. Effective CDI processing also enables identification of records which have been incorrectly merged in the past and will identify additional customers available for cross-sell and up-sell marketing. The presence of CDI links across all key product and marketing data systems enables more up-to-date data to be shared to support customer management activities.

Customer retention and win-back

The availability of up-to-date cross-database information improves the quality of retention model development and the accuracy of predicting customer attrition. Customer retention activities can be more effectively implemented using outbound customer communications.

Call centre operation

CDI enables faster customer identification in the call centre, leading to faster call handling and enabling pre-population of customer details for application processing and response capture. Faster customer identification also enables more effective call routing to agents and areas of specialist support based on the details retrieved for the customer, eg VIP customer management, routing to Save teams.

Privacy enablement (data protection)

The current UK Data Protection Act 1998 gives individuals the right to access all information held about them by a company. By implementing CDI links across all product, operational and marketing data systems, companies can satisfy this requirement in an automated manner, delivering faster and less costly compliance. This is very important for organizations with many relationships with each customer.

Single customer view

CDI enables the development of a real-time single customer view (SCV), allowing significant savings in the development of a SCV solution and for the continuing maintenance and enhancement of the application. Hardware savings may also result from the implementation of a 'virtual' as opposed to a 'physical' SCV.

E-mail addressing

Capturing and correcting e-mail information is difficult. There are no directories of e-mail addresses, so companies rely totally on customers to enter them correctly. For example, a credit card company found the quality of e-mail addresses supplied to be generally very poor. They were often spelt incorrectly on the original application form, or keyed incorrectly when entered into the data capture screens. This made e-mail marketing a less than perfect channel. However, it is possible to ensure that the verification of the syntax is correct, but this is of limited use. The fact that many people have more than one e-mail address adds complexity for e-mail marketers. With around 20 per cent of UK employees moving each year, addresses are changing all the time. However, e-mail marketing has its attractions. Response rates are usually high compared with traditional direct marketing. It is also much easier to change messages quickly. In addition, e-mails can have cookies attached to them to collect data that can then be used to refine future campaigns.

DATA ANALYSIS

For new businesses, the emphasis is usually on acquiring customers. Data analysis is seen as a secondary problem. However, understanding the data that is collected and how to make the most out of it is fundamental to making the business work in the longer term. Although the concepts of customer segmentation, geo-demographics, etc, have been around for many years, many companies have still only scratched the surface of what is available and the analyses on customer data that can be performed. Approaches include:

- customer profiling – comparing a group of customers with a larger group, such as the overall UK population, or all customers for a particular product or service;
- customer segmentation – dividing customers into different segments based on a given criteria, such as age, income, etc;
- customer value analysis – developing a value for each customer based on a combination of internal and external data;
- model building – extracting data from a segmentation or value analysis to determine the expected reaction to a particular offer or product.

For example, data analysis techniques might be used to identify those customers more likely to leave the company, and develop a retention strategy to retain high-value customers. Figure 19.2 shows the different types of customer in the retention matrix and the approach that needs to be developed to deal with them. Developing models based on the data that has been captured can be used to identify which customers need to be addressed in this way.

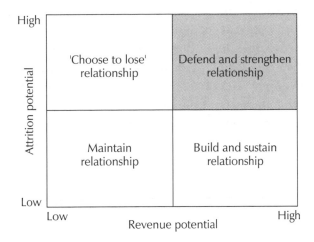

Figure 19.2 Customer retention matrix

For example, an insurance company used a customer value analysis approach to build models of their customers. From this they were able to score each customer with a value representing that customer's value to the company. This value was then used to assess the profitability of each customer. Around 43 per cent of customers were unprofitable. Based on these results, they were able to devise customer management strategies to improve profitability, including:

- increasing cross-sales/up-sells to profitable customers at appropriate customer life stages;
- reducing the number of profitable customers lapsing;
- reducing the number of unprofitable customers recruited.

The building of models to understand customer behaviour is nothing new. However, in an e-business environment there are new elements:

- the type of data that is available;
- its volume;
- its timeliness – real-time delivery of personalized offers based on real-time behaviour is possible. By building event-based models, real-time event-driven marketing can take place if the data is collected and processed that way.

Automatic reporting tools

Many CRM systems have front-end reporting tools that will report in a variety of ways. However, beware of investing too much in new customer-orientated database systems without fully understanding the process of turning this customer data into customer knowledge. One can find out what customers did, how they acted and reacted to the Web site, for example, the route that they took through the data, but one cannot automatically assess why. A front-end statistical solution gives the basic metrics, but will not be able to explain customer behaviour in depth. To do this one needs bespoke segmentation systems, based on a combination of the data collected over the e-channel, whether clickstream data, customer data from completed application forms, or purchase information. This data can in turn be matched to external data from lifestyle companies, market research and other data to develop a wider, more detailed picture of each customer and their potential value to the company.

DATA SECURITY

E-business increases security risks, potentially exposing hitherto isolated systems to open and risky environments. There have been many stories where access has been inadvertently obtained to other people's accounts. Security breaches can be defined as:

- those with serious criminal intent (eg fraud or theft);
- casual hacking;
- flaws in system design.

Many companies still store their data on the Web server, where it is open for hacking. It also opens up the possibility of working through the server into other systems with less stringent security set-ups. Some companies are now employing ethical hackers – consultants who hack into their own systems in search of weaknesses. Most of the problems that are found tend to be basic errors, such as not changing default passwords. All of these threats have potentially serious financial and legal implications. So how should companies approach them? Suggestions include:

- having an up-to-date data security policy, which is communicated through the company;
- building best-practice security controls into systems and networks as they are developed, rather than adding them on at a later date;
- being proactive – actively testing security systems on a regular basis;
- developing a rapid response approach to security breaches;
- using all of the system-based tools that are provided to you.

Not only are there financial and legal issues. Reputations are at stake. Financial institutions must ensure that their crisis management processes also include PR. Rapid dissemination of information, particularly bad news, can change customers perception quickly.

For more on risk, see Chapter 20.

Data privacy

As in the physical world, so in the virtual world – companies need to ensure that individuals' rights and information are adequately protected. This also extends to the way in which their data is held and used. This topic is dealt with in detail in Chapter 22.

Data protection principles are designed to ensure that individuals have a right to know where data is being stored about them, what data is held, how it is going to be used, and have the right to view, change and correct that information as appropriate. For privacy to work, we must give: 1) notice of how information about people will be used, and; 2) a choice regarding whether it can be used.

This applies just as much to online companies as to traditional companies and care needs to be taken to ensure that these principles are not being breached. Data protection requirements in e-mail addressing are still very unclear. Although in many countries governments have not finalized their policies, good practice favours opt-in, and certainly this seems to get better responses from customers. Although in the UK one is precluded from sending unsolicited e-mails for sales or marketing purposes, this is widely ignored in practice. With viral e-mail campaigns, where e-mails are copied from one person to another, e-mail addresses may get into the public domain by being passed from one person to another. However, it is good customer management practice, as well as accepted global online practice, to ensure that the person's permission is obtained before adding them to an e-mail list. This includes business as well as consumer contacts. Also, blind copying should be encouraged wherever possible.

CONCLUSION

Data management is a vast area, and this chapter has only scratched the surface. However, the key message is that good data management is fundamental to a business's success. In an e-business world, data becomes even more important because there is so much more of it. Holding, sifting and analysing it to find out about customers is more important than ever. The pace of change in this area is unlikely to slow down. As companies start to come to terms with the data collected from the Internet and e-mail, so SMS, interactive-TV, WAP and other m-commerce activities are beginning to grow. To be competitive it is essential that e-businesses realize early on the need to manage their data effectively.

Various activities can be carried out to review data management activities. These include:

- **Data capture** – assess the ROI on data: what there is, how it is collected from all touch-points, its usefulness to the business against the cost of collecting and processing.
- **Data systems** – ensure systems are delivering the data needed for maintaining competitive advantage. Remember, systems include people.

- **Data quality and maintenance** – review data quality procedures and ensure that data held is up to date and relevant.
- **Data analysis** – check the availability of data analysis skills to hand to make the most of this rich company resource.
- **Data security and privacy** – evaluate data security and privacy policies to ensure that they are adequate and appropriate.

Part 6

Risk and compliance

20

Managing customers in a world of risk

David La Bouchardière, Maureen Madden, Greg Scorziello and Merlin Stone

INTRODUCTION

We live in a world of increasing risk, and companies have, of necessity, become expert at dealing with, and building into their business processes provisions for certain types of known risk. However, companies now find themselves faced with a complex amount of issues that need addressing if they are to protect themselves and their customers and, at the same time, maintain their valuable customer relationships.

UK companies were already burdened with the necessity of understanding the 12 volumes (over 3,000 pages) of the Financial Services Authority's (FSA's) handbook, in order to comply with recent legislation and be prepared for N2, the date on which the FSA received their full powers, midnight on 30 November, 2001. Now, as a result of the events of 11 September 2001, companies have to be prepared for, and take action to protect themselves and their customers from, acts of terrorism.

Business is playing its part in the fight against terrorism, and the financial services industry, in particular, is firmly engaged in this fight. An unfortunate reality that has emerged, and that needs careful consideration, is that not only do companies have to ensure that their customers are dealt with fairly and reasonably, but they are also now placed in the position of having to protect themselves from certain customers who may be responsible for carrying out what is now being called 'cyber-crime' against them.

ISSUES

Data protection

In the UK the Data Protection Act 1998 requires companies to prevent unauthorized or unlawful processing of information they hold. They also have a duty to prevent accidental loss or damage to the information. The Act requires companies to ensure that information held on people is safeguarded adequately. The Act pertains to personal data, ie information about living identifiable individuals or 'data subjects'. Organizations collecting, holding and processing data about people are expected to safeguard the information and to get it right, and keep it right. For more on this, see Chapters 19 and 21.

Cyber-crime

No company can be certain that its systems are 100 per cent secure as financial services firms are under constant, 24-hour, threat of attack and the most disturbing fact is that they don't know who the enemy is – the threat could come from an employee, an ex-employee, or even a valued customer.

In the wake of 11 September, the risk for the finance sector of becoming a victim of cyber-crime has grown. A group of European hackers, Young Intelligent Hackers Against Terror, claims to have extracted data connected with transactions between bin Laden's al-Qaida network and the al-Shamal Islamic Bank in Sudan. Reprisals by pro-Taliban hackers have led the US and UK governments to warn business to secure against hacking.

Money laundering

The events of 11 September have caused governments to focus on efforts to tackle money laundering. The G7 group of industrialized nations is examining whether the Financial Action Task Force, an anti-money-laundering body set up in 1989, should add hunting for terrorists' funds to its remit. The USA, France and Britain have all called for the task force to scrutinize the use of legitimately acquired funds for terrorist purposes – a marked change from its traditional focus on the proceeds of crime. The European Union aims to curb money laundering within its 15 Member States. EU-wide legislation to combat money laundering is currently being hammered out by the European Parliament and the EU finance ministers.

When the Financial Services and Markets Act took effect in December 2001, the FSA became able to prosecute for breaches of the Money Laundering Regulations. The FSA also became able to enforce its own rules, which set standards for the anti-money-laundering procedures that financial institutions must maintain. These standards are higher than those that were in place under the regulations, and the FSA has powers both to fine and 'name and shame' banks that do not comply.

The FSA is not just focusing on banks. The Authority says it is working with building societies, fund managers, and insurance companies as well as banks and stockbrokers as it hunts for terror funds.

For more on money laundering, see Chapter 23.

Security

As the Internet is used increasingly as a platform for business transactions, security becomes a primary issue for Internet applications. Over the years the amount of business being conducted on the Internet has been growing dramatically. Companies started to allow their customers to order goods or request services via the Internet. Banks introduced home banking and online brokerage applications using basic security functions for the Internet such as server authentication and the Secure Sockets Layer (SSL). For identification and authentication, the user had to enter an identification string and a password. However, this traditional level of security is not sufficient for such sensitive business transactions on the Internet as payments and legally binding contracts. The European Union and the United States have passed legislation to establish the conditions for making a digital signature the legally binding identification and authentication mechanism for contracts on the Internet. The legislation requires that the technology employed not allow secret keys to be copied or used by non-authorized parties. The consequence of this requirement is the need for a secure secret-key storage, if the digital signature is based on public key cryptography. It is believed that the recent worldwide government focus on security will make smart cards more important as tools to protect the integrity of Internet sites.

Business continuity and disaster recovery

Since the tragedy of the World Trade Center (WTC) attack, business continuity and disaster recovery have moved to the forefront of CEOs' and CTOs' minds. One fact that has emerged is that financial services companies, while having disaster recovery plans in place, had failed to test their plans on a regular basis and were not ready to deal with a disaster on such a momentous scale. The first test of the plan should not be on the occasion of an actual disaster – tests should be held regularly in order to work efficiently and effectively when the actual disaster hits.

The magnitude of the WTC attack means that firms need to revisit their disaster plans Within a few blocks of the WTC, IBM had about 1,200 clients. Rather than focus on disaster recovery – where CIOs and CTOs worry about systems and data – the emphasis must be shifted to business recovery across the organization. In the WTC attack, the centralized IT computing fabric remained largely intact, but employees could not access it. So while firms may have great plans for recovering their information technology, the WTC incident shows that they need to expand it to include the human element. Power failures and fires are the old way of thinking about disaster interruptions. A disaster of the WTC size shows that although employees may be safe (and sadly many were not), psychologically they may or may not be in a condition to return to work. So the business continuity plan needs to address those issues.

Another element of a business continuity plan should be a check of the supply chain. If the key people with whom a company does business upstream and downstream are ill prepared and unable to function, then the company's efforts at business-continuity planning may have gone to waste.

The important thing is to get help in developing the plan. This includes attention to issues like whether the supplier engaged to provide backup IT will be syndicating the computer space. If the servers are not dedicated, will the supplier have capacity in the event that several companies require it at the same time?

SOLUTIONS

Business, although challenged by the need to comply with legislation, to deal fairly with customers, and at the same time protect itself from attack, should not be daunted by this challenge. There are many excellent tools and solutions that can be employed to minimize the risk of exposure.

Technology – not the only solution

Besides ensuring they have the best possible technological solutions available, companies also need to be aware of other aspects of security that need to be considered. Everyone that comes into contact with personal data in the workplace must understand the implications of security, risk and data protection legislation. Staff involvement is the key to effective management and can best be implemented through clear, accessible policies and structured training. As Chapter 22 shows, awareness of data protection and compliance with it is low. As Chapter 21 shows, compliance with regulatory reporting requirements is low. We believe the same applies to all other areas of risk. While senior IT managers may perceive legislation as a burden, we believe that good practice in the handling of information can actually benefit the running of the business, as well as reduce the risks that the organization may be exposed to through non-compliance. Companies should also consider appointing an IT security manager; although some companies may consider this a waste of resources, there are many benefits to be reaped from such a move. Although, with the international adoption of BS7799, the UK became a world leader in the definition of security policies, very few companies have a formal policy in place. The value of having a professional individual dedicated to maintaining the security of a company's assets from attack by disenchanted individuals, whether from inside or outside the company, must surely justify the salary the IT security manager commands. Employing an IT security manager, however, does not absolve a company's directors from their ultimate responsibility for managing the risk.

Ethical hacking

When a company provides a service to users over the Internet, extranet or intranet, it exposes its organization to risks. Every service opens a new path into the organization. 'Intruders' can exploit these paths into the organization's network and data. Some disreputable organizations may even deliberately set out to steal intellectual assets or create distrust amongst customers. The organization can be embarrassed or interrupted in the best cases, and can lose customers and money at worst. So, ethical hacking can detect vulnerabilities that leave clients open to attack. It ensures that environments are tested using a range of tools and in ways that 'black-hat' hackers use to penetrate Web sites and e-commerce environments. 'Ethical hackers' can simulate a real intruder's attacks but in a controlled, safe way. They will tell a company what they find and how it can fix it to keep them out.

Anti-money-laundering

Companies also need to ensure they have the most up-to-date and leading-edge technology in place to minimize the risk of attack. On 8 January 2001, Searchspace, an IBM business partner, launched the first artificial intelligence business operating system that will, among other things, automate compliance and financial reporting. Intelligent Enterprise Framework will link into all firms' existing legacy systems and intelligently monitor every single transaction to build an evolving picture of the organization and its customers. The system can continually expand its understanding of each particular business and its customers, automate core business decisions and at the same time treat electronic customers as real individuals. IEF has six key processes, including sentinels. Sentinels are trained to monitor particular types of transactions and activities, such as audit concerns, operational risk, compliance management or fraud detection. They patrol all the transactions across the enterprise, looking for activity that requires further investigation or action. The sentinels also provide a full audit trail by breaking down their decision path as well as the reason and context for their decision.

Risk assessment

One of the first things companies should do to test the efficiency of their systems is to carry out a risk assessment, focused on assessing the current state of information security within the organization. The aim of the assessment should be to:

- gain an understanding of the business environment and business goals;
- identify weaknesses in processes, awareness and working practices that affect information security;
- review relevant documentation and assess general compliance;
- assess information security policies and guidelines;
- review change management procedures;
- review incident response and management;
- review asset classification;
- review business continuity planning;
- assess the effectiveness of the information security organization and any existing security programmes.

Smart cards

Many existing Web applications protect the confidentiality of communication through encryption using the well-established SSL, Transport Layer Security (TLS) or Wireless Transport Layer Security (WTLS) protocols. This protection of confidentiality is efficient and considered adequate. For user authentication, the currently established method employs a user identifier and password. A password provides only limited security because it can be stolen in many ways. An additional means of authentication, for example, through biometry ('what you are') or through additional cryptographic hardware ('what you possess'), provides additional protection. A smart card used as a mobile personal cryptographic token is optimally suited for this purpose. To secure an individual transaction, a password by itself is not sufficient. Less common methods have been applied in using passwords so far, for example one-time passwords or Transaction Authorization Numbers (TANs), both of which have to be manually fetched and entered by the user. To secure individual transactions and to achieve non-repudiation, a smart card is an attractive option.

Business continuity and disaster recovery

When it comes to backup and disaster recovery, most companies focus too much on protecting IT equipment and not enough on protecting their overall business. In the wake of the WTC disaster, IBM business partner BI-Tech Solutions conducted a series of Business Continuity and Recovery workshops for their clients – senior IT managers in financial services institutions. BI-Tech Solutions (Business Impact Technology Solutions) is a company dedicated to simplifying the management and security of distributed business information assets, providing solutions for business continuity, business recovery and enterprise storage as well as infrastructure design and implementation, service and support.

Amongst the findings were the following.

PRESENT PROBLEMS

- Off-site delayed recovery – focused on limited server platforms and limited user population.
- No real-time list of key users who must be recovered in a disaster recovery situation.
- Would not meet business expectation of recovery.
- Staff resources insufficient to cope with manual recovery.
- Depends on human intervention.
- Business not prepared for loss of key disaster recovery staff.
- Key vendors not integrated into the disaster recovery plan and have no contracted service level agreements.
- Maintenance of disaster recovery plans not consistent.
- Interfaces/feeds not replicated.
- Insufficient real estate for use in disaster recovery situation.
- Telephony/fax/telex not fully replicated.
- Desktop technology in disaster recovery not maintained.
- No audit of server recoverability.
- No understanding of risk profile or metrics for disaster recovery.
- Data is backed up on legacy media, legacy servers, legacy database, legacy applications.
- Disaster recovery plans are not located off site.
- Incomplete disaster recovery plan and limited testing.
- Political restraints inhibiting delivery of disaster recovery plan.
- Geography not far enough apart.
- Public infrastructure dependency (national).
- Cost to maintain is high.

- Country / city dependent.

Desired state

- No loss of continuity of business in event of disaster.
- Seamless transfer of service (no human intervention), with self-sensing automated failover.
- Acceptable level of cost to maintain and invoke appropriate disaster recovery.
- Disaster recovery based on documented and signed-off business requirements.
- One hundred per cent availability in case of capability – people / technology / buildings.
- Mobility.
- Immune from virus attack or hacking.
- Affordable / measurable.
- Verifiable and regular testing.
- Global compliance.
- Full capability (100 per cent business solutions).
- Integrated with day-to-day business.
- No data loss.

CASE STUDY

One of the leading financial services organizations in Europe realized a need to deliver risk management through an enterprise-wide system, while continuing to manage operational costs. At the same time the market was becoming progressively more unpredictable – and this, coupled with an increasingly knowledgeable and accessible customer base, required the bank to seek out a system to automate its business process and provide strong 'know your customer' functionality.

This visionary institution implemented the Searchspace enterprise-wide IEF framework and appropriate sentinels to comply seamlessly with regulatory requirements and in turn realized significant operational savings through the re-engineering of internal controls. The bank is now an intelligent, automated enterprise that is able to streamline its business processes and operate at a level of maximum efficiency, handling both risk and opportunity in a seamless manner.

Prior to installing the Searchspace solution, the bank relied completely on manual methods to deal with regulatory compliance and operational risk management tasks, requiring substantial internal resources to be continually applied. In addition to the significant resources needed to effectively monitor its operational business activities, the numerous review points introduced inconsistencies to the overall process and significantly increased error rates. Since the installation of the system, many instances of suspicious activity have been detected and dealt with accordingly. IEF also provides the bank with a consistent and systematic level of regulatory compliance, and regulators now regard the institution as an example for other financial service organizations to follow.

Owing to the increasingly service-centred nature of their business, combined with the bank's customers' increasing utilization of online and other electronic banking methods, the institution needed the Searchspace system to systematically monitor all of its clients' behaviour, both to scrutinize for suspicious activity and to ensure each customer was benefiting appropriately from the bank's services. The technology from Searchspace continually monitors each of the millions of transactions that flow through the organization on a daily basis, regardless of their origin, enabling analysts to receive notifications of suspicious behaviour immediately. The intelligent lifestyle triggers generated in the system enable the bank to closely monitor the services used by each customer, prompting cross-selling and up-selling situations.

Eliminating manual controls and implementing a system that enables continuous monitoring of transactions allows the bank to reduce its overall headcount and ensure that each employee is performing the tasks most conducive to overall business efficiency. As the market changes and therefore demands new solutions and processes, the institution is empowered to use the data collected to modify its business plans automatically without the need for human intervention.

The business process that results from implementing the system ensures that notifications are sent proactively to the appropriate user, activity is analysed and actions initiated in a fraction of the time when compared to manual monitoring, with virtually no error rate. This decreases the cost of additional employee hours and the loss in profitability associated with events such as false alarms.

CONCLUSION

Business is challenged by the need to comply with legislation, to deal fairly with customers, and at the same time protect itself from attack. However, as already outlined, there are many excellent tools that can be employed to minimize the risk of exposure. To summarize, companies should consider:

- conducting a risk assessment;
- hiring the services of ethical hackers;
- purchasing a cutting-edge system to prevent money laundering;
- ensuring all staff dealing with personal data understand the implications of data protection legislation;

- appointing an IT security manager;
- employing the use of smart cards;
- reviewing business continuity and disaster recover plans and conducting a periodic test of the plans.

21

Customer service, complaints management and regulatory compliance

Joy Terentis, Fabian Sander, David Cox, Merlin Stone and Maureen Madden

The aim of this chapter is to investigate the current state of complaints management in the UK financial services industry and identify what it needs to do to become compliant with the regulatory requirement. It examines the regulatory requirements for the management of customer complaints in financial services. It describes the outcomes of new research, which shows that most financial services companies are some way from being able to meet these new regulatory requirements. It identifies the processes that must be followed to fulfil these requirements, and outlines the type of system that is likely to be able to support meeting these requirements. Finally, it identifies that the probable reason for the neglect of this area is the heavy involvement of most financial services companies' customer service functions in meeting the needs of the sales process (before, during and after the sale) rather than the more traditional role of customer service – listening to customers and solving their problems.

INTRODUCTION

The Financial Services Authority (FSA) became the single regulator for financial services in the UK at midnight on 30 November 2001, when the Financial Services and Markets Act

(FSMA) 2000 was implemented. The FSA requires firms to have in place an appropriate written complaints procedure and to ensure that this is operated effectively. This requirement is supplemented by specific rules setting out the minimum standards these procedures are expected to meet, including:

- publishing complaints procedures and making them easily available to consumers;
- investigating complaints promptly, within appropriate timescales;
- offering appropriate levels of redress where complaints are upheld;
- keeping records of complaints and reporting aggregate data to the FSA;
- cooperating with the Financial Ombudsman Service (FOS) in its investigation of complaints.

Complaints for FSA-authorized firms for which record keeping and reporting are required are those that involve allegations of financial loss and/or material distress or inconvenience (ie those handled by the ombudsman).

IMPACT OF THE FSA COMPLAINTS REQUIREMENTS

One of the first effects on firms was the need to revise their existing literature so as to improve consumer access to complaints procedures, and to ensure compliance of literature by 1 January 2002. Firms are also required to publicize their membership of the FOS. Secondly, firms need to introduce new systems to capture data and to report to the FSA bi-annually (first report due 31 March 2003) on:

- the number of complaints received;
- the percentage of complaints resolved within the four-week and eight-week period stated in the rules;
- a breakdown according to the subject matter of those complaints (a list of approximately 20 categories has been drafted with views being sought from the industry).

The FSA also proposes that certain types of 'small business' be treated as private consumers with the same rights to register complaints. The key issues are how 'small businesses' are defined (the FSA will introduce a common definition) and whether a common definition is appropriate for all sectors of the industry. Companies that participated in the research for this chapter believe that the 20 categories now included in the definition of an FSA complaint will significantly increase the volume of communications considered to be complaints and thus the workload of customer services and complaints handlers.

There are five main areas of focus on complaints:

1. Time limits – firms must either resolve complaints within four weeks or explain why the complaint has not been resolved, in which case an additional four weeks' processing time applies.
2. Access – firms must publish details of their complaints handling procedures and make them easily available to consumers. In particular, firms should publicize the availability of their complaints procedures and their membership of the Ombudsman Scheme at the initial point of sale and should send complainants a copy of these procedures when a complaint is first made
3. Reporting – twice yearly reports on the level and types of complaints received by firms should be provided to the FSA (this requirement now also applies to firms subject only to prudential supervision).
4. Recording – firms should make and retain records on any complaints received for a set period (six years).
5. Handling – firms should investigate all complaints promptly and ensure they are adequately reviewed, and that consumers are kept informed of the progress.

For each of these, firms are likely to have some kind of procedure in place, either because of regulatory requirements or their own internal control arrangements. Responses by firms to the FSA requirements could be anything from upgrading / revamping an existing system to installation of a new bespoke system.

OTHER FINANCIAL SERVICES COMPLAINT STANDARDS AND REQUIREMENTS

Companies that have signed up to the General Insurance Standards Council (GISC) and the Strategic and Long Term Risk (SALTR) standards will need to meet the complaints requirements of those bodies to gain the necessary approvals and accreditation, designed to improve customer confidence in the industry. For those firms also regulated by the FSA, meeting FSA requirements is likely to mean compliance with GISC and SALTR. A key aim of SALTR is to improve customer service. An accreditation scheme run by the Pensions, Protection and Investments Accreditation Board (PPIAB) has been established to focus on improving customer service. The central intention is to raise standards throughout the industry on a voluntary basis, complementary to the role of existing legislation and statutory bodies such as the FSA. One SALTR standard is designed for complaints management. There are related standards for customer service. The requirement is for yearly statements, clear and comparable information, and presentation of charges. Forty-five well-known financial services brands have signed up for SALTR accreditation and the first successful applicants were announced in September 2001.

In the *FSA Handbook* there are rules and guidance on the subject of 'Senior Manager Arrangements, Systems and Controls' which support the FSA's Principle for Business number three, 'A firm must take reasonable care to organize and control its affairs responsibly and effectively, with adequate risk management systems.' In practice this has major implications for the CEO and a firm's directors to adapt current processes and systems to meet all the new regulatory requirements, including managing cross-departmental/functional risks and contingency planning in the event of a regulatory failure. For example, the customer services director and head of customer complaint handling 'must take reasonable care to establish and maintain such customer services systems and controls as are appropriate to the scale, nature and complexity of its business'. Senior and middle managers in customer services must ensure that those in the customer services department/team responsible for the control systems are sufficiently qualified, competent and experienced. In addition, they must take particular care regarding:

- anti-money-laundering;
- compliance training programmes;
- systems of supervision;
- risk assessment.

The regulator requires that the business and affairs of the firm, including customer management, are adequately monitored and controlled by the directors, relevant senior executives and the governing body of the firm. Compliance with the regulatory requirements is to be taken very seriously as the consequences of failure are individual censure by fining, and/or exclusion from the financial services industry. The people, processes and technology involved in customer management, customer service, and complaints handling, in the financial services industry, need to be of the highest calibre and best quality appropriate to the particular business. The FSA's Principle for Business number seven on communications with customers states that 'A firm must pay due regard to the information needs of its customers, and communicate information to them in a way which is clear, fair and not misleading.'

CUSTOMER SERVICE AND COMPLAINTS MANAGEMENT SURVEY

Major changes in regulation of the industry by the GISC and the newly empowered FSA raise challenges, especially for customer service and customer management, around data storage and protection, reporting and other issues related to compliance to regulatory issues. In July 2001 IBM sent out a survey to more than 50 companies mainly operating in the insurance sector; however, major players in other sectors of financial services were also included. The survey contained questions about customer service processes, technology and complaint-handling issues, providing a good overview of what is currently in place in the industry. The data has now been analysed, identifying main issues and likely areas of improvement; main conclusions have been included in this report.

The purpose of the survey was to:

- ascertain the degree of centralization of customer service and complaints management functions;
- identify the main channels in which customer feedback and complaints are received;
- establish the level of formalization and use of customer service/complaints management processes;
- establish the existence and extent of performance measurements in different categories;
- identify the current state of technology and e-enablement in the industry;
- consider the likely impact on customer service management and standards, of the impending new requirements from the FSA and GSIC;
- identify main areas of improvement in order to meet a company's strategic goals.

Additional data was derived from the scores database from QCi's Customer Management Assessment Tool (see Chapter 3 for more on CMAT). For the analysis of this report a range of questions related to customer service and in-bound client contacts has been selected. The scores represent the average extent to which companies are compliant with good practice – a company scores 0 for very poor compliance for an individual attribute, up to 100 for having an attribute that represents best practice. The average CMAT score for all companies, all attributes, is around 40 per cent.

CENTRALIZATION VS DECENTRALIZATION OF CUSTOMER SERVICE

Our survey shows (Figure 21.1) that customer service functions are distributed throughout most organizations, rather than centralized in a single department. Seventy-seven per cent of companies use a decentralized approach to customer service, which could impede the consistency and quality of data and have an effect on the continuity of processes throughout the whole company, and also the use of the customer data base for data analysis and data mining.

Mergers and acquisitions can lead to a decentralized structure for the business as a whole and also customer service, including complaint handling. However, among survey

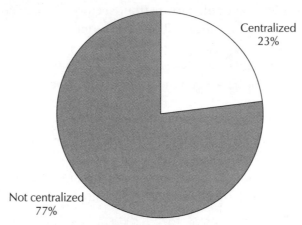

Figure 21.1 Proportion of centralized customer service among survey respondents

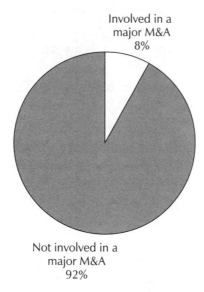

Figure 21.2 Mergers and acquisitions activity among respondents 1999–2001

respondents, only 8 per cent had been involved in a major merger or acquisition in the previous two years (Figure 21.2).

As a result, distribution of data and access to relevant information for customer-facing staff is not always guaranteed. The average CMAT score for the question 'Is the customer database accessible to all staff whose role involves significant customer contact in a way that matches their needs?' was only 42 per cent – not even half the points achievable with a system enabling all relevant staff to use data as required.

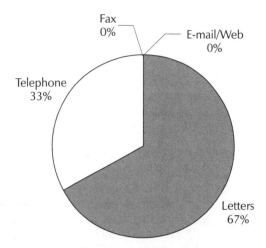

Figure 21.3 Most commonly used channel for incoming customer contacts

CHANNELS OF COMMUNICATION FOR INBOUND CUSTOMER CONTACTS

Our survey found that letters are the most commonly used method of communicating complaints to companies (see Figure 21.3). For 67 per cent of businesses, this is still the main channel. E-mail and the Web were not major channels. Interestingly, of the companies whose customers communicate mostly by letter, only 50 per cent have systems capable of scanning documents. Manual processing is still widespread in the industry.

CUSTOMER SERVICE AND COMPLAINTS HANDLING PROCESSES

Amongst most survey participants, customer service procedures are documented and kept up to date, but although one respondent made them available over the intranet, they are mainly in paper manuals, and often not indexed for ease of use (see Figure 21.4). As mentioned before, every customer-facing employee should have full knowledge of the service process, and also have access to updated information. Non-electronic storage of process information makes it more difficult to update and distribute process information.

When we examine in detail how process documentation is created and stored, it seems that most companies do not have easy access to, or measurement of, the process. CMAT scores within financial services averaged 28 per cent. Also, processes for incorporating customer feedback into new product development are not well developed in the industry. The average CMAT score of companies operating in the financial services industry is only

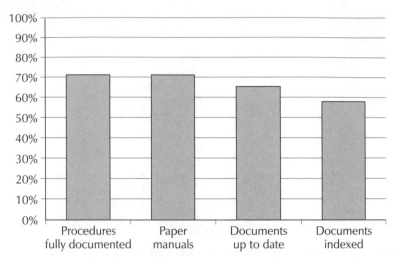

Figure 21.4 State of customer service process documentation

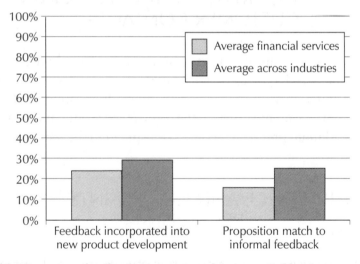

Figure 21.5 CMAT scores – feedback incorporated in essential business processes

24 per cent (see Figure 21.5). Interestingly, that score is also less than the average of all industries – 29 per cent. Another CMAT question, asking if the customer proposition is constructed to reflect informal feedback from prospects and customers, did not give a better picture. Here the average score amongst players operating in the financial services industry is only 16 per cent of possible points achievable, compared to 25 per cent across all industries (see Figure 21.5).

CMAT analysis also shows that there is a lack of integration between customer service processes and business processes. Companies are failing to put processes into place, and to make it easy to communicate the results of enquiries back to their point of capture (see

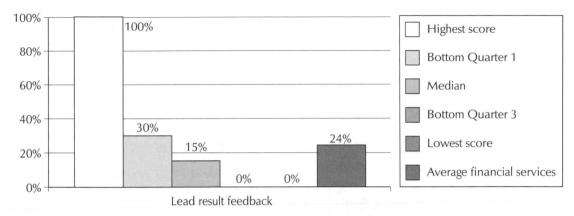

Figure 21.6 CMAT scores – process for enquiries results feedback

Figure 21.6). The average score ranged at only 24 per cent, while 41 per cent of companies could not achieve any score and 50 per cent of businesses scored 15 per cent of points achievable or less.

COMPLIANCE AND DATA PROTECTION

Implications of current and planned data protection legislation are not well understood in the industry. The average score amongst companies in the financial services industry was only 41 per cent. International companies in particular find themselves facing chaos, with the different sets of legislation being imposed (see Chapter 22 for more on this).

CUSTOMER SERVICE AND COMPLAINTS HANDLING – PERSONNEL ISSUES

Nearly all our survey respondents stated that a trained employee could pick up a complaint, even if another employee originally handled the complaint. Only one participant stated that this was not possible. The CMAT analysis draws a different picture. Asking for clear visibility of the status of a complaint, 50 per cent of companies scored 30 per cent or less of achievable points (see Figure 21.7). This feature is obviously required to pick up a complaint in process, but 29 per cent of companies scored zero on this question, and the average score lies at only 37 per cent.

Process continuity requires a long period of training. It usually takes over a week to train an employee on a customer service and complaints handling system. It emerged that businesses that only require several hours to train their employees on their systems have very

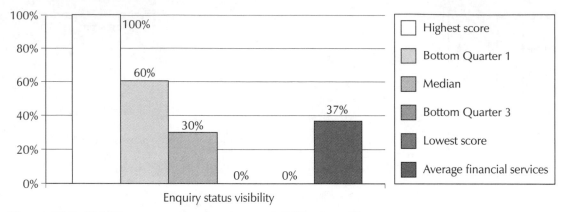

Figure 21.7 CMAT scores – enquiry status visibility to staff

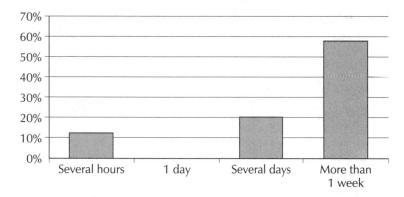

Figure 21.8 Time required for staff training

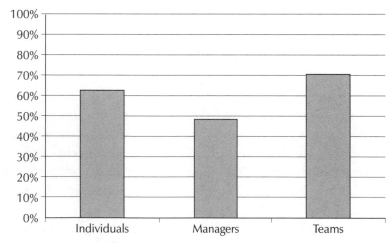

Figure 21.9 Proportion of performance measurement in current systems

basic systems in place (see Figure 21.8). These systems cannot offer the functionality required for good practice customer service and complaints handling.

The survey identified the proportion of companies that measure the performance of individuals, managers or teams in this area (see Figure 21.9). Individuals and teams are usually measured to a greater extent than managers, but that could be dangerous bearing in mind that support from senior management is crucial to successful customer management and customer service.

CUSTOMER SERVICES AND COMPLAINTS HANDLING TECHNOLOGY

Various databases and spreadsheets were the prevailing technology for customer service and complaints handling among respondents (see Figure 21.10). Such methods can hardly be used for customer data analysis or data mining, and they were usually widely spread throughout a department or, as most of the respondents had no centralized customer service department, throughout the whole organization. Also, the structure of ownership is mostly vast and complicated, making it difficult to organize campaigns or coordinate contacts between different parts of the organization. After systems built in-house came specialist bespoke software. From a security and unique requirements point of view, you might instinctively approach your own IT department to build a system for handling customer-controlled contacts, but some of the companies in our research that took this approach regretted it. They believed that the software would be easy to build, but this turned out not always to be the case.

We mentioned the current inability of businesses to cope with the increasing load of complaints and enquiries they face. The structure and technology used for customer service systems are simply not able to cope with the growing demand, and communication through a restricted number of channels is the result. CMAT data underpins this impression with the results from the question on convenient access to organizations through communication channels. Here the average score amongst companies in financial services ranged at 44 per cent – less than half of the points achievable for businesses that are completely accessible to their customers (see Figure 21.11). CMAT analysis also shows that companies do not really check the level of performance and acceptability of their technology to their customers. For this question, the average score amongst businesses operating in the financial services industry lies at only 21 per cent, and 47 per cent of companies failed to score at all.

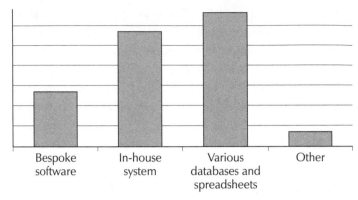

Figure 21.10 Currently used technology for customer services and complaint handling

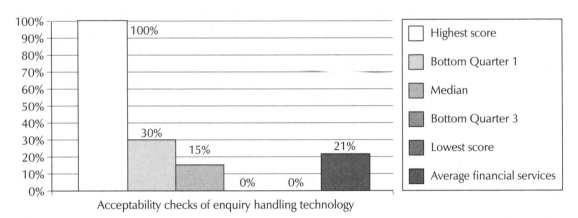

Figure 21.11 CMAT scores – regular enquirer acceptability checks for implemented technology

FUNCTIONALITY PROVIDED BY SYSTEMS

Together with its partners, IBM has developed the following set of essential functions for improved customer service systems and complaints handling:

- scanning of documentation;
- creation of documents from templates in order to make workflow electronic;
- analysis of customer satisfaction;
- root cause analysis in order to find original reasons for complaints;
- feedback to other organizational units in order to integrate processes and the customer service department into the organization;
- activity analysis for customer service for ability of performance measurement and cost analysis;

- reporting to the board in order to maintain informational function and integration into the organization and to reinforce senior management commitment;
- reporting to the regulator in order to satisfy regulatory requirements;
- regulatory tracking in order to satisfy data protection and compliance issues.

On average, 53 per cent of those surveyed had systems capable of implementing the functions suggested above. In our view, all functions are essential for good customer service and complaints handling (see Figure 21.12). One problem throughout the financial services industry seems to be getting the right technology in place. Some businesses have tackled the systems issue well, and are now able to leverage the advantages of a system providing full functionality, but the overwhelming majority are still behind, or at worst their systems do not provide any functionality at all. The CMAT data suggests that most systems provide only basic analysis features. Businesses scored on average only 28 per cent of points relating to the question (see Figure 21.13). If they had put the information held on customers into a data warehouse (or similar) and used data mining (or similar) techniques to identify trends and patterns, they would have been able to benefit from the advantages previously mentioned.

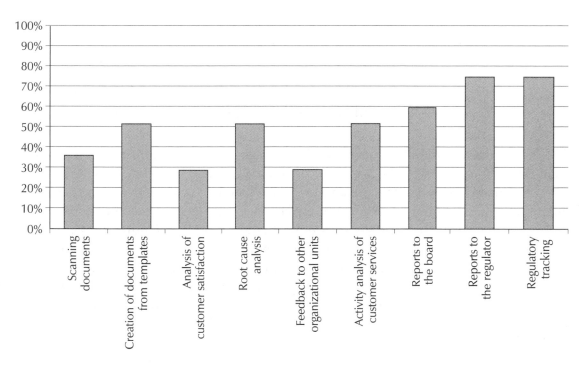

Figure 21.12 Essential functionality available in current customer service systems

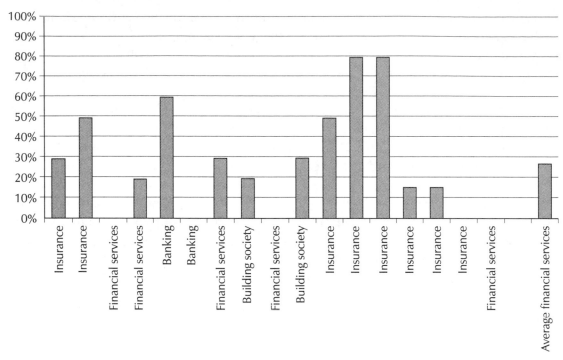

Figure 21.13 CMAT scores – combined customer data analysis – financial services

USE OF NEW MEDIA

CMAT analysis also reveals issues around the usage of new communication technologies such as e-mail or the Web. The average score on the question 'Has the customer database been developed/upgraded to store and use information on customers which enables full benefit to be gained from the World Wide Web?' was only 26 per cent, and 47 per cent of companies could not achieve any score on this question (see Figure 21.14). Another question was related to regular consideration of new media for customer contact. Here the average score looked a bit better, 41 per cent, but still less than half the points achievable. Also, 24 per cent of companies scored zero on this question. Businesses do marginally better in handling Internet enquiries. The average was 52 per cent, over half of the available points.

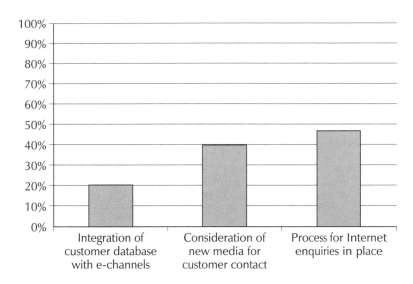

Figure 21.14 CMAT scores – usage of new media

CUSTOMER SERVICE – IMPROVEMENT AND STRATEGIC GOALS

Almost all respondents are aware of the necessity to improve, and 92 per cent stated that they plan to improve their customer service and complaints handling operations. This seems reasonable, considering the systems on which their operations are based. However, only 17 per cent of those companies that plan to improve are willing to use third-party assistance.

We asked survey participants to rate the importance of different aspects of customer service and complaints handling to their strategic goals. The issues they were asked to rate were:

- speed up complaint resolution time;
- increase accuracy of complaint resolution;
- increase customer service quality;
- reduce costs of customer service and complaints handling.

The main priority was to increase accuracy of complaint resolution, followed by the overall improvement of customer services quality (see Figure 21.15). The industry is fully aware that action must be taken.

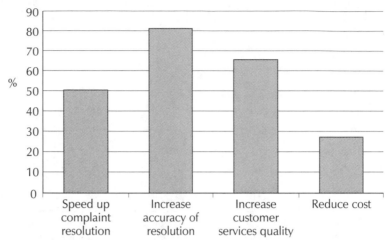

Figure 21.15 Importance of customer service to the strategic goals of survey respondents

BEST-CASE SCENARIO

A bank reached the highest score in our survey (see Figure 21.16). Although its customer service functions are not centralized, its system provides the full range of functionalities essential for quality customer service and complaints handling. The bank uses a bespoke software package alongside various databases and spreadsheets, which is possibly the reason for its achievement.

The proportion of complaints that had to be referred to an Ombudsman in the best-case scenario was 3 per cent, representing only a fifth of the maximum 15 per cent (see Figure 21.17). It is also less than the average proportion identified by the survey.

The quality of data entered into and produced by the system is checked weekly which is also above average. However, even though they are running a system close to the state of the art, they still plan to improve their customer service and complaints management.

WORST-CASE SCENARIO

A life assurer reached the lowest score amongst respondents. Its current system, consisting of various databases and spreadsheets, doesn't provide any of the functionality that we see as essential for good practice customer service and complaints handling. Customer service and complaints handling processes and procedures are neither fully documented, nor is the documentation up to date, or indexed for ease of use. Documentation exists in the form of paper manuals. Another employee cannot pick up previously entered complaints, and

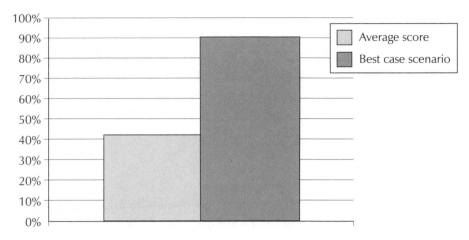

Figure 21.16 Functionality provided by the average and best case system

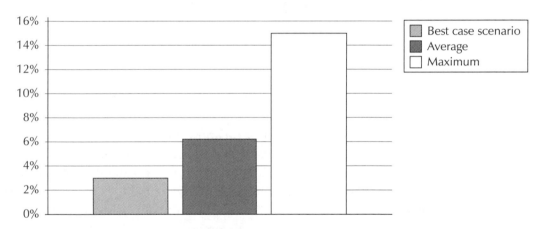

Figure 21.17 Complaints being referred to Ombudsman

quality of entered data is not checked at all. Also, performance measurement is only possible for individuals and managers; teams are neglected.

RECOMMENDATIONS

Strive for good practice customer service and complaints handling

As we saw, customer service, and especially complaints handling, can have a crucial effect on satisfaction, loyalty and retention of customers. That's why good practice customer service and complaints handling are a vital requirement for companies operating in a marketplace characterized by fierce competition and increasingly powerful customers. Using documentation in the form of paper manuals, and closing down communication channels because your company is not able to cope with the load of customer-initiated contacts, obstructs the way to good practice customer service. There is a need for most companies surveyed to change processes, procedures and technology, and invest in a system that enables them to provide top of the range service to their customers.

Customer retention

As a result, improved customer service and complaints handling would lead to a higher customer retention rate. Instead of switching companies for no particular reason, customers might be motivated to stay, encouraged by their experiences when dealing with the customer service department. Even if customer retention doesn't have a direct impact on the ROI, increased sales to a growing customer base will have.

Direct effects on ROI

Additionally, implementing the right system is likely to lead rapidly to a positive return on investment. Our success stories are good examples of this. The positive impact on employee productivity and motivation, as well as on knowledge about their customer base, enables companies to improve the way business is done. Cross-selling opportunities can be identified, and fewer full-time employees are required to serve a greater customer base in a more effective and efficient way. The reduction in time and staff allows for immense cost cutting. A faster response time when dealing with enquiries allows companies to strengthen their customer base and acquire new customers.

Centralization without changing the organizational structure

A sophisticated system can also fundamentally change the way customer service departments work. Almost all respondents to our survey had decentralized customer service and complaints handling functions in place. That doesn't necessarily have to change; implementing the right system can still make a vital improvement. Different workgroups and teams could be enabled to work on one central customer database, while the different departments and functions are distributed throughout the company. Centralization of customer data is key to enabling advanced data analysis, data warehousing and data mining. A system that embraces all customer service functions in a company, and collates all relevant information about customers, contacts, campaigns, etc, would also enable better integration of customer service and complaints handling processes into those of the rest of the organization. In general, centralized data management, which does not have to result in centralized data storage – a distributed DBMS could do the job – is vital for learning from customer contacts and improving product and service offerings.

Integrated business processes and procedures

Good practice customer service and complaints handling is not achieved only by integrating systems and data into a single, possibly distributed architecture. Another primary objective of customer service, apart from achieving customer satisfaction and thus loyalty, should be learning from the customer contact experience. This is enabled by opening communication channels, processing gathered information throughout the company, and incorporating valuable data about customer preferences and wishes into value propositions. Additionally, business processes have to be adapted and integrated in order to increase the accuracy and speed of dealing with customer complaints. Customer service should not be seen as a necessary attachment to the company, but an integral part of business, especially as it deals with customers – the real assets of companies operating in a fiercely competitive market.

E-enablement – another key to success

Customers can establish contact with companies in only a few seconds through new channels and enabling technology. However, many companies still do not use similar technology to organize and, more importantly, speed up their processes and procedures. E-enabled customer service and complaints handling is a vital requirement. A quick response to enquiries is dependent on electronic handling of these enquiries; on documentation of processes and procedure being updated and distributed in a much easier and precise way, and on information for customer-facing staff being distributed to anybody who needs it. Also, complaints can be resolved with increased accuracy due to the immediate availability of the required information and case history, as well as possible root cause analysis, which gives additional clues about the reasons for complaints.

Address regulatory issues by choosing the right system

Compliance with regulatory issues is a hot topic for boardrooms today. We have already mentioned the requirements which affect customer service and complaints handling. The right system can, and should, help companies meet these requirements. Compliant data storage, retrieval and protection have to be addressed. The system should warn the operators prior to regulatory deadlines, and reporting to the regulator should be enhanced and simplified using powerful data-warehousing mechanisms. Best-of-breed products are more likely to be able to build the internal reports required by the regulator and, being easier to use, can assist in preparing for, and dealing with, high and / or fluctuating volumes of customer contacts. Speed and efficiency gains can be made through systems that provide full audit trails, online monitoring, audit and review by the firm's compliance department. Safety in terms of regulatory compliance is a vital requirement for companies, especially in the context of the all-embracing power the Financial Services Authority gained on 30 November 2001.

Ultimately, complaints which are resolved to a complainant's satisfaction do not get referred to the Financial Ombudsman Service, which not only charges a firm by case, but is also likely to require further redress to be paid. In our survey, between 3 and 15 per cent of cases are resolved by the Ombudsman, which could be reduced to zero by better practices and systems, simultaneously reducing costs and improving customer satisfaction. A full audit trail of a complaint also means that if referred to the Ombudsman, he or she is more likely to agree with the firm's findings and not require further redress.

Bespoke or 'off-the-shelf' software vs in-house design

This is normally one of the most difficult decisions to make. From a security and unique requirements point of view, a company might instinctively approach its own IT department to build a system for handling customer-controlled contacts. Some companies in our survey took this approach and regretted it. They believed that the software would be easy to build, but this is not always the case. There are now several good products on the market. Here are some reasons why it may be better to take the product route:

- A good product will incorporate many features that are standard to all customer service operations, irrespective of the industry sector. Why reinvent the wheel? Such a product will be based on the many actual experiences of other major companies running effective customer service operations, and the system may therefore add considerably to current procedures.
- A good system can be purchased as an 'off-the-shelf' package with 90 per cent functionality, and can be further customized or tailored by the supplier to meet a company's exact requirements.
- A company's IT department may not have the right programming skills, or sufficient time, to develop easy-to-use customer service systems. They may be more focused on developing and maintaining the company's core transaction processing systems, and customer service systems might take a lower priority.

Also, it is usually more cost-effective to purchase a product than develop in-house.

CONCLUSION

This study shows that the customer service function, as traditionally defined, is at the back end of the queue when it comes to systems and processes. It seems to us that because call centres have (not incorrectly) become a key focus for CRM, with as much emphasis on their ability to sell (whether or not the customer is calling with this in mind), complaints management has been neglected. Our survey shows just how bad the situation is. As our chapter on data protection shows (Chapter 22), companies must be careful not to let too large a gap emerge between what regulators want and what they are achieving. The gap is *very* large in complaints management.

22

Data protection[1]

Genevieve Findlay, Merlin Stone, Matt Leonard, Martin Evans and Barry McEnroe

INTRODUCTION

There is increasing international focus on data protection. Although different countries have taken different stances, leading to an inconsistent set of rules, there is increasing pressure to work together to protect the rights of consumers as personal information crosses international borders. Data protection under European legislation is particularly stringent. This chapter shows that when it comes to managing customer data, many companies still need to do a lot of work on quality. It also shows that senior management is not focusing enough on the issue of data quality. The popularity of CRM lies behind these issues. CRM strategies usually involve a company gathering much more customer information from various sources, placing it in a central repository for segmentation, analysis and reuse. A 'single view of the customer' is a frequently cited aspiration of many CRM projects. But it is this very bringing together of information into a single database or several databases that can potentially be at odds with the law. The data chaos caused by the scramble for customer data has led many companies to be in direct contravention of these strict laws because they lack the rigorous processes required to keep them compliant. In most cases:

- there is no process for ensuring that the customer has full access to all personal data;
- there is no process for reviewing, refreshing and discarding data on a regular basis;

- there is inadequate protection of data being transferred between countries with different data protection standards.

Many companies are ignorant that they are breaking the law in this way. However, the issue is broader than compliance with legislation. For while the threat of prosecution, fines or closure of a Web site is very real, the loss of customer confidence and trust is more alarming. This chapter shows what companies can do to improve the quality of their customer data and how it is used. The focus of this chapter extends beyond financial services, not only because this issue is a general one, but also because many financial services companies are involved in other sectors and need to be aware of the data protection issues that affect these sectors.

The research for this paper was carried out using a number of sources: 1) results of a Data Protection Questionnaire sent to key CRM representatives in over 20 blue-chip companies and CRM strategists, and; 2) customer management assessment scores (70 companies in many sectors were evaluated using QCi's Customer Management Assessment Tool – see Chapter 3 for more on CMAT).

OVERVIEW

Data protection and privacy issues are coming to the fore again in the age of the Web. Citizens are concerned about the use of data they give on the Web, reinforcing an old concern first raised in classic direct marketing contexts (telephone, mail). These concerns were never really completely resolved, although the introduction of mail and telephone preference schemes, together with the improving control of major marketers over their direct mail and telemarketing activities, have in general reduced the public attention focused on problems associated with errors and intrusiveness. However, the introduction of three new channels to the world of customer relationship management – interactive digital TV, mobile telephones and the Web – has created the need to re-examine the extent to which companies are in control of their customer data. This is because these three new media have much greater potential for intrusiveness and for gathering data from the customer than older media, and also for gathering it when the customer is not conscious of its gathering.

Whether citizens are surfing the Internet, using a mobile phone or exploring the interactive pages of digital television, they are producing data for the companies that supply them. They are also open to being targeted with commercial offers. The issues discussed in this chapter should be of interest to government, citizens/consumers and companies, because in these new environments, the potential for customer data to be used illegally is much greater. How well are companies prepared for this new era of interactivity, when it comes to how they manage customer data? The answer, as this chapter shows, is – not very well. The reason – senior managers are not focusing on quality issues in customer data management.

So desperate are companies for better customer information that the overall spend on CRM projects has risen dramatically and is set to rise further. However, in the scramble to acquire more customers and to implement more and more data-driven applications to collect even more detailed customer data to help retain and develop them, 'data chaos' has ensued. Data is being gleaned from the ever-increasing number of different channels without any secure process for maintaining that data to an appropriate quality standard. Often multi-channel strategies fail because what is right for one channel cannot be replicated across all the others. Ownership of data is frequently spread across many different departments and business units, making management and responsibility for the integrity of the data as a whole almost impossible.

Where senior management is focused on topics relating to customers, it is on classic CRM topics, such as customer retention, and not on customer data. This is despite the fact that that our work indicates that: 1) the quality of customer data management is not strong, and; 2) attention focused on customer data is not wasted.

The various studies we have seen about senior management priorities in related areas indicate that the main topics exercising senior management are these:

- deregulation;
- competitive entry;
- merger and acquisition;
- risk;
- e-business and (in some cases) wireless aspects;
- CRM;
- marketing and sales efficiency;
- distribution channel uncertainties;
- long-term shifts in demand patterns.

In many cases, these issues are combined. For example, the impending further deregulation of the motor industry (the end of the European Union Block Exemption allowing motor manufacturers to specify that motor dealers deal solely in a single brand) is leading to a strong interest in CRM, e-business and a search for alternative distribution channels. The risk associated with changing climate patterns is causing property insurance companies to consider how to modify their CRM efforts to ensure that they do not attract too many customers with recently enhanced levels of risk. Competitive entry by e-banks is causing traditional banks to bolster their own e-operations, but also to focus their CRM efforts on customer retention and development. Retailers and airlines who have failed to address longer-term shifts in demand patterns are reconsidering their CRM efforts – in some cases enhancing them, but in others reducing them in favour of a stronger focus on the core offer.

Of course, management focus is not just a question of underlying forces. It is also directed by the efforts of companies marketing relevant products and services. For example, the enormous budgets dedicated by CRM software suppliers and their partners to advertising and exhibitions have undoubtedly helped sustain the salience of CRM. The same can be said for a variety of systems companies in relation to e-business. Publicity from major management consultancies and research companies reinforces the agenda, although at least in the latter case some are now focusing on reasons for failure. Paradoxically, in some cases it is senior management's drive in other areas that is reducing compliance with data protection laws. Every new channel that is added, every merger or acquisition that takes place, means that different data sets are acquired or developed, often about the same or overlapping sets of customers. Old data sets may need to be combined with new ones. Indeed, the ability to manage the same set of customers more efficiently or to gain improved value is often cited as the reason for a merger or acquisition or for the development of a new (often electronic) channel. Where this is so, failure to comply with the law also implies failure to manage data properly – or at the very least risks alienating customers. This in turn raises doubts about whether a company will be able to achieve the proposed gains in areas such as:

- marketing and sales efficiency;
- competitiveness;
- customer acquisition, retention and development;
- customer service.

RESOLVING THE PROBLEMS

Total anonymity is almost impossible in today's society. Basic necessities in life such as earning a living, holding a bank account, driving a car, receiving medical treatment and schooling children all require giving out pieces of information about oneself. Successful CRM strategies rely on gathering this and more sophisticated information on current and potential customers. The value of holding customer data has been recognized universally and those companies that do not understand their customers find themselves increasingly disadvantaged. Demand predictions are driven by the amount and quality of customer information held. Revenue and profit rely on accurate supply chain management based upon customer forecasts. Customer data is no longer a 'nice to have'; it is absolutely critical for commercial success.

However, consumers are becoming increasingly concerned about how personal information is used. They dislike being exposed to irrelevant advertising ('junk mail' and 'spam' e-mail being perfect examples of this). Whilst this phenomenon is annoying, the real issues that bother consumers are twofold: 1) Who knows what about me? (there is a real fear about repositories of personal information held without the individual's knowledge); 2) Could this information be used against me? (for example, individuals do not want to become the victims of fraud, to be fired from their jobs or to be denied insurance based on a set of data held without their knowledge or permission).

Any attempt to protect customer data has at its heart these two questions, which together deal with the mutually dependent issues of privacy, security and trust.

CURRENT TRENDS IN DATA PROTECTION

The Internet has brought new focus to the issues surrounding the protection of data. Never before has there been such freedom of access to an immense amount of personal information on a global scale. Countries, such as the United States, that value their open society and personal freedoms and find any bent towards totalitarianism deplorable are being forced to rethink how to deal with the balance between privacy and freedom of information. By contrast, Europe, which spent 20 years working out the finer details of the EU's 1995 Data Protection Directive, is beginning to realize that its ability to legislate is being outstripped by the speed of technology and that some form of self-regulation is desirable. Table 22.1 gives a quick overview of the two different approaches to data protection.

The success of a business depends upon the trust of its customers. Individuals will not choose to do business with companies they do not trust. Trust cannot be won unless privacy is respected and security is assured. Respecting privacy and protecting personal data mean much more than mere adherence to laws and regulations. A company must put in place the standards and disciplines required to meet customer expectations; it must practice the art of self-regulation. Those companies that harness their understanding of their customers' data protection requirements will demonstrate integrity to their customers. Their customers will have confidence that their privacy is protected and their transactions are secure. Treating people the way they want to be treated can give companies a significant competitive edge.

In the United States there are no statutory rules. Codes of practice exist within the industries but little is known about their effectiveness. There is also some sector-specific legislation. But data protection laws are not the decisive factor when it comes to consumer trust in data protection. Jennifer Barrett, Chief Privacy Officer of Acxiom, says:

> If companies are merely making investments to comply with privacy laws and regulations, they are missing a huge opportunity if they do not recognize it as a dual investment in building trust, increasing customer loyalty, and creating a competitive edge. The most forward-looking, customer-centric companies recognize that compliance with the law and the related communications is a platform for entering into a positive dialog with the

customer about how the company treats their personal information, honours their preferences, and cares enough to listen.

Opting in separately to all the possible uses of customer information would be virtually
impossible. So, this makes it very important to be a trustworthy business. No matter what a
company promises, if it deceives customers or uses information about them incompetently,
it will pay in the court of public opinion and eventually in revenue and profit. This suggests
short and general notices are more likely to work, the more complex the relationship.
However, re-solicitation of important permissions (eg to use particular communications
media, to promote major product areas) may be worth considering.

There is also a big difference between the business-to-business and business-to-
consumer environments. Companies in the former are entrusted with complex and
sensitive information about their client companies and about many individual managers in
these companies. This means that business-to-business companies need to work particularly hard to maintain high standards in the management of customer data.

In the business-to-consumer area, there has been consumer uproar about the data-gath-
ering practices of online companies such as DoubleClick and Toysmart.com. DoubleClick
planned to combine the names and addresses of consumers with their Web surfing and
shopping habits. It planned to use cookies to track individuals without those individuals
knowing they were being watched. Public outrage forced the company to rethink its

Table 22.1 Data protection trends in the United States and Europe

	United States	**Europe**
State regulation	• Federal law protecting the citizens of the USA against the collection, processing and use of data by the government is comprehensive and relatively restrictive • No federal law for commercial data protection passed, but with increasing examples of abuse of personal data, increasing pressure is now being brought to bear on the government to do so • Thousands of individual pieces of privacy law being created by individual states in response to local concerns (eg in 1999, over 7,000 pieces of state legislation on data protection and privacy were made state law)	• Data Protection Directive created in 1995 • Individual countries of EU have own laws in compliance with Data Protection Directive. For example, the UK Data Protection Act 1998
Self-regulation	• Long history of industrial self-regulation • Series of codes of practice within industry, but no ultimate means of enforcement. Little evidence as to how effective the self-regulation is • Non-profit privacy groups are finding alternative ways to protect data (eg the Privacy Foundation based in Denver is testing a tool to identify surveillance tags too small to see) • Safe harbour agreement between USA and EU	• Much legislation cannot match emerging technology (especially anarchic nature of the Internet) • Self-regulation becoming increasingly prevalent, eg FEDMA has created a series of codes of practice which set standards for data protection (encouraged and supported by the Directive)

practices. It hired a chief privacy officer, shelved its master data-collection plans and invited an external auditor in to look at its business practices. In another case, Toysmart, the online toy retailer, filed for bankruptcy and wanted to sell its extensive list of consumer information as an asset. Again, public outrage forced it to reconsider the sale. The fear of such public relations disasters has meant that companies are trying harder to comply with the new rules. There has also been a bipartisan push in the USA to see federal laws passed on privacy protection.

HOW DO CUSTOMERS FEEL ABOUT THIS?

Privacy is clearly an issue for some customers, with physical privacy (the intrusion of direct marketing into their homes) representing an annoyance and information privacy (relating to the information available on consumers) representing a more substantial worry. In terms of the latter, respondents' level of knowledge varies substantially. People react in different ways. For example, some are pragmatic and recognize that the provision of personal details may improve targeting. However, those who feel particularly strongly attempt to minimize the information held on them, and rarely, if ever, provide direct marketers with personal details or request communications from them. Interestingly, privacy concerns feature most strongly when respondents perceive that they are targeted with irrelevant marketing communications. The emotive response to this can vary from a general annoyance to overt concerns, and the strongest reaction is to actively withdraw from direct marketing communications. Direct mailers do not like the term 'junk mail'. It applies to mail that is perceived by the recipient as being uninteresting or irrelevant.

Research carried out at Bristol Business School showed that there are several dimensions to the relevance issue, the four variations being interest, timeliness, repetition and the information-processing effect. Relevance can only be achieved through improvements in targeting, improvements that require the use of personal data on individuals by companies. Control is an important consideration for consumers. Indeed, control issues underpin concerns with regard to both privacy and relevance and, as such, must be taken seriously. Here are some examples of what consumers said to the Bristol researchers:

> I would prefer it if I didn't see anything in the post unless I had specifically requested it.
>
> (Female, 25–34)

> Personally, if I've got something that I want to do financially, I would look into it and go to my own people. I would search them out myself rather than look at something that came through on the carpet because generally you just pick it up and throw it away.
>
> (Female, 25–44)

It's just it's annoying to be sent things that you are not interested in. Even more annoying when they phone you up… If you wanted something you would go and find out about it.

(Female, 45–54)

HOW TO IMPROVE THE QUALITY OF CUSTOMER DATA MANAGEMENT

Data quality has always posed problems. Incorrect or incomplete data leads to internal frustrations, inaccurate marketing campaigns, incorrect segmentation, etc. Our research shows that the majority of CRM managers feel that there still needs to be significant improvement in the quality of data management. Despite spending considerable sums of money on CRM software and the resource to implement it, most of them stated that there have been few major improvements to the quality of customer data in the past few years. However, until now this has, for the best part, been considered an internal issue. As a result of this customer data management issue, they risk damaging publicity leading to lack of trust by customers.

Trust is the foundation for maintaining good customer relationships. It was clear from our expert survey (the details of which are presented in the appendix) that the retention of best customers is the top priority for most companies (acquisition of new customers, though rated highly, is not considered to be as important to the success of the business). It is not surprising then, that when the respondents were asked to state their priorities in marketing, customer service and related areas, we saw an emphasis on those activities which involved developing the relationship and trust of the customer. For example, ensuring security of customer data and ensuring the customers' rights to privacy were cited as key concerns.

Issues of security, privacy and trust are growing in importance, particularly with the coming of age of the Internet. Companies that will succeed over the next decade will be those capable not only of understanding who are their best customers, but nurturing that relationship and providing those customers with the comfort that their data will be used with integrity. This can only be achieved by taking a holistic approach to the processes and procedures for good data management. Most companies need to take a close look at how customer information flows into the company, how it is managed internally and how it is passed out of the company. They also need to look at the processes that focus on the customer experience. Customers must be allowed full access to their information should they require it and the company should frequently check that customers are comfortable with how their personal information is being used.

MANAGING THE CUSTOMER EXPERIENCE

The customer experience begins with the acquisition of data (even at the prospect stage – when they have yet to become customers) and continues until the company no longer holds any personal data on that individual.

Customers should be made aware of what information is being recorded about them. There should be complete visibility at the point of capture. Companies are weak in recording declarations made to customers when customer data is captured. Our research shows that even blue-chip companies with good internal customer management processes have poor knowledge of exactly under which declaration data from a given customer is held. Many companies do not even record declarations made to customers when they capture customer data. If a company does not know, it should refresh the declaration by sending the data to customers and asking them to sign a new declaration, or it should restart its data collection process with clear separation between old and new data.

The *type* of data gathered must be relevant. In an Internet bank that wanted to be seen as a market leader in customer service, the CRM team felt that there was no such thing as 'irrelevant' data, and that any information gathered about a customer, via whichever channel, should be kept for future analysis.

Customers should be made aware if personal information is to be used for purposes other than that for which it was collected. This has fundamental implications for any CRM programme. Most CRM databases were designed with a wider use of combined data in mind. Customers should be informed of these wider uses at the point of data capture, or consent should be obtained subsequently. Companies must therefore ensure that they monitor the use of customer data and seek permission when the use is outside the original remit for acquiring the information.

Many companies are also poor at maintaining up-to-date records for marketing purposes. While most are diligent about canvassing new customers with regard to their willingness to receive marketing information from the group and partners, very few of them regularly check to ensure the opt-out clause is up to date. Companies should consider putting a process in place that can, at regular intervals, automatically check that a customer is happy to continue receiving marketing literature.

Companies must be able to track customer data and allow their customers to access it if they wish. The capability to track customer data as it is used and stored in different parts of the organization is critical if data is to be protected. Data is often moved to more centralized repositories so as to get a 'single view of the customer' – said to be essential for the customer to experience consistent treatment by all parts of the company. In our survey we asked CRM managers, CRM consultants and other relevant experts whether their companies could quickly and accurately recognize a customer at any of their contact channels and access complete and up-to-date information for that customer. With a few notable exceptions, most respondents had to agree that it was currently impossible in their organization or those of their clients, despite a declared aspiration eventually to attain the holy grail of a 'single customer view' . However, a single customer view has implications for data protection. To comply with legislation, a company must maintain high quality records of the source of all the data it holds about its customers. Real-time updates of customer information across all channels make data extremely difficult to track.

Most of the respondents to our questionnaire on data protection (see appendix) stated that they had problems with keeping track of the source of the data, especially with inbound e-mails. At the same time, most of our expert respondents saw achieving a single view of the customer as being a priority. We wonder whether a sense of reality needs to dawn. A 'less fragmented view' rather than a 'single customer view' might be easier and less costly to manage, whilst having the added benefit of allowing better management of the data and therefore compliance with the Data Protection Act. This is especially important given that there are constant pressures that cause 're-fragmentation' of the customer view in many of the industries that are big users of customer data, such as financial services, utilities, telecommunications, travel and leisure. These pressures include mergers and acquisitions, launch of new ventures targeted at existing customers, and proliferation of channels of distribution and communication for managing the same set of customers.

MANAGING CUSTOMER DATA INTERNALLY

In Figure 22.1, Bar 1 shows how comprehensively the industries surveyed understand the requirements of the Data Protection legislation in all the countries in which they have customers. By contrast, Bars 2, 3 and 4 reveal the extent of customer data management processes in place to manage customer data:

- Bar 2 shows the existence of a customer information plan covering information value, acquisition priorities, information management and usage.
- Bar 3 reveals the extent of clearly documented customer information quality standards that apply to customer-related data.
- Bar 4 shows the degree to which the information quality is formally measured against the information plan, with measures being stored and used to monitor improvement.

Although overall understanding is quite good, it is worrying to note that though the understanding of the law in financial services industries is better than in other industries, it is still not very good. Also, despite an understanding of what is required, companies are neglecting to put in place the practices and processes they need in order to be able to manage their customer data to the standards expected by the legislation. This suggests that companies need to introduce a number of disciplines, suggested below.

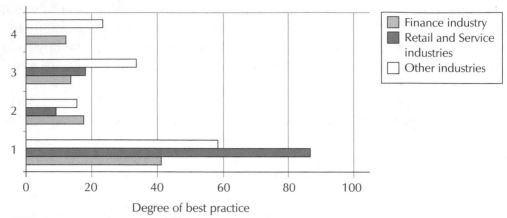

Source: CMAT Scores

Figure 22.1 Data Protection: Understanding versus Activity

INTERNAL DATA AUDITS SHOULD BE UNDERTAKEN AT REGULAR INTERVALS

An internal data audit is one way for a company to understand how well it is managing customer information. This will reveal:

- the amount of data kept on individuals;
- where the data has come from (and where it has been across the organization);
- the consistency and accuracy of that data across different channels and databases;
- the relevancy of the data (eg has excessive data such as 'hobbies' been recorded for an individual?);
- how long the data has been kept;
- whether the data should still be kept (ie is the original purpose for collecting the data still valid?);
- whether the data has been processed in accordance with the individual's rights;
- how secure the data is (ie is it open to internal/external fraud?).

Through such an audit, companies discover the full extent of the customer data they hold and the quality of that data. When companies undertake an audit, they usually discover that they are holding far more data than they thought, at far lower quality. The data is rarely concentrated on one database, except in relatively simple businesses (eg single product or single channel). If, as a result of doing an audit, a company becomes compliant (or nearly compliant) with the new Act, a year later it may well have become non-compliant. This is likely to be because another customer database has been set up that is not properly tied to the first and has records that overlap with it. The chances are that either or both customer records are incorrect, but the company will not know which.

Internal principles for managing data must be set

To attain high quality data management, it may help if data privacy guidelines and principles to be set are published and communicated to relevant parties – particularly to those members of staff who have customer-facing roles. Business practice can then be evaluated against these privacy guidelines and principles to ensure continuity of quality. They might include:

- published quality guidelines for all imported data;
- clear policy with third-party channels regarding the customer information they provide;
- documented customer information quality principles that apply to customer-related data; these principles should be set using a customer information plan that covers information value acquisition priorities, information management and usage.

Enlisting staff help to improve data quality

With increasingly complex systems interfaces to contend with, the employees' contribution to the quality of customer data management can be great. There are a number of steps a company can take to ensure that the employees' contribution is maximized:

- Staff can be given incentives and sanctions to ensure the information quality on the customer database. Very few companies subscribe to this way of thinking. In no sectors are CMAT scores here over 26%. Interestingly, it is the finance industry (where mistakes can be extremely costly and where staff are typically given financial incentives to produce the desired result) that is the worst culprit, scoring an average of only 8.9%.
- Our research also shows that there is a problem with the way that customer information is being recorded. Rarely is core customer information clearly documented in a way that can be understood by non-systems staff. All industries, it would appear, have a problem with this, since no sectors achieve a higher CMAT score than 32%.
- Minimize keeping of records on paper. In our questionnaire to CRM managers, we discovered that there are a large number of companies whose customer-facing staff keep some records on paper. This puts the quality of customer data at risk, and should be minimized.
- Regular checks should be made on key customer/prospect records to validate their existence. CMAT scores show that most companies do this rather infrequently.

There must be a clear archiving strategy

Figure 22.2 shows that, with the exception of the retail and service industries, most companies do not have a coherent and well-managed archiving strategy. Data should not

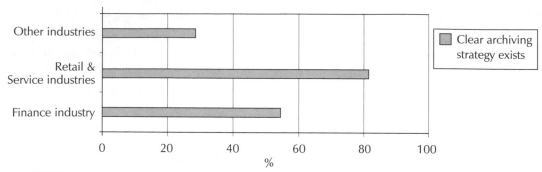

Source: CMAT scores

Figure 22.2 Archiving strategy

be stored for longer than its purpose requires. It effectively has a shelf-life. Even with a clear strategy on what information can be archived at what stage, there needs to be mechanism in place to alert the company that the information has gone out of date and needs to be either deleted or refreshed (with the customer's permission).

Summarizing the results from using the CMAT data gives a stark picture:

- Only 15 per cent of companies have clear and published data standards for imported data.
- Only 26 per cent comply fully with the terms of list rental agreements.
- Only 30 per cent consistently store the source of their customer data on the customer database, for each new record added.
- Only 17 per cent could demonstrate complete understanding of data protection legislation.
- Only 7 per cent have comprehensive and clear customer information quality standards.
- Only 7 per cent give proper incentives to relevant staff concerning customer information quality.
- Only 10 per cent document core customer information in such a way that relevant non-systems people can understand it.
- Only 7 per cent formally validate customer records once a year or more often.
- Only 20 per cent have a clear policy for archiving customer information.

Building an infrastructure to avoid problems

Most companies' problems with compliance with data protection laws arise from not paying close attention to their data infrastructure – the processes by which customer data is gathered, maintained and supplemented, and the systems on which it is held. It is now possible to ensure that data gathered from and used by different channels, products and subsidiaries is unified and maintained to high quality standards.

HOW TO BECOME COMPLIANT – AN EXAMPLE

IBM's Client Information Integration Solution (CIIS) is an operational client data management system that consolidates client information into a single, enterprise-wide view, and makes it available through all customer contact points. It operates as the operational client management system for the organization. It provides many important business benefits that ultimately derive from the availability of accurate, consolidated and complete client data to online business applications. It also ensures that a company can quickly implement compliance to new data protection directives in a cost-effective way.

While the many legal and administrative issues surrounding data protection directives are not always clear, we can be certain at least of some of the requirements it places on client information management. Companies need to:

- Provide accurate, complete and consistent client information to their business systems. Without this, compliance to data protection directives will prove difficult and costly to provide.
- Provide accurate information on relationships. For example, key relationships such as legal guardian, spouse, parent are obviously important as these may determine who is entitled to access a party's personal information.
- Provide complete and accurate information on the services and products that a client has purchased. For example, a client's credit may be withheld due to an inaccurate account balance.
- Ensure that operational business systems have a common enterprise view of the client and that any updates to client information are reflected across the whole enterprise.
- Ensure that rules relating to the creation of new client information are applied in a consistent way. This may include enforcing the capture of certain mandatory information such as privacy and non-solicitation status.
- Ensure that new client data is captured, accessed and updated in a consistent way so that the conformance of client data to regulations is maintained. This means that client information will continue to be accurate as rules are enforced in relation to its use.
- Understand what personal information is captured, why it is captured, who can create it, who can update it and who can delete it.
- Be able to demonstrate compliance with data protection directives to the relevant statutory bodies.

CIIS provides a centralized client management solution that meets these key requirements. It helps ensure compliance to new data protection directives in the following way:

- It provides a centralized client information repository that provides operational business systems with their client data needs. As client information is centralized, its compliance with data protection guidelines can be more easily maintained and assured.

- It enforces centralized rules for client information management that ensures that client information is created, accessed and updated in a consistent way. This means that companies can be certain that business applications process personal information in a way conforming to data protection guidelines.
- It provides a single enterprise view of the client that is accurate, complete and current. The result is reduced errors in client data that potentially could lead to infringement of data protection guidelines.
- It is integrated with channel and legacy applications. Therefore CIIS ensures that all client information changes are synchronized and that information is up to date irrespective of the channel through which it is accessed. Again this avoids another potential source of data protection infringement.
- Its business model dictates the way in which client data and relationships are stored and accessed. This model resolves many of the data-modelling and analysis challenges in implementing an enterprise-wide client management system. This business model is ideal for managing relationships such as guardian, parent, spouse and right of attorney where access to data may need to be provided to other parties.
- It allows capture of the status of the customer preferences with respect to privacy and non-solicitation. This may also include different particular preferences with respect to different roles, names, contact points and financial products. For example, it may capture a client's request not to send marketing information to a holiday home address but allow it to a work address.
- It allows the consolidation of older sources of client information. This enables the transformation of existing client data to meet new data protection guidelines.
- It records the details and the history of all data changes to client-related information. This captures the source system and person who made the update. This provides protection from fraudulent claims.
- It can be tailored to restrict and secure access to information.
- It provides a comprehensive methodology that defines the changes required to provide a business with a single enterprise client view, analyses existing sources of client data and determines how they can be consolidated and suggests the best strategy for integrating client management with existing applications.

CONCLUSIONS

Customers have a right to expect companies to manage their data professionally. This is not just a marketing question – financial issues are at stake too. Fraud is the most obvious risk, but there are other financial risks, eg the recent case in which many customers of an insurance company were asked to return demutualization bonuses because they were not qualified to receive them but had done so because of data problems. It is therefore important for companies to review the extent to which their own practices match best practice, and to establish strategies and targets to improve their practice.

APPENDIX: EXPERT OPINION

Respondents were asked the question, 'In terms of your company's priorities in marketing, customer service and related areas, how would you score the following (score 5 for top priority, 4 for very important, 3 for quite important, 2 for not very important, 1 for not important at all)?' The answers are given in Table 22.2, ranked by priority. The table shows that data security and protection issues are important, being 2 among the top 5. However, our analysis of CMAT scores shows how far companies are from achieving their desires. An inspection of the standard deviation column shows that although coping with different kinds of change was less of an issue, the higher standard deviations indicate less of a consensus.

A second set of questions was asked, concerning the current status. Respondents were asked to state their degree of agreement with the statements listed in Table 22.3, using 5 to

Table 22.2 Business priorities

	Mean	Standard deviation	% Agreeing or agreeing strongly
Retaining our best customers	4.14	0.99	78
Ensuring security of customer data	4.05	0.90	70
Improving quality of CRM	4.05	0.79	70
Developing our relationship with existing customers	4.05	0.84	65
Ensuring our customers' rights to privacy	3.91	0.97	65
Acquiring new customers	3.73	0.88	74
Improving the quality of customer data	3.68	1.04	57
Compliance with Data Protection Act regulation to provide data to individual customers on demand	3.68	0.95	43
Implementing e-business	3.64	1.05	61
Coping with shifts in demand patterns	3.59	0.85	52
Making customer management more cost-effective	3.41	1.18	43
Coping with structural change – deregulation, mergers and acquisitions, competitive entry	3.27	0.94	39
Coping with changing patterns of customer risk	3.09	1.15	39
Coping with distribution channel uncertainties	2.90	1.07	30

Table 22.3 Current status

	Mean	Standard deviation
We still need to make significant improvements to the quality of our customer data	3.76	1.48
We always ask our new customers about their willingness to receive marketing information from our group company and from our partners	3.62	1.24
We still have a long way to go when it comes to identifying the preferences of our customers for communication with particular media	3.52	0.93
The customer data that results from our customers' transactions with different business units is held on separate databases	3.48	1.50
Our company has made major improvements to the quality of its customer data in the last few years	3.43	1.12
We have found it difficult to keep to our normal data quality standards when dealing with inbound e-mails	3.40	1.10
The addition of new channels of communication and distribution means that my company is finding it difficult to bring all its data about customers together	3.38	1.43
Members of staff who deal with customers still keep some of their records on paper	3.38	1.47
Our company maintains a high quality record of the source of all data it holds about customers	3.19	1.03
We still have a long way to go when it comes to identifying the interests of our customers in particular products or services	3.19	1.08
Our company can quickly and accurately recognize a customer at any of our contact channels and access complete and up to date information for that customer	3.05	1.40
Our company knows exactly under which data protection declaration it holds data from any given customer	3.00	1.18
Our company's policy is to ask our customers regularly about their willingness to receive marketing information from us, so as to ensure that our Data Protection Act opt-out and customer preference information is up to date	2.75	1.21
We do not believe that it would be cost-effective to develop a single view of the customer	2.33	1.11
My company does not believe that a 'single view of the customer' – in the sense of having a comprehensive, rapidly updated view of all its interactions with a given customer – is really achievable	2.29	1.15

indicate agreeing strongly, 4 agreeing, 3 for neither agree nor disagree, 2 for disagreeing, 1 for strongly disagreeing. In Table 22.3, these are ranked in order of agreement, so the statements at the top of the list are the ones that most respondents agreed with. Note that the strongest positive consensus was about the need to improve the quality of customer data. Note too the agreement concerning the distribution of customer data on different databases, despite the general disagreement about sceptical statements about single view of customers.

Notes

[1] The research for this chapter was sponsored by Acxiom. None of its content should be construed as offering legal advice

23

Money laundering

Kevin La Croix

WHAT IS MONEY LAUNDERING?

According to Article 1 of the draft EU Directive of March 1990, money laundering is defined as:

> the conversion or transfer of property, knowing that such property is derived from serious crime, for the purpose of concealing or disguising the illicit origin of the property or of assisting any person who is involved in committing such an offence or offences to evade the legal consequences of his action, and the concealment or disguise of the true nature, source, location, disposition, movement, rights with respect to, or ownership of property, knowing that such property is derived from serious crime.

Although the above definition refers to 'property', much of the illegal activity occurring in this area is the 'processing of cash' from illegal sources into legal assets. Legal prohibitions against this activity are relatively recent, with the first US legislation appearing in the 1980s. The origin of the term 'money laundering' is disputed. It may come from a description of the activities of the Al Capone crime organization in Chicago during the US Prohibition period. In order to make use of the proceeds of illicit whiskey and beer, prostitution and gambling, the Capone organization purchased many coin-operated laundromat facilities. Illicit funds were easily mixed with revenues from a completely legal cash business. As the value of this process grew, organized crime increasingly penetrated other cash-based businesses, especially the vending machine market.

There are not reliable figures on the total volume of laundered money on a worldwide basis. However, estimates run from $600 billion to $1 trillion per year. The range of opportunities for this activity is far wider than the domestic banking system. Organizations that are prime conduits for the money launderer also include currency exchanges, stock brokerages, gold dealers, casinos, automobile dealerships, insurance and trading companies, free trade zones, wire systems, trade financing suppliers and private banking facilities.

For much of the past 25 years, anti-money-laundering legislation was introduced to eliminate domestic crime and tax avoidance efforts. However, with the internationalization of the financial system and of the major crime cartels, the control of illicit transnational cash movements has become a significant issue.

There are typically three steps in the 'money laundering process':

1. Placement or insertion – the process of placing the illicit proceeds of criminal activity into financial institutions through deposits, wire transfers, and the purchase of negotiable instruments, eg traveller's cheques, certified or counter cheques, etc). In this step, many relatively small transactions may be performed to launder the funds in batches that fall under regulatory thresholds. Given the number of entry points for placement or insertion around the world and the daily number of retail and business transactions conducted, the monitoring and recognition of this first step is an extremely complex problem.

2. Layering – the process of separating the proceeds of criminal activity from their origin through the use of layers of complex financial transactions. The purpose of this step is to provide the initial disguise as to ownership of the money, disrupt any attempts at establishing an audit trail and provide layers of anonymity over a series of transactions. The 'layers' are typically provided by moving funds between offshore accounts, the use of bearer shell companies, stock, commodity and futures dealing, fraudulent bills of exchange, inflated bills of lading and false billings.

3. Integration – the process of using an apparently legitimate transaction to disguise illicit proceeds after layering into an otherwise legitimate ownership. The purpose of this step is to allow the ultimate 'owner' of the illicit funds to benefit from the use of those funds in a manner that is legal. The money is integrated into the legal economy and assimilated into all of the other assets of 'the system'. This step is often accomplished through the use of anonymous companies (allowed in certain jurisdictions), false export–import invoices or the transfer of funds from a 'shell bank' to a legitimate bank.

THE CUSTOMER PROPOSITION FROM THE CRIMINAL'S POINT OF VIEW

For the money launderer, there are three key design points that must be satisfied:

1. concealment of the origin and true ownership of the assets being laundered;
2. maintenance of control of the assets as they proceed through the process;
3. conversion of the form of the asset (typically large amounts of cash) into a legitimate and more portable format (deposits, stocks and bonds, bills of payment, etc).

Obviously, there are dependencies for the delivery of these 'key design points' that the money launderer will attempt to take advantage of. These can include:

- lax enforcement of customer and/or counter party identification procedures;
- poor or ineffective systemic audit trails;
- collusion on the part of employees within the financial system;
- ineffective training for the employees within the financial system;
- volume of legitimate transactions within which to mask illegitimate transactions;
- confusing and/or conflicting procedures, regulations and oversight standards.

THE IMPACT OF ORGANIZED TERRORISM

Historically, the 'end-to-end process of money laundering' operated primarily on a one-way trajectory. The beginning of the process was the accumulation of very large amounts of cash raised from illegal operations. Whether this cash was in the form of coins and small bills (eg from the 'numbers racket') or in large denomination bills (eg from drug and organized crime cartels), the intent of the process is to transform the asset from illegal to legal and, often, from cash to other, more portable forms of assets.

The movement of international terrorist funds may represent a reversal of that trajectory. The beginning of the process may, in fact, be the accumulation of large amounts of cash, cheque and electronic transfer-based assets that represent, in and of themselves, legal operations. These may include honest contributions to apparently legitimate charities, transfers of money from governmental agencies, operation of non-governmental organizations (NGOs), or other licit sources. The intent of the money laundering process in this case is to transform those assets into an untraceable medium that can be spent on illicit activities – often that medium is cash. The money launderer's objectives change in the following way:

- reduced importance of concealing the origin and true ownership of the assets being laundered;
- increased importance of controlling the assets as they pass through the process;
- increased importance of converting the asset into a readily disbursable and untraceable format (US dollars, euros, precious metals, gems, etc).

THE EFFECT OF MONEY LAUNDERING

The obvious impact of money laundering is to enable individuals or organizations to benefit from or engage in illicit activities. However, with the current scale and reach of money laundering activities, there are significant collateral impacts far beyond criminal or terrorist activity:

- Front companies that are used to shelter illegal funds can operate at costs far below market rates, undermining legitimate private sector enterprises.
- Financial markets and financial institutions can be undermined and, in cases such as BCCI, the institution can be fatally affected.
- Countries may lose some control over their economic policy and, in some emerging market countries, illicit fund operations may be larger than legitimate operations. The IMF estimates that the magnitude of total money laundering in 2000 was between 2 and 5 per cent of world gross domestic product.
- Economies may be distorted as illicit funds are invested in uneconomic activities or industries that are primarily used as a holding mechanism for the money.
- Countries may lose significant tax revenues and the cost of tax enforcement can be substantially increased.
- Countries may find that privatization of national assets is distorted as criminal organizations have access to unregulated capital in bidding for these assets. There is an old saying attributed to Meyer Lansky, the CFO of US organized crime for 30 years: 'If you want to get rich, rob a bank, if you want to get seriously rich, buy a bank.'
- Successful large-scale money laundering can significantly increase national and institutional reputational risk, even if the government or institution is not in active collusion with the launderer.

THE 'CHOKEPOINTS' IN THE MONEY LAUNDERING PROCESS

There are at least three points in the process where controls can be put in place to respond to this activity:

- cash (and potentially other bearer value instruments) in and out of the system;
- transfers within the domestic financial system;
- cross-border flows of funds.

Whether the objective of money laundering is to 'wash' the proceeds of illicit activity or to distribute and use the proceeds of legal activity for illicit means, the range of activities that are coming under increasing global scrutiny is expanding well beyond the traditional banking system. These include:

- acceptance of deposits and other repayable funds from the public;
- lending;
- financial leasing;
- money transmission services;
- issuing and managing means of payment (eg credit and debit cards, cheques, traveller's cheques and bankers' drafts...);
- financial guarantees and commitments;
- trading for account of customers (spot, forward, swaps, futures, options...) in:
  - money market instruments (cheques, bills, CDs, etc);
  - foreign exchange;
  - exchange, interest rate and index instruments;
  - transferable securities;
- commodity futures trading;
- participation in securities issues and the provision of financial services related to such issues;
- individual and collective portfolio management;
- safekeeping and administration of cash or liquid securities on behalf of clients;
- life insurance and other investment related insurance;
- money changing.

IMPLICATIONS FOR FINANCIAL SERVICES SYSTEMS INVOLVING CUSTOMERS

The Financial Action Task Force (FATF) is a 29-nation organization that sets standards in regard to money laundering issues and coordinates the activities of regional organizations that account for approximately 130 jurisdictions and represent about 85 per cent of world population and 90–5 per cent of global economic output. It has identified that the systems required to combat money laundering include:

- customer identification technology;
- customer information management;
- CRM;
- transaction profiling and archiving;
- document verification and archiving;
- pattern analysis;
- data modelling and warehousing;
- online real-time or near-real-time reporting;
- distance learning in support of compliance training and updates.

Many of the actions that financial institutions will need to take in combating money laundering will be governed by a complex and changing set of business and process rules. These rules are likely to be set according to a range of criteria:

- institution rules based on management's responsibility to protect the brand value, compliance position and financial integrity of the enterprise;
- regulatory rules based on the oversight responsibility of national and international industry regulators to protect the stability of the financial system;
- law enforcement rules based on the enforcement responsibility of national and international policing bodies to detect, interrupt and prosecute money launderers;
- intelligence rules based on the responsibility of international intelligence and defence agencies to detect and interrupt potentially dangerous – particularly terrorist – activities.

Although some of these rules are likely to remain relatively fixed over time, some will certainly change according to circumstance and are subject, in some cases, to rapid changes in their parameters. Whilst it is likely that the methods for customer identification will remain generally constant, the types and patterns of transactions that are classified as 'suspicious' may change daily or hourly. It is therefore important for companies to develop robust business processes that can respond to a variety of fixed and changeable rules in this area. If money laundering can be defined as an end-to-end process, the tasks and actions that need to be taken to recognize, track, report, and ultimately prevent it can also be described as an end-to-end process.

APPENDIX

This appendix includes the full list of FATF recommendations in the interest of completeness.

Recommendation 1

Each country should take immediate steps to ratify and to implement fully the 1988 United Nations Convention against Illicit Traffic in Narcotic Drugs and Psychotropic Substances (the Vienna Convention).

Recommendation 2

Financial institution secrecy laws should be conceived so as not to inhibit implementation of these recommendations.

Recommendation 3

An effective money laundering enforcement programme should include increased multi-lateral cooperation and mutual legal assistance in money laundering investigations and prosecutions and extradition in money laundering cases, where possible.

Role of national legal systems in combating money laundering: scope of the criminal offence of money laundering

Recommendation 4

Each country should take such measures as may be necessary, including legislative ones, to enable it to criminalize money laundering as set forth in the Vienna Convention. Each country should extend the offence of drug money laundering to one based on serious offences. Each country would determine which serious crimes would be designated as money laundering predicate offences.

Recommendation 5

As provided in the Vienna Convention, the offence of money laundering should apply at least to knowing money laundering activity, including the concept that knowledge may be inferred from objective factual circumstances.

Recommendation 6

Where possible, corporations themselves – not only their employees – should be subject to criminal liability.

Provisional measures and confiscation

Recommendation 7

Countries should adopt measures similar to those set forth in the Vienna Convention, as may be necessary, including legislative ones, to enable their competent authorities to confiscate property laundered, proceeds from, instrumentalities used in or intended for use in the commission of any money laundering offence, or property of corresponding value, without prejudicing the rights of bona fide third parties.

Such measures should include the authority to:

1. identify, trace and evaluate property which is subject to confiscation;
2. carry out provisional measures, such as freezing and seizing, to prevent any dealing, transfer or disposal of such property;
3. take any appropriate investigative measures.

In addition to confiscation and criminal sanctions, countries also should consider monetary and civil penalties, and/or proceedings including civil proceedings, to void contracts entered into by parties, where parties knew or should have known that as a result of the contract, the State would be prejudiced in its ability to recover financial claims, eg through confiscation or collection of fines and penalties.

Role of the financial system in combating money laundering

Recommendation 8

Recommendations 10 to 29 should apply not only to banks, but also to non-bank financial institutions. Even for those non-bank financial institutions which are not subject to a formal prudential supervisory regime in all countries, for example bureaux de change, governments should ensure that these institutions are subject to the same anti-money-laundering laws or regulations as all other financial institutions and that these laws or regulations are implemented effectively.

Recommendation 9

The appropriate national authorities should consider applying Recommendations 10 to 21 and 23 to the conduct of financial activities as a commercial undertaking by businesses or professions which are not financial institutions, where such conduct is allowed or not prohibited. Financial activities include, but are not limited to, those listed in the attached annex. It is left to each country to decide whether special situations should be defined where the application of anti-money-laundering measures is not necessary, for example when a financial activity is carried out on an occasional or limited basis.

Customer identification and record-keeping rules

Recommendation 10

Financial institutions should not keep anonymous accounts or accounts in obviously fictitious names: they should be required (by law, by regulations, by agreements between supervisory authorities and financial institutions or by self-regulatory agreements among financial institutions) to identify, on the basis of an official or other reliable identifying document, and record the identity of their clients, either occasional or usual, when establishing business relations or conducting transactions (in particular opening of accounts or passbooks, entering into fiduciary transactions, renting of safe deposit boxes, performing large cash transactions).

In order to fulfil identification requirements concerning legal entities, financial institutions should, when necessary, take measures: 1) to verify the legal existence and structure of the customer by obtaining either from a public register or from the customer or both, proof of incorporation, including information concerning the customer's name, legal form, address, directors and provisions regulating the power to bind the entity; 2) to verify that any person purporting to act on behalf of the customer is so authorized and identify that person.

Recommendation 11

Financial institutions should take reasonable measures to obtain information about the true identity of the persons on whose behalf an account is opened or a transaction conducted if there are any doubts as to whether these clients or customers are acting on their own behalf, for example in the case of domiciliary companies (ie institutions, corporations, foundations, trusts, etc that do not conduct any commercial or manufacturing business or any other form of commercial operation in the country where their registered office is located).

Recommendation 12

Financial institutions should maintain, for at least five years, all necessary records on transactions, both domestic or international, to enable them to comply swiftly with information requests from the competent authorities. Such records must be sufficient to permit reconstruction of individual transactions (including the amounts and types of currency involved, if any) so as to provide, if necessary, evidence for prosecution of criminal behaviour. Financial institutions should keep records on customer identification (eg copies or records of official identification documents like passports, identity cards, driving licences or similar documents), account files and business correspondence for at least five years after the account is closed. These documents should be available to domestic competent authorities in the context of relevant criminal prosecutions and investigations.

Recommendation 13

Countries should pay special attention to money laundering threats inherent in new or developing technologies that might favour anonymity, and take measures, if needed, to prevent their use in money laundering schemes.

Increased diligence of financial institutions

Recommendation 14

Financial institutions should pay special attention to all complex, unusual large transactions, and all unusual patterns of transactions, which have no apparent economic or visible lawful purpose. The background and purpose of such transactions should, as far as possible, be examined, the findings established in writing, and be available to help supervisors, auditors and law enforcement agencies.

Recommendation 15

If financial institutions suspect that funds stem from a criminal activity, they should be required to report promptly their suspicions to the competent authorities.

Recommendation 16

Financial institutions, their directors, officers and employees should be protected by legal provisions from criminal or civil liability for breach of any restriction on disclosure of information imposed by contract or by any legislative, regulatory or administrative provision, if they report their suspicions in good faith to the competent authorities, even if they did not know precisely what the underlying criminal activity was, and regardless of whether illegal activity actually occurred.

Recommendation 17

Financial institutions, their directors, officers and employees, should not, or, where appropriate, should not be allowed to, warn their customers when information relating to them is being reported to the competent authorities.

Recommendation 18

Financial institutions reporting their suspicions should comply with instructions from the competent authorities.

Recommendation 19

Financial institutions should develop programmes against money laundering. These programmes should include, as a minimum:

- the development of internal policies, procedures and controls, including the designation of compliance officers at management level, and adequate screening procedures to ensure high standards when hiring employees;
- an ongoing employee training programme;
- an audit function to test the system.

Measures to cope with the problem of countries with no or insufficient anti-money-laundering measures

Recommendation 20

Financial institutions should ensure that the principles mentioned above are also applied to branches and majority-owned subsidiaries located abroad, especially in countries that do not or insufficiently apply these Recommendations, to the extent that local applicable laws and regulations permit. When local applicable laws and regulations prohibit this implementation, competent authorities in the country of the mother institution should be informed by the financial institutions that they cannot apply these Recommendations.

Recommendation 21

Financial institutions should give special attention to business relations and transactions with persons, including companies and financial institutions, from countries which do not or insufficiently apply these Recommendations. Whenever these transactions have no apparent economic or visible lawful purpose, their background and purpose should, as far as possible, be examined, the findings established in writing, and be available to help supervisors, auditors and law enforcement agencies.

Other measures to avoid money laundering

Recommendation 22

Countries should consider implementing feasible measures to detect or monitor the physical cross-border transportation of cash and bearer negotiable instruments, subject to strict safeguards to ensure proper use of information and without impeding in any way the freedom of capital movements.

Recommendation 23

Countries should consider the feasibility and utility of a system where banks and other financial institutions and intermediaries would report all domestic and international currency transactions above a fixed amount, to a national central agency with a computerized data base, available to competent authorities for use in money laundering cases, subject to strict safeguards to ensure proper use of the information.

Recommendation 24

Countries should further encourage in general the development of modern and secure techniques of money management, including increased use of cheques, payment cards, direct deposit of salary cheques, and book entry recording of securities, as a means to encourage the replacement of cash transfers.

Recommendation 25

Countries should take notice of the potential for abuse of shell corporations by money launderers and should consider whether additional measures are required to prevent unlawful use of such entities.

Implementation and role of regulatory and other administrative authorities

Recommendation 26

The competent authorities supervising banks or other financial institutions or intermediaries, or other competent authorities, should ensure that the supervised institutions have adequate programmes to guard against money laundering. These authorities should co-operate and lend expertise spontaneously or on request with other domestic judicial or law enforcement authorities in money laundering investigations and prosecutions.

Recommendation 27

Competent authorities should be designated to ensure an effective implementation of all these Recommendations, through administrative supervision and regulation, in other professions dealing with cash as defined by each country.

Recommendation 28

The competent authorities should establish guidelines that will assist financial institutions in detecting suspicious patterns of behaviour by their customers. It is understood that such guidelines must develop over time, and will never be exhaustive. It is further understood that such guidelines will primarily serve as an educational tool for financial institutions' personnel.

Recommendation 29

The competent authorities regulating or supervising financial institutions should take the necessary legal or regulatory measures to guard against control or acquisition of a significant participation in financial institutions by criminals or their confederates.

Strengthening of international cooperation: administrative cooperation/exchange of general information

Recommendation 30

National administrations should consider recording, at least in the aggregate, international flows of cash in whatever currency, so that estimates can be made of cash flows and reflows from various sources abroad, when this is combined with central bank information. Such information should be made available to the International Monetary Fund and the Bank for International Settlements to facilitate international studies.

Recommendation 31

International competent authorities, perhaps Interpol and the World Customs Organization, should be given responsibility for gathering and disseminating information to competent authorities about the latest developments in money laundering and money laundering techniques. Central banks and bank regulators could do the same on their network. National authorities in various spheres, in consultation with trade associations, could then disseminate this to financial institutions in individual countries.

Exchange of information relating to suspicious transactions

Recommendation 32

Each country should make efforts to improve a spontaneous or 'upon request' international information exchange relating to suspicious transactions, persons and corporations involved in those transactions between competent authorities. Strict safeguards should be established to ensure that this exchange of information is consistent with national and international provisions on privacy and data protection.

Other forms of cooperation

Basis and means for cooperation in confiscation, mutual assistance and extradition.

Recommendation 33

Countries should try to ensure, on a bilateral or multilateral basis, that different knowledge standards in national definitions – ie different standards concerning the intentional element of the infraction – do not affect the ability or willingness of countries to provide each other with mutual legal assistance.

Recommendation 34

International cooperation should be supported by a network of bilateral and multilateral agreements and arrangements based on generally shared legal concepts with the aim of providing practical measures to affect the widest possible range of mutual assistance.

Recommendation 35

Countries should be encouraged to ratify and implement relevant international conventions on money laundering such as the 1990 Council of Europe Convention on Laundering, Search, Seizure and Confiscation of the Proceeds from Crime.

Focus of improved mutual assistance on money laundering issues

Recommendation 36

Cooperative investigations among countries' appropriate competent authorities should be encouraged. One valid and effective investigative technique in this respect is controlled delivery related to assets known or suspected to be the proceeds of crime. Countries are encouraged to support this technique, where possible.

Recommendation 37

There should be procedures for mutual assistance in criminal matters regarding the use of compulsory measures, including the production of records by financial institutions and other persons, the search of persons and premises, seizure and obtaining of evidence for use in money laundering investigations and prosecutions and in related actions in foreign jurisdictions.

Recommendation 38

There should be authority to take expeditious action in response to requests by foreign countries to identify, freeze, seize and confiscate proceeds or other property of corresponding value to such proceeds, based on money laundering or the crimes underlying the laundering activity. There should also be arrangements for coordinating seizure and confiscation proceedings that may include the sharing of confiscated assets.

Recommendation 39

To avoid conflicts of jurisdiction, consideration should be given to devising and applying mechanisms for determining the best venue for prosecution of defendants in the interests of justice in cases that are subject to prosecution in more than one country. Similarly, there should be arrangements for coordinating seizure and confiscation proceedings that may include the sharing of confiscated assets.

Recommendation 40

Countries should have procedures in place to extradite, where possible, individuals charged with a money laundering offence or related offences. With respect to its national legal system, each country should recognize money laundering as an extraditable offence. Subject to their legal frameworks, countries may consider simplifying extradition by allowing direct transmission of extradition requests between appropriate ministries, extraditing persons based only on warrants of arrests or judgements, extraditing their nationals, and/or introducing a simplified extradition of consenting persons who waive formal extradition proceedings.

Part 7

Channels and value chain issues

24

Managing customers in retail bank branches

Merlin Stone, Chandra Kiran, Tamsin Brew and David Selby

Banks are working hard to change how they manage customers. This chapter explains the general background to changes in how customers are managed in branches, and how banks are trying to change in this area. It will give examples of successes, and also summarize the results of a recent global study that shows that in some countries customer management in branches is making great progress, while in others it is not. It explains that the main reasons for failure are a lack of management focus on what makes anything successful in branches – people and process – and too great a focus on data and systems.

The financial services industry is experiencing fundamental changes caused by deregulation, customer dynamics and technology which are all having a profound impact on distribution. Although we are no longer expecting a complete structural bypass, ie Internet-enabled structural bypass of the current business infrastructure, the Internet and of course intranets have nonetheless made a big difference to the way branches are evolving, not just in changing the economics of distribution (CRM and transactions management), but also in terms of enabling partnerships with everything from retailers to Internet-enabled aggregators. We are still expecting continued reinvention of customer relationship-based value capture through aggregation, event-mediation and agency offerings. Combining e-business techniques with other developments in marketing and service technology (such as advanced analysis and profiling techniques) has enhanced the ability of distribution channels to focus on the financial needs of different target customer segments and hence to align customer and channel interests. In parallel, dramatic reductions in traditional infrastructure and process costs and the emergence of functional-based e-business processes have allowed big improvements to be made in the productivity of all channels.

In general, current distribution channels (a combination of branches, call centres and e-channels), in spite of being the largest operating expense, are not delivering results that banks require to meet their current and future growth and profitability objectives. However, physical branches are still attracting more than half of the customer base in the UK. Even for customers who rarely use them for transactions, they are still seen as the embodiment of the bank, and often the place at which significant changes in the relationship take place (eg account openings, serious problems resolved). They are changing and mostly not closing – with most banks having more or less finished their big programmes of branch rationalization (in rural and certain suburban locations). So, despite the prediction of the branch's demise and the forecast of branches being overtaken by the Internet and mobiles and call centres, many institutions plan to increase their number of branches over the next years, sometimes in joint ventures with, for example, retailers.

CYCLES OF CHANGE

Branch delivery of service has developed through several stages, from the old 'bricks and personal service only', through introduction of self-service branches, to sales branches with transactions handled in other channels. In the future we may see proliferation of the so-called branch portal, combining the best of all approaches but still clearly centred on the branch. This approach will include:

- reviving the human touch;
- empowering sales and advice;
- matching strategy to business models;
- integrating e and call centre channels with the branch approach.

However, some customer types will migrate fully to the e-model and abandon the branch altogether, and banks will still continue to be challenged by the fact that these will tend to be higher-value customers. For example, in the UK, the number of adults conducting online banking rose by around a million in the six months from September 2000 to April 2001, and nearly 5 million people have bought or serviced a financial product online. This is about a third of Internet users and around a fifth of bank customers. Two-thirds of them are male. More than a third of the population now uses digital television – partly because the main providers are ending their supply of analogue TV. Investing online is rare – only 7 per cent of UK Internet users have done it. But many more customers say they would be happy to do it. Surprisingly, there is strong evidence that customers will not use this technology to switch banks – although they will use it to spread their banking and investment business around more suppliers.

Similar Internet penetration levels in financial services are being reported in most countries, so we can be certain that the Internet will take a key role as a channel of communication. How far it substitutes for other channels of distribution remains a moot point. The success of Internet-only banking in some countries (albeit with in some cases a suspect value model) indicates the customer-acceptability of the approach, and in general, where customers like it, capitalism will find a way!

THE REQUIREMENTS OF THE BRANCH PORTAL ERA

One of the most interesting questions is whether customers will relate better to what they see as a national Web site or one that relates to 'their' branch of the bank. Here, the jury is out. However, the motor industry provides an interesting example of where the equivalent of the branch (albeit in most cases independent of the manufacturer), motor dealers, have greatly extended their reach. In financial services, the main justifications of physical retail presence are cash management and the requirements of certain usually difficult transactions (either difficult because they are complex or because they involve dealing with sensitive issues such as financial problems, security, fraud or the like). Banks have an opportunity to build on this by creating branches on the Internet. Indeed, for those banks that are creating franchises, it could be argued that having a branch portal into the offerings of the 'parent' is essential.

The requirements for success are as follows:

1. a revenue/profit model which creates a cost-effective channel – not just a necessary expense;
2. a sales culture and incentives and processes to match – for staff and managers;
3. 'personalization' to the location and customer segment served.

We are not sure which way banks will move, but as most banks are moving steadily to extended hours of operation, fewer and smaller sites, smaller numbers of staff, and are continuously integrating self-service into their business models, we foresee at least a period of experimentation with the virtual branch or branch portal as at least a channel of communication for the branch.

BRANCH STRATEGY AND BUSINESS MODELS

The branch strategy must map to the business models of the lines of business. Different models may be required across the institution. The above requirement may move branches

390 Channels and value chain issues

to a new model, that of the financial resource centre. We may see evolution to four types of branch centre, depending on the strategic business model of the bank. These are listed below, and are based on the methodology described in Chapters 4, 6 and 39.

Wealth centre: customer centric

This offer will focus on the following:

1. wealth management;
2. life-cycle event management;
3. product events;
4. customer education.

Its success factors are advisory skills, excellence in customer experience. Most major banks are focusing on this offer.

Sales office: production centric

This offer will focus on the following:

1. speciality shops;
2. sales skills, focus;
3. white label partners.

Its success factors are sales skills, incentives, product knowledge. This offer is a classic in retailing, and is normally offered by higher quality retailers. However, mid-market retailers have made significant headway with this offer too.

Service centre: fulfilment centric

The offer will focus on the following:

1. self-service;
2. delivery efficiency;
3. multi-channel integration.

Its success factors are scale, flexibility, efficiency. Many broking firms are offering this.

Marketplace centre: market centric

This offer will focus on the following:

1.   business, consumer centres;
2.   many companies' products.

Its success factors are alliance skills, open strategy, control points, destination. This offer may develop from any of the others.

Common to all of the above will need for security, flexibility, migration strategy, and training

INITIATIVES FOR DISTRIBUTION RE-ENGINEERING

High distribution costs have forced banks to focus on the question of re-engineering distribution. One response has been the creation of separate business units for distribution and manufacturing operations. The performance of each unit has then been managed with aggressive targets on revenue and costs. These targets have sometimes been contradictory, with the drive to achieve high volumes of customers and/or products leading to higher levels of bad debt or at a minimum to many customers with a cost to serve which is high relative to revenue. This is because of a lack of focus on customer value. The outcome of this has been that while some of the targets may have been hit, overall the distribution channels as separate business units have not delivered the required productivity or growth. An additional reason for this has been inherent conflicts in multi-channel environment – put simply, when banks extend additional channels of communication and/or distribution to their customers, customers respond by using all the channels without necessarily committing more of their budget.

Banks have succeeded to some extent in shifting transaction processing to lower-cost channels (call centres and the Web). There has been a relatively successful transition for retail banking and retail brokerage (for investments and general insurance), but the life and pensions sector has achieved only marginal success with call centre operations due to fragmented channel operation.

Some banks have gone for partnerships and alliances (eg with retailers and insurers) to create new channels, with some success. However, where the financial model for these alliances was based on achieving very aggressive cross-selling targets for the whole combined customer base, these targets have generally not been achieved, resulting in failure to meet financial goals.

Some banks have focused strongly on trying to make CRM work – in terms of revenue and profit – within existing branches, while adding new channels of communication for cost-reduction and customer services. This requires strong alignment of channel and customer interests – meaning that high-cost low-revenue customers need to be managed out of the branch, and high-revenue low-cost customers into the branch. In general, a lack of understanding of customer needs, poor segmentation, poor profiling and lack of changes to the way branch staff are trained and motivated to manage customers have meant that in all but a few exceptional cases, their has been continued misalignment of distribution channel objectives and customer needs.

SUCCESS STORIES

If the above analysis sounds full of doom and gloom, there are some stirring success stories, showing what companies are able to do today. It is worth noting that most of these involve combining classic direct marketing with a customer-oriented view of what technology can do. Here are a few of them.

La Caixa, Spain

To maintain its lead in the savings market, 'la Caixa' relies heavily on its branch network – which today runs to 4,300 outlets – to retain and attract customers. But many transactions are undertaken by third-party agents, partners and mobile staff, and it is crucial that the support they receive is the very best possible. In 1999, la Caixa invested in a new financial teller transaction framework from IBM that is already streamlining operations, improving customer service and producing cost savings. In the years since the Spanish government deregulated the sector so that banks could operate outside their home areas, la Caixa has opened 3,000 new branches across Spain. It has a continuing policy of opening on average more than one branch every day. By judicious investment in systems and the associated business programmes, la Caixa has achieved the following benefits:

- **Stronger channel** – in addition to 4,300 branches, there are 1,000 points from which people need regular access to the financial teller system. The browser-based solution allows platform-independent access to the host, providing a homogeneous interface.
- **Lower operating costs** – tellers are more productive, and the system is cheaper to maintain and upgrade than previous systems.
- **Faster to market** – because the only software on the remote computer is a Java applet, new products can be introduced quickly and simply.

- **Better customer recruitment/retention** – transactions are processed quickly and accurately, and the new system has already had a positive impact on the monthly customer satisfaction surveys.

All the information about customers gained from the branch is kept in a data warehouse and used for segmenting and profiling, and ultimately for marketing and selling. The challenge is in bringing together similar information from other channels to create a single CRM resource. All products need to be distributed to any channel under a common customer view at any moment to any of the enterprises of la Caixa group in an efficient manner.

A US credit union

Formed in 1931 and with around 140,000 current customer accounts in some 50 US states, this is a case study of a mid-western credit union. The client's management team is very far-sighted. They have made a conscious decision to rely on technology to cut infrastructure and servicing costs. This puts them on an equal footing with larger commercial financial institutions positioned in the same market space. The credit union, with its 9 branches and 16 ATM sites, is one of the top 100 credit unions in asset size in the country. The key difference between a credit union and a bank is that a bank can invest cheque funds into other investments such as equities. A credit union may not, because of legislation, undertake such a practice. This means that in the credit union's business model, cheque funds represent the main lifeblood of the economic equation. So, stimulating new cheque accounts and the general growth of funds provides one of the key enablers. The other key driver in the business model is profitability. Although the charter of the credit union does not allow it to make a profit per se, the institution must be profitable to allow it to best serve its members.

One of the fundamental changes in management that has taken place over the years has been to establish a customer profitability data warehouse. The technology allows customers to be monitored on a real-time basis to glean actionable information about members. This helps the credit union's team understand which products are most popular and which members bring the credit union the most profit. Additionally, insights into members' behaviour and trends helps the credit union design promotions that will elicit positive responses from appropriately targeted members. Aggregates of this information underpin a more advanced forecasting model which models cash flows, the implications of new product introductions, 'what-if's, and other variables such as the increase in membership and downturn in the marketplace.

The credit union is under continual business pressure from other large national banks that constantly send marketing materials to the most desirable members in the member base. In order for the credit union to successfully service all of its members, overcome this marketplace threat, and take on the large banks in a latter-day David and Goliath battle, they invest in technology. The credit union operates an electronic banking service for around a third of its total population. This presents one of the most interesting real-time marketing areas in the bank's infrastructure.

One effect of being able to better combine customer understanding with research led to the realization that the credit union was constrained by its own brand. The longer-term forecasting models demonstrated that growth was hampered by the size of the catchment area and the market perception of the original brand as being associated with a trade association. The original name of this credit union was therefore clearly constraining its market. Although the original charter positioned it in a niche market position, it soon became clear that if it were to be efficient it would need to expand its member base. So, it went about re-branding itself. This raised many difficult issues. The well-established base had a set of expectations and permissions associated with the existing brand. It had sensitively not only to select a new brand, but to communicate that brand in order to migrate the existing customer base in such a way that they felt there was no loss in brand values, loyalties and permissions associated with the existing brand. Once the new brand was chosen and approved by the legislature, a careful programme was undertaken to communicate the change to the existing community. The main aim of the new branding was to improve the catchment area of the credit union in order to facilitate significant growth in the number of members it could attract. This would directly improve its profitability by increasing its cash flow.

Before the profitability warehouse was deployed, marketing campaigns tended to be incredibly limited. The focus was on marketing to the whole base with a single message rather than targeting profitable customers with good cross-sell and up-sell offers, which addressed their wants and needs. The system also affords the ability to study and administer delinquency models. This facilitates the identification of members who may need special assistance in avoiding problems. Members currently in delinquency are profiled and then their early behaviours are matched to those of other members who appear to be moving into that profile group. From this the credit union can truly add value by attempting to help these members become financially healthy again.

Perhaps it's worth starting with one of the strangest findings that has come from profitability analysis. It is the investment structure for Web devices. It turned out that some of the most profitable customers desired the support of WebTV, probably one of the more difficult devices to support on the Internet. But the profitability analysis allowed a business case to be made for investing in the device and support is now in place on the home banking site. Profitability utilizes some innovative mathematical techniques to determine future value based on the products held, tenure, and cash flows. These variables are aggregated to provide an indexation of value. This quotient is used to drive investment in the customer from a marketing point of view. It is also used in aggregate for higher-level planning decisions.

Another interesting area that has come from implementing the profitability warehouse is understanding the right staffing levels. It is essential to have enough employees working in a branch at any given time, but the credit union must avoid overstaffing. The data warehouse assists this with tools/reports necessary to allocate part-time employees effectively to cover peak traffic times. The same has also been found true for the Web site. Web analytics has led to a clearer understanding of customer traffic. This has made it easier to understand when to schedule system changes to minimize customer impact.

Business rules are the lifeblood of all marketing organizations. Every campaign is underpinned by some set of rules about who will be targeted. In the case of electronic commerce, these rules are turned into something we can programmatically implement in a rules engine. This piece of software allows business rules such as *'if life_time_value is over x and customer has more than two products and propensity_score_to_attrite > 0.6 then offer_tax_adviser_service'* to be expressed in an auditable and computer-executable way. One of the real-time target marketing solutions figures heavily in the Internet marketing initiative. When members log on to the credit union's Web site to access the home banking service, they will receive individual targeted messages. It will immediately be obvious that these offers have been chosen specifically for that member at that exact point in time. This is undertaken by using a combination of the customer behaviour profile, an ever-evolving set of key variables about that customer, and the rules engine.

The credit union has invested in a high technology approach to drive down costs and better manage its portfolio of customers. Overall analyses led to an understanding that the catchment area was too small. The only way to address this was by a re-branding exercise that has been skilfully undertaken so as not to alienate an existing loyal customer base. Some other interesting side effects of having a profitability warehouse have been illustrated by the revelation of business issues such as staffing levels and Internet device support.

Bank of Montreal, Canada

Three months after implementing its new customer knowledge database, Bank of Montreal's executives were already equipped with the facts necessary to make changes. First, the bank's team leveraged the data in the system to make informed decisions about pricing product bundles, channel migration, resource planning and a host of other key business areas. Next, the bank looked at distribution – branch openings and closings. Analysis helped the team to determine that it was necessary to close some of the bank's 2,000 branch locations. By studying customers' spatial relationships to remote locations, recommendations were made to close several hundred outlets. However, by identifying the customers the bank wanted to keep and taking the appropriate actions, the bank retained virtually all its balances and best customers one year after closure. The custom analytical capability also helped the bank refine its marketing campaigns. With more insight about customer segments and their specific patterns, the marketing department is able to tailor offers to the customers most likely to be receptive. By using insight gleaned from the system in this way, campaign response rates have increased.

The solution enabled the marketing team to uncover several surprises, too. A case in point is that the number of additional products sold to a given customer (cross-sells) is not directly related to that client's profitability. The average number of products held by top-tier versus bottom-tier customers is about the same. There are other more significant profit drivers at work – like balances, channel preference and transaction frequency. With low decile customers, understanding the determinants of 'unprofitable behaviour' is the first step in raising profitability levels. Such factors as unwise mortgage pricing and overly flexible 'multi-transaction' plans often contributed to lower profitability levels in some customers. Armed with this information, the bank repriced for value delivered to the client. Some customers were price protected or saw price reductions. Other customers had price and fees increased. These changes ultimately resulted in a better bottom line for the bank. The most important result was the special measures the team was able to design to retain the institution's best customer segment. This initiative, a national retention campaign known as 'Trusted Advisor', targeted high-profit customers and clients that had tripped a 'risk of diminishment/defection model'. Current account customers who had a plan that was inappropriate were a prime example. Some of these customers, it turned out, were actually spending more on their plans than was necessary. Many were offered the opportunity to convert to lower priced plans that delivered the same level of service. This campaign was one of the bank's most successful, netting a several thousand percent return on investment. To test the long-term validity of this approach, a test group of customers was set aside. The test set consistently received plan advice from bank representatives. Their balances and their loyalty continued to increase. Not surprisingly, the control group, a segment of customers not receiving the Trusted Advisor service, did not show the same types of balance increases. Admittedly, for some clients, the monthly savings in fees resulting from the Trusted Advisor programme were insignificant.

The bank also is piloting a programme called Rapid Cycle Customer Retention (RCCR), in which data from the system is used to determine a customer's propensity to diminish or defect. A mechanism is in place to flag the bank's retention managers 90 days prior to the predicted defection. Marketers call these individuals and offer them services or products to increase the chances that they will stay with the bank. Call centre staff are empowered to remedy many types of problems, adjust rates and handle service issues on the spot. This type of immediate action helps the bank gain higher loyalty rates, as well. The bank's new strategy is to deliver a consistently superior client experience for its core target segments. The institution does this through a wide range of relationship technologies and personal interactions. This new style of dealing with customers crosses whatever channels the customer chooses – from the branch to the call centre to Web-enabled ATMs. The key to the success of this type of marketing lies in getting the customer's permission, to be appropriately familiar, but not betraying privacy, confidences or trust.

Garanti Bank, Turkey

The executives at Garanti Bank have learnt that the most effective interpretation tools are business intelligence technology and CRM techniques. Over the past several years, Garanti not only recorded a continually increasing customer base, but also came to understand the importance of increasing customer satisfaction. The effect of mutual fund test campaigns on sales was dramatic. The bank experienced a 214 per cent increase in mutual fund sales in the four pilot branches, while the bank as a whole grew by only 6 per cent during the period. A similar credit card campaign also showed impressive results. The four branches in the pilot achieved a 132 per cent increase in credit card sales. Implementing CRM capabilities had an immediate and direct affect on profitability per customer.

The bank's customer profit model, now accepted by all parts of the bank, takes into account revenue, transaction and maintenance costs that are allocated at the customer level to reach an individual profit figure. The model reflects 'relative' rather than 'absolute' profit. Small groups of retail customers, the team has determined, have a major impact on both profit and transaction loads in the bank. Segmentation also contributes to having a better knowledge of customers. Previously, Garanti's retail segmentation was based on account balances. The new criteria incorporate age, education level, wealth, overall life stage, full demographic information, the transactional data of customers and the average bank balance held. Credit card limits, spending habits, and other specifics are also part of the critical information mix. This new segmentation model was developed and validated by branch and marketing staff and proven by the profit model. Nine new customer segments resulted from the team's efforts. The bank concentrates its sales efforts on the top ones. The sophisticated custom analytics in the system helped the Garanti team uncover the fact that these top four segments represent about 6.5 per cent of Garanti's overall customer base. The institution earns about 56 per cent of its profit from these segments alone.

While some customers do not fall into the top four segments, analysis unearthed the fact that they are, nonetheless, still quite profitable for the bank. With that in mind, the team set an unpublicized 'minimum customer profit limit', which enabled this additional segment of profitable customers to be nurtured. For other customers who fall outside both the top four segments and the additional profitable customer segment, the team planned a cost management strategy. These lower-tier customers were directed to a mass-market branch and alternative banking channels that were offered fee-free for a short time. Garanti Bank promoted the mass-market bank for these lower-tier segments. It has special products and branches that are designed for them.

Abbey National

Abbey National is betting on franchising. It launched its franchising scheme in August 2000, and since then one-third of its UK branches have been 'internally franchised' – meaning that ownership remains with the company. Franchised branches have produced sales productivity increases from 15 to 25 per cent above those of non-franchised branches. The bank plans to extend this approach to the majority of branches by 2002. This is expected to generate up to £45 million pa extra in revenue gains and cost reductions, helping to keep the bank's cost to income ratio down to 37 per cent, one of the lowest in the industry. The franchising model does not require the franchisee to have an equity stake. Instead, the franchisee accepts greater risk in terms of future income, and also relinquishes benefits such as the company pension. In return, franchisees can earn greater rewards, which are shared amongst franchise staff. Abbey National retains the infrastructure and responsibility for credit policy and regulatory compliance, while franchisees have responsibility for local marketing priorities and resources. Results include improved customer and staff satisfaction. The results have been so successful that Abbey National is experimenting with giving partial ownership to franchisees. Four local markets (branches are organized into local markets – there are 750 UK branches organized into 91 local markets) are being used for this pilot, and will become 51 per cent subsidiaries of Abbey National.

Supermarket banking – changing the definition of branch banking?

Banking has traditionally been based on a current account, which formed the centrepiece of the relationship with the customer. Supermarket banks have broken this paradigm, offering customers banking with a different type of relationship. The threat that this presents to the retail banks should not be underestimated. They have been forced to push products at their customers to cover the cost of providing free current account banking. Many of the new 'wealth management' propositions have been attempts to sell more products to wealthier customers. If supermarkets can offer quality financial products, which can stand alone competitively, retail banks could conceivably be left holding the unprofitable current account with no means of cross-subsidizing it.

Supermarket banks are in a strong position:

- **Customer base** – they have a large, loyal base of customers, who identify strongly with their brands. This reduces the cost of customer acquisition. They should also know their potential banking customers well, through analysis of their purchasing patterns, through research they conduct for branch location, through data they obtain from their product suppliers, and of course through data obtained from potential or actual banking and other financial service partners.

- **Brand** – strong brands that are not tarred with the legacy of certain other financial services brands or even the poor legacy of suppliers of whole categories of product. The brands are also established, so they do not require investment (or price discounting) to raise awareness or to gain commitment. Supermarkets are generally positioned as family friendly in financial services.
- **Economics** – low cost (especially distribution) of adding financial services to retailing. Retailers have the advantage over Internet banks of having a physical presence, without the overhead of a branch network. They also outsource and white label to reduce the costs of servicing and processing.
- **Competitive products** – supermarkets have shown that they can achieve good market shares, compared to other players, for several types of product (eg credit cards, short-term savings, general insurance).
- **Society** – consumers have money but are increasingly time-poor. They are more willing to buy financial products from non-traditional channels, eg supermarkets, if this saves them time. Supermarket banks can use their retail expertise to understand which products consumers will be willing to buy in a retail space and which they won't.

The opportunities for supermarket banks are large:

- **Leveraging customer loyalty** – retail banks are investing huge sums in CRM but super-market banks have a different approach: they use their retail experience to adopt a more customer-focused approach at the product development phase. They aim to offer a range of relevant, quality, accessible products which allow customers to choose or shop for the products which best suit their needs. For supermarket banks, customer choice or 'shopping', backed by brand loyalty, is the big opportunity – not CRM. Banks have been trying to increase customer loyalty, and some have succeeded, but not at the speed with which supermarkets have established and then developed their customer bases using retail techniques.
- **Moving into 'lifestyle enablement'** – this includes affinity programmes and home delivery. Customers want to simplify their lives and save time – using a single organi-zation for various types of shopping, financial services and the like meets the needs of some customers.

Of course, supermarkets need to keep their product strategy very focused. There are many financial services products that so far do not 'fit' into the supermarket basket. However, with increasing government pressure for low charges and simplification, we can expect a gradual 'basket drift' in favour of supermarkets. This does mean that supermarkets must be careful not to overstep the mark at any moment, while gradually increasing their financial services offer.

Points that supermarkets will need to watch include:

- **Overcoming customer apathy/inertia** – this is what keeps many customers from deserting their banks. This so far has not been a problem for supermarkets, but will be if they try to push too quickly.
- **Building/buying the capabilities** necessary to translate their brand values into a good financial services experience. For example, different capabilities are required for customer service in financial services, compared with traditional retailing (although the loyalty card experience has greatly increased the frequency of named interaction and the depth of contact, eg in call centres and now on the Web). This is likely to be very important for retailers who decide that they need to break with their financial services partners because of conflict of interest, perhaps using a variety of third-party suppliers instead or taking some operations in-house.
- **Multi-channel distribution** – physical bank branches still attract about half the UK customer base. Even if rarely used for transactions, customers will often visit a branch for major 'events' (eg taking out a mortgage). Banks that adopted a purely Internet strategy are now finding it necessary to establish some sort of physical presence. The implications for supermarkets are that some customer types may prefer face-to-face distribution for some or all products. They might consider evolving to a true multi-channel distribution model, which would allow them to capitalize on their economics.
- **Stretching the brand** – knowing where to stop. Some financial products need to be backed up with a certain level of expertise or advice. Customer trust may not extend this far, eg mortgages, advice.
- **Segmentation** – financial services customer segmentation is likely to be different from retail segmentation. Managing two different segmentation frameworks adds complexity to the business, but will enable supermarket banks to understand their customer needs and align their product and channel strategies with those needs. However, as we have pointed out above, the retail approach in which customers drop a product in a basket (albeit figuratively) requires less segmentation (none for outbound purposes if followed to the extreme).

CONCLUSION

Branch CRM is not magic, and some companies are doing it well. Companies that rush at it are not. Banks that have used absolutely classic database marketing and retail techniques – cleaning databases, profiling, targeted cross-selling, combined with appropriate staff policies (remuneration based on customer value rather than product, branch scorecards balancing product, customer and cost indicators, motivation and training focused on customer value and customer service), have had great success in moving away from the awful situation where 10 per cent of customers produce more than 100 per cent of the profits. In this respect, the UK banks are some way behind certain Canadian and Australian banks. In the United States, perhaps surprisingly, the exceptions prove the rule – there, most banks are emerging from a period when they dominated their individual state, and learning to compete for customers using these classic techniques.

However, banks will continue to spend significantly on making their branches work. There will be an estimated US $7 billion spent by banks on a worldwide basis in 2002 in this area. They will spend this money on:

- branch transformation – modernizing the branch as the primary delivery channel to the retail and small business customer segments of banks, to increase sales and decrease costs;
- retail merchandising in the branch – ensuring that the branch is arranged to deliver the transformed service;
- business case justification of a transformed branch – making sure that the financials are right;
- establishing the bank brand across channels, using marketing, service and systems techniques to ensure consistency of business focus, presentation and delivery;
- e-banking: ensuring that what is delivered in the branch is matched and/or complemented by the e-channel, and establishing a long-term scalable infrastructure for e-banking, now that many e-applications are in place, and performance and server management issues are becoming more of a concern as more individuals use the Web interface. This includes using e-banking to reach the self-directed Web-oriented customer in brokerage and insurance. With aggregation and wealth management now available via PC and the Web, there is a whole new level of function available to the self-directed customer.

Getting these various initiatives into balance will be the key to successful banking CRM.

25

The impact of e-commerce on UK financial services product providers and their intermediary relationships

Philip Aitchison

INTRODUCTION

The UK financial services sector is undergoing a period of profound change, including the advent of e-commerce and intermediary depolarization, coupled with demographic changes and government regulation. This chapter explores the nature of these industry trends in relation to UK product-providers, mainly pensions and life assurance product-providers and their most important organizational stakeholder, the independent financial adviser (IFA). It discusses how this relationship has evolved to date and recommends how UK product providers might restructure their operations in light of the industry trends. The chapter concludes firstly that the advent of increasingly sophisticated consumers implies that UK product providers must develop products/services more tailored to the end-user and distribution channels. Secondly, business models must be restructured to more closely reflect organizational core competences, distribution channel relationships, strategic alliances and outsourcing opportunities. Thirdly, the IFA/product provider relationship will change greatly, affecting the delivery of financial product/services to consumers. Finally, the strategic and tactical challenges resulting from these issues are discussed in some depth.

The financial services sector has been revolutionized to become a more technologically driven, fiercely competitive service-oriented market.[1] Financial services are increasingly regarded as quasi-commodities that serve a complex market in which organizations of markedly differing business models use diverse marketing strategies and different technologies to service a multitude of consumer segments. Technology is now facilitating cost-effective mass customization.[2] This is reflected in the customization of the ideal product, the aggregation of services, the targeting of the right product for the right buyer, immediate transactions and the availability of progress information.[3]

The Internet has virtually eliminated the information arbitrage opportunities that many financial services firms have traditionally relied upon. The number of online users of financial services is increasing. In terms of the distribution of financial services business, IFAs and direct sales operations still handle the largest proportion of transactions but it is anticipated that the Internet has 17 per cent whilst ATMs/call centres and point-of-service venues will account for 12–13 per cent by 2003.[4] These statistics illustrate the importance of new technology to the future of global financial services and implies that in order to prosper, significant changes in strategic thinking, market organization and consumer understanding are required.

In the New Economy, consumers have (for a price) the same access to the information sources as intermediaries (ie IFAs) and therefore need not rely on their 'expertise' to locate the best financial opportunities, eg over 10 per cent of the UK population searched for financial products online.[5] This implies that consumers now want customized assistance in analysing requirements, the reassurance of strong brands, and the convenience of straight-through processing (which means that information is entered once and used throughout the decision-making, transaction and servicing process without human contact interfering with data integrity, leading to fewer mistakes, less duplication and efficiencies in data storage, sharing and processing). Consumers also want better access to financial intermediaries and an all-round more intuitive customer experience. However, Forrester research indicates that a much larger percentage of online users are only browsing for life assurance or investment products than are actually purchasing online. Furthermore, 23 per cent of users have searched for financial services online, whilst only 2 per cent have purchased.[6] Accordingly, with regard to the three stages in the overall sales process – namely research the marketplace and provide generic information, understand clients' needs and offer advice, consummate the sale – only the information search process currently adds value, despite being a commodity.

UK PRODUCT PROVIDERS IN EVOLUTION

The evolution of business models

There is no doubt that e-commerce and e-business are changing the marketplace by transforming how firms conduct business, stakeholder relationships and market structures.[7] An organizational business model expanded to encompass the nature of e-business may be defined as 'a collaborative enterprise that establishes a close partnership amongst its stakeholders, employees, customers and suppliers, leveraging technology to minimize distance between its business and its partners and to automate transaction processing, strengthen relationships and reduce costs'.[8] This definition suggests that organizational boundaries are becoming less distinct and increasingly flexible to accommodate a wider network of strategic partnerships.[9] The advent of e-commerce allows companies to reorganize themselves in a virtual context. Many traditional business models have been successfully adapted to the online world, eg the subscription-based content provider, direct marketing, free trial and a number of new models such as the freeware model, information barter, access provision or active service provider model.[10]

Product provider business model design

UK product providers operate both business-to-business and business-to-consumer models. Thus, Scottish Amicable acts as the business-to-business division of the Prudential and so deals mainly with the independent financial adviser market. Other examples include Scottish Mutual as part of Abbey National plc or Scottish Equitable as part of the Dutch conglomerate Aegon. However, companies such as Standard Life or Fidelity Investments act as a single entity serving both consumers directly and professional intermediaries.

There are three main channels of distribution:

- Tied agents, who are contractually obliged to sell the products of the parent company.
- Direct channels such as telesales or direct selling have traditionally been key distributional channels, although use of sales forces is declining due to cost inefficiencies. For example, Prudential has recently significantly reduced its direct sales force.[11]
- The intermediaries, ie independent financial advisers (IFAs), are a key distribution channel which is increasing relative to the others as the proportion of business transacted through IFAs has increased from 38% to 54%.[12]

These channels of distribution are serviced by several delivery mechanisms such as branch networks, call centres, Internet portals or digital TV.

The impact of e-commerce and Internet technology

E-commerce and the Internet have had a significant impact on product-providers' business. According to Datamonitor (2000),[13] online banking is the most popular financial service in the UK. Figures 25.1 and 25.2 illustrate online financial services behaviour.

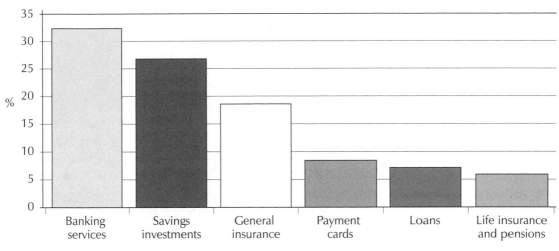

Datamonitor (2000)

Figure 25.1 Financial services browsing by product group

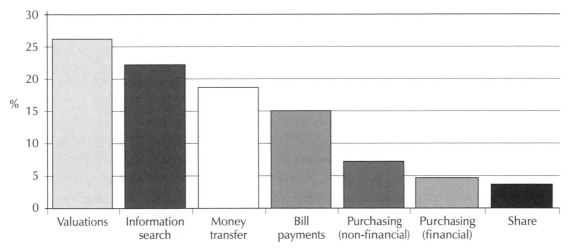

Datamonitor (2000)

Figure 25.2 Popularity of banking services

These graphs show that there is still a big discrepancy in terms of the product category viewed via the Internet. This should come as no surprise as there remain significant differences between bank accounts / credit cards and personal pensions. This suggests that there is a clear need for research into the category of product most suitable to be viewed and transacted over the Internet. Indeed, the distinction between valuations and actual transactions is crucial because as the next graph demonstrates, consumers appear currently to use the Internet for viewing financial information and data, etc, as opposed to transactions. Figure 25.3 shows the factors that consumers value in financial services.

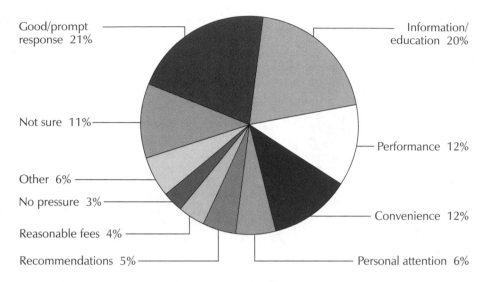

Good/prompt response 21%

Information/education 20%

Not sure 11%

Performance 12%

Other 6%

No pressure 3%

Convenience 12%

Reasonable fees 4%

Recommendations 5%

Personal attention 6%

The Economist, 18 May 2000

Figure 25.3 What customers value in financial services

This chart controversially claims that consumers may be more interested in the provision of accurate information and prompt service than personal attention. However, the balance of personalization and functionality is a complex issue that product providers have yet to resolve.

THE INDEPENDENT FINANCIAL ADVISER MARKETPLACE

IFAs represent a significant distribution channel in the UK financial services sector, as there has been a 33 per cent increase in new life and pensions premiums from $5.8 billion to $7.3 billion during 1995–99.[14] It is anticipated that the importance of the IFA as a key distribution channel will continue, for several reasons. First, by 2005 over 5 million people will have investible assets over $75,000, with aggregate wealth growing from $1 trillion to approximately $3 trillion.[15] Second, the increasing complexity of financial products implies a need for independent advice on a personal level; for example, there are now over 1,200 different ISA plans available to consumers. Third, the increasing emphasis on personal financial responsibility, decreasing State provision and the increasing interest in share ownership further re-emphasize the need for advice. Finally, there is also an increasing recognition on the product provider side that the use of a widespread direct sales force is more cost-effectively utilized in conjunction with IFAs.[16] The IFA sector employs around 50,000 people with around 9,000 IFA organizations – the vast majority (in excess of 80 per cent) are SMEs. IFAs handled $37 billion of new medium and long-term savings business in 1998. It is estimated that by 2005 IFAs will account for over $3 billion of GDP.[17] IFAs have become increasingly important in providing investors with impartial advice and are now responsible for approximately 60 per cent of the market in many business categories.

IFAs fall primarily into four main categories:

- national IFAs (eg Towry Law, Inter-Alliance);
- networks (eg DBS and Burns Anderson);
- large regional IFAs (eg Aitchison and Colegrave Group);
- small IFA sector.

A constantly changing marketplace presents significant ongoing opportunities for IFAs able to adapt their marketing strategy quickly and efficiently. For example, consider the current UK political drive to make individuals responsible for their own financial future.[18] This emphasis on financial independence, coupled with demographic trends such as the increasing elderly population, ie 'grey market', increases in the proportion of people pursuing professional and managerial careers, and increases in financial literacy plus associated increases in inherited wealth, present significant opportunities for personal financial planning.[19]

The IFA sector growth has been higher than the national average for 15 years and is anticipated to grow faster than the economy for the foreseeable future.[20] Accelerating technological development, continuing changes in regulation, introduction of stakeholder pensions and an increasing emphasis on client servicing and retention, together with a 1 per cent charging structure leading to lower profit margins for both product-providers and IFAs, are seen as the most important influences on future trading conditions.[21] The marketplace presents major opportunities for IFAs who can not only offer a comprehensive range of investment, tax shelter and financial planning services, with the emphasis on wealth management, client service and relationships, but, as importantly, are structured and managed on a professional basis.[22]

New virtual competitors and intermediaries

Although dot.coms are not replacing existing market players, the number of Internet trading firms has rocketed from 12 in 1996 to 170 in mid-2000.[23] Established companies such as Prudential (Scottish Amicable as IFA provider), Abbey National (Scottish Mutual as IFA provider) are using multi-distributional channels to emerge as formidable competitors in the financial services market, eg companies such as American Express subsidizing the cost of online dealing. UK players such as Motley Fool, IFAonline and FT.com are now offering free investment research and are consequently significantly altering traditional lucrative market positions. Traditional players are increasingly modifying business models in light of these pressures whilst barriers to entry are simultaneously declining. For example,

Inter-Alliance, a leading IFA, is now transacting business online in conjunction with traditional face-to-face sales processes. A further example is an international product-provider that has just launched a new product-provider operation, which intends to deal with IFAs solely via the Internet.

The UK independent financial adviser performs an important role; it is unclear how this role will change as market forces affect their business model design, remuneration models and intermediary functions. e-commerce, e-business and the Internet have led many industry commentators to suggest the demise of the intermediary.[24] It is suggested that the proliferation of information, the increasing sophistication of consumers and increasing direct communication between buyer and seller imply that the added-value role of the future stereotypical intermediary is limited.[25]

The evolution of the intermediary

The traditional intermediary plays an important role in the function of contemporary markets. Indeed, according to Jallat,[26] this role may be categorized into four separate functions:

1. Aggregation – Intermediaries bring together a number of buyers and negotiate business on their behalf with seller(s). This achieves economies of scale, cuts costs and increases the bargaining power of buyers.
2. Trust – Intermediaries introduce a middle ground that protects both sides. This creates a common, fair trading platform from which an intermediary may charge a premium.
3. Facilitation – Information transfer across value chains may be complex and costly; therefore intermediaries can facilitate access to information and validate common standards. This is termed lowering coordination costs, and intermediaries may supplement this with added-value services such as financing.
4. Matching – Intermediaries may locate buyers or sellers and thus create a marketplace suitable for transaction. Here, intermediaries may actually create/stimulate demand, thus pursuing a self-fulfilling role for product comparison, etc.

Impact of e-commerce and Internet technology

Whilst intermediaries have been historically recognized as performing an important role in markets requiring massive information flows between buyer and seller, some authors have suggested that intermediaries will become a relic of historically inefficient markets. The advent of electronic data interchange (EDI) and the Internet has allowed more widespread inexpensive access to information and buyers to locate, communicate and transact directly with sellers.[27] Coupled with the creation of electronic markets, this has led to many fore-casting the demise of intermediaries (eg Kieft[28]). This disintermediation has been argued in the following way. First, radical operational efficiency improvements in the cost of obtaining, processing and storing information have led to changes in market structures and organizational design.[29] This has led to the rise of the 'networked organization' and carries the implication of improvements in an organization's value chain and company inter-linkages.[30] As a result, manufacturers increasingly use IT to perform traditional interme-diary functions themselves, making intermediaries redundant. Malone et al [31] suggest that electronic integration creates a cost advantage, which implies the disappearance of inter-mediaries. Following this logic to its natural conclusion, manufacturers will find it increas-ingly cheap to interact directly with consumers and consumers will utilize the ability to customize products/services directly with producers. Accordingly, Sarkar et al [32] question how far these improved electronic links between companies threaten the existence of inter-mediaries.

This logic has been criticized on the grounds that it assumes that companies and consumers are sufficiently sophisticated, have the necessary time/flexibility/attitude to risk to undertake lengthy comparisons and transact by themselves.[33] Some authors argue that this is not necessarily the case and that electronic markets create opportunities for the re-intermediation of electronic intermediaries. Re-intermediation recognizes that buyer/seller interests must, by definition, conflict and that roles such as needs analysis, product information dissemination or producer risk management require some form of intermediary body. Sarkar et al [34] note that these bodies may be termed 'cybermediaries' in that a network-based intermediary offers a range of functions such as product search or product distribution over the Internet. A useful example of this argument in practice is the existence of Auto-By-Tel.[35] Auto-By-Tel acts as information broker matching vehicles with client preferences and matching buyers with suitable car dealers through access to a contin-ually updated information base, thereby creating a more efficient search and negotiation process.

With increasing Internet usage and an increase in awareness of and access to infor-mation, end users may continue to do their own information searching.[36] It seems equally likely that an element of disintermediation will occur. However, the advent of electronic markets and associated technologies does not necessarily imply the demise of the interme-diary. Rather, the traditional form of intermediaries is liable to change, giving rise to the likelihood of new intermediary models in the future.[37] Bailey et al note, 'new roles for inter-mediaries seem to outweigh any trend toward disintermediation'. Indeed, key functions of aggregation, matching and market facilitation seem to be critical to both buyers and sellers, albeit with varying importance in differing contexts. Bailey et al [38] surveyed 13 markets and contrasted the role of electronic intermediaries with that of more traditional, physical inter-mediaries. Table 25.1 shows the differing roles attributed to the two categories of interme-diary.

Table 25.1 Categories of intermediary (Bailey and Bakos, 1997)

Role of market intermediaries	Physical-oriented intermediation service	Information-oriented intermediation service
Aggregation	Combination of customer orders in wholesale orders	Provision of one-stop shopping
Trust	Provide legal contracts to govern market participation	Provision of authentication and secure communications
Facilitation	Provision of market-specific infrastructure	Exchange of messages between customers and suppliers
Matching	Provision of rich product information	Provision of marketing information to suppliers

Bailey and Bakos [39] found that although the traditional role of intermediaries was in most cases reduced, there were new roles for new types of intermediary to fulfil. Thus, although the aggregator role was reduced, the reduced coordination costs produced by market infrastructure improvements created opportunities for mobilizing consumer bargaining power. Another example is matching in the financial services sector. Here, although the plethora of information reduces search costs, this carries the concurrent importance of navigating, filtering and matching of financial products with individual requirements.

The IFA – an evolving intermediary

As a result of the trends affecting the financial services sector as a whole, the IFA sector faces many complex issues that could alter its place in the marketplace forever. Depolarization is of fundamental importance. So far, the distinction between agents operating on a 'tied basis' (contractually obliged to recommend products of a particular product-provider) and those operating on the foundation of 'truly independent' advice (operating without contractual stipulations binding them to any product-provider) has been clear.[40] However, depolarization introduces the concept of 'multi ties' whereby an IFA would abandon the 'independent advice' mantra and adopt a formalized panel of several product-providers for each aspect of financial planning, eg protection, pensions, investment bonds, unit trusts, ISAs, etc. The implications for consumers are that IFAs choosing the multi-tied route would no longer be able to offer completely independent advice based on a process of due diligence, but would be forced to offer a limited range of products albeit on a discounted, priority basis.[41] Some national IFAs and networks would welcome this approach as it implements a model arguably in tacit practice today, whilst other players such as large regional IFAs view depolarization as a serious threat to their niche status as 'free agents'. It has been suggested that the widespread prevalence of multi-tied agents remains inevitable, whilst others believe that scope remains for both independent and multi-tied agents to co-exist.[42] If the ability to remain truly independent means that IFAs are obliged to change from being fully remunerated by commission, then many IFAs will probably switch to multi tie or perhaps adopt a two-tier approach, ie operate a multi-tied agency alongside a fees-only IFA company.

The process of depolarization has important implications for business model design. IFAs may be faced with pursuing a discount broker house model focusing on volume-dependent consumer markets,[43] or else focusing on the affluent market, ie high net worth individuals (HNWIs) and blue-chip corporate clients as a more attractive opportunity, working through personal relationships and concentrating on providing added value based on expertise and ongoing client service.

A further implication for IFAs is how closer relationships with product providers, depolarization and governmental regulation affect revenue streams. Commission-related remuneration has traditionally compensated the IFA sector. The advent of the stakeholder pension charges, the so-called '1 per cent world', has depressed the margins that product providers extract from new business generation.[44] This lower margin has implications for IFAs in the form of cost-cutting exercises and the advent of fee-based remuneration. Increasing use of technology will be essential to reduce operating costs of IFAs and to improve the service to clients. It is unclear how this will affect IFAs and their traditional revenue models.

OUR RESEARCH

To probe further the issues described above, we carried out some empirical research. This consisted of 15 in-depth interviews with intermediaries, product providers and experts (consultants, journalists and systems providers involved in the industry). Here are the results.

Industry structure

The most common suggestion was that government has played a key role by firstly reinforcing regulation, ie the Financial Services Act in 1986, and subsequently increasing the burden of regulation in an endeavour to protect consumers. More recently, this has been due to an ideological shift in terms of the current government's role in relation to its citizens' financial expectations. According to a leading national IFA, demographic changes such as the 'exponential increase in the elderly population, ie the so-called grey market' forced the government to explore potential solutions to the perceived inability of the State to finance state pensions on an ongoing basis. According to this respondent, this shift, coupled with a general increase in disposable income and financial sophistication, led to a policy change geared toward the 'importance of individual responsibility for financial planning'.

Further, the government reacted to the pension mis-selling debacle during 1992–94 with the Pension Mis-selling Review, the Disclosure Review and the Evolution Project to provide the consumer with greater clarity in terms of the how much financial products actually cost. New initiatives such as the advent of (commission) disclosure together with the introduction of the stakeholder pension and the 1 per cent world in 1997 led to a general increase in awareness associated with financial planning. In addition, the ever-increasing complexity of financial products led to the recognition of the importance of specialist advice associated with the growth of the equity culture. It was suggested by a third-party commentator that the '[1 per cent world] implied more margin in distribution as opposed to manufacture' and that a paradigmatic shift in the balance of power from product-providers to intermediaries and aggregators was under way. A product provider also suggested that 1 per cent charging structures will expand from 'merely pensions [to encompass all] financial products in the future'. A management consultant commented that this transparency coupled with 'the rise of exotic investments such as hedge funds had led to [distribution] channels preferences… IFAs have made a strong comeback as consumers now appreciate the breadth of choice and [consequently] want advice'.

A further important factor is the uncertainty surrounding regulatory constraints in terms of the 'polarized versus depolarized world', according to a technologist source. This factor refers to the Financial Services Authority (FSA – a new super-authority replacing the now defunct PIA) review on the introduction of multi-ties in relation to IFA depolarization, transparency of revenue models and CAT standards (imposed charges caps) throughout the product sector. This issue impacts on the intermediary business model design of IFAs and has concurrent product provider stakeholder implications, which will be studied later in this section.

Consolidation in the sector refers to the acquisition of UK product-providers such as Clerical Medical (acquired by Halifax in 1996), Scottish Amicable (acquired by Prudential in 1997) and Scottish Mutual (acquired by Abbey National in 1992) by financial conglomerates seeking to introduce a business-to-business distribution channel to their business model. This period of consolidation has reflected a product-provider's opinion that there was 'recognition that mutual companies could not exist profitably by themselves in the long term and needed to be acquired [by a financially strong conglomerate]'. This trend has also affected the IFA sector, for example the Misys £75 million acquisition of DBS Management on 18 June 2001 to create a network of 7,250 registered IFAs and 3,700 member firms. This consolidation should, however, be regarded in the context of increasing fragmentation in terms of companies specializing in product manufacturing, marketing, servicing and delivery. This is exemplified by the existence of companies such as the Exchange FS, fund supermarkets such as CoFunds or Fundsnetwork, Screen Pages, Yodlee and

Synaptics Network who exist to fulfil specialist functions in the financial services value chain.

There has been a rise of innovative products such as hedge fund investments and a rapid rise of price-driven product such as simple term assurance or individual savings accounts (ISAs) bought direct or delivered through discount brokers. For example, the retail bank HSBC offers several types of ISA according to consumer risk profile. One IFA respondent suggested that this variety and complexity may 'bewilder people', which in turn created a broader role for his IFA role from a mere product focus to 'a financial planning strategy tailored to their specific requirements'. A further qualification added by a third party was that the continued volatility in equity and currency markets would imply that product providers must become more 'receptive to change' in consumer tastes and preferences. The impact of reduced margins will ensure a continued drive to reduce costs (by up to 50 per cent suggested by many product providers) leading to increased use of technology and the Internet by both product providers and IFAs.

The introduction of capped charges affects product providers' ability to differentiate themselves, leading to resultant tacit product commoditization together with a decreasing ability to extract profit from depressed margins. Equally, IFAs are affected since depressed margins imply that reduced commission levels may become insufficient, therefore leading to the possibility of pursuing a hybrid model constituting a mix of fee-based services and commission charges. Indeed, a leading IFA noted that it seemed 'inevitable that fees would become the greater part of the overall remuneration model'.

Impact of e-commerce upon UK product providers

Opinion was divided as to the impact that e-commerce has had on UK product providers to date. On one hand, e-commerce has played a relatively minimal role in product providers' business to date. According to a leading technologist, product providers have 'largely paid lip service [to e-commerce] and the delivery [of e-commerce] has failed'. He suggested that product providers have regarded e-commerce and e-business as opportunities to achieve cost efficiencies as opposed to electronic valuations or commercial transactions. He cited Skandia as an example whereby the Internet and e-commerce allowed it to create a front-end graphical interface connecting multiple legacy systems. A leading product provider explained why the uptake of e-commerce has been slow: 'the reality has been at odds with analysts' expectations and traditional models have been challenged – but not as people expected'. He elaborated further by suggesting that 'product providers struggled to find ways to use technology which forced them to work more closely with IFAs in sales, new product development (NPD) and training'. Another product provider argued that use of e-commerce and e-business had been largely confined to product comparison in commoditized markets and for the dissemination of information, eg pension applications.

Finally, a management consultant suggested that e-commerce and e-business had neglected areas such as 'Web enablement of sales online – this will continue due to the need for advice in the market'.

On the other hand, some respondents indicated that e-commerce has played a significant role in product providers, although the potential still remained unrealized. A leading IFA suggested that product providers were now able to 'design new products with [creative use of] new distribution channels, but that is not the case with old policies'. A technologist remarked that e-commerce and e-business has had an 'impact upon day-to-day operations with IFAs, but that relationships with consumers remained unaffected'. The example of electronic quotations obtained via the Exchange FS was highlighted, but in contrast relatively few products available to consumers via the Internet were given as an example. However, a leading IFA respondent noted the existence of Fundsnetwork (offered by Fidelity Investments) and CoFunds as examples that opportunities offered by e-commerce and e-business were being addressed, albeit remaining in the minority. One industry commentator noted that some companies had adopted the 'head in the sand approach due to the increasing costs of compliance, coupled with the inherent threat to their sales forces and IT budgets being spent on reducing costs rather than business model [redesign]'. A technologist believed that the impact had in fact been significant in business-to-business relationships in terms of EDI, etc, but that business-to-consumer e-commerce remained in an embryonic stage.

Opportunities resulting from e-commerce, e-business and the Internet have been received with a mixture of procrastination, suspicion and lukewarm acceptance by a number of companies. This reinforces our earlier suggestion that the financial services sector had failed to embrace the potential offered by e-commerce. Indeed, one leading product-provider suggested that e-commerce had been approached in time-honoured fashion, which was no different to any organization witnessing the prospect of radical change. He suggested that the approach could be viewed as following discrete 'phases such as identification, initial denial, recognition, rebellion and acceptance. Three years ago, the challenge was getting e-commerce on the corporate agenda. This took around one year. Then companies recognized e-commerce as a way of saving money and committed resources... [Organizations are now] struggling with integrating e-commerce projects with existing projects and shifting legacy systems/policies/projects to the new model'. The next section advances this argument by establishing the strategic vision of product-providers as a foundation for assessing their progress to date.

UK product providers' strategic vision

There appears a lack of long-term strategic vision in product providers' depiction of how e-commerce would be used in their business. In our research (described later), respondents

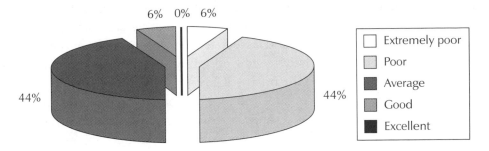

6% 0% 6%

44%   44%

	Extremely poor
	Poor
	Average
	Good
	Excellent

Figure 25.4 UK product providers' strategic vision

were asked to describe UK product providers' strategic vision. The results are shown in Figure 25.4.

This shows that UK product-providers' strategic vision is thought to be poor or at best average. A third-party commentator elaborated by suggesting that 'most firms are trying to put old business models online – but that Prudential with Egg and the Halifax with Intelligent Finance were exceptions'. One technologist noted that his poor opinion 'wasn't necessarily an indictment of the industry as it varies dramatically'. A further third-party commentator noted that the financial services industry had improved in its 'commercial awareness' but qualified this comment by suggesting that its 'strategic vision was good but that implementation [systems infrastructure] was not so good'. The next section establishes what role respondents attributed e-commerce in relation to UK product provider business.

The role of e-commerce for UK product providers

All respondents were united in their opinion that e-commerce had a major role for UK financial services. However, there appear significant discrepancies in the precise nature of this role. A leading international product-provider suggested that e-commerce had three constituent applications:

● 'information search and transaction via the Web;
● business-to-business communication and value chain integration;
● e-trading between product provider'.

Most product providers regarded e-commerce as offering potential for cost efficiencies and value chain compression. Most respondents emphasized the role e-commerce and e-business had in generating more productive relationships with IFAs or in gaining further cost efficiencies in the 1 per cent world, eg stakeholder pensions. Respondents believed that the advent of the Internet, increasing efficiencies of IT and the accessibility of technology had led to internal cost efficiencies and associated benefits to market. One third-party respondent noted that product providers were adopting 'a bolt on, piecemeal approach' to the integration of e-commerce into the business. He suggested that e-commerce would be used to achieve 'a multi-manager architecture for his company that would allow it to offer a range of financial products across a range of consumer and corporate markets using a single systems platform'. Further, he cited the possibility of e-commerce, e-business and the Internet offering the possibility of tailoring products more specifically to individual requirements. Interestingly, one product provider did suggest the possibility of e-commerce pursuing an 'all-encompassing role in the business, sales, service and communication [value] chain'.

One respondent from a technology background suggested that a key factor was the identification of new channels to deliver e-commerce. He suggested that alternative channels such as digital television have potential for massive growth and, if successful, would carry a host of external companies from retail, media or telecommunications industries into further revolutionizing the UK financial services sector. Third-party commentators' and IFAs' views appear to have more strategic focus, indeed one commentator suggested that e-commerce would lead to 'portfolio valuations 24 by 7, top-up pensions online, fund switching, etc, online' for both intermediaries and consumers.

The general consensus is that technological improvements have led to a general increase in consumer convenience in terms of portfolio valuations/amendments/transactions and which also carried concurrent challenges/opportunities for business. The Internet was suggested as a new delivery channel through which both product providers and new intermediary players could transact business. It was noted that there was a need to utilize technology but that must be set against increasing costs associated with training, compliance and administration which also required significant investment.

There is therefore no doubt that the Internet is viewed as a viable medium for IFA/client/policy servicing. However, opinion remains divided as to the viability of product providers to sell products online. On one hand, several respondents suggested that product providers could transact online, both by offering a direct sales route via the Internet and through participation in third-party portals such as the Exchange. One management consultant emphasized that 'all products can be sold online – despite the fact that only 25 per cent of UK households have Internet access, this segment is sophisticated'. The only barriers to achieving this would be 'understanding the [relevant] demographics and buyer behaviour and [problems associated with] electronic signatures'. A technologist suggested that purchasing financial products would become possible using new media such as via digital TV, eg 'the Coronation Street ISA' offered by companies entering into traditional financial product providers' territory, such as media or telecommunications companies.

However, one product provider suggested that it 'would be difficult for product providers to sell over the Internet'. This may be due to the fact that consumers are 'too savvy to go to them [product providers] over the Internet'. One respondent suggested that transacting online was 'dubious, as sales carries a [concurrent] role for advice... [In the future] this may be face-to-face, but technology advice [eAdvice] is three or more years away'. Most respondents agreed that such business may be confined to certain simple commoditized products such as term assurance or ISAs aimed at more price-driven market segments. It was suggested by a management consultant that questions such as 'How complex is the product? or What is the requirement for advice?' would dictate the extent to which products could be transacted via the Internet. Accordingly, more complex products such as mutual funds or stakeholder pensions would always require advice.

A national IFA noted that 'transacting business for HNWIs or owner-managed business' required 'total financial planning' where the 'personal touch, trust and face-to-face contact' was important. He believed that the Internet was an 'extremely effective marketing tool, thus creating added value for information and communication'. A third-party commentator noted that 'consumers are unlikely to rely on a passive medium – a combination of distribution channels' was a more attractive proposition. The importance of the personal touch administered through personal contact was underlined by the suggestion of Web-based assistance (eg live chat or 'call me back' facilities). This multi-channel approach, made available to carefully chosen market segments, could include face-to-face advice, electronic distribution, mailer and possible direct contact with product-providers via some form of intermediary body.

Priorities for UK product providers

Respondents were asked to suggest key priorities for UK product-providers to consolidate/capture market share. One industry commentator suggested that there should be an organizational drive to assess opportunities. He recommended three courses of action. 'Firstly, undertake extensive segmentation modelling in both customer and IFA markets to understand each player's contribution to the business. Second, launch a separate business operating alongside the existing firm via the Internet. Third, conduct several company experiments offering relatively simple products such as ISAs over the Internet.' Several third-party respondents who suggested that the use of stakeholder profiling was crucial to future survival endorsed these comments. Here, estimating 'the total lifetime value of all customers' was deemed important. One provider noted that 'for too long financial services companies have committed the cardinal sin of ignoring their client base'.

A further priority for UK product providers was to establish commonality throughout the industry in terms of standards, mass-subscription to 'portals such as the Exchange to provide real-time access to client data' and 'support development of legal frameworks such as electronic signatures'. Projects such as ORIGO and EMX were supported but received criticism due to their slow progress and incomplete support. One industry commentator noted that 'the government or FSA had a role to play in this issue'.

Where systems were concerned, the common suggestion was to 'integrate legacy systems with current e-commerce projects, marketing programmes with a front-end Web interface'. This view was reflected in the form of an innovative Web-based concept called 'Open Finance' which seeks to provide a technological solution to develop a common multi-product platform, 'so-called eArchitecture', for product-providers. Another leading industry commentator suggested that 'consistent information to customers and partners across all contact points' was an important priority to all product-providers.

Where value chain alliances were concerned, one leading IFA suggested that a key priority for UK product providers was 'to work more closely with IFAs and develop systems to monitor the cost of doing business with IFAs, eg the cost of acquiring new business'. A leading third-party commentator endorsed this sentiment by suggesting that understanding the intermediary market would prove important. One IFA respondent noted that product providers are 'currently going through the motions' and that streamlining IFA access to back-end new business processes and quotations with front-end interfaces was critical. This IFA also suggested that 'although product providers were keen to develop and refine technology integration between their business, some product providers were less than forthcoming'.

These findings build upon the main thesis of the review of the literature, which suggested that e-commerce and e-business had potential for wide-reaching improvements in UK product provider business. Interestingly, however, the findings also indicate that opinion appears to be confined to tactical value chain efficiencies as opposed to the addressing the possibility of lateral strategic thinking. The next section explores how these opportunities affect the product provider's relationship with its most important organizational stakeholder, the independent financial adviser.

UK product provider and IFA relationships

Here, the consensus was that the 'larger national IFAs and networks were establishing closer ties with selected product providers [at the expense of] smaller one-man bands'. Indeed one technologist commented, 'national IFAs have the power to drive e-commerce strategies for product providers'. A third-party commentator noted that 'the relationship has got much closer with increased cooperation' as selected IFAs became 'involved in product providers' decision making processes'. However, the point was re-emphasized that this proactive relationship applied only to IFAs with specific qualifying criteria as 'product providers had undertaken a profitability analysis' to determine potential candidates. This view was substantiated by a further IFA suggesting that 'product providers were holding IFA hands as strategic partners'.

Most respondents noted that IFAs were crucial to the development of product provider business but it was noted that this may change due to the changing mix of alternative distribution channels. One technologist suggested that 'the cost of serving IFAs is unsustainable' and that 'focusing on new business generation was a mistake in light of the transfer from commission to fees'. This is particularly important as it highlights the apparent conflict of interests between product providers and that of IFAs. Product providers appear primarily concerned with new business generation whilst according to one IFA, 'the thinking IFA is concerned with serving existing clients better with the addition of added-value services'. This conflict indicates that both parties have not fully reconciled their differences and are not as yet effectively collaborating to achieve their respective objectives.

One IFA suggested that 'different products would be designed for different IFAs – badged and priced on a bespoke basis'. Further, the IFA suggested that 'there was more margin in manufacturing than distribution so some IFAs would manufacture their own products'. This view conflicts with an earlier view that suggested the precise opposite. This issue illustrates how the industry is in a profound state of flux to such an extent that industry players harbour conflicting views as to their own future. A noted industry consultant suggested that 'the uncertainty of how market structure [will be affected with respect to] the product provider relationship in a tied world' was an issue currently perplexing the industry. Although most respondents realized that multi-ties may be inevitable, opinion was divided as to the attractiveness of the concept.

Perhaps naturally, IFAs were convinced that the concept was flawed. One IFA suggested that this would 'confuse the public more if they introduced a middle ground – [it would lead to a] sort of semi-independent advice'. Another IFA suggested that some people 'would take multi-tied advice thinking it was independent', alluding to the possibility of mis-selling similar that of 1992–94. His position was that his company would maintain its independent status but would consider launching a separately branded multi-tied venture should circumstances require it. A further IFA suggested that although he was against the concept since it did not offer consumers 'best-of-breed advice', the majority of IFAs would become multi-tied due to wider trends such as sector consolidation, etc. One IFA source suggested that 'no more than 10 per cent of IFAs would go multi-tied' as HNWIs, blue-chip corporate clients, would continue to demand truly independent advice, particularly specialist expertise. However, a technologist suggested that 'multi-ties should happen for the right reasons – some IFAs would rather be dead than go multi-tied whilst others may have no choice' due to increasing pressures to join a wider national network.

Some respondents favoured depolarization, leading to the prospect of multi-tied agents. One product provider suggested that it would respond to a general consumer change to more price-driven financial products and 'couldn't see why IFAs wouldn't want to [pursue this direction]'. Indeed, he suggested 'although it would be difficult to explain to consumers – it merely formalizes existing practices'. This alludes to the practice of many IFAs using tacit product panels for each aspect of financial advice. IFAs emphasize that this semi-formal panel exists as a result of research, analysis and due diligence but others argue that it offers a poor option for consumers as they receive semi-independent advice. A technologist commented that 'independent financial advice is flawed – there is no such thing as independent advice'. Accordingly, one respondent asked 'what will really change?' One product provider reasoned further, noting 'consumers are more educated... and have an increasing ability to distinguish' between advice given by tied agents. This logic was extended by a third-party commentator when he suggested 'what consumers really want is good value... IFAs and product providers feel that consumers want a higher level of advice than they really do'. These arguments would suggest that there is considerable scope for self-segmentation in the UK financial services market – namely that under a multi-tied environment, consumers will be able to choose whether they prefer 'table d'hôte or à la carte' advice.

UK product providers – future direction

A common view was that the market would become more transparent, in effect 'more professionalized', and that the impact of further government regulation would catalyse a new era in which IFAs would prosper. This is despite the fact that increasing bureaucracy would prove 'counterproductive, as it would impose further regulatory burdens for IFAs and product providers'. Further, the impact of operating in the 1 per cent world would 'provoke further consolidation as product providers struggled to operate within the 1 per cent capped charges' and this was qualified by the fact that this applied 'in terms of both manufacture and distribution' since both required significant scale economies to achieve sustainability. Further, it noted that the current drive for common standards, eg ORIGO and EMX, would prove stillborn unless product providers established sufficient ground upon which to negotiate much-needed industry standards in order to achieve substantial progress. It was reluctantly suggested that this might be a useful role for the government to pursue as existing industry endeavours were failing.

One industry commentator rather controversially suggested that this emphasis on capped charges 'could bankrupt some life companies' and that this was 'doing fundamental harm to the UK economy'. The balance of power within the sector was anticipated to change further as product providers 'struggled to understand how to incentivize IFAs' and more interestingly, a technologist suggested that 'current distribution channels would expand to encompass both independent and tied agents' as both product providers and IFAs would strive for client ownership. A technologist suggested that 'smaller IFAs would face increasing pressure to join networks to put purchasing power behind them' but that there would also be 'a requirement for national IFAs and there were people manoeuvring to do that'.

It was suggested 'the impact of decreasing interest rates would make traditional products such as with-profit funds less attractive'. This is further exemplified by the introduction of stakeholder pensions as it was anticipated by one respondent that 'non-pension markets would grow as they were more profitable'. However, several respondents pointed out that an emphasis on investment performance would continue, although there would be a clearer distinction between price- and performance-driven products in response to more efficient segmentation. A product provider's comment qualifies these observations on the sector by noting that 'relationships now last for around 5 to 7½ years for product providers' and that the drive to control costs for the duration of that relationship would compel the search for partners in a bid to achieve financial strength. A national IFA respondent added that the sector now had 'the ability to transact, access mainframes and reduce administration costs' – a combination that had previously appeared unlikely.

A respondent from a leading consulting firm suggested that 'European markets were becoming increasingly saturated and there would be greater segmentation of markets'. Further, he suggested that a concurrent increase in customer relationship management (CRM) technologies appeared likely to transform relatively static and under-utilized databases to produce more useful behavioural information. Finally, he noted that product design would become more creative to take account of the seemingly conflicting requirements of an increasingly aged population and increasing sophistication of the mass affluent market. This was qualified by a respondent noting that 'European and UK retail companies would try to establish an IFA brand' in a bid to deliver this sophisticated product strategy. This renewed emphasis on 'tailoring brands and propositions to client segments' would increasingly become the preserve of conglomerates with both business-to-consumer and business-to-business operations functioning from a single product platform.

Nearly all respondents agreed that the advent of new entrants appeared increasingly likely. Attention was drawn to recent entrants such as www.virginmoney.com – 'they have turned their attention exclusively to consumer markets focusing on price'. One IFA noted that 'barriers to entry are reduced by the Internet and may give rise to execution-only type firms' which will 'give consumers the opportunity to use these firms in conjunction with IFAs'. Consumers may soon be able to take advantage of an integrated portfolio, which contains best-of-breed services from a range of financial services product providers. Although a leading third-party commentator suggested 'consumers aren't yet ready for clicks only', www.yodlee.com and other such information aggregators would soon enter the marketplace. Respondents also agreed that new entrants might originate from other industries such as media and entertainment, telecommunications and overseas markets such as the USA. 'Retail brands such as that of BSkyB or Microsoft Life partnered with BT might have a go' since communications and technology are so important in financial services.

Business model reconfiguration

One respondent suggested that 'big change was imminent with the arrival of fund super-markets which could mean the abolition of commission' – this would herald a fundamental shift in how product-providers deliver products, receive revenues and remunerate inter-mediaries. Should 'product providers start connecting capital markets with consumers themselves and go direct' as a third-party commentator suggested, then the role of inter-mediaries will be affected in two ways: first, in terms of how they sell product and second, how they get remunerated. These issues will be addressed in the next section. Respondents agreed that both 'back office re-engineering' and the support of industry initiatives such as ORIGO were important. Respondents suggested that changes to the product provider revenue model appeared likely. 'More income will come from increasing recurring income' was suggested as product providers come to understand the 'lifetime value of a client and are increasingly able to tailor products to suit evolving client requirements'.

For product providers, one respondent noted that 'it is going to be easy to drive margins down to oblivion' in a 1 per cent world. Anticipating a multi-tied world, the implications for the product provider business model are that they must 'gather five business partners and try to integrate services' amongst these partners. The key question is to understand 'what mass do you need to optimize profitability at low margins'? Accordingly, product provider business models should concentrate on either 'manufacturing or distribution'. A third-party commentator suggested 'that products would continue to be multi-channels – with some "e", some direct and some IFA'. One product provider noted 'companies such as NU would get the chequebook out and buy distribution, take the hit up front and reap the long-term benefits in a multi-tied situation'. Respondents agreed that the larger product providers such as the Prudential could turn their attention to consumer markets, offering an 'e-commerce model, not the mail order approach', but that this would probably be under a separate brand, as 'advice will account for 90 per cent of their business'. It was suggested that 'channel-specific product providers should stick to their own channels but that the development of a common service infrastructure' would facilitate different brand opera-tions. Accordingly, the solution appears to lie with careful product analysis to determine precisely which products are most suited to which distribution channel.

One IFA noted that he 'wouldn't dismiss the thought of going multi-tied but that would be under separate company and separate brand' but that 'our own clients would expect completely independent financial advice'. This would suggest that the IFA sector would, as a whole, have to undertake a profitability analysis of their client base since perhaps the HNWIs, blue-chip companies and the general mass affluent market would expect truly independent advice, as products would be increasingly focused on investment performance and the demand for quality ongoing service would increase. One product provider noted that IFAs 'should not be disconcerted [by the advent of technology, fund supermarkets, etc] as the role of advice is crucial'. One product provider suggested 'psychology not business model design was the cornerstone of the IFA' which implies that as long as consumers perceive that they are getting good advice at an acceptable price, the possibility of a multi-tied agency business model is not a major threat.

Respondents were asked to assess the prospects of an IFA pursuing two separate business models, that of a transaction-oriented discount broker house or a relationship-oriented advice and service-based approach focusing on wealth management, ie 'a total asset management and financial planning service' for the mass affluent sector, HNWIs and blue-chip corporate clients. Most respondents noted that there would be scope for both, citing the decreasing barriers to entry in volume-driven broker houses. One respondent said, 'opportunities exist in both, but also in the middle segment (neither very rich but have money)'. This indicates that a role for multi-tied agents appears well founded as a significant proportion of the market may require quality, value-driven advice from a company representing a number of reputable, solid investment performance achieving product-providers. As expected, however, the client-relationship-driven model based on quality advice and service received most support as, according to one IFA, 'client relationships are stronger and offer best hope for recurring income'. However, if, according to another IFA, simply selling products is not the *raison d'être* for the company, then this model appears most likely for long-term profitability.

The IFA revenue model will be subject to radical change as 'the existing reliance on indemnity commission can be no longer sustainable'. Indeed, the IFA consensus is that adoption of fees must be considered and that it has to further refine its own fee-based remuneration model. One respondent suggested that 'consumers should be given a choice', empowered to determine whether to pay fees or to permit commission as remuneration, since fees may not necessarily be appropriate in differing situations.

These findings suggest considerable difference of opinion as to how product providers and IFAs should operate in the future. It is clear that product providers must address the value chain efficiencies and strategic opportunities afforded by e-commerce. One the other hand, opinion is split as to how they may conduct business. The research highlighted that product providers should regard consumer markets, multi-tied IFAs as well as truly independent IFAs, as opportunities. The research also suggested that the future of the truly independent IFA as a market intermediary was in doubt, as the review of the literature suggested. The research highlighted the differing roles attributed to IFAs in the future and emphasized a number of priorities for product providers to consider.

RECOMMENDATIONS AND CONCLUSIONS

UK product providers

As a result of dealing with an empowered and increasingly sophisticated and discerning customer, companies will become more focused on delivering tailored customer solutions. The coordination of products/services, systems infrastructure and strategy will be geared to conducting relationships with individual customers. Certainly, the existing product/technical focus is decreasing, but discussions with product providers such as Scottish Equitable, Scottish Amicable and Scottish Mutual reveal that all efforts are still focusing on value chain efficiencies rather than stakeholder management. Accordingly, the evolution of truly CRM-oriented financial services organizations may be still some distance away, perhaps three to five years in the future.

Further consolidation in the industry is likely as financial requirements (ie capital adequacy and free asset ratios), brand strength, access to global markets and customer trust are becoming difficult and expensive to establish/maintain. Traditional financial services company core capabilities such as technical skills and resources such as financial strength will allow larger players such as Merrill Lynch, Prudential and Royal Bank of Scotland further M&A opportunities. Some companies will use their scale to become commodity or infrastructure providers, churning out products in volume (ie as commodities). Other companies will aim for niche positions as innovators or superior performers offering asset or risk management services.

Opportunities for outsourcing and strategic alliances in areas such technology, CRM and product delivery will be significant. *Business Week* speaks of 'technology on tap' in its annual report on technology and this example proves the synergy potential for the pooling of resources and capabilities. An example of distribution channel alliances is the partnership of Tesco with the Royal Bank of Scotland. This partnership allows Tesco to outsource the infrastructural (including technical expertise) aspects of its personal financial planning operation whilst the Royal Bank benefits from exposure in a separate but complementary area of its consumer market. The renewed emphasis on CRM, strategy and associated non-technical skills, the so-called 'soft skills' of the future, will place exhaustive demands on organizations. Traditional expertise in areas such as investment management, technical knowledge, deal-making and systems development may become less important with the resultant demand in favour of soft skills such as customer support – see Figures 25.5 and 25.6 for evidence of this. So, training, recruitment and associated consultancy will also be needed.

On the consumer side, increasing familiarity with technology and new concepts such as self-service financial planning (involving simple decision trees) look increasingly likely, particularly as the young people of today grow ever more comfortable with technological innovation. As the industry is currently burdened by complex product specifications and

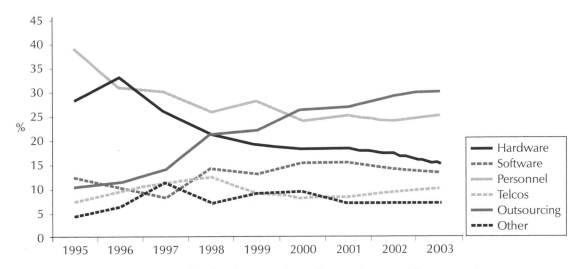

Figure 25.5 Percentage (%) of technology budget allocated to specific categories

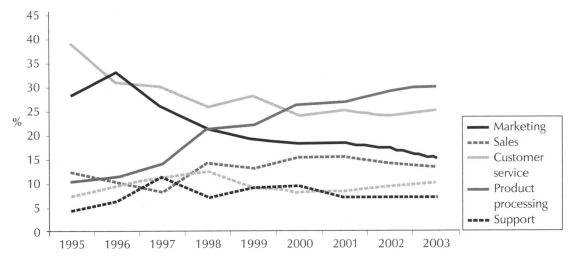

Figure 25.6 Percentage (%) of technology budget allocated to function

ever-increasing industry regulation, this will not be easily achieved. A further extremely important trend for consumers is the increased prevalence of traditionally non-financial providers. For example, business-to-consumer financial portals coordinated by the likes of AOL-Time Warner, Yahoo and Tesco will bring financial services to a new tier of consumers that will combine to make products simpler to understand, more accessible, flexible and attractive to groups traditionally ignored by many financial services companies, such as the retired population (the grey market) or lower income families, in addition to the consumer segments that will readily embrace technology.

To date, UK product providers have justifiably been concerned with internal efficiencies (eg new business processing) and continued profitability by focusing on areas such as increasing sales productivity and perhaps less interested in the provision of added-value services and client retention. Product-providers are prime candidates for a 'bricks and clicks' e-business strategy. Gulati and Garino (2000)[45] suggest that traditional companies combine their core competences with modern e-business skills to develop a hybrid business strategy, thus servicing established traditional markets together with electronic markets. However, the analysis above demonstrates a requirement for strategic thinking detailing how product providers may reorganize themselves to take advantage of the opportunities afforded by e-business.

Product providers should consider the reorganization of their value chain to encompass the efficiencies, cost savings, added-value services and opportunities afforded by e-business. Indeed the notion of straight-through processing is similar to Rayport and Sviokla's (1995)[46] virtual value chain in that traditional business processes or market positions are circumnavigated by technology. We have explained some of the options for product providers in Chapters 4, 6, 10 and 39.

One option is that of relationship manager – a mediator between customer and product provider. This model requires detailed understanding of consumer preferences and habits, whilst facilitating the possibility of premium pricing in return for customizing the 'customer experience'. It is also expensive to implement, as sustained investment in systems, human resources and company culture is required. Further, this model requires a long-term horizon due to the difficulties associated with establishing/maintaining close customer ties. Table 25.2 summarizes the main differences between the transaction and relationship approaches.

This model requires product providers to consider carefully their value chain activities and relationships with intermediaries. A key question is whether product providers wish to consider effectively transferring ownership of clients to themselves and away from IFAs. Product providers should assess whether it is more profitable to engage end consumers more directly in the management and administration of their financial affairs or to maintain the manufacturer role and rely on distribution via intermediaries. Which choice they should make depends partly on the outcome of depolarization and any resulting industry

Table 25.2 Transaction versus relationship approach

Transaction-based style	Relationship-based style
• One sale	• Many sales
• Commission bias	• Fees bias
• Low service level	• High service level
• Sales orientation	• Service orientation
• Product focus	• Solutions focus
• Product promotion	• Brand promotion

consolidation. If many IFAs evolve as multi-tied agents and commence contractual relationships with a limited panel of product providers, then this permits a greater degree of systems and service integration than is currently in existence. Accordingly, as product providers provide end consumers with greater access to their policies such as valuations/amendments/transactions/investment performance/general information, the possibility of product providers maintaining more direct relations with consumers appears increasingly likely. However, should the majority of IFAs remain truly independent then client relationships will continue to be considered their specific domain. This business model is further complicated by the fact that most product providers will have to operate with both multi-tied agents and IFAs and should therefore strive for the middle ground.

Indirect channels – IFA/product provider relationships

The existing preference by consumers for face-to-face contact will probably continue for the foreseeable future. IFAs will continue to play an important role in the distribution of investments, life assurance and pension products, despite the continued increase in direct channels such as telephone or new media, ie the Internet and digital TV. Indeed, Datamonitor predicts that IFAs will increase their market share of the distribution of life/pension products to around 57.3 per cent by 2004.[47] Table 25.3 shows how product provider channels of distribution are expected to evolve. It is clear from these projections that the IFA/product provider relationship in terms of investments, life assurance and pension products will continue to form the most important role for product providers. It is expected that this will change with the introduction of depolarization. Depolarization holds both opportunities and threats for product providers in that they must commence informal negotiations with 'candidate multi-tied' IFAs to gain access to the clients most suited to their products, but risk harming close ties with larger IFAs who intend to remain independent regardless of depolarization. Accordingly, decisions must be made as to how UK product providers view multi-tied firms and truly independent financial advisers. The author is of the opinion that both types of IFA should be accommodated, thus necessitating differing product/service offerings. It is recommended that product providers should undertake extensive analysis of their entire product/service portfolio and cross-reference these results against a profile of the IFA that is most suited to these characteristics. This involves identifying key IFA accounts that require superior service levels compared to relatively low priority IFAs who simply require a telesales approach. This exercise should seek to establish each component's requirement for personal advice and specialist assistance and whether this form of advice/assistance is best administered via an IFA or multi-tied agent. Further, the author recommends that product providers commit significant resources to the establishment/maintenance of closer electronic integration with selected IFAs. This exercise should view subsequent value chain efficiencies as of paramount

Table 25.3 Life and Pensions Distribution, 2000–04

Datamonitor (2001) *eConsumers in Financial Services*

£Million	2000	2001	2002	2003	2004	CAGR 2000–04
IFAs	2992	3251	3545	3725	3961	7.3%
Direct sales force	1290	1291	1272	1279	1299	0.2%
Bancassurance	624	704	808	904	995	12.4%
Tied agents	258	277	295	301	309	4.6%
Other direct	209	227	249	273	301	9.5%
Affinity marketing	9	15	32	38	47	49.1%
Total	5382	5763	6200	6520	6912	6.5%
%	2000	2001	2002	2003	2004	+/-2000–04
IFAs	55.6	56.4	57.2	57.1	57.3	1.7
Direct sales force	24	22.4	20.5	19.6	18.8	-5.2
Bancassurance	11.6	12.2	13	13.9	14.4	2.8
Tied agents	4.8	4.8	4.8	4.6	4.5	-0.3
Other direct	3.9	3.9	4	4.2	4.3	0.5
Affinity marketing	0.2	0.3	0.5	0.6	0.7	0.5

importance, yet these should also be regarded as hygiene factors, ie as prerequisites for successful IFA relationships.

The major source of innovation in the indirect channels of distribution is expected to lie with the introduction of information aggregators such as the Exchange, Yodlee and Fidelity's Fundsnetwork. This new form of intermediary will assist in the analysis, evaluation and purchase of relatively simple financial products and will act as a medium accessible via the Internet to both consumer and corporate clients. UK product providers should view these new entrants as a major opportunity to dilute their historical reliance on IFAs and engage consumers more directly in the transaction process. Product providers should regard such intermediaries (portals, infomediaries, etc) as the opportunity to match products with clients more efficiently. Product providers should undertake both product and profitability analyses to understand precisely which products are best suited to each distribution channel. For example, stakeholder pensions hold the possibility of being administered online using the technological capabilities offered by 4th Contact, for example, and their online project entitled 'Working Wealth' which offers the potential for viewing pensions, health insurance, stock options and other benefits schemes online.

We recommend that product-providers should also consider greater product customization in light of fast-approaching depolarization and dominance of national IFAs and networks. Here, more complex products such as self-administered pension schemes (SIPPs) or inheritance tax mitigation plans could be customized to more closely reflect the client base requirements of the larger, more profitable IFAs.

Direct channels

Many providers are using this approach, and although the share of business is low, it is growing. Success here implies use of the telephone to move from a purely execution-only to a more advice-driven basis. Growing consumer sophistication and the increasing ability for information search implies that product providers must offer consumers a range of products and services suitable for delivery over the telephone. At present, Scottish Widows and Standard Life offer this service but use it as a method of backing up IFA business as consumers are encouraged to retain an IFA. The author believes that relatively simple products such as term assurance or ISAs should be available via the telephone due to the decreasing costs associated with maintaining a telesales operation. Accordingly, the telephone should be used as a direct channel of distribution supporting other channels but clearly has the capability for increasing transaction levels, as Virgin has clearly demonstrated (although profitability has yet to emerge).

The Internet is perhaps the most important opportunity for direct consumer interaction with product providers as it offers the potential not only for increasing the frequency and quality of value chain communication, reducing cost and offering new marketing opportunities, but also for transaction capability. However, product providers must engage in product analysis, in essence, redesign products to become more streamlined and suitable for distribution via the Internet. An example of product providers establishing an alliance with a corporate client is Prudential's venture with Sports Fitness and Leisure Ltd whereby Prudential provides an online education service with the intention of eventually launching a transaction-based operation. Since government has already initiated price/charge transparency, product providers should seize this opportunity to refine their entire product-range.

Depolarization offers the opportunity of more closely aligning product providers across different product specialisms so the cost of this exercise could be shared across all partners. Indeed, the advent of depolarization indicates that product providers will be selected on the basis of their systems/IT infrastructure. Therefore, although provider allegiances will prove cost-efficient, the author believes that they will also prove to be a strategic necessity. An example of such partnership is Legal and General working with Standard Life and the Printing Industry Pension Scheme to deliver policy information account statements online. The author would also encourage the enthusiastic support of industry initiatives such as

ORIGO to achieve the establishment of industry standards such as the widespread adoption of public/private key identification, standard proposal forms and new business processing.

Product providers should also increase efforts to transact online. This should be through relatively simple price-driven products to be delivered via the Internet effectively as commodities. The advent of Fundsnetwork and CoFunds further demonstrates the viability of using the Internet to transact online and the author believes that there are significant opportunities for product providers to transact online to both corporate (eg in connection with stakeholder pensions) and consumer markets (eg ISA products).

Traditional product provider revenue models

UK product providers are under increasing pressure to provide products within a 1 per cent capped charge. They will need to find ways of radically reducing costs associated with processing and administering business. It increases pressure on IFAs to move from a primarily commission-based revenue structure to a more fee-based model. UK product providers may consider moving to a dual pricing structure, paying IFAs greater remuneration for operating electronic administration than that of traditional, labour-intensive and paper-based methods. IFAs would probably experience declining margins in commission-oriented transaction-intensive activities such as fund switching and may be inclined to launch their own fee-based remuneration structure until administration costs are reduced. Product providers must find ways to motivate IFAs to join in cost-cutting value chain efficiencies whilst adopting a more anticipative, proactive stance toward industry trends.

The functions of new business processing, client servicing, administration, communication and collaboration will need to be progressively migrated on to the Web. New systems such as that offered by 1st Software, adopted by many leading IFAs, facilitate electronic reorganization of systems, but there is a clear need to develop the notion of straight-through processing across the product-provider value chain. This will span both the internal departmental lines and, across the intranet/extranet, product providers or large corporate clients. This internal process integration will allow product providers to reorganize their organizational boundaries to follow a more flexible, semi-permeable membrane organizational model. The flow of communication between product providers and external stakeholders will become more frequent, structured and flexible to facilitate access to a variety of internal services.

Product providers need to recruit more customer-oriented staff with softer skills such as customer relationship management or alternatively outsource this requirement. A balance between the technical expertise, administration quality and the CRM-oriented focus of the workforce is required, if product providers are to foster new and strengthen existing relationships with stakeholders. This implies that significant resources be devoted to the recruitment of new staff along with retraining of existing employees. Organizational culture is an important managerial challenge.

The financial services sector as a whole is contemplating the arrival of e-business-related technology with considerable concern, as these issues do not rest easily with the traditional product-oriented focus adopted by many companies. Product providers currently have strong cultures based on technical knowledge and expertise, investment performance and product-oriented sales norms as introduced and reinforced by legacy systems and industry trends spanning decades. How may this be changed to encompass the latest attitudes towards stakeholder relationships, technology, etc, required at board level and at all levels throughout the organization? Many product providers appear restricted to a relatively myopic view of e-business, believing it impossible to attempt anything more than value chain efficiencies for at least two years ahead. It is therefore up to progressive IFAs to spearhead developments in straight-through processing and business model design by exemplifying/pioneering innovations and aligning themselves more closely with similarly progressive product providers. So, current criteria for selecting a product provider (namely, investment performance, charging structure, financial strength) should expand to include e-business capabilities.

One of the key external managerial challenges is concerned with strategic alliances and outsourcing of technological development, systems infrastructure and technical expertise, eg IBM's links with the Bank of Scotland as a pioneering example, which proves the possibility of pooling resources whilst avoiding conflicting cultural problems, training costs and compensation disparities associated with the introduction of new system/business processes. Outsourcing and alliances increase the speed to market of in-house developments and allow the opportunity to expand the customer base at minimal cost. However, relationships with third parties require change management programmes coupled with information sharing and collaboration arrangements. These pose significant problems in an industry used to clear organization boundaries and unambiguous market relationships underpinned by complex service-level contractual obligations. Alliances will only work if undertaken with an open-minded, flexible managerial/entrepreneurial mindset.

A final managerial challenge is the myriad of technological innovations, which further hinder clear strategic thought. In addition to common development tools such as XML, and communication/collaboration standards such as Rosettanet, there is a wide variety of access devices, which open the delivery of financial products and services to a new market-place. The advent of mCommerce, iTV and wireless connectivity and broad bandwidth offer significant opportunities. The implications of this relate to the delivery of location-non-specific services allied with more complex insights into consumer preferences. The development of the universal device (music, video, telephone, Internet access) also lends credence to the increasing diversity/dynamism of marketing as cross-selling opportunities and potential for individual customer relationships increase exponentially. For example, Royal Bank of Scotland currently works with Orange and Woolwich with Nokia to deliver

WAP services throughout the UK. It seems likely that consumers may soon become less concerned with technology and access devices and more concerned with seamless access to information and personalized transactions. Accordingly, as explained earlier, the author recommends that product providers seriously consider the customization of financial products and value-added services to more closely reflect the idiosyncratic characteristics of distribution channels and, of course, the end consumer.

Notes

1. Shelton, D (2001) Life in 2005, *Money Management*, June
2. Shelton, D (2001) Life in 2005, *Money Management*, June
3. Shelton, D (2001) Life in 2005, *Money Management*, June
4. Shelton, D (2001) Life in 2005, *Money Management*, June
5. Datamonitor (2000) *eConsumers in UK Financial Services*
6. Forrester Research (2000) *UK Supermarkets Arrive*, June
7. Moreton, R and Chester, M (1996) *Transforming the Business: the IT contribution*, McGraw-Hill, London
8. Venkatraman, N and Henderson, J (1998) Real strategies for virtual organizing, *Sloan Management Review*, Cambridge, Autumn
9. Burgess, L and Cooper, J (2000) E-commerce – a report on emerging business models, University of Wollongong, New South Wales, Australia
10. Bambury, P (2001) *A Taxonomy of Internet Commerce*, First Monday
11. (2000) Don't discount the discount brokers, *Money Management*, June
12. Datamonitor (2000) *UK Independent Financial Advisers*
13. Datamonitor (2000) *The UK eConsumer – Impact 2000 Report*
14. Lombard Street Research, London, United Kingdom, 2000
15. Cap Gemini Ernst and Young (2000) *Electronic Commerce – A Need to Change Perspective*
16. Datamonitor (2000) *UK Independent Financial Advisers*
17. Lombard Street Research, London, United Kingdom, 2000
18. (2001) Goliath falls, *Money Management*, June
19. Shelton, D (2001) Life in 2005, *Money Management*, June
20. Lombard Street Research, London, United Kingdom, 2000
21. Datamonitor (2000) *UK Independent Financial Advisers*
22. Datamonitor (2000) *The quest for value in eFinancial Services*
23. Lombard Street Research, London, United Kingdom, 2000
24. Datamonitor (2000) *eConsumers in UK Financial Services*
25. Janssen, M and Sol, H G (2000) Evaluating the role of intermediaries in the electronic value chain, *Internet Research: Electronic Networking Applications and Policy*, **10** (5), pp 407–417
26. Jallat, F (2001) Disintermediation in question – New Economy, New Networks, New Middlemen, *Business Horizons*
27. Sarkar, M B, Butler, B and Steinfield, C (1996) Intermediaries and cybermediaries: a continuing role for mediating players in the electronic marketplace, *Journal of Computer-Mediated Communication*, **1** (3)
28. Kieft, R K (1995) The death of the librarian in the (post) modern electronic information age, in *Information for a new age: redefining the librarian*, compiled by Fifteenth Anniversary Task Force

Library Instruction Round Table American Library Association; Englewoord, CO: Libraries Unlimited, pp 15–22

[29] Sarkar, M B, Butler, B and Steinfield, C (1996) Intermediaries and cybermediaries: a continuing role for mediating players in the electronic marketplace, *Journal of Computer-Mediated Communication*, **1** (3)

[30] Porter, M E and Millar, V (1985) How information gives you competitive advantage, *Harvard Business Review*, July–August, pp 149–60

[31] Malone, T, Yates, J and Benjamin, R (1987) Electronic markets and electronic hierarchies: Effects of information technology on market structure and corporate strategies, *Communications of the ACM*, **30** (6), pp 484–97

[32] Sarkar, M B, Butler, B and Steinfield, C (1996) Intermediaries and cybermediaries: a continuing role for mediating players in the electronic marketplace, *Journal of Computer-Mediated Communication*, **1** (3)

[33] Jallat, F (2001) Disintermediation in question – new economy, new networks, new middlemen, *Business Horizons*, March **1**, p8

[34] Sarkar, M B, Butler, B and Steinfield, C (1996), Intermediaries and cybermediaries: a continuing role for mediating players in the electronic marketplace, *Journal of Computer-Mediated Communication*, **1** (3)

[35] Jallat, F (2001) Disintermediation in question – new economy, new networks, new middlemen, *Business Horizons*, March **1**, p8

[36] Fourie, I (2001) Should we take disintermediation seriously?, *The Electronic Library*, **17** (1)

[37] Bailey, J and Bakos, Y (1997) An exploratory study of the emerging role of electronic intermediaries, *Internal Journal of Electronic Commerce*, **1** (3), Spring, pp 7–20

[38] Bailey, J and Bakos, Y (1997) An exploratory study of the emerging role of electronic intermediaries, *Internal Journal of Electronic Commerce*, **1** (3), Spring, pp 7–20

[39] Bailey, J and Bakos, Y (1997) An exploratory study of the emerging role of electronic intermediaries, *Internal Journal of Electronic Commerce*, **1** (3), Spring, pp 7–20

[40] 2001 IFAs will have to fight for a piece of the cake, *Money Marketing* () 21 May

[41] (2001) Collaborate or consolidate?, *Money Marketing*, 7 April

[42] (2001) Looking back in the review mirror, *Money Marketing*, June

[43] (2001) Looking back in the review mirror, *Money Marketing*, June

[44] (2001) Looking back in the review mirror, *Money Marketing*, June

[45] Gulati, R and Garino, J (2000) A mix of bricks and clicks, *Harvard Business Review*, June

[46] Rayport, J F and Sviokla, J J (1995) Exploiting the virtual value chain, *Harvard Business Review*, November–December

[47] Datamonitor (2000) *eConsumers in UK Financial Services*

26

Deconstructing the value chain: property and casualty insurance servicing

Paul Greensmith, Peter Routledge, Stuart Degg, Cathy Pickering and Merlin Stone

INTRODUCTION

For several years, there has been speculation on value chain deconstruction in the property and casualty (P&C) insurance industry. This chapter examines whether such deconstruction might take place in the servicing side (ie excluding manufacturing and distribution). It is highly relevant to the topic of CRM, as it shows that we cannot assume that customers will always be managed by the same kind of supplier. The pressures of deconstruction run completely counter to the ideas of 'single source' and 'comprehensive relationship' that form the basis of so many CRM programmes. Indeed, if deconstruction leads to very great cost savings, it is hard to resist the conclusion that many consumers will be better served by doing business with companies that know how to combine low-cost providers. Many brands that consumers are used to dealing with as integrated suppliers may turn out to be distributive fronts for a range of outsourced suppliers.

This chapter argues that a strong economic rationale for deconstruction exists. Standardization is a key force behind deconstruction, since it increases the attractiveness of outsourcing. Three drivers accelerating standardization are identified:

1. the emergence of new technologies;
2. corporate and industry drive toward efficiency;
3. reduction of regulatory barriers.

A consequence of increased standardization is the rise in credible external options that provide functions within the value chain. The growing presence of business process outsourcers (BPOs) proves that the P&C insurance industry is contemplating this. Structural profitability pressures will further fuel deconstruction. These profitability issues have structural, not just cyclical origins, being primarily related to over-capitalization within the P&C insurance industry. As a result: 1) P&C insurers must focus on developing their core sources of economic value where they can most readily differentiate themselves from the rest of the market, and; 2) P&C insurers are considering their strategic options with regard to the servicing element of their business. Some smaller P&C insurers lacking scale and expertise are already pursuing deconstructive strategies through the use of outsourcing utilities. Whilst larger insurers have more time to consider their strategic options, defending vertically integrated business models is likely to become an increasingly challenging strategy in the long term

Evidence from other industries supports the case for responding proactively to the forces of deconstruction. In other deconstructing industries, those players who first pursued strategies in support of deconstruction tended to be more successful than those defending traditional value chains. However, P&C insurers' response to deconstruction should vary depending upon the complexity of the product and its strength in given markets. Any decision on the strategic direction of an insurance servicing function is likely to be made within the context of a broader strategic debate, including both the manufacturing and distribution functions. While this process of evaluation and resolution is ongoing, it is likely that we will see the growth of stronger, more robust BPOs, offering increasingly credible outsourcing alternatives in the servicing of insurance business

WILL VALUE CHAIN DECONSTRUCTION EMERGE?

In January 2001, Abbey National appeared to support a vision of a deconstructed P&C insurance industry by divesting itself from its non-life-insurance joint venture with CGNU plc. Rather than using a vertically integrated business model to provide its customers with insurance products, Abbey contracted with Norwich Union for its underwriting product and Capita Group for its policy administration and claims servicing. Is this an anomaly or an early sign of value chain deconstruction in the P&C insurance industry?

This kind of deconstruction is not new to the P&C insurance industry. Insurance brokers and third-party administrators are outward manifestations of the forces and economic logic of deconstruction. Yet, larger P&C insurers have remained vertically integrated, despite predictions from industry analysts to the contrary. The P&C industry, however, is exposed to significant forces of transformation, such as the growth of standardization, existing market profitability pressures, and the emergence of new business models. This chapter, therefore, will examine whether a clear economic rationale combined with industry-wide profitability pressures will compel large, vertically integrated P&C insurers to deconstruct the servicing segments of their value chains.

Since the industrial age, managers have wrestled with the issue of which inputs to produce themselves via vertical integration and which inputs to purchase from the market. For example, early in the 20th century Ford Motor Company owned its own rubber plantations in Brazil from which it acquired the raw material to produce tyres for its automobiles. Since divesting itself of its rubber plantations (and thereby deconstructing part of its value chain), Ford has chosen the market as the most effective means of organizing the production of rubber for its tyres.

The key question underlying the deconstruction issue is whether to obtain a good or service from the market or within the firm (ie vertical integration) Let us consider some of the economic arguments.

Transaction costs and asset specificity

Two simple economic ideas help managers determine whether to produce a good/service on the open market or within the firm (vertical integration) – *transaction costs* and *asset specificity*.

Transaction costs

The Nobel Prize-winning economist, Ronald Coase, examined why companies opted to integrate vertically along their industry's value chain, rather than purchase these goods and services from focused specialists on the open market. He determined that firms choose to integrate vertically because of the existence of transaction costs. Transaction costs, broadly defined, are the costs of using the market to organize the production of a good or service. Coase reasoned that, in using the market, firms incur transaction costs that are not present when they organize these functions in-house.[1] He, and his successors, identified three types of transaction costs:

- **search costs** – the cost of finding the product/service that a market participant needs from a vendor it can trust;
- **coordination costs** – the cost of coordinating activities, resources, and processes between two market participants who agree to an exchange;
- **negotiating costs** – the cost of negotiating a contract between two market participants.

Therefore, when managers decide whether to organize internally (via vertical integration) or externally (via the market), they must economize on the combined production and transaction costs. In a world of relatively high transaction costs, it is still uneconomic to obtain that good/service from the market. Firms will therefore choose to produce that good/service internally. In a world of relatively low transaction costs, it is economic to obtain that good/service from the market. Firms will choose to use the market to obtain that good/service rather than develop the capabilities to produce it themselves. In both cases, the market is the more efficient mechanism for producing the good/service.

Asset specificity

Asset specificity refers to the degree to which a particular good or service is specific to a firm (ie custom-made) versus how general it is. If a particular good or service is highly specific to a firm, its asset specificity is high. In the case of an insurance company, the detailed methodology and data underlying its pricing of risk has a high asset specificity, while its payroll management system has a low asset specificity. A good or service with high asset specificity is typically native to the particular firm – it has attributes not relevant outside the firm, it cannot be easily obtained through alternative sources, nor can it be easily redeployed in alternative situations. It is an asset that is close to the core of the firm and, as such, it is a source of economic value. Asset specificity is the most important factor influencing transaction costs, so when it is high, transaction costs tend to be high. This is due to the fact that goods and services with high asset specificity are unique to the firm and the information flow related to their production is typically very rich, requiring regular attention from management. Less amenable to standard practices/procedures, the transmission of rich information to parties outside the firm is very costly. Therefore, when asset specificity is high firms will tend to organize production internally; when it is low, firms will look to the market.

The choice between organizing internally and organizing via the market, however, is not discrete. Each form of organization is, in fact, an end point on a continuum that includes networked forms of organization (including equity carve-outs, long-term servicing contracts, and joint ventures), outsourcing, alliances, long-term supplier relationships, and licensing arrangements. When asset specificity is moderate, firms will often find the optimum solution to be one of these networked forms of organization (see Figure 26.1).

CURRENT FORCES DRIVING THE ECONOMIC RATIONALE

Within the past decade, there has been increased standardization across virtually all industries. Industry standards reduce information richness and, therefore, asset specificity. As the asset specificity is reduced the good or service is commoditized and becomes more available in the marketplace, reducing transaction costs. The factors causing this increase in

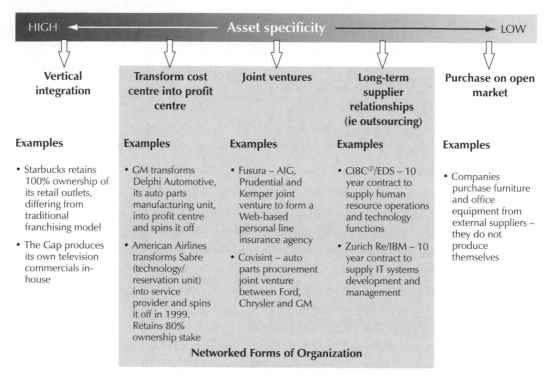

Note: (1) Not an exhaustive list of networked forms of organization. Others include licensing arrangements, franchising, strategic alliances, etc.
(2) CIBC: Canadian Imperial Bank of Commerce

Figure 26.1 Continuum of organization forms

standardization can be attributed to advances in technology, a reduced regulatory environment, and a common drive towards efficiency. The following factors are accelerating change and the likelihood of deconstruction:

- **Advances in technology** – the speed of change of processing power and software development has had a noticeable impact in almost every industry. Computers have rapidly evolved from data collection, to processing, to managing the flow of information and finding patterns within it. This development of expert systems is a result of simplifying a lot of the previously complex processes and procedures. By defining parameters around which information is collected and exchanged, there is more opportunity for interaction with third parties and for the outsourcing of a variety of functions.
- **Reduced regulatory environment** – two main forces at work here are globalization and deregulation. Governments are keen to enter free-trade pacts, which bring with them regulatory standards for policies and procedures. Similarly, as deregulation is introduced, so are criteria around service levels and reporting. Again the reduction of artificial barriers of entry (regulatory, tariffs, quotas, taxes, etc) allows the entry of more companies, in turn providing more market options and directly lowering transaction costs.

- **Drive towards efficiency** – as companies seek to gain efficiencies internally there is a realization that there needs to be commonality among units and across countries. The advantage is that best practices and infrastructure development costs can be shared and ultimately reduced. Additionally, firms are agreeing to cooperate on elements that improve the operation of the industry as a whole. For instance, the acceptance of the Online Financial eXchange (OFX) is a good example. Developed by technology and financial services firms, it sets comprehensive parameters for transmitting personal financial information over the Internet.

Consequently, over the past decade, the world witnessed a trend towards standardization, led by great advances in technology. Standardization reduces the richness and complexity of information, and lowers both the asset specificity and transaction costs. Given the complexity of this transformation, the precise implications are hard to predict, but, for our purposes, some practical observations are emerging:

- **Vertical integration will become less attractive** – as transaction costs fall, firms will be able to reap the benefits of specialization by looking outside their boundaries for many goods and services.
- **Horizontal integration will become more attractive** – falling transaction costs will allow firms that are successful at a particular activity to realize economies of scale and scope by expanding their productive capacities to a wider variety of goods and services and to a greater number of customer groups.
- **Networked forms of organization will continue to proliferate** – while asset specificity will decline for many goods and services, in many cases it will not weaken enough to make them amenable to market forms of organization. Instead firms will experiment with a wide variety of organizational forms to economize on the combined production and transaction costs. Such forms will include outsourcing, long-term relationships, joint ventures and strategic alliances – we have already witnessed this in the UK corporate partnership arena for a number of years.
- **Those industries whose products are largely digitizable will be most at risk** – industries such as software and financial services, whose products are largely information based, will be amongst the first and most significantly impacted, since the financial and qualitative costs of transferring data are generally low.

APPLICATION TO INSURANCE SERVICING

How does this apply to the world of P&C insurance? Claims processing and policy administration are functions entirely based on information. They take data from customers or prospective customers, process it using rules and formulas, and output a resolution satisfactory to both policyholder and insurer. Traditionally, the information processed was rather rich as these functions often lacked uniformity of process and insurers relied heavily on individual expertise for their successful execution. As a result of this information richness, claims processing and policy administration had typically high levels of asset specificity and firms organized them internally.

Technology leads the way

Today, IT innovations are driving standardization of insurance servicing functions, as seen in Figures 26.2 and 26.3. As a result, perceptions about what processes are truly core to creating value are changing as insurers realize that these processes do not vary much from firm to firm. Given these facts, trusted third-party specialists are becoming better positioned to perform these services, achieve scale economics, and thereby make them their own core sources of economic value.

Traditionally, the industry had resisted the argument of possible outsourcing through the use of two key lines of reasoning: 1) this does not apply to the entire P&C insurance

Standardization drivers	Rating and quoting	New policy issuance	Policy adjustments	Policy cancellation	Policy renewals
Internet/call centre technology	• Creates standard interface for presenting policy information	• Creates standard interface for distributing and binding policies	• Creates standard interface for policyholders to update their policy records	• Creates standard interface for policyholders to cancel their policies	• Creates standard interface for notifying policy-holders of renewal • Standardizes renewal interface
Workflow systems	• Standardizes processing of quotations	• Standardizes processing and issuance of new policies	• Standardizes insurers' response to amendments to policy coverage	• Standardizes cancellation process	• Standardizes renewal procedures
Expert systems (eg credit scoring, CRM)	• Creates standard rules for quantifying the risks of individual policyholders • Automates the validation of quote information	• N/A	• N/A	• N/A	• Standardizes analysis of existing claims and policy data • Creates standard rules for approving renewal
Advanced database technology	• Standardizes storage and utilization of quotation data	• Standardizes collection of and structures new policy data	• N/A	• N/A	• Standardizes collection and analysis of policy and claims data

Figure 26.2 Standardization drivers for policy administration

Standardization drivers	Notification	Adjudication	Negotiation to agreement	Indemnification	Recovery
Internet/call centre technology	• Creates standard customer service levels and operating procedures • Ensures standards for data capture	• Allows adjudicators and customers access to standard, sanitized information	• Standardizes resolution of some disputes by providing parties with standard interface (eg Cybersettle.com)	• E-procurement technologies standardize communications with vendors and enforce expenditure rules	• Action sites (eg CGNU's BlueCycle.co.uk) standardize resale of recovered items
Workflow systems	• Forces initial handler to follow standard operating procedure	• Provides set parameters for handling claims • Implements mandatory procedures, authorizations and audit trails	• Standardizes dispute resolution times at each stage of negotiation process	• Establish and enforce rules for indemnification process	• Establish and enforce recovery rules
Expert systems (eg fraud detection)	• Automatic segmentation of claims – separates out claims requiring enhanced level of scrutiny	• Automatic identification of potential fraud	• Gives standard guidelines for negotiation as to indemnity and quantum (eg CSC Colossus)	• N/A	• Automate identification of recovery opportunities
Advanced database technology	• N/A	• Structures claims information according to standard criteria • Facilitates easy sharing of information across firm or industry (eg CUE)	• N/A	• Structures expenditure data to facilitate standard management reporting	• Structures recovery data to facilitate standard analysis

Figure 26.3 Standardization drivers for claims processing

industry, and; 2) these processes are mission critical and should be kept internal. Regarding the former, there is some validity in arguing that complex commercial P&C insurance (eg major global programmes), where regular human intervention and negotiation are mandatory, tend to be better suited to internal organization of insurance servicing. However, other product categories – such as auto, homeowners, fleet, and workers' compensation – that are more prone to standardization do lend themselves substantially to external organization.

Regarding the second critique, while *ensuring* accurate and effective policy administration and claims processing are mission critical, they may not be core to the insurance carrier's own economic value-add. Many processes critical to business operations – data centre operations, call centres, application development – are frequently outsourced by insurers and other large corporations. Networked forms of organization such as long-term contracts and detailed service level agreements (SLAs) help mitigate the risk of such action.

Deregulation plays a hand

The increasing power of non-traditional insurance distributors (eg bancassurers) is also leading to deconstructive pressures on the servicing side of the value chain. Traditionally, maintaining a consistent relationship with the customer, from policy sale through to claim, supported vertical integration. However, large intermediaries dictate the separation of functional responsibilities. Thus for the past few years Royal & Sun Alliance (R&SA) has been involved in a disaggregated value chain with regard to the Halifax. Halifax as the distributor has opted to service its claims in-house. This leaves R&SA as the product underwriter and risk carrier.

As underwriters decouple from distribution, there is less logic for always maintaining ownership over the entire claims process, unless that underwriter possesses a 'genetic superiority' in claims activity, on which he or she relies for competitive advantage. The customer may be better serviced, with focused experts meeting their very different distribution and servicing needs, while customer confusion from dealing with separate vendors can be mitigated through a single brand (likely the distributors').

Industry initiatives

Information technology is not just driving standardization and lowering asset specificity at the firm level, it is also doing so at industry level. Via industry associations, insurers are collaborating to bring standardization to insurance servicing. The most relevant example is the Data Standards Work Group, established by the Insurance Data Management Association (IDMA) in 1999 to create policy and claims data standards. Its objectives are to:

- create a claims data exchange standard and implementation guide to facilitate easy exchange of claims data;
- develop and document data element specifications in a 'Policy Data Element Dictionary' which will be used to build policy data exchange standards;
- collaborate with other associations to promote the development and adoption of data standards in the insurance industry.

As outlined earlier, industry standards aid IT in reducing asset specificity. Therefore, standards initiatives like the IDMA's will increase the attractiveness of external organization of insurance servicing.

BPO service providers are a sign of deconstruction

An early harbinger of reduced asset specificity in insurance servicing is the rise of the business process outsourcing (BPO) industry. The insurance BPO industry has its roots in the information technology outsourcing (ITO) industry as well as the captive/self-insurance market. ITO began from the simple premise that companies expended too much time and resources focused on running data centres and applications development – functions with low levels of asset specificity. As a result, a large industry sprang up to provide these services more efficiently and effectively than individual firms could. P&C insurers have capitalized on this trend. The companies that provide services to these segments are now turning their attention to the insurance BPO market. These players are focusing on small and medium-sized insurers that do not have sufficient scale to maintain cost competitiveness and make large technology investments. At present, service providers are not attacking the large insurer segment, as BPO solutions do not presently lend themselves to large carriers with proprietary processes that require industrial-strength solutions. However, as these players win business from small to medium-sized carriers, a great deal of knowledge and expertise will flow to these specialized service firms and position them to provide industrial-strength, cost-effective solutions in the medium term.

Therefore, the migration path that these service providers are likely to follow includes these milestones – after establishing market presence and building capabilities, these players will: 1) target small to medium-sized insurers to enhance scale, and; 2) attack the large insurer segment. Progress towards these milestones is likely to accelerate as the BPO sector is growing rapidly.

Conclusion

Fusing the advancements in information technology with the economic rationale for deconstruction, we find that asset specificity, and therefore transaction costs, are declining within the servicing segment of the P&C insurance value chain. This will place increased pressure on P&C carriers to consider networked forms of organization for this function (such as organizing it as a profit centre, creating a servicing utility joint-venture, or outsourcing). The rise of BPOs and developments within the distribution segment of the insurance value chain further support this trend. Therefore, we assert that deconstructive forces will exert significant pressure on the value chains of P&C insurers to seek new business models. A key assumption underpinning our argument above is that combining the servicing volume of multiple P&C insurance carriers will drive down the average cost of that service. An insurance servicing utility would derive its benefits from enhanced buying power and process efficiencies enabled by new technologies and increased scale.

STRUCTURAL PROFITABILITY PRESSURES AND OPTIONS FOR P&C CARRIERS

Above, we argued that the industry has an economic rationale, technological stimulus and the emergence of standards to offer deconstruction an opportunity. The question remains whether it is likely that a deconstructive force will emerge from within the industry to transform that opportunity into reality. Now let us look at the forces generally at play in the P&C sector to see if they offer an answer.

Structural profitability issues

Returns on equity within the P&C insurance sector consistently trailed other financial services sectors and industries in the 1990s. This is primarily due to the persistently high combined ratios in the P&C industry over the past 20 years. These profitability problems have structural, not just cyclical origins. Supply of risk capital within the P&C insurance market greatly exceeds demand. This has created an environment of chronic under-pricing where the majority of insurers utilize their excess capital to erode their own, and the industry's, operating margins.

Implications of profitability pressures on P&C insurers

The structural profitability pressures to the P&C insurance industry makes the drive towards becoming 'best in class' a fundamental one. Faced with these profitability issues, P&C insurers must wholeheartedly acknowledge that they can't be 'world class' at everything. Acceptance of this principle obliges P&C insurers to make challenging decisions across the entirety of their current activities. Insurers will have to become effective at selecting those activities where they have the capabilities and depth to become truly market leading. Those activities must then become 'core' to the strategic direction of that organization. In short, insurers must undergo a process of evaluation to select which activities they should invest in to win, and which activities they should divest to more efficient organizations on the open market.

To effectively decide the scope of their future activities and strategic direction, we believe that insurers are asking themselves three key strategic questions:

1. **What do I want to be?** This would clearly define the future focus of their business – product lines, geographies and leveraged skills.
2. **How good can I get at performing those activities?** Insurers must objectively assess their chances of becoming world class in the manufacturing, servicing and distribution elements of their business. The level of shortfall between their current capabilities and a world-class performance will enable insurers to decide the migration path and effort required to become market leading, or indeed the realization of their aspirations.
3. **How can I organize myself to win?** Once questions 1 and 2 have been successfully answered, insurers can then understand how they implement the construction of their

organizational model. The critical question here involves the degree to which they will vertically integrate activities or look to the marketplace.

While in the longer term we believe that some companies will face the issue of 'outsourcing' such hitherto 'core' activities as underwriting and claims policy, in the near term the more likely target is insurance servicing – policy and claims administration functions.

Within the P&C marketplace, some P&C insurers are adopting a similar approach to banks and retailers and deciding that the servicing of insurance business is not particularly attractive or essential to their business model. Therefore in order to reallocate resources into areas of strategic focus they are experimenting with the benefits of enhanced efficiency, comprehensive expertise and in-depth data mining capabilities provided by the consolidation of policy and claims processes within outsourcing utilities.

We believe that a number of these insurers will attempt to reduce operating costs by specializing in highly asset-specific elements of the value chain while outsourcing their servicing functions. As this trend develops, we believe it is unlikely that there will be wholesale deconstruction of the servicing, manufacturing or distribution elements of the P&C value chain. More probable is that insurers will pursue a variety of different strategies in response to profitability and deconstructive pressures. These variances will stem from the different organizational configurations of insurers, eliciting different responses from each organization to the three key strategic questions outlined above.

The future adoption of deconstructive strategies is further clouded by a series of inhibitors, which will slow the process of deconstruction within the industry:

- **Conservatism and regulatory constraints** – as it provides financial protection to individuals and organizations against harmful events, the P&C insurance industry is by nature risk averse. We expect both purchasers and carriers to embrace change cautiously. In addition, regulatory bodies are primarily concerned with maintaining the financial security of insurers rather than their operational efficiency, and will slow down industry transformation.
- **Scale and expertise** – critical success factors in both high and low complexity insurance products are scale and expertise. New entrants to the insurance industry will not be able to develop these competencies quickly.
- **Tax issues** – in many countries, market transactions are subject to consumption taxes (eg VAT in the UK). For example, BPOs will have to achieve efficiencies and quality improvements greater than the value of these taxes in order to be truly competitive. Furthermore, their advantage must also make it possible for BPOs to realize a sufficient profit margin. While daunting, the existence of these taxes was not enough to impact the growth in IT outsourcing in the 1990s.

While these inhibitors partly explain why the adoption of deconstructive strategies has been somewhat slow, experience in other industries teaches us that deconstructive forces will ultimately affect every P&C insurer. However, the majority of insurers must take the time to assess their strategic options and develop prudent migration paths to realize the opportunities that deconstruction presents.

Strategic paths for P&C insurers

Lowering asset specificity and transaction costs combined with acute profitability pressures are set to alter both the shape and dynamics of the current P&C marketplace. Depending on their current strengths, weaknesses and strategic direction, insurers will pursue one or more of the following broad strategic paths:

1. **Strategies based on the development and expansion of sources of core economic value** – insurers must decide on their core sources of economic value and invest to develop market-leading capabilities within those functions. Once those functions have reached a sufficient level of market superiority, the insurer must seek to leverage those strengths to successfully expand their business activities. That expansion could be through the creation of a servicing utility, or alternatively an expansion that leverages genetic superiority in other elements of the value chain. For example, it could be through the micro-segmentation of markets by leveraging new technologies (eg CRM, expert underwriting systems), innovating new products (eg securitization, enterprise risk management solutions), executing M&A strategies and pursuing geographic expansion.

2. **Strategies based on experimentation with alternative organizational structures** – this path does not imply a radical and immediate deconstruction of a P&C insurer's value chain, but rather a focused experimentation with networked forms of organization. This could mean creating a product/geography-independent claims group within the existing organization, outsourcing to a credible third party, turning a claims organization into a profit centre, or establishing a joint venture with a BPO or other large insurer to provide policy administration and claims processing services to targeted segments in the P&C industry.

3. **Protect existing organizational strategy by enhancing current capabilities** – this would require significant incremental improvement in product areas, markets and competencies that are central to the organization's current operating framework and book of business.

We argue that, given the economic logic of deconstruction and the structural profitability issues faced by the industry, large insurers should at minimum pursue path 3 as an interim measure. Furthermore, they should begin to consider initiatives based on strategic paths 1 and 2 as ignoring them is likely to be costly.

Conclusion

Structural profitability pressures will combine with the economic forces of deconstruction to strain the vertically integrated value chains of large and small P&C insurers. The implications for P&C insurers will vary according to their current size, performance and strategic direction. All P&C insurers must seriously reconsider their strategic options and critically undertake an audit of their current capabilities in order to identify their core sources of economic value and market differentiation. Singularly protecting an existing organizational strategy is probably not the most advantageous strategy for these players, as underlined by the experiences of other deconstructing industries.

OVERALL CONCLUSION

In closing this chapter, we reiterate that the broad outlines of deconstruction are very apparent within the servicing segment of the P&C value chain. The economic rationale for vertical integration, namely asset specificity and transaction costs, is reducing. This is a result of the acceleration of standardization by the emergence of new technologies, reduction of regulatory barriers, and a corporate and industry drive towards efficiency. Not only have these necessary economic preconditions for deconstruction appeared, but companies are emerging (in form of BPOs) that are actively encouraging this reality. Significant structural profitability pressures will fuel deconstruction and present vertically integrated insurers with three broad strategies – those based on vertical deconstruction, horizontal expansion, and defending the status quo. Evidence from other industries indicates that players aggressively pursuing strategies based on vertical deconstruction and horizontal expansion are more successful than those defending the status quo. The ultimate conclusion we should draw from this analysis, therefore, is that the forces of deconstruction are real. The companies that effectively identify their core sources of strength, and act earlier to leverage those strengths, will be better positioned for success.

From the perspective of CRM, if companies are to combine the supposed benefits of deconstruction and CRM, strong emphasis will have to be placed on the information systems that allow companies to manage customers coherently, however deconstructed the value chain that supplies them.

Notes

[1] 'Outside the firm, price movements direct production, which is coordinated through a series of exchange transactions on the market. Within a firm these market transactions are eliminated, and in place of the complicated market structure with exchange transactions is substituted the (manager), who directs production.' Coase, Ronald H (1988) The nature of the firm, in *The Firm, The Market, and The Law*, University of Chicago, p 35

27

Direct insurance

Bryan Foss, Merlin Stone and Roy Sheridan

For some time, we have understood[1] that the financial services area is one where consumers *most expected to have relationships with brands*. In the UK, the structure of the entire financial services industry has been placed under immense pressure by a variety of forces – the most important of which has been deregulation. This created the preconditions necessary for the consumer direct insurance industry to be created as a laboratory of experimentation for the financial services industry. In this laboratory, companies have tried to apply the principles of customer acquisition, retention and development in a highly competitive environment. The special characteristics of this experiment have been its focus on: 1) direct relationships between underwriters and customers, attempting to replace the traditional system under which underwriters marketed their products through agents (brokers), and; 2) one of the most volatile and short-term of all insurance products – private motor insurance.

Initially, the direct experiences were confined to general insurance, which therefore provides the most mature 'laboratory of change'. However, the marketing practices of direct insurers have been transferred to other product areas, such as investment and pensions. The key question facing most insurers is whether some of the relationship marketing achievements of direct insurers do provide lessons to be learnt for the entire industry. To answer this, we need to understand some of the detail of how the industry works.

The consumer property and casualty or general insurance industry consists of all insurance which is not life or pensions. Life and pensions is often called assurance, because it assures a return to investors or their beneficiaries. The three most significant categories of general insurance are motor, house and home contents – all relating to property. The difference between these two categories is that assurance normally involves very long-term contracts (10–25 years), while general insurance is sold mostly on an annual contract. The value of each sale is therefore much smaller. In between these two categories are various other products. Some – such as critical illness, employment protection and permanent health – are similar to life and pensions in that they insure the individual rather than property. However, the value of each contract is similar to general insurance, though their persistence, ie the length of time before cancellation, normally falls between the two. As a result, many insurers are uncertain in which category to place these products.

In frequent insurance decisions, eg motor, consumers get rapid feedback on whether they made the right decision. In life and pensions, consumers do not know until it is too late, ie when the policy matures. For the former, consumers use what they see as relatively 'hard' information to decide, eg price, detailed peer recommendation on ease of adminis-tration or claiming. For the latter, consumers probably need advice, due to the complexity and value of the decision, and therefore the purchase is more dependent on trust and rela-tionship. Between these two ends of the spectrum there are many intermediate points and products. For example, although health-related policies can be renewed or switched like motor, rumours and publicity about ease of claiming and disqualifications have made the decision for some consumers more like life and pensions.[2]

Many insurance companies are heavily involved in selling additional investment products – not just endowments (which are insurance linked) but unit-linked policies and tax-efficient products. Some companies sell mortgages, and one or two insurance companies are now deposit takers, planning to become banks. Meanwhile, companies that tended to specialize in life and pensions or general have crossed the formerly quite well-established boundary between the two. Much of this broadening of the product range has taken place in the past few years, and has caused many insurance companies to re-evaluate their marketing approaches. From the time when – after the initial sale – the company could rely on persistence of seven years or more, insurance companies now have to manage customer bases where average persistence ranges from five to two years. This means a much stronger focus on:

1. customer retention, to prevent loss of customers to competitors targeting their acqui-sition;
2. customer acquisition, to replace valuable customers lost through attrition – cancel-lation, switching, etc, and to grow the business;
3. customer development – broadly, cross-selling the new wider range of products, to increase the volume of business and to defend customers against acquisition by other companies. Customers who have bought additional products are normally less vulnerable to competitive attempts to switch the initial product.

However, as we shall see, the traditional organization of the industry made it hard to focus in this way. The arrival of direct insurers led existing insurers to question whether they had a structural handicap in managing customer relationships.

THE DIRECT INSURANCE VALUE CHAIN

The industry has traditionally made a distinction between:

- direct writers – companies which handle the whole process, from customer recruitment and underwriting through to claims management;
- brokers and other intermediaries – who recruit and retain customers, and contract the underwriting to traditional insurance companies;
- the traditional insurance companies, who marketed entirely through brokers and large financial services retailers such as building societies and banks, none of whom originally owned insurance companies.

The distinction between direct writers and traditional insurance companies is not to be confused with the distinction between direct marketing and other methods of communicating and managing customers – although it is true to say that direct writers originally reached their customers through direct marketing techniques, mainly direct response TV, inbound telemarketing and direct mail.[3]

In fact, it is clear that insurance customers do not make the distinction. Most customers distinguish between large companies that use direct marketing approaches – whether they are direct writers or direct brokers – and smaller brokers, with whom they may have local contacts, sometimes face to face, sometimes over the phone. Even this distinction blurs, because some large brokers have urban offices, while many retail marketers of insurance also use direct methods. Put simply, many consumers regard general insurers as they do retailers of own-label groceries – they are not interested in who made the product. What they like is that they only have to deal with one company if there are problems. However, some consumers are interested in product branding when they buy through a broker. A bank's insurance policy sometimes highlights the supplier insurance company – as this can add security. This is especially the case when the intermediary has little security (eg the local sales person of another product).

A simplified picture of the market structure, as it was at the beginning of the 1980s, is shown in Figure 27.1.

In the early 1980s, much general insurance was sold by high street agents or brokers, some of which were national chains, professional practices (eg solicitors), accountants, and by calling sales people, some of whom combined this work with other work involving

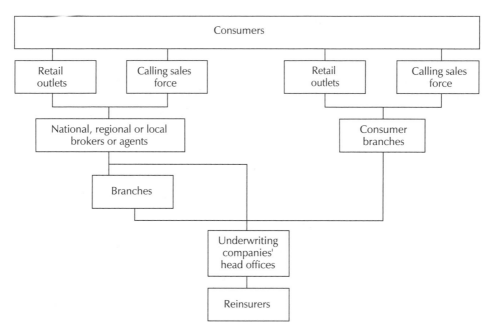

Figure 27.1 The market structure – simplified

frequent calling on their customers, either as consumers or as small businesses. In the motor insurance sector, the rates charged were agreed and published in a Rate Book. For property insurance, a great deal was (and still is) sold by building societies, 'bundled' in with the mortgage payment – although this link is now looser as many insurance companies have targeted this market, encouraging consumers to ask their building societies for explicit quotes and then buying on price.

The role of reinsurers is to handle excessive risks, eg a large value of claims in one day, very high individual liabilities. 'Excessive' is a relative term, defined largely in terms of the underwriters' own risk management policies. New areas of risk are particularly likely to be contracted to reinsurers and reinsurers are always involved in some manner, including in the provision of advice to new and established companies.

THE NATURE OF THE INSURANCE VALUE CHAIN

The direct insurance industry is a very good example of how value chains can split, be brought together, and then perhaps split again. The key steps in the insurance value chain are:

- customer acquisition;
- underwriting;

- customer relationship management;
- claims management and service.

The four can be split or combined in one company. The advantage of splitting is the traditional advantage of focus and economies of scale. The greater the number of companies that encompass the whole value chain, the smaller the opportunity for companies that specialize in one link in the value chain. However, the integrated provider's advantage depends critically on matching the cost-effectiveness and quality of the best of the specialist 'one-link' providers at each link in the chain, or on being able to achieve a better overall effectiveness by re-engineering the value chain, eg by simplifying the processes that connect each link.

Expressed in terms of relationship marketing, the most cost-effective value chain is the one that can acquire and then retain a critical mass of customers, with a risk profile that is more than covered by the premium paid by those customers. If too many customers are acquired at a particular premium level, this will normally be because some customers who have been acquired cost more to manage than is warranted by the premium. If there is insufficient understanding of costs, then poor segmentation and pricing results. If the total costs of managing customers (including claims) are invisible to those responsible for recruiting customers, this can lead to exposure (as has traditionally occurred when agents recruit and insurance companies underwrite). This is illustrated in Figure 27.2.

Premium	Large relative to the expected claim	Profitable if customers carefully selected for risk, but business may be too small	Very profitable, but hard to identify large segments
	Small relative to the expected claim	Probably not viable	Only viable if risk is carefully controlled
		Low	High
		Volume	

Figure 27.2 The premium/volume balance

The costs of managing a customer broadly consist of: 1) claims, ie do customers claim often and/or for large amounts? and; 2) acquisition and retention costs, ie is the process of acquisition too expensive, or are customers highly likely to switch? One reason why these costs can be too high is fraud, which is why insurers of all kinds are most willing to share data on fraud.

The main activities that take place in the value chain are broadly as shown below. In the case of direct writing, both underwriting and agency functions are carried out by the company:

- **Actuarial** – the main function of the underwriter, with the reinsurer handling risks outside the normal for the underwriter:

- risk database creation / maintenance;
- risk analysis and assessment;
- actuarial product development;
- assessment of individual risk;
- pricing;
- fraud identification.
- **Marketing** – mostly done by agents, with the cooperation of underwriters, who see agents as their customers:
  - customer and prospect database creation / maintenance;
  - marketing infrastructure development and management;
  - marketing mix decisions and implementation – product policy, pricing elements not determined by actuaries, marketing communications, distribution channels, customer service etc;
  - customer management – targeting, enquiry management, recruitment, retention and development.
- **Policy administration** – mostly initiated by the agent and completed by the underwriter:
  - quotation documentation;
  - policy documentation;
  - payment receipt.
- **Finance and treasury** – by underwriters and reinsurers – to handle premia before they are required to cover underwriting losses:
  - assessment of future cash and capital requirements;
  - raising capital;
  - investment management to meet requirements.
- **Claims management function** – led by underwriters, involving reinsurers where necessary:
  - claim receipt;
  - claim validation;
  - claim payment;
  - fraud identification.
- **Repair** – by underwriters:
  - cost assessment;
  - organization of cost-effective repair or replacement.

In addition, there are also government and regulatory activities carried out by all participants in the value chain. These include liaison with industry bodies and government to ensure conformance and influence their activities, laws and regulations.

One of the major weaknesses of the value chain as traditionally organized was that risk assessment and marketing were separated. Agents might target customers for recruitment, only to find that their risk profile was too high to be insured by any one of the underwriters on the broker's panel of insurers. This is a disadvantage usually not experienced by direct writers, who can manage their claims data together with their marketing data. We place fraud identification at the beginning and at the end of the value chain, although traditionally insurers placed it only with claims management (ie at the end of the chain). Placing it at both ends enables insurers to avoid taking on fraudulent customers in the first place, rather than waiting until a claim arises – and all the costs that it involves even if the claim is refused because of fraud). In the USA, cars are sometimes photographed before being insured (to prevent insurance after crashes), and in the UK, companies try to identify whether the car was actually written off before the insurance started. In the UK, frequent claimers can be identified through the CUE database. This helps prevent a variety of frauds, eg staged crashes.

Case study – the advent of Direct Line

In the USA, the direct insurance model is well developed. So we have taken as a good case study one that shows the impact of the arrival of the first direct insurer in a market – the UK. In 1985, Direct Line, a joint venture between the Royal Bank of Scotland and Peter Wood, entered the market. Its strategy was simple but clever. Arguably Direct Line was the first UK financial services company to have a clear strategic view about the kind of customers it wanted to attract and retain and to translate that view into a complete strategy for marketing, administration and information technology.

The structure of a directly insured market is much simpler, as shown in Figure 27.3.

Broadly speaking, Direct Line's entry strategy – which was copied with some modifications by several successful later entrants – could be described as follows.

Clear market targeting

Initially, the company targeted what was known as the 'vanilla' or 'Cortina/Sierra' (now Ford Mondeo) customer – the family motorist with a reasonable claims record, a solid

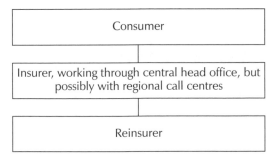

Figure 27.3 Stucture of a direct insurer

record on personal probity (eg no County Court judgements), a car that was not too expensive, and a good residential and occupational history.

Simplified products

Clear market targeting enabled the company to specify a product that was likely to appeal to the average, lower risk customer. The customer was not given many options, eg a limited excess possibility – which also reduced the amount of self-insurance. Payment options were also limited. For Direct Line, the key was to get all the money up front. Avoidance of direct debit reduced exposure to 'direct debit cancellers', who would get a cover note by direct debit, and cancel the direct debit – the cover note remaining valid.

Simplified and very rapid initial sales and confirmation processes

Computing and call centre technology and a simple product range enabled the company to allow operators to gather all the details required to write a policy very quickly, and get the documentation to the customer quickly. There was no need for two mailings, ie cover note followed by policy.

Simplified and very rapid after-sales claims service processes

A similar approach was taken here, with most details being collected over the telephone in a structured way, ensuring low-cost entry of details and rapid authorization.

Direct response television

The use of television as a prime device for initiating the customer recruitment cycle, by gaining customer attention and establishing branding, was considered innovative at the time.

Inbound telemarketing

Direct Line was one of the first financial services companies to use inbound telemarketing as a cornerstone of its fulfilment strategy for customer recruitment. Previously, most financial services companies had assumed that at some stage there would be a 'counter-service' transaction. This change required consumers to trust the telephone as a device for doing business with a financial services company – hence the branding and customer service emphases discussed below.

Advanced US call centre technology and practice

Direct Line was one of the first UK financial service providers to really understand how to deploy the call centre approach to customer recruitment. This approach, closely linked with its media buying and IT approaches, ensured very rapid and low-cost processing of customer calls. Customers were quickly identified through their postcodes. Having full data available on customers allowed a very rapid risk assessment to be carried out, the quotation to be given instantly and the business secured.

Tried and tested mainframe computer systems

Direct Line was probably the first UK financial services company of any kind whose IT systems were designed to support completely their business processes, rather than to support just the operational process, ie policy issue and claims management. At this time, most of Direct Line's competitors still had many uncomputerized processes, with much customer handling still based on manila files, with payments and other transactions put through later. Direct Line was and still is in many respects a very conservative company, preferring to combine tried and tested approaches in innovative ways, rather than operating at the leading edge or, as it is known in the world of IT, the 'bleeding edge'.

However, the approach Direct Line took to adjusting quotations according to current data on customers (eg enquiry levels), risks, was innovative. In the USA, this would not be permitted as prices must be state-approved. Other insurers have proved that a 24-hour continuous learning process is possible, collecting data from trials one day, analysing and taking a varied approach the following day. This needs tight processes, certainly daily and perhaps even 'real time'. Direct Line were always believed to have known the balance of risk vs price taken on as the hours of the day progressed – taking resulting pricing actions to balance prices and risk for profit. This hourly and daily approach to customer acquisition can be contrasted with traditional insurance companies, for whom it can be two months after new customer acquisition or renewal that an insurer with intermediaries knows the state of business sold or renewed.

Strong branding

As a new entrant into the market, where customers were known for their conservatism and inertia, Direct Line had to come up with a strong marketing proposition that would persuade a very large number of customers even to pick up the telephone. Direct Line chose the red telephone as its branding device, and demonstrated its use in all forms of advertising, but particularly powerfully in its direct response television advertising.

Direct marketing campaign techniques and media

We have already discussed several components of this – television, telephone, rapid mail fulfilment. But rather than being treated as a tactical approach to win a few more customers, the whole philosophy of Direct Line was based upon classic direct marketing campaign management practice.[4]

Excellent media buying

The key to effective call centre management, but also to learning the most cost-effective approach to acquiring customers, is media buying. Direct Line brought in the best media buying expertise available on the UK market at the time. This enabled the company to keep the right kind of enquiries flowing in. Built into the company's computer systems were reporting techniques allowing the company to identify which media approach resulted in the right type and volume of enquiries.

Measurement mechanisms

Direct Line used measurement mechanisms that enabled it to measure progress against its objectives almost immediately, eg costs and benefits of using particular media, of recruiting particular kinds of customer.

Staff management

This is an area which has always created problems for the traditional insurance industry. One significant difference was that Direct Line had very few managers, and concentrated its staffing at the point of contact with customers, mainly in the call centres. This facilitated the emergence of a strongly customer-oriented culture Also, motivation systems were designed to ensure that staff were not driven to sell against the customer interest, an area which created severe problems for the life and pensions industry a few years later. Of course, the absence of intermediaries removed a whole set of management problems, while being a new company enabled Direct Line to avoid the rather complex staffing and remuneration practices and internally oriented culture that characterized traditional insurance companies.

The effect of Direct Line's entry

This approach revolutionized the UK market. In the early 1990s, Direct Line had captured around 2 million of the 20 million UK motor policies and took over from Norwich Union (now combined with CU and GA) the title as the largest personal motor insurer at that time. Initial estimates were that this new method of direct writing, in which the company selling the policy handled nearly all the risk, was the inevitable way forward, as it led to such immense economies.

The direct approach, which after four or five years was taken up by many other insurance companies, resulted in administrative expense levels of around 10 per cent, compared with the 20–30 per cent which is still not uncommon in more traditionally organized channels. The big differences between direct and indirect companies persisted for some time, probably because few insurers had any breakdown of their internal process costs, and found it very hard to analyse them according to relationship marketing metrics (customer acquisition, retention and development). In most cases, their information systems simply could not deliver the information, eg which customers for product X had also bought product Y. This of course has changed under competitive pressure.

However, marketing costs for direct writers are higher. They are a closely guarded secret – we estimate them at around 5 per cent of premium income in the UK (3–5 per cent in the USA). These marketing costs are mainly focused on customer acquisition. However, if agents are used, marketing costs are effectively even higher because of agents' commission.

To keep marketing costs under control, retention must be high, or the company will need to spend more on 'recycling customers'. In the earlier years of direct writing, customer retention by direct writers was very high, but started to fall due to the increasing number of competitors. Customers seem to switch between insurers, at one broker or between brokers, often after one year, otherwise after three or four years when they may feel it is time for a change. Brokers may see this coming and switch the customer themselves, rather than the customer switching brokers too! Retention rates can be over 80 per cent for direct writers (in the USA the best achieve over 90 per cent), and even higher for affinity groups, eg Saga. Broker retention rates are often lower – some lower than 50 per cent. This causes real problems, as the customer acquisition process must fill the bucket faster than it leaks.

Effectively direct insurers pay for 'business won and lost', but indirect insurers only pay brokers for business won, through commission on policies. The acquisition cost must be amortized over policy life for direct – but with the indirect approach commission is paid every year. London & Edinburgh were first to start a scheme where the broker gets reduced commission for renewals, with the insurer taking all the work from them. However, this is unusual and not a widely accepted approach.

Direct Line has pushed harder into managing repair outlets, broadening its direct and intermediated financial services business and other non-motor insurance sectors (now including travel, pet and other lines). However, like most motor and other general insurers, it is preparing for the time when rates are expected to harden, as the rate of new entrants into the industry slows, brand recognition becomes more important, and insurers are more careful about the pricing of the risks they accept.

As we saw earlier, the disadvantage of direct writing is the need to be very good at all links in the value chain in order to be the best. In fact, what has happened is that companies that were originally pure direct writers have discovered that their relative strengths are not the same. So some have also taken on the role of traditional underwriters, but working very closely with national brokers to emulate the integrated marketing and systems approach that they know so well. Meanwhile, traditional insurers and brokers have understood that to compete with direct writers, they must develop processes which 'bridge the value chain seamlessly and inexpensively', so that they can operate 'as if' they were direct writers.

However, this does require complete transparency of marketing and risk data, and some companies feel that they expose themselves to commercial risk by sharing this data with companies that are also dealing with their competitors.

There has been widespread realization in the industry that the strong focus on customer acquisition that created the initial success of direct writers could not sustain the market in the long term. While this appeal is still very strong, there is increasing focus on managing customer retention, particularly through smarter management of the claims and repair cycle. Direct Line's own advertising has switched to the red telephone as a device for making stress-free claims rather than for seeking cheaper quotes.

THE ADVENT OF OUTSOURCING AND SHARING DATA

Outsourcing

Like many other service industries, there is active exploration by many companies of the possibilities of outsourcing some key operational aspects in order to reduce costs. In some cases, this outsourcing can be contracted to a common third party, leading to sharing of data and enabling companies to focus on other competitive strengths. This can neutralize the data advantage apparently possessed by direct writers. Major insurers are increasingly turning to systems partners to guide them to the new opportunities constantly being presented through technology. For example, network computing may help insurers take a big slice out of their systems budget, as their expenditures on PCs and support are usually enormous. Traditional general insurers, operating through agents, are increasingly considering how they might use outsourced data providers to counter the main data advantage of direct writers, ie the use of total customer information (marketing, risk, etc) at the point of sale. Note, however, that this may mean actually outsourcing the process of customer acquisition.

In the area of telemarketing, outsourcing companies have specialized in handling very high volumes of inbound calls stimulated by mail-shots and media advertising for insurance companies, filtering customers so that only those qualifying for the second contact need to be handled by the insurance company. The outbound customer service calling supplied by such companies, using predictive dialling techniques to ensure maximum efficiency, has become an essential weapon in the insurance company's battle for customer retention.

Using 'best of breed' third parties can result in cost savings, eg in claims management. In some cases where traditional insurers use third parties, it is effectively a way of introducing more efficient practices. These are the same practices that the direct writers with their fresh approach introduced as a matter of commercial good sense, but which the traditional insurers simply could not find ways to drive through their complex organizations and administrative processes. If third parties can attract enough clients, they can develop economies of scale that can easily outdistance those of the direct insurers.

Sharing data

The industry is keen to share data about bad customers, but less certain about sharing data about good customers. Yet this is shared all the time via financial and similar profiling techniques, both in this and other markets. The form of sharing, however, is indirect, by confirming that a particular profiling technique or set of data was useful in a particular targeting exercise. Has the industry made an arbitrary decision? If survey data were made available on non-switching customers, would the supplier of such data be trampled in the rush or quickly made bankrupt? Customers who are known switchers might be avoided by some companies, while being targeted by others who were confident that they had the price/service combination to make the customer loyal. Loyal customers might be avoided because there is little chance of switching them.

The US and UK claims and underwriting exchanges are good examples of sharing data. In the UK initiative, nearly 30 companies initially entered claims data for household buildings, household contents and motor policies. This was later extended to other lines of business. Early on, one insurer identified a claimant with a history of undeclared claims, moving from insurer to insurer making similar claims. A police investigation showed that he was also making fraudulent benefit claims. The original weakness of this approach was that this knowledge was applied too late in the process, at the claims end and on a batch basis, rather than for online customer acquisition, ie to decide whether to accept a customer. This was because traditional insurers preferred this rather cumbersome solution. Initially the direct writers did not join, as they wanted a solution that worked online at the stage of customer acquisition, and so eventually developed an enhanced system and approach. This forced the traditional insurers to move too, as it set new standards for pricing and accepting business.

This question raises all the issues characteristic of game theory. It can be presented as shown in Figure 27.4, which describes a situation in which companies pool data on propensity of customers to be loyal or to switch. It shows that the balance of advantage lies in sharing, although a company that is confident that its data set is better than that of the 'sharing group' would still find it sensible to go it alone. It also shows that the decision is not about the principle of sharing, but about the assessment of competitive strengths. Obviously, there are other relevant factors, such as marketing strategy, which need to be taken into account in this analysis, but it provides an initial framework for decision making.

The essence of successful application of game theory to identify cooperative strategies is repeat games. In this case repeat occurs over many transactions and many years, so there is no killer or end-game action which can be created by breaking trust with each other.

		What competitors do		
		All share data	**Some share data**	**None share data**
What the company does	**Share data**	• The advantage goes to the company that is best at using information for customer management • Other companies suffer	• The advantage of sharing goes only to a few companies	• The advantage goes to the company which is best at using the 'classic marketing mix'
	Not share data	• Competitors avoid the costs of targeting 'difficult' customers • Or they develop services which suit these customers best, and may even change these customers' behaviour	• Only a few competitors gain the advantage	• All suppliers suffer from customers with a high switching propensity

Figure 27.4 The effects of sharing or not sharing data

The data concerned is not just current data – history of customer behaviour is important too, and those who have either larger numbers of customers or large amounts of data or a longer history may not be prepared to share. For example, take the NHBC, an insurer of major building repairs occurring after construction. It only covers costs for the first few years. Repairs could come many years after buildings are built. It can eventually inspect and match all claim types to changes in building techniques over many years. How can a new entrant, with no access to historical data, compete? Price matching is only possible if competitive quotes are visible or where price structures are simple, ie not in most insurance, where most quotes are individual and offered direct. Before long, a company may find its claims are nothing like expected, especially if its risk portfolio is very different from its competitors'. In motor insurance, personal injury is 'long tail', ie a long period after the incident, and this adds to the problems facing the new entrant.

If those who benefit from openness get together, does this force those who benefit from closed communities to join in? Of course, the answer depends partly on their initial market shares and associated economics. Some companies are aware that there are benefits in sharing data and techniques relating to good and fickle customers, as this might help them to cut marketing costs.

INNOVATIVE TECHNIQUES FOR OBTAINING CUSTOMER FEEDBACK

One of the risks of going direct is losing touch with customers. Today, new developments in information technology have provided ways of avoiding this. Today there is such strong pressure on companies to be much more cost-effective in gathering the data needed to *sell now* that customers in some sectors are finding it even harder than usual to give data about how they feel about the company, whether they are happy with its service or products, and what the company can do to serve them better.

In fact, many research projects have shown how contemptuous customers are about the clumsy attempts companies make to manage them through call centres. A key problem is confusion between gathering information and agreeing action. If companies could separate clearly between the two, encourage customers to do the same, and then provide very cost-effective channels for customer feedback, could the whole process be carried out more efficiently while keeping customers satisfied? In particular, would things be easier if information could be gathered at very low cost?

The answer to the last question is 'yes, if managed properly'. Web enthusiasts will no doubt point out that the ability to capture information at virtually zero marginal cost has been with us for some time. The problem is that very few companies have really made a success out of it. The same applies to the Web's wireless cousin, SMS (with WAP success still mostly in future). The mechanism for gathering information is only one aspect of this. It is important that customers are free to use different media and that they can access those media when they feel like it.

Consider the situation of companies with many millions of paying customers – this applies to most companies in financial services, passenger transport, energy, telecommunications, retailing, grocery products, etc. They are faced with a difficult choice. Their heart tells them that it is always good to hear from customers. Their brain tells them that the cost of managing feedback from so many customers could be very expensive. But their brain also tells them that if they don't make it easy for customers to tell their company what it's like to do business with them, they may not only lose individual customers or miss the opportunity to sell more to them, but they may also miss wholesale shifts in attitudes or perceptions. They may also miss news that can be turned into value straight away. For example, I recently had dealings with a company that knows that it is experiencing a temporary boom in business but has no way of finding out how many customers have tried but failed to do business with it.

The ordinary call centre provides no answer to this problem. The cost of every customer calling a call centre can usually be reckoned in pounds rather than pence, unless the interaction is very limited. Many customers will give up when they can't get through. Mail questionnaires are great for detecting longer-term shifts in attitudes and perceptions, but not for tracking short-term changes. What about the Web? Web questionnaires have been effective in narrowly targeted markets, especially when prompted by e-mails. But companies with 'mega' customer bases would benefit from the ability to handle tens of thousands of inbound contacts – by all media – every day, at virtually zero marginal cost – with the bonus that such feedback would, under certain criteria and subject to customer permission, feed individual queries into the company's CRM system or, if many customers had the same view, trigger alerts to warn the company of an impending surge (of problems, opportunities, etc). Fortunately, providers of such products and services are beginning to step forward. One of them is ViewsCast.

ViewsCast offers, in the form of a managed service or as software, the ability to obtain real-time customer or employee feedback on satisfaction, perceptions and preference. It provides immediate browser-based access to results and the ability to enhance CRM systems by incorporating direct customer feedback. Just as important is the ease of set-up. Survey scripts are created in a simple Windows drag-and-drop program. The whole process can be done in a couple of hours, and modifications take minutes. The output from this program is independent of the medium in which it is deployed. Currently these are phone and Web, with e-mail, WAP and digital TV under development. As soon as a customer completes a ViewsCast survey, the results are available for analysis and download via a Web browser.

A leading bank needed real-time evaluation of its customer service and satisfaction levels. Its existing methods of market research (postal questionnaires, face-to-face and Internet) did not allow for this level of speed and flexibility. The bank is using ViewsCast for various new and developing departments within the organization. Real-time results from surveys are defining new benchmarks for customer care. ViewsCast also allows feedback direct from customers to influence changes in company-wide customer care policies and helps identification and correction of weaknesses in call centre scripts. The company is also using data obtained through ViewsCast as a guide to identify training needs.

A leading insurance company is using ViewsCast for two clear distinct purposes – to measure levels of service within its claims department, and to ensure compliance with recent legislation. It is also using ViewsCast's real-time surveys to improve team motivation and morale, by focusing on positive as well as negative aspects of customer service. ViewsCast is also being used to enhance existing research methods, particularly for gaining immediate insight into customer opinions. The company is also planning to conduct employee surveys with ViewsCast.

Another leading insurer has integrated ViewsCast's service into its helpdesk operation. The company was convinced that real service improvement could only be driven by accurate analysis of continuous customer feedback. It wanted a way to provide the feedback that its customer service and training departments needed to review and modify communication and telemarketing processes. The ViewsCast approach focuses attention on customer satisfaction, highlighting any deficiency in the communication of product and service details or terms and conditions. This is important for general insurers, who must ensure compliance with the guidelines of the General Insurance Standards Council. ViewsCast also collates valuable statistical information that shows the service standards reached.

The company also needed to convince its helpdesk personnel that ViewsCast would help to identify training needs, leading to enhanced performance and job satisfaction. So it incorporated ViewsCast into an incentive programme that highlighted the benefits of structured training and coaching. Training is now more accurately targeted, relevant and beneficial to both employer and employee.

Call centre agents might be tempted to pick and choose which customer comments are recorded and remove any comments that are uncomplimentary. The company addressed this by instructing its agents to offer all customers the option of having their say. To ensure that this happens, team coaches closely monitor calls. So, all customers are offered the opportunity to leave comments on the service they receive. If they accept, the call is transferred to a server that gives them brief instructions before running a customer satisfaction monitoring script. The majority of customers accept the offer.

Here is an example of a script:

- Thank you for agreeing to take part in this brief survey. We will ask you some questions about the service that you received from our customer service agent. Use the keys on your telephone to answer the questions. To repeat questions, press the hash key. If you need help at any time press the star key. When you are ready to start, press the 'one' key.
- On a scale of 1–5 , where one is the lowest score and five is the highest score, how would you rate the courtesy of the agent who handled your call?
- Where 1 is 'not at all', and 5 is 'completely', how well did the agent deal with your call?
- Where 1 is 'not at all confident' and 5 is 'very confident', how confident was the agent who handled your call?
- We value your thoughts on how we can improve our service. If you would like to record a message for us, please press 'one' now.
- Thank you for your time – your feedback is greatly appreciated. Goodbye.

The script takes just a minute or two to run, depending on whether or not the customer leaves a message. The script was designed, recorded, tested and ready to run in a couple of days, and can be amended to include new or revised questions within hours. The company's employees have continuous access to performance updates via their intranet. Call centre managers and team leaders use the information to:

- monitor and review individual and team performance in terms of call volumes and customer satisfaction;
- help individual agents understand their strengths and weaknesses and develop commitment to training and development;
- review the impact of peak workload periods on customer satisfaction;
- monitor the impact of training on service quality.

The company also plans to use the approach to structure a reward and motivation package for call centre agents. This will not only help to ensure that customers receive excellent service, but will also help the company to recruit and retain agents in a competitive labour market.

ISSUES RAISED BY THE SUCCESS OF DIRECT INSURANCE

The success of the true direct writers and their subsequent history raises two interesting issues.

Firstly, disintermediation – the removal of intermediaries in the value chain – seems to be associated with using direct marketing techniques to access final customers and manage the relationship with them. However, when direct writing first arose, and perhaps even today, the key weakness in the traditional route to market was not that it split the value chain between too many companies, but that the split was badly managed. Neither agents' nor underwriters' information systems or business processes were designed for efficient and effective end-to-end customer management, and in many cases were nearly archaic.

Indeed, in the UK, Virgin, one of the most challenging new entrants in a number of sectors, believes that intermediation is the key to success. From a marketing point of view, Virgin Direct financial services is just a brand and a strongly customer-oriented culture. Its policies were initially outsourced to Norwich Union, and then to Australian Mutual Provident Society/Pearl. Probably few customers have noticed!

It can be argued that brand and culture are the key differentiators, as many of the other characteristics of direct writing can be copied. Direct writers who have learnt how to manage the entire value chain properly and to manage relationships with customers are now working with national brokers to achieve the same effect. However, the advantages of 'data control' possessed by the direct writers are being eroded by data cooperation.

With shared (state of the art) systems and data and efficient processes, there is no reason why an underwriter and broker should not achieve the same cost-effectiveness as a direct writer. Indeed, that is the target of some of the major underwriters. However, such an approach does require a long-term agreement and mutual commitment – something we are starting to see as major brokers rationalize their panel of suppliers and develop deeper relationships with their remaining suppliers.

Also, it will be difficult for the agent/writer chain to use processes that are as efficient as direct writers. However, agents do have the advantage of local (or special) market knowledge and close customer relationships – still an advantage in many areas of insurance.

However, there are many opportunities for reallocating marketing and service responsibilities across the value chain. In the UK, as was mentioned above, London & Edinburgh (now no longer trading under that name) took all servicing and administration away from their brokers after a sale was made. It piloted the payment of a reduced commission for renewals where there was no work required by the broker. NU has a scheme for local industry marketing with brokers, creating leads for it through targeted campaigns.

Secondly, relationship marketing – in which all aspects of managing the customer need to be reasonably well attuned to the needs of the customer and managed according to a coherent strategy and over the life cycle of the relationship – might seem to militate against splitting the responsibility for managing the customer between two or more parties. Even with a strategy that is shared between two organizations, aren't there just too many opportunities for coordination to fail? Here, the jury is out. We can certainly point to many examples where relationship marketing does fairly well in an intermediated environment. Examples of this include:

- frequent flyer programmes, in an environment in which most ticket purchase is through agents;
- charge card management, in which most transactions are undertaken through third parties, principally travel agencies, hotel, car hire and retail companies;
- the customer management programmes of most automotive manufacturers, where most transactions take place through dealers.

However, in all these cases, there is a clear leader in the relationship management process, and agreement on how mutually generated customer data is to be accessed and used by the parties concerned. We believe that the leader needs to be the company that best knows the customer and how to manage the relationship. As soon as one of the value chain partners tries to follow its own independent customer management objectives, there is the possibility of conflict and inefficiency. This can only be prevented by clear agreement between the parties on 'rules and rights' concerning marketing, data and systems. In some cases, using independent third parties as data hosts for open or closed user groups may be the key to success. Of course, we should remember that this is not always a monogamous marriage. The broker has other partners, as does the insurer. A joint venture is different perhaps, as one of the terms may be exclusivity.

CONCLUSIONS FROM THE DIRECT INSURANCE EXPERIENCE

The direct insurance sector represents the state of the art in mass marketing of financial services – a laboratory of change that the financial services industry is still watching, as it applies its skills outside its home territory of motor insurance. Managers in the sector are confident that their focus and skills will help them to make inroads into all consumer financial services markets. They have also realized how great their power is to influence consumers. The next few years will show whether this special combination of relationship marketing, technology, culture and management skills will continue to revolutionize the world of financial services.

Notes

1   The Henley Centre (1994) *The Loyalty Paradox*
2   For more on this, see Dawes, J (1986) Selling a relationship: personal selling in retail financial services, *Journal of Financial Services Marketing*, **1** (1), pp 48–55, and Ennew, C T (1992) Consumer attitudes to independent financial advice, *International Journal of Bank Marketing*, **20** (5), pp 13–15
3   For more on this, see Swiss Re UK (1994) *Customer Direct*, and Thwaites, D and Lee, S C I (1994) Direct marketing in the financial services industry, *Journal of Marketing Management*, **10**, pp 377–90
4   See, for example, Mounsey, P and Stone, M (1990) *Managing Direct Marketing*, Croner, for a complete description of the processes and systems involved in this kind of direct marketing approach

28

CRM partnership between banks and insurers in practice – a case study

Vince Mason and Merlin Stone

INTRODUCTION

This chapter examines the role of CRM within an intermediated business environment, ie where the relationship between supplier and consumer ('customers') is through intermediaries or third parties ('partners'). In this case – a major UK insurance company ('the insurer') – the partners are banks, building societies and major retailers. Their customers are supplied insurance services either on behalf of or in tandem with the partners. Figure 28.1 provides a simple picture of the arrangement.

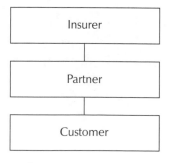

Figure 28.1 Simple picture of partnership

Much of the literature on CRM assumes that the supplier–customer relationship is direct. In an intermediated situation, CRM techniques are not only relevant but vital for generating improved value for all parties: suppliers, partners and customers.

COMPANY BACKGROUND

As one of the UK's biggest insurance companies, the insurer operates in most sectors of the market and via most channels. The insurer provides insurance through partners in financial services and some leading retailers, many of whom have added financial services to their traditional product range. The insurer provides a wide range of insurance products and services. These include household (buildings, contents and joint), motor, travel (single trip and annual), health (personal accident, hospital cash and private medical insurance), extended warranty and creditor. These products are typically marketed under the partner's own brand. The insurer 'manufactures' the products and these are then 'retailed' through partners' existing channels or through channels set up specifically to support their personal financial services product range.

The relationship between the supplier and end customer depends on the type of agreement between the insurer and partner. The supplier–partner relationship takes the form of either 'block' or 'individual' contracts. These terms refer to the way the insurance business is written. In the case of block business, a household contract might relate to insuring 100,000 properties associated with individual mortgages provided by a bank or building society partner. In this case the insurer does not know the names of customers until they make a claim, and consequently full CRM by the insurer is not possible. The customer has virtually no direct contact with the insurer. For individual business, the customer contracts directly with the insurer, who holds all customers' personal details. For example, the partner gives the customer a call centre number, and the insurer runs the call centre. This allows normal CRM to take place by the insurer, although normally only with the permission and usually the cooperation of the partner.

In either case, it is knowledge of customers – their behaviour (responsiveness, buying and claims patterns), their needs, and so forth, that provides the foundation of CRM. The customer database is the source of this customer knowledge, as it is where information on the customer is stored. Proper use of the database not only allows individual customers to be managed better, but also allows suppliers and partners to evaluate market potential, assess market penetration and match their products to their customers or prospects. Of course, both supplier and partner may have multiple customer databases. For example, the supplier and the partner may have separate customer databases for each line of business that they do. The supplier may also have one or more customer databases for business done through other partners.

CRM is important to the insurer because it can achieve greater profit by improving the value of the business to the partnership (both the supplier and the partner). Many partners have several insurance service suppliers (for example, banks and building societies often employ a panel of insurers), so suppliers compete to get more business within each partner. The supplier needs to demonstrate to partners that partnership with them offers a commercial advantage.

ROLE OF THE CUSTOMER DATABASE

The customer database has a central role to play in the development of CRM. The processes identified below indicate the main activities that contribute to understanding the customer and profiting from this understanding:

- **Data management** – this refers to the process of capturing, cleaning and updating the customer data. Within the insurer this includes bringing together data from the various transactional systems and from partner systems. The insurer also overlays geo-demographic data to enhance the database with information not captured by the internal systems.
- **Understanding the customer** – statistical analysis of the database allows the insurer to profile customers exhibiting particular behaviours, identify distinct segments and differentiate customers based on their relative value.
- **Market intelligence** – this helps the insurer to understand external factors affecting customers, eg political and economic factors, social trends, unemployment, wealth, National Health Service, social exclusion.
- **Customer communication** – the database can be used to determine whom to contact (prospect, customer or defector), how to contact them (telephone, mail or e-mail), what to say and when to say it. It can then be used to track the communication and later analyse the effect it had.
- **Sales management** – the database can provide 'triggers' for up-sell, cross-sell and 'save the sale' activities for telephone or mail activity in support of customer acquisition, development and retention.
- **Customer service** – the database can also be used to track which services customers have experienced – claims servicing, complaint handling, loyalty programmes, satisfaction surveys, etc, and the impact these have had on the relationship. If 'cost to serve' data is available, the database can be used to track the costs of providing these services at an individual customer level.
- **Management information** – the database provides information for the supplier and partners. In addition to the financial and operational information from other systems,

unique customer information can be generated from the customer database. The customer database is typically the only repository where all customer information is available in one place. This is especially true where partner and insurance data are combined.

- **Campaign management** – the database helps supplier and partners determine which campaigns work best and then to build on them. For example, campaign A has the highest response and conversion rates but it also has the highest attrition in terms of customer defections, and it is less profitable than campaign B which generated a lower response from a higher quality population with a lower subsequent defection rate. Such analysis can help to improve future campaign activity.
- **Product planning** – the database allows identification of customers' insurance needs and how best to serve them. Careful analysis can help identify customer segments that are not well served by the current product offerings.

THE INSURER'S DATABASE INITIATIVE

For a major insurance supplier, justifying investment in a customer database covering policies sold through partners is not easy. During the past few years companies have not only had the challenges of Year 2000 compliance, the introduction of the European Monetary Union and the 1998 Data Protection Act, but several have also had the additional challenge of accommodating mergers and acquisitions. During this period competition for scarce IT resources has been tough. All these factors applied to the case study company. However, a business case for developing a partnership database was put and accepted and the database built. Given the nature of the relationships with its partners, the insurer felt that it was best first to segment customer data by partner. Most analysis is undertaken within the context of a partner relationship and consequently the concept of data marts has had appeal. Indeed several data marts dedicated to specific partner customer portfolios are maintained. The database model used combines customer and transaction data pulled from the insurer's operational systems into its data warehouse. This is merged with data provided by partners and overlaid with external data, for example geo-demographic data. These latter offer additional ways of classifying customers. Out of this database comes the analysis that can drive customer-facing processes such as cross-selling and up-selling rules, retention initiatives and other 'triggered' activity.

The insurer's market intelligence systems are mainframe based and are linked to the numerous transactional systems supporting the various insurance operations. The customer database system is LAN based, employing several database servers and a number of workstations. Various selection and analytical software packages enable the insurer to undertake simple counts, line of thought enquiries and ultimately to develop

Table 28.1 Partnership customers and cross-selling

Partner	Percentage of customer base by contract		
	Buildings	Contents	Building & Contents
A	26%	25%	49%
B	7%	74%	19%

more complex models using CHAID and linear modelling techniques. A good example of the application of the customer database is to compare the effectiveness of cross-selling household insurance between partners (see Table 28.1). For example, the insurer has a sole insurer relationship with Partner A and is free to engage in cross-selling additional lines of cover to the customers. With Partner B the insurer is simply one of a panel and therefore subject to whether the customer is best served by them or by one of the other panellists.

The customer may have both buildings and contents insured with the partner but only the contents may be placed with the insurer. The fewer the restrictions that are placed on the insurer by the partner, the greater the opportunity to practise CRM and to engage in cross-selling and up-selling. However, achieving volumes of business is not the primary objective. The insurer should also be striving for business that represents value for supplier, partner and customer. Of course, partners may have different (even incompatible) strategies on customer selection and pricing. For example, one bank may not want the insurer to reject any applications, another may want attractive pricing or special terms and conditions for particular segments. Block policies hide many of these factors from the underwriters. A shared-data relationship will need these to be openly discussed and managed.

IMPROVING CUSTOMER PROFITABILITY

Within each partner portfolio, the insurer wants to know who are the most and least valuable customers, how can more higher value customers be attracted, retained and developed, and negative value customers avoided. Customer value is defined as the product of all contributions made by the customer (in this case premiums paid) less all expenses incurred (acquisition, renewal, claims and other servicing costs). In the case of one partner's customer portfolio, graph (a) in Figure 28.2 shows the sum of contributions made by decile (10 per cent) bands of customers ranked from the most valued on the left to the least valued on the right.

The best decile (20,000 customers in this portfolio) contributed 58 per cent of the total value of the portfolio. The best 20 per cent here contribute approximately 80 per cent of the total value of the portfolio. The worst decile makes a 28 per cent negative contribution. But what do these profitable and unprofitable customers actually look like? How can they be

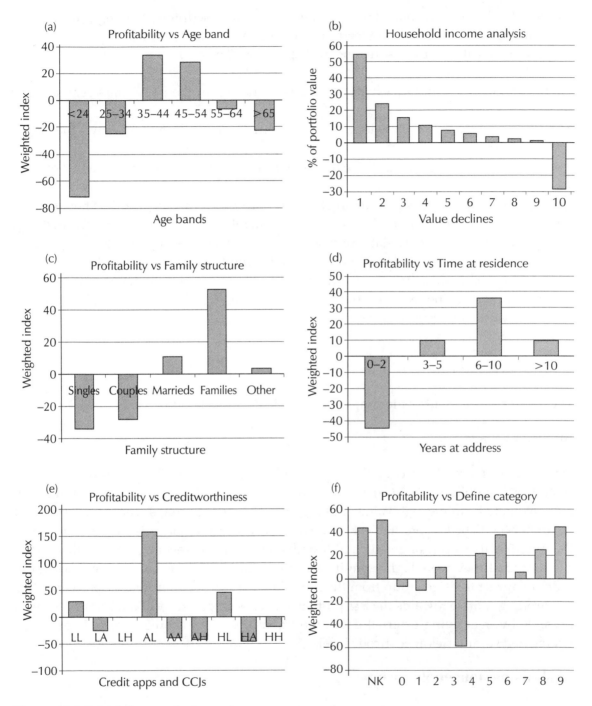

Figure 28.2 Initial data analysis

identified? The transactional data provided very few descriptors, making it difficult to differentiate between 'good' and 'bad' customers in any meaningful way.

Customers' value to the insurer and partner is determined by:

- the amount of cover requested, which affects the size of the premium – generally the more the better;
- the length of tenure or how long the customer remains with the company – the longer the better;
- the size and frequency of claims experienced – the smaller and less frequent the better.

However, knowing this is only the first step to improving profitability. But how do you predict these behaviours from the information available about the customer? The first step was to analyse customer profitability by a series of variables (see Figure 28.2 (a), (c), (d), (e), (f)). The analysis carried out was simplistic, and could have been improved by the use of data mining techniques. At the same time, because many banks' marketing processes are very weak, introducing more complex analytical techniques – leading to complex targeting rules – may be counterproductive.

Single variable analysis

The insurer started with some simple single variable analysis, shown in Figure 28.2.

Analysis by age

Firstly, the insurer looked at the relationship between the 10 value scores and the customer's age (Figure 28.2 (a)). It discovered that the 35–54 age bands were significantly more likely to be in the high value deciles than the other age groups. The insurer expected the under-35s to be less profitable than the rest because historically this was true. However, the over-50s had been targeted as a desirable segment for several years on the understanding that they were highly profitable. In fact, due to the heavy discounts needed in order to attract this age group from their existing insurers, a significant proportion of this age group gravitate towards the less profitable deciles. The next set of analyses were made possible by overlaying external data onto the individual customers' records based on aggregated summaries at post-code level.

Analysis by household income

Perhaps not surprisingly, the better-off households were most likely to fall into the most valuable deciles – this makes sense in that they have more possessions to insure and therefore carry higher premiums but do not necessarily experience higher claims costs.

Analysis by family structure

Postcodes where households are predominantly occupied by families are significantly more profitable than those with either married or unmarried couples; where residents are predominantly singles the households tend to be unprofitable to insure (Figure 28.2 (c)).

Analysis by tenure

The time a customer has spent in his or her present home has a strong influence on value and it is interesting that the value is highest at 6 to 10 years, with value rising to this peak and then dropping off again (Figure 28.2(d)).

Analysis by creditworthinesss

Creditworthiness is measured by applications for credit and the level of County Court Judgements (CCJs) by postcode. A low level of CCJs is a very positive attribute for insurance profitability, but for credit applications low and high are both less attractive than an average level of activity. This analysis is of particular significance as many partners are credit-providing institutions (Figure 28.2(e)).

More complex analysis

Some of these single variable observations are probably reflecting a similar phenomenon. For example, younger age groups are more likely to be single, low paid and to have recently moved house. Therefore the insurer employed a more complex classification tool where a combination of variables could be simply applied.

Geo-demographic overlays provide postcode-based summaries using a combination of the variables used above (or proxy variables) such as occupation, affluence and home ownership. Here, group 0, 'affluent, professional families', group 8, 'rural dwellers', and group 9 'residential homes/institutional accommodation' correlate with the higher value deciles whilst group 4, 'younger rented council', group 6 'younger mixed tenure' and group 5, 'older rented council' are more likely to be lower value.

This analysis is quite interesting and does shed a little light on who customers are, how they behave and how valuable they are. However, by itself it is a risky basis for either predicting customer behaviour or planning activity (eg pricing, customer targeting). The next stage is to combine the variables and undertake modelling. This was done, but the results are considered too confidential for publication.

Customer characteristics vary from one insurance product to another and between partner portfolios. For example, the determinants of profitability in personal accident insurance customers are very different from those for household insurance customers. This can be explained partly by the fact that household insurance is almost universally required and in many cases (for mortgaged homes) mandatory, whereas personal accident is usually a discretionary product.

One bank's customers may behave quite differently from another despite the basic similarities of the insurance product. This may be explained by the relative importance of a particular channel, say the branch network, which may dominate one bank's activities but play little part in the other. The socio-demographic character of partners' customer portfolios can also differ markedly. However, it is not difficult to build propensity scoring models which take into account explicitly the interactions between geo-demographic variables and channel use.

MAKING USE OF THE ANALYSIS

It was in the call centre that the insurer found greatest initial application for these findings, by deriving cross-sell and up-sell rules (ie whom to sell to, based on their profiles). However, much more could be achieved. The key issue is how the supplier and partner can work together to maximize joint profits.

This could only be applied where the insurer had the participation and cooperation of the partner. This is particularly difficult in the case of a bank, say, employing a panel of insurers. Also, the partner's principal activity may not support CRM applied to the insurance proposition. For example, the partner may be more interested in developing credit or loan business with certain customers rather than offering them insurance services. As a consequence the partner may prefer to communicate offers of loans to the customer and restrict mailing of insurance propositions. In most insurer–client partnerships, the partner 'owns' the customer and as a consequence the insurer's dealings with customers must be consistent with the partner's overall contact strategy. The level of collaboration depends greatly on the strength of the supplier–partner relationship. For example, if there is a profit-sharing arrangement, both parties have much to gain from exploiting CRM. If the partner makes commission on every sale, irrespective of its profitability, and uses several suppliers, then it is less likely to agree to in-depth CRM with one. In some cases, the partner may not be committed to CRM. Or it may not have the capabilities that enable it to play its part in joint CRM.

Of course, all the normal insurance CRM principles apply. Customer knowledge helps the insurer achieve better results in terms of getting profitable customers to renew their policy, buy additional cover or recommend the company to a friend. The ability to target customers with a propensity to lapse or cancel allows the company to undertake profitable retention campaigns. Differentiating customers and prospects in terms of their value helps the company focus its acquisition and retention activity towards the most profitable segments, those really worth recruiting and keeping. An indiscriminate retention programme could result in an increase in the proportion of unprofitable customers. Further, by identifying and analysing groups of customers currently not well served by the company's product range or unprofitable to insure it can highlight the opportunity for product development.

CASE STUDY OF A SPECIFIC BANK PARTNER PORTFOLIO

Where a partnership exists it makes a great deal of sense to explore the two companies' experience with the same customer. If the partners are operating within the same business sector, it is probable that the customer will display similar characteristics in both relationships.[1] There are also specific factors that apply to the way banks market insurance.

For example, the Table 28.2 highlights the importance of the strength of the relationship with the bank in determining the rate at which customers convert their quotations to a policy. A customer taking out buildings insurance in association with a bank mortgage is nearly four times more likely to convert than if the customer requested a quotation after seeing a newspaper or other advertisement without any other relationship.

Where the partners operate in sectors that are not primarily financial, say retailing, it is still worth exploring the relationship. Here, however, the retail predictor variables for 'goodness' in insurance are likely to be more complex. They might include:

- merchandise buying behaviour (eg product types, frequency);
- payment behaviour (eg credit card, cash, cheque);
- finance behaviour (eg how purchases are funded);
- complaint and merchandise return behaviour;
- loyalty (ie share of wallet spent at store);
- loyalty card behaviour (eg use, fraud, etc).

Table 28.2 Relative conversion rates split by source of enquiry and policy cover

		Cover held		
		Contents	Buildings	Joint
Source of enquiry	**Mortgage adviser**	3	1	2
	Branch referral	4	5	7
	Newspaper or other advertisement	6	8	9

Banks commonly measure their customers' behaviour in terms of number and types of bank accounts held, account balance, credit card activity, credit scores and how well the customers manage their accounts. These measures have been used for some time to help guide bank staff as to how to treat the customer, eg whether to grant new loans or extend existing credit.

The insurer believed it was worth testing whether positive bank scores correlated with profitable insurance behaviour, ie to answer the question, 'does a good bank customer make a good insurance customer?' Common sense suggests that there is a good chance that a relationship will exist. The problem is to prove it and then, if proven, to capitalize on the fact.

Privacy legislation as interpreted by the Information Commissioner, The Banking Code of Practice and the Association of British Insurers does not allow companies to share personal customer information. So a procedure had to be devised to merge insurance and bank data to create a complete picture but in such a discrete way that the identity of the individual customer was not known and could not be derived. The exercise then went on to test the relationship between the individual bank scores and the various insurance behaviour we wished to encourage or avoid.

Positive banking characteristics include:

- surplus balance on account, ie in credit;
- no or few unauthorized overdraft withdrawals;
- multiple bank accounts – loan, savings, current, credit card.

Positive insurance characteristics are:

- low claims history or a low propensity to claim;
- low sensitivity to size of premium;
- multiple lines of insurance cover (eg buildings and contents);
- long-term relationship or a tendency to renew or extend each year.

The following general results were discovered:

- Conversion rates for new business are higher for customers with positive banking indicators and are lowest where negative banking indicators are present.
- Customers are significantly more price sensitive when negative banking indicators are present.
- Customers are more likely to renew their policy if they have positive banking indicators, leading to higher retention rates.
- Claims experience is worst where banking indicators are negative.

The conclusion we reached was that the best insurance customers also have good banking and credit experience.

The insurer then had to implement processes or procedures to capitalize on this knowledge. Where bank staff provide insurance quotations, it is possible to provide prompts to them to offer incentives to desirable customers to drive up their take-up rate. Typically, where banks measure their customer behaviour, an indication of their value is displayed on the customer contact screen.

THE CORE ISSUE – GAINING COOPERATION

Of course, none of the techniques described above are new. They are just the application of classic direct marketing. The difference is that the approach involved cooperation between two big companies with a shared customer base. How was this cooperation achieved? In another research project completed by one of the authors[2] it is clear that such cooperation is contingent upon the existence of trust between the two parties.

Arguments for sharing customer knowledge

The main arguments for sharing customer knowledge include:

- improved targeting of marketing strategy;
- improved targeting of marketing communications;
- improved/more relevant content of marketing communications;
- improved product planning;
- improved pricing;
- reduced costs of data acquisition;
- reduced costs of data processing;
- reduced media advertising;
- reduced direct mail expenditure;
- increased responsiveness to changing market conditions;
- gaining an advantage over competition at the same level of the value chain;
- bargaining more effectively with other value chain partners (eg divide and rule);
- reduced market risk;
- learning/skills transfer.

Our respondents focused primarily on improved targeting, cost reduction and competitive advantage.

Arguments against sharing customer knowledge

The main arguments against sharing customer knowledge include:

- increased complexity of the marketing process;
- increased marketing costs;
- increased problems with data management;
- conflict caused by mismatch in types/pace of marketing /sales process;
- general conflict of interest;
- conflict of interest over customer ownership;
- conflict of interest over data ownership;
- systems incompatibilities;
- legal complexities (regulatory, data protection);
- data security;
- political difficulties;
- skills shortage – data analysis;
- skills shortage – data management;
- accentuated marketing skills difference between partners.

In this research, which consisted of seven in-depth case studies, most respondents stressed issues relating to lack of alignment – skills, processes, systems. Conflict of interest was also raised.

The reasons for or against sharing include the following.

Sector-specific issues

These may be regulatory, but can also be cultural, eg a history of conflict, or to do with the product, eg an intermittent purchasing cycle can give the retailer the upper hand because the supplier becomes more remote from the customer.

Competitive situation

This includes factors such as how many major companies are competing on each side of the market, their size distribution, their relative competitive strengths (eg products, distribution, branding). These factors tend to determine the risks if competitors get hold of information that has been shared. For example, if the customer list of a weak company gets into the hands of a strong company, then the latter will be in a good position to mount a competitive attack.

Relative strengths and weaknesses of different partners

This can apply to areas such as customer knowledge management or information technology – where sharing with a partner perceived to have a greater or lesser capability could lead to a perceived risk of better/worse exploitation of data and consequent problems with customers or competitors. Skills and systems compatibility problems can have their origin here.

Particular marketing/sales approach of the different companies in the supply chain

This includes in particular the extent of use of targeted marketing. In many distribution chains, it is not uncommon for the level nearest the customer to be involved in direct marketing. However, this is changing, particularly as the economics of managing high volumes of customer data are not necessarily favourable to this approach.

Perceived costs and benefits of sharing

These are usually determined by the partners' views about the above factors. Our research shows that there is little doubt about the general benefits – the issue is whether it pays the particular companies, and whether the partners can work with one another cost-effectively.

Availability of trusted independent intermediaries to help with process of sharing

Our research shows that third parties are generally trusted with demographic and lifestyle data, some of which may have been contributed or collected on behalf of specific partners. In financial services, this trust extends specifically to transaction data (eg credit cards).

Relationship between prospective partners

This includes strategic agreements to meet other objectives, and of course trust. The research showed that:

- in general, companies are happy to exchange data about general customer characteristics, but reluctant to do so about topics such as sales and promotional response;

- where exchanging this kind of data, companies are likely to do so only in the context of a strategic agreement, backed by trust;
- the role of third-party suppliers in supporting data exchange is important;
- the main benefits of exchanging data were targeting, competitiveness and cost reduction;
- the main barriers were perceived differences in analytical skills and to some extent process skills, plus perceived problems with systems incompatibility;
- in one case perceived legal barriers were important;
- the quality of the respondents' systems and business intelligence capability varied significantly, with some claiming an ability to report in nearly all areas, with others admitting significant limitations.

In the case of the two companies featured in this section, the trust did exist. In fact, the insurer had taken a consultant's advice about which of the banks to approach. The advice was simply – approach the one with the best track record of cooperation, and where it is felt that trust is well established.

CONCLUSION

CRM can be done successfully within an intermediated environment. In such an environment a partnership rather than a supplier–client approach will give most benefit. The more parties involved in the relationship with the customer, the more complex the challenge. But this is worth looking at because joint ventures, mergers and collaborations are becoming more common and customer demands are growing. If partnership is mismanaged, then conflict of interest can occur, as insurers may end up cannibalizing their own base by targeting their own direct customers through a partner.

By employing CRM techniques as described in this section, significant business benefits were achieved. Improvements in customer value were made following customer development activity (retention and cross-sales). By focusing acquisition strategies upon particular prospects (segments) within the bank customer base, the quality of new recruits improved.

The types of analysis described in this section are only of value if they remain current. Customers can and do change over time. It is therefore important to recognize that the analysis must be repeated periodically in order to track the dynamics of the customer portfolio. Further, the results presented here are from a specific group of customers purchasing particular financial services products through a unique set of channels. Although the methodologies employed may be useful and interesting for those elsewhere, the general findings should not be adopted without thorough reassessment.

Much of the value in insurance companies today is in long-term savings, life insurance and pensions. Most of this value is intermediated. The question is whether these findings, derived from the general insurance market, are equally applicable for life and pensions. We believe that similar patterns are likely to emerge, whereby customers with positive characteristics in terms of multiple purchases, length of tenure and claims experience would continue to demonstrate these qualities and should therefore be targeted, but at an appropriate life stage (ie not after they have committed all their value). The problem is likely to be a shortage of adviser intelligence material that can be used for modelling purposes.

Notes

[1] Stone, M (1999) Managing good and bad customers, Part 1, *Journal of Database Marketing*, **6** (3) pp 222–32, and Part 2, *Journal of Database Marketing*, **6** (4), pp 299–314

[2] See Stone, M, Virdee, T and Condron, K (2001) Sharing customer data in the value chain, in ed B Foss and M Stone, *Successful Customer Relationship Marketing*, Kogan Page

29

Managing customers with direct mail

Merlin Stone, Brian Scheld and Bryan Foss

INTRODUCTION

This chapter is based mainly on a research project sponsored by the Royal Mail. It aims to help marketing managers in companies in financial services to determine: 1) where they should put their emphasis on developing customer management in practice; 2) how direct mail can help them manage customers better.

This chapter covers:

1.   best practice in developing and implementing strategies for using mail in managing customer relationships, including:
    *   marketing and sales strategies as applied to relationship cycles and life cycles;
    *   integration between marketing, sales strategies and technology decisions, including development of approaches in association with strategic suppliers, including the media;
    *   operational issues, ie how strategies are delivered, monitored and controlled, and how information about performance feeds back to influence policy;
2.   the nature of the gap between best practice (of leading edge users) and actual practice (of most users – distinguishing between faster followers and laggards);
3.   the difference between practices in different types of company, eg by sector and size;

4. the barriers to improving practice – what holds companies back;
5. practical steps that financial services companies can take to develop a mail strategy for relationship marketing.

BACKGROUND

Financial services direct mail in the UK and some other countries continues to dominate direct mail. The main causes of this high volume are:

-   the entry of many new suppliers from other markets (eg utilities, retailers, travel companies, affinity groups);
-   the advent of many new direct-only financial services businesses;
-   the attempts by many established suppliers to market new categories of product or to develop new routes of access to customers.

Typically, companies have focused their direct marketing efforts on mailing as a way of attracting new customers. Most mailings to existing customers have traditionally been administrative mailings (eg statements), with cross-selling through these mailings taking the form of relatively untargeted 'statement stuffers'. However, cross-selling efforts are rising quickly as companies start to develop customer databases which enable them to identify with reasonable certainty which customers have which of their products. In recent years, there has been something of a frenzy of prospecting mailings by financial services providers, and in most cases these campaigns prove profitable at relatively low response rates (eg around 1 per cent). The only area where mailing profitability is suspect is where customers recruited by this route have high early attrition rates, eg in motor insurance, where with acquisition costs of anything between $30 and $140, it can take up to three years of non-claiming retention for a customer to turn profitable.

However, the intense use of direct mail under these conditions has probably affected consumers' attitudes to direct mail. Consumers' concerns include issues such as access to their personal data and invasion of privacy. However, it is not clear whether consumers extrapolate from their experience of prospect mailings from companies they are not customers of, to mailings they receive from their existing suppliers. Sometimes, these mailings are received not because of their status as existing customers, but because their supplier has sourced a list that contains their name, and is not capable of de-duplicating it against a list of existing customers. Worse, a company may hold several customer databases, built over the years for the management of each product line or strategic business unit. It may not realize that prospects for cross-selling a given product on the database for another product are already present as customers for the first product on the appropriate product database. To avoid this, and obtain better results, financial services providers are increasingly focusing on identifying 'warm prospects' across the entire customer base, and focusing efforts on up-selling and cross-selling on these. A key part of this is to identify within the overall prospect universe which ones should be targeted as being in the 'prospect pool' for particular campaigns.

The extent to which suppliers know their customers must not be overestimated. In many cases, companies are still doing what might seem quite basic work in improving knowledge of their customer base, enabling them to target existing customers for specific purposes. This includes not only the creation of data warehouses to provide a single view of the customer, to avoid the kind of error mentioned above. It also includes gathering data about 'life stage' events – or even anticipating them, for it is these life-stage events that often trigger financial services purchasing decisions. Perhaps most significantly of all, just a few companies are making serious attempts to 'household' their data. As many financial services decisions are household-based rather than individual, this makes obvious sense, especially if a company is trying to develop a high quality relationship with the family over, say, a decade or two. This process is made much easier if the company has one or two products that are family based, eg private health care or travel insurance. In its most advanced form, this helps a company estimate the future value of a family as it goes through its life cycle.

A central idea of CRM is that it pays companies to focus their attentions on customers with future value. In fact, most companies focus on current value, or even past value. For example, most life and pension companies make their commissions from the first few years of the customer relationship, so targeting existing customers with high value policies who have not bought anything for many years does not constitute targeting higher future value customers. However, companies are starting to address this issue, and models for predicting customer value are now being used.

One key to success here is to identify customers of low current value who are likely to have high future value, and try to retain or even increase one's share of their business as they buy more financial services. One way to do this is to examine the histories of current high value customers – usually only possible if the company has a 'time-sliced' data warehouse containing customer value history. Identifying the triggers that lead to value shifts is important, and regrettably many financial services companies have a history of 'arriving too late on the scene', ie after the customer has become more valuable.

One reason for this is that most do not see the various kinds of data they hold (eg policy and service transactions, producer, product and customer satisfaction survey data as well as third-party demographic and life event data) as sources of information on when customers are passing through life or relationship stages. This in turn is often due to failure to adopt a holistic view towards data collection and analysis. Companies that have been through the process of warehousing of customer and related data from a variety of sources usually understand better how data can 'tell stories about customers'.

IMPROVING THE SITUATION – WHERE SHOULD COMPANIES START?

Given the wide range of practices, recommending that a company move to best practice immediately in all areas is not sensible. This can create severe stresses within the organization and counterproductive results with customers. Suppose that a composite insurer decides to move to best practice direct marketing to support its efforts across all its channels (eg direct – mail, telephone; own sales force; brokers). It develops a customer database and recruits managers with strong direct marketing qualifications and experience. It begins to target its marketing efforts much more precisely, but does not consider the organizational problems of integrating direct marketing with its other marketing and sales efforts. Irrespective of the channel through which customers were originally acquired, customers receive mailings related to their propensity to respond and their predicted net value (including risk). The sales force does not pay proper attention to the leads, and brokers object that 'their' customers are being targeted. Customers become confused as they are subject to approaches for the same products from an additional direction. This company should have moved more slowly, sorting out a long-term customer management strategy and the rules and rights for working across different channels, based on the benefits for all parties – customers, brokers, sales force and other customer-facing staff. The company would have done better to aim for a steadier across-the-board improvement in practice, perhaps piloting or testing different approaches and allowing time for adjustments to be made in the practices of different channels.

To help companies identify the appropriate direction and speed of movement, we have developed a simple overall classification of stages of development of good practice in the use of mail in customer management. This is based on the detailed CRM analysis that we provide later. In this inevitably simplified classification, we identify three stages of development – basic, good and excellent (see Table 29.1). In our view, a balanced approach to improvement to the next stage of development is likely to yield the best results.

The benefits of moving from stage 1 to stage 2 are normally:

- substantial savings in costs of customer communication, as duplicates are removed, contact frequency is more attuned to customer needs, so response and conversion rates and value per conversion rise;
- after initial investment, steady reduction in systems costs due to removal of duplication and poor inter-working of different systems;
- ability to sustain substantially increased volumes of marketing activity through improved marketing and systems infrastructure;
- improved image with customers, as mailing tends to be more appropriate and timely;
- small improvements in customer retention and development (cross-sell).

Table 29.1 Stages of development of direct mail

	Basic	Good	Excellent
Customer management policy and implementation process	• Between non-existent and used only as tactical and inconsistent approach to achieve other marketing objectives. Implementation left to individual managers' initiative	• Process under development, parts of it agreed and some being tested in practice in some areas of the business • Customer segments are identified, recognized and analysed	• Process agreed and implemented, but also continually tested and researched for revalidation • Marketing programmes based on clear market segmentation, with various ways offered to customers to opt-in to programmes
Organizational adjustment to use of mail in customer management	• No consideration of organizational change implications	• Some of organizational implications identified, and recognition that more work needs to be done. Some organizational changes made, balancing customer management with product and channel management	• Organization model balancing customer, product and channel dimensions fully developed, implemented and periodically reviewed
State of customer database(s)	• Multiple databases, often on inconsistent platforms and no common data model • Customer data embedded in policy or product systems • Distinction between operational customer database and data warehouse not even considered • Constant difficulties updating customer databases from operational databases (ie transaction systems)	• Databases being merged and single data model being developed but not yet implemented • Customers are 'householded' • Distinction between operational customer database and data warehouse understood and development plans being considered or agreed and being implemented. Problems of updating customer databases from operational systems largely resolved	• Appropriate numbers of customer databases exist, with clear relationship to operational databases and data warehouse • Database provides holistic view of the customer • Feedback loop is used to link contact and response activities back to database
State of customer data	• Highly variable quality (errors, duplicates, etc), frequent problems with overwriting of key data. Many quality problems still to be fully documented. Ownership of data quality not allocated	• Quality problems mostly fully understood and process being put into place to resolve them and prevent recurrence. Ownership of data quality being allocated	• Ownership of data quality fully allocated. Data quality very good, and although occasional problems recur, these are swiftly identified through well-established processes and quickly resolved
Degree of understanding of customers	• Poor – marketing information is not company-wide but retained by individual deaprtment/ product lines • Understanding focused on products, risk and economics of channels of distribution and communication, rather than on customers	• Good understanding of customer being developed – needs, buying and communication behaviour, own and competitive product holdings, life and relationship stage behaviour. Processes being established for improving and maintaining understanding	• Good understanding of customer and strongly established processes for maintaining this understanding and translating it into action – across all channels and customer types

Table 29.1 Stages of development of direct mail *continued*

	Basic	Good	Excellent
Use of direct mail	• Largely tactical, to promote particular products. No rules concerning frequency or type of mailing to be sent to particular customers. No longer-term views about developing mail channel – overall or to particular segments	• Role of mail in retaining and developing customers understood and tests on improving performance under way	• Role of mail in retaining and developing customers firmly established in practice, and kept under review by well-established processes
Extent of integration of direct mail with other contact media	• No integration other than at tactical campaign level as part of contact strategy	• Role of mail channel relative to other communication channels defined clearly for retaining and developing some key market segments and now being tested	• Clear role of different media acting together for customer retention and development and established process for keeping relative contributions in balance, using return on investment criteria
Direct mail measurement and reporting processes	• Patchy – many campaigns not thoroughly measured, and results often not permanently documented, so much learning is lost	• Process designed and being implemented	• Process fully implemented and integrated into senior management reporting mechanisms
Senior management situation	• Little understanding of role of mail and of importance of strategic decisions in mail area • Poor understanding of importance of contact management and of relationship between customer contact management and customer data	• Good understanding of role of mail and emphasis being placed on work to improve strategic returns to mailing	• Excellent understanding of role of mail and required involvement of senior management in improving strategic performance of mail

The benefits of moving from stage 2 to stage 3 are mainly in the areas of:

• much more precisely targeted activities of all kinds – up-selling, cross-selling, retention – with much higher returns on marketing investment;
• much better inter-working between different media – particularly mail and telemarketing;
• better understanding of the balance between customer retention and yield per customer;
• better understanding of the relationship between customer profitability, retention and satisfaction;
• much improved customer satisfaction and profitability due to the above.

USING MAIL STAGE BY STAGE

In this part of the chapter, we provide detailed recommendations for mailing policies, based on the best practice that we found in our research. The use of mail in managing existing customers can usefully be viewed in terms of almost the same CRM stage analysis that forms the foundation of the QCi CMAT CRM assessment process described in Chapter 3.

This chapter describes each stage in detail, and then identifies three phases of the use of mail, as follows:

- basic – what most companies are doing;
- good practice – what a few more advanced companies are doing;
- best practice – what we consider to be the best example of cost-effective use of mail.

In this analysis, we have used two sets of issues to classify our results. The first are what we call policy issues. They cover:

- objectives during stage;
- branding objectives of mail;
- communications content, eg offer, pack, creative.

The second set is what we call technical issues:

- length – how long does the stage typically last (note that early stages may be completed very quickly for some customers, but may take much longer for others);
- key questions customers want answered at this stage;
- key questions companies want answered at this stage;
- data collection objectives;
- key analyses required.

In each case we identify:

- standard practice;
- good practice;
- best practice.

There is no implication that a company should do everything that we cover in this chapter. In our work in every sector, we have found that prioritization is the key to success. For example: companies with high early-stage customer attrition problems normally need to focus on their targeting process (have they targeted the right customer in the first place), and their welcoming process; customers with problems in developing additional customer value (up- and cross-selling) normally need to focus on their getting-to-know stage, in which they identify whether they should be trying to sell more to existing customers, and if so, what. They also need to beware that they are not trying to do this to customers who consider themselves in intensive care or pre-divorce.

Also, in many cases the tasks can be carried out by a combination of channels of communication and distribution – Web, sales force, telemarketing, intermediaries. The media and channels used are determined not solely by the cost of contact, but also by more strategic issues like the ability of the company to use the channel competitively for other customer management tasks. Companies that use a variety of channels should therefore use this analysis more broadly, taking into account their communication and distribution strategies.

RELATIONSHIP POLICIES

Welcoming

Objectives during stage

- Ensure customers are safely on board, ie know what they need to do, eg if there are problems.
- Minimize as far as possible the risks of early stage attrition due to poor welcoming, and later stage attrition due to discovery, for example, that product did not match customer needs from the beginning.
- Ensure customer knows how to minimize risk (for insurance).
- Reinforce branding, mainly to confirm to customer that decision to choose this supplier was correct.
- Identify early stage opportunities for up-selling and cross-selling – perhaps due to fact that initial sell was too little.
- Gather data essential for the above.
- Validate data used/given during targeting and recruitment.
- Identify timing for contacts during relationship.
- Create culture of communication between customer and company.
- Confirm readiness to move to getting to know.

Branding objectives of mail

- Deepen branding already achieved by the media through which the customer came to company.
- Create expectation that any communication received is first in a series that aims to help customer.

- Demonstrate a relevant range of products and services (but probably not too broad).
- Highlight the accessibility of the brand, and the benefits for the customer of giving information.
- Reassure the customer of the care that will be taken over any data given, and the relevance of the uses to which it will be put.
- Show case studies of satisfied customers, to personalize the brand.

Communications content, eg offer, pack, creative

- Welcoming pack that actually focuses on welcoming – ie ensuring customer is safely on board and gathering information needed to manage the customer safely towards account management, rather than early stage cross-selling.
- This includes branding, as customer may have bought for other reasons, eg inertia, price.
- Not just print, but video and audio tape, and digital/audio compact disk.

Standard practice

- Simple welcome pack explaining product features and benefits, not asking for response, with additional cross-selling inserts.
- No check to see if understood, or even read.
- No involvement device.

Good practice

- Welcome pack contains explanations and cross-sell inserts, but also strong involvement device, eg video or audio cassette.
- First copy of customer magazine.

Best practice

- As above, plus response device to ask for confirmation that pack read and understood.
- Company asks for customer to make activation call (so product can be used or additional benefit achieved), in which welcoming process is quality checked and additional data is sought, or...

- Questionnaire asking for additional details of customer and family, perhaps with small incentive to complete (ideally with element of incentive a benefit deferred until renewal where appropriate).

Getting to know the customer

Objectives during stage

- Improve understanding of customers, their nature and their needs.
- Identify any changes in the above since recruitment.
- Analyse pattern of interaction (usage, claims, additional purchases, responses) to determine appropriate future treatment, including best benefit/cost media for each customer group.
- Separate good and bad customers and allocate to different treatments (eg divorce if pattern completely bad, remedial treatment if good long term value but poor current performance).
- Early cross/up-sell (also to other family members).
- Deepen brand – maintenance of coherence and understanding of brand and its benefits.
- Avoid early stage attrition.
- Secure transition to account management.

Branding objectives of mail

- Keep broadening and deepening brand.
- Extend brand to other family/business members discovered during early stages of relationship.
- Where questionnaire is used to gather more data, to show how company is interested in the company and keen to meet needs.
- Through style of questionnaire, to show that company has considered how to make it easy for customer to give data.

Communications content, eg offer, pack, creative

- In-depth questionnaire, exploring further needs in this and related product areas, as well as relationship needs and other individuals, eg family, business. Should also test awareness of other products and services, and readiness to move to account management stage.

- Carefully targeted cross-selling and up-selling, based on data given in recruitment/welcoming questionnaires and on customer-profiling (in transactions-based businesses, early transactions patterns hold the key).

Standard practice

- Little recognition that this stage exists – most companies assume smooth transition from welcoming to account management, ie that simple welcoming programme enough to secure customer for ever.
- Standard mailings and inserts driven by product events, with relatively low response rates and little understanding of what determines which customers respond, and why they respond.
- Untargeted cross-selling.
- Little recognition of customer events (or indeed gathering of relevant customer data).

Good practice

- Second questionnaire to identify in-depth needs and any issues with product, service, or company.
- Second contacts triggered by timing identified in welcoming, and not just by product timing.
- Broadly targeted cross-sell.

Best practice

- Analysis of all data (particular response, transaction and customer) to identify opportunities.
- Closely targeted cross-sell.
- Retention risks identified and relevant information sent to customers to reinforce branding/benefits.

Account management – retention and development

Objectives during stage

- Retain customer and his or her family as long as they are profitable or likely to be so in the future.
- Develop loyalty and recommendation.
- Up-sell and cross-sell.

- Retain customers in this stage for life of product, and then transfer to other appropriate products or re-sell same product.
- Stimulate usage (for transaction products).
- Keep view of customer updated, by staying in touch with the customer to facilitate giving of data.
- Keep customer informed of new developments by the supplier or in the market.
- Remind customer of features, advantages and benefits of doing business with the supplier.
- Reinforce branding.
- Achieve right long-term balance between costs and benefits for both parties, eg channels, streaming for managing customers in different value categories, identification of micro-segments for different offers.
- Agree longer-term life-stage management process with customer (especially for life/pensions products).
- Optimize contact media.
- Explore options of communicating with customer through new media.

Branding objectives of mail

- Maintain breadth and depth of brand, especially as family/business changes over time.
- Use questionnaire to demonstrate continuing interest in customer.
- Ensure continued relevance of offer is demonstrated to customers.

Communications content, eg offer, pack, creative

- Targeted cross-selling and up-selling offers, with clear benefit to customer of deepening existing relationship.
- Continued reminder of benefits of brand and product.
- Regular questionnaire to detect key changes on customer side (needs and their causes).

Standard practice

- Basic customer databases, now mostly with cross-product holdings properly identified (or being built).
- Drive to increase product holdings by mailing all non-holders.
- Broad insert programmes.
- No attempt to identify customers with propensity to leave.
- Poor integration between mail and other media.

Good practice

- Drive to increase product holdings by targeting customers who fit crude profile of holders of other products.
- Customer base segmented by value and responsiveness, and standard mailings to each segment.
- Occasional questionnaires, but not as structured dialogue.
- Newsletter experimented with, but effect on increasing customer value not understood.
- Mailing programmes mainly product-event driven.
- Integration between mail and other media now partly understood and actioned.

Best practice

- Customer-event driven mailing programmes (eg life-stage).
- Regular questionnaire.
- Segmented newsletter, with effect on improving customer value and retention properly tested through use of control group(s).
- Strong integration between mail and other media – joint effects understood and programmes managed in integrated way.

Intensive care – service problems and customer change

Objectives during stage

- Make it easy for customer to signal changes in needs that make product unsuitable.
- Maintain approachability of brand, so that customer does not see product being unsuitable as reason to move away from company, but as reason to approach it to adjust portfolio.
- Achieve cost-effective and accurate re-diagnosis of customer need.
- Facilitate adjustment of portfolio.
- Identify patterns of change, to allow likely move into intensive care to be predicted.
- Make it easy for customers to signal problems – their nature and their precise requirements for resolution.
- Achieve cost-effective resolution.
- Identify patterns in problems and prevent recurrence.
- Reassure customer that past problems are recognized and affect the way current problem is handled.
- Secure rapid return to account management, where appropriate focused on higher predicted value customers.

Branding objectives of mail

- Ensure outbound messages take into account indicators of intensive care, as ignoring them will weaken brand.
- Continue to reinforce benefits of brand, particularly those aspects which seem not to have been well communicated to the customer.

Communications content, eg offer, pack, creative

- If complaint, apologise, explain and compensate, where appropriate.
- If product deemed unsuitable because of customer need change, offer to migrate to more suitable product with appropriate incentive.

Standard practice

- Stage not normally recognized – customer readjusts portfolio or moves straight to pre-divorce.
- Customer service questionnaires analysed for general issues, but impossible to identify customers with specific problems as questionnaire conducted by market research and not database departments, so customers at this stage not individually identifiable.

Good practice

- Stage recognized implicitly but not explicitly.
- Regular customer questionnaire aims to pick up signs.
- Questionnaire sent by database department, so customers with problems are identifiable.
- Regular tracking of customer perceptions of each interaction helps pick up signs of problems.
- Professional complaints management process, with rapid bounce-back of mail acknowledgement.

Best practice

- Stage recognized explicitly.
- Regular customer tracking of named individuals takes as a main task identification of customers at this stage.
- Strong emphasis in call centres on likely existence of this stage and training in how to handle it.
- Mail packs developed to bounce back to customers in this situation.

- Win-back/retention team call centre and mail process deployed at this stage rather than later.

Pre-divorce

Objectives during stage

- Identify customers who have decided to leave and persuade those that are predicted to be 'good' to stay, while letting those predicted to be 'bad' leave.
- Gather any information about reasons why customer decided to leave that was not collected during intensive care stage, and also about their feelings about the process of leaving.
- Change product or service to reduce attrition at this stage.
- Re-orient or reschedule communication to prevent recurrence of this stage for this customer (media used, frequency of contact, segment customer is managed in).

Branding objectives of mail

- Continue to reinforce benefits of brand, particularly those aspects which seem not to have been well communicated to the customer.

Communications content, eg offer, pack, creative

- As per intensive care, but with incentive to customer to communicate alternatives being considered.

Standard practice

- Nothing done.

Good practice

- Telephone retention team for one-time save of customer, with mail confirmation.
- But no change to communication stream, ie customer is treated as if immediately returned to normal account management.

Best practice

- Customer is placed in re-welcoming and getting-to-know treatment.
- But with special stream 'intensive care' philosophy.

Divorce

Objectives during stage

- Identify that customer has in fact left (not always self-evident).
- Identify whether customer has switched or has stopped using the category.
- Identify reason for leaving, and whether due to brand, product, service or other reasons.
- Identify whether remediable, and if so how.
- Apologize for reasons for leaving, if due to supplier failure of any kind.

Branding objectives of mail

- Maintain brand for those customers who are predicted to be able to be won back.

Communications content, eg offer, pack, creative

- Letter of regret, with win-back offer.
- 'Sign-off' questionnaire.

Standard practice

- Often not sure if customer has gone.
- So keep contacting the customer until well after the customer considers self to be divorced.

Good practice

- Clear indicators that divorce has taken place.
- But no clear strategy for predicting optimum time for re-contact, so simple replacement in prospect pool.

Best practice

- Clear indicators of divorce and of propensity to re-buy from supplier.
- Questionnaire to identify precise reasons and to collect data indicating propensity to re-buy.
- Planned contact stream by mail and telephone for customers indicated as likely good prospects for win-back.

TECHNICAL ISSUES

Welcoming

Length of stage

- Depends on typical life cycle of product, but for transaction products (eg cards, bank accounts), is time for first few transactions to be shown. For policy products, this is usually best measured by period during which most 'front-end' attrition takes place.
- We suggest up to three months for general insurance and credit/charge card, up to six months for bank account and life/pension/health.

Key questions customers want answered at this stage

- Have I got all the right documents?
- Do I understand them?
- How do I sort the policy documents out from additional promotional documents and other material?
- Is there anything else I need to do?
- Did I make the right choice – price, features etc?
- What do I do if I'm not happy with the choice I made?
- Who do I write to, call or e-mail?
- If I have already made an additional contact, how does the impression I got compare to the impression I had before I made the choice?
- Can I do all the things I chose this product to allow me to do?
- Am I properly covered?

Key questions companies want answered at this stage

- Is the customer safely on-board?
- Are there any early indicators of likely additional value or risk (marketing or financial)?
- Can I immediately cross-sell anything?
- Have I understood the basics of the client's family or business situation, and can I see any additional opportunities arising from this?
- Am I handling this stage in the most cost-effective way possible?
- Are my customers satisfied with their treatment in this stage?
- Have I reinforced my branding in this stage?
- When is this customer ready for the next stage?
- Have I identified by which media this customer would prefer to be contacted or to contact me and how frequently?

Data collection objectives (where not already collected during targeting or recruitment)

- Holdings of other products.
- Identity and needs of other family members.
- Referral issues (whether have referred or were referred).
- Preferred contact media and frequencies.
- Financial and domestic plans.
- Qualitative data on how customer perceives this stage is managed (eg via customer service questionnaire and text mining of complaints).

Key analyses required

- Newly collected data by customer and product type, to refine opportunity analysis.
- Re-prediction of attrition.
- Communication streaming.

Getting to know

Length of stage

- Typically at least as long as welcoming. Must include renewal of short-term contracts (1–2 years).
- For frequent claiming products, must include first claim.
- For transaction products, period determined by typical speed of evolution of transaction patterns.
- Partly determined by speed at which life events develop – this is normally also period before any major life-change events expected.
- Period could be considered as long as 5–7 years for 25-year life/pension/mortgage products, as up to 50% of customers leave before this period without ever reaching account management stage, eg straight from welcoming to intensive care/pre-divorce.

Key questions customers want answered at this stage

- Is the company keeping in touch with me as problems emerge or as my needs change?
- Does the company allow me to tell them about problems or need-changes?
- Does the company know and understand my priorities?
- Is the company using data I have given previously to make relevant offers to me?
- Is the company asking me for data that I have already given it?

- When I contact the company, am I recognized?
- When I contact the company, does it respond quickly, in the way that I want?
- Does the company value my business?
- Does the company want more of my business?
- If so, is it prepared to make me any special offer?

Key questions companies want answered at this stage

- Do I know what additional data this customer is prepared to give to help him/her meet his/her needs and to help me identify his/her additional potential?
- Do I know by which medium this customer would most like to give this information? Have I given this customer the choice?
- What are the customer's usage and response patterns telling me about this customer's additional potential, retention prospects and financial risks?
- Am I handling this stage in the most cost-effective way possible?
- Are my customers satisfied with their treatment in this stage?
- Have I reinforced my branding in this stage?
- When is this customer ready for the next stage?

Data collection objectives

- Depending on length of this stage, reconfirmation of data given during welcoming.
- In-depth data on usage, response, etc.
- Qualitative data on how customer perceives this stage is managed (eg via customer service questionnaire and text mining of complaints).

Key analyses required

- Identification of additional sales opportunities through profiling of 'good' early-stage users and motivating others with similar profiles to achieve good profile.
- Identification of risk patterns.
- Identification of which contact media are most cost-effective.

Account management – retention and development

Length of stage

- Ideally for ever, but actually determined by distribution of persistence.
- If welcoming and getting to know last up to a year, then this period is typically another 3–4 years for general insurance, 5–6 years for transaction products, mortgages, banking, life and pensions.

Key questions customers want answered at this stage

- Is the company keeping in touch with me as problems emerge or as my needs change?
- Does the company allow me to tell them about problems or need-changes?
- Does the company know and understand my priorities?
- Is the company using data I have given previously to make relevant offers to me?
- Is the company asking me for data that I have already given it?
- When I contact the company, am I recognized?
- When I contact the company, does it respond quickly, in the way that I want?
- Does the company value my business?
- Does the company want more of my business?
- If so, is it prepared to make me any special offer?
- As I, my family and my needs all change, does the company monitor these changes in any way?
- Does the company help me manage my long-term financial future?

Key questions companies want answered at this stage

- Is the customer satisfied with every aspect of my dealings? If not, which aspects are causing dissatisfaction and how important are they to the customer?
- Have I understood the most important opportunities presented by this customer – individual, family, business, whether as buyer or recommender, and am I managing them to the satisfaction of this customer?
- Is this customer profitable or not? Was he or she ever profitable, and will he or she be? If not currently profitable, how can I restore profitability? (this question might be asked by customer group, of course)
- Am I handling this stage in the most cost-effective way possible? In particular, have I got the right balance between communication, response, revenue and profitability?
- Are my customers satisfied with their treatment in this stage?
- Have I reinforced my branding in this stage?
- When is this customer ready for the next stage?

Data collection objectives

- Usage, contact, response, claim, cancellation and additional purchasing patterns.
- Changes on customer side – family size, income, location, housing type, product holdings, risks.

Key analyses required

- Gaps in product holdings.
- Additional potential for up-selling.
- Emergence of additional good or bad customer traits, attrition risks

Intensive care – service problems and customer change

Length of stage

- In customer's mind may last for months, but supplier may miss it completely as customer apparently goes straight to divorce.
- In practice, length often increases the longer the relationship has lasted – ie customers are slower to switch from suppliers they have used for a longer time.
- Can be a matter of hours or days if due to a severe service problem, eg a mishandled claim.

Key questions customers want answered at this stage

- Does the company recognize that my situation has changed?
- Has it offered me a way to deal with this that makes sense to me?
- How will it benefit it me to stay with the company while I change my portfolio, as opposed to switching?
- What should I do to ensure I get the best deal out of the company when I switch?
- Does the company recognize that I have a problem, and how serious it is?
- Is the company responding quickly and seriously to my problem?
- How does the company's performance in resolving my problem compare with what they promised me, with my last experience of it, and with what I and my friends experience from other companies?

Key questions companies want answered at this stage

- Do I know whether this customer is in account management or intensive care?
- Do I know whether I want to keep this customer?
- If in intensive care, what are the general and detailed reasons (need change or service problem)?
- Is my process for changing my dialogue with this customer understood by the customer?

- Am I handling this stage in the most cost-effective way possible? In particular, have I identified the probability that this customer will be saved?
- Are my customers satisfied with their treatment in this stage?
- Have I reinforced my branding in this stage? In particular, will the likely intensification of dialogue with the customer be seen as too little, too late?
- When is this customer ready for the next stage?

Data collection objectives

- Nature of change in customer, needs, etc.
- Text of complaints.

Key analyses required

- Predictive profiling of customers likely to show persistence problems.
- Categorization of complaints.
- Text mining to identify overt and hidden issues.

Pre-divorce

Length of stage

- May be almost instantaneous, but can also last six months to a year.

Key questions customers want answered at this stage

- What do I do if I am keen to leave – to whom do I write, where do I call?
- Has the company made it easy for me to know what to do?

Key questions companies want answered at this stage

- Have I identified the key indicators for this stage?
- Do I collect these indicators from this customer?
- Do I know that the customer has moved into this stage?
- If I deployed retention activity in intensive care (if I caught the customer at this stage), why did it fail?
- Am I handling this stage in the most cost-effective way possible?
- Are my customers satisfied with their treatment in this stage?
- Have I reinforced my branding in this stage?

- When is this customer ready for the next stage?

Data collection objectives

- As per intensive care.

Key analyses required

- What customer retention strategies work at this stage?
- Can I gain additional clues at this stage as to whether customer is worth saving?

Divorce

Length of stage

- This is state of not buying, so may last forever.
- However, experience has shown that customers who divorce for reasons other than extreme service dissatisfaction can be won back after a period, the length of which needs to be tested.
- Minimum period for this is determined partly by policy type (eg annual policy, winback can start after 6 months).

Key questions customers want answered at this stage

- Why did they let me go (so easily)?
- Why do they keep harassing me with irrelevant details?
- Is it worth my while staying in touch with this supplier?
- Is it sensible to try this supplier again?
- Does this supplier have any products or services that might ever interest me?

Key questions companies want answered at this stage

- Has this customer actually left (in his or her mind)?
- Am I unhappy or pleased that this customer has left?
- Should I place this customer back in my prospect pool?
- Am I handling this stage in the most cost-effective way possible?
- Are my customers satisfied with their treatment in this stage? Have I understood how this customer felt about the entire process of divorce and how I handled it?

- Have I reinforced my branding in this stage? In particular, does this customer think more or less of me because of the process of leaving?
- When is this customer ready for the next stage?

Data collection objectives

- Transaction cessation indicators.
- Absence of renewal.

Key analyses required

- Any departures from transaction pattern.
- Response propensities.
- Identify whether worth replacing in win-back pool.

RECOMMENDATIONS

1. By following a CRM stage approach, companies can greatly improve their use of mail in customer management.
2. To do this, companies should consider what data they need to estimate what stages their customers are in, and what contact mechanisms they use to allow customers to say what stage they are in (see the chapter on transparent marketing for more on this).
3. This approach should be prioritized, based on a CRM assessment (see Chapter 3). This shows at which stages the opportunities are greatest or the problems most severe.
4. All the best practice ideas suggested in the CRM stage analysis are testable. So companies should ensure that they do set up proper tests.

Part 8

Implementation

30

Managing value in e-business

Emma Cullen, Merlin Stone, Martin Hattenbach and Ted Strader

In today's cluttered environment, financial institutions search for ways to differentiate themselves with the myriad of software and services collectively known as business solutions. Many solution implementations fail to create value, largely because they have expected technology to do the job. Winning companies, by contrast, think about business issues first, linking technology capabilities to a focus on creating customer value. They recognize that technology alone won't create value. In this chapter, we pose and hopefully help answer some of the difficult questions that chief executive officers and chief financial officers pose to those who spend big budgets on trying to manage their customers better.

THE NASTY QUESTIONS

CRM has captured the attention of today's managers because customer-centric policies can pay big dividends. However, many companies have discovered that installing an off-the-shelf CRM software package does not by itself lead to improved customer relations. Many executives find it hard to show how investment in CRM will help improve their business. Some large companies are spending as much as $100 million on CRM investments, making them significant enough to warrant board-level explanations for return on investment.

So, if you've finally finished rolling out that new CRM system, can you say by how many thousands it will increase the bottom line in FY 2004? How about your Web initiative – you just had to have it, of course, but is there any way to state specifically and accurately how it increases shareholder value? For that matter, just what is information technology worth to your organization? Some CIOs and technology champions say that such a broad question is preposterous, but others are not so sure anymore. For an increasing number of executive and financial officers, vague promises of productivity enhancements and cost cutting are no longer enough to justify IT's ever more voracious budgets. Suspicious over the Y2K doomsday that never happened and bowled over by the costs of CRM, sales force automation and other multi-year, multimillion-dollar systems, executives want to know just what they're getting for their IT dollar.

The challenge for financial services firms today is to focus their IT investments in ways that enable them to devise new value propositions for customers, invent new ways of creating and capturing profit and ultimately to engineer a business model that is not only superior but unique.

CURRENT LACK OF STRATEGIC FOCUS

Most organizations have not done a good job of quantifying what they can deliver from IT projects. Most projects overrun, and most companies cannot estimate correctly the costs incurred. That drives executives to say, 'If IT people are always late and always coming back for more money, what's the value of IT?'

However, there is not always a simple relationship between IT investment and financial outcome. Investment in IT typically has an indirect financial effect, in which technology improves some intermediate valuation, like customer service, which in turn boosts customer confidence, which finally results in increased sales for the company. What is required is an investment appraisal technique to make visible those intermediate steps, in ways that can be quantified, measured and tracked. At the very minimum, the CIO should be able to say exactly what he or she is trying to derive from a valuation system. Is it the cost of e-commerce? The justification for new hires? Building a defence against budget cuts? There has to be a business driver for valuation. Before you begin, you need a reason to quantify – you need to understand why you're doing it.

ACHIEVING SUSTAINABLE BENEFITS FROM IT INVESTMENT

There are five practical steps that should be taken to ensure successful investment decisions. These are:

1. Develop a compelling business case, with in-depth understanding of revenue growth and/or cost reduction potential, using a range of techniques (please see later for more details).
2. Develop metrics for success to assess progress and gate investment – know when and how to rework the plan or pull the plug.
3. Determine optimal organizational structures to support full growth and cost control potential.
4. Use existing competencies and technical assets to maximize success. Know what you are good at and build from your experience.
5. Employ a strong project management approach to ensure appropriate resource allocation, leading to faster implementation cycles.

DEVELOPING THE BUSINESS CASE

The business cases for most strategic investments are often incomplete, unacceptably inaccurate or even missing entirely. When they are in place, they tend to focus only on technology costs, project delivery logistics and related risks. When they deal with the benefits, the focus is usually restricted to the immediate quantifiable cost avoidance, cost displacement or revenue impacts of traditional return on investment. This approach is valid in terms of identifying immediate savings, particularly where hard costs can be identified. In our experience this approach to a business case is rarely adequate for today's complex and sophisticated environment, particularly where there may be a lack of existing data. In many cases, additional business improvements take place, resulting in more benefits than were initially expected. However, if these benefits are not being tracked or managed the result is that investments are evaluated and deployed with a very weak link to any business gains.

A well-developed business case helps you to make the right decision. However, in our experience, key information is often lacking from the business case. Specific areas of concern include:

*   **Business** – do you have a thorough understanding of business model options? Do you know where you want to be? Do you know what you want? Does your understanding of the underlying issues enable you to effectively prioritize each business opportunity?
*   **Financial** – can you qualify and quantify all benefits associated with each opportunity? Do they demonstrate the realistic business opportunity, the potential risks and corresponding risk mitigation strategies? Have you calculated the P&L implications of a project? Do you know how this will effect shareholder equity?
*   **Operational** – have you analysed the detailed impact of each opportunity on the existing business, both during and after implementation?

- **Technology** – can you validate the accuracy of the business case for major technology investment? Do you understand the risk / reward trade-off for different technology solutions?

WHY DEVELOP A BUSINESS CASE?

A well-defined business case is critical to understanding the implications of large IT investments. Managers must have a through understanding of the profit and loss implications of an action before putting shareholder equity to work. A business case will help senior management evaluate and make well-informed decisions relating to strategic investments. For example, a business case should be applied to support decisions regarding: 1) new business opportunities (eg digital marketplaces); 2) new business applications (eg CRM, ERP).

Areas of focus within the business case will typically include:

- opportunities for improvement in the organization;
- potential benefits, costs and associated risks;
- the effect on organizational stakeholders;
- the effect on organizational profitability.

BUSINESS CASE PLANNING APPROACH

There are three basic approaches to business case development, as shown in Table 30.1. The effort needed to create the business case can vary widely from project to project. Discussions must be held between the sponsors / programme manager and the other project team leaders during the planning phase to assess the need, desire and value for generating a business case. These discussions will dictate the scope and depth of the effort and that will drive the hours and task duration for business case generation. On a large transformation engagement, a full business case can involve 1–4 project members for the duration of the project. Typically 5–10 per cent of the project cost should be used to quantify expected value and measure progress against value targets. The sponsor should be prepared to assign the CFO or other high-level financial director / manager to own the business case and work with the project team to assist and verify the financial calculations, since they will be presented to the management committee and possibly the board of directors. Communicating to the enterprise, organizations that manage their investments effectively should have a powerful message to convey to the employees, the board of directors and outside financial analysts about what has been achieved by the investment. This communication also becomes an essential tool for refining the decision process in the future.

Table 30.1 Different approaches to business cases

Approach	Description	Benefits	Costs/Risks
Top down	Financial focus: little involvement from management	Quick answer, direct translation to bottom line	Little cultural buy-in, weak link to required operational changes
Bottom up	Operational focus: significant involvement from middle or line management and staff	Significant cultural buy-in	Long business case development cycle, time, lack of consensus
Hybrid	Operational focus: with defined link to bottom line; includes representation from executive and middle line management: outcome validated by staff where needed	Line managers, utilized as change agents, buy-in at local level	N/A

THE CRITICAL PATH FOR A BUSINESS CASE

Our approach to business case development consists of five comprehensive, typically over-lapping steps as shown in Figure 30.1. By following the five phases as shown below, a full business case can be developed for a transformation project. However, it must be noted that when preparing for the business case, the business case team must take notice of the impacts from the relevant business environment plus have an understanding of critical legal and regulatory requirements.

Phase 1 – Value proposition

What distinguishes the few firms that are using CRM effectively is a clear focus on growing customer value, building customer relationships that enhance the long-term flow of profits to the company. These organizations begin by understanding and articulating their customer value proposition and developing a customer-centric strategy that defines the growth objectives, the key business leverage points and the appropriate role of technology. Every move should be based on its potential to create value; initiatives should be priori-tized by their contribution to the overall financial performance.

Over time, gaps exist between the business strategy and the ability to affect it through the business structure. The goal of the business case is to determine which steps the client should take to eliminate the gaps between the business strategy and business structure. This is where value propositions come into the picture. A value proposition starts with an opportunity for improvement. This opportunity is then researched for:

- potential benefit;

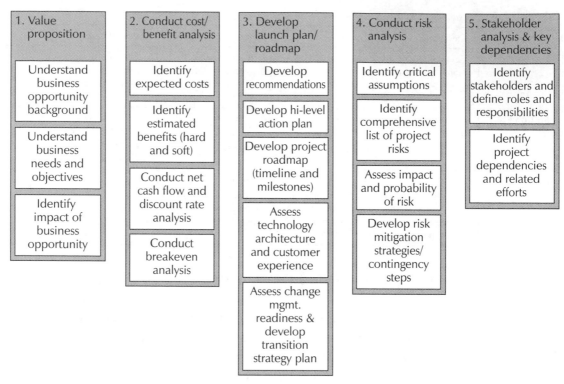

Figure 30.1 Business case development stages

- potential cost;
- potential risk;
- probability of success (organization's ability to make the change).

The business case then:

- outlines all value propositions;
- defines the organizational enablers that are needed to support the change;
- analyses their financial and cultural impact;
- defines which value propositions will be implemented.

The business case becomes an enabler of the continuous improvement process as seen in Figure 30.2.

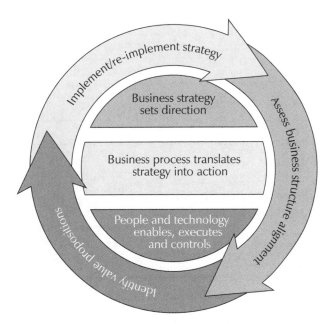

Figure 30.2 Value proposition development and use

Phase 2 – Cost/benefit analysis

During Phase 2 a rigorous cost/benefit analysis is conducted. Here, operational and financial analysis skills are used to drive out tangible and intangible benefits. Once the opportunity has been clearly defined, a cost/benefit analysis is conducted to identify expected results and capital and resource requirements for implementing the opportunity. Here the financial and the economic benefits are qualified and quantified. For CRM investment, measuring and collecting the right value metrics can help identify the most 'valuable' projects. In Table 30.2 we have included some of the costs, which we expect to form a major part of the CRM cost–benefit case. Typically there are two types of benefits: revenue enhancement and cost reduction (see Table 30.3). Whereas revenue benefits reflect the net increase in cash flows that result from the implementation of the initiative, cost benefits reflect the net expenditure decreases from the same implementation.

However, CRM can do much more than improve service and save money. It can change the way a company does business. For example, a few years ago a number of companies assumed that only simple products could be sold over the Web. However, innovative companies demonstrated that the greater the complexity, the better the product can be handled over the Web. Vendors can now allow their customers to be the buyer and configurator for their products.

Often termed return on investment (ROI), net cash flow analysis using discount rates permits the concise computation of the value that the marketing initiative will create for the

Table 30.2 Cost categories

CRM investment costs – one-off costs	CRM non-investment costs – ongoing costs
Hardware costs	Marketing development, production and delivery costs
Software licensing	List/name acquisition costs
External consulting costs	List/name enhancement costs
Internal resource costs	Outsource costs associated with the development, production and delivery of the CRM communication
Business reorganization costs	Internal costs associated with the development, production and delivery of the CRM communication
Marketing resource costs	

Table 30.3 Benefit types

Revenue enhancement	Cost reduction
Increase in response rates	Decrease in charge-off rates
Increase in cross-sell ratio	Decrease in marketing programme cycle times
Decrease in account attrition rate	Decrease in data mining time
Increase in fees	Fewer account closing costs
Increase in price	Reduced business planning time
Increase in interest earned	Fewer IT support costs

enterprise. ROI is the profitability determined by the amount of net revenue or operational cost reductions that exceed investment. Using a discount rate, this enables the organization to calculate the expected future net cash flows at the current value.

Table 30.4 gives an example of the revenues and expenses associated with a CRM project. The project shows a net loss for the first year and then net gains for the next two years. The NPV calculation, discounted at 10 per cent, returns an NPV of over $7 million. This means that this project should be accepted, because the revenues outweigh the costs over the life of the project. An important step is to provide a breakeven analysis, which will allow the investors/shareholders to understand the length of time the organization will take to recover the cost of the project.

Table 30.4 Simple example of NPVcalculation

	Year 1	Year 2	Year 3
Revenue			
Number of purchases	500,000	1,000,000	1,000,000
Revenue from purchases	$5,000,000	$10,000,000	$10,000,000
Expenses			
Project cost	$10,000,000		
Project costs/product	$2.50	$3.50	$3.50
Total project costs	$11,250,000	$240,625	$120,313
Net revenue	$(6,250,000)	$9,759,375	$9,879,687
Discount rate	10%	10%	10%
NPR	$(6,250,000)	$8,065,609	$7,422,596
Cumulative NPV	–6,250,000	1,815,609	9,238,205

Phase 3 – Develop integrated launch plan and roadmap

To capture the full value from CRM, an integrated improvement approach is required. Thus, the CRM project could be divided into several programmes (see Figure 30.3), each focusing on developing specific capabilities required for the overall project. Overall success depends on successful completion of programmes. To help deliver these phases a launch plan and roadmap (see Figure 30.4) are created to help guide the organization in implementing the business opportunity. This helps in understanding the key project activities, outcomes and implementation timeline. Each project phase should be broken down into key initiatives and action steps. The critical paths have been identified, and time lines and responsibilities defined.

Phase 4 – Conduct risk analysis

There are several risk analysis methods. For each opportunity for improvement identified, we need to identify risks (internal/external) that could be posed if that opportunity is or is not exploited. These include financial risk (eg cash flow, capital investment), regulatory/compliance risk, operational risk, market risk (impairment to market competitiveness) and implementation risk.

Phase 5 – Stakeholder analysis and key dependencies

This is probably one of the most important elements for a business case and should be completed and verified throughout the project. Strong ownership needs to be identified

INTEGRATED LAUNCH STRUCTURE

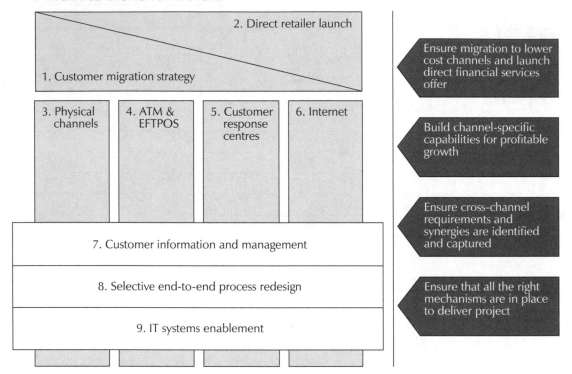

Figure 30.3 Example of programme plan summary

OVERALL PROGRAMME TEMPLATE STRUCTURES

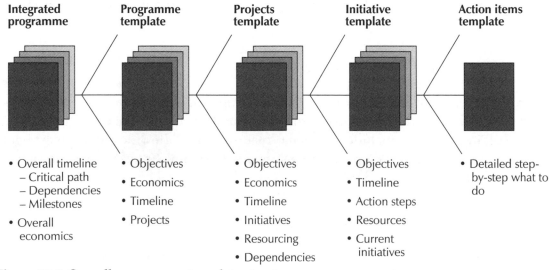

Figure 30.4 Overall programme template structure

across the project, with regard to costs, benefits, resources, risks and project milestones. No initiative or project is an island and nowhere is this more true than in CRM efforts. Getting initiatives and projects approved throughout the life of the CRM programme will require collaborative efforts with affected stakeholders to address their concerns and ensure their support.

SOME FINAL THOUGHTS

Speak the language of stakeholders

Because you have defined value in terms of business performance measures, you will be able to state ROI in terms most relevant to each group of stakeholders. For example, the CRM team will usually identify best with productivity expressed as an increase in customer retention or customer value (eg achieved by cross-sell or retention or by increased value per product). However, the CEO will often be more concerned with financial effects, although the wise CEO will also focus strongly on human resource indicators. It is important to define value in both performance measures and cash terms, since all stakeholders will be able to understand the impact of the new technology in terms of what they deal with most often. Ultimately, the people who use the solution determine its effectiveness.

Time matters

With larger transformation projects, the resulting value does not always occur immediately. Although some benefits of IT begin when the system is turned on, most are dependent upon the productive use of the tools in practice. Success depends on effective user training programmes and on overcoming human resistance. Weigh all these delay factors in determining when achievement of the performance targets can be expected. Be as realistic as possible to develop a believable and achievable timetable. A monthly grid outlining the 12–18 month period following implementation will help all stakeholders identify when the benefits are captured.

Keep score

By developing performance measures and estimates that define the value of the new technology, you've assembled the elements of a project scorecard – a vehicle for tracking results. Organized by processes or areas affected by the new solution, the various measures that constitute a scorecard should indicate both the baseline performance for each measure as well as the performance scorecard. Project scorecards do not need to be complex – a simple measuring system is better than none at all, since tracking the value of a transformation project is the only way to know what you did right and what needs more work. This information is not only critical to demonstrating the success of the project but also serves as extremely valuable input into any future investment decision process.

Pay for it

It is important to build value analysis and measurement resources into the project budget. Too often the project team does not spend sufficient time developing a detailed value analysis and therefore the benefits are not well understood and cannot be measured. Even when benefits are measurable the entire project team is typically deployed immediately to the next project and achieving the results is left to the user community. A good rule of thumb is to dedicate 5–10 per cent of the project budget to quantifying expected value and measuring progress against the value targets.

CONCLUSION

Hopefully with the information provided in this chapter you are ready to compute the ROI for a CRM initiative or project. Along with understanding the customer value proposition, the business case provides the bedrock for investment decision making and for continuing measurement of the value of CRM efforts. However, you need to understand that major CRM projects usually result in significant learning by both your staff and your customers, so the expected benefits may accrue faster or slower than you expect, and some not at all, so recalibrating the business case may be needed. Also, if there is anything you can do to test cost-effectively and quickly the assumptions in your case – do it!

APPENDIX: A CASE STUDY

Here is an extract from the benefits side of a business case developed for a US life insurance company. The numbers are not disclosed – the only numbers given are the assumptions made for improvements resulting from the CRM investment.

Current situation

- $x billion in annual premiums;
- y% lapse rate;

- z% new business growth rate;
- Profit margin is w% per dollar of premium.

Business case assumes these assumptions are static, only changing from quantifiable improvements from CRM individual projects.

Improvement projections basis

These are based on:

- industry studies;
- judgment based on business gap analysis;
- internal activity-based costing study;
- a major improvement is lapse rate improvement which results from common front-end interface and operational customer data store.

Detail of improvement projections

- Required customer service functionality and operational data store access provides lapse rate improvement of 2%.
- Conservative – industry average is 2.5% per industry study, due to a 5% increase in customer satisfaction.
- We modelled a 0.5 % increase in 2002, 1% increase in 2003, and 0.5% increase in 2005.
- This translates into saving $n million in premium from 2003 through 2007.

Other individual projects will also contribute to this benefit:

- call centre technology projects;
- customer service realignment project;
- workflow management integration;
- middleware integration.

Another improvement will be a reduction in training expenses that will result from the common front-end interface.

Employee turnover in customer service should go from y per cent to z per cent gradually over three years (2003, 2004, 2005). This is a very conservative estimate – best of breed is 6 per cent turnover in customer service. For z employees, and average training cost of $m, this saves w employees a year and translates into training expense savings of $n per year.

There were other employee/distributor benefits that were not quantified in the model:

- Telemarketing turnover should fall (currently z% turnover).
- Agent and broker turnover should also improve as sales automation is rolled out.
- Reduction in training time and time to become proficient in front-end skills (as opposed to learning a number of different systems as in today's environment).
- Employee (and subsequently agent/broker) satisfaction will increase, leading to many other benefits (ie satisfied customers).
- The common front-end interface with sales functionality for direct marketing will improve the new business growth rate 10% per year each year for three years (per industry study).

Benefits are realized in 2003, 2004, and 2005, and were based on direct marketing premiums. This equates to m additional sales per telemarketer per year (currently average telemarketer sells y policies per year) each year for three years. This translates into generating $x million in premium from 2003 through 2007.

Other individual projects will also contribute to this benefit:

- call centre technology projects;
- sales process realignment project;
- leads interface to predictive dialler.

The common front-end interface with cross-sales functionality for customer service reps will also improve the new business growth rate. Customer service efficiencies will allow for v full-time equivalent (FTE) employees (about 22 per cent of current customer service front-office FTE) to focus on cross-sales activity launched from a customer service transaction (per IBM estimated improvements based on the activity-based costing study and efficiency opportunities discovered in the business gap analysis). Using current average premium generated per telemarketer per year ($y), and modelling gradual improvement, a 0.6 per cent new business growth improvement will be realized in 2002 and a 1.2 per cent improvement in 2003. We believe this is conservative because we consider a satisfied customer a hot lead for a cross/up-sell. This translates into generating $x million in premium from 2003 through 2007.

Premium growth from freed-up resources results in higher NPV than realizing the expense savings (not to mention the other benefits of premium growth, such as increased market share), even with the conservative estimate.

An integrated voice response unit (IVR) for self-service will result in expense reduction in customer service. Twenty-five per cent of general inquiries and premium-related inquiries will be handled in IVR (very conservative, compared to 70 per cent estimated at another insurer). $x million is currently spent on these activities per year for FTE-related expenses (per activity-based costing survey), translating to a $z million expense savings per year. We modelled a gradual benefit realization of $y million expense savings in 2003 and $x million each year after.

There were other benefits that were not quantified in the model:

- Customer satisfaction will increase due to new contact method choice being offered for routine inquiries.
- Employee satisfaction will increase due to the customer service role migrating to handling more complex inquiries and requests and expanding to other activities (cross/up-sells).
- An IFS-wide campaign management system and a lead distribution and management system will result in significant new business growth.

There is expected to be a 12.5 per cent improvement in new business sales due to more value-added sales activities, measuring and planning occurring with same resources:

- If half the agents and half the brokers were subject to this benefit, the effect is an 8% improvement in new business sales.
- Equates to y additional sales per agent per year (currently average agent sells z policies per year).
- Also equates into generating $n million in premium from 2004 through 2007.

Other benefits not quantified in model:

- Employee and distribution channel satisfaction will increase due to the ability to sell more policies and spend less time on non-value-added tasks.
- Customer data warehouse and/or data marts, segmentation and prospect scoring will improve the lapse rate and new business growth rate.

Scoring will provide a five per cent increase in sales per year for three years (2004–06). This translates into generating $x million in premium from 2004 through 2007. Customer service efficiencies will allow for n full-time equivalent (FTE) employees (about y per cent of current customer service front-office FTE) to focus on retention activities (per estimated improvements based on activity based costing study and efficiency opportunities discovered in the business gap analysis).

Segmentation and scoring-driven retention activities will provide a one per cent lapse rate improvement each year for two years (2004 and 2005), which translates into generating $y million in premiums from 2004 to 2007. Premium growth from freed-up resources results in higher NPV than realizing the expense savings (not to mention the other benefits of premium growth, such as increased market share).

Calculating the lifetime value of a household and using it for analysis will improve expenses and premium growth. Lifetime value analysis will allow for optimizing marketing, sales and servicing resources by targeting increased efforts on high and potentially high lifetime value customers and prospects. Profit margin should improve by 0.5 per cent on the premium dollar in 2005 and 0.5 per cent in 2006 (total of one per cent, per industry study). This translates into bottom-line benefits of $x million in 2005, $y million in 2006 and $z million in 2007. All customer-facing processes – marketing, sales and servicing strategies and systems – should use lifetime value to realize this benefit. LTV will enable the company to achieve the ultimate financial goal of profitable growth, lowering unit cost per policy in force from $x to $y.

Providing a common front-end interface with sales functionality for agents and brokers will improve the new business growth rate. Common front-end interface implementation with sales functionality for agents and brokers will provide a new business improvement of 10 per cent per year each year for three years (per industry study) for agents and brokers that are affected. Benefits are realized in 2004, 2006 and 2007 and are based on agent and broker premiums. This equates to y additional sales per agent per year (currently average agent sells z policies per year) for each of three years. This also equates into generating $n million in premium from 2005 through 2007, assuming only half of agents and brokers are affected and a 10-phase rollout during 2003. This project, along with many of the other projects up to implementation time of this project, should effect agent and broker retention.

The business case developers commented that to maximize the chances of the business case being achieved, the following were needed:

- A project cost–benefit monitoring process to compare actual costs and benefits to projected costs and benefits.
- Establish the timing of comparisons (monthly, quarterly).
- Reporting process to ensure necessary information is available in a timely manner.
- Monitoring process to review progress towards projected benefits and comparison to control groups.
- Research variances between actual and projected numbers, and set up action plans where necessary.
- Document unforeseen benefits and constraints, and set up action plans where necessary.
- Adjust models as necessary (ie population basis changes).

31

Implementing CRM

Merlin Stone, Bryan Foss, Neil Woodcock, Michael Starkey, John Mullaly, Liz Machtynger, Rich Harvey and Brian Scheld

INTRODUCTION

This book has described a financial services world in which very little stands still. In the world of property and casualty insurance, the storms caused by weather and terrorism have filled the headlines. Mergers and acquisitions have created serious problems for companies, whether in bringing together the way they work (in particular operational systems), the way they present themselves to the world (brands, channels, products, etc), or the way they work with customers (databases, marketing and service policies, etc). There have been significant geographical shifts, as companies have turned their attention from the over-served and/or overly competitive developed markets to under-served and only recently deregulated markets in developing countries. Despite this, it can be argued that there has been little real change in the competence of financial services organizations – most would recognize that they are only at the beginning of a long road of change. This applies to CRM too, so this chapter looks at the specific implications of implementing CRM in financial services organizations.

Many financial services companies are aiming to implement more complex, more comprehensive CRM strategies. This carries with it a high risk of failure. The chances of achieving success can be increased if a company follows some simple guidelines. Plans are often inflexible. They are often based on little accurate knowledge of the company's situation – hence the importance of using an assessment tool such as CMAT (see Chapter 3). Activities should be prioritized from the beginning. They should build on the strengths and remove weaknesses. Prioritization should be based on factors most likely to affect business performance. Projects should be kept short with a clear business focus. The programme should be managed, not just individual projects. Above all, it should be recognized that success in CRM is achieved through people. Beautifully crafted plans, excellent CRM systems, brilliant customer database analysis tools – all these are virtually worthless without the people who have to use them to manage customers.

CRM PROGRAMMES DO FAIL!

Many CRM programmes will fail. Very large programmes are particularly vulnerable to failure. Companies often end up with systems that are poorly aligned with business needs. This is usually due to an unclear definition of requirements (possibly due to an unclear business model) or poor project control, leading to 'scope creep', so that system requirements are never actually finalized.

The commonest reasons for failure appear to be:

- failure to think through the business strategy and model;
- not dealing with the basic problems of the organization (listening to employees would help here!);
- too much focus on technology, too little on data and skills;
- objectives unfounded on knowledge of the organization today, its capability to change, and receptiveness of customers to different ways of being managed;
- absence of skills to deliver the programme;
- not having done it before, so no knowledge of how and where to start;
- choice of wrong partners to support the project;
- failure to integrate the different aspects of CRM in a 'joined up' approach – partly because senior managers do not view the idea holistically, and because organizational structures create problems;
- setting aggressive time-scales.

Companies can increase the chances of successful CRM programme implementation by:

- taking a phased, steady approach to CRM development, not big bang;
- developing a vision of the future, but not making it too detailed too soon;
- knowing the starting point – understanding how well customers are managed today;

- focusing on a few easy actions that will lead to increased profitability quickly – cherry-pick key actions and quick wins;
- listening to staff – remove what they see as the basic barriers to managing customers better;
- from the beginning, managing the programme by outputs as well as inputs, to ensure that what the company expects to happen with customers does happen, and if it does not, to ensure that the reasons are understood;
- using the learning from initial phases to plan and implement later phases;
- accepting willingly and unemotionally any challenges to the longer-term vision – whether from competitors, market developments or from within others in your organization – based on their analysis or ideas, or performance challenges identified during the early stages of implementation.

Phased, steady approach CRM development

In our work over the past 15 years, we have identified the following two basic models of programme planning for implementing customer management (CM) or customer relationship management (CRM): 1) **Big bang** – moving as rapidly as possible to implement CM principles across the business. This generally only works for 'greenfield' businesses. Success is very rare, and normally only works in businesses that are direct-only or single distribution channel businesses, usually with simple product ranges, where strong central control can be used to ensure implementation. 2) **Steady progress** – moving steadily towards a CRM vision, while recognizing that the vision will continue to change. For larger companies, often with a background of several partly successful CRM initiatives, this is usually the better option. Very strong programme management disciplines are required as the series of projects are rolled out across the business. It is usually best to start with pilot projects to establish possibilities and capabilities, before rolling out CM activity to the rest of the business. Tough choices have to be made about where to start, and indeed whether parts of the business should be left untouched.

Develop a vision of the future, but don't determine the detail too soon

Establishing the vision is normally the starting point. This should cover markets (segments), competitive positioning and the broad approach to distribution channels. Unless the company is a start-up, or is changing its CRM approach as part of a much wider change programme, it need only be in outline. Here are some questions that need to be answered early on:

- What is the relative attractiveness and size of different segments?

- What is the company's competitive differentiation in each segment?
- What communication and distribution channels will be needed to cover each segment? Will this change for different product groups?
- What proposition is needed to find and keep target groups?
- How will the organization need to change so it can deliver the proposition?

Know the starting point

The value of doing a customer management assessment (see Chapter 3) is that many senior managers do not know what their company is capable of today, in CRM terms. Companies that do not know their starting position build future corporate competencies on shifting sands rather than a solid foundation. It is usually only companies that are good performers already that know what is wrong and what needs to be done. One of the commonest findings in CMAT assessments is the difference between management intention (and belief) and reality. We call it the great **customer management illusion**. Just as alarming is the fact that the majority of senior managers do not give clear, visible leadership in achieving excellence in customer management. Lack of clear visible leadership is particularly evident in poor performing companies. Those that perform the worst are the ones most likely to believe that they are good, and the ones least likely to welcome 'bad' or critical feedback.

Cherry-pick key actions and quick wins: use a clear prioritization process

To select the components of the first phase of a programme, it is important to prioritize the activities or tasks identified in the business case. The prioritization process involves examining the following elements:

- expected net *value* of benefit over three years;
- expected *timing* of benefit;
- *probability* of benefit being achieved, taking into account ease of implementation.

The first phase should contain a blend of quick wins and longer-term capability development. The quick wins will give confidence to the sponsor, senior team, project team and others, help engage doubters, and encourage sponsorship for longer-term investments.

Manage the programme for outputs from the beginning

The first phase of the programme should last no longer than about six months. Costs should be limited before some payback is witnessed. This applies even in the largest companies with the largest programmes. Some may find this controversial, but the strong evidence of project failure justifies this.

Listen to staff

Ensure that enough resource is allocated to training, coaching and measurement. In many financial services CRM programmes too much time and resource is spent on systems development and formal training. Companies should consider more post-implementation coaching. People should be coached to ensure they understand and can apply the new ways of working. Management must listen to feedback as to why people find it difficult to deploy, and then make changes to ensure more effective programme deployment.

Measure and build on the first phase

Measurement should cover employees' and partners' behaviour and attitudes towards the required change. This may involve researching people and partners, as well as customers. The same measurement process that identified where the company was starting from should be used to identify whether improvements actually have been made.

Prepare for future phases

Later phases of the project cannot be planned in detail at the outset. Future phases should be relatively flexible – based on the vision and actual performance in earlier phases.

Manage the programme, not just the project

Here is a programme management checklist for determining the likelihood of programme success and for identifying where changes are needed.

Programme scope

- Clear objectives overall.

- Realistic deliverables / accurate reflection of business case.
- Real change to business.
- Adequate focus for change management.
- Areas for potential conflict.

Programme financials and business case

- Robust business case? Accurate financials?
- Access to sufficient budget? Short-term budgetary constraints?
- Short- and long-term deliverables / parallel strategies.

Programme team

- Senior and supportive programme leader.
- Supportive senior champion.
- Coordinated by a steering group of senior managers? Clarity of roles? Full buy-in?
- Overall delivery entrusted to senior experienced programme manager.
- Programme team have full implementation authority?

Project management

- All main stages in programme identified and planned? Sub-projects?
- Right programme structure?
- Clear and unambiguous business measures in place?
- Clear prioritization process?
- Current position benchmarked?

Managing implementation

- Informal network to identify blocks / barriers?
- Dependencies identified?
- Key influencers identified? Are they advocates?
- Right skills mix internally?
- Too much outsourcing of skills?
- Sufficient skills to maintain project momentum?
- Have we identified the right supplier(s)?
- Are formal procedures for supplier selection in place?
- Is momentum maintained by documentation and communication?
- Internal communication in place?
- Benefits identified for all key influencers?

- Thought given to holistic implementation?

Performance management

- Right balance between coaching and training? Skills being passed on?
- Is attitude and behaviour research planned relative to implementation?
- Scope within the programme to test and refine alternative approaches?
- KPIs being developed relative to programme needs?

Accept challenges to the longer-term vision

Very few markets are stable or predictable enough for a company to be certain that the first phase of its programme is 100 per cent correct, especially if the first phase includes research and analysis of customer behaviour and value for the first time. The findings from the latter will be likely to change future phases of the programme.

PROJECT SPONSORSHIP

One of the more difficult issues to resolve in CRM implementation is how the CRM change programme should be constructed and led. To implement anything other than tactical approaches, the programme sponsor must be senior, visible and totally supportive. The sponsor of any large programme must be a senior person with cross-functional responsibility. Normally this person should have a board-level role and needs:

- executive team authority;
- access to a significant budget;
- to be a great communicator / motivator;
- to have considerable experience in customer management;
- to have clear measure against which to benchmark progress.

Sadly, the reality is often that the board-level person does not really own the project and is just a sponsor in name only. Sometimes this is due to the fact that the board-level person is not experienced in CRM, or does not really believe it is his or her responsibility. This lack of commitment leads to common problems such as:

- limited project visibility;
- non-attendance at key meetings;
- slow to respond to emerging blocks to the project;

- loss of momentum in the project;
- de-motivation of project team.

The champion of any programme should be a senior manager. This is not the project manager of course, but a programme champion who is there to chair the steering group and become involved in steering direction and helping to solve key 'blocks' to project success. Sometimes this is the 'sponsor'. Common pitfalls are:

- This person does not allocate enough time to ensure that the project is progressing along the lines of the points in this checklist.
- The programme is just skin-deep for the 'champion'. He or she does not really champion it and the programme team feels he or she does not really understand the issues.

A programme manager should be appointed to be responsible for delivery. The qualities the person requires are:

- experience;
- understanding of the business;
- vision;
- not to be locked into legacy thinking;
- strength – will not be dominated by 'concept touting' consultants.

The programme manager should work closely with the work-stream leaders and with the programme manager to ensure that the programme is on track. Key functions and responsibilities of the programme manager ought to include:

- communication to ensure that the organization is fully 'engaged' in the process;
- quality control to ensure that the output is well thought through;
- managing commitment, ensuring that users, or non-core programme people, involved in some work-streams provide appropriate commitment to the programme.

The programme manager may have to import some key skills, but the priority should be to train current employees. New people coming in may have a different culture that alienates staff who must do the actual implementation.

Often the programme manager will appoint an independent consultant adviser, with experience of managing similar projects, to work with him or her. Most companies will require some independent expert help to guide them through an implementation, but be mindful of the impact of having an alien culture of 'consultants' or system integrators being seen to 'own' the programme. The external team should clearly be led internally. If the programme manager is external, as is often the case because of the skills and knowledge required, it is important to make sure they quickly become part of the team and that their 'culture' and work behaviours fit with the organization's.

WORK PLANNING

The team must have the authority to ensure that individuals in suppliers or functions not under their direct 'control' make time for and contribute to the programme in the ways required. The programme manager should develop a clear outline of work to be done and output required, and provide realistic guidelines as to how much time it will take. If team members are unclear about the time commitment required, this will become frustrating for the others involved. The programme manager should monitor the quality of the work, focusing on the most important tasks or those being carried out by 'at risk' teams (those with less obvious commitment). Where the work is clearly rushed as the deadline approaches, the resulting output may not be well thought through. The programme manager should counsel team leaders to ensure that their issues and worries are resolved and also be able to change people involved in the programme if required. If the scope of the programme implies significant potential change, the team must have the authority to implement organizational change.

The steering group should be chaired by the champion, as above, and attended by managers from each of the functions impacted by the strategy (often IT, marketing, sales, service, finance, HR, analysis and research). The programme managers should also attend along with the managers of individual projects. Others may be asked to attend depending on the work carried out and the stage in the programme. A common problem is that the business functions nominate lightweights – the people with time on their hands. The members miss meetings and do not read programme status reports. They are 'named' members only and people in their function or department quickly pick this up and become unresponsive to meeting and work requests from the programme team.

Failure is more likely when core or non-core team workers have hidden issues / worries (some genuine, some not, but all perceived) concerning the programme that go 'un-listened to' and unresolved. This will affect the quality of their output and the mutterings within the organization may grow into significant barriers to change. Setting up an informal network designed to raise early issues with the programme manager is a key success factor here. There may be very valid reasons why the programme plan may need to change.

COMMUNICATION

Communication is key in programmes that involve organizational change. People are used to ways of working, want to protect their and their staff's future security and position in the organization. At a more mundane but nevertheless critical level, they may have personal issues against members of the team and will always be looking for the programme to fail. The programme manager needs to win the hearts and minds of the organization. This requires an internal marketing campaign using appropriate, relevant and timely messages that people will accept. Aims and objectives, likely benefits, or key messages are usually not repeated often enough. As in any marketing or propaganda activity, the repetition of a message is central to the message being understood and remembered.

One of the key change roles is that of senior sponsor and champion. This person needs to have powerful influencing skills, and must make them available to the programme manager. The programme manager needs to work with this person on the CRM programme's positioning and both of them must listen to the organization's reaction to it. The senior sponsor and champion plays a key role in communicating.

Communication during the programme, in different ways, with different messages, is vital. This is usually forgotten. People who are in other ways really expert at customer management often ignore the importance of internal communication to users and influencers. In one key account management process, we identified pan-European user-influencers within the organization and involved them in the implementation process. They returned to their local organizations and trained/advocated the approach to their immediate account teams and peers, who then came on the training. This networked the implementation into the organization very successfully.

Attention should be paid to:

- the type of people who need to be communicated to;
- the type of messages they need to hear;
- the contact strategy applicable: looking in particular at media (face-to-face, telephone, e-mail, newsletter, posters on wall, etc);
- the frequency (eg daily updates, weekly, monthly, at key trigger points).

Different types of content will require delivery to different people in different ways at different frequencies with different messages. Key targets include:

- business unit managers;
- personnel/HR managers;
- finance managers;
- marketing and sales personnel;
- operations personnel;

- stakeholder (including partners and customers).

It is important to select key influencers at grass-roots level and work with them to turn them into advocates. Winning advocates is yet another key programme management point. The programme team should determine who in the 'user' organization are key influencers of others. They should be brought into the programme and encouraged to provide input. It is important to demonstrate that their contribution is valued and that it is being listened to. Another possibility is to get them involved in user testing of the process or system, and designing the training so that they feel as emotionally involved in its success as the programme team.

ENCOURAGING CHANGE

People are naturally resistant to change, but many will be prepared to change if they are encouraged and reminded. An implementation plan needs to:

- consider ways to reduce the constant pull-back by old world behaviour 'magnet', for example making existing processes, systems obsolete, or managers requesting to see regular 'output' of new ways of working;
- consider ways to pull (carrot-led) to new world desired behaviour, for example recognizing 'new style working' in coaching and appraisal systems, and making appropriate comments or giving appropriate rewards, providing real benefit to all in using the new system, ensuring that senior and line managers 'live the vision', reinforcing it through their behaviours;
- consider ways to push (stick-led), for example, identifying 'old style working' in coaching and appraisal sessions and taking appropriate action, using charts and targets that rank people's 'new system' behaviours and performance, making sure that senior people insist on the new way of doing things.

The usual practice is to rely on pull (carrot-led) tactics, but this is often done in an insular and not holistic way.

It is important to try to ensure that there are real benefits for all users that save them time, really help them achieve their targets, and add some other value to what they do. This may change the scope of the programme a little. For example, in a sales management systems project, this meant building in additional functionality ('what if?' management information reporting) to encourage the sales managers to use the system and encourage their teams to use it. If there are no obvious benefits that users can buy into, then the change required of the user will be harder to enforce. If the user has a choice, they will naturally revert back to the old way of working. This is not because they are being obstreperous or deliberately malevolent, but because it is human nature.

Changes need to be introduced carefully in a multifaceted way. Training has an important role to play, of course, but implementation does not end there. Coaching on site normally has a large influence on the success of change programmes. This reinforces training concepts, and helps individuals apply them in the real world. This can be supported by:

- management reinforcing the concept through behaviours and attitude;
- peer influence;
- building the concept into performance contracts;
- changing personal targets and objectives to reflect the need for the desired behaviours;
- maybe changing remuneration structures to encourage behaviours;
- providing short-term incentives;
- changing appraisals to look for the hard and softer aspects of the change required;
- online training reference courses;
- online coaching consulting.

We have already mentioned coaching. Coaching is an essential part of the change process. Here are some examples of its deployment:

- An organization that found out that a group of its call centre people had over 90% success rates in retention developed a programme to transfer this group's successes through call observation, using the key people in other teams and gaining customer feedback – this improved overall retention by 5% overall.
- An organization that had developed targeting models in one business unit transferred some of the team to a completely different business unit to coach the team in the second unit on how they had achieved success in targeting.
- Most successful organizations have a policy of coaching less experienced team members in direct customer contact methods.
- Some companies extend this coaching practice across company boundaries to partners.

THE ROLE OF STAFF AND CUSTOMER RESEARCH

It is very helpful to carry out research into employee attitudes and behaviour (just as with customers) during the implementation programme. This helps you:

- identify weak areas;

- determine training and support needs;
- improve results.

Research should also be carried out to understand change in customers' attitude and behaviour as a result of the programme, and the two sets of research should be compared. A similar approach can also be applied to other stakeholders – intermediaries, suppliers, sponsors and shareholders. This helps a company identify whether any problems are likely to emerge later.

THE CHANGE IMPLIED BY CUSTOMER MANAGEMENT

CRM means change. Management of change is a key capability. Here are some examples:

- Business units traditionally aligned to selling product now have to realign to focus on customers.
- Marketing focuses on retaining, developing and acquiring the right customers.
- Sales becomes relationship orientated.
- Service becomes multifunctional and more proactive.
- Products become solutions or propositions.
- Pricing policy is more focused on customers rather than one-off product sales.
- Information technology becomes embedded in change programmes rather than a separate, distant function.
- Information about the effect on customers of any of the company's activities becomes an important new ingredient in many decision-making processes.
- Measures – whether marketing, finance, operational, logistics – add a customer dimension.

All this, means a real need for strong and sustained management, and a lot of trust and support from the organization.

MEASUREMENT

'What you cannot measure you can't manage' applies very strongly to customer management. It is through new sets of measures that staff will understand whether they are making progress. However, most companies have large numbers of measures in place – many of them longstanding – which can stand in the way of CM progress. For example:

- For call centre staff, the total focus on time on call can distract from a broader relationship and development.
- For sales staff, the focus on acquisition can result in acquisition with little focus on what happens to those customers acquired.
- For marketing, the focus on acquisition cost can drive towards acquisition of the wrong customers.
- For service staff, the focus on service efficiency (speed or cost of processing) can drive towards the prioritization of the wrong things and customer dissatisfaction.

The lack of linkage between these measures and the overall goals of the company can lead to inconsistent treatment of customers – eg when costs need to be cut, they are cut across the whole of marketing activity rather than specific activity for certain customers. It is therefore important to undertake a separate measurement project, evaluating how existing measures work and how they need to change at different stages of the customer management cycle, from targeting to win-back, to allow the company to meet its overall customer management objectives.

PEOPLE ISSUES

One of the most difficult questions facing all companies interested in improving their customer management is: 'I've decided what customer management strategy to put in place. I've decided which model(s) of customer management to use. I've bought my systems. I've decided on my implementation programme. Now, where on earth do I get the people to manage it all?'

This is the wrong question. Leaving the people area until last is not a good idea. Indeed, companies that succeed in implementing new approaches to customer management tend to appoint much of the team first, and leave the team to develop plans. This follows the excellent principle of not expecting people to implement plans that they had no hand in shaping.

Of course, it is not possible to appoint a complete team before deciding what to do, as the decisions about what to do, and where and when to do it, affect decisions about the nature and size of the customer management team. Indeed, it is this 'chicken and egg' interdependence between appointing the team and developing and implementing a customer management plan that causes such stress in many companies trying to improve their customer management.

But if it's a people thing, what should companies to do to manage their people so that their CRM initiatives deliver better results?

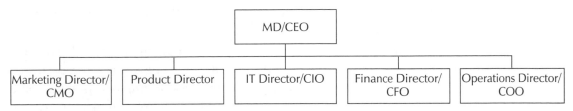

Figure 31.1 Typical organization structure (simplified)

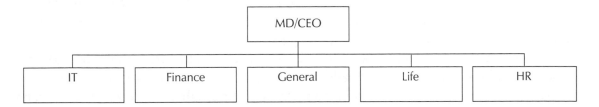

Figure 31.2 Typical insurance organization structure

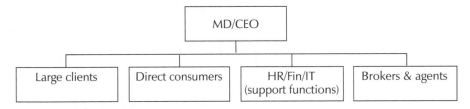

Figure 31.3 Customer-focused organization

STRUCTURING THE ORGANIZATION FOR CUSTOMER MANAGEMENT

Some of the problems of implementing CRM derive directly from the way financial services organizations are organized. Figure 31.1 gives a typical organizational structure. In insurance, a typical structure would be as in Figure 31.2. In either of these structures, the two main problems – from a CRM point of view – are as follows: 1) Results are provided at the business level – so that performance with customers is hidden. 2) Skills and competence areas are functionally defined – IT, finance, human resources, marketing, etc, and there is little cross-fertilization.

Very few would advocate changing the whole organization just for CRM, but it does seem clear that managing customers better is supported by board ownership of the issue, cross-functional working at different levels of the organization. However, some organizations have found that reorganizing helps CRM. In Figure 31.3, the focus is by customer groups. Here, the key is to ensure that the other dimensions of performance – particularly product propositions and profitability – are also measured differently to take into account the customer dimension.

While we have pretty solid models of how customer management should work in a direct-only environment (eg mail order), these models cannot be simply imposed on a company with a 'real' business. Because customer management cuts across many other dimensions of marketing (and indeed business) management, there will always be arguments about the status and accountability of customer management versus other lines of authority in a business. This is no different from the arguments that relate to the relative positions of product, channel or area. There is one simple rule – if a particular dimension (such as product or customer) is absolutely critical for competitive success, then this dimension must be relatively important in the organizational hierarchy. But where several dimensions are considered to be equally important, then it seems that the best approach is to have them equally important organizationally, reporting to the chief marketing officer or marketing director (provided that the latter is responsible for marketing, sales and service). Quite frankly, if a company is unable to determine the relative importance of these different dimensions, and leaves it to fighting between managers responsible for these dimensions, then structural decisions will not solve the problem. However, CRM is likely to thrive if clear criteria for success with products, areas, channels or customers are allocated to different managers, and a good conflict resolution process exists (based not just on estimated profit – often hard to determine – but also on the aim to achieve balance and compromise).

Organizational dotted lines thrive in the world of successful customer management! However, these need to be created if they do not exist already. Charts of influence need to be drawn up to see from the beginning where people are at and where they need to be. This helps to reduce the barriers between functions. The planning of hot-houses, workshops, pilots and projects, and programme management should take into account the need to create connections between different parts of the organization. Involvement and inclusion are key.

The most serious problems we have seen in CRM programmes are often political. Here are a few examples:

- Setting up a CRM department that can be considered to be in competition with other departments is not a good idea, though many companies have done this.
- CRM can threaten many existing functions, so if there is not a real intention to make it work from the top it will fail.
- Changing staff can also cause problems – newcomers arrive with different views and approaches, and new things to prove. This can alienate existing members of the team.
- Consultants – and a variety of other supplier organizations – can cloud the situation further, as they may have different views on how they would like the organization to be structured and to work.

- When the going gets tough – and it usually does, and the results are not yet visible, most senior managers will revert to areas of comfort (eg classic product-line reporting). It is difficult to make customer management an area of comfort in a short period of time.
- CRM can make traditionally 'junior' people become more powerful, ie those dealing with customers, database managers. Those whose relative authority declines obviously do not like it, while others are not sure how to cope with it.
- Given the possibly very broad nature of a CRM programme, it is easy to dilute responsibility, and this opens the door to blame cultures and activity.
- The skills mix is wrong, because people are allocated roles in CRM by power-sharing rules, not according to competence.
- Often there is no measurement at all, or if there is, there are tensions between contact, conversion and quality.
- Non-customer-facing roles get left out – database management should be measured on customer measures too!
- It is not understood how to motivate people/teams. Not all are the same, and not all are motivated by money alone. Recognition is important.
- Partners or suppliers are not trusted. CRM requires interaction and trust between partners, in particular if the partners are intermediated. In insurance, this means building relationships with brokers. Trust is very important for social well-being as well as for organizational culture. Trust is one of the fundamental principles outlined in many companies' cultural statements. In a knowledge-based society, trust is critical. If people believe knowledge is power and to share it is to lose power, particularly to those who will misuse it, then knowledge sharing and creation will be limited.

These problems can usually be moderated (if not solved) by:

- managing and influencing the unofficial organization as well as the official organization;
- establishing clear measures and responsibilities – for progress with the programme and for interim and final results, and of course for success with customers;
- communicating – clearly, often and relevantly;
- keeping the *customer* and *business* aim visible at all times;
- bringing in some new blood from other organizations/industries, but managing them into the culture carefully while allowing them to change it gently;
- setting up a series of battles that must be won and focusing on these rather than ones that can never be won;
- moving carefully towards measuring and rewarding staff primarily for their success with customers, supported by appropriate data, systems and processes. Culture can rarely be changed quickly. Many financial services companies have anything up to 300 years of tradition and practice – which cannot be broken. In a survey in one large

insurance company, of all those interviewed (100 interviews) 80% described themselves as belonging to an organization with strong underwriting values and more than 50% actually wanted to be underwriters! The organization had not described what CRM meant for underwriting, so there was no real route to begin to break into the product and pricing mentality which had been in place for many years.

Here are some more detailed examples of ways that companies are using to deal with and overcome structural problems:

- **Segment teams** – some organizations have set up customer segment teams containing all elements of the marketing sales and service competencies, eg the 'young family' team.
- **Time-boxed** – a few organizations are now setting up the concept of continual 'programme management' around customer management solutions launches. No element of the programme takes longer than three months or it's out! This forces more creative thinking across teams to shorten time-scales.
- **Cross-functional** – one organization sets up cross-functional mini-teams tackling specific issues, eg 'retention in first year', including 'unlikely suspects', eg delivery drivers.
- **Linked measures** – organizations that are successful manage to link measures across marketing, database, sales and service processes, and measure individuals accordingly.
- **Overview of the customer** – a single view of customer data established across the areas dealing with customers, including past and planned communications, tends to promote more proactive and cooperative behaviour around the customer.

An increasing number of senior managers now own one or more aspects of CRM. The role of the senior CRM 'champion' varies across organizations from IT director to customer services director or marketing director. This tends to indicate the focus of the programme within the organization. In the best examples, a company director or similar owns the customer experience, and develops and owns the business case for the implementation. This is then implemented through 'steering groups' or teams combining marketing, IT, service, sales and HR. This can mean taking every company decision on investment or cost cutting through the 'customer check' – eg how could it impact on the customer experience? However, few organizations have the strength to sustain this strategy and many breakages occur due to senior management changes.

PROGRAMME MANAGEMENT AND PEOPLE

Large organizations have to make some difficult changes to the traditional structures and ways of working in order to achieve what they want to in CRM. This is made difficult because the organization has often been sliced into departments or areas of competence that directly impede a positive experience for customers – this has to be changed. Core measures and reward systems tend to promote customer acquisition activity and distract from sustained relationship building with the customer base – these have to be changed. Senior leadership is critical to the drive and continuity of the strategy. All those involved have to see how they have an impact on successful delivery of customer management – and should be rewarded accordingly. Partners will necessarily play a key role; as such they need to be managed and measured in line with the strategy. How is all this to be achieved?

The critical people factors determining whether CRM programmes succeed or fail are these:

- Restructuring current teams to create the right environment can be extremely difficult – old frames of reference constantly creep in. For an established company, a team that understands the history of the company and the pockets of people that really make a difference to customers should drive the change.
- Strong programme management is absolutely critical. This requires senior business management responsibility, with a strong human resources component. If this fails, companies end up with great project plans and strong processes and systems, but the people leave or are disenfranchised.
- The management role needs to change too. New metrics and competencies are required. Many managers find it hard to adjust, and benefit from sharing their experiences with their peers in other parts of the company and in other companies.
- Using consultants too much can create dependency in critical areas or lack of buy-in from the troops. In some areas it is critical to gain expert input and an external view. These include strategy formulation, programme design, quality management, information technology architecture/design, analysis/profiling, system supplier/product selection, database construction. In some areas, external help is needed to plug resource gaps temporarily, particularly IT implementation, service/contact centre. However, it is always important to be clear why external suppliers are being asked to take over essentially internal roles, and to manage the input well.
- Keeping people is probably the most difficult thing once the organization has developed them. There seems to be a 70–80% loss rate of senior programme managers in this area after two years. There is enormous demand for them. The pay and other rewards they receive often fail to match the stress involved.
- Financial services companies have realized that customer management cannot be owned by the IT or marketing department alone. So good customer management programme managers are getting even harder to find as the competition for them is

becoming more international. However, the balance between creativity and structure in the change programme varies.

- There is a need for more focus on working with partners to provide sound customer management propositions and to implement customer management. This should take into account the culture of the organization and the fit of people working together. Exchanging staff with suppliers and other business partners can advance programmes greatly.

- Knowledge management is at the heart of customer management. People developing and sharing knowledge about customers, how they behave, how they react to the company's proposition, what works and what does not – these are all critical elements of a customer management programme, and require the appropriate infrastructure, measures and technology to support them.

- It is important to link pay and rewards to customer management where possible. For example, if a data model has been built to support retention activity and the retention activity based on the model works well, has the database team been rewarded for its success?

- Though it is hard at the beginning of a customer management programme to be clear about roles and accountabilities and how they need to change, it is important to define certain key roles and accountabilities and keep them under review. Key responsibilities that must be allocated include those for customer acquisition, retention, development and for the cost-effectiveness of customer management.

- Building teams around customer groups is a good way to motivate people. One company built a centre team around acquisition sales and service for regions of the customer base and watched the conversion rates soar by 12%.

- Achievement/recognition is often the area that has the greatest impact. It is not all about money. The best example of this is an organization that gains key customer input on individuals' performance and creates monthly, quarterly and annual communications around these. Based upon this feedback, individuals and teams are provided with additional development roles.

- Don't forget the emotional aspect. The ideal (though difficult) objective is to change feelings in the hearts of customers and staff. There is a fine line between motivation and emotion. If you can create more positive customer emotions, and the impact of this emotional change is demonstrated to staff, this can have a really positive effect on how staff think and work. It can also reduce some of the stress and conflict that customer management programmes can lead to if conflict with other policy areas is not resolved. Being part of something that is different in the marketplace and is recognized as being successful also promotes a buzz. When a company succeeds in creating this kind of emotion, it is immediately obvious in the tone and content of e-mails from customers, for example. It is just as important to recognize that negative customer emotions can have a serious effect on customer-facing staff. For this reason some companies create 'mentoring' networks for those dealing with very difficult complaints or claims processes.

THE CRM TEAM AND ITS MANAGEMENT

CRM missionaries make poor programme managers. They are usually so committed to CRM and its core ideas of customer focus that they do not pursue a balanced approach to developing a company's CRM capability. They may be impatient – not recognizing that it is hard to simultaneously develop a new customer management capability and start to use it. Missionaries tend to alienate senior managers in charge of areas such as products, marketing communications, operations, channels of distribution and information technology. A good programme manager builds a team including managers from these other centres of power, and insists on a steering group of senior management from the same centres. Good programme managers always involve at the earliest possible stage managers and staff from the customer service function, who usually have to cope with the increased frequency and complexity of customer contact that normally results from CRM programmes. Finally, attention should be paid to the balance between individuals in the team – a good mix of line managers (who know how to manage achievement), technical experts (eg data quality, analysis), classic marketing management, and project management skills is required.

Senior managers often give lip-service to ideas of CRM, but the way they are managed forces them to compromise customer management objectives when faced with pressure in other performance areas, rather than allowing a degree of balance. Commitment that is both genuine and long term is critical. If it is absent, the jackals will pounce, and the CRM programme will fail.

Often, an unrealistic (in terms of timing and/or results) business case for CRM investment is agreed by the board, and then the task is 'thrown over the wall' to a manager appointed to head the CRM effort. A team is quickly appointed and money is spent like water in building a CRM infrastructure, with no clear basis for deploying it. This is the wrong way round. A general case can be made for improving customer management, and the team should then determine which aspects need improving, how and how fast, and what objectives and strategy would be appropriate. A global company that did it the wrong way round found that the whole initiative produced no results except expenditure, because a centralized view of objectives, strategies and timing did not match what could be achieved in most business units.

CRM programmes – if and when they work – require many people to behave differently, and work with different colleagues. They need to understand the world they are moving towards and then to function within it. So a structured programme is required – including work on job definition, assessment of competence, appraisal, coaching and mentoring and culture change. Organizational design is key. The organization required to run CRM is not the same as the organization to set it up. Performance criteria need to be changed. New kinds of measurement are needed, eg retention, customer value. Getting staff to experience the company as a customer is a helpful way of creating a customer-focused culture.

Often, suppliers are viewed just as providers of specific services. But suppliers can be an integral part of the team, working on customer management in areas such as analysis and planning, actually managing customers, supplying supporting data and systems, and of course measuring the results. The highest scoring company in our CMAT work so far fired its advertising agency because the agency found it difficult to work within the company customer management strategy. CMAT has a section on supplier management, and interestingly it is part of the people management section, because the two are so closely related.

A company's customer management history will partly determine the attitudes of staff and the skills they have. If a company has only just started using customer management, or if it is slowly increasing its use of customer management techniques, there will be a variety of attitudes towards customer management. Attitudes will also differ if customer management is seen as having a basically tactical role to play, as opposed to being the fundamental basis for a company's competitive strategies.

People's attitudes are also be affected by the state of development of customer management processes. These may be quite rudimentary monitoring and control procedures, perhaps aimed at ensuring that campaigns yield some profit, sales or information. As a company gets more sophisticated in its use of customer management, it may develop sophisticated management systems for ensuring that objectives are achieved. They may use scheduling processes and systems, for example, to ensure that campaigns do not overlap, and to ensure that markets are covered by the right campaigns.

KNOWLEDGE MANAGEMENT

Some organizations attach great value to customer knowledge, and to the people (human capital) who have this knowledge and the expertise to use it. Knowledge management can fall to the bottom of the list as a 'nice to have', but leading insurers such as Skandia base their strategies on knowledge creation and management, while Royal & Sun Alliance has made knowledge management one of the main foci of its CRM programme. Understanding the knowledge base of the organization and the motivations of people who use it is a key to implementing CRM programmes. How this works in practice is strongly linked to the background of the organization and of the individuals involved.

In many property and casualty insurance companies, much of the knowledge base relates to underwriting. This knowledge base is organized mainly by product, not customers. Knowledge of, for example, how customers behave or benefit from their relationship with the organization is often weak. The result – customers are unhappy because they do not see any benefit in joining or staying with the company, while underwriters ignore any CRM programme because their knowledge has not been included in the process. Those that are having success in CRM are introducing customer underwriting alongside product underwriting, challenging the current knowledge base and creating new knowledge. Some companies are actively building networks of practice, but, in some cases, this only amounts to a series of 'show and tell' meetings, often only within a country.

Here is a checklist of questions concerning use of knowledge management techniques in CRM:

- Have you outlined the areas of expertise around the customer (competence)?
- Do you know who the experts are?
- Do you create forums for people to bring these areas of expertise together?
- Do you make the most of intranets/extranets to transfer/exchange and apply knowledge?
- Do you create forums to develop knowledge of the changing circumstances of your customer base/technologies/environment etc?
- Is there strong input into knowledge development from partners, intermediaries and customers?
- Do you promote and reward good ideas?
- Do you transfer your ideas and expertise to customer propositions (eg content on the Internet)?
- Are you forced to relearn through loss of CM knowledge and prior experience?

THE FIVE KEY ELEMENTS OF SUCCESS REVISITED

We have identified five key elements required for success in CRM, as follows:

1. customer management strategy – which customers are to be managed, for what products or services, through which channels;
2. customer management models – how these customers are to be managed, eg through classic segmented CRM or through a top 'vanilla best service for all' approach;
3. infrastructure – systems, data, operational customer management capabilities (eg call centres);
4. people – who is to develop the new capability, who is to manage it, and how;
5. programmes – how new customer management capabilities are to be installed.

One of the most common errors general managers make in this area is to confuse these elements.

The worst error is to confuse the organization required to *implement* CRM with the organization required to *manage* CRM – although continuous change tends to blur any boundaries here. We describe this as confusing 'getting there' with 'being there'. The former is a combination of strategic and programme management. It involves determining what kind of capability is required to manage customers and changing the organization's capability in the area of CRM. The latter is best described as a functional task, one of using a newly developed or modified capability to manage customers differently. However, both tasks involve managing teams of people to do things, so neither should be given to managers who are poor people managers. A common mistake is to give one or other (or worst of all both) tasks to a 'CRM advocate', someone who is a 'true believer in CRM'. Because the

Table 31.1 CRM programme approach

Overall task	Detailed task	People requirement
1. Strategy and planning	• Review approach to customer management, including current strategies and models • Determine requirement for any change, and urgency, size and general scope of change • Develop business case and obtain approval	• Generally best done through combination of routine corporate strategy process, perhaps combined with special task force consisting of cross-section of involved functions/departments, marketing/customer service suppliers, and possibly consultants • May require in-depth assessment of current approach – what the company does, what the results have been (eg net value and persistence of customer base – perhaps using data warehousing and data mining techniques), and what customers feel about it (using market research techniques) • Probably best to have board-level sponsor(s) and steering group
2. Detailed programme planning and implementation	• Plan and implement programme details	• Programme manager appointed. This person then works with senior sponsors to appoint team, allocate tasks, recruit suppliers, etc. Included in this list of appointments is customer management leader • Organizational sub-project determines structure, size, accountability and outline budgets of customer management department • Steering group composition may change to reflect functions most affected by change
3. Capability in use	• Programme manager hands over capability to be used by customer management leader	• Customer management leader implements new approach to customer management • Starts by appointing team and suppliers • May be relatively high level of outsourcing of some operational tasks until full capability developed, as company may require that capability comes into use before complete (indeed programme management approach would suggest this)

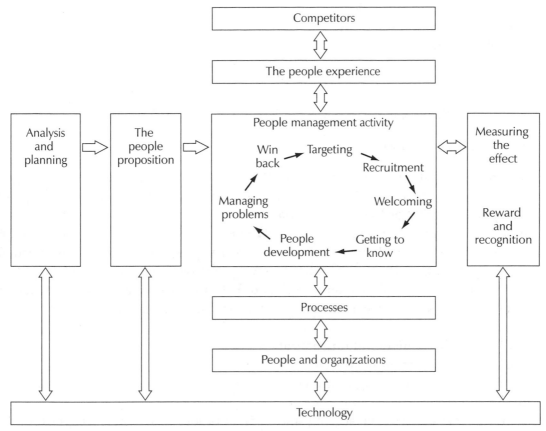

Figure 31.4 People relationship model – based on CMAT model terminology

customer management dimension usually cuts across other dimensions of the customer-serving organization (eg products, channels), such a person usually alienates senior managers responsible for these other dimensions. The net result is usually either a failed CRM programme or a customer management capability that can never be properly used because it has lost a battle for authority that should never have been started.

Companies are more likely to succeed in improving their customer management if they adopt an approach similar to that described in Table 31.1. It is obviously highly simplified, but makes the distinction between programme management and using the new capability very clear. Obviously, if a company wishes to deploy its capability before it is completely ready, then tasks 2 and 3 will overlap.

ADAPTING THE CMAT MODEL FOR PEOPLE MANAGEMENT

It is possible to adapt the CMAT model (see Chapter 3) for managing people for CRM purposes (see Figure 31.4). It shows the importance of 1) developing a strategy for acquiring, retaining and developing different groups of people required for CRM and 2) setting up a proposition/process and infrastructure to deliver it to them.

This helps to link the language and approach of the human resources area firmly with the business strategy.

CASE STUDY: GLOBAL CRM PROGRAMMES IN INSURANCE

The merger and takeover frenzy

The insurance industry has been characterized by a frenzy of global takeovers and mergers. As we move into the new millennium, we see an industry dominated by a few global players, plus a number of regional participants.

The first steps after a merger usually involve the creation of a common infrastructure, covering all the 'overhead' functions such as treasury, personnel, and IT. This is usually accompanied by rationalization of brands (AXA is perhaps the most aggressive example of this). In the most successful companies, this tends to be followed by a series of well-defined global programmes, along the lines described later in this briefing, such as the following:

- call centre enhancement and rationalization;
- e-business introduction and development;
- standardization of campaign management processes and systems, for both direct and intermediary customers;
- data analysis – customer scoring and segmentation, sales analysis, product and customer profitability analysis;
- product improvement, risk pricing and rating;
- claims and fraud analysis and improvement – smarter determination of current and future good and bad customers.

Not all these initiatives are successful, and only in the best companies can these be described as truly global programmes, with sharing of information, common development of knowledge, and rapid transfer of good practice. However, given the proven gains that can be achieved by such programmes within countries, we expect that the companies that take the strongest line on globalization of these initiatives will in the end emerge as the most profitable.

One area of strong focus after many mergers or acquisitions is identification of common business processes and infrastructures that can be merged or at least shared (eg in information technology and communications, common hardware, reuse of tools, sharing call centres), to reduce costs and complexity. This is usually done without changing the different business models that operated independently prior to the merger. It may be that the initial focus apparent in some companies on securing a common customer is not appropriate, given the demonstrated gains that can be made from infrastructure and process commonality.

Perhaps the most widely referenced example of mergers undertaken mainly for a customer-centric purpose is CitiGroup's bringing together of Citibank and Travelers. Conseco is another US financial services conglomerate that has grown quite rapidly through acquisition. It faces issues of business organization, process and data integration each time it absorbs a new acquisition. These companies and others are discovering that achieving one 'operational' view of the customer is much more difficult than was first thought. Other companies following the same direction are the major European companies Zurich, Allianz, AIG and ING. The race is on to achieve a holistic view of the customer in an industry fraught with 'silos' – business units operating with different data sets, processes, systems and customer management models, all focused on the same or overlapping sets of customers. However, some of these companies have decided that integrating without prioritizing is dangerous, and are now prioritizing their integration efforts.

Another issue that companies are facing after merger/acquisition is the branding issue. This is very important to multinationals because while there are significant economies of scale in global branding, there is also a risk that customers will see reduced rather than increased value. AXA, Zurich and Allianz specifically have faced this as they have merged their Equitable, Farmers and Fireman's Fund brands into their more worldwide-known parent companies. Each of these companies is in a different stage of branding and brand acceptance.

One consequence of mergers is that putting together diverse brands also means putting together a diverse customer base, which is more difficult to understand and manage as a whole than they were when managed by separate companies. Because of the size and number of many of the resulting databases the customer management implementation focus has often become blurred and energies diverted to technical (eg database and data) rather than customer issues. There is still a divide between the life and general divisions of most insurance companies. Not surprisingly, most customers fail to see the benefit of being served by one company in these two areas, because there is no clear joint proposition or benefit. The differing cultures of merging organizations have caused great difficulties for global programmes. In some cases, there has been a clash between short-term results and programme orientation and longer-term relationship orientation, and the merger has created setbacks for the customer management implementation process. In the worst case, the customer management programme has been destroyed, sometimes because it was at too early a stage to have identified the business benefits clearly.

When a merger or acquisition is announced it normally gives rise to cost-reduction commitments to the stock market. The race is then on to achieve these by the next results announcement. There is a tendency to slash costs through layoffs, channel reduction (fewer agents, consolidation of call centres), product reduction (allowing usage of fewer admin systems, therefore fewer operating costs, etc). However, the impact of these changes is often to drive customers away – especially those customers who bought from and stayed with the company due to the products and/or channels that are now being slashed. In very few cases do companies devote the time and resource first to merge their customer data to understand common customers, cross-product holdings and even estimate customer value *before* taking action to reduce products and channels. Having shown cost reductions, a company then needs to demonstrate to shareholders that it is more valuable as a single company than as two. This is the 'value add' phase that some major European insurers are now in, but some others are struggling with it. At this stage the focus is on common standards, shared value through reuse of data, infrastructure, processes, etc, even though the customers of each company/country may be entirely separate (so there is little direct value in sharing customer data, only the indirect value of learning and shared development cost).

Meanwhile, new entrants using the best of new technology have challenged the merging companies. New entrants are finding the insurance model a particularly easy one to approach via the Internet, eg Quotesmith.com in the USA, Mysis in Europe. The visibility of price and the simplification of questions are making the shift to commodity purchase inevitable, with the absence of any real value being offered to customers who stay with or buy more from traditional insurers.

To meet this challenge and improve profits, a number of companies are now embarking on global initiatives to create and implement a model of customer management, which helps them increase market share while reducing costs. Some global players have global/international customers, but others have different customers in each market/country. Where this happens the local market companies usually own the budgets for customer management projects (and other major marketing initiatives) and need to form a corporate board to agree on standards for prioritization and reuse, as central management power and the global use common systems are usually diminished.

This corporate board (or similar group) can assist programme design and execution by developing and promoting standards and/or processes that relate to areas such as: 1) a common programme management capability and project method; 2) understanding of the interdependencies of projects carried out in different areas, eg call centre development, warehousing, skills development, customer research. This avoids the projects simply being 'handed out'

The central group can also help by:

- assessing (or helping different country operations assess) the CRM 'maturity' in each country, and the improvements in maturity and ROI resulting from each prioritized local programme, or reuse of developments from other programmes;
- setting common systems standards where appropriate (for example, a common data model on which applications are developed or integrated);
- conducting global negotiations with suppliers, as a global licensing arrangement can often be achieved for the equivalent price of a small number of major country implementations.

Where these issues are not tackled, the company is likely to have a lower ability to execute its CRM programmes on an international basis. Programmes are likely to result in smaller benefits through lack of scalability or integration with programmes that are interdependent.

In the insurance industry, following the wave of mergers and takeovers, several companies are developing and deploying these capabilities right now, usually in close cooperation with one or more international suppliers (to ensure consistent availability of services and support). Our research indicates that those companies that do not see the importance of or cannot develop these capabilities will be operating sub-optimally.

The global insurance players seem to have strategies that are too similar, and which do not take into account their differing abilities to execute those strategies. Some of our clients have expressed the view that consultants appear to reuse 'standard CRM visions', without an understanding of the customer base of the company, or of the company's ability to develop new capabilities.

SUMMARY OF IMPLEMENTATION ESSENTIALS

If this chapter is to leave you with just a few points, they should be these:

- Ensure senior management ownership and active leadership of people management in CRM.
- Create cross-functional working around customers/groups where possible and focus on smooth customer experience across functions.
- Ensure that a people motivation and development programme is in place – based around measurement and reward, team-based approach, recognition programmes including the customer.
- Focus on promoting trust and sharing in the organization.
- Recognize the importance of coaching – using those who are good at CRM activity.
- Link individuals' measures to CRM performance (retention, development and acquisition of customers) and to the ROI measure.
- Promote knowledge sharing and creation programmes.
- Understand the core areas of competence and develop and recruit around these.
- Set up service level agreements/game plans for partners/suppliers relating to customer performance, and monitor closely.

32

Motivating people to manage customers – through their pay

David Port

INTRODUCTION

Financial institutions around the globe are working hard to improve the effectiveness of their distribution. As more products are distributed through more channels, the need for cooperation across the channels, product groups and business units has become a critical success factor. Companies are looking for a consistent management device that can work across organizational boundaries and broadly align the organization towards executing its strategic objectives. Incentive compensation is a powerful means of corporate alignment because it reaches down to all levels and across all groups in the organization. Incentive compensation represents the ligaments and tendons of the organization. The effective use of incentive compensation allows the organization to perform in a unified and consistent fashion, ultimately offering the customer a coordinated, common experience. Of course, incentive structures must be well conceived and they must reside in a flexible system backbone that can ride on top of the organization's data-streams. The result should be a uniform tracking mechanism that can monitor referral programmes, cross-sell behaviour, strategic sales programmes, transaction profitability, etc and provide management with a new set of tools for directing and managing the business.

Fortunately, a new category of enterprise application software, referred to as enterprise incentive management (EIM), is helping financial institutions around the world to overcome the challenges associated with efficiently distributing financial products to consumers. EIM software enables the large enterprise to optimize the use of its incentive resources towards distributing the organization's products. One of the key drivers for this class of software is the need to coordinate and motivate staff involved in the distribution of products and services across multiple channels to market. Most enterprises today attempt to manage incentive compensation, in all its forms, via error-prone tools such as spreadsheets or via inflexible and outdated in-house systems. Neither of these approaches meets the demands being placed on enterprises today to deploy more products, more efficiently, through more channels. EIM also acts as a link to close the loop between the selling activities tracked in CRM systems and the actual products sold and tracked in the traditional financial systems. EIM provides the feedback to management as to sales effectiveness, product profitability, channel activity and product mix. EIM applications represent a powerful new capability to enhance both top-line revenue and bottom-line profitability.

In this chapter, we describe some of the business drivers behind the broad movement towards a new generation of incentive compensation solution in financial services. Whenever appropriate we augment our findings with short case studies of actual financial institutions that have elected to implement packaged solutions to automate their incentive processes. It is now well within the ability of any financial institution to use incentive compensation not only to ensure the success of their CRM applications, but also to significantly enhance competitive position and profitability.

INCREASED COMPETITION AND MARKET SEGMENTATION

The financial services industry is undergoing significant structural change (see Figure 32.1). Regulatory barriers between different segments of the industry (insurance, banking, investment management, capital markets) continue to come down in most major markets. Consolidation through mergers and acquisitions is accelerating as companies seek economies of scale and more efficient distribution models. New types of intermediaries and new business models arrive almost daily. Examples of this are discount securities brokers, the direct sale of personal lines of insurance to consumers via the Web, or the distribution of investment products through unconventional retail chains such as grocery stores. One result of this innovation and market segmentation is an increase in the number of new products being created and a reduction in margins received. As margins come down, financial institutions look to optimize their investments in branch networks, call centres, the Web, and direct and indirect sales organizations by motivating these organizations to work cooperatively in distributing the firms' products. Creating compensation structures that foster and reward cooperation and joint selling can be a significant challenge as well.

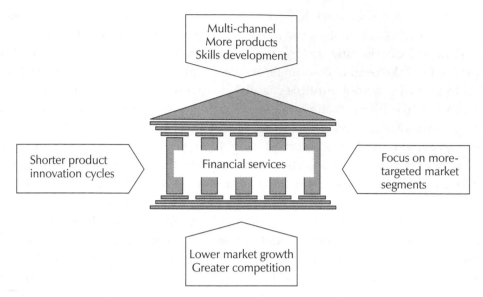

Figure 32.1 Structural change

CASE STUDY 1: GLOBAL INVESTMENT BANK DRIVES MORE BUSINESS, MORE PROFITABLY

This top investment bank offers a variety of financial services to most classes of investors. Its securities unit offers securities underwriting, merger and acquisition services, and other corporate finance services, as well as a full-service retail brokerage with premium services for wealthy individual clients. Its asset management unit provides both individual and institutional investors with investment products and services, while its credit services unit oversees its card operations. The firm has some 600 branches in more than 25 countries. The bank's credit card division has automated its incentive compensation process, initially for its 500-person field sales organization. In subsequent phases, the bank plans to extend this pay-for-performance system to both its outbound and inbound call centres – representing an additional 5,000 personnel. These are the reasons why the bank automated in this area:

● **More sophisticated compensation schemes** – the bank needed to be able to deploy more sophisticated compensation schemes that could help motivate the greatest value for the bank. For example, the bank currently offers bonuses to the reps if they can retain a customer that has called in to cancel his/her credit card. However, the reps had no disincentive to offering other services for free in order to save that customer. Being able to compensate reps according to the overall profitability of a transaction provides a strategic value to the business.

- **More motivation** – tying rewards more closely to behaviour is motivational. This solution allows the bank to reduce the payment period from semi-annual to monthly. This is more competitive and coincides with the industry norm. It also helps the bank to attract the best talent available.
- **Management and sales performance information** – improving the type and style of reports used by employees throughout the company to view sales and compensation information was a key objective of the bank. Providing the sales organization with visibility into its performance allows for valuable course correction.
- **Administrative efficiency/reduced error** – a key goal of the project was to reduce the time spent by account managers, team leaders, product sales teams, department managers, and regional operations directors on tracking, auditing, reporting and correcting transactions within the incentive compensation process. Automation has allowed the bank to reduce the errors caused by having to track and accumulate sales results manually.
- **Rapid new product deployment** – to remain competitive, the bank wants to be able to create and deploy new credit card products without having to rewrite or modify support systems.

THE NEED FOR EFFICIENT MULTI-CHANNEL DISTRIBUTION

As an increasing number of products are being distributed through a growing number of channels, new pressures are being placed on the incentive and commission systems that support the variable compensation process. These systems are typically inflexible, error prone, administratively expensive, and often based on difficult to maintain technology and platforms. They usually provide insufficient audit trails and rarely provide quality management information to the organization. As new products or channels are developed, there is a tendency to build one-off piecemeal or poorly integrated solutions that eventually become unwieldy and difficult to scale. These inefficiencies and exposures are particularly acute in institutions that have grown through acquisitions and mergers and that suffer from a plethora of non-integrated systems. A common example would be the result of a merger between an insurance company and an investment management firm. Clearly it would be desirable to offer the full range of products through one set of channels. Often the application and technology barriers to accomplishing this goal are substantial.

The greatest pressure on existing commission systems is found where collaborative or consultative selling is required, where different channels are used, or where several divisions are involved in the sale. In these circumstances, a company may require either significant revamping of the system itself or in some instances an entirely new system. This is because many commission systems are designed for simple sales process, operating through single channels, for the benefit of one part of the company.

CASE STUDY 2: DELIVERING INTEGRATED MULTI-CHANNEL DISTRIBUTION

As one of the global leaders in financial services worldwide, this European-based bank's activities include investment banking and asset management – savings, life insurance, pension and investment products, as well as other banking and insurance services. The channels to market include a network of tied financial advisers, a call centre to support the less complex products, an Internet-based application (ePortal) for pension funds management and whole life insurance, and geographically distributed investment centres.

The European investment and insurance market is undergoing a period of structural change. Governments are removing regulatory barriers and opening the market up to increased global competition. In many countries consumers are being incentivized to invest directly into the market for their personal pension requirements. This bank has created a new organization focused on delivering a full range of investment and insurance products to an affluent segment of the consumer market.

The following are the reasons why the bank decided to select a new generation packaged solution:

- **Integrated multi-channel strategy** – the central strategy for this new business is to provide an integrated multi-channel solution to clients. This includes the financial advisers, the call centre, the ePortal, and the investment centres. Each of these channels needed to work closely with the others. A single incentive compensation system with corresponding incentive structures was the key to achieving this.
- **Cross-divisional cooperation** – from the outset, this bank had intended to leverage the distribution arm of its sister insurance company. Likewise, it intends to distribute that company's insurance products through its field advisers. This requires that both organizations share a common compensation system with sufficient power and flexibility to meet both sets of requirements.
- **Attracting the best talent** – in order to attract, motivate and retain the highest calibre of banking, insurance and asset consulting experts, the bank has developed a very competitive compensation package with a strong pay-for-performance element. The compensation scheme is quite complex and takes into consideration all of the parties that cooperate to sell a particular piece of business. It also anticipates the rapid growth in the size of the sales organization, making sure that all parties are fairly treated as clients and are passed between advisers. This sort of incentive complexity is a key ingredient to achieving the bank's strategic objectives.

CURRENT COMPENSATION SCHEMES ARE INADEQUATE

Acquiring new customers is more expensive than selling more products to existing customers, especially where the company is distributing a diversified set of financial products. Once a relationship of trust is established, the opportunities to cross-sell and up-sell financial products are significant and this can have a very positive impact on the margins yielded from the relationship over time (see Figure 32.2). The ideal situation is for advisers to be in a position to make recommendations and thereby actually direct the sale. The primary issue here is the compensation scheme. Most financial institutions incentivize new business sales heavily and often ignore the value to the firm of penetrating the client further over time. The reasons for this are historical and often based on the limitations of inflexible commission systems.

Many financial institutions are looking to move to a more value-based model of compensation – no longer treating every dollar the same as every other dollar. They look to create more sophisticated incentive structures around such measures as:

- net increase of total assets under management;
- achievement of cross-selling ratio targets;
- loss ratios and margin contribution, for insurance products;
- reward cooperative selling and lead passing;
- charging for and paying commission on the generation of a financial plan;
- reward success in targeted high-value market segments.

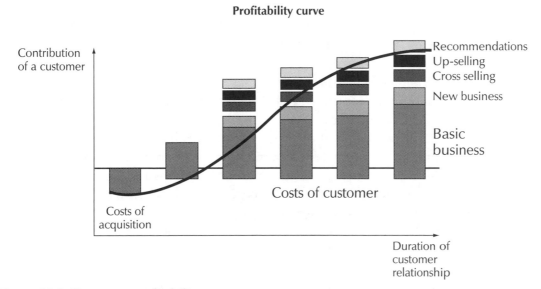

Figure 32.2 Customer profitability curve

It may be necessary to compensate a broader group within the company for the booking of business – including marketing, product specialists, call centre staff, business development, etc. Regardless of whether a financial institution is focused on penetration selling or relationship selling, at a particular point in time, incentive structures need to become more comprehensive and complex in order to motivate the optimum organizational behaviour. An important by-product of a comprehensive compensation scheme that considers territory changes, team selling and margin contribution is its ability to help attract and retain the best talent in the marketplace. Paying people correctly, on time, and in more frequent pay periods, builds trust, confidence, and productivity.

CASE STUDY 3: DRIVING PERFORMANCE THROUGH THE BRANCH NETWORK

This Asian-based banking group is one of the world's largest banking and financial services organizations, with major personal, commercial, corporate, investment banking, and insurance businesses operating in Europe, the Asia-Pacific region, the Americas, the Middle East and Africa. It employs over 170,000 employees in 78 countries and territories. In Asia, the bank provides a full range of personal banking and wealth management services, including current and multi-currency savings accounts, home finance and personal loans, term deposits and credit/debit cards, financial planning, investment services such as unit trusts and securities, mandatory provident fund investment options and insurance products. These are distributed through various electronic channels and branch networks. The personal financial services division employs around 2,000 sales staff in the branches to support its customers. Of these, about 450 are financial service executives. These represent full-time sales staff that receive basic salary, commissions and bonuses for selling individual life insurance, group insurance, retirement scheme, non-life insurance, unit trust, and mortgage products.

In the past, four full-time staff members administered sales compensation. This administration team collected Excel spreadsheets and reports from other systems, consolidated them to validate that individual and departmental targets had been met, calculated the incentives to be paid, and compiled these numbers into various Excel spreadsheets for reporting. They also manually prepared payment instructions for the in-house payroll system to administer the payments. The bank has plans to extend the pay-for-performance principle to more branch-based job classes in the future.

The following are the key business drivers that moved the bank to install a variable compensation package to automate the process:

● **Deploy new, more complex plans** – the bank wanted to deploy more sophisticated compensation schemes based on such new factors as:

- three-month moving average approach to performance measurement;
- paying on qualitative measures such as campaigns and customer satisfaction;
- considerations of customer churn factors;
- rewarding performance consistency over time.

● **Add more job classes to incentive compensation** – as mentioned above, the bank wanted to compensate more job titles within the branches in an incentive manner. The current Excel-based system simply will not scale to that degree.

● **Administrative inefficiencies** – the bank had a mostly manual process with very limited audit-ability or trace-ability. The bank wanted to centralize all transaction and compensation information through automation.

● **Quantitative analysis of compensation decisions** – the bank wanted the ability to make informed analytical decisions about compensation plan changes using real historical data.

THE ENTERPRISE INCENTIVE MANAGEMENT APPROACH

Given the heavy reliance today on legacy and CRM systems to manage the compensation process in financial services companies, any packaged solution must provide very strong data integration capability. Advanced data profiling, extract, transform and load/update tools are provided with most systems to provide batch integration with the many legacy systems. More recently, near-real-time and trickle feed updates are provided to ensure that employees can be motivated through continually tracking their compensation against achievement of personal targets. Clearly, data integration is always a significant task and one that should not be underestimated in the achievement of a successful project and early ROI.

All logic associated with credit allocation, performance measurement, incentive calculation, and payments should be maintainable by the business users. The EIM system becomes a single overlay system that often spans multiple instances of commissions-related systems – thereby consolidating the compensation process across multiple product lines or groups. All information about product families, channels and field hierarchies are maintained within the packaged EIM system. In many cases, the implementation of an EIM solution enables the retirement of entire legacy systems. This approach effectively delivers a console through which business managers can control all aspects of the compensation process. Through role-based security, a complete audit trail is maintained of all changes, adjustments and modifications made in the system. This class of automation can reduce administrative overhead to a small fractions of its current level.

An important by-product of the consolidated view is a repository of some of the most valuable information in the company – sales and commission data broken down by product, geography, channel, etc. This management information can be easily distributed to executives across the organization. All personnel in the field or in management are provided Web-based access to that portion of the information that they are authorized to see.

CASE STUDY 4: INFLUENCING PRODUCT MIX WITHIN TARGETED MARKET SEGMENTS DELIVERS VALUE

This US bank has more than 2,200 locations in 24 mid-western and western states along with nearly 5,200 branded ATMs. The bank offers consumer and business banking services, as well as brokerage and investment management services; private, corporate, and institutional trust services; mortgage banking; consumer finance; lease financing; and insurance sales. It also provides venture capital and merger and acquisition advisory services. The bank recently acquired a packaged incentive compensation solution to pay its 1,400 loan officers, loan processors, branch managers and regional managers more efficiently and effectively.

The following are the key business drivers that moved the bank to automate:

- **Influence product mix** – some loans are more strategic and more valuable to the bank than others. Product mix is important to this company. The bank has segmented its market and is targeting specific types of loans to those segments. For example, the bank is willing to pay more commission on home loans to first-time homebuyers because those customers are more strategic and valuable to the bank in the long run.
- **Compensation plan flexibility** – the mortgage lending service is interested in having more flexibility in its compensation plans as well. For instance, they need to be able to offer different compensation plans or plan components for loan officers in different regions in the country. The previous system did not offer that level of flexibility.
- **Sales productivity and effectiveness** – the bank is looking to Web-based reporting to increase the productivity of its loan officers. Internally developed return-on-investment studies quantified more than $500,000 of improved sales productivity resulting from the loan officers' ability to see their compensation data in a timely and accurate manner.
- **Administrative inefficiencies and exposures** – today, branch managers keep track of the sales achievements of their loan officers and submit this information manually to corporate head office. This process is error prone and expensive to administer. The bank estimates that it overpays commissions by at least 2 per cent due to errors – this equates to the loss of millions of dollars to the bank. Further, the process offers only very limited audit-ability, which represents an exposure to the bank as well. The bank expects that automating this process will result in greater employee retention within the groups affected.

CONCLUSION

Financial services companies are being challenged by increased competition from more players selling a changing set of products into smaller and smaller market segments and through more channels. The incentive management process is a critical success factor for these businesses and is one that is under increasing pressure to adapt to the new distribution models. Companies that understand how to deploy new products more quickly, attract and motivate better talent, and distribute products efficiently through multiple channels will experience higher margins and greater market share. Upgrading the incentive compensation system is key to achieving these goals. Deploying the newest class of enterprise incentive management software solutions has become a strategic imperative for customer relationship marketing in the financial services industry. Successful and rapid deployment is reliant on excellence in business change and rapid but reliable data integration.

Part 9

Making the most of your
(most valuable?) customers

33

Managing wealth? Are you? Really?

Kevin La Croix, Merlin Stone and Rohitha Perera

'Wealth management' has become the new mantra of much of the financial services industry. Banks and insurers are investing millions of pounds into the establishment and marketing of a variety of wealth management propositions. Just as with many other 'fashions' in financial services and in marketing, senior managers are beginning to wonder whether, and if so when, these investments are going to pay off. In particular, they are starting to wonder whether the wealth management propositions their staff are developing really do help their customers manage their wealth, or whether they are just another way of selling the same old products and extracting commissions from customers. They understand that this might lead to a severe mismatch between what customers and suppliers understand by the term. If either or both of these is true, these new propositions run the risk of developing a poor market reputation as well as government disapproval, with the possibility of the same damage done in the areas of pensions and endowments in the past 10 years. Also, they are wondering what, if either is true, can be done to ensure that their companies obtain a good share of the emerging market, and how to protect their existing investment businesses.

This chapter focuses on the definition of wealth management, and some of the major strategic issues companies should address when getting involved in wealth management. Specifically, this chapter considers questions such as the following:

- Whose wealth is at issue?

- What is 'wealth' anyway?
- Can it be managed?

A new class of 'mass affluent' customers is emerging. They are a potential source of revenue and sustainable profit for the financial services industry, which has therefore adopted wealth management strategies with a vengeance. Clearly, banks, insurers, brokers and fund managers see this as a way of managing their own wealth.

Much of the discussion in the financial services industry is of the usual 'prescriptive' kind, ie what companies want to do to customers. However, as we are marketers at heart, we thought it would be sensible to try to define the concept of wealth from the perspective of customers. They are likely to understand many different things by the term. What they understand may change as they grow older and richer (or poorer). Once we have probed this, we shall be more able to understand why a person would want his or her wealth to be managed – or not. In this chapter, we cannot probe all possibilities, so we try to demonstrate these points by example.

To a young person, wealth may be seen as the amassing of 'money'. Whether the money is in the form of equities, cash, precious metals and gems or the latest luxury goods, wealth is often defined as having and having more; it is a 'numbers game' in which the biggest numbers win. An ancient role model for this attitude toward wealth is King Midas. Poor Midas asked the gods to give him the gift of turning anything into gold simply by touching it. His request was granted and he went off, merrily touching everything in sight in order to be the biggest winner of the numbers game in the world. Of course, the king found that his miraculous touch also turned everything he ate and drank into gold and rapidly realized that in winning the game he might die of thirst or starvation. He quickly begged the gods to remove the curse that he first saw as a blessing.

Standing out from the 'young crowd' are three groups of young people. One group – let's call them the young entrepreneurs – see wealth as the potential value (if sold) of the business assets they are creating or about to create. Their wealth lies in a combination of their ideas, their energy, their contacts (sponsors, financiers, current and potential customers), and hopefully in their sense of self-preservation (a determination not to destroy their assets by spending on cars or other less tangible ways of rapidly depreciating their assets).

Another group, perhaps closely related to the above, see wealth as their lifetime stream of earnings and associated savings. Those amongst this group, interested in maximizing their wealth, are likely, for example, to seek careers in high earning professions or trades. They may also seek, from an early stage, to associate themselves with such people, perhaps adopting them as role models.

A third group may see wealth in classic sense, the sense of personal well-being – a combination of health and happiness and possibly assets (to the extent that they perceive possession of the latter to lead to the former).

This latter view may also be common at the other end of the life cycle. Here, wealth may be seen much more as 'security against unknown and uncontrollable events'. Extensive property and investment holdings might not be of value on their own; but the protection they are seen to afford against helplessness can be of primary importance. An ancient role model for this attitude toward wealth is the Greek lawgiver, Solon. The fame and wealth of the splendid court of Croesus at Sardis attracted many visitors. One of these, according to legend, was Solon. The king proudly displayed his treasures and asked Solon who was the happiest man that he had met. Solon named two or three obscure men who had lived and died happily. Croesus was surprised and angry and said: 'Man of Athens, dost thou count my happiness as nothing?' 'In truth,' replied Solon, 'I count no man happy until his death, for no man can know what the gods may have in store for him.'

Whether a customer is or wants to be as 'rich as Croesus' or have 'the Midas touch', the successful management of his or her wealth should be based on a common understanding of what wealth means to the customer at any particular point in their life cycle.

Perhaps new mass-affluent customers are not really interested in 'wealth' at all! Perhaps they actually value wealth for the things it can enable. Wealth enables a comfortable, even a luxurious, lifestyle. Wealth enables power. Wealth can enable the creation of a family dynasty or the fulfilment of ego. Wealth can enable influence on social change, an honest desire to do charitable works, or a need to control the lives of others. Wealth can be used to buy companionship in old age or can cushion the pain of a lingering death. Would-be wealth managers should ask, 'what is this wealth we are managing for a given customer, and what are their intentions in amassing, maintaining and growing their wealth?'

One way to look at wealth management is to see it as a constant balancing of a portfolio of outcomes and assets that are held by customers over the various stages of their life cycle. Economists might be happier with this view – in which the outcomes are expected drawings upon the assets. This introduces the question of risk. For it is unlikely that an individual will make steady progress throughout his or her life, gradually improving all positive measures. Some will regress some of the time, and health is almost certain to. The worry for the individual is whether a regression establishes a trend and whether the trend will return to positive. As the poem goes:

A trend is a trend is a trend.
The question is – will it bend?

Therefore, attitude to risk is an enormously important part of wealth management (see Chapter 36 on wealth management in the UK). Risk must be interpreted not only in an absolute sense (cg absolute rises or falls in value or health) but also in a relative sense (unexpected changes relative to an expected trend). For if wealth is psychological, only partly based on financial assets, then how does the individual feel about a regression on one or more fronts? For how long will this retreat have to continue for the individual to feel damaged? If damage does take place (eg through a general fall in asset values), will the individual 'mourn' the loss for a certain period by abandoning normal behaviour (eg by stopping investment in equities), before recommencing investment? Will the retreat lead to a revision of objectives (if the individual had any), so as to make the situation more tolerable ('I didn't really want it anyway')?

Of course, the retreat may not be a financial retreat. Indeed, for the individual who has made the right choices, and can hold to them through short-term market-based fluctuation in financial assets, the most severe fluctuations are likely to be caused by factors associated with health (until and whenever it really becomes possible to forecast health, and even then accidents will happen), society (eg illness or death of relatives and friends, neighbours from hell moving in, children failing to meet educational aspirations) or employment (unexpected promotion or demotion, bonus or lack of it, loss of job or offer of an unexpectedly good job). Also, changes in mental or social state can lead to imprudent financial decisions, eg switching of assets that attract high switching costs, which, as shown in Chapter 36, is destructive of financial wealth.

It could be argued that many people are not subject to these changes. Perhaps this is a middle-class perspective – based upon the writers' feeling that they are in control of their own lives – a perspective which might not be shared by those who haven't been fortunate enough to receive the education or parental wealth boost that gives them choice.

Let's consider this point in more detail. The wealthy professional childless couple may have a 'portfolio' of outcomes that include social status and acceptance, fashionable possessions, charitable works, shared financial decision making and long-term post-career comfort. The wealthy single-earner couple with adolescent children may value outcomes such as access to education and opportunity for their children, protection of their estate at death, practically useful possessions and convenient financial decision making for one of the couple.

As life cycles progress and the portfolio of outcomes – and the risks associated with that portfolio – changes, so the portfolio of assets – fixed, liquid, low risk, high risk, debt based, credit based – should change as a result. If 'wealth' can be defined as the ability to realize outcomes, then wealth management can be defined as the skill to match assets to outcomes over time – in the light of probable risks over time.

The good news for financial services providers is that they have the individual and segment-based data that can be analysed to identify the optimum match of outcomes to assets and risks over time. Perhaps no other industry has the experience and skills to assess individual financial habits and goals, segmental profiles of behaviour and risk, and the ability to design offerings that create the linkages between them. The bad news for financial services providers is that they are often unable to recognize or understand the value of the outcomes to the customer. The building society that believes the customer wants a mortgage rather than a home, the bank that assumes that the automobile loan is more important that the automobile, the insurer that thinks that the pension is the objective rather than a comfortable post-career lifestyle – each of these providers demonstrates an ignorance of outcomes that can make their offer of wealth management irrelevant. The wealth manager may want mortgages, automobile loans and pensions. The mass affluent may *need* mortgages, automobile loans and pensions – what they want are homes, cars and beaches! They want these things because they contribute to their feeling of well-being, but of course as we have seen, they are only one contributor.

So far, so good, but what are the practical implications of all this for financial services providers? They are simple, but revolutionary.

The first point is that suppliers should recognize that wealth is not just a question of money, or indeed financial assets, but a question of how the customer perceives well-being. To claim to be managing wealth rather than the financial support for wealth is to over-claim. It exposes suppliers to accusations of failure in wealth management when customers' wealth suffers for reasons that are actually nothing to do with failure of investments or returns, eg health. The focus should be on a wider range of variables, and the customer benefits associated with their changing values, not the values themselves.

The second point is that if the distribution channel through which the customer buys financial assets is incapable of engaging with the customer on issues such as those covered in this chapter, the probability of failure of the channel to meet customer needs will be high. The question is – do most people ever receive the kind of guidance and support that helps them manage their wealth? Or has the fragmentation of society, and in particular the lack of support from a family or a social network, exposed most people to having to make decisions with no other advice than that from biased parties? For financial services providers, the suggestion is that the way in which staff who give advice are trained should be very different from today. If customers are given the broader counselling that this note suggests, they may make better financial decisions which are more balanced and less destructive of wealth.

The third point is that there is a serious problem of inter-agency and intra-company failure. This is a recognized problem in the public sector – most distressingly obvious in cases of acute cases – health, child abuse, murder. When so many agencies (police, health, social services, education, etc) have their own view of the customer, failure to deliver the right advice and care may occur. When it comes to managing wealth – whether in the restrictive financial or broader personal sense, the probability of poor service is very high. The different financial providers do not talk to each other – indeed they may be forbidden by data protection legislation and/or specific financial services regulation to do so unless the customer permits it. They may also have conflict of interest – they may see the customer as a zero sum game, in which business that they get is denied to a competitor, rather than a cooperative game, where more than one company can cooperate in increasing the customer's wealth. If they see the customer as a zero sum game, they will try to obtain as large a share of the customer's expenditure as possible. However, this problem is not insuperable, and companies should try to work with each other where possible, and not always assume that they can only meet customers' needs by controlling all their financial assets. This is possible particularly when one company, eg an insurer, uses another (eg a bank) as a channel (see Chapter 28). Even within companies, the different business units that can affect the customer's wealth, as defined in this chapter, do not talk to each other much. In a typical large provider, different units offer pensions, investment services, life assurance, health insurance and the like; full householding – in the sense of putting data about the family and household together for advisory use – is rare, though increasing. Of course, many customers may not want an integrated proposition. Indeed, few customers would really recognize such a proposition if presented with it, so product-focused has been their past dialogue with the industry. So we are not recommending a U-turn – both sides need to make steady progress along a learning curve.

The fourth point, which follows directly from the third, is that presenting a true wealth management offer may require a complete re-evaluation of business strategy and implementation. It may change everything from the products a company produces or sources, the channels of distribution it uses, its customer management processes from marketing and sales through to claims, and indeed its branding in real and virtual worlds.

The fifth point is that governments themselves conspire in creating possible confusion. Financial service regulation forces a focus on rates of return, with a more misty focus on charges (transparency is still weak, but sharpening). There is rarely any measure of the quality of advice. Nor do governments insist on quality standards for the provision of advice, other than quality of diagnosis and appropriateness of financial recommendation. Governments rarely intervene to support initiatives that aim to educate customers as to the above issues. However, this should not stop companies aiming higher.

Our conclusion for prospective or actual suppliers of wealth management services: do not slow down the development of your services, and the appropriate systems, data and process support. But do pay close attention to the broader definition of wealth management suggested in this chapter, and consider how you can really manage your customers' wealth, not just their free financial assets!

34

Bridging the wealth management gap

Tamsin Brew, Rohitha Perera, Merlin Stone and Ica van Eeden

INTRODUCTION

This chapter examines the early history of a new phenomenon – wealth management. It discusses whether it really is new, and how much of what we are seeing is a case of 'the emperor's new clothes'. It explains why the phenomenon has become so important to financial services companies and what they are doing about it. Finally, and perhaps most importantly, it discusses the real changes that customers are expecting and should expect in the services they are being offered.

The feeding frenzy of financial services companies is evident, but consumer enthusiasm is not. This is, we believe, because of the restrictive definition of wealth management adopted by most of these suppliers, and the lack of clear benefit for the consumer.

In this chapter, we first define the idea of wealth management. We then review quickly the well-trodden ground of the evidence of market size. We then discuss the concept of the family office, which is the nearest we have seen to comprehensive wealth management, and go on to suggest what kind of company is likely to lead the wealth management market in the future.

DEFINITION

In Chapter 36, we explore the state of wealth management defined in terms of the management of discretionary and free financial assets, ie those assets a customer can set aside for longer-term purposes. We explored the extent to which customers were paying high charges for performance that was no better than if they invested in a 'lightly packaged' service. However, our research indicates the need for a broader definition – the nature of which was explored in Chapter 33. In that chapter, we took a view that wealth includes a lot more than assets, and could even be extended to include current and predicted well-being, ie health, and the financial products that underpin it.

In this chapter, we define wealth management as an integrated and structured approach to caring for and managing a client's financial affairs and relationships. It typically involves a high-touch, enabling, multi-product consultative relationship with wealthy individuals and depends on a collaborative customer relationship through a combination of technology and personal contact.

THE MARKET

In a climate of growing affluence, a combination of factors has increased the complexity of customers' affairs, making management of wealth more important – and anxiety producing – than ever. These include the following:

- More inherited wealth – trillions of dollars of wealth will be transferred between generations over the next few decades. In many cases, this will be the first substantial inter-generational transfer for the family and will increase the demand for financial and estate planning.
- Increasing real disposable income and assets among the upper middle class.
- The retirement funding 'crisis' and the shift of the responsibility for and risk of retirement funding adequacy from the government/employer to the individual.
- Changing world of work (greater job mobility, more self-employment, etc).
- An ageing population and lengthening life expectancies – by 2030, 25% of Europe's population will be more than 65 years old.
- Changing gender roles – with women playing a much more active role in long-term finance.
- The changing structure and roles of households and families – divorce rates remain high and women are having children later, extending the period for which households have to maintain high incomes.
- Consumer financial behaviour becoming more complex and less homogenous – customers have become more demanding, more sophisticated, less trusting, keener to manage their affairs themselves, less loyal, more interested in wealth and how they should be managing it. Investors are more knowledgeable and sophisticated, though many are still naïve, and it can be argued that wealth is still outrunning wisdom.

- Lower interest rates and inflation have made it harder for individuals to fund their retirement by buying property on a mortgage – they now need to get a better real return on investments.
- The government has promoted the introduction of a range of more complex, tax-efficient savings products.
- Deregulation – the current polarization rules, which dictate that regulated products sellers must be either 'tied' (selling only their own products) or 'independent' (selling the products of any provider), are being reassessed. A new category of 'multi-tied' providers may emerge.

Globally, an estimated 7.2 million people hold over $1 million in financial assets, totalling approximately $27 trillion. By 2003, 25 million investors are expected to manage $1.9 trillion online, generating approximately $20 billion in industry revenue. Few organizations have been able to ignore the scale of this opportunity and a huge number have turned their attention to the wealth management market.

THE RESPONSE OF SUPPLIERS

Many different types of financial institution are trying to capitalize on the opportunity by stretching their offerings and capabilities. There are examples in all the categories shown in Figure 34.1 of organizations trying to adapt their current business models, existing brands and offerings to capture the wealth management market. The result has been a lot of 'noise' and confusion over what wealth management really means. There has also been much neglect of fundamental management principles, which many financial services companies are still getting to grips with:

- targeting the right customers and serving them through appropriate, cost-effective channels;
- objectively understanding customer financial needs using financial planning disciplines;
- developing the right tools and capabilities to support a 'trusted' relationship.

Figure 34.1 shows the two key dimensions – customer behaviour, ie need for depth or quality of advisory service – and amount of customer wealth at which these services are targeted. Those in the top right corner are institutions that deal fully with the very wealthy – the private banks, such as Credit Suisse and SG Hambros. They are targeting the next layer down of the wealthy (the affluent), but because of the high costs of their advisory services, they are also having to offer several tiers of advisory services to achieve margins

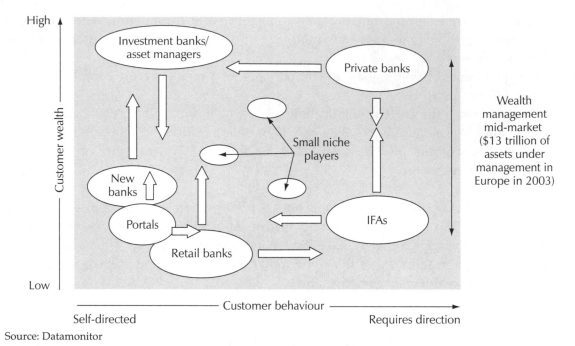

Source: Datamonitor

Figure 34.1 Wealth management market map

that are appropriate for each. In the top left corner are the investment banks and asset managers – companies such as Goldman Sachs, Merrill Lynch HSBC and JP Morgan Chase. They too are seeking to broaden their base, but have realized that in order to help the new wealthy manage their assets properly, they have to both offer advisory services themselves and broaden distribution of their products through other wealth management organizations. They also face the problem of private banks – how to offer these advisory services cost-effectively.

At the bottom right are IFAs, ranging from the one-man band to companies such as Hargreaves Lansdowne. Responsible for the wealth of very large numbers of mid-worth individuals, they are under threat from all the other institutions, partly because of the commissions they receive for their work, which consists largely of configuring highly complex products to simple needs (see earlier chapter). They evolved largely to cope with the complexity of the market created by past regulation about what is possible, poor regulation in the area of clarity over charges, and an over-complex industry structure. However, IFAs are starting to respond by putting greater focus on efficiency, and by becoming tougher with their suppliers. Mergers have also increased their average firm size, facilitating this application of pressure. In the USA, Charles Schwab's creation of the mutual fund no-fee supermarket virtually created the IFA fee-based business model and allowed high quality wealth management services to be delivered to the upper-middle class. Once viewed by the other players as a fad, IFAs in the USA are now actively courted by virtually all product manufacturers.

At the bottom left of the diagram are the new entrants (eg Egg, Virgin, iii.co.uk). Using direct marketing and Web technology, they are aiming to capture more of the assets of the wealthy through efficiency. Just to the right of these are the traditional retail banks (eg Barclays, Lloyds TSB), which are trying to spread their influence in all directions (though some of them also own companies that work elsewhere in the diagram). Somewhere in the central space are small niche players, such as Close Wealth Management, which offers highly efficient advisory services, which provide comprehensive advice and education up front and hence reduce the ongoing advisory requirement.

All of these players have been attracted to the wealth management market by the financial opportunity they perceive there.

THE ECONOMICS OF WEALTH MANAGEMENT

The key driver for organizations moving into the wealth management market has been the attractive economics illustrated in Table 34.1 by the return on equity (ROE) achieved by different types of organization.

There are several reasons why a 'high street bank' would want to move into the wealth management market:

- It is big – total assets under management of $27 trillion in 2000 and expectations of $40 trillion in 2005. Revenues represent about $100 billion pa.
- It is growing – 10% compound annual growth rate (CAGR) for whole market, with even faster growth in the onshore European market – 12%.
- It is profitable (see ROE figures in Table 34.1) – very high returns compared to other markets, driven by low regulatory capital requirements, and annuity-based commission income.
- It is stable – once established, a 'trusted' advisory relationship experiences little attrition.

Table 34.1 Average return on equity for different banking propositions

	Average ROE
Private bank	87%
European Universal Bank	22%
UK retail	30%
US commercial	29%

Source: Morgan Stanley Dean Witter, *Private Banking in the 21st Century*

- It is fragmented – the top five private banks in the world hold about 5% market share between them (UBS, Credit Suisse, Merrill Lynch, Deutsche Bank, JP Morgan Chase, CitiGroup).
- It is low risk – private banks carry few assets, so little asset risk. Most risk is operational.

The JP Morgan data in Figure 34.2 appears to demonstrate that the need for products grows with wealth:

- About 40% of private clients hold four or more products, compared to 6% of basic (retail) clients.
- Private clients are typically 22 times more profitable than basic clients.
- A private client with four or more products will generate profit of approximately €868 pa, compared to €162 pa for two or fewer products.

Unfortunately, organizations have responded to this by throwing more products at the wealthier customer, seeing the opportunity for cross-selling. This misses the key fact that as they get wealthier, the complexity of customer's lives also increases and they need more help. It is these economics that seem to have motivated all of the competitive moves demonstrated in Figure 34.1, not customer needs. Table 34.2 summarizes the main reasons why organizations have entered the market.

Different types of financial institutions had different expectations when entering the wealth management market. Most of the institutions expected to leverage their existing capabilities and customer base in order to gain market share and grow profits. In addition, external factors, such as shrinking margins and increasing competition, have pushed

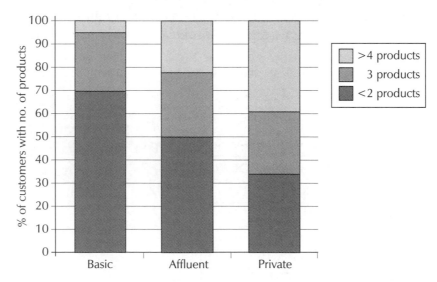

Figure 34.2 Product holdings grow with wealth

Table 34.2 Reasons for entry

Type of institution	Reason for entry
Investment banks, asset managers and retail banks	Leverage existing customer base and capabilities – cross-selling Economies of scale Increase profits and market share Gain competitive advantage
Private banks	Attract growing mass affluent Protect high net worth base Increase profits and market share Gain competitive advantage
Insurance companies	Leverage existing customer base and capabilities – cross-selling Increase profits and market share
Brokerages	Acquire high margin wealthy customers Increase shrinking margins Cross-sell
Non-financial institutions	Acquire high margin wealthy customers Leverage existing customer base Diversify into more profitable areas

financial institutions in the directions shown in the wealth market map in Figure 34.1. However, noticeably absent from the list of drivers and expectations is any mention of customer needs. This is because of the different views of wealth management held by financial institutions and by the customer.

THE WEALTH MANAGEMENT GAP

Organizations define wealth management as a very wide range of products (see Table 34.3), all broadly in the area of advice, relationship management or financial planning, rather than a comprehensive service for customers. Relationship management tends to be fragmented and focused on one or other of the individual services.

This has become the traditional view of the wealth management market. No company has really created a truly comprehensive service, though some would claim to have done so. Instead, they have tried to create wealth management by adding services, which essentially help them to sell more products.

This means that there are two very different wealth management models now in existence: 1) supply side – providers using traditional product push over multiple channels using a 'trusted adviser' positioning which exists in name only; 2) demand side – customers want someone they can trust to help objectively define their needs, recommend the right products for them (vs the provider's needs) and pay a fair price for the service.

Table 34.3 Product definitions of wealth management

Banking	Current account, money transmission, bill payment
Brokerage	Research, advice, trading, settlement
Lending	Mortgages, credit cards, loans
Personal trust	Estate asset management, trusts, foundations, charities, agencies
Mutual funds	Research, trading, settlement, valuation, record keeping
Investment management	Research, advice, trading, settlement, management
Tax	Personal finances, offshore, tax advice, tax preparation, wrappers
Life and pension	Life, home, travel, health, retirement

Today, the customer's needs are not being met, while other service characteristics are irritating and frustrating. Many, if not most, customers remain confused. Most suppliers seem to define wealth management as clustering products around generic financial needs and pushing these through different channels, including the Internet. This leads to customer dissatisfaction. Customers are:

- disappointed about their past experiences with poor investment performance, high sales charges, lack of transparency, etc;
- frustrated by having to provide the same personal details to different parts of the same organization;
- frustrated with low levels of resident knowledge in traditional channels, where advice can be poor and/or not objective;
- tired of turnover in advisers and providers, which makes it difficult to establish and maintain long-term relationships;
- very sceptical of promises; 'High quality service cannot be sold; it must be demonstrated.'

The definition of wealth management that customers have, on the other hand, revolves around 'making the right decisions about my life, my finances'. They:

- want to be recognized as valued customers;
- believe they have more sophisticated needs than their providers recognize;
- want empowerment, help, information, suggestions and attention;
- prefer to make their own decisions, but need help understanding how different solutions might affect them individually.

Customers are crying out for someone to get wealth management right, and when a provider does, the benefits will be large because of the unmet demand in the market and the marketing advantage of being the first mover. Customer needs are poorly met at the moment, hence the emergence of the 'wealth management gap', where the greatest opportunity now lies.

LOOKING MORE CLOSELY AT CUSTOMER NEEDS

For the customer, the objective of wealth management is not to purchase a financial product. It is about defining and meeting their emotional and lifestyle needs, using financial products simply as an enabler. The range of these needs is illustrated in Table 34.4.

Most customers have an unwritten and often vaguely recognized personal mission statement which reflects their goals, such as 'I want to retire at 50 and live my life to the full'. Table 34.4 attempts to provide a blueprint of all the key needs. Our hypothesis is that these needs do not vary with wealth level, although the ways of satisfying them might. Different people may have different priorities, but basically all human beings have similar needs, around which the key life events and goals can be grouped. This is a perspective that, almost without exception, organizations have not recognized in designing their wealth management offerings.

THE FAMILY OFFICE

So far, we have encountered only one business model which recognizes the full range of wealth management needs as described above – the family office. This truly customer-

Table 34.4 Customer needs

		Customer's Mission Statement			
	Secure my future Reduce my risks	Give me peace of mind	Help me enjoy life, achieve my aspirations	Simplify my life	Save me time
Emotional needs	Retirement Birth/adoption Business start-up Childcare Divorce, separation University education	Job loss Property loss Death Birth/adoption Home Illness	Cars Charity Birth/adoption Wedding Furniture/consumer goods Family celebrations Sports, hobbies Arts/entertainment Luxury goods Vacation	Transport Shopping Vacations Home	Transport Shopping Business start-up Home Childcare

centric organization provides advice/oversight/aggregation over a full range of all financial assets and liabilities, regardless of the product provider. The sorts of services routinely provided by a family office include:

- asset enhancement services/strategic advisory, eg:
  - ownership;
  - structure;
  - wealth/estate transfer planning;
  - investment policy;
  - trusteeship;
  - asset allocation;
  - philanthropy;
  - financial education.
- risk management and cost control services/compliance and overseeing, eg:
  - customized financial reporting;
  - investment manager research and selection;
  - investment performance monitoring;
  - trust accounting and reporting;
  - tax planning and compliance;
  - cash flow management;
  - budgeting and financial planning;
  - custody oversight and securities settlement;
  - insurance coverage and claims;
  - charitable foundation administration.
- convenience services/personal service, eg:
  - bill payment;
  - travel planning;
  - administrative support;
  - property management;
  - domestic service management.

The strength of this model lies in the range of services that it can provide – an aggregation capability, third-party sourcing and advisory role. The model is completely customer-focused, ie starts with the customer need and identifies suitable products, not the reverse. Because they are created by the customer, family offices are focused on translating customer needs into exactly those value elements which reflect the added value sought by customers and they build the capabilities they need to provide this value. Most financial services organizations would claim that they are customer focused, but how many have actually been designed by their customers? The family office concept is entirely relationship based and as a consequence, the costs associated with delivering this type of service are high. However, we believe that through using technology, the concept of the family office can be applied to the lower end of the market.

THE 'WEALTH MANAGEMENT LOOP'

This process of translating a customer's emotional needs into value elements, which are then delivered by a series of capabilities, which, in turn, satisfy the emotional needs, is encapsulated in the model illustrated in Figure 34.3. This shows how each of these elements are related to each other and are part of an iterative process.

This model reflects the notion that: 1) wealth management is about more than just financial services, and 2) for that reason, existing financial services organizations cannot just stretch their current business models – they need to transform their organizations to put the client first, understand what customers want and develop organizational capabilities accordingly.

To illustrate the range of a customer's emotional needs, consider the following scenario:

Oliver is 35, married with two children, aged 8 and 10. Oliver is a lawyer in Leeds and has just got a new job with a large London law firm, which means uprooting his family and moving to London. The job is a big step up for him, with a large salary increase, which will enable him to buy a bigger house. His needs go far beyond a larger mortgage, though. As his wife also works, time for organizing the move is at a premium, and neither can afford the time for frequent trips south to house hunt. What they really need is someone to go through the details of the vast number available and

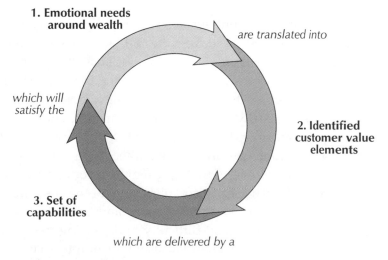

Figure 34.3 The wealth management loop

provide them with a short list which reflects what they are actually looking for (Emotional need (EN): save me time; Value elements (VE): non-financial needs, prompt service, convenience, one stop shop; EN: secure my future; VE: lifestyle needs, a home) and then to arrange visits over one weekend. They also need a trusted adviser to examine their financial situation and objectively advise them on how big a mortgage they can afford to take on, bearing in mind the higher cost of living in London (EN: give me peace of mind; VE: trust and integrity, demystified guidance; EN: secure my future/reduce my risks; VE: long-term relationship, lifestyle needs, life-stage needs, financial planning, a home; EN: help me enjoy my life/achieve my aspirations; VE: flexible options, financial planning). Once the size of the mortgage is decided, they need to decide on the best mortgage product and how to increase their life cover (EN: give me peace of mind; VE: best-of-breed products, transparency of charges, demystified guidance; EN: save me time; VE: convenience, one-stop shop; EN: secure my future/reduce my risks; VE: financial planning, security, tailored products).

Once they find a suitable property in Islington, they need someone to handle the purchase process (conveyancing, including dealing with the estate agent, arranging the new mortgage, finalizing dates, booking the removal company, arranging for utilities to be connected, insurance, etc) as well as organizing the sale of the property in Leeds (EN: save me time; VE: convenience, non-financial needs, one-stop shop, prompt service; EN: simplify my life; VE: long-term relationship, simple administration, banking services, product aggregators; EN: give me peace of mind; VE: choice of suppliers, trust and integrity, best-of-breed products, emergency and disaster planning; EN: help me enjoy my life; VE: performance and value for money, non-financial needs, flexible options; EN: secure my future/reduce my risks; VE: security, tailored products, lifestyle needs).

To deliver a full wealth management service successfully, financial institutions must possess all the capabilities needed to address the full range of customer value elements. There are many examples today of organizations not possessing the right capabilities, which illustrate the likely consequences for the customer. Many financial institutions do not possess a 'consolidated view of the customer' capability because they remain organized into product 'silos' (eg insurance division, mortgage company). Consequently every time a customer buys a new product, he or she has to deal with a different part of the organization. If the customer buys an insurance product, the insurance division does not have access to the customer data held by other areas of the bank and the account-opening process is effectively repeated. No one in the bank has a complete view of the customer's affairs – much less the means to understand the implications of a customer's holdings on his or her needs.

Many financial institutions have great difficulty in delivering the trusted adviser-type relationship they promise. Poorly trained advisers, incomplete customer knowledge, adviser turnover, commission-based compensation and product push are elements working against building trusted relationships with a financial services organization. To a traditional organization striving to meet the emotional needs of the wealth management customer, the challenge of delivering the comprehensive range of required capabilities requires a true transformation of the entire culture and operation.

ESSENTIAL WEALTH MANAGEMENT CAPABILITIES

The family office model is built upon just such a range of capabilities. An overview of the full range of capabilities required to meet the emotional needs blueprint is shown in Table 34.5.

At first glance, many organizations that currently offer wealth management services would argue that they do have such capabilities, for instance a relationship management capability. However, when these are measured against the benchmark of the family office, they fall a long way short. Table 34.6 provides an analysis of current wealth management players' capabilities. This analysis can then be extended by taking three of the most important capabilities for wealth management – relationship management, a consolidated view of the customer and true asset management – and identifying the key characteristics associated with them. These are perhaps three of the most common weaknesses identifiable in existing wealth management propositions. Critically, it is not good enough to have some of these capabilities – they all work together. So, for example, you cannot provide really good relationship management if your relationship manager hasn't got a complete view of all the customers' affairs. In addition, you cannot be a true wealth manager unless you have the resources to manage *all* of a customer's assets. To do that the customer must trust his or her relationship manager, who must have a consolidated view, etc.

CASE STUDY: A SOUTH AFRICAN PRIVATE BANK

The case study below illustrates the importance of possessing all of these capabilities.

At this bank, relationship management has been part of the culture and philosophy since inception. However, the company recognized that to be truly effective at managing relationships, it needed a single view on its customers. The information this provided would allow it to give better quality advice to its customers and deepen the relationships.

The bank subscribes to the philosophy that CRM is a technology-assisted approach to creating a holistic view of the customer relationship and that a CRM approach is the cornerstone of a customer-centric organization. The technology should enable the relationship manager to interact more effectively and efficiently with the customer, as well as with the rest of the organization.

Table 34.5 Value and capabilities

Value element	Capabilities	How capability helps in		
		Simplification	Enjoying life	Saving time
Convenience	Empowered staff	Fewer handoffs		Shorter transaction time
	Physical presence	Easy face-to-face access		Easy face-to-face access
	Proactive service		Range of needs	Anticipation of needs
	Flexible robust processes			Fewer errors
	Contact management	Easy access to right people		No need to repeat request
Complete delegation of assets and liabilities	Relationship management	Trust, long-term relationship	Better understanding, good customer care	Act as integrator
	Contact management	Easy access to right people		No need to repeat request
	Independent experts		Range of needs	Quality advice
	Trained staff	Better understanding		Shorter transaction time
	Interpersonal skills		Better understanding	
	True asset management		More time spent on personal things	
Product aggregation	Access to customer data	Quicker service	Access all information in one place, single password	No need to use different providers
	Third-party alliances and sourcing		Broader range of providers, more options	No need to shop around
	Secure and safe infrastructure		Increased customer confidence	
	Cross-border agreements	No need to deal with different providers	Range of needs	No need to use different providers
	Capture customer data	Viewing customer the whole customer picture		Shorter transaction time
	Consolidated customer view	Viewing customer the whole customer picture	Includes non-financial, lifestyle products	Shorter transaction time
Non-financial needs	Contact management	Easy access to right people		No need to repeat request
	Third-party alliances and sourcing		Broader range of providers, more options	No need to shop around
	Flexible robust processes			Fewer errors
	Capture customer data	Viewing the whole customer picture		Shorter transaction time
	Proactive service		New ideas	Anticipate needs

Table 34.6 The capabilities of different types of player

Value element	Capabilities	Retail banks	Insurers	IFAs	Players Investment banks	Private banks	Portals	Niche Players
Convenience								
	Empowered staff	L	L	H	M	H	L	L
	Physical presence	H	H	M	M	M	M	M
	Proactive service	L	L	M	M	H	L	H
	Flexible robust processes	M	M	M	M	M	M	M
	Contact management	L	L	L	M	M	L	L
Complete delegation of assets and liabilities								
	Relationship management	L	L	M	M	H	L	H
	Contact management	L	L	L	M	M	L	L
	Independent experts	M	M	H	M	M	M	M
	Trained staff	M	M	M	H	M	M	H
	Interpersonal skills	L	L	H	M	H	L	H
	True asset management	L	L	M	M	M	M	M
Product aggregation								
	Access to customer data	M	M	M	M	M	M	M
	Third-party alliances and sourcing	L	L	L	M	M	M	M
	Secure and safe infrastructure	M	M	M	M	M	M	M
	Cross-border agreements	M	M	L	M	H	L	M
	Capture customer data	M	M	M	M	M	M	M
	Consolidated customer view	L	L	L	L	L	L	L
Non-financial needs								
	Contact management	L	L	L	M	M	L	L
	Third-party alliances and sourcing	L	L	L	M	M	M	M
	Flexible robust processes	M	M	M	M	M	M	M
	Capture customer data	M	M	M	M	M	M	M
	Proactive service	L	L	M	M	H	L	H

KEY
H   Full capability   They have it and it is good
M   Medium capability   They have it but it is not good enough
L   Weak capability   They either have it but it is very weak or they do not have it

The bank aims to provide its clients with a suite of financial services that will cater for their total wealth management needs, ranging from transactional banking to investment management and specialized wealth advisory services. The products and services are 'manufactured' by third parties, and delivered through the relationship manager supported by a client service consultant.

A number of factors increased the pressure on the bank to deepen its relationship management capability:

● Its customers had become increasingly demanding in the service they were seeking, as well as the ways in which they wanted to communicate with the bank (ie email, Web, face-to-face, etc). Managing all these different interactions, together with capturing the information they generate, had become increasingly challenging.

- Its product offering spanned three areas: transactional banking, asset management and financial planning. It was not possible to identify the complete picture of a customer's holdings across these three areas, making it difficult to manage the customer's affairs holistically.
- It needed to mitigate the risk of losing a relationship manager, with all the information on its customers, to a competitor. The risk is that customers move with their relationship managers, because they have developed a relationship with them, rather than the organization.

The bank identified the need to implement a CRM solution to help its customer-centric organization deliver holistic wealth management, centred on strong relationship management and built upon a consolidated view of the customer. This presented challenges of change management (educating staff in the use of new technologies, processes and procedures), as well as organizational restructuring, to provide better focus on the customer relationship and a technical architecture that could support the customer-centric organization and the new CRM strategy.

Table 34.7 identifies these key characteristics and provides examples of providers whose current service displays the characteristic, if not the full capability. This illustrates the complexity and sophistication required to meet the complete range of a customer's needs, as well as illustrating why it is that it is not possible to leverage existing financial services capabilities. Clearly, wealth management is a complex business, which demands a broader view of customer needs.

NEW COMPETITORS AND POTENTIAL THREATS TO FINANCIAL SERVICES ORGANIZATIONS

To achieve the holy grail of 'true' wealth management, financial service organizations must develop new capabilities to meet the challenge of addressing the broader needs of their customers and to go further than just pushing products.

As Figure 34.4 illustrates, the family office model represents an ideal, equating to 'true' wealth management. Between that ideal and the proliferation of financial services players in the wealth management market are two types of intermediate player who are well positioned to develop towards 'true' wealth management. These organizations are more closely aligned with customers' emotional needs than the financial services organizations in the bottom left corner, which will require the most transformation before they can hope to succeed. These players present a new competitive threat. They have recognized that customers buy to satisfy their emotional needs, such as 'Save me time' and 'Simplify my life'.

Table 34.7 Which players have which capabilities

	Relationship management	Successful example	Consolidated customer view	Successful example	True asset management	Successful example
Key characteristics of capabilities	Acts as integrator	Yodlee, Kinexus, Zisto, AccountUnity, Cymric, Pictet Family Office	Single customer database	Charles Schwab, JP Morgan Chase	Management of full range of all financial assets and liabilities	Pictet, Bessemer, UBS, Merrill Lynch, Cymric
	Long-term relationship	Cymric Family Office, Pictet, UBS, Credit Suisse	Channel integration	Charles Schwab, JP Morgan Chase	Consolidation and management, regardless of provider	mycfo.com, Cymric
	Advice not commission linked	Adviceonline.co.uk	Contact management	First Direct	Non-financial asset management (art, property, antiques, wine, etc)	UBS, Pictet Family Office, Bank of Bermuda
	Advisor has stake in advice	Tenuk, Pictet Family Office	Access to third-party information	Yodlee, Kinexus, Zisto,	Third-party product sourcing (best of breed)	Funds supermarkets Coutts Bank of Bermuda
	Generates trust	Pictet Family Office, Bessemer Trust, UBS, Credit Suisse	Aggregation	Yodlee, Kinexus, Zisto, AccountUnity	Wide range of market/product information	Merrill Lynch, iii.co.uk,
	Transparency	Tenuk, Cymric, Pictet, Bessemer, UBS,	Robust, integrated platform and infrastructure	First Direct	Performance management and measurement	Pictet, Merrill Lynch, Bessemer
	Advice reflects personal circumstances	Pictet, Bessemer, UBS, Merrill Lynch, Cymric	Availability of data is key to consultative relationship	Yodlee/Corillian	Processes for managing external managers	Bank of Bermuda, Inscape, Coutts
	Understands individual's needs	Pictet, Credit Suisse, Bessemer				
	Willing to educate individual	Charles Schwab Cymric, Credit Suisse				
	Has a track record or backed by strong brand	Merrill Lynch, UBS, JP Morgan Chase				
	Proactivity	Pictet, Bessemer, UBS, Merrill Lynch, Cymric				

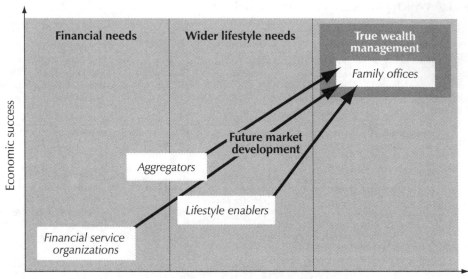

Figure 34.4 Future market development

LIFESTYLE MANAGERS

Like family offices, the lifestyle manager focuses on the lifestyle needs of the customer, not on selling products. They are becoming increasingly popular in the UK and directly address the needs of the customer *outside* financial services. They promote their services with statements such as:

- 'We will do anything the customer wants, as long as it is legal.'
- 'Managing our member's lives... by building personal relationships based on trust.'
- 'Bringing balance to your life.'

These organizations offer what is essentially an extension of the concierge service, which has proved very successful in the United States. They claim to go beyond concierge services, by providing a dedicated relationship manager and building up a trusted relationship, with only 20–25 clients per manager. For an annual fee of between $1,700 and $2,200, they will help 'rebalance your life' by taking care of all those things that you don't have time to do (they'll find you a plumber and then wait in to supervise the work; they'll get you theatre tickets; they'll manage your rental property; they'll book you a holiday; they'll find you a dog psychologist!). Their charging policy is totally transparent, helping build a trusted image.

Other key features include:

- They deliver value for money, because their database of researched suppliers will never charge more than market rate.
- The customer decides what services to use, and how much he or she wants to trust the organization.
- The limitation is that they don't provide an advisory service. They will find an adviser, but will not provide advice. This is the key difference from wealth management services.
- They are completely independent and source third-party products and services – unlike many financial organizations. Their incentive is to retain the customer year on year. (At least one of the three companies has a tiered pricing structure, so that as customers trust the company more and use it more, they pay more.) They are therefore only as good as the suppliers that they provide and so have a vested interest in identifying and managing good suppliers, something relatively rare in the financial world, although there are instances: IFAs (whose charges are commission-based and not transparent), fund of funds.

Table 34.8 shows how it is that lifestyle managers meet many of the emotional needs that fall outside the traditional wealth space and the capabilities they demonstrate to support the customer value elements.

Table 34.8 Emotions, values and capabilities

Emotions	Value elements	Capabilities
Simplify my life	Convenience Simple administration One-stop shop Product aggregators Long-term relationship	Relationship management Third-party sourcing Interpersonal skills Consolidated view of customer Capture and access customer data
Save me time	Convenience One-stop shop Non-financial needs	Proactive service Third-party sourcing Interpersonal skills Consolidated view of customer
Help me enjoy my life	Lifestyle needs Non-financial needs Performance and value for money	Proactive service Interpersonal skills Capture and access customer data
Give me peace of mind	Trust and integrity Performance and value for money Best-of-breed products Choice of suppliers	Relationship management Third-party sourcing Interpersonal skills
Secure my future/ reduce my risks	Lifestyle needs Long-term relationship	Relationship management Proactive service Interpersonal skills Capture and access customer data

There are several key differences between the services of lifestyle managers and financial services organizations:

- Few financial service organizations can demonstrate the sort of independence required to truly save customers time. Very few people would take a first opinion from any financial services organization, without shopping around to check that they were getting the best price / performance / features, etc.
- If you compare the capabilities of the two types of provider, they appear to be very similar, *but* few banks offer ratios like 25 customers to 1 relationship manager (even private banks rarely achieve less than 75:1; family offices are more like 5:1); few financial services organizations offer advice that is not linked to a product sale / commission; because lifestyle managers operate on a fee basis, they have a stake in the recommendations they are giving.

This unique combination of capabilities, and the fact that they are not bound by selling products, means that the service lifestyle managers provide covers a much wider range of customer emotional needs.

PRODUCT AND ACCOUNT AGGREGATORS

Product and account aggregators are another type of new competitor specifically addressing the customers' need for saving time and simplifying their lives. Product aggregation involves providing different products from different suppliers to clients. For example, from zisto.com, a client can trade shares through an E*Trade or TD Waterhouse brokerage account, without leaving the zisto.com site. Account aggregation, which is particularly popular in the USA and Australia, saves the customer time by removing the need for multiple logons to different sites, using different user-ids and passwords. Currently the only example of this in the UK is AccountUnity but US players such as Yodlee, Kinexus, Corillian and CashEdge are actively looking at entering the UK market.

Table 34.9 summarizes the customer value elements and capabilities of account and product aggregators. Product and account aggregation is still a very new concept in the UK

Table 34.9 Aggregator services

Emotional needs	Simplify my life, save me time
Value proposition	Consolidation of information from multiple online accounts on a single screen with one password
Value elements	Convenience, product aggregation, trust and integrity, speed and ease of access to information
Capabilities	Security, alliances and integration with service providers

market. Whilst there is clearly a demand for it, many of the issues presented by it have yet to be completely resolved, particularly in the technical, legal and regulatory areas.

THE REVISED WEALTH MANAGEMENT MARKET MAP

These new competitors are well positioned to successfully fill the gaps in the market left by financial service offerings not focused on customer needs. Figure 34.5 shows where these three types of new competitors will fit into the market. Family offices are common in the USA, and a relatively new concept in Europe (though many of the major European players, particularly private banks, have recently developed, or are in the process of developing, their own family offices). They serve ultra high net worth families, managing their wealth and the extended needs of their family. Generally they only serve families with an excess of $25 million, hence their position in the top right-hand corner.

Lifestyle managers target self-directed people. These people usually know what they want, but lack the time, or the interest, and would rather delegate as much as possible to other people, without losing control over key decisions. Companies like Tenuk (www.tenuk.com), Entrust (www.entrust-net.com) and Liberate (www.liberate365.com) do not have any advisory services, but can locate advisers, if required. They are located towards the upper left because the average annual fee is between $1,700 and $2,200, which is a significant outlay for most people for the luxury of delegating everyday tasks.

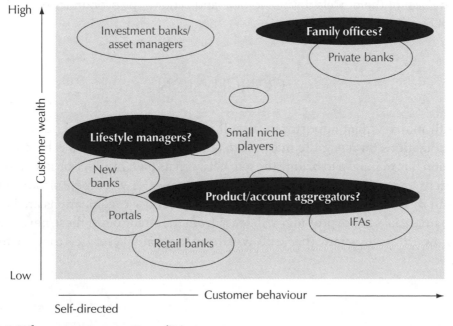

Figure 34.5 Where new competitors fit in

Product and account aggregators are positioned lower down the affluent scale, as they do not charge for their services. These companies both serve the self-directed and require direction as some of them offer advisory services. The advent of these new competitors signals a challenging future for those financial services organizations that wish to capture a slice of the market.

THE FUTURE OF WEALTH MANAGEMENT?

To achieve the holy grail of true wealth management, there are a number of guiding principles that financial services organizations must embrace. 'True wealth managers' will be those organizations that can:

- break out of the mould of just selling their own financial products;
- fulfil the position of trusted adviser by taking a complete view of the customer's affairs and advising them honestly and objectively on all their assets and liabilities;
- help manage a customers' risks;
- get to grips with the idea of customer emotional needs;
- develop the capabilities to serve those needs;
- look at the family office model and find ways of making it economic, fair and transparent for the affluent market;
- take the best of the models discussed here and achieve the economics of a private bank, but not be driven by this alone.

CONCLUSION

The wealth management opportunity is still very much in evidence, but it appears that most organizations targeting the market are failing to capture it. This is because no single organization has managed to bridge the gap between its own product-based view of wealth management and customers' lifestyle needs-based view. New competitors are entering the market and displaying the capabilities that financial service organizations are lacking, and the astute financial service provider will learn from the strengths of these new entrants and build its own offerings into the 'true wealth management' service that customers are seeking.

35

Building the private banking customer experience

Rohitha Perera and Tamsin Brew

INTRODUCTION

Private banks have traditionally viewed themselves as exceedingly 'customer centric', offering what they believe to be highly personalized services to the high net worth (HNW) customer. However, changes in customer behaviour and accumulation of wealth are resulting in the needs of HNW customers becoming more diverse and complex in terms of the sorts of products they want, the channels through which they want to access them and the associated range of advice. This is an increasingly difficult proposition for many private banks to deliver in a way that satisfies customers and is economically viable. We believe that it is possible to achieve both a satisfied HNW customer base and a focused, efficient business serving their needs by using a structured approach to defining a hierarchy of customer experiences, which can then be used to identify and prioritize the capabilities that the organization will require to deliver that experience.

THE MARKET – ATTRACTIVE BUT DEMANDING AND EXPENSIVE TO SERVE

In Chapter 34, we showed that private banking is an attractive market, with most private banks achieving the sorts of return on investment (ROE) that other bank executives can only dream of. The reasons that it appears so economically attractive include:

- A large and growing market – total assets under management of $27 trillion in 2000 and expectations of $40 trillion in 2005. Revenues represent about $100 billion pa. Also, an impressive market growth rate – 10% CAGR for whole market, with even faster growth in the onshore European market – 12%.
- Low concentration – the top five private banks in the world hold only about 5% market share between them (UBS, Credit Suisse, Merrill Lynch, Deutsche Bank, JP Morgan Chase, CitiGroup).
- Private banking clients are more profitable than retail or affluent customers – about 40% of private clients hold four or more products, compared to 6% of retail clients. Private clients are typically 22 times more profitable than retail clients.

Although these factors suggest that profitability is easily achieved in private banking, this is a long way from the truth. The wealthier the customers, the more demanding they are – and clients increasingly expect more and more from their banks. Competition for these supremely profitable customers is increasing, from traditional private banks, investment banks and asset managers, and new 'onshore' competitors.

Therefore, those banks that do not address customers' needs in a structured, prioritized manner will quickly find that either their customer bases are shrinking or they are failing to acquire new customers. In both scenarios, the consequence will be an unsustainable cost base from which to service customers. Compared to their retail counterparts, private banks may display impressive ROE, but their cost–income ratios are quite different – private banks can have cost–income ratios of around 60 per cent (eg Julius Baer 61 per cent in 2000), compared to retail banks' 40 per cent (such as Lloyds TSB 43 per cent in 2000). This represents perhaps the biggest test for private banks – how to meet diverse customer needs economically, without diluting the customer experience.

CHALLENGES FACING PRIVATE BANKS

The challenges implied by this test for private banks if they are to maintain profitability in the face of growing customer demand include:

1. Identifying similar customer needs groups through effective segmentation. We have seen a number of major private banks such as UBS, Coutts, ABN AMRO Private Bank , and HSBC Republic moving towards needs-based segmentation in the last year.
2. Creating economic value propositions to meet the needs of these segments.
3. Identifying and developing the necessary capabilities to successfully translate these value propositions into a 'tangible' yet economic customer experience that meets customer demands for increasingly multi-channel access and complex, tailored products.

This last point is, of course, the most difficult to achieve. A recent IBM survey of the industry found that executives were happy to define strategy but frequently struggled to implement the change it entailed (see Chapter 2). IBM's experience suggests that one reason is because they fail to appreciate the structure of creating a compelling customer experience.

THE HIERARCHY OF CUSTOMER EXPERIENCES

The first step towards successfully winning, retaining and growing the profitability of private banking customers is to understand what their wants and needs are, so that the organization can be built around serving those needs. Only when an organization has done this and incorporated this into its strategy can it start to design its value proposition and a customer experience that will enable it to achieve a differentiated competitive position in the private banking market, and more importantly, do so in an economically viable way.

The basic customer experience

There is a basic 'generic' customer experience that many private banking customers are seeking. To be a credible player in the market, a private bank must be able to deliver this 'base' experience. This represents a common set of needs that are shared by most HNW customers. Therefore, the private bank must have the capabilities required to meet these needs for the majority of its customer base.

All customers, regardless of wealth level, have similar emotional needs, which drive their need for advice and their purchase of products (see Figure 35.1). Different wealth levels impose different priorities on meeting these needs and open up new avenues for doing so. For instance, HNW customers can afford to take higher risks with some of their money, because they are not depending on it to fund their retirement, so their priorities may be associated with growing wealth, rather than preserving it, allowing them to choose a product option with a higher risk/reward ratio. If this is true, it means that all HNW customers start with a basic, common set of what they want and need from a private bank, which might include:

- personal, long-term relationship;
- advice combining industry expertise and knowledge of personal circumstances;
- high quality, consistent service;
- security, privacy, confidentiality.

At this basic level, grouping together these core wants and needs produces a set of generic characteristics that an HNW individual seeks from an organization before he or she will

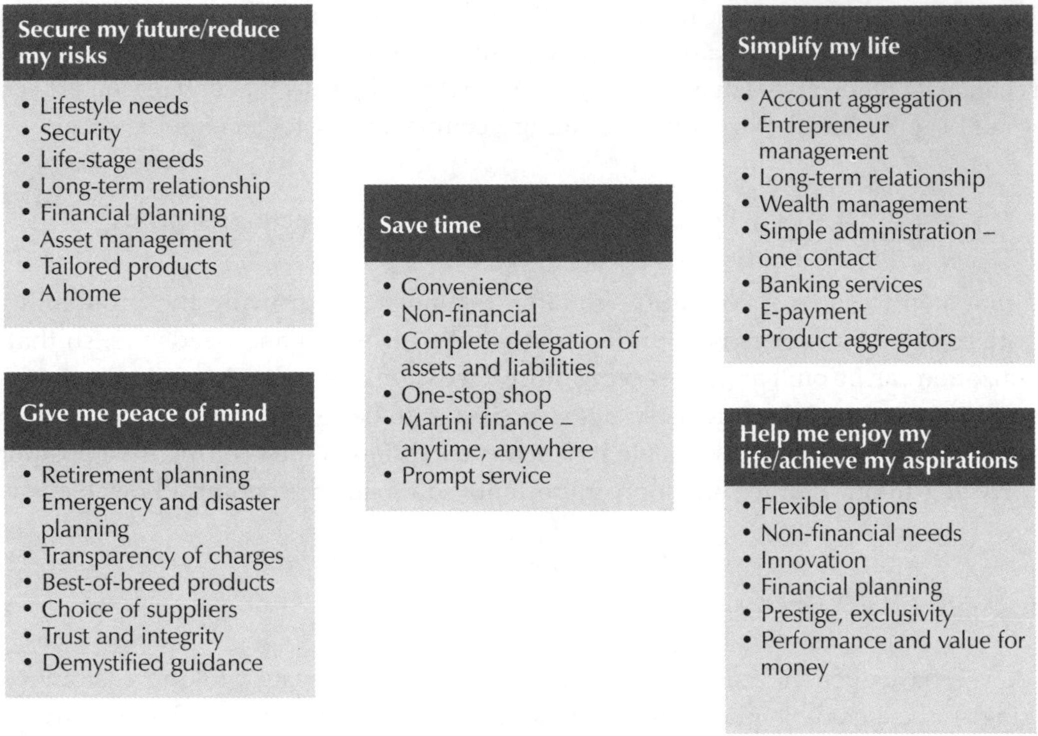

Secure my future/reduce my risks
• Lifestyle needs
• Security
• Life-stage needs
• Long-term relationship
• Financial planning
• Asset management
• Tailored products
• A home
Give me peace of mind
• Retirement planning
• Emergency and disaster planning
• Transparency of charges
• Best-of-breed products
• Choice of suppliers
• Trust and integrity
• Demystified guidance
Save time
• Convenience
• Non-financial
• Complete delegation of assets and liabilities
• One-stop shop
• Martini finance – anytime, anywhere
• Prompt service
Simplify my life
• Account aggregation
• Entrepreneur management
• Long-term relationship
• Wealth management
• Simple administration – one contact
• Banking services
• E-payment
• Product aggregators
Help me enjoy my life/achieve my aspirations
• Flexible options
• Non-financial needs
• Innovation
• Financial planning
• Prestige, exclusivity
• Performance and value for money

Figure 35.1 Customers' emotional needs – blueprint

Advice and expertise
• Give me independent advice specific to my circumstances
High-quality service
• Provide consistent, high quality, error-free service
HNW customers
Personal relationship
• Provide me with a single adviser to manager my affairs
Performance
• Provide me with the best possible return on my assets

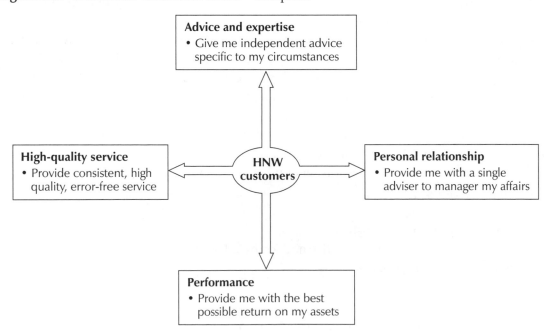

Figure 35.2 Components of the basic HNW customer experience

even consider placing any of his or her wealth with it – this is 'the basic customer experience', shown in Figure 35.2.

Underlying these generic characteristics is a set of capabilities covering organization, process and technology, which the private bank must possess to operate in the high net worth market.

The segment-specific experience

To build on this 'base' experience, private banks also need to consider the segment-specific needs of their target customers. This in itself requires a capability to identify and justify target customers and understand their needs beyond banking, to ensure that their emotional needs are met. It is here that the customer is made to feel like an individual, but it is also at this point that costs and infrastructure can spiral, as customers' needs start to diverge. The segmentation process identifies groups of customers with similar wants and needs, who are seeking a similar experience from the provider. Importantly from the organization's viewpoint, this means that they can also be served by similar sets of capabilities.

The experience at this level is made up of:

- the channel preferences of each segment and associated channel experience – for example, a self-directed group of customers will use the Internet for transacting, information gathering and even some advice, whereas advice seekers and less financially sophisticated segments require more access to an adviser / relationship manager and a more basic experience over the Internet;
- the product and service preferences of that segment – for example, the more sophisticated customers are more likely to demand more complex products such as alternative investments, whilst others may prefer discretionary portfolio management.

Figure 35.3 shows what the customer experience for a specific group of customers might look like – in this case, sports / media personalities. Not only are new components added to the experience (in this case 'flexibility' and 'discretion') but the 'base' experience elements (eg advice and expertise) become defined in more depth, according to the specific needs of the customer segment.

Once the segment experiences have been defined, the associated capabilities must again be identified. The hierarchical approach to defining customer experiences helps to filter these capabilities as: 1) it is possible to identify experience elements that are common to more than one segment – these will carry a higher priority for development as they will benefit more customers; 2) the segmentation exercise will provide comparative sizings for the target segments. Capabilities required for the larger, more profitable segments take precedence over those needed for smaller segments.

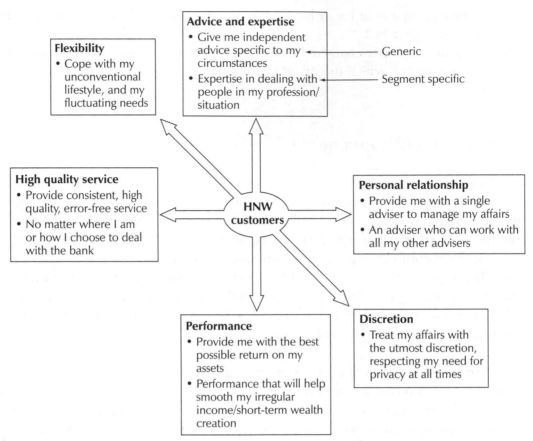

Figure 35.3 Example elements of a segment-specific experience – sports/media segment

The organization-specific experience

The final step, having identified the base and segment-specific elements of the HNW customer experience, is to identify how the experience that each organization offers its customers is distinct from the experience offered by all other private banks. This means clearly identifying the components of the experience that are only associated with a particular private bank, delivering a clearly differentiated experience. This process will define: 1) elements of the organization's style and culture that are embodied in the brand; 2) products and services to be provided.

In the same way that every brand is different, so the experience of dealing with every bank is different – Pictet stands for something very different from Credit Suisse in the mind of the customer, as well as delivering a very different offering in reality. This means that there is no blueprint for an organization-specific customer experience, but there are broad areas that will play a part in the experience offered by organizations such as:

1. **The size and scale of the organization** – is it a global giant with worldwide representation (like UBS or CitiGroup) or a smaller niche-focused bank with expertise in a local market (like Julius Baer or Lombard Odier)?

2. **Independence** – does the private bank operate as an independent entity (like Pictet) or is it a division of a much larger organization (like CitiGroup Private Bank)? In the UK, independence also refers to the regulatory status of the bank – is it tied or an IFA (like Coutts)?

3. **What jurisdictions does the bank operate in?** – can it provide both onshore and offshore services to its customers, with the necessary separation and privacy?

4. **What kind of image does the bank have?** – is it a progressive, innovative organization or a more traditional, understated bank with a strong history?

5. **Service** – does the organization embody service excellence and professionalism? Is it synonymous with long-term personal relationships and continuity?

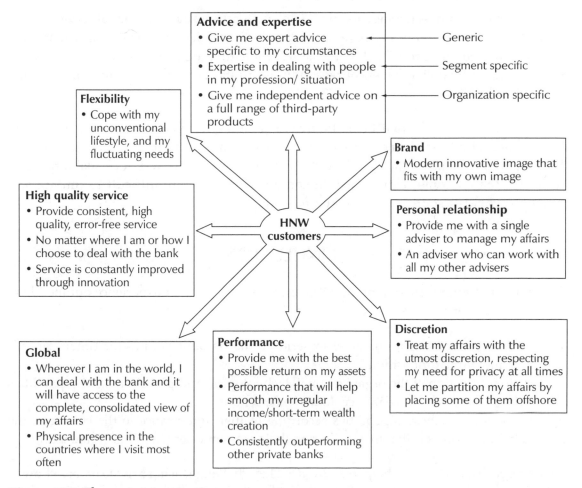

Figure 35.4 The customer experience

6.   **Product range** – does the bank offer a broad range of third-party products or access to wider Group product capabilities (eg corporate finance, structured products and derivatives)?

Having identified the key components of the organization's unique customer experience, the private bank must build these into an experience. Figure 35.4 shows what such an experience might look like for a modern private bank, which has identified sports and media personalities as one of its target segments. Again, the other components of the experience can now be defined in greater depth, according to the organization's characteristics.

The next step is to identify the key capabilities required to deliver this experience. They may include capabilities such as:

- physical representation (for instance, in target markets, or specific offshore jurisdictions);
- the processes and technology required to consistently ensure exceptional service;
- the technology to allow international customers to seamlessly receive a consistent experience and personal relationship, no matter where they are in the world;
- a remuneration policy that encourages advisers to stay and develop long-term customer relationships.

The organization now has a list of definitive capabilities, which it must possess in order to deliver the desired customer experience. As with the components of the experience, it is not the individual elements that produce the experience, but the 'web' of capabilities that underlies the customer experience. In combination, they are difficult to imitate and therefore provide a source of competitive advantage.

CONCLUSION

The structured approach to defining different levels of customer experience outlined here delivers a number of benefits to a private bank:

- a distinctive, consistent customer experience that is built around the organization's brand and value proposition;
- clear identification of the organizational, technological and process-related capabilities required to deliver the desired customer experience;
- prioritization of these capabilities according to their importance to the customer, the number of customers that they affect and their economic benefit to the organization.

This approach can therefore help to address the key challenge facing private banks – how to meet diverse customer needs economically, without diluting the customer experience.

36

Managing wealth – a new approach in the UK

Merlin Stone

INTRODUCTION

This chapter investigates how well 'mid-worth' individuals are served by the investment management community. This chapter defines and analyses the new phenomenon of 'mid-worth' individuals – the rapid growth in the number of people with significant liquid assets available for investment. It then considers how well these individuals are served by the most common investment products. It concludes that most individuals are so poorly served that the result is seriously damaging to their long-term financial health. It then investigates the main reasons for this – a lack of understanding of the relationship between risk and return, and what can only be described as a conspiracy of 'mystification', resulting in customers standing even less chance of understanding the risk–return relationship. The consequence of this is that investors end up paying far too much for 'heavily packaged' investment products. The result of this is that investors may find they have much less money available to them when they need it most – in old age.

The chapter then describes a new approach to low-cost wealth management that has been introduced into the UK market by Close Wealth Management (CWM) and other companies. It shows how this approach is likely to produce much better returns over the long term for most investors. It then investigates some of the issues involved in managing financial services customers, and uses QCi's Customer Management Assessment Tool

(CMAT) to assess CWM. The conclusion is that CWM has made a classic start, with a very strong focus on a customer-friendly proposition, and strongly targeted marketing. However, if it is to remain true to its charter of offering very good returns combined with excellent service, CWM's service processes will need to be tightened up as its customer base grows.

The aim of the chapter is as follows:

- to show why a new generation of mid-worth customers is emerging, and explain their need for wealth management services;
- to show why most mid-worth customers have been so poorly served by the financial services industry;
- to explain and assess the principles on which wealth management works, both in terms of investment management and customer management;
- to show why investors who invest with the help of wealth management companies are almost certain to do better in the long run than those who invest in packaged financial service products.

WHO ARE THE NEW 'MID-WORTH' CUSTOMERS?

Mass-market wealth management as a proposition serves investors with liquid (ie available for investment) assets of around $70,000 to $7 million. Before inflation did so much damage to the value of sterling, many of these investors would have been regarded as 'high net worth' (HNW). Today, we could call all those with liquid assets within this range 'mid-worth'. Nowadays, HNW is a term better applied to customers with wealth of more than $7 million, while 'rich' is a term that might be better reserved – at least from the point of view of the financial services community – for people with $15 million or more.[1] This is because these two groups of customers have very different financial needs, and also because they can be served cost-effectively in very different ways, as Table 36.1 shows.

Traditionally, investment management companies have segmented the market by the amount of assets available – the more the assets, the more expensive the service provided, usually because it is more dependent on people and poorly automated processes. Wealth

Table 36.1 Wealthy customers

Customer type	Capital available	How they are served today	How they are best served
Mid-worth	£50,000–£5m	Packaged, some direct, some bespoke investment management	Wealth management
High net worth	£5m+	Private banking plus direct investment	Private banking plus direct investment

management as described in this paper makes high quality service available to virtually all customers.

There are of course many definitions of high and mid-worth individuals. This chapter is not a statistical study – we know the market is large and growing rapidly. Many of today's mid-worth investors achieve this status relatively late in life. This can be through:

- inheritance from parents at middle age or later;
- receipt of a lump sum at time of retirement;
- yield from a long-term savings policy, such as an endowment;
- proceeds of a divorce settlement – particularly for women;
- sale of a larger family property in order to move into a smaller 'empty nest' property.

Most mid-worth customers will have stopped accumulating wealth by the time they are 55. For example, the average police constable receives a lump sum of $140,000 on retirement, and often retires at around 50. The next step is often another job. The lump sum must then work for 10 years or more to provide the kind of retirement that the officer has a right to aspire to. This 'retiree–employment' syndrome is becoming more common in all sectors, with many employees contracting back to their employers as 'consultants'. This means that the lump sum will not be needed, and should be put to good use, as the last few years of earning will not be pensioned unless the new 'consultant' sets up an additional pension scheme.

Many managers approaching retirement have pursued flexible careers, rather than working for one company. This became more common from the 1980s onwards. Most have taken some responsibility for their pension plans, though not all have exercised this responsibility well. Many will have several lump sum payments arising from various private pensions. Some will also have accumulated assets from lump sum payments from one or more redundancies. Their management of all these lump sums will determine whether they have a good or bad retirement. Their former employers are no longer as paternalistic as they once were, and are more likely to cast them off with a little help, rather than treat them as 'company pensioners', which many of them will not now be.

One of the consequences of the post-war baby boom is that large numbers of employees are approaching retirement. Many of them, whether in the public or private sector, will be receiving a lump sum payment as part of their pension settlement. For those that retire early (and there are many), this lump sum is often enhanced. Employers of these baby-boomers have a special duty to these employees, who will have to live much longer than their predecessors on the proceeds of their retirement saving, with much less government support. Given that the children of this generation will have to save harder than previous generations to ensure that they in turn will retire on good terms (because of the current government's more punitive tax regime towards pension funds), we would not advise them to rely on their children for support.

Most people in the pre-retirement age bracket feel good about the various sources of money that start to yield at this age (inheritances, endowments, lump sums, proceed from property down-sizing). However, it also shows that most are very anxious about money, knowing they need the proceeds to last for up to 40 years. They are afraid of what might be 'around the corner'. They know that they lack financial expertise. This tends to drive them to highly conservative risk positions, which paradoxically destroy their long-term wealth. They are aware that they do not understand risk, but do not know how to deal with it. Worse, most have few sources of 'impartial' advice, and do not know where to get it – they are 'un-networked'.

In the UK, around 600,000 people each year come into the pre-retirement planning market, defined as those aged 47–61. From 62 onwards, very large numbers of people are retired. This number is rising by about 1 per cent a year. Putting it another way, there are over 9 million people in this age bracket now, but in 10 years' time there will be well over 10 million.

Another way of looking at this is to look at the number of people currently retiring, which is around 500,000 a year, of course also rising around 1 per cent a year. This compares with 600,000 being made redundant and 1.5 million receiving an inheritance.

The 600,000 people will be likely to receive on average around $24,000 in tax-free lump sum from their pension fund (this calculation is based on distribution to them of the permitted 25 per cent of the available pension fund). However, this amount is likely to be unevenly spread, with half having around $45,000 and half around $6,000. Of this top 300,000, at least one-third work for larger companies. Their tax-free lump sum is likely to be larger.

Other mid-worth customers achieve their wealth earlier in life, perhaps through business success (their own earnings or share options), or through private dealings in property, or for the really lucky a Lottery win or similar. In all cases, there is a very pleasant time in their life when they realize that they are in the business of wealth management. However, the decisions that they take during this period can affect whether the dreams of pleasant retirement turn into a nightmare.

WHAT DO MID-WORTH CUSTOMERS DO WITH THEIR MONEY?

Most mid-worth individuals are seriously under-invested in equities, usually because they find the process too complicated or consider it too risky. Both of these can be considered a consequence of lack of provision for mid-worth investors. Many mid-worth customers have assembled what can best be described as a ragbag of PEPs, ISAs, unit trusts, with-profits bonds and cash. These return long-term growth well below what these customers could get, often because each is bought and managed on a risk-reduced basis, rather than through considering risk over the whole portfolio. Such a portfolio is best described as unmanaged. Indeed, many wealth management customers come from the 'disillusioned', customers who have used packaged investments for years and have been disillusioned with their performance over time. Other customers are fairly sophisticated but simply do not have the time to manage their direct investments themselves. Others still are virtual novices, who have some packaged investments but really do not know how to manage them, and may just vaguely suspect that they could do better. Just a few customers see mortality approaching quickly and are terrified of leaving their situation in a mess, so that their surviving partner cannot cope, or so that their children benefit much less than they could.

Were it not for the emergence of the mid-worth customer, governments all around the world would be facing much greater problems in funding the health and accommodation of the old. It is therefore important for governments that the wealth of these individuals is properly managed. This money is not that of the super-rich – it is not what some call 'funny money', money that can be invested with indifference as to its long-term return. It must therefore be put to work with the maximum effectiveness if it is to provide for the investor as required.

If we assume that most of these mid-worth customers achieve their wealth by the time they are 60–65, their life expectation is typically at least another 10–15 years, and in the case of couples, the female is likely to live for another 15 years. This point is significant because it means that, subject to income withdrawal requirements, there has been no 15-year period in the last 50 years of British investing history when it would not have paid these individuals to invest directly in equity markets. For those who are fortunate enough to acquire their wealth even earlier, the costs of not investing in this way are much greater. Taking a longer-term view, there were 15-year periods ending in the 1940s when bonds outperformed equities (this period includes the great crash of 1929), but even during these periods equities outperformed cash. So it would have paid to be in equities over any 15-year period in the last hundred years, providing the basis for comparison is cash.

With many more people retiring earlier, and with more wealth to fund their retirement – but with lower state pensions – it is essential for retirees to look hard at the sacrifice to their wealth (and that of their inheritors) that they are certain to make by choosing heavily packaged and/or low risk investments, regardless of their real return.

The financial services industry has devised many products to meet the needs of mid-worth customers. They include:

- unit trusts;
- single premium endowments;
- insurance-linked bonds.

These products are sold through a variety of channels – independent financial advisers, banks, direct from their providers, affinity groups and the like. These products attract large sales commissions, which from the customer's point of view are paid for by large initial deductions before the remainder is applied to investment. Then the providing company levies significant charges for investment management and administration. The net result is that customers get a significantly worse deal than if they had invested directly (in any asset).

In addition, as this chapter shows, in order to optimize their wealth management, the relationship between the investor and the wealth manager must be both close (in the sense that the customer is helped to diagnose his or her needs very fully) and efficient, so that the client does not effectively pay too much for the services of the adviser.

In most cases the relationship is distant and inefficient, because the way that most advisers are trained does not give them the full expertise either to diagnose the client's needs properly or to make the right recommendations. However, it can reasonably be argued that people with busy lives do not always have the time to develop the expertise to invest directly, which is why they turn to 'trusted' financial service providers for help. As we shall see shortly, this decision is extremely expensive for them.

However, the reason for so many customers making the decision to go for packaged investment bought through IFAs is that discretionary fund management has in the past been the province of the rich and famous. The new generation of wealth management companies is changing this. They bring discretionary fund management to the many rather than the few.

Why do most investors make such a severely sub-optimal decision? The situation in the UK contrasts with that in the USA, where direct investment is more common, and where 'thinly packaged investment' (eg mutual funds) is also more common. The new mid-worth investor has been successfully confused into believing that the optimal strategy for the long-term investor is always to invest in heavily packaged investments. This is not to say that heavily packaged investments are never the right thing to do. There are sometimes tax reasons for choosing a more packaged investment, because capital gains are only taxed when the investor sells the packaged fund, not when the investor sells a share. However, with proper management of disposals and the better performance of directly invested funds, this is unlikely.

Of course, this chapter does not imply that using the services of a financial adviser is always the worst option. Some financial advisers give excellent service and advice. However, unless the client is paying a fee for the advice, the long-term performance of the packaged investment, net of all the fees that must be charged to meet the adviser's commissions, is unlikely to beat a wealth management approach, unless the performance of the packaged investment company beats the market by some way. The larger and more successful the packaged products supplier, the more likely its performance is to be close to that of the market, *even before deduction of commissions*. This is because the large providers effectively constitute the market, and as all major providers try to match each other, they are likely to be making similar decisions – more on this later. This of course excludes smaller funds, which may be deliberately high risk, high return plays – more on this later. One cannot argue in general against such funds, as some have demonstrated excellent performance. However, for mid-worth customers, such an approach can be over-risky.

RISKS AND RETURNS

Investment is at the same time a subject of great excitement and great fear for mid-worth customers, particularly if they are new members of this category. Dreams of making enormous returns by investing very successfully are combined with fears of losing everything in a stock market crash. For many new mid-worth customers, the sum that they have available for investment can make all the difference to their lifestyle, particularly in their later years. It is therefore quite natural for such investors to be conservative. This conservatism expresses itself in various ways, for example:

- The thought of losing money may weigh on them more heavily than the prospect of making an excellent return excites them.
- An investment which grows steadily in money value may seem more attractive than an investment which is almost certain to grow much faster over the long term but may have swings in value in the shorter term.
- The idea of a defined income, in the form of a cash withdrawal option, may make the investment seem more like a safe fixed-interest investment, even if the income actually offered over the long term is much less than what could be earned and withdrawn by a more effective investment.

It can be argued that this conservatism of investors is simply a consequence of fear of the unknown. But it can also be argued that it is a response to the confusing range of products that are proposed to investors so as to help them overcome their uncertainties about investment. These uncertainties are really due to failure to understand that big investment decisions can be explained quite simply.

The mid-worth investor usually invests a lump sum, with occasional additions over 10–15 years. The resulting sum must then be available to provide capital or income for another few years. In these circumstances, the principles of wealth management for the investor are based on three key factors:

1. budgeting: determining the investor's likely need for funds (amounts and timing) and thus the period for which the investment is to be made;
2. selecting the type (ie stocks, bonds or shares) of investment, taking into account the investor's attitude to the likely rate of growth in value but also the variability of the value;

3. the quality of the company managing the process for the investor – in terms of its cost-effectiveness, its service level, its process for agreeing a strategy with the investor and its success in adhering to that investment strategy.

Let us look at the first two factors in more detail. The last is covered in the second part of the chapter.

THE FIRST WEALTH MANAGEMENT PRINCIPLE – LOOKING INTO THE FUTURE

Once mid-worth customers have acquired their sum to be invested, they need, perhaps for the first time in a long while, to re-examine their budget. They may have last done this as a struggling young couple deciding how large a mortgage they could afford, or slightly later when deciding on their children's school or university education. If their wealth is a result of a long-term savings plan, they may have budgeted when considering how much they could afford to commit to it. Typically, for the re-budgeting needed for wealth management, they need a realistic estimate of:

● remaining years of income earning (anything from 30 to 0 years);
● likely income levels during these years;
● likely level of pension, including what will happen to pension if one partner dies before the other;
● likely level of expenditure, not just running the house and holidays, but also maintenance of children, educational costs, health, helping grandchildren;
● future value of the family home;
● predictable medium-term requirements, eg new car, home improvement, extensions;
● possible contingency requirements, eg hospital expenses, weddings;
● how much they want to leave to their families (unless this is just a residual, ie what happens to be left).

Some investors do serious budgeting for the first time only when they have wealth to invest – until then it might have been a question of 'hoping and getting by'. Many mid-worth individuals – even quite wealthy individuals close to the high net worth category, whether or not they have budgeted before, get into bad habits. This may be because they have had a period of high earnings, in which income has so far exceeded outgoings that they have not had to budget. With this budgeting laziness often comes investing laziness, with very poor decisions made. This includes substantial amounts held on short-term deposit, paying amounts after tax that barely beat inflation. It also includes tax-inefficiency, eg making too low contributions to pension plans. This even applies to investors who have access to all the latest computing tools. It also happens to professionals such as solicitors who advise their clients to make sure they are well provided for.

This chapter does not explain how to budget. However, budgets can be developed with simple computerized spreadsheets, allowing various options to be considered, eg early retirement, variations in house price value, or unforeseen expenditures on health. Constructing such budgets for clients can transform their lives. This may be because conservative investors tend to be over-conservative, even pessimistic, in forecasting their future. Correspondingly, investors who are over-optimistic in estimating returns may also be imprudent in budgeting.

Budgeting for them is even more important. More advanced tools may help correct this. These are being developed in great numbers in the USA. For example, financialengines.com asks users to pay for a service that uses a variety of forecasts and assumptions about the state of the economy and investment returns to allow the customer to determine the size of their required retirement funding.[2]

Now let us turn to the assets that make this wealth possible.

THE SECOND WEALTH MANAGEMENT PRINCIPLE – UNDERSTANDING FINANCIAL ASSETS

Any financial investment, whether direct, packaged or derivative, must be based on one or more of the following assets:

- money markets;
- fixed income;
- equities.

Their characteristics are described in the Table 36.2. This table excludes domestic and rental property and more sophisticated financial investments such as futures. Most mid-worth customers own their own property, but many do not want to extend their property ownership because of the work and risks involved. The return yielded by rental property is somewhere between that of equities and fixed income. Although it provides an income, it is obviously less liquid (ie saleable in the short run), and will therefore only meet the needs of investors wishing to continue to build assets for eg their children. It is also liable to both capital gains tax (unless owner-occupied) and income tax (on rent).

The most obvious point in this table is the relationship between risk and return. So, for the investor, it can be seen that the biggest decision is what level of risk the investor is prepared to take, in order to gain a particular return. However, this assumes that the investor knows what is meant by risk, and that he or she can establish his or her own attitude to risk.

Table 36.2 Characteristics of investments

	Money markets	Fixed interest	Equities
Definition	Short-term lending to banks or other companies	Longer-term lending to governments, companies or financial institutions, in form of bonds which investor purchases	A share in the profits of a limited company
Example	Bank or building society savings accounts	Treasury stock, corporate bonds	Shares in big companies, eg Unilever, Shell, which tend to make steady profits, or shares in small companies where main prospect is growth in share value
Level of risk to capital	No risk to capital	None if stock held to maturity date, but price fluctuates in short term as market interest rate changes	Higher risk of short-term loss
Long run return	Inflation + 2%	Inflation + 3%	Inflation + 8%
Income yielded	Usually varies with bank rate, though can be fixed for specified periods	Fixed for term of bond	Low but with potential to grow
Capital growth	None	Low	Usually some dividend income, but capital returns provide most of gain. Further income can be derived by selling shares
Access	Easy/instant	Easy – bond is tradable	Easy – shares are tradable
Management cost	Minimal	Low	Higher

For most mid-worth customers, the first time they are faced with questions about risk may be when a financial adviser asks them, 'Do you take a high-, medium- or low-risk attitude to investment?' Most investors are never confronted with the true financial consequences of making this statement, so their answers may be meaningless. A customer who buys a lottery ticket probably has a better view of the risk involved in that particular decision. This might be expressed as 'I am almost certain not to win anything, and my chances of winning anything are pretty low, so I might as well regard it as a donation to charity (and to government) which brings me a bit of excitement.' An investor in an investment packaged to yield income withdrawal of 5 per cent might only be able to say, 'I know I am going to get 5 per cent tax-free return, but I have no idea how this will affect the long-term value of my investment, although I believe I shall get my cash back and more.'

For customers new to the world of investment, their attitude to risk cannot be properly captured by asking them to choose between products described as low, medium or high risk. For example, with-profit bonds would be described as low risk as bonuses once added can't be taken away and there is a 5 per cent annual tax-deferred withdrawal facility. However, these bonds are based on investments in fixed income, equities and sometimes in commercial property. According to a recent Institute of Actuaries report, they under-perform the market by an average 4.5 per cent pa. If this is not risk, what is?

The strengths and weaknesses of different approaches to investing are described in Table 36.3.

Volatility measures are sometimes produced using advanced statistics and published in the more specialist financial press – but this is probably too complex for the average mid-worth investor. For this reason CWM uses worst-case scenarios. This helps mid-worth investors establish the true level of risk they are prepared to tolerate, given their good reasons to err on the side of caution, by focusing on the maximum loss they would be prepared to sustain over particular period. For this reason, CWM illustrates the choice between different asset classes in terms of the worst return that they might sustain over a one-year or a consecutive two-year period (see Table 36.4). These are gross actual returns, ie not including fees or tax but gross of inflation. Note that for most people, the tax position would make the equity return relatively much better.

Figure 36.1 – a simple compound growth chart – illustrates how long-term investments are compromised by avoidance of risk. It shows what happens to an investment of $100

Table 36.3 Strengths and weaknesses of different investment approaches

	Packaged Products	**Trackers**	**Direct**	**Wealth management**
Positives	Diversification Consistency Professional management	Cost Diversification Risk control/ predictability	Transparency Advice Personalized Advisory service	Transparency Advice Choice Cost Diversification Professional management Consistency Upside potential Risk control Accountability
Negatives	Cost Transparency Accountability = poor performance No personalization No advice on structure	No upside vs benchmark transparency	Accountability	Limited personal interface No advisory service

Table 36.4 Market performance

Return	Money markets	Fixed interest	Equities
Worst 1 year 1983–99	+5%	-3%	-16%
Worst 2 consecutive years 1983–99	+6%	+5%	+3%
Long-term return over inflation	+2%	+3%	+8%

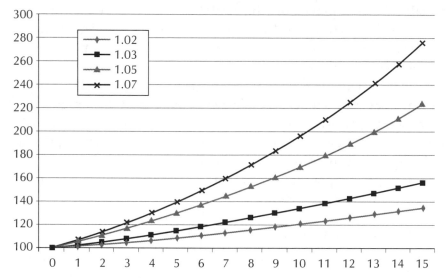

Figure 36.1 Compound growth of investment

over 15 years when invested in cash at 2 per cent net of inflation, bonds at 3 per cent, typical packaged investments at 5 per cent and equities at 7 per cent (these figures are with assumed commissions of 1 per cent for wealth management, 2.5 per cent for heavily packaged investments).

The next stage is to ask a customer what is the maximum loss that he or she is prepared to tolerate over any one- or two-year period and his or her required return over an agreed period (see Figure 36.2). This then leads directly to the construction of a desired portfolio in terms of the mix between equities, fixed interest and money markets.

Note that this chart shows that only the most conservative investor, with no tolerance of loss over any one-year period, would ever hold money market investments except those needed for short-term expenditure. The actual choice an investor makes should be determined by his or her likely capital requirements as determined by his or her budget.

Note too that the actual performance figures are based upon published benchmarks of performance. CWM takes the view that the individual investor's benchmark should be the one determined by the desired mix of investments. For example, investors who deliberately choose a portfolio that carries less risk of a short-term decline should not benchmark their

Linking risk (worst case return) to the types of investment

Worst-case returns between 1983 and 1999

Rolling *1 year* %	5	–3	–5	–6	–11	–16
Rolling *2 years* %	6	5	6	7	6	3

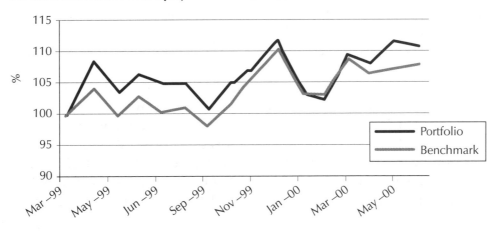

Figure 36.2 Tolerance of risk

CWM performance

Benchmark: FTSE 100, FTSE All Stocks and FT/S&P World ex UK

Portfolio: 25% Bond / 75% Equity *March '99–June'00*

Figure 36.3 Performance against benchmark

portfolios against an index that is 100 per cent equity. This is because they have agreed that they do not want to take the risks that making such a return would bring with it. For this reason, CWM provides its customers with their performance reported against the benchmark that is appropriate for the level of risk they have chosen (see Figure 36.3). This ensures that CWM's clients can see how well their investment performs against their chosen benchmark and review the effect of their chosen benchmark on their investment performance. (Please note that these returns have declined more recently.)

However, as CWM aims to serve a large number of customers efficiently, it would not be feasible to provide the high level of reporting to which CWM aspires if it also gave its customers completely free choice of their target portfolio. It has therefore decided to offer

Table 36.5 Model portfolios

Fund allocation		Historic benchmark annual returns 1983–99			
Fixed income %	Equity %	Worst 2 yr %	Best 2 yr %	Worst 10 yr %	Best 10 yr %
100	0	5.4	17.9	10.5	13.1
75	25	6.4	24.1	11.5	15.3
50	50	6.5	29.8	11.9	16.7
25	75	5.5	35.0	12.3	18.1
0	100	2.8	42.3	12.3	19.2

its UK clients five portfolio benchmarks, to give a broad choice of risks and return ratios. These are as shown in Table 36.5.

CWM selects the investments to match each of these, and holds them in client nominee accounts. The dividends from these investments are transferred to a high interest bank account provided by the Bank of Scotland. CWM also provides a tax return completion service to enable customers to keep their personal affairs simple by delegating their entire tax management to CWM.

The table of risks and returns assumes that the currency in which the assets are bought is the same as that in which the investor's likely future expenditures are denominated. The reason for this is that CWM believes that there is no point in a mid-worth investor taking unnecessary risks. However, although buying investments investing in other currencies has not historically increased returns much above those quoted in the table for any of the above classes of investment, it can reduce risk while maintaining the return. CWM has therefore concluded that for a UK investor, the non-UK equity proportion needs to be 20–50 per cent (currently 30 per cent).

Within each of these portfolios CWM decides which investments to make. However, as a relatively small though rapidly growing player, Close has an advantage, in that it is not so large that its own buying and selling of assets affects the market. The giant packaged investment firms do suffer from this disadvantage. As CWM grows it will add new portfolios with different risk/return profiles, eg high tech, to meet clients needs.

An efficient, transparent approach to wealth management has the following benefits:

- It allows CWM customers to understand very quickly the true nature of the decisions they are taking, and the consequences of these decisions for their financial lives.
- It allows CWM to manage customers very efficiently, thereby keeping down charges.
- It avoids the needs for high initial charges, so that even if the customer needs to extract cash earlier than was planned, the penalty will be very low.

- Lower continuing charges mean that the investment has a better chance of outper-forming the market, as with heavily packaged investments, high charges reduce the net return significantly.
- It avoids the situation in which high costs have been extracted in order to create apparent liquidity or lack of risk, eg as with unit trusts or with-profit bonds.

The costs to the customer of opting for a heavily packaged product are as follows:

- the initial charge for taking up the package;
- large spreads between bid and offer prices (the prices at which customers can buy more or sell units back);
- charges levied on the value of the fund;
- early cancellation penalties.

Charges are also hidden by burying them in small print. Customers may be misled by use of terms such as 'no explicit charges'.

However, an investor can invest directly without help, so avoiding all charges other than those involved in buying and selling shares. Why does this chapter not suggest that individuals do this? The answer to this is simple. Most mid-worth investors are unlikely to have the time or expertise to dedicate to the selection of investments and buying and selling them to match the target risk/return. Moreover, the transactions needed to maintain the desired portfolio may be small, and this may result in relatively high transaction fees as a proportion of the wealth to be managed, because most brokers charge a minimum level of commission. Finally, smaller investors are more likely to make decisions based on emotion, not adhering strictly to the ideas of efficient investment. They are therefore more likely to buy and sell at the wrong time. Missing just a few good days in the market can be disastrous for long-term performance.

The approach that CWM has developed is to:

- help the customer make the correct choice on risk and return;
- provide a cost-effective means of investing in a well-diversified portfolio;
- provide such high quality reporting on each individual's portfolio (which is held in a nominee account for them) that investors have as much control over their portfolios as if they were directly investing themselves, without incurring the costs and stress of so doing, for relatively low charges.

ASSESSING RISK

Investors do not get much help with assessing risk. This section explains the main technical measures and why simpler methods must be used to help customers understand risk.

The best help that seems to be available is from a company called RiskMetrics (see http://www.riskgrades.com/). RiskMetrics offers a service that helps investors calculate what they call the 'RiskGrade' of an investment. It does this by: 1) calculating how much variation there has been in an asset's price, weighted by the recency of the variation (ie later variations count for more than earlier variations); 2) comparing the asset's variability to the variability of a basket of global equities.

The ratio of these volatilities is called the RiskGrade. It can vary from 0, for cash, to values well over 1,000 for highly speculative investments. However, most mid-worth investors are unlikely to be able to make sense of this measure in terms of what it implies for their assets, for reasons cited earlier. Would a simpler statistical measure help?

Standard deviation is the most commonly used statistical measure of variability. It measures how widely the value of a variable varies from its average. This variability may be over time, as with the value of a given investment over time (time series variability). Or it may be of the dispersion from the mean of a group or sample at a particular moment in time (eg how investment returns of different stocks in one period vary from the average of all returns of those stocks), which we call a cross-section analysis. The simple standard deviation does not take account of how long ago variations took place. There is evidence that recency of a variation does influence likely future variation. For example, if a stock varied wildly for a year five years ago, and then stabilized, then its pattern of variability is not likely to be as great as a standard deviation unweighted for time would predict. However, while this is certainly true for individual stocks, and is therefore a relevant factor for investment management, it is not true for sectors or markets, so this issue does not need to be covered in detail by individual investors. For them the issue is the difference in variability between stocks and bonds, for example. The other difference is that RiskGrade is expressed as an index, with 100 being set for global equities. This enables relative variability to be easily understood by investors. For the mid-wealth customer, who is much less expert than the average US investor for whom RiskGrade is designed, it is easier still to understand risk in terms of how much could be lost over a one- or two-year period, ie the worst-case scenario.

Beta measures how much a stock moves with the general market. A Beta of 1 means that a stock moves exactly with the general market. A Beta of 1.5 means that on average a stock rises 1.5 per cent for a 1 per cent rise in the market, and falls 1.5 per cent with a 1 per cent fall in the market. Beta is therefore a measure of relative risk, not absolute risk. Once again, this is a complex point for individual investors to understand, and one that most mid-wealth individuals do not need to understand. But it tells investment managers how much a stock contributes to the risk of a portfolio.

These methods are not easy for any but the most sophisticated investor to understand. It is therefore not surprising that CWM opted for the idea of using tolerable minimum performance as described earlier in this chapter.

DEMYSTIFICATION – AND WHY HAVE WE HAD TO WAIT SO LONG?

Now that we have covered the essential simplicity of wealth management for mid-worth customers, it is time to return to one of the central questions of this chapter: 'Have most UK mid-worth customers become so confused by what is on offer that they have managed to follow an investment policy which is deeply destructive of their own long-term value?'

The answer to this question is that the UK financial services industry is, like any other industry, self-maintaining. That is to say, so long as customers go on buying from it when it supplies in a certain way, they will go on buying from it! This 'stable state' situation is of course encouraged by companies that benchmark against each other rather than against the benchmark of what customers could have achieved if they had invested in their own best interests.

The UK packaged financial services industry achieves this by mystifying customers. It does this by:

- confusing customers into thinking that low risk investment can only be achieved by packaging and 'guarantees of returns', many of which are not real;
- combining insurance and investment, so that what the customer gets is effectively expensively provided insurance, if measured in terms of the sacrifice in return paid to get the insurance;
- using strategies to create smoothing of returns, which actually are not required by customers because they hold investments for much longer periods, so that unsmoothed investment combined with careful disposal could yield a much higher return;
- confusing income yields with the potential to provide money over the long term, which can be achieved simply by disposal of shares.

The reasons for this mystification are very simple. They are: 1) to hide the performance of investments such as with-profit bonds, which in the long term have performed much worse than unpackaged investments; 2) to hide the process of destruction of customer value that is created by very expensive sales and service channels, supported by poor systems and high commissions.

If this story of poor performance is successfully hidden, then many well-paid people in the financial services industry will continue to receive their large salaries and remuneration packages. Put simply, mystification costs the customer money, in serious amounts. Yet, far from mystification withdrawing in the face of consumer challenges, it has if anything intensified. Successive UK governments have devised new ways of encouraging consumers to commit to packaged investments (eg ISAs), and also biasing taxation in favour of packaged investments (eg capital gains taxation only paid when a customer withdraws a packaged investment). Let us have a look at the reasons for this.

'Mystification' was a term that first came into common use in the 1960s. It referred mainly to how professionals of all kinds – doctors, teachers, lawyers and, yes, university lecturers – developed an approach to managing their customers (clients, patients, students) in which the 'expert' used a special and hard-to-understand vocabulary to describe situations. This made it impossible for customers to understand what was supposedly being done to benefit them. A famous book, *Deschooling Society*, was written by Ivan Illich, in an attempt to get society to reject this 'rule by experts'. Fortunately, over the years, throughout the Western world, the extent to which experts are allowed to use their expertise to claim the right to manage customers in particular ways has declined, although in the UK we are still victims of this in certain areas. Of course, we invite this victimization by over-respectful behaviour towards these professions. It is particularly dangerous where our own well-being is concerned, and where performance measurement is not public (bringing bad practice to account). Not surprisingly, it is in healthcare where the UK customer suffers particularly badly from lack of public performance reporting, and politicians have partly conspired in this (political parties and doctors have much in common!). This contrasts strongly with the United States, where choice of specialist by the customer is often determined only after inspecting the doctor's performance record. However, as we shall see, past performance is only useful as an indicator if you know what benchmark performance should be. Putting it another way, you can't expect a brilliant doctor to reduce lung cancer among heavy smokers to the level experienced by non-smokers. His performance can only be judged according to whether *his* heavily smoking patients have a better survival rate than all heavily smoking patients.

Interestingly, the US commitment to performance reporting in health is mirrored by a similar commitment in financial reporting. Avoiding damage to health and to wealth can involve similar solutions. While UK managers often criticize the quarterly reporting on US companies, it is not hard to see why the strong US commitment to performance produces better returns in stock markets and less mystification in financial services products. In the UK, we train our financial services advisers to become expert in complicated packaged products, and suggest that advisers cannot do their job properly without being able to manage the complicated processes and forms required. In the USA, advisers focus more on performance and risk, usually with portfolios that are lightly packaged, ie the underlying assets visible to the client.

Interestingly, in the UK it is the generation that revolted against mystification in the 1960s that has now come up most sharply against financial services mystification as they approach retirement. The mystification is being compounded for those who first require wealth management as they approach retirement by employer laxity in recommending 'classic' IFAs. Employers should ethically at least consider recommending the wealth management option to their employees, rather than driving them into the hands of an industry that will give them poor value for money over the long term. However, it seems that corporate customers have also been mystified, perhaps because the human resource directors who make these recommendations have so many other priorities that they are happy to believe that they are doing the right thing, especially if it means just doing what everybody else does.

THE CONCEPTUAL BASIS OF THE CWM PROPOSITION

CWM's proposition is so simple and radical that it can be hard for customers – and the media – to appreciate, because it goes counter to much of what is currently written and broadcast about investment. The proposition can be summarized as a series of simple statements. Each one of these seems very sensible and backed strongly by evidence. When they are put together, the resulting argument is compelling. Here are the statements. They are grouped into a number of areas, as follows:

- How the game has changed.
- But the investor's interest has stayed the same.
- The roles of client advisers and investment managers are very different.
- The role of the client is even more important.
- The implications for the mid-worth investor are clear.

How the game has changed

- Western stock markets are now dominated by big institutions, with typically around 80% of stocks owned by them, and most trading dominated by them.
- The market and the institutions are therefore no longer separate – the institutions are the market.
- To help them make the 'right' decisions, the institutions employ large numbers of highly qualified, intelligent and experienced stock analysts.
- Around them has grown an enormous information-provision industry so the quality of information they have available to assess companies is very good.
- With so many experts and such good information, it is much harder to 'beat the market' than it used to be, and this is shown particularly well in the performance of funds over the longer period – most funds do not outperform the relevant benchmark.

- In addition, there is the possibility that analysts who recommend stocks do not do so in an unbiased manner. If they downgrade their stock recommendation, they may be deprived of information by the company. If the analyst is attached to a company with broad corporate finance interests, their company may not get business from the company in question. The rarity with which analysts produce negative recommendations (less than 1% of recommendations according to a US survey) supports this point (for more on this, see Charles Batchelor, Analysts' reports: to be taken with a large pinch of salt, *Financial Times*, Wednesday 26 July 2000, p 24).

- There are conventionally four ways in which it is supposed to be possible to beat the market – timing of purchases, selection of specific stocks that seem likely to beat the market, portfolio strategy (selecting particular types of stocks that seem likely to produce better value than others), or developing an investment philosophy or specialization that is supposed to give greater insight than others have.

- Past performance is in general no guide to future performance, for funds or for individual shares. Indeed, it can be argued that as the values of shares and funds tend to fluctuate randomly around the trend for their reference group (sector, risk category, etc), past performance is positively misleading.

- This convention has been stimulated by the financial media, whose audience is boosted by continuing to generate excitement about short-term trends of markets and stocks, despite the fact that these have little effect on longer-term returns.

- None of these four ways works in the long run, and many of these approaches work for some and not for others, in an unpredictable way, indicating that the returns to the approach are randomly distributed.

- Some of these approaches seem to produce higher returns than 'the market' in the long run, but this is nearly always because they have a different risk profile (eg high-tech stocks).

- Focus on short-term news can generate unstable investment behaviour (witness the recent boom and slump in Internet stocks) and, it can be argued, risks diverting economic activity into areas where news affects value, rather than where value is news.

- This short-term focus also draws the financial services industry's resources into services that are supposed to help investors 'beat the market'. As identified above, this is not possible overall. But a consequence of this is that investors as a group pay more for the investing process, and therefore get less value in the long run. This trend is very strong in the UK, but weaker in the USA, where the preference for direct investment is much higher, and there is better understanding of risk. The wealth management approach as described in this chapter will take the UK more in the direction of the USA, where it is clear that industry benefits from more direct investment. It can also be argued that the US economy benefits in the long run from this more mature approach to wealth management, even if sometimes it takes leave of its senses!

- Stock investment has therefore turned from a winner's game, in which winners beat the market by excellent decisions, to a loser's game, in which failure to keep up with the market is caused by bad decisions.

The investor's interest has stayed the same

The investor is still interested in the same things as always, to make the best return that is compatible with the period for which the investment is to be made and the degree of risk that the investor is prepared to accept:

- The acceptable degree of risk is not just determined by the period, but also by the investor's ability to accept the falls in value associated with different degrees of risk.
- Investors, however, tend to be impatient, and in particular react wrongly to short-term falls in values by, where possible, putting pressure to sell or reduce risk. Support for this comes from positions taken in the current debate on pension transparency stimulated by Paul Myners' inquiry into pension fund management.
- It has been said that greater transparency might lead to poorer quality decisions, and that trustees who might become excessively influenced by what members might think might tend to become more conservative in their decisions and therefore take less risk than needed to ensure the long-term health of their scheme (see William Hutchings, Pension funds fight disclosure, *Financial News*, 24–30 July 2000, p 10). However, surely the response to this is that scheme members – whether companies or individuals – need to understand the relationship between risk and return, and how optimal strategy is affected by the period until retirement. In fact, it is arguable that even with members having little awareness of what goes on in a fund, fund managers are overly conservative. This is because in many cases liabilities, ie pensions and lump sums, can be paid for out of current contributions, particularly for the foreseeable future, as individuals increase their contributions to pay for a future in which the state will support them less.

THE ROLES OF ADVISERS AND INVESTMENT MANAGERS

- The role of the adviser is to work with the client to identify clearly both the level of risk that the client is prepared to accept and the right time horizon.
- This should be based on realistic budgeting and contingencies.
- This information should then be translated into a return/risk profile that is achievable given the historic performance of markets.
- The required risk/return profile is then specified as a benchmark to the investment manager.

- The role of the investment manager is to deliver the client's return/risk profile over the specified period. This is best measured by performance against the agreed benchmark.
- Assessing investment managers by general performance benchmarks is worse than useless, as this is not based upon what the investment manager is hired to do – ie manage returns and risk for individuals.
- The investment manager will best be able to meet the benchmark by selecting stocks according to their individual risk/return profiles to build a portfolio of stocks that is most likely to match the benchmark, not by trying to beat the benchmark. This is also a special, information-supported activity, but with a different objective from 'picking winners'.

The role of the client

- This is no longer to select the world's best investment manager, as this is a fruitless exercise. Even the investment manager with an excellent record in the past is unlikely to maintain it in the future, as the evidence shows.
- The role of the client is to keep the required risk/return profile under review at regular intervals, and only to change portfolio objectives when this profile changes.
- If the client puts pressure on the investment manager to improve performance, performance is likely to get worse, not better. For example, if stock prices have fallen, the client may put pressure to reduce risk, making it less likely that the portfolio will benefit fully from recovery, while if stock prices have risen, the client may suggest more risk, which increases the likelihood that the portfolio will fall.

Implications for the mid-worth investor

- The mid-worth investor does not have enormous sums to invest, and therefore must use cost-effective channels to place the investment.
- This investor also does not necessarily have access to the information or skills required to pick the stocks to achieve the right mix of risk and return.
- The amount of money available to invest does not usually allow the customer to cost-effectively purchase individual stocks which, put together, match the portfolio requirements. This is changing with Web-based services, but still the commission charged on smaller transactions will be relatively high.
- This client often has clearly defined needs over the foreseeable future, which can be expressed in terms of a required risk and return.
- However, if a client buys a packaged product, entry and exit fees are likely to be high. This client is likely to be much better served by a direct investing approach.

- For this to work, the client must be able to select from a broad range of target risk / return profiles.
- This is subject to the conditions that the client first receives the education necessary to ensure he or she understands why this approach is best for him or her, and then that the help is cost-effective, with small initial commission and recurring charges, plus high quality information about performance against an agreed benchmark which helps the customer avoid making the wrong decisions (his or her own loser's game).
- With pure Web-based investments, without an adviser to help clients stick to their required risk / return profile, overall performance could be worse over the longer run because the client loses at the loser's game. It is therefore important for clients not to confuse simplicity of access and ease of transaction with delivery of the long-term value, which comes from not panicking, good diversification and low costs. This is the winner's game. A Web site that allows investors to happily destroy their own value just allows them to lose faster at the loser's game.
- In this situation, the role of regular, clear reporting is to confirm with the client that investment performance is matching the agreed benchmark. This helps the client avoid panicking if the current value of the investment falls, even though its prospects over the term as agreed by the adviser remain good. This makes it much easier for the client to take the longer-term perspective that enables maximization of returns.

SIMPLIFYING WEALTH MANAGEMENT

The aim of this part of the chapter is:

- to explain why CWM came into existence, and provide a profile of CWM – the company and its people;
- to assess CWM in terms of how it manages its customers, using QCi's CMAT to compare CWM both with other financial services companies and with other organizations in more general markets, recognizing that as some aspects of CWM's approach are still being developed, this picture will not be perfect;
- to thereby help all those involved in the world of investment to understand what it takes to combine excellent service to customers while delivering good investment returns.

Is it possible to so simplify the investment process while ensuring a good long-term return? This was the belief of Close Brothers in setting up CWM. It follows what I have called the 'top vanilla' principles of customer management. This involves providing the best, most cost-effective service to all customers in the target market.[3] The use of the term 'vanilla' comes indirectly from the world of ice-cream, via the use of the term to describe the 'vanilla product', the standard product which was at the base of every product line. The top vanilla argument reverses this, with the idea that all customers in the target market should get excellent, cost-effective service.

The top vanilla approach was first demonstrated in the UK in 1985 in the motor insurance market by Direct Line. Faced with an expensive distribution channel that added little value and forced a complex process upon customers, Direct Line simplified the process quite dramatically, and in doing so gave a much better deal to customers in its target market, at a much better price. Today's best example of top vanilla is probably easyJet, a company that has dramatically simplified and cheapened airline travel for customers who do not want all the frills that airlines have traditionally foisted upon them. Both of these companies achieved their success by combining clarity of strategy and business vision with a strong commitment to process and systems innovation. They both avoided risk by using established technology that was known to work, but in innovative ways that accelerated and simplified marketing and customer service to reduce the need for manual intervention because the proposition was so clear.

CWM aims to make the same sort of difference to mid-worth customers that Direct Line and easyJet made to their markets. However, the difference is that the decisions made by mid-worth investors seem to be more complex, and have much greater longer-term significance than those taken by customers of Direct Line or easyJet. But the corporate values are the same – making best value available combined with, not instead of, good customer service. The principle is also the same – minimum intervention between the customer and the source of value. Of course, investors who are very experienced and with greater levels of wealth than mid-worth individuals may do better buying shares directly. The proposition that CWM has designed and is implementing is specifically aimed at those who want best value but don't know how to get it. In order to allow customers to get best value, as each customer has a particular risk/return requirement, CWM has had to adopt some of the principles of mass-customization. This requires that customers' investments are assigned to an individual portfolio, which is then managed by the smartest systems and reporting so that customers get a better service than if they were managed manually.

In order to understand why CWM decided to offer this service to investors, one needs to understand their backgrounds and experience. They have all come from the same financial services industry whose practices they seek to change. They have seen the enormous costs associated with the marketing and selling of packaged products, with administering the complex outcomes, and also with using investment managers whose focus is on 'beating the market' rather than executing an agreed risk/return strategy. They have witnessed how the packaged financial services industry works through its bias towards insurance-based investments with complex and opaque structures, wrapped around with arcane and subjective language used to promote their own ends.

For this reason, CWM's managers decided to use their expertise to create a different option. However, this expertise means nothing unless it is transformed into excellent customer service and investment performance that meets client risk / return objectives. The strength of their commitment to the challenge, and the passion they feel for their business, is hard to convey in print. Their passion for change, and their commitment to it, stems from their knowledge that the poor returns that investors get are not just a consequence of strong marketing by some big financial services businesses. It is that these businesses are working to a business model that is destructive of customer value. That is why the propositions of companies such as Virgin Direct are so misleading for customers. The products that Virgin Direct sells are typical packaged products, supplied by a typical package provider, AMP (Australian Mutual Provident). Virgin Direct may have done a good job trying to simplify the un-simplifiable, but its business model is just that of another intermediary. Just putting Direct in the title does not make the dealing direct, as it is not in the case of Virgin. Indeed, the use of Direct, presumably referring to direct marketing methods, can be misleading. The Virgin business model is usually to set up a business with a partner, to exploit the Virgin brand, and then sell the business to the partner concerned. To make that business profitable, the partner then has to raise prices. Simplicity of access and ease of purchasing can, as I have already mentioned, make it easier for customers to destroy their own value. This kind of simplification actually works not by simplifying the investment, but just by simplifying the sale. The rest is simplified by not mentioning it!

The CWM senior management team is still working on many aspects of the CWM vision – the company was only launched in June 1999. Let us examine some aspects of that vision in more detail.

The vision – close to senior management's hearts

CWM's vision of a top vanilla approach, combined with mass-customization to give excellent personalized service, drives the way that systems and processes are set-up at CWM. With a passion for being with customers – both corporate and private, CWM senior management are often to be found at CWM's sales seminars explaining the essential simplicity of the approach, and how it achieves cost-effective results for the customer. They also play a key role in working with corporate clients, explaining CWM's strongly ethical, pro-customer approach, and the duty of the employer to ensure that their employees are well served, particularly as they approach retirement.

Marketing

The CWM commitment to customer value meant that the marketing director was not given a large marketing budget to throw at the problem of making enough potential clients aware of the CWM proposition and then to give it the required attention. Close Brothers set up CWM on the basis that it would have to stand on its own two feet, not by having access to the Close Brothers customer base, although there have been some referrals from this source. CWM's strategy has been to work with corporate clients, to help them assist their retiring staff, while pursuing a very focused approach to attracting individual clients, using classic direct mail and seminar techniques. Because CWM rejects the high commissions involved, CWM cannot go through IFAs. Instead, therefore, CWM uses a combination of national and local public relations work, direct mail, seminars and account management to build its client base.

The target market is of course broad, and customers are new to it only once. Then typically they become clients of IFAs. The better IFAs retain a strong hold on their clients. However, many clients become 'orphaned'. This means they receive no active servicing by the IFA. This may be because the IFA loses interest. 'Sell and run' is not uncommon practice, as if the first sale absorbs most of the client's spare cash and future spare cash flow, there is not much prospect of making more commission. Even if the client cancels, the bulk of the commission will still be paid, as set-up charges paid by clients are not refundable. Or it may be because the client moves.

The marketing process therefore has two main parts to it. The first is public relations. The launch of CWM was by far the most successful element of this. Coverage in a quality weekend paper resulted in a very large number of leads, a high appointments to leads ratio, and a high conversion ratio of appointments to signing up (obviously the figures are commercially confidential). In parallel to this process is the seminar programme. This focuses on inviting the client to a seminar, where the CWM approach is explained. Investment consultants attend the seminars to handle client questions, although senior management are often present. There are currently only eight investment consultants, as once again CWM's commitment to cost-effectiveness implies using a few investment consultants cost-effectively across the entire country.

The economics of this process are simple. Once a seminar venue has been selected, a carefully targeted mailing of around 9,000 produces enough response to run a seminar, with around 80 per cent of those responding actually attending, and with a good conversion rate (again confidential) from attendance to appointment. The conversion rate from appointments to signing up is high, and is often as high as 100 per cent, but averages about 40 per cent. This process is the most cost-effective in terms of cost per client, and was beaten only by the PR work at launch. Continuing PR results in a slightly higher cost per client acquired. For this reason, CWM has decided that seminars will be the main client acquisition process, with some PR work.

This commitment to cost-effective client acquisition is critical if CWM is to maintain its low-cost approach to wealth management for mid-worth clients. It also ensures that investment consultants and account managers spend the time with clients that is appropriate to their needs, rather than using sales pressure and dubious arguments to persuade clients to part with money. It also ensures that prospects who are not appropriate do not become customers and cancel early. This creates customer dissatisfaction and also increases costs.

The marketing department is responsible for specifying how the CWM Web site works. The first stage of development here has been to:

- display the CWM's offer and provide information on its people;
- give information and guidance on investing;
- provide market commentaries;
- allow e-mail response;
- give clients secure access to standard investment portfolio reports.

In future, it will provide:

- online enrolment, trading and funds transfer;
- personalized reporting;
- comparison with competitors' performance and charging;
- delayed stock price information from external links;
- access to market returns database and cash flow analysis model.

Pre-retirement planning

Pre-retirement planning seminars are an important part of the process of explaining to employees what their options are and how to handle them. These seminars, when run by large companies, often attract as high a proportion as 95 per cent of eligible employees, indicating the level of uncertainty felt about the financial implications of retirement. If these employees are to make the most of the finance available to them, they really do need to understand the importance of budgeting and of how decisions about the type of investment they make can have an enormous effect over the 20 or more years that they have left. This is almost as long a period as some of them will have been contributing to pension funds. As some of them will be retiring earlier than expected, with less State help, even if the employer tops up their fund, it will still need to be managed optimally if they are to enjoy their retirement fully.

Curiously, although most employers in this situation do not want to be seen to be recommending a particular course of action, their very choice of adviser usually has an implicit bias to heavily packaged investments. This may be due to the same misunderstandings about risk and return that exist with employees. Many employers use the same financial adviser that advises them on pension plans, and only a few use a panel of companies, with formal reviews. Some employers seem to make the recommendation on a random basis. It seems that few seriously check for bias in recommendations. Although CWM's research indicates that employers aim to avoid sales pitches and biases towards certain asset classes, they themselves do not know how to check for this, and may confuse lack of bias in the sense that no particular packaged provider is favoured, with overall lack of bias.

Investment management

Senior management's commitment to a realistic investment strategy has driven CWM's approach to investment. This is based upon: 1) determining the individual investor's attitude to risk and return; 2) developing a benchmarked approach to strategy and reporting, so that the investor could set and stick to a strategy without being deterred by short-term market movements.

Initially, the focus has been on the markets that UK investors need in order to meet their basic risk/return needs – UK stocks and bonds. For, as this chapter has made clear, the key requirement is the ability to build a portfolio which accurately reflects the risk and return needs of clients. If other investments are required (as they are), they can be dealt with by outsourcing, eg technology funds, overseas funds.

CWM's senior management believes that the institutional fund market has peaked, and a new generation of companies such as CWM will start to gain share at the expense of old-style fund management, simply because of the poor value that the latter offer. In many cases, investment consultants develop their own views about individual stocks and implement these inconsistently with their various clients – often on the basis that the clients who make the most noise get the most attention, even if this is not appropriate. Today, CWM's investment strategy is based on the idea of giving excellent and appropriate value to all clients, following modern ideas of risk management.

As much as possible of the CWM process is automated, from share dealing to client management, and in particular the buying and selling of shares to match them to individual client's portfolio needs. This allows the investment management team to focus on ensuring that the right stocks are selected to meet client strategic needs, and ensuring that the team shares knowledge.

Account management

CWM's director of account management has a team of six managers and support staff. CWM believes that in most businesses clients leave because of absent or poor communication. For this, the critical period is the first 3–6 months. This is the period after the client has joined CWM. The investment consultant has done the adviser's job of sitting down with the client, helping the client set time-frames and budget within them, identifying the right risk/return profile, and managing the client's funds securely into CWM's care. This may include existing packaged investments which client and consultant agree should not be touched – CWM 'babysits' these at no charge. Individual direct investments – stocks and bonds – can also be warehoused in a similar way. Both of these are important because reporting on the value of the client's portfolio means that valuations of all investments must be obtained by CWM.

Once the client is properly set up, the account management process can take over. This ensures that the client gets high quality reporting on their individual portfolio, and other information as required, eg newsletters. The investment consultant is brought in as appropriate, eg when there is a need to re-budget or re-diagnose risk/return requirements.

A client has the right to expect the level of service that CWM provides, namely:

- advice, information, and help in making decisions;
- high quality of customer service;
- a clear statement of their charges, their competitiveness and impact upon returns;
- full evidence of performance – whether in terms of reports or customer references, closely linked to agreed benchmarks;
- performance reviews;
- access to other financial services – tax, wills, pensions, trusts and mortgages;
- control – including baby-sitting and personal holdings;
- security – investments are held in nominee accounts.

A requirement that CWM will be meeting is the demand for budgeting tools.

A key part of the account management process is the investment seminar for existing clients. CWM believes that too many companies ignore their existing clients' needs for face-to-face contact in groups, where they like to discuss investments and also their experience of being managed by the wealth management company.

CWM very rarely loses customers. But when it does, a critical part of the process is the exit interview with senior management. This helps CWM understand where it is not meeting client expectations.

CWM's account management work is supported by a system based on Lotus PrimeTime. The data is currently being restructured to allow more data about client contacts to be kept. The customer is of course the family, not just the individual, and the database allows a full set of data to be kept about the family. As CWM's Web reporting is developed, this will free up some account management time that was dedicated to routine reporting, and this time can be allocated to ensuring that new customers are managed well as the business grows.

The success of the proposition is not only demonstrated by the initially very low attrition rate, but also by the good proportion of referral business (between 10 and 40 per cent depending on the consultant – this figure is rising).

IT

CWM's objective is to have everything processed in real time – an objective that is common to most top vanilla companies. In order to do this, CWM has focused on building a strongly business-oriented IT team, many of whom have backgrounds in accounting rather than IT. Their job is to integrate a number of best-of-breed systems to provide an excellent investment and customer management process. In addition, CWM insists that all of its staff are or become IT-literate, so that they are able to use the best systems for managing customers. Training is provided to ensure this.

Needless to say, high quality client reporting is an essential element in strategy, and this will eventually be via the Web where the client wishes. Seamless banking integration is also part of the plan, as client monies generally pass into and out of the high interest check account operated for CWM by the Bank of Scotland. The client management database is being worked on. At the moment, with a relatively small client base, the emphasis here is on computer/telephone integration. CWM is currently evaluating its options for a client management database to serve as a central database for its marketing and client management activities.

Critical functions are deemed to be:

- effective contact and follow-up management for prospective clients;
- contact management for existing clients;
- client information storage;
- client reporting management;
- document management;
- integration with portfolio management system;
- integration with the CWM telephone system.

It is proposed that all client documents currently held on file will eventually be transferred to the client database. All new clients will be set up on the system as they are signed up.

ASSESSING THE QUALITY OF CWM'S APPROACH TO CUSTOMER MANAGEMENT

QCi's CMAT measures the quality of customer management. It is described fully in Chapter 3.

How CWM scores

A mini-assessment of CWM was carried out. This was based upon a subset of 60 questions out of the full 260-question set – those questions that we have found to be most important in assessing a company's customer management capability. Table 36.6 shows the results.

Table 36.6 CWM CMAT scores

	Close
Analysis and planning	55
The proposition	77
People and organization	65
Information and technology	50
Process management	22
Customer management activity	40
Measuring the effect	64
The customer experience*	3
Average (rounded)	**47**

*This 3 means that Close gets no structured feedback from its customers on their experience – it does not mean the experience is bad. It can be worded as 'Understanding the customer experience'.

CWM was the second equal highest overall scoring financial services company (only beaten by a mutual bank), and the fourth equal highest of all companies. By category, the performance was not surprising. It showed the great strength and simplicity of the proposition and the involvement of people in delivering it. I expect that if we had analysed Direct Line in 1985 we would have had a similar result. The analysis and planning strength comes from the fact that the success of the company is acutely linked to cost-effective customer acquisition. Its business plan is directly translated into cost-effective customer acquisition targets. Indeed, when I asked the marketing director what the target number of new customers for 2000 was, he replied immediately with the number.

On the other hand, we identified two areas of weakness which are typical of a new company. The first is processes. We identified a number of areas where customer management processes will need to be greatly strengthened as the customer base grows. Today, the commitment and quality of staff make up for lack of process. Finally, the customer experience measurement, which focuses on the extent to which the company formally measures its customer experience through research, benchmarking, formal processes of becoming the company's customers, and the like, was also weak. This will need to be much strengthened as the company grows. In our experience, just as CWM has done, new companies often research their initial proposition to customers very carefully and build high quality delivery into their systems and processes. This means that the customer experience for the first few years is very good. However, as the company matures and grows, and with it the customer base, its mechanisms for understanding the customer experience must be strengthened, as it is at this stage that the strong initial focused offer and its delivery through a committed small team is at risk from complacency and bureaucracy. Maintaining the customer focus becomes key, and a high quality process for understanding the customer experience is an essential enabler of this continued focus.

Consequences for customers

These are in a way very simple. CWM offers a very focused proposition, so a new customer can expect to get a clear explanation of what the proposition is. The CWM system is designed to help a customer transfer assets smoothly into CWM management, and then to ensure that the customer gets regular reports on the state of those assets. The proposition is relatively sophisticated for most mid-worth individuals, so much effort has been devoted to explaining it in everyday terms.

Once the customer has been assigned to the CWM function, the strong focus on people at CWM will ensure a high level of customer care. As the CWM customer base grows, more formalization will need to be introduced into customer management processes, otherwise there will be a risk of inconsistency of treatment. This will, in any case, be necessary as CWM develops new ways of allowing its customers to be managed and manage themselves over the Web. However, it will have to ensure that this helps keep the customer to the proposition that he or she has bought, ie performance that is appropriate given the risk/return choice.

CONCLUSION

CWM is one of a new breed of companies dedicated to giving much better value to mid-worth investors with less experience and/or time. It offers a focused proposition to a focused target market – but one that is fairly large. Its success will be determined by its ability to explain to large numbers of investors that they need to take their understanding of risk and return slightly beyond the confused presentation offered by packaged investment companies. The early signs are that it is succeeding.

Notes

[1] The *Financial Times* Supplement on Private Banking (7 July 2000, p IV) defines high net worth individuals as those having liquid assets of more than $1 million. There are 2.2 million of them in Europe

[2] See Bethany McLean (2000) *Mutual Funds*, May, pp 53–56 for more on this

[3] Stone, M, Woodcock, N, Foss, B and Machtynger, L (1998) Segment or succeed – the new 'top vanilla' culture in financial services marketing, *Journal of Financial Services Marketing*, **2** (2), pp 107–21

Part 10

Strategic implications

37

Competitive advantage analysis

Kevin La Croix and Bryan Foss

BEATING THE OTHERS

An important aspect of developing an holistic view (mentioned in Chapter 40) is identifying and understanding the positive differences in a financial services organization that enable it to meet or exceed competitors' capabilities, industry norms or 'best of breed' organizations. In the world of management consulting, there is a strong bias towards fixing what is wrong in a company or industry. Business transformation, total quality management, process re-engineering and economic value add are all well known and tested corrective approaches used to uncover and 'fix' problems in an organization. These methods often start by identifying the negative differences in the enterprise. However, unless the enterprise is on the verge of complete failure, there are also positive differences that must be recognized, protected and developed.

Below, we focus on identifying and understanding those positive differences. We discuss an approach (competitive advantage analysis) to preserving what is right in a financial services enterprise, describing a five-step method that can be used to analyse the positive elements of a business and to place them in a competitive advantage framework that can be used to evaluate long-term business strategies. A final, sixth step should also be taken to identify which of the remaining negative differences should be eliminated by using an appropriate corrective approach.

HOW COMPETITIVE ADVANTAGE ANALYSIS WORKS

Differentiation has become one of the magic formulae of modern business management. Companies are advised to set themselves apart from the pack and find unique elements within their business model – elements that competitors cannot or will not copy. Being different can be valuable. It can also be costly, embarrassing and lonely. If the objective of the business is to capture more market share and increase profits and returns to the shareholder, there is little value in being different if the difference does not result in a competitive advantage.

When Eddy Shah launched *Today* newspaper in March 1986, he created a paper with a distinct difference. The prominent and frequent use of colour photographs made the paper stand out from the other 'red tops'. However, the other tabloids simply invested in colour printing themselves and wooed their readers back, as there were no other significant difference in any of the tabloids any more. *Today* newspaper (from 1987 part of the Murdoch stables) ceased publication in 1995, the first British newspaper to cease printing in nearly a quarter of a century. Differentiation must be maintained to have any value.

Retailers and some financial service companies now have processes in place to identify new product or service differentiation from their competitors, and to replicate this in a very short time, even days. This approach is developed with the belief that no differentiation is really sustainable, and that using common suppliers (in retail) and very flexible products (in financial services), almost any differentiated offer can be replicated very quickly. As a key part of retention of differentiation, at least one UK financial services company has maintained a high level of secrecy of its internal processes through speaking and sharing only in very limited ways at industry conferences and contracting with suppliers to maintain confidences for substantial periods.

A valuable differentiator provides competitive advantage if the marketplace values it and is willing to pay in terms of money, loyalty or forgiveness; or, it enables the company to do something that is valued by the marketplace. This advantage may be limited or sustainable for some longer period, depending on ease of replication by others.

The successful enterprise can be identified by all three of the measures of 'payment':

- It can price its goods and services at a profit and still attract sufficient customers to meets its market share objectives.
- It can market and sell to its chosen customer segments efficiently because they are loyal to its brand.
- When the inevitable mistake occurs, its customers will give the successful enterprise an opportunity to remedy the error.
- Ultimately, such an organization will develop advocates – customers who recommend the company to the people they care about. These customers become an extended

marketing and sales team and although their value is difficult to measure in real terms, the impact can be enormous.

Competitive advantages may be significant or small. They can affect both the perception of the enterprise and the measurable results achieved. Understanding their characteristics and durability can, in itself, be a significant competitive advantage for an enterprise.

COMPETITIVE ADVANTAGE ANALYSIS – THE FIVE-STEP METHOD

The method is summarized below:

1. Identify the characteristics that make an enterprise different from its competitors.
2. Determine which differences provide competitive advantage to the enterprise.
3. Rank the advantages according to their contribution to success.
4. Analyse the characteristics of the competitive advantages.
5. Determine the advantage horizon of the enterprise.

Protecting and extending what is right with a business is as critical to future success as improving on those capabilities that do not meet a competitor's abilities.

STEP 1: DIFFERENCES ARE NEITHER GOOD NOR BAD – THEY ARE JUST DIFFERENCES

Every enterprise has characteristics that distinguish it from its competitors. These differences may be trivial or fundamental. They may be valuable or destructive. They may also lose their value over decades – or overnight, and, until they are identified, they cannot be managed.

By the late 1980s IBM had developed differences from its competitors across the whole range of company activity. 'Big Blue' was very, very big. In terms of number of employees, product and service range, geographic reach, market penetration, and capitalization, IBM was different to any of its competitors. Its unique abilities in developing intellectual capital were proven by its Nobel laureate staff members and unique portfolio of patents. Perhaps, most different of all, IBM had a unique organizational culture. By 1990, a 'federation of businesses' was envisioned by IBM – a corporate 'family of nations' that would continue to dominate the information technology industry.

Although some of these differences were valuable and some were trivial, many of them had become costly and irrelevant to the marketplace. Competitors copied some of IBM's differences and developed their own unique ones. By 1990, many of IBM's differences had lost their value to the market IBM operated in. Over the next several years, the company bathed in billions of dollars of red ink and, painfully, started to reinvent itself. The reinvention is not yet complete, but its objective is clear and others are now starting to follow the same route of reinvention. New differences are needed and their only value lies in the value that IBM's chosen markets place in them. If IBM's new differences do not provide competitive advantage, the reinvention process will fail.

In the same way, successful financial services companies are considering the differentiation that can be gained by their existing competencies and customer base, developing strategies which provide a unique exploitation of this combination of capabilities, market and asset base. Unfortunately, too many consultants offer a similar vision and strategy to each individual financial services company. In the event, this process proves to be inappropriate for most of them, making their planned journey impractical to achieve. In comparison, a well-grounded approach to the development of competitive advantage (eg the CMAT approach as shown in Chapter 3) provides a development route that is both appropriate to provide substantial differentiation, and also achievable by the specific company.

In any enterprise, the following question should be asked: In what ways are we different from our competitors? The differences may be tangible and measurable or perceptual and ill defined. Whatever the nature of the differences, the first step in understanding the strengths of an enterprise is to identify them.

Results of Step 1: A defined list of significant differences from the competition without regard to their positive or negative qualities, based on a realistic and verifiable assessment of the company's capabilities and customer base.

STEP 2: FROM MANY DIFFERENCES A FEW ADVANTAGES MAY BE BORN

Not all differences are created equal. Some are more critical to business success than others, while some are easier or more difficult to achieve and/or sustain. In all cases, it is likely that an enterprise will not derive a large number of true competitive advantages from its differences. There may be many differences between one enterprise and its competitors. Management may view these differences as benefits; however, if they do not deliver or enable market value, they should not be considered as advantages.

Examples of basic differences between financial services companies, which may or may not result in advantage, can include the size and scope of a company, the variety of channel and product mix, brand strength, pricing policies, etc.

A list of differences that could be observed in a specific financial services enterprise might include the following:

- We can introduce a new product faster than the industry average.
- Our executive compensation scheme is the lowest (or highest) among peer enterprises.
- We have a superior price/earnings ratio.
- We have the most effective distribution network (niche or integrated).
- Our employee productivity is well below (or above) competitive standards.
- Our CEO is the most visionary executive in the business.
- Our budget for external consulting is larger than any of our peers'.
- We are protected by the government from foreign competition.
- Our offices are located in a city with the best climate.
- Our cost/income ratio is well above the industry average.
- Our annual shareholder meetings are better attended than our competitors'.

All of these characteristics can make one enterprise different from competing enterprises in the same market. Their value and importance in providing competitive advantage will depend on the business plan of the enterprise and the dynamics of the marketplace. Speed to market, speed of product development and a healthy price/earnings ratio are likely to be valuable differences that yield competitive advantage in financial services. Poor productivity and high costs are likely to be differences that would be very apparent and will need to be eliminated.

Some of the other differences may be positive or negative based on the objectives of the enterprise. Well-attended shareholder meetings may reflect loyal investors or strong shareholder discontent. Low levels of executive compensation may be a positive difference in an enterprise that is a member-owned, mutual organization, but could equally demonstrate a limited ability to attract new management talent. Heavy usage of consultants may be positive if the services provided are used properly and worth the price. A visionary CEO may be a negative difference if the fundamental direction of the enterprise is changed repeatedly based on instinct and short-term planning.

Finally, some of the differences above may just be differences, neither supporting nor threatening competitive advantage. The climate of the head office location may be critical to attracting people with the right skills, or it may just be a nice city to have offices in.

From the list of differences about the enterprise, the competitive advantages that exist should be developed. The following elements might be found on a financial services company's list of competitive advantages:

- ability to use a recessionary economy to make profit;
- superior understanding of consumer behaviours;
- good working contacts with regulatory bodies;

- ability to make profitable and early use of leading-edge technology;
- recognition of the danger of complacency and / or indecision;
- ability to control operational costs in almost any circumstances;
- understanding of how to take advantage of demographic change;
- superior ability to learn and deploy;
- the best integrated distribution capability in the industry.

In any financial services enterprise, the following question should be asked: What appropriate competitive advantages do we possess based on the differences between our enterprise and our competitors? Where this has been achieved in the strategy development phase of financial services companies, unique strategies have been developed which are both appropriate and achievable. As an example, a globally acquisitive financial services company (conducting many mergers and acquisitions) will decide to emphasize its differentiators as advantages against in-country or niche players.

In combination, making full use of the enterprise's competitive advantages will be critical in maintaining success while the work to eliminate the negative differences continues. They may even need to be consciously protected (guarded through secrecy or prepared for more consistent deployment through formal process development) while other problem areas are 'fixed'.

Results of Step 2: A defined subset of significant differences from the competition that provide competitive advantage.

STEP 3: DOMINANT, IMPORTANT AND USEFUL COMPETITIVE ADVANTAGES

The ranking of competitive advantages will depend on the strategy and objectives of the enterprise and on the external marketplaces in which the enterprise operates. It is unlikely that these advantages and their respective ranking will stay constant over time, especially in the rapidly changing financial services marketplaces.

Dominant competitive advantages

These are the primary, strategic advantages that an enterprise has over its competitors. They are also often the main catalyst for profit creation in the organization. The loss of a dominant advantage would severely damage the organization's ability to meet its objectives and, ultimately, could cause its failure.

Financial services companies constantly monitor (through external market research) their relative positions by product and customer or market segment. Significant changes in the role of specific competitors can indicate their development of a new dominant advantage, or the depletion of the advantages of others. Underlying measures, including customer satisfaction, advertising spend and PR visibility, can provide insights into the advantages they aim to develop.

Dominant competitive advantages can only be replaced with significant planning, skill and effort, or in the event of major marketplace or economy shifts that benefit the company substantially. The effect of dominant competitive advantage (sometimes by a small group of companies) can change the market for a long period. During the UK pension boom, a few fast-reacting companies grew very substantially in just a few years and have retained their positions since, relegating others much further down the rating list by premium income.

Important competitive advantages

These are the tactical advantages that an enterprise has over its competitors. The loss of an important advantage would limit the organization's ability to meet all of its objectives and would relieve pressure on competitors. Important competitive advantages can be replaced but often at significant expense.

Useful competitive advantages

These are the day-to-day transactional advantages that an enterprise has over its competitors. The loss of a useful advantage might not, in itself, prevent the organization from meeting its objectives. However, its loss might prevent the organization from becoming best of breed in its industry.

Useful competitive advantages can typically be copied, purchased or developed at relatively low cost – however, they require attention because they are so easily overlooked and/or lost rather than exploited.

In any company or market, the following question should be asked: What is the relative importance of each of our competitive advantages?

Results of Step 3: A ranked list of the advantageous differences based on contribution to meeting the objectives of the financial services enterprise.

STEP 4: THE CHARACTERISTICS OF COMPETITIVE ADVANTAGE

Competitive advantage can be viewed from two different but complementary viewpoints. In one view, the advantages an enterprise has over its competition can be based on internal or external factors. A dynamic and visionary CEO, a unique technology, an extremely effective corporate culture, a highly respected brand, a strong view of customer needs, long-term experience of customer management and measurement, or a sufficient amount of capital are all internal factors which may be competitive advantages. Internal advantages can be managed and used as direct assets, in fact many financial services companies now consider their customer base and customer knowledge as a substantial asset. This example and other assets may be unique to the enterprise. Inept competition, a favourable regulatory regime, socio-economic trends, national demographics and infrastructure, and environmental conditions are external factors that provide differences that can be competitive advantages. External advantages may be available to all competitors and are more difficult to control and manage. Each competitive advantage can be controlled to a greater or lesser degree by the enterprise depending on whether it is an internal or external advantage, and depending on its management abilities.

In the second view, the advantages an enterprise has over its competition can be described as stable or unstable. Stable competitive advantages are valuable differences that are likely to endure for the strategic period of the company's planning and investment horizon. If corporate experience and knowledge about a particular business process are a competitive advantage, it is likely to endure for some time. The belief in the brand by a company's customers and the ageing trends in a consumer marketplace are unlikely to change radically in the short term. However, competitive advantages can also be highly unstable. Massive and unexpected changes in the financial services market or general economy, the introduction of new analytical or contact point technologies or the loss of one or more key executives can all eliminate competitive advantage – in some cases overnight.

Each competitive advantage can be depended on to a greater or lesser degree by the enterprise depending on whether it is stable or unstable, and the company's ability to influence or take advantage of its stability.

In any financial services company or market, the following question should be asked: Which of our competitive advantages can we control and which of them can we depend on?

Results of Step 4: A description of each of the ranked advantageous differences based on their key characteristics: internal vs. external and stable vs. unstable.

Visualizing competitive advantage

In order to take an organized view of competitive advantage, Figure 37.1 may be useful. The graphic is not a rigid tool to be applied blindly. It can, however, provide insights into the complex subject of competitive advantage. The practical value of this model is that it allows the business to evaluate the durability of its inventory of competitive advantages over time. Just as the historic differences that gave IBM competitive advantage eroded during the 1980s, any company or industry can lose valuable competitive advantages if the company or the environment in which it operates changes. The loss of competitive

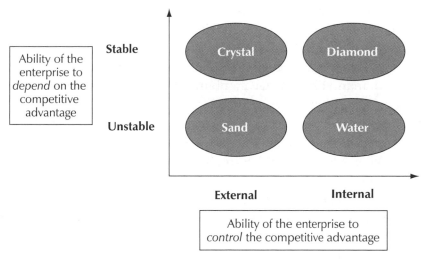

Figure 37.1 Visualizing competitive advantage

advantage can be a slow, barely recognized process or it can happen with alarming speed and without warning.

The major restructuring and rapid growth of personal pensions in the UK during the early 1990s provide such an example. Life companies that focused on their traditional strengths, rather than taking advantage of this new opportunity from rapid market change, lost competitive advantage and substantial share in the redefined UK life and pensions market.

In general, competitive advantages will fall into one of four categories:

- unstable and external: highly likely to change and beyond the control of the business – 'sand';
- stable and external: less likely to change and beyond the control of the business – 'crystal';
- unstable and internal: highly likely to change and within the control of the business – 'water';
- stable and internal: less likely to change and within the control of the business – 'diamond'.

A business built on sand...

Sand is one of the most common materials on earth. Vast quantities of it at the seaside offer a comfortable and inviting place to rest and relax. However, sand is an unstable material; a structure built on a foundation of sand is likely to fall. There is not much value in a house built on sand – unless it is a fantasy sandcastle. Companies and, in some cases, entire industries depend on some competitive advantages which are both external to the business and highly unstable. Where the dominant advantages have these attributes, they will, over time, become competitive disadvantages.

The Native American casino industry depends on a variety of advantages for its success. There is a market demand for legalized gambling in the USA. However, this is not in itself a competitive advantage for casinos operated by Indian tribes. Casinos located on public or private land are as capable of meeting that demand as casinos built on Indian reservations. A dominant competitive advantage that Native American operated casinos have is their legal position. Taking advantage of US treaty law that placed the native populations on reservations, various tribes have established what would otherwise be illegal gambling casinos on their lands. These businessmen have turned the historic injustice of the reservation into a dominant advantage. Aside from a limited number of areas where gambling is legal (eg Nevada and Atlantic City, NJ), the Native American entrepreneurs have a virtual monopoly on casino gaming.

This dominant advantage is, however, both external to their business and potentially highly unstable. The advantage does not come from expertise in casino management or cost control. It is not based on brand loyalty or asset base. It is based on the state and local laws (which typically do not apply to Indian lands) that prohibit casino gaming in much of the USA. The instability in this advantage comes from the potential for states and counties in the USA to change their gambling laws. As local tax bases continue to be under pressure, legalized gambling may become an attractive source of public revenue. Government-operated lotteries are already established in many states. A change of law in several key states would dramatically and rapidly reduce or eliminate the competitive advantage of reservation-based casinos.

Howard Lutnick, CEO of Cantor Fitzgerald, built a successful bond brokerage based on a range of competitive advantages. Among these were several that proved to be tragically beyond the company's control and disastrously unstable. The company's culture was 'family like', with key employees working closely together. Staff members were encouraged to recommend potential candidates for employment – among them siblings, spouses and children. The company's location was also an asset. With offices high atop Manhattan, they operated in the heart of New York's financial district with personal access to key decision makers and market influencers. These advantages were destroyed in a matter of minutes when a jet aircraft slammed into the World Trade tower that was their corporate home. Cantor Fitzgerald lost two-thirds of its US staff, 95 per cent of its US bond traders and 170 of its 425 partners. After an earlier terrorist attempt failed to bring down the tower several years before, a handful of international terrorists succeeded this time and the company saw two of its advantages turn to horrible disadvantages.

A business that depends on external and unstable factors for its success is not only at significant risk. The protection of the external status quo becomes a primary objective. The exporter who depends on government subsidies, the state bank that depends on lenient regulation, and the casino owner who depends on neighbouring state law are all driven to argue against change. Their reliance on the external and unstable advantages becomes complete. Rather than identifying new competitive advantages, they become addicted to the old ones. In attempting to block change rather than recognize and take advantage of it, these enterprises turn their backs on the development of new advantages; traditional advantages turn into competitive disadvantages. Inwardly focused and culturally rigid, these enterprises are truly built on foundations of sand.

Keep the company crystal clean and safely put away...

Crystal is a relatively durable and valuable material that graces the tables of many homes in the form of glasses, goblets and decanters. When polished it gleams, when struck lightly, it rings true and when cut, it sparkles. Crystal is also fragile; when dropped or hit hard enough, it shatters. There is not much practical value in shattered crystal.

In some cases, dominant competitive advantages can be external to the company but will be relatively stable. A stable competitive advantage, whether it is internal or external to the company, is a valuable weapon. It can be relied upon to add value to the business and, over time, it becomes part of the competitive culture of the enterprise. However, when the stable advantage is external to the company, outside its direct control, a significant threat can develop. When that advantage is a dominant one, the entire business may be at risk. This is because the pace of change affecting external advantages is not only beyond the control of the company; it may be beyond the ability of the company to anticipate and understand.

From the end of World War II through the 1960s, the American auto industry encouraged and responded to the market demand for larger and more powerful cars. Wheelbase, engine power and weight were all increased and autos the size of pre-war limousines were parked in front of homes across the country. Foreign imports were seen as small 'starter cars' for the less affluent or as second or third cars for the growing middle class. An apparently stable and external competitive advantage that US auto manufacturers enjoyed was reliably plentiful and inexpensive gasoline. Fuel efficiency was not an issue at 29 cents per gallon of gas – even if the new monsters of the motorway consumed fuel in massive amounts.

This competitive advantage was shattered like a fine crystal glass by the first in a succession of oil crises. Both the availability and price of fuel were affected. Americans found themselves sitting in their massive cars in long lines at the gas station. When they finally arrived at the pump, they were shocked at the cost of filling the huge fuel tank their car depended on. The foreign competitors came into ascendance. They had never enjoyed the luxury of designing a car based on plentiful and inexpensive fuel. Once they gained a foothold in the market, Americans began to realize that the imported cars had qualitative as well as economic advantages over domestic autos. The US auto industry descended into a deep and extended crisis as a result.

For generations, the population of the UK looked to building societies for home loans. The concept of 'membership', mutual ownership, and of providing a personal rather than business service became ingrained in the provision of mortgages and, as a result, in personal savings. Although the building society movement became used to viewing this advantage as a permanent state of affairs, it ultimately proved to be as fragile as fine crystal. The benefits of 'membership' became increasingly unclear, mortgage products became commoditized and therefore price sensitive, 'carpetbaggers' made convincing arguments for de-mutualization, and, in some cases, the industry showed an arrogance based on its belief in the permanence of the perceived value of 'being mutual' for the customer. In the end, the customer's beliefs and perceptions proved to be beyond the ability of the industry to take for granted or manage. As a result, most converted to banks and only a very few remained as mutual, each aiming to make this status more permanent.

In relying on dependable advantages that are beyond the control of the enterprise, an attitude can develop that there is a 'natural right' to the advantage. Whether it is the ideal climate of Southern California, continuing inflation in Latin America, or cheap and plentiful gasoline in the USA, companies that assume that these advantages will always be available do so at their own risk. El Niño can empty the tourist sites of the US West Coast. A determined government can reduce the rate of inflation. Gasoline can cost $2.00 per gallon.

Even if the water isn't leaking, it's probably evaporating

Water covers three-quarters of the surface of the earth. It sustains and takes life. People drink it, wash with it, swim in it and travel on it. Complex water storage and distribution systems have been critical to man's organized survival from pre-historic times. These systems must be maintained and the water supply must be renewed. Over time, a slow leak or the process of evaporation may deplete the water supply to dangerously low levels.

Competitive advantages can be internal and unstable. An internal competitive advantage can be a powerful business weapon because it is owned and managed by the business. However, when the advantage is unstable, its value will likely erode over time. Time is the great enemy of competitive advantage. The brilliant, highly effective general manager ages and either loses some of his or her ability or retires. The exciting new process or product is copied or improved on by others.

In the late 1960s banks discovered a new and cost-effective way to provide teller transactions to their customers. The ATM (automated teller machine) was born. The new device had several competitive advantages: many teller transactions could be done at a fraction of the cost and customer convenience could be dramatically improved. Leading banks developed and marketed their ATM networks as a dominant strategic advantage. The networks were clearly branded with names like 'Mr Cash' in Belgium, Toronto Dominion's 'Green Machine' and First Hawaii's 'Honolulu Lulu'. There was no question of inter-bank cooperation as each organization reminded the market that it had ATMs and its competitors did not.

By the early 1990s, ATM networks were not providing dominant competitive advantage to their owners. They had become a cost of doing business. If a bank did not own ATMs it provided the service to its customers through pool agreements with banks that did. By the mid-1990s ATM networks in countries as different as Finland, the USA and Australia were virtual public utilities. Customers could use any bank's card in any machine. The names of Visa, MasterCard, the pool operator and the ATM manufacturer had become more visible than the name of the bank that paid for and maintained the machine. The competitive advantage inherent in providing ATM services has slowly evaporated over 20 years – it has become the price of admission to a large part of the retail banking marketplace, therefore protecting against new entrants rather than existing market competitors.

In relying on advantages that can be copied or trivialized over time, the enterprise must understand the 'life cycle' of the advantage in their market. While it is not always best to be first, it is almost always bad to be late in introducing an internal/unstable advantage. It can be very easy and very dangerous to assume that an internal/unstable advantage can be depended upon indefinitely.

Diamonds are an enterprise's best friend

Because of its rarity and beauty, a diamond is one of the most valuable of gemstones. It can be cut and shaped by a master craftsman, but it is also one of the hardest and most durable substances on earth. In many families, diamonds are handed down from generation to generation and if one is lost, there is a sense of true wealth, value and heritage gone forever. Some competitive advantages are both internal to the enterprise and stable over time. Unless an enterprise is very skilled or very lucky, such advantages are likely to be quite limited in number. Internal and stable advantages allow a company to determine its own future. They are 'owned' by the company and can be deployed and adapted to respond to competitive threats and to proactively set the rules of competition. They are difficult for competitors to copy or replace and cause them to expend valuable energy and resource in reacting to imposed rules of competition. A company that owns no 'diamonds' is likely to be left behind in the market or fail completely.

'There is no other article for individual use so universally known or widely distributed. In my travels, I have found it in the most northern town in Norway and in the heart of the Sahara Desert.' Those words are not taken from a recent advertisement or press release. In 1926, King C. Gillette used them to describe the global reach and recognition for his company's flagship product, the Gillette Safety Razor. Seventy-five years later, the company's ability to distribute a consistent product line from 'Boston to Bangladesh' has resulted in a dominant position where over 1 billion consumers use at least one Gillette product every day.

Over three-quarters of a century, the company has developed and protected a difference that provides significant advantage: a unique view of the global nature of its market and a unique ability to distribute effectively to the world. Unlike many other 'global players', Gillette puts its organization where its mouth is. The company consists of three operating groups:

- Global Business Management with worldwide responsibility for all research and development, manufacturing and strategic marketing for all product lines;
- Commercial Operations, Western Hemisphere responsible for all trade marketing and sales for all products in North and Latin America;
- Commercial Operations, Eastern Hemisphere responsible for all trade marketing and sales for all products worldwide except for North and Latin America.

Gillette's ability to take a global, single market view is an internal competitive advantage that has shown remarkable durability. The company has clearly shown that it can establish the management systems and organizational culture to protect this diamond, and that, as with any good diamond, this difference has maintained its value across generations of customers, employees, managers and shareholders.

Washington Mutual Savings Bank of Seattle, Washington, USA (WAMU) is an example of a financial institution that understands its 'diamonds' and admits to its 'crystal'. Owing to its unique heritage and licensing structure, WAMU had a unique advantage in its market. It was legally allowed to market banking, brokerage and insurance products long before its larger competitors. However, the management of the bank realized that this advantage, based in regulation, was beyond its long-term control. It did, however, develop an advantage within its control that has served it well for at least 10 years. This was the ability to identify, understand and manage the truly critical business processes necessary for success and to bring continuous executive focus to them. As a result, Washington Mutual has not only built a successful and effective outsourcing strategy, but they have consistently been able to engage in successful merger and acquisition activity with rapid integration of acquired institutions into their core processes with maximum cost savings. WAMU knows the difference between a shining crystal decanter and a shining diamond ring.

On the surface, there is little apparent risk in owning 'diamonds'. In fact there may be three severe risks to the enterprise that is lucky enough to have a stock of this precious commodity:

- Diamonds require regular attention and maintenance and there is the risk the company will take its internal/stable advantages for granted. MGM, NBC and Pan American all either lost their 'diamonds' or gave them away.
- Diamonds can be worn in poor taste. The possession of these powerful advantages can be abused or can lead to such market dominance that external agents such as regulators

or governments intervene in the operations of the enterprise. Standard Oil, IBM, AT&T and Microsoft have all been accused of market abuse or inordinate dominance. In the case of the first three, huge resources were expended to defend their positions and eventually reorganize themselves in the face of legal and governmental pressure.

● Diamonds can make their owner smug. Enterprises that enjoy internal/stable competitive advantages can become arrogant. Customers do not necessarily care about the level of skill and ability that an enterprise has. They care about how well those capabilities are used to deliver the products, services and results that they want and need.

People may be envied or respected for their diamonds; they are rarely loved because of them.

STEP 5: THE COMPETITIVE ADVANTAGE HORIZON

It is highly unlikely that an enterprise will be fortunate enough to have any competitive advantages that last indefinitely. Companies and countries, enterprises and empires have all enjoyed relatively durable competitive advantages, only to see them disappear or erode over time. Sustainable competitive advantage comes from understanding the probable duration of current competitive advantages and from the ability to replace them with new ones as the current ones fade or disappear with little notice.

In order to develop the competitive advantage framework for an enterprise, the ranked list of advantages needs to be reviewed for its likely durability. Depending on the mix of 'sand', 'water', 'crystal' and 'diamonds' in the advantage portfolio, that horizon may be very near or reassuringly far off. Each advantage should be examined to understand what factors exist that might cause its loss and the likelihood of these factors occurring should also be understood.

The competitive advantage horizon chart (Figure 37.2) is divided into four areas of risk:

● Zone I represents the relatively higher risk for the dramatic loss of value of a particular competitive advantage in the near term.
● Zone II represents the relatively lower risk for the dramatic loss of value of a particular competitive advantage over the strategic period.

These two quadrants include the fragile advantages that may be lost due to either external or internal changes.

● Zone III represents the relatively high risk for the dramatic loss of value of a particular competitive advantage over the strategic period.

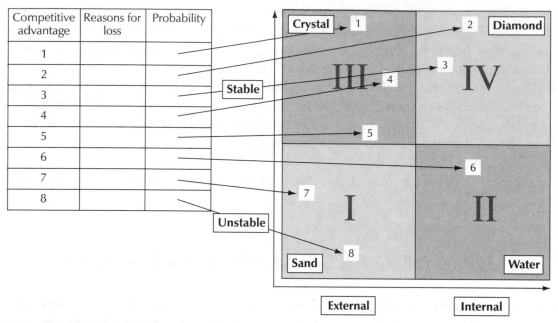

Figure 37.2 The competitive advantage horizon

- Zone IV represents the relatively high risk for the dramatic loss of value of a particular competitive advantage in the near term.

These two quadrants include the more durable advantages, likely to survive changes in the environment or within the enterprise.

Based on an analysis of the durability and threats to the value of each of the competitive advantages, they are located in the appropriate zone. The overall chart represents the competitive advantage framework of the enterprise. In the example above, an enterprise has been found to have a total of eight unique competitive advantages on which it primarily depends for success.

Advantages 7 and 8 are at high risk. They are not within the control of management and the environmental factors that support them are liable to short-term change (eg regulation, macro-economics). Advantage 6 may be under the control of the enterprise but still shows symptoms of unreliability (eg the current large branch network as consumer attitudes change). Advantages 1, 4 and 5 appear to be stable; however, as they depend upon the external environment they are at risk of disappearing (eg telecommunications and postal reliability). Finally, advantages 2 and 3 are viewed as highly durable and under the control of the enterprise (eg brand distinction, detailed and effective understanding of customers and markets).

Regardless of the outcome of the analysis, there are likely to be forces at work within and outside the enterprise that are destabilizing the competitive advantage framework.

Depending on the volatility of markets, business environments and competitive trends, the competitive advantage framework may need to be re-evaluated continually. Stable and internal advantages are being destabilized as skills and capabilities are lost in the inevitable turnover of employees and managers. Decisions about investments, resource allocation and business alliances can all destabilize internally based advantages. Stable and external advantages are being destabilized as forces in the broader environment change the rules of business and competition. Unstable and internal advantages become externalized as competitors copy them and develop new ones. As if in some vast desert, competitive advantages eventually disappear into the sand.

Results of Step 5: Recognition of the relative risk of loss of the competitive advantages of the enterprise over time.

FIXING THE PROBLEMS OF THE ENTERPRISE

The method described in this chapter concentrates on identifying what is right with an enterprise, assessing the importance of the things that are right and understanding the degree to which they can be relied on to provide competitive advantage over time. There will inevitably be things that are wrong in an organization and they too can be identified by understanding the ways in which the enterprise differs from its peers, from industry norms or from 'best practice'. Once these 'negative differences' are identified and analysed, there is a wide variety of methods and approaches for eliminating them. From small repair projects to massive re-engineering and transformation programmes, the solutions almost outnumber the problems. It is the fact that these methods concentrate on fixing what is wrong that poses a threat to what is right. A balanced look at what is right and its contribution to meeting the objectives of the enterprise may prevent the tragedy of throwing the advantages out with the bath water! Recognizing and eliminating negative differences in an enterprise can be of significant value in meeting business objectives. Recognizing and maximizing positive differences can also be a major contributor to success. However, recognizing the life expectancy of positive differences and planning for their replacement may be the ultimate definition of 'sustainable advantage'. To paraphrase John Maynard Keynes, in the long term all competitive advantages are dead.

38

The customer service gap

Kevin La Croix

THE WEAKNESS IN THE CUSTOMER PROPOSITION

In Chapter 30, we showed that one of the major weaknesses in how financial services companies manage their customers is the formulation and delivery of their proposition to customers. It is perhaps too easy to forget that financial institutions are service companies, and often judged for their service against mass-market retailers. Of course, some financial services companies have recognized the competitive advantage in providing high quality service to their customers. Significant investments have been made in providing the training, tools and information to the customer-facing employees so that they can deliver the 'right' level of service. To the frustration of executive management, the results have often been disappointing. The employees on the front line do not feel that they can give the intended level of service. Customers see little or no change in the treatment they receive. After pouring significant amounts of money and effort into the *service gap* (see Figure 38.1) that exists between what customers expect and what they perceive that they receive, little or no return is realized from that investment. Perhaps the problem is that the service gap is not actually at the point of customer contact. There are other points in the company where service gaps can be found. These gaps are the real causes of customers' dissatisfaction with the service the company provides.

The fact that customer service has a high degree of *perceived value* should be remembered in analysing the ability of the business to meet its customer service objectives. It may, in fact,

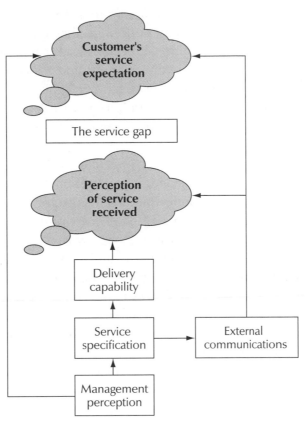

Figure 38.1 The service gap

not be necessary to provide the best objective level of service. It may be sufficient simply to have your customers believe that you do. Four elements of a company's customer service strategy should be evaluated to understand the causes of the service gap.

SERVICE GAPS START AT THE TOP – SERVICE GAP 1

In defining a customer service strategy for a company, there are often significant changes required in the corporate culture, employee training, technology infrastructure and measurement systems. These fundamental changes and the associated investment of resources and personal commitment depend on the clear leadership of the executive management. It is here that we should look for the first *service gap*.

Simply stated, too often senior management does not know or understand what the customer expects or perceives in terms of service. How often do the owners, CEOs or general managers of businesses actually purchase or use the goods and services that their businesses deliver to the market? Unfortunately, the answer is not often enough. Senior executives often delegate their personal affairs to subordinates or personal assistants. If they do make use of their own company's offerings, they typically have an experience that no ordinary customer would recognize. Procedures are streamlined or ignored, middle-level managers rush to accommodate their request and the normal departmental boundaries within the company are temporarily torn down. After all, 'the boss' deserves special treatment! Protected from the normal operations and frustrations of the customer service process, even the most committed general manager can fail to understand the normal treatment a customer receives.

In an attempt to overcome this lack of personal experience, many senior executives commission market research studies and 'mystery shopper' campaigns. They depend on surveys and statistical analysis to understand what customers want and how satisfied they are. Clearly, organized and rigorous research can provide valuable information on customer requirements. It is much less useful in gaining an understanding and clear insight into the perceptions in the customer's mind regarding service. Here is an example of how not to do it. A consultant was asked to visit 35 branches of a major UK bank and report on his impression of customer service. On the first morning of the work, he reported to head office where he was provided with a chauffeur-driven Mercedes to transport him to the first three branches. Just before arrival at the first branch, the chauffeur telephoned to announce their arrival. The branch manager met the consultant at the front door. So much for understanding the point of the study – or the use of honest, customer service evaluation.

There are examples of executives who recognize the need to experience the same treatment that their customers get. Sam Walton, the founder of Wal-Mart, was famous for his commitment to visit every store in his network once a year. During those visits he never failed to ask customers and employees 'how am I doing?' He did not ask how his company was performing; he wanted a personal appraisal. He listened to complaints and suggestions and acted on them. An airline in the USA has a policy of every senior executive spending one week a year either checking-in passengers or loading baggage. The chairman of a large bank does his own banking on Saturdays in casual clothes and at suburban branches where he is not recognized. The general manager of a UK building society publishes his home telephone number in the annual report. His intention is to allow customers to call him directly if they have a problem or question. While these examples are not necessarily the right approach for every company, they all have a common theme. These executives realize that they need to experience customer service at first hand if they are to understand the perceptions of their customers.

Several questions should be posed in evaluating the presence of Service Gap 1 in a business:

- What is the quality of the market research, if any?
- What use do senior executives make of market research?
- How often do senior executives meet with members of key customer segments?

- How often do executives meet with frontline, service delivery staff?
- How many layers of management are there between senior executives and frontline service staff?
- How often do you and your senior executives act as 'anonymous customers' of your own business?

Understanding what your customers really want and whether they are actually satisfied with the service they receive can be a humbling experience. If the president of an airline only flies in the company jet, if the head of a bank has his secretary handle his accounts, or if the CEO of a manufacturing firm does not meet with and listen to his service staff, Service Gap 1 will make a mockery of any 'customer service strategy'.

SERVICE GAPS ARE CLOSED BY SENSIBLE STANDARDS – SERVICE GAP 2

Let us assume that the senior executives of the business understand the expectations and perceptions of the customer regarding service. This understanding is based on personal experience, face-to-face discussions and a sense of the perception issues that exist in the minds of target consumers and frontline, service delivery staff. If this understanding is not communicated to the people responsible for developing the customer service strategy, the measures and standards of service quality are likely to be inappropriate. Businesses tend to limit the ways they measure themselves to criteria that are important to the business, or criteria that are easy to measure. Neither of these criteria is necessarily relevant to customers.

A major UK bank launched a new service strategy built on its telephone call centre. Millions of pounds had been invested in the technology and staff recruitment to build a 'state of the art' facility. A major advertising campaign introduced this new facility and a promise was made to the customers: *'We will answer the phone in four rings or less.'* This promise was based on two criteria. The business believed that it was meaningful to customers and, given the advanced technology, it was easy to measure. Unfortunately, the customers were not impressed by either of these factors. For many years, customers of UK banks had been trained to go to their branch to get information and resolve problems. This was time-consuming and often frustrating, but service expectations were traditionally low and at least they had a chance to talk to a familiar person face-to-face.

Although the prospect of convenience that was promised by the new service programme sounded positive, in reality it was a disappointment. The phones were indeed answered in four rings or less. However, there were no obvious measures of the *quality of the conversation* once the phone had been answered. The impersonal operator could not execute the customer's request with any more quality than the branch staff member. Follow-up conversations were invariably with another operator who needed to start from the beginning. The customer's call was transferred to a variety of 'service points' and, at times, was disconnected. *'Four rings or less'* became known as *'four rings* and *less'*. If the telephone service centre was used, the four rings led to the perception of less service.

Contrast this poorly thought out and somewhat arrogant measure of quality with a simple measure that Southwest Airlines introduced. Southwest operates in the highly competitive 'no-frills' airline sector. Its customer proposition is based on low cost and no extras. There are no meals or movies and all passengers fly economy class. The Air Florida crash in Washington, DC and the Valuejet disaster in Florida raised significant concerns in the press regarding the potential for low safety standards among the low-cost carriers. After these disasters, the president of Southwest realized that customer perception might associate low-cost air travel with low safety air travel. As a part of managing this perception, a new standard was established by the airline. The contract cleaning company employed to clean Southwest's aircraft was told that 100 per cent of the fold-down tray tables must be spotless on every flight. Failure to meet this service standard would result in cancellation of their contract. The president of Southwest understood a key to his customer's perceptions. Coffee rings on the tray table might indicate low maintenance standards for the aircraft itself. This potential customer perception could cause the company to fail and it was addressed through a standard that was directly designed to manage that potential perception.

Service Gap 2 is the failure to translate the understanding of the customers' service expectations into service standards that are *relevant to the customer*. In evaluating your service standards, several questions can be asked to spot Service Gap 2:

- Is there a belief in the company that customers cannot actually be given the level of service they want?
- Is there a relationship between the customer perceptions that need to be managed and the customer service standards that are set?
- Are there service standards that customers simply do not care about?
- Do your service standards imply a promise that is not fulfilled in practice?
- Have you personally reviewed your company's service standards and thought about the effect they will have on customer perception and satisfaction?

Understanding the service promises you make to your customers and the way your management will measure your progress on meeting those promises is vital to executive management. If service standards are exclusively *quantitative*, they may be irrelevant to the marketplace. Often, it is the *qualitative* measures that your customers care most about.

COMPANY RESOURCES MUST BE OBSESSIVELY FOCUSED ON SERVICE STANDARDS – SERVICE GAP 3

Again, let us assume that Service Gaps 1 and 2 have been closed. Executive managers have an intimate understanding of customer expectations and perceptions and have ensured that service standards are relevant and meaningful to the marketplace. To enable the delivery of the service standards, many resources may need to be allocated to that specific objective. The culture of the organization must be aligned with the objectives. This can be accomplished through a wide range of activities, including recruitment, training, appraisal and rewards for service staff. Physical premises may need to be assessed and information tools will need to be provided. Techniques for accurately sampling customer attitudes will need to be in place and a clear cost–benefit plan for the customer service strategy will be needed to justify the effort.

One example of implementing this set of resources can be found in the USA. Pizza Express offers a home delivery service for its product and has worked for some time to differentiate its brand based on service. The company recognized that product differentiation was increasingly difficult in what was becoming an overcrowded and commoditized market. Pizza Express committed specific resources to its home delivery telephone operation to enable it to set its brand apart from the rest of the industry. When a customer calls the Pizza Express home delivery telephone number, the following events take place:

- The operator is furnished with the caller's number, name, information on their last order and the caller's favourite order based on history.
- The operator answers by saying 'Yes, Mr Smith. Thanks for calling us again. Was the cheese pizza you ordered last week satisfactory?'
- As an alternative, the operator may say 'I see that you prefer our sausage pizza. Would you like to order one of those? Do you want your usual litre of cola included with this order?'
- After entering the order into the system, the operator is given the delivery instructions to the customer's home by the system.
- The operator may ask the customer 'are you still at the same address? Will the 1996 Ford be parked in the driveway and do you want our driver to deliver to the kitchen door as usual?'
- As this conversation is being conducted, the kitchen processes the order and the most direct route to the customer's house is being printed for the driver.

Based on customer research, Pizza Express discovered that service in its market was defined by ease of placing an order over the phone, and reliable and timely delivery of the product. It also discovered that meeting those two criteria were the most important factors in developing brand loyalty.

When looking for the existence of Service Gap 3 in your business, it may be useful to ask the following questions:

- Do customer service employees have clear roles and the authority and the information required to deliver the planned level of service?
- Are employees rewarded in such a way that customer service staff are in conflict with other staff members?
- Is there a problem with the matching of service staff skills and the tools they are provided?
- Does the measurement and compensation plan encourage adherence to the customer service strategy?
- Do service staff believe that they can control the 'service interaction'?
- Is the organization a cultural team, working together to deliver the service strategy?

In almost all cases these questions should be asked by the senior executive in face-to-face discussions with the employees who actually deliver the service promise.

BRAGGING ABOUT THE RIGHT THINGS – SERVICE GAP 4

The final service gap that may exist within a company is created by misdirected marketing and advertising programmes. These programmes create both explicit and implicit promises in the mind of the customer. When these promises are not fulfilled, customer satisfaction will suffer.

A large British bank launched a major campaign several years ago to demonstrate its innovation and creativity. The advertisements were built around the fact that it had been a pioneer in Britain in launching an ATM network, providing revolutionary levels of convenience to its customers. Over the 25 years since their launch, ATMs had become commodities in the market. Today, any bank card in the UK can be used in any bank's ATM. The real breakthrough that this bank launched is now a virtual public utility, taken for granted by the marketplace. The unintended impression created by this campaign was that the bank had not had a creative idea in a quarter century. At least the customer's service expectations were not raised as a result.

Compare this with the marketing campaign of a competitive institution in the UK. It based a marketing communications campaign on a proposition of attentiveness to customer needs. Coupled with this launch of a new image, a new call centre was opened so that the bank could make it easier to be attentive to its customers. With the inevitable start-up problems associated with the new call centre, the bank did not demonstrate an ability to react to its customer requests and complaints. Inevitably, the bank became known as being attentive but never following up. In this case, raised expectations were not met by better service.

There are many examples of good and bad financial services marketing and advertising campaigns around the world. The best ones manage both the implicit and explicit service promises they make and ensure that those promises can be kept. One area of the business that can be an excellent source of marketing and advertising material is operations. This is the area that handles the day-to-day, repetitive tasks that are combined to deliver the product or service that the customer is paying for. Taken together, these tasks can present a picture of excellence that is relevant to a customer. Whether it is a manufacturing firm, a bank or insurance company, or an airline, the cumulative record of success can be a powerful promise backed up by actual performance. '100,000 tires without a defect', '2 million claims settled within 72 hours', or '25 million passenger miles flown without a delay' are operational statements that can be taken for granted by the company. They may not be taken for granted by the customers – customers may value them.

In looking for the existence of Service Gap 4 in a company, it may be useful to ask the following questions:

- Do we use overblown or irrelevant advertising?
- Is there executive visibility in the implicit or explicit service promise?
- Is there good communication between the sales department and operations?
- Is there good communication between the marketing and operations departments?
- Is the entire organization aware of the customer service strategy and its impact on the business?

Making a promise to a market can be a powerful or a dangerous move. If that promise is relevant and if it is met, business volumes and profits may improve. If the promise is meaningless or, even worse, if it is broken, not only financial measures will be affected. Both customer service staff and customers may develop a cynicism that attacks the basic brand value of the business.

THE COMMON ELEMENT IN CUSTOMER SERVICE

A common theme in finding and closing Service Gaps 1–4 is the commitment on the part of executive management to the job. This commitment starts with a willingness to understand the attitudes of customers regarding what they expect and what they get. It is useful to know the 'facts' of the service strategy and performance of the company. It is critical to share the perceptions that the service strategy and service performance create. As shown in Figure 38.2, this is the first of four key tasks for the CEO, General Manager or owner.

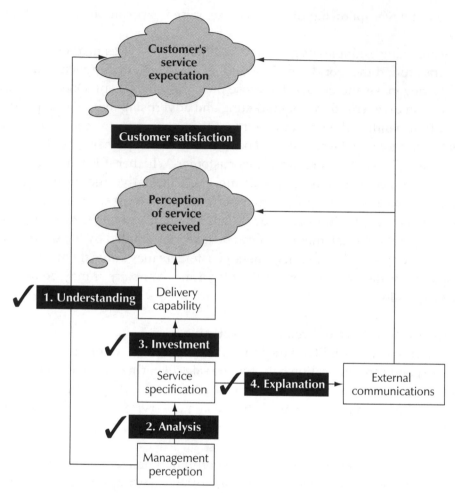

Figure 38.2 The importance of understanding

The second responsibility of the executive is to ensure that customer expectations are managed and expressed in the terms of the measurable service standards that the business sets. It may be possible to delegate responsibility for implementing these standards. Establishing the standards should be the responsibility of an informed and understanding executive team. The analysis of the fit between perceptions and measurements is the second job of the executive team.

The investment plan that supports the customer service measurement system is the third job of the executive team. Significant resources are probably required to enable the business to meet its service objectives and to measure and verify acceptable performance and results. These resources should be applied within a clear cost–benefit case and there should be clear business objectives associated with it. This discipline gives the entire organization a reason to meet the service standards as well as the skills and tools to achieve them.

The final customer service responsibility of the executive is explanation of the strategy to the market and to the staff. Communication of the strategy in relevant terms, clearly understood and supported by the top of the company, and continuously evaluated at the highest level will provide the example and prove the commitment to the market.

A bank in Hong Kong wanted to develop a customer service strategy. It held a three-day executive session on the subject. For the first two days, one of the participants remained silent. He took lengthy notes but did not contribute to any of the discussions. At the start of the third day, the workshop leader asked the CEO who this person was and what his role was in the meeting. The response was very revealing. The CEO said, 'Oh, that's Charlie... good guy... been with the bank for years. He will be responsible for customer service.' The workshop leader than asked, 'What will you be doing while Charlie is running customer service?' The CEO answered, 'Me?... I have a business to run!' Perhaps Charlie can 'run customer service' while you run the business. However, if customer service is critical to your commercial survival, you may not have a business to run if you don't run customer service yourself.

39

Competing for customers in an era of change

Vikram Lund

INTRODUCTION

The financial services industry is undergoing sweeping change in virtually every area – from the kinds of products and services customers are seeking to the ways those offerings are delivered. As executives confront these shifts and chart their path for growth in this new environment, they must ask themselves a key question: What do our customers pay for now, and what will they pay for in the future? While management comes to grips with this issue, corporate leadership will be called upon to determine the following:

- What are our core strengths?
- Do these strengths put us in a strong position for the future?
- Do we need to develop (organically or through acquisitions) new competencies for leveraging opportunities in a changing marketplace?
- Is the technology in place to manage these changes?

Addressing these issues effectively and expeditiously can help ensure alignment with marketplace trends, while providing customers with the goods and services for which they are willing to pay.

Although managers across industries must face a similar set of issues, the pressure is clearly on the financial services sector, an environment in which many companies pursue short-term gains in lieu of longer-term growth strategies. Currently, the industry has a number of compelling opportunities to use technology to exploit competencies and serve a larger number of customers. Today's leading-edge financial firms understand the importance of capitalizing on this opportunity and are learning to balance short-term financial performance with long-term approaches for maximizing their portfolio of businesses.

Over the next five to ten years, market factors will force most traditional lines of business in the financial service industry to reinvent themselves. This will result in dramatic shifts in revenue sources and market share. For example:

- The Web and its related technologies will affect significantly virtually every aspect of brokerage, banking, insurance and trading – both institutional and retail.
- Traditional delivery systems will give way to new models that leverage technology to reduce costs, improve customer service and maximize efficiencies.
- Multiple points of access and service will be increasingly key to enhancing and maintaining customer relationships.
- Companies in other industries will use their brands, capabilities and customer bases to expand into the financial services sector, creating a new breed of potent competition (and, in many cases, driving the need to build new competencies).

Financial services senior executives need to deal with some difficult issues in the areas of customer needs, their company's ability to meet them, competitors' strategies and their company's core capabilities. They need to incorporate next-generation technologies and prepare for an inevitable shift in business models that can strengthen their value propositions, sharpen their competitive edge and increase profitability.

WHERE DO YOU STAND TODAY?

IBM has developed a 'three-wave' model that demonstrates how various e-business dynamics combine and interact. This model is part of a larger analytical framework that strategists can use to understand how e-business is evolving within a particular industry and is discussed in more detail in Chapters 4 and 6.

In the financial services sector, the factors associated with evolution are forcing companies to abandon traditional organizational silos built solely on relationships, products, portfolios and processes. This in turn is prompting a shift to business models and core capabilities designed to improve end-to-end business performance.

Today, the financial services industry functions within distinct business clusters that reflect limited and diminishing value propositions. The first wave of e-business has seen financial institutions employ technology to enable new operating efficiencies, enhance distribution systems and improve customer service while leaving the existing business model intact.

A second, e-business-centric wave has also emerged, with dot.coms and new-media units competing against traditional entities. Players in this wave have ushered in new business models and value propositions that focus on creating online brands and employing new forms of customer acquisition and service. While many dot.coms have failed recently, the need for business-model reinvention has not disappeared. Casualties uncovered the inefficiencies of traditional structures and opened the door for well-established brands to reinvent their businesses and revitalize their relationships. A hybrid model of waves one and two, leveraging both physical and virtual businesses for the benefit of the customer, has also surfaced.

To develop their business structure as a whole, financial services executives must first identify where their business is currently positioned on the continuum of technology waves. Then they can determine which new business models should be leveraged as the foundation for each operating unit.

WHERE WILL YOU STAND TOMORROW?

As the balance of power shifts from producers to consumers, the next wave of e-business will surface, characterized by the realignment and redefinition of entire industries. In wave three, enterprises will attempt to build dynamic e-businesses capable of rapidly accommodating and participating in a range of value chains with a variety of new partners. In the process, organizations will face a series of challenges centred on what customers will pay for and how best to align the business to meet their changing demands. This will require launching some significant initiatives, including:

- migrating existing businesses and operating models to a defensible competitive position;
- applying brands across multiple businesses and industries;
- assessing prospective economic opportunities (and threats) from emerging technologies;
- leveraging next-generation technologies to create competitive advantage;
- gaining customer acceptance and loyalty.

FOUR 'CENTRIC' BUSINESS MODELS

Successful financial services enterprises will go to market armed with a combination of four new 'centric' business models (see Figure 39.1) that will empower management to:

- Replace the traditional product-based value proposition and compete on the basis of core capabilities (customer point of contact, fulfilment, production or market knowledge). As management engages in this process, it is important to avoid segregating the business. Although one model may be selected as the primary approach, leaders will weave together key elements from each centric model to achieve maximum results.

- Leverage next-generation technology platforms that allow management to focus on core capabilities, outsource non-essential functions and align all lines of business in a given enterprise.

- Identify new revenue sources that map to the company's core competencies (both existing and acquired).

In exploring the four centric models, it is important to view them not as precise paradigms in which to structure and manage a business, but as symbolic of the options available. By doing so, managers can realign their companies to address changing marketplaces and position themselves to provide 'what customers will pay for'.

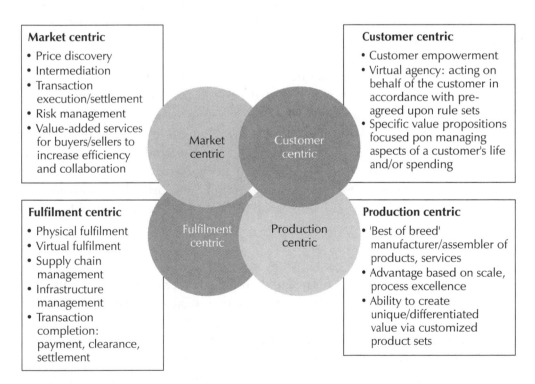

Market centric

- Price discovery
- Intermediation
- Transaction execution/settlement
- Risk management
- Value-added services for buyers/sellers to increase efficiency and collaboration

Customer centric

- Customer empowerment
- Virtual agency: acting on behalf of the customer in accordance with pre-agreed upon rule sets
- Specific value propositions focused pon managing aspects of a customer's life and/or spending

Fulfilment centric

- Physical fulfilment
- Virtual fulfilment
- Supply chain management
- Infrastructure management
- Transaction completion: payment, clearance, settlement

Production centric

- 'Best of breed' manufacturer/assembler of products, services
- Advantage based on scale, process excellence
- Ability to create unique/differentiated value via customized product sets

Figure 39.1 Different models of centricity

THE CUSTOMER-CENTRIC MODEL

Businesses operating under this model have a pervasive influence on the customer relationship. By providing customers with a gateway to a network of industry-relevant product and service vendors, these entities act as an agent – controlling the point of customer interaction and empowering customers through education, knowledge and convenience.

By focusing on a specific customer base and providing access to a tailored set of financial planning products and services, myCFO has adopted an early form of the customer-centric model. The company, which affords customers convenient access to personal financial management via on–line interaction, is currently developing brick-and-mortar locations across the USA to offer in-person service delivery to those who prefer that option. Although the financial services giants may view myCFO as a niche player in a highly targeted market, the business has a proven track record, and has invented a business model that promises to be a harbinger of the future.

This model puts a business in a strong position to offer customers precisely 'what they are willing to pay for', even as their demands evolve with the marketplace. More often than not, they will turn to such businesses to explore and acquire new offerings. The customer-centric model often appears to be the most natural – everyone knows that building on customer relationships is a key to further success. It is also likely to attract the greatest numbers of competitors.

Sony, a long-established manufacturer and marketer of high-end electronic products, recently announced plans to open an Internet bank in the Asia-Pacific market. Working with J P Morgan to provide personal financial tools and with Sakura Bank for industry expertise and access to the latter's ATM network, Sony is leveraging its capabilities to exploit a new market. This move represents a threat to traditional financial services companies as a new breed of competitor – with roots remote from this market – enters their space. Such customer-centric virtual agency offerings will provide significant customer value through 'peace of mind' creation, enabling the creation of defensible positions of market advantage.

Customer-centric companies:

- act on behalf of customers and represent their wants and needs in marketplace;
- manage aspects of a customer's life and/or 'spend' in accordance with pre-agreed rule sets and level of delegated authority;
- provide personalized advice and counsel regarding alternatives via an ongoing dialogue with customer, capturing decisions and preferences;
- enterprise economic interests exactly align with/centre on customers' interests.

Their core competencies are:

- understanding, anticipating and reacting to customer needs;
- acting as customer advocate with access to the total marketplace, independent of specific product-providers;
- continuous learning about customers, markets, and providers;
- ability to build strong and loyal customer relationships by providing 'peace of mind';
- highly focused personalization/customization, while upholding the highest standards for privacy and security;
- providing full customer access, wherever and however they want to interact;
- partnerships with strong fulfilment organizations.

Their revenue sources are:

- customer fee for services;
- percentage of customer's savings.

Their success metrics are:

- customer profitability;
- percentage of customer spending and/or selling;
- customer referrals;
- customer acquisition costs;
- satisfaction indicators: retention/loyalty;
- increased delegation;
- supplier/fulfilment effectiveness ratings.

THE PRODUCTION-CENTRIC MODEL

These players either meet customer needs directly, or serve as a resource for companies adopting other centric models. These businesses compete on the basis of price, quality, and/or convenience.

Folio FN enables investors to choose their personal investing preferences (risk, industry, etc), then directly invest in portfolios that match those selections. Folio FN's value proposition is in helping clients eliminate the unnecessary risk, cost and guesswork inherent in investing in one stock at a time. Folio FN takes advantage of the fact that investing in a portfolio of stocks can provide investors with a lower level of risk for the same expected rate of return, or the potential for a higher expected rate of return for the same level of risk. Because Folio FN investors directly own the stocks in their portfolios, they can avoid the high fees often associated with mutual funds. Unlike mutual fund investors, Folio FN investors always know exactly which securities are in their portfolio, and can customize and tailor these holdings to reflect their preferences and values.

Since the production-centric model involves intense competition on price, financial services firms should continue to look for ways to offset any potential revenue loss by turning their core 'production' capabilities into new revenue streams.

The Royal Bank of Scotland Group plc (RBSG) makes its back-end banking functions available to companies wanting to offer banking services without engaging in the logistics of operating a bank. RBSG furnishes its back-office capabilities as a production-centric line of business. RBSG is now engaged in such a transaction with Norwich Union. As part of this arrangement, the two businesses will seek to further their commercial cooperation by identifying opportunities to develop their respective businesses. Such production businesses will optimize market and financial performance through 'perfected' traditional and hybrid business models, most of which will compete on scale and unique capability

Production-centric companies have these characteristics:

- cost-effective manufacture of products and services;
- advantage based on scale and process excellence / capability;
- ability to sell into the marketplace or direct to customers;
- ability to create unique / differentiated value via customized product sets.

Their core competencies are:

- streamlined business processes;
- supply chain integration / virtualization;
- understanding, anticipating and reacting to intermediary needs and end customer needs;
- portability of operation to compete on a global basis;
- development of strong relationships with selling partners;
- dynamic pricing;
- collaborative demand planning / forecasting.

Their revenue sources are product / service sales.
Their success metrics are:

- customer satisfaction;
- quality control;
- inventory analytics;
- activity costs / return on capital;
- product profitability;
- process efficiency;

- R&D analytics;
- new product introduction;
- supply chain efficiency;
- revenue by channel/partner.

THE MARKET-CENTRIC MODEL

Market-centric companies offer buyers and sellers value-added services that provide a context in which both parties (or their agents) can conduct commerce.

Their capabilities include:

- mechanisms for price discovery;
- functionality to enable transaction settlement;
- mechanisms to mediate risk;
- orchestration of necessary fulfilment;
- collaboration features.

E-Bay, the popular online auction house, is moving towards the market-centric approach by understanding the needs, concerns and relationships among buyers and sellers, and utilizing next-generation technology and partnerships to create a loyal community of users. To address its growing number of customers and the resulting fulfilment tasks, E-Bay created an option so customers can shop within their local market using the site's advanced search option. This gives buyers peace of mind knowing that they can personally examine the item for sale, as well as reduce shipping costs and delivery time. E-Bay patrons are also given the opportunity to rate the seller. This model helps create a sense of loyalty to E-Bay on the part of online buyers – and a new form of customer relationship management. Such next-generation market-centric models will reach further into buy and/or sell business functionality to secure customer relationships.

Market-centric companies carry out the traditional customer-facing roles. In helping customers by making it easier for them to find and compare prices, they perform a role that encourages customers to switch between companies. The smarter these companies are at reducing the costs of setting up relationships, the less it costs the customer to switch between suppliers. So, paradoxically, the better these companies perform, the lower loyalty may be in the market. In financial services, if customers move frequently between suppliers, risk can be greatly increased, so the more effective a company is at relationship set-up, the smarter it has to be in risk management.

Market-centric companies' core competencies are:

- attracting qualified buyers and suppliers, locally and globally;
- providing robust commerce infrastructure and matching engine;
- truly understanding needs and processes between buyers and sellers;
- focusing on understanding product, the related integrated supply chains and environment within which the product is positioned to provide collaboration and integration services;
- maintaining neutrality between buyer and seller;
- having functionality to interact with virtual agents;
- understanding complexities of differing geographical 'end points' for fulfilment;
- using risk management to understand fully risk and its mitigation as part of buy/sell transaction process;
- understanding who fulfilment partnerships are and gauges their performance.

Their revenue sources are:

- transaction fee/percent;
- fees for value added services.

Their success metrics are:

- buy/sell business process outsourcing revenue;
- number of qualified active buyers/sellers;
- volumes (bids/ transactions);
- risk measures (eg losses);
- customer ratings/feedback.

THE FULFILMENT-CENTRIC MODEL

Fulfilment-centric businesses create economic value by identifying and fulfilling the needs of buyers and sellers. They achieve this through:

- distribution conveniences, such as geography and availability;
- 'fair' price relative to speed of delivery;
- reliability and dependability;
- post-fulfilment services.

This model requires – at minimum – superior physical and virtual fulfilment capabilities and the necessary infrastructure. Key differentiators will be the degree of supply chain and infrastructure efficiencies and the intelligent use of next-generation technologies to enable enhanced payment and transaction processes.

As one of Japan's largest retailers, Ito-Yokado operates about 8,200 7-Eleven stores in Japan and more than 400 other businesses that include superstores, supermarkets, discounters and speciality stores. The company's new venture, IY Bank, will enable customers to deposit or withdraw funds to IY Bank and other financial institutions at ATMs installed in Ito-Yokado stores – 24 hours a day, seven days a week. Customers will also be able to settle transactions for their securities accounts, pay credit card and utility bills and make insurance payments. What's more, IY Bank will provide small lines of credit for customer purchases at its stores. Since IY Bank will only offer small loans for shopping and will borrow space from Ito-Yokado group retail outlets, it will operate with few additional assets.

Fulfilment-centric models offer compelling advantages. They can help assure access to the customer while exercising a high degree of control over which products and services they offer – and the terms upon which they will do so. The more robust their fulfilment capabilities, the more they can strike favourable distribution agreements. Such fulfilment businesses are capital intensive and leverage their scale to provide an optimal combination of virtual and physical 'delivery' for their customers, based on the product/service being delivered.

Fulfilment-centric companies provide one or more of the following:

- the physical infrastructure to deliver products and services between buyers and sellers;
- the technology infrastructure to enable the interaction between buyers and sellers in the marketplace;
- the capabilities, process functionality, and information to enable transaction completion and settlement.

Their core competencies are:

- leverage of capital investments and physical infrastructure;
- capable of full integration into buyer/seller supply chain management;
- robust infrastructure (24/7/365);
- providing a two-way interchange between the buyer and seller (delivery and return);
- fully understanding the dynamics of channel integration;
- providing 'perfect' visibility/trackability of orders;
- value-added information services;
- global scale capabilities/operations.

Their revenue sources are:

- delivery fees (transportation, related services);

- fees for customization/packaging/information services;
- fees for business processes performed for customers.

Their success metrics are:

- return on infrastructure costs;
- customer ratings/satisfaction;
- delivery time/channel performance;
- inventory levels/turns;
- supply chain efficiency.

ARE YOU READY?

To survive in the emerging e-marketplace, financial services enterprises need to plan and manage a 'business portfolio migration'. To do this, executives must be ready to ask themselves some difficult questions, such as:

- What are my revenue streams? What sources can I maintain, and which ones will disappear or change?
- What are the strengths and weaknesses of each business within the organization?
- What are the potential e-business opportunities and threats?
- Which lines of business lend themselves to reinvention?
- What are the possible unique value propositions?
- What is the current maturity profile of each line of business?
- Who are our competitors and how can we position our company strategically to gain more market share?
- What are the needs of each of the target customer segments?
- What offerings can be crafted to meet those needs?
- How can we leverage next-generation technology to deliver those offerings?
- What will be our best marketplace position? What will be the best processes and structure to effect these changes? How can we reorganize business capabilities to meet the new offerings and marketplace position?
- What current and new business capabilities and assets can be leveraged to generate new synergistic revenue opportunities?

PREPARING FOR THE FUTURE

We believe that the following steps can help companies answer these questions and determine which model or models they should adopt.

Build a comprehensive 'franchise profile'

- Take a snapshot of where each business unit is now (in terms of maturity).
- Identify which businesses will be subject to reinvention.
- Define target customer segments that require an alternate strategic position (ie customer-centric).
- Evaluate existing processes, plus the strengths and weaknesses of each business line.

Plan the transition

- Make decisions regarding the market position, target customers and core capabilities of each unit.
- Identify the architecture, processes and core capabilities that will be needed to meet customer needs.

Execute

- Generate efficiencies in core processes through next-generation technologies and outsourcing of all non-core processes.
- Leverage combined skills and assets to create new revenue streams.

The challenges companies face as they seek to transform and align themselves to 'what customers will pay for' are complex. Channel conflict, structure development, integration of culture and management models – all must be addressed as the business evolves and adopts new business models. But the advantages of change far outweigh the risks of doing 'business as usual'. New market entrants, the expansion of existing companies and growing customer empowerment are compelling reasons to apply fresh and creative thinking (and the execution that follows) to assure a vital future for the company.

40

Managing change

Kevin La Croix, Merlin Stone and Fola Komolafe

CHANGES AND TRENDS

No managers in financial services need to be told that their world is changing quickly. No managers in financial services need to be told that managing change is difficult. No managers in financial services need to be told that short-term success is no guarantee of long-term success or even survival, or that short-term failure is not a guarantee of demise. However, we believe that all managers in financial services need to understand that balancing change for tomorrow and change for the day after tomorrow is probably the best trick that they can pull off – for their own careers, for their shareholders or stakeholders, and for their customers.

In considering the current and future trends that are likely to shape the financial services industry, two criteria are important. The first has to do with *relevance* – what trends actually have a bearing on the industry's evolution? The second criteria concerns *predictability and permanence* – what trends are highly likely to continue and perhaps increase in velocity, and which trends are subject to potentially dysfunctional interruption? Depending on the selection criteria used for 'relevance' and the assumptions of 'permanence', dramatically different scenarios can be envisioned for the industry.

There are several trends that have clear relevance and that are already affecting the development of the industry. These include:

- a lowering of regulatory barriers between the banking, insurance and brokerage sectors of the industry;
- increasing globalization of the industry and its corporate customers, supporting increasing cross-border capital flows;
- shifting demand for services and products on the part of retail customers;
- dramatically increased access to the offerings of the industry and information about them through technological innovation and particularly through the Internet;
- increasing occurrences of insourcing, outsourcing, 'white labelling', co-branding and new entrant business models;
- growing merger and acquisition activity in national and international terms.

Although these trends affect the industry in different ways and to different extents in various countries, regions and within different trading zones, they generally have had important and consistent effects on the industry. The opportunity for choice delivered by new entrants and new technologies has generally increased the power of the customer. Evidence of this effect can be seen in the growing resistance to product and service fee structures, decreasing loyalty to primary providers, acceptance of non-traditional brands and propositions, and the willingness to 'shop' for a better offer and self-select the solution. The opportunity for integration enabled by regulatory change, emerging business models and technology has generally increased the power of the supplier. Although there is limited evidence that there are compelling economies of scale or scope in financial services, the industry is pursuing both strategies aggressively. Merger, acquisition and alliance agreements tend either to reduce the number of provider choices, or to complicate choice as products are bundled, package priced or cross-subsidized.

ARE THESE TRENDS PERMANENT?

Whilst these trends are relevant, can it be said that they also have the quality of permanence? Or are they becoming even stronger?

Regulatory barriers

The lowering of regulatory barriers between the sectors of the industry is gaining momentum in much of the world. Even in the United States, where the 'fire walls' between insurance, brokerage and banking had over 50 years of authority, these barriers are being eroded. There is not, however, an inevitability to this regulatory trend. The concentration of investor, depositor and systemic risk implicit in this trend could result in a deceleration or partial reversal of industry integration. If the economic catastrophe of the early 1930s provided justification for sector separation in the United States, could a similar catastrophe, perhaps in Japan, South America or Central and Eastern Europe, be the cause of a similar reaction?

Globalization

The increasing globalization of the industry and the resulting increase in cross-border capital flows is becoming an increasingly politicized phenomenon. The most evident opponents of this trend are the various anarchistic and protest-driven groups who argue against it on a variety of grounds. However, there are many respected non-governmental organizations that are expressing concerns on political, moral and indeed religious grounds about the 'unethical' concentration and movement of global capital. There are also concerns being raised by international and national parties, including the United Nations and the government of France, and the 'Tobin Tax' on cross-border capital movement has become a relevant issue. If the results of globalization are perceived to be an increasing polarization between rich and poor countries and regions, if the socio-economic tragedies of poverty, child death, disease and mass unemployment are seen to be caused by unrestricted capital flows, a populist political response may dramatically affect this trend.

Shifting demand

The shifting demand for products and services on the part of retail customers is based in much of Europe and North America on conflicting satisfactions and concerns. Undoubtedly, the past 10 years have produced a sense of well-being and security in the minds of the majority of these customers. Their world is largely at peace, their environments are largely orderly, and the institutions and infrastructures upon which they depend are largely reliable. This set of present satisfactions is countered by longer-term concerns. In these countries, there is recognition that government cannot supply the needs of the retired, the aged and elderly helpless. If the present is comfortable and secure, the future is threatening and that threat stokes the desire to invest for the long term and to demand surety as well as return on that investment. Compare that scenario with the Japan of today. The past 10 years have not produced a sense of well-being. To be sure, Japan has been at peace. However, the environment has hardly been orderly as many social systems have eroded, employer–employee relationships have been redefined, and corporate structures have proven unstable. Their institutions and infrastructures, including political parties, government ministries and the banking and insurance industries, have proven to be inflexible and non-responsive. A set of present dissatisfactions has combined with the long-term concerns of a rapidly ageing population to cripple consumer demand and intensify short-term savings. If the sense of present-day well-being is heavily eroded, if the 'wealth effect' is replaced by a perceived 'loss effect', might the wants and needs of US and European customers reflect more closely their Japanese counterparts?

ACCESS

Dramatically increased access to the offerings of the industry and information about them has had a profound impact on the financial services industry. As consumers take up technology-driven channels there has been the opportunity to reduce costs dramatically. The old adage that the branch is open when it should be closed and closed when it should be open has been replaced by extended or 24-hour availability. Information aggregators have developed 'multi-provider storefronts'. Switching costs in terms of cost, convenience and reliability have been dramatically lowered. Finally, the new technology has enabled the providers to amass ever-increasing amounts of data about their customers and markets and to derive additional information from that data.

It is quite surprising that in the development of these new capabilities there have been few, if any, catastrophic events. The potential for fraud on a massive scale, the opportunity to wreak havoc on the Internet, and the temptation to abuse the vast new amounts of information gathered about individuals and enterprises have not resulted in events that call into question the present applications of technology in the industry. To be sure, billions have been lost in the bursting of the 'dot.com bubble', 'third generation mobile dream', and 'multi-media miracle'. However, these billions are certainly more the result of poor management, flawed business planning or herd instinct. If, however, significant examples of abuse or loss are attributed to the industry's use of technology, either customers or governments, or both, may take a very different attitude to the value of convenience, lower costs and ease of comparison. In such a scenario, might legislative limitations or lower customer acceptance make the investment in these technologies less economic?

New business models

The evolution of new business models has been particularly evident in the financial services industry. As financial enterprises have defined and selected their core business processes, they have been able to de-emphasize certain activities or abdicate them to other specialist firms. At the same time, as they have invested in further strengthening of core processes they have been able to 'sub-let' these to others, including their competitors. Human resources, information technology, premises, and other 'ancillary' functions have been given over to specialists as credit management, treasury operations, underwriting, claims handling and portfolio management have become points of competition and cooperation.

Taken to the extreme, this functional granularity may intensify two factors that can ultimately work against providers – commoditization and de-branding. If many core functions of the industry are operated by a few specialist enterprises but offered by many players, features, service levels, accessibility and reliability may become relatively consistent across the market. In such an environment, even relatively complex offerings may be viewed as commodities where price is the major determinant. In addition, if customers perceive that a valued traditional brand can be accessed though any number of new providers and entrepreneurial brands, all of the offerings within that market sector may be viewed as more of a 'public utility', with little provider differentiation. These two effects are already clearly developed within the narrow set of offerings delivered through the combined ATM network in many countries. Users are unlikely to know or care who owns and operates the machine; they are likely to assume that Visa or Carte Bleu or Link plays that role. They are not likely to remember which financial institution supplied the last machine they used, and they are very likely to assume that 'someone else' will pay for the cost of ownership of the equipment. There may come a point at which the loss of differentiation, brand loyalty and identity outweighs the gains of functional granularity.

Mergers and acquisitions

The growth in merger and acquisition activity in national and international terms seems likely to continue. In the developed world, penetration of financial services into available markets is relatively high and organic growth often results in trading one's customers for the customers of a competitor. Acquiring market share one customer at a time can be very expensive and disruptive of relationships with current customers. Acquiring a large group of customers by buying their supplier has not only potential market share, but also cost advantages. The concentration of the industry may yield positive results for investors through improved returns on equity and assets. It may also provide improvements to customers through improved reach and range. However, it may create issues of sovereignty and be challenged by local loyalties. Governments at the national and state level may increasingly look unfavourably at mergers and acquisitions that appear to threaten their ability to govern or that are inconsistent with competition, social inclusion or employment policies. New local providers may increasingly appeal to customers based on their 'local character', 'home-grown culture', or civic participation.

Socio-economic factors

Consider then the financial services industry that might result from a dysfunctional evolution of the major trends first introduced in this chapter: although each of the trends introduced at the beginning of this chapter are arguably relevant to the development of the financial services industry, each of them is also unpredictable. They largely depend on socio-economic stability, politically based decisions, perceived values and beliefs and individual preference. These factors are, to say the least, fragile. Barring a cataclysmic event, these trends are likely to have their predictable impacts on the shaping of the industry. Over the longer term, however, these trends become increasingly unpredictable.

Finally, there may be several additional relevant trends that are perhaps more predictable:

- socio-demographics;
- pressure group activism and the 'democratization' of the industry;
- the rise of complementary currencies;
- denationalization.

Socio-demographics

The socio-demographic nature of a country or region is embedded in its history and, barring epidemic, war or invasion, is relatively fixed over a long time period. Of course, different countries and regions present different socio-demographic profiles. At the risk of generalizing, Turkey is young, Italy is old. Denmark is healthy, Bangladesh is unhealthy. Canada is urban, Sudan is rural. Such comparisons can be made across a number of factors. As they are applied to the financial services industry, their primary implications are on what services and products are most appropriate and what is the capability of the market to absorb those services and products. The very reliability over the relatively long term of 'youth' in Turkey, illness in Bangladesh, or agrarianism in Sudan may demand the development of financial institutions whose capabilities and strategies are more based on broad socio-demographic profiles than on local or global opportunities.

Pressure groups and protests

The rise of the pressure group phenomenon, so visible at recent World Bank, G8 and IMF meetings, is unlikely to abate. Single-issue organizations such as the Anti-Vivisectionists have been able to deny Huntington Life Sciences domestic bank funding and services. It is not appropriate here to argue the merits of the case for any of the hundreds of groups that have adopted a 'cause' or objective. It is, however, clear that the Internet, combined with relative affluence, social services policies and leisure time, has enabled thousands of individuals to combine in voicing their beliefs and positions. At the heart of many of their perceptions is the role of the financial institution in supporting the evils against which they fight. As these various protests grow (sometimes unfortunately stimulated by obviously inhuman conditions or unethical behaviour), they are likely to gain resonance in the elected governments of North America and Europe. Boycotting a German bank in support of Holocaust victims or disinvesting from a fund that invests in multinationals with poor Third World employment records is increasingly politically effective. In the long term, this interplay between individuals, politicians and the financial services industry is likely to grow in intensity. For good or bad, banks, insurers and brokerages may be at the forefront of the democratization of industry.

Complementary currencies

The rise of complementary currencies is likely to continue and to present the industry with a new set of opportunities and challenges. These currencies are developing in two broad forms: corporate scrip and community scrip. In the former, companies around the developed world have introduced loyalty point schemes, frequent mileage offers and purchase reward vouchers. However, these plans have increasingly ceased to be a 'closed system' benefit, issued by the seller and spent with the seller. More and more, these schemes have taken on the characteristics of 'money'. They provide a store and measure of value, they are accepted in an ever-widening number of unrelated transactions, and they are transferable to a third party in lieu of an obligation. If it is possible to earn the majority of frequent flyer miles and spend them without ever boarding an aeroplane, to what extent is that company's scrip becoming a wider currency?

Unlike company scrip, community scrip tends to be developed locally and is intended to support some perceived civic or societal benefit. Japan, Switzerland and some cities in the USA all have developed alternate currencies to encourage people to volunteer time and skills to care for the elderly, teach the young and perform defined good deeds. In some cases this alternative currency can be spent within the city or region, can be given to another as charity, and can even be used to pay local taxes.

It is not likely that any complementary currency system will take the place of the national fiat currencies that governments issue. However, it is likely, particularly if incomes, lifestyle and generational gaps widen, that these currencies will coexist in greater number and volume in the future. To the extent that they thrive, they will need to be managed, cleared, protected and accounted for as traditional currencies are today. To the extent that the financial services industry is responsible for the 'value management' within the economy, this new form of value may present a significant opportunity or challenge.

Denationalization

Denationalization appears to be a growing phenomenon that may have profound and trau-matic effects on the financial services industry. Its most obvious example is the increasing political and financial integration of the majority of EU countries. The abandonment of their legacy currencies is a significant step in the process. There are, however, other symptoms of denationalization that will redraw political and economic boundaries. In times of extreme macroeconomic chaos, countries look to a currency board, in affect adopting the currency of another country. Ethnic groups look to secede from what they believe to be their existing 'synthetic' country and to return to a historic dream or myth – the Balkans provides a tragic example. Countries and regions whose borders are the result of former colonial rule contain forced collections of ethnic and religious groups that remain together with unease at best. The widening gap between 'have' and 'have not' countries has created a hunger for migration that is likely to increase as information becomes more available to more remote populations. All these factors will put increasing strains on governments, political systems, global financial institutions and central bankers. The long-term results of the combination of these elements of denationalization are extremely difficult to predict. However, the results are likely to powerfully shape the financial services industry and the regulatory, legislative and commercial systems that underpin it.

THE OVERALL RESULT

So, we come full circle to ask which trends are relevant and which are predictable in the attempt to draw the future shape of the financial services industry. Few, if any, of these trends would have been recognized in 1975. The industry coped with them as they emerged and fundamentally changed itself in the process. There is no reason why it cannot continue to do so – except for two issues: 1) the speed and impact of these trends is likely to increase, demanding ever more agility and ever more diligence over risk; 2) the impact of the socio-demographic, democratization, complementary currency and denationalization trends are particularly challenging because they are each external to and largely out of control of the industry and the governments that regulate it.

The business environment of the industry continues to accelerate and grow, driven by more external factors. Perhaps, if the traditional financial services industry is to survive, the most likely trend is not that it will make better use of data and information; not that it will be smarter or more knowledgeable; but that it will develop wisdom.

MANAGING CHANGE

Much of the focus of management thinking today is on how financial services companies should cope with the changes described above – regulatory, technological, customer behaviour and needs, etc – it is on where they should aim to get to. This thinking is traditionally conducted using the two approaches mentioned below:

- Scenario planning – This approach describes the major changes to the structures of industries and markets, supply chains, technology, and so on. Likely scenarios of combinations in different areas are developed, and the resulting overall scenarios are often radically different from each other. Suggestions are made as to the timing of phases of evolution from scenario to scenario. There may be big discontinuities between the situation today and some of the scenarios of tomorrow.
- Trend-based planning – This approach starts with the situation today and extrapolates already visible trends into the future. Of course, some of the scenarios arising from scenario planning may be arrived at in this way.

Both approaches imply a highly rational approach to how companies evolve. They imply that companies are working from a secure base, in which they are well managed today, and know what they do. It also suggests that companies are in full control of the direction of change. If so, it is argued that understanding possible future scenarios and likely trends is useful because armed with this understanding, a company can securely plan its own path to the future. As scenarios and trends are often derived (at least partly) from observation of the current actions of other companies, there is also an assumption that other companies are making their way rationally to the future. In fact, there is very strong evidence from many sources that managing change is a very, very different process. Here are some examples of the evidence:

- Major systems-supported change projects have very high failure rates, just like those conventionally cited for new products. This implies that the companies that make it to the scenarios of the future will be the few survivors of a fairly chaotic process of movement.
- Most companies are also not really certain about what they can achieve today, and take much longer to come to grips with and then exploit today's technology and today's management best practice (details from report).

The reasons for this are not that managers aren't trying – it's that managing change in a changing environment is hard to do well. If you focus too much on getting things right for today, you may do very well in the short term, but be completely undermined by a new business approach from a competitor. If you focus too much on far horizons, you risk falling off the cliff right in front of you, because you aren't using today's best practice to ensure that you remain competitive. The conclusion of this is that anything you can do to improve (not necessarily optimize) the balance between improving today's business and adjusting the business for tomorrow's scenario is going to increase your chances of meeting your own, your shareholders' and your customers' needs in the next few years.

THE NEED FOR BALANCE

Let's use a simple diagram to explain what we mean (Figure 40.1). In this diagram, the upper curve is the strategic change curve. It shows the leading edge of change in a company. For example, IBM's E-Business Innovations Institute has developed some well-articulated descriptions of financial services markets evolving in their use of e-business (see Chapters 4, 6 and 39). The most advanced version (Wave 3) involves complete redefinition of value chains, emergence of new kinds of intermediaries, splitting of roles between buy-side and sell-side aggregators, and the like. This is described in Chapter 39. At any one time, the participants in the market may be using the models implied in any scenario. Current (Wave 1) practices may survive long into the Wave 3 era, simply because of market (customer and/or supplier) inertia, which may be associated with the innovativeness or market dominance of buyers and/or sellers. A given buyer or seller may buy or sell using different practices. Companies on either side of the market may combine current (Wave 1) practice with future (Wave 3) practices, across or within divisions.

However, companies vary in their success in implementing the business model implied by a particular 'wave'. This leads to the idea of the trailing edge, which reflects the extent to which a company is using today's best practice. For example, many retail financial services companies are still learning how to improve their use of direct mail and call centres. Corporate finance houses are still learning to apply basic technology for managing sales people to improve their chances of major wins in, for example, issue of financial instruments or merger and acquisition deals. So, a company might take a view about its 'outer envelope' – the pace at which it is moving its 'leading edge'. This is the upper curve in Figure 40.1. The trailing edge is represented in the lower curve.

The spread between the upper and lower curves we define as the 'change span'. It reflects the breadth of focus that senior management needs to achieve. This diagram can be drawn for a company as a whole, or for divisions within it. The diagram shows a company

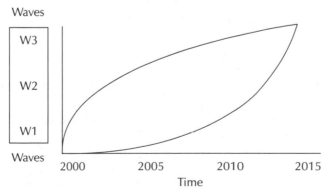

Figure 40.1 The envelope of change

aiming to move from a Wave 1 model in 2000 to a Wave 3 model in 2015. In such a situation both curves would tend to show a series of steps as the company implemented its new capabilities and withdrew from old models. In practice, the curves are rarely smooth, and they are subject to constant readjustment. They may shift down as well, as a company fails in operational implementation, or as it realizes that its plans were too aggressive. The curves may shift over time, upwards or downwards.

In most financial service companies, the change span is very broad. This creates particular problems, because of the very different processes required to manage the upper change line, which means changing business models, while managing the lower line – implementing models which may have been first committed to some time ago.

What happens when companies show competence in one area (changing models) and not in the other (improving within models), and vice versa? Let's answer this first by having a look at some examples of what tends to lead to success or failure (see Table 40.1).

Broadly speaking, success in changing models is mostly related to major programme management capabilities and innovativeness. Success in model improvement is mostly related to functional disciplines and team working over long periods.

Most large companies in financial services have little choice but to be good in both ways. Of course it is possible to envisage a strategy in which a company deliberately abandons today's model and migrates to another. It is also possible to envisage a strategy in which a company decides to focus on within-model improvement, relying on acquiring or being acquired by 'new model' companies, or indeed planning to withdraw from business, having made good profit for shareholders by being ultra-efficient. A common strategy is to give up all attempts at moving a business with a well-entrenched current model, and to set up a separate unit with the aim of integrating it with the main business at a later date. This often proves to be very difficult.

Following the dot.com debacle of 2000, it seems that the period in which a company could attract funding for new models of business irrespective of its record in managing 'real' business operations is drawing to a close. We therefore believe that major players in the financial services market must balance their focus between moving towards tomorrow's business models and optimizing today's. To achieve this, these players will

Table 40.1 Changing or improving models

A company good at changing models	A company good at improving within models
• Understands broad characteristics of current model, and how they need to change • Knows how to move resources between units/businesses with different models, adapting them where necessary • Knows how to manage parallel projects, understanding the risk of failure in some of them	• Understands the detailed operating and information requirements of each model • Has a disciplined approach to measuring performance within each model • Has a disciplined approach to investment case for improvements, including piloting and testing • Has a strong commitment to involving all relevant departments in improvement programmes

need to devise change programmes that encompass change to existing business models while modifying those models that deliver most of today's business.

What does this mean for senior management? Table 40.2 looks at the problem from the perspective of the company as a whole and the five key officers, the chief executive officer (CEO), chief financial officer (CFO), chief marketing officer (CMO), chief information officer (CIO) and chief operating officer (COO). We have tried to identify the three or four most important points each of them should understand, points which will as near as possible guarantee that each is not going to be caught out by an imbalance between optimizing current operations and moving to new models. We've added four points for the company overall.

Of course, if the prize for each of the chief officers is eventually the CEO's job, they may try to perform across the board – being good at strategy and operations. We wonder if this is like positions on a sports field – team members who are excellent in one position can be lousy in another. If it is true that strategists make lousy operators and vice versa, then it is critical that those who govern the company ensure that CEOs who are strategists are supported by good operators, and vice versa.

Managing change is difficult! However, financial companies that take a more holistic view are more likely to get where they want to go, and to be able to change to new destinations as their environment changes in ways that they can't anticipate.

CASE STUDY: CHANGES IN THE UK FINANCIAL SERVICES INDUSTRY – LIFE AND PENSIONS

When managers in the UK financial services industry look back on the beginning of the new millennium, the wiser ones will laugh at the panic over Year 2000. However, the wiser ones will realize that the good work that was done all through 1999, and earlier, was responsible for the smooth transition. Those who held that the true millennium started on 1 January 2001 might feel that if there is any correlation between calendars and auspicious events, their choice of millennial commencement is the right one. In one year, financial services companies in the UK have had to face the challenges of:

- The 1 per cent world and the stakeholder pension, causing many companies to consider what business they really wanted to be in, and whether their cost structures were sustainable, while providing a field day for better-off customers to provide an excellent tax-sponsored investment for themselves and their families.
- Depolarization – recognizing the reality that many IFAs already pre-select suppliers, but giving legal basis to it, thus leading the life and pension industry towards a scenario where the business-to-business (manufacturer to IFA) supply chain comes under a brighter spotlight, particularly in relation to pre- and post-sales customer service.

Table 40.2 Managing change – perspectives of different corporate officers

Company as a whole	• Make sure that the CEO has the strategic understanding to steer the business through changes in business models and also has the operational skills to maximize results using the company's current business model. Make sure also that the company has a management team that in itself exhibits all these skills – almost two management teams each of which focuses on its own 'curve' • Ensure that all senior managers realize that moving operating models forward by strategic change requires long-term programme management, which combines innovation and insight with thoroughness and attention to detail • When faced with any major decision, senior managers should be required to identify how the decision would look under the company's next business model, and whether the sums may look funny because the model is in the middle of changing • Consider whether the fact that the various chief officers' progress in the company took place under earlier business models means that they take a certain view about newer business models, whether they are feasible, and how they are to be implemented. Chief officers should try to see change from the point of view of the younger managers whose jobs will rest on whether the change succeeds and whose skills, energy, motivation and experience will make it happen – or not!
CEO	• Build a team with the different skills required to manage a broad change span • Managing change in silos is sub-optimal, just like managing customers or risks in silos • Make sure that all chief officers pay attention to their points
COO	• Identify when changing strategy means making a major change to operating methods, and when it can be contained until it can be included in a wider change in operating model (version control) • Make sure that your reporting approach which supports your drive for efficiency can be transferred to your company's new business models • The size of what you manage is less important than its contribution to profit. If you have to outsource more to make more profit, do it with the thought that this can greatly reduce your paycheck/stress ratio
CIO	• Although you'll always be spending most of your budget on system maintenance, budgeting for change is important • Don't assume that change is stable – you're briefed to provide many new kinds of information management capabilities that will never be used, at all or properly • Learn to interrogate the briefs you are given by functional counterparts – don't accept them as they are
CMO	• A CMO's job is to deliver value to customers, shareholders and company people, as your business model changes • The latest fashions in marketing won't work for all your customers, all the time. If you want to be remembered for adding rather than subtracting value, work closely with the CFO, the CIO and the COO to develop business models that are sustainable no matter how innovative the approach to the value chain • Balance your work on strategic change in channels, products, customers, etc with work aimed at ensuring that marketing efficiency is measurable and manageable
CFO	• Your job is to identify – ahead of your colleagues – what the financial parameters for success are for new business models, and what financial performance will look like under your company's chosen span of change • You must maintain a clear, quantified and updated view of all your assets and liabilities and be aware of their changing relationships and changing inherent value as the business environment changes. Use this to identify as early as possible the risks entailed in your company's chosen span of change, and how these risks can be managed • Understand that most business cases for change are based on inspired guesswork, and that the more you can test, the better. Look for evidence that something is likely to work, rather than polished figures that are divorced from reality

- The possible restructuring of the life and pensions industry (where the above two initiatives could be regarded as recognizing existing pressures for restructuring, rather than driving). This is most likely if margin pressure outruns the growth of assets under management.
- A new approach to regulation, with combined regulatory powers not necessarily meaning coordinated, and some lack of clarity as to what compliance requirements are. Put bluntly, more meddling is already here, and more seems to be on the way.
- Government realization that many of its objectives in terms of transferring the burden of the state to the individual will not be realized through voluntary means, with the possible emergence of compulsion.
- Declining levels of customer service, not just in financial services and not just in the UK, and apparently declining levels of competence in managing it (as documented in Chapter 3).
- Failure of general management to take control of how it manages its customers, and how its image is presented to the different types of stakeholder.
- A new Data Protection Act coming into force in a world in which mergers, acquisitions and new business launches were taking many companies way from compliance with the old Act.
- Big advances in genetic research, which bring us even nearer to a situation where genes will be one of the main determinants of the individual's optimum approach to insurance and investment.
- Admission by over-confident governments throughout the Western world that they got their sums wrong, with emerging, though for the time being reasonably mild, recessionary pressures causing companies to view new approaches to management (such as e-business and CRM) as much in terms of their ability to save cost as their ability to generate improved performance.
- The events of 11 September 2001, sadly making government sums even more wrong, while reminding businesses of the breadth and variety as well as the depth of risks against which they need to make contingency plans, and confirming the need for reinsurance on a global scale.
- Trivialization of most of the above issues by the media, forcing a focus on spin rather than substance, encouraged by the success of certain governments in management by spin.

Meanwhile, in the background are the longer-running events that are already stimulating their share of market change, such as:

- The post-war population bulge passing into maturity, with its proceeds of inherited properties, businesses sold, maturing endowments, and tax-free lump sums. This includes the retirements of the massive intakes into the public sector of the 1960s and

1970s, as well as the maturing of the Thatcher generation into their hedonistic middle age.

● The development and use of many new ways of managing customers, such as e-business, the mobile phone and interactive TV.

● The rise of a new generation of young people who seem to be an interesting blend of Thatcherism and environmentalism – happy to take on responsibility for their own future, to spend on mobile phones and fashion wear, but with a residual concern for what all this might be doing to their health and well-being.

● The survival into a distressing longevity, marred by Alzheimer's and other chronic illnesses, of the parents of the post-war bulge. They signal a warning to their successors, in terms of provision for old age.

All these developments together seem to constitute almost a 'witches' brew' of problems. However, this book argues the opposite – that these events provide an opportunity for: 1) capitalism in the best sense of the word to show what it is made of, and why it has become the dominant economic form in the world; 2) companies to use this situation to gain share over their competitors, and lay the ground for much improved profitability in the future.

In these circumstances, most life and pensions companies have focused on reducing costs and increasing market share in this slightly less stable but interesting world. What should they be doing? The simple answer seems to be – don't be hit by analysis-paralysis. In all the business-driven work that IBM does in financial services – such as consulting, outsourcing and systems implementation – a common set of messages seems to be coming over.

CONCLUSION

The above messages are ones companies ignore at their peril, because if they are not understood, they lead quickly to a company drowning in a mass of detailed decision making. They are closely related to how IBM now runs its business, and explain why IBM has performed well, in an atmosphere of tough, managed prudence in which managing the future features as a key part of its activities. Here are our conclusions:

● You may have to run your business in separate business units, divisions, silos (or whatever consultants decide to call them), but you must have a simple overview at senior management level. Your information systems should provide support to this process, but not drown senior managers in data. These should cover not only the classic financial variables such as profit, capital investment, working capital, cash flow and revenue, not just the older and newer marketing, sales and service measures such as orders, customer wins and losses, customer satisfaction and service delivery, but also areas of risk such as operational risk, economic/financial risk, capability risk and compliance risk.

- That overview is not best generated by complex scorecards, but by simple scorecards at each level, with extremely tough, measured and disciplined delegation of performance, with the right data delivered to manage it at each level, and responsibility for performance and contribution to higher-level measures delegated and measured. This can only be done if you manage people issues well.

- Business performance cannot be measured just by current value (eg sales, profits, cash, headcount, inventory, working capital), for these only tell you about the past and present. Managers manage the future, and in most businesses the present is determined by others (customers who decide to buy now, sales people who are motivated to sell now, workers who are motivated to work now, etc). Managing near-term performance requires developing a clear picture of what it is, and this includes not only the likely future values of the measures mentioned above, but risks around them.

- Risk is everywhere, and is normally badly managed when different categories of risk emerge and are detected but are not raised to the level at which they can be managed (or raised at all). Particularly dangerous are risks which multiply when combined (as we sadly saw on 11 September, when operational, physical and market risk combined).

- Personal accountability is the key to long-term success. The board is accountable not just for performance, but also for image, customer service, and risk management. Ownership of these issues can only be achieved if they are properly understood and the information on their status and how they interact is taken to the level where it can be managed – at the top. From there, it can only be transferred to the people who can do something about performance – from senior middle managers downwards – if you make sure that these people understand what the company is trying to do and what their contribution is to achieving it. This depends upon motivating, measuring and rewarding people by relatively simple sets of incentives and measures, which are transparent to the individuals.

- You must be very clear about which models you run your business by. Many managers do not understand what is meant by model. It is simply a picture of the main entities or factors that account for how the business is run, and of how they must relate to each other for the company to succeed. For example, in the CRM area, a business which gets most of its profit by selling through intermediaries who influence final customers strongly in their choice of product must determine what makes for successful relationships with intermediaries. There is no point in developing a strong relationship with final customers without a strong relationship with intermediaries (unless no one has a strong relationship with them). In risk management, a company whose business depends upon customers, suppliers or other business partners located in particular locations must understand what it risks if these locations come under physical threat. Most businesses experience problems in the 'models' area when they are 'tunnel-visioned' about exploring different views of their business. This prevents them seeing threats posed by different models used by competitors, or by factors that they have not taken into account in their modelling.

- Intermediation is changing. New technologies for handling relationships between businesses are permitting new market models to evolve. These often involve the introduction of new intermediaries between companies and those they formerly regarded as their customers. In some cases this intermediation is only partial – for example, the partial outsourcing of the service they deliver. This is because these new systems reduce the cost of inter-organizational communication. Pretending that these opportunities do not exist is no solution, as competitors who use these opportunities to reduce the costs of dealing with customers, or to increase the focus on specific aspects of service, will win away customers based on level of service or cost.

- Value is becoming a focus, but most companies are very confused about value. There are many different kinds of value – here are some examples: value of customer to the company (present and over time), value of the company's offer as perceived by customer, stakeholder or shareholder value, and allocation of value chain tasks between customers, the company and its business partners. These different values can be related in a positive way, but the relationship may be counter-productive. For example, allowing customers to extract much more value than they return can create problems, unless this is a prelude to the reverse taking place (investment in customers). Similarly, not understanding the full value chain costs of a particular way of dealing with customers can lead to a whole value chain becoming uncompetitive.

- Understand what you're doing today. In many situations, we at IBM have the benefit of being 'well-connected' outsiders, with the privilege of looking into a company from outside. We see many interesting things, but perhaps our main value is perspective – we have the same view of many companies, and we can see recurrences of patterns. One of the commonest patterns is what we call 'the board illusion' – a situation where the board of a company does not really understand what is going on – in all the areas mentioned above. In most cases, this weakness can be resolved by use of one or other more or less structured audit methodologies, sometimes involving a comparison with a database of practice. These are not easy to interpret, but they are pretty well guaranteed to remove the illusion.

- See your company from outside – from the point of view of customers, business partners, suppliers, government and other interested parties. See it also from your staff's point of view – for they are your inside people who have to manage your outside people. Unless you understand the inside view and the outside view, you won't be able to manage either.

Index